THE GERNSBACK DAYS

A study of the evolution of modern
science fiction from 1911 to 1936

by

MIKE ASHLEY

and

ROBERT A. W. LOWNDES

Hugo Gernsback. in 1959.

THE GERNSBACK DAYS

A study of the evolution of modern
science fiction from 1911 to 1936

by

MIKE ASHLEY

and

ROBERT A. W. LOWNDES

WILDSIDE PRESS

THE GERNSBACK DAYS

Published by:

Wildside Press
P.O. Box 301
Holicong, PA 18928-0301
www.wildsidepress.com

First Wildside Press edition: 2004

ACKNOWLEDGMENTS

Acknowledgments for source material from private or academic collections are as follows:

Forrest J Ackerman for copies of hundreds of letters from many authors in the period 1930-1935.

George Arents Research Library, Syracuse University, Syracuse, New York, for copies of selected text and illustrations from Gernsback's magazines in their Hugo Gernsback Collection; and for copies of correspondence between Will F. Jenkins [Murray Leinster] and Robert Hardy, and between Hugo Gernsback and David H. Keller. [My thanks to Ms. Carolyn A. Davis and Diane L. Cooter for their unfailing assistance.]

Brown University Library, Providence, Rhode Island, for copies of correspondence to Clark Ashton Smith from Hugo Gernsback, David Lasser, August Derleth, Charles D. Hornig, Julius Schwartz, Ione Weber, and Donald A. Wollheim. [My thanks to Mark N. Brown.]

Eastern New Mexico University Library, Portales, New Mexico, for copies of correspondence to Jack Williamson and Edmond Hamilton from Hugo Gernsback, David Lasser and Miriam Bourne, and for copies of issues of *The Bulletin of the American Interplanetary Society* and *Astronautics*. [My thanks to Mary Jo Walker and Leone Reynolds.]

University of Illinois at Urbana-Champaign, Urbana, Illinois, for copies of correspondence between Hugo Gernsback and H. G. Wells. [My thanks to Gene K. Rinkel.]

Temple University, Philadelphia, Pennsylvania, for copies of correspondence between Lloyd Arthur Eshbach and Hugo Gernsback, Miriam Bourne, David Lasser, Julius Schwartz, Raymond A. Palmer, and Harry Bates. [My thanks to Thomas M. Whitehead.]

The State Historical Society of Wisconsin, Madison, Wisconsin, for copies of correspondence to August Derleth from Clark Ashton Smith and David H. Keller. [My thanks to Harold L. Miller.]

The University of Wyoming American Heritage Center, Laramie, Wyoming, for copies of miscellaneous papers from its Hugo Gernsback Collection. [My thanks to Emmett D. Chisum.]

Science Fiction Foundation, Dagenham, Essex, for access to original magazines and a wide range of reference material, plus a plentiful supply of photocopying paper. [My thanks to Mrs. Joyce Day.]

This book is dedicated to

Forrest J Ackerman,

for his help and for keeping the spirit of wonder alive;
to

David Lasser,

for bringing realism to science fiction;
and to all of those authors, artists, fans and editors
who raised science fiction from
infancy to maturity.

CONTENTS

Yesterday's Worlds of Tomorrow by Robert A.W. Lowndes

Appendices

PREFACE

In recent years there has been a resurgence of interest in Hugo Gernsback, and the start of a serious study of the contribution he made to the development of science fiction. But when I first considered writing this book, Gernsback was almost a dirty word in science fiction, having achieved a notoriety that had made him the *bête noir* of the field. Critics, led most vocally by James Blish and Damon Knight, had castigated Gernsback for creating a "periodical ghetto[1] for science fiction. The most damning inditement, and probably the most harmful, came from the internationally respected writer and critic Brian W. Aldiss, who, in his *Billion Year Spree*, published in 1973, wrote:

> It is easy to argue that Hugo Gernsback was one of the worst disasters ever to hit the science-fiction field. Not only did the segregation of science fiction into magazines designed especially for it, ghetto-fashion, guarantee that various orthodoxies would be established inimical to a thriving literature, but Gernsback himself was utterly without any literary understanding. He created dangerous precedents which many later editors in the field followed.[2]

Aldiss maintained that argument in his book's successor, *Trillion Year Spree*, published thirteen years later, with other international critics supporting his case, most notably Sweden's Sam J. Lundwall. The young American writer and reviewer, Darrell Schweitzer, then entered the ring with his own vitriolic attack upon Gernsback in "Keeper of the Flame" (*Algol*, Winter 1977/78). He came to the conclusion that "I doubt anyone else could have been a *worse* influence on the field."

In simple parlance, it became the in-thing to "knock" Gernsback. I almost found myself doing it, starting to accept what respected critics were saying. When, one day in 1978, I caught myself doing it, I stopped to think. I soon came to realize that, beyond the writings of Sam Moskowitz, I knew little about Hugo Gernsback, and certainly very little about his work prior to the appearance of *Amazing Stories* in 1926. Whilst I had much respect for Moskowitz as a researcher and, most especially, as science fiction's premier archeologist, it can be dangerous to accept without question the research and opinions of one man, regardless of his reliability. It seemed to me that the time was due to reinvestigate the Gernsback era and dig into the facts surrounding the origins of *Amazing Stories*. I wanted to find out exactly why Hugo Gernsback had launched the magazine, what he was trying to achieve, and to consider what effects he had—good and bad.

To do this I needed to get back to first-hand sources. It was my original intention to edit a volume of essays about the Gernsback days, written by his contemporaries, including Jack Williamson, Raymond Gallun, Charles D. Hornig, Donald A. Wollheim, and others. This volume was going to be a mixture of new articles, specially commissioned from those still living, plus reprints of pieces written during the Gernsback period by writers no longer with us.

9

It was some while before I could get my thoughts together sufficiently to prepare a proposal for the book, but during 1978 and 1979 I made contact with many writers from the Gernsback days, including Neil R. Jones, Stanton A. Coblentz, Raymond Z. Gallun, Curt Siodmak, Jack Williamson, Manly Wade Wellman, and others, and started to gather reminiscences from them about their early work. At that stage, having no publisher for the book, I did not directly commission any articles. Charles D. Hornig, however, whom I was delighted to contact in February 1980, was keen to put his memories in print, and submitted to me the article which, in a slightly revised form, appears as Appendix I to this book.

Eventually, early in 1981, I submitted a proposal to a publisher who rejected it on the grounds that they only published new material, not reprints. I found their argument a little spurious, but did not pursue the point. I'd mentioned my activities to Neil Barron, editor of *Anatomy of Wonder*, and it was Barron who suggested that instead of a rag-bag of reminiscences I make the book "a narrative history and critical analysis," integrating the reminiscences into the text.

That approach began to appeal to me, and it is to Barron that the credit should go for most of the final format of this volume. At the time, I felt I could probably work it both ways, by having the main history plus a set of appendices containing the full text of the various authors' reminiscences. However, whilst I was gathering a fair amount of recollections in communications with writers, I still did not feel in a position to expect them to write anything for publication without the immediate prospect of a publisher. Since I was also, then, heavily involved in my research for and writing of *Science Fiction, Fantasy, and Weird Fiction Magazines*, I did not have the time to pursue my Gernsback research, especially in tracing some of the lesser-known writers, or their relatives, from the period.

At that stage an answer seemed to present itself. Charles Hornig mentioned to me that he'd been interviewed by Jeffrey M. Elliot. I'd noticed Elliot's interviews in a variety of magazines, and knew that he'd also been contacting other old-timers. I thus contacted Elliot in August 1981 to see if he'd be interested in collaborating with me on the project. He was, and during 1982 we worked out an arrangement between us, whereby Elliot would do the groundwork in contacting and interviewing writers, and tracing articles in contemporary magazines, feeding that data to me to prepare the first draft of the book, which we would then polish up between us. Elliot leapt into the project with enthusiasm, and soon found an interested publisher. Unfortunately it was the same publisher who had rejected my original proposal, and I was not too keen on the arrangement. Fortunately, Elliot very rapidly interested Ted Dikty, and a contract was soon drawn up and signed. I must thank Jeffrey Elliot, therefore, for securing a publisher.

All during this period I had been in correspondence with Robert A. W. Lowndes. At the time Lowndes was working for Gernsback Publications as Managing Editor of *Sexology* and *Luz* magazines. When those magazines were sold in 1978, Lowndes became Production Associate at *Radio-Electronics*, a position he retained until his retirement at the end of 1989. I had originally asked Lowndes whether I might be able to reprint his series of editorials, "Yesterday's World of Tomorrow," from *Future Science Fiction*, in the Gernsback book. This idea gradually metamorphosed into Lowndes writing his own section, surveying the fiction throughout the period. I was much relieved at Lowndes's willingness to do this. As I expressed to him in a letter dated 11 February 1983: "It's worried me that I started the ball rolling on this and now feel I won't have the time to get it all done." Lowndes helped me out of a spot. With his ever-friendly willingness and interest he began work re-reading all of the old issues, and writing his section. His first draft was finished in March 1985.

During this time I found myself swamped in several very large projects. Not only was I completing the work on *Science Fiction, Fantasy, and Weird Fiction Magazines*, but I was also helping Frank Parnell on his index to weird fantasy magazines, *Monthly Terrors*, and striving to research the life of Algernon Blackwood, and produce a bibliography of his works. All this, plus other, shorter projects, left me no time to pursue the Gernsback research, but with Elliot and Lowndes playing their parts, I felt reasonably content.

It was not until 1987 that I was able to get to grips with *The Gernsback Days* once and for all. By then Jeffrey Elliot and I had gone our separate ways over the book. I was sorry about this and I also felt a little guilty about my own lack of research in the intervening years and that during that time many authors whom I had hoped to contact had died and valuable memories had been lost forever.

In late 1987, therefore, I resumed work on the project, finding that I still had an awful lot of work to do. In addition to the ever-present encouragement of Robert A. W. Lowndes, I was helped through this situation by the much-welcomed assistance of three generous people: A. Langley Searles, the editor of *Fantasy Commentator*, and one of the most perspicacious, erudite and knowledgeable scholars of the field; Eric Leif Davin, who gave freely of his own research and provided a fresh insight into the period; and Forrest J Ackerman, the legend of the fantasy field. I was especially grateful for Searles's assistance in providing details and texts from small-press magazines and writers' journals of the period, and from other research conducted at the New York Public Library. Without his help this book would be considerably less detailed. Major credit and laurels must go to Forrest Ackerman, though, who sent me copies of all of his correspondence with science-fiction writers throughout the thirties containing a wealth of material unavailable elsewhere. Ackerman also unstintingly provided copies of rare Gernsbackian magazines and other associational material and there is no doubt that this book would never have been completed to my satisfaction without his help.

I am also much indebted to Terry Hill who made available to me his complete bound run of Gernsback magazines. This helped fill in the gaps in my own patchy collection, and allowed me to read all of the stories, which was valuable in placing the stories in the perspective of their period. I was also grateful to Joyce Day at the Science Fiction Foundation, who helped me with research into the letter columns in the magazines (which were not in Terry's bound copies), to the point where I obtained photocopies of them all, and was able to read and catalogue them. My thanks also to Alistair Durie who, with unstinting kindness and remarkable keenness, always responded to my odd queries and requests, usually for illustrative material, from his voluminous collection. Alistair helped provide many of the illustrations of the magazine covers reproduced here.

Throughout 1988 and 1989 I contacted many archives and libraries, repositories of various papers and correspondence from the Gernsback days. These provided the prime source of documentation that formed the core of my research and helped bring the book into its final shape. The librarians I contacted were always helpful and, without hesitation, provided the voluminous photocopies I requested. I must record my especial gratitude to Carolyn A. Davis and Diane Cooter of the George Arents Research Library at Syracuse University, who made hundreds of photocopies for me from their Gernsback collection.

I was especially pleased to contact, at a late stage in the proceedings, Jean-Claude Muller of Luxembourg, who had undertaken original research into Gernsback's early days. It was with his help that I was able to obtain the information provided in chapter one, and which was the final link in the chain that allowed me to complete the manuscript.

Inevitably my research has unearthed more than I could contain within this book, and this has resulted in several incidental articles which flesh out data not covered in such detail here. These are listed in the bibliography at the back of the book. There will be other such articles: indeed, I feel I have more data than I could do justice to, even if I drew upon it for articles for the rest of my life!

If I were to list everyone who provided help or information on this project it would become an exhausting list. Yet I feel I cannot leave out those, whose kind words and share of memories added an extra dimension to the research in bringing the past back in to focus. Walt Dennis and Conrad H. Ruppert, for instance, responded to my letters of enquiry, with a wealth of material about their early days in fandom. It was a pleasure to contact Clifton Amsbury, one of the earliest correspondents to *Amazing Stories*, whose memories of those days were as clear as if they had happened yesterday. Will Murray was always able to provide some help and advice from his astonishing depth of knowledge on the pulp magazines. I only wish that, despite his help, we had been able to make contact with Desmond W. Hall, the one important name from the Gernsback days whom I was unable to trace. My thanks also to Arthur C. Clarke and Ray Russell who responded to my request in *Locus* with their personal anecdotes about Hugo Gernsback.

At the risk of an impersonalised and incomplete list, I must also thank the following, who provided helpful advice, guidance or information on various aspects of Gernsbackian history, not all of which I could use in this book, but which will certainly surface in some form or other. Thomas G. L. Cockcroft (for letting me tap his encyclopedic memory of the fantasy pulps), Arthur Jean Cox (with data on Charles Schneeman, Ross Rocklynne and Clifton B. Kruse), Elizabeth Starr Hill (with background on her father, Ray Cummings), Lloyd Arthur Eshbach (who made available much prime documentation now housed in the Temple University Libraries), J. Harvey Haggard, Ryerson Johnson (whose ever-youthful memories of the pulp days are always a delight to read), Neil R. Jones (whose bundle of correspondence with Gernsback, Lasser, Tremaine, and Hall, which he sent me in February 1980, was the first major step in making this book possible), Paul Spencer (who provided much helpful material on David H. Keller), Frank K. Kelly (whose memories helped provide a key to the past that had hitherto eluded me), David A. Kraft (for his help with Otis Adelbert Kline), David A. Kyle (whose memories clarified a mystery about the final issue of *Wonder Stories*), Dennis Lien (for his research into magazine circulation), Richard Lupoff (for his help, advice and wisdom), Sam Moskowitz (for his help, advice, wisdom and patience), Mary E. Drake (with helpful data on her brother, P. Schuyler Miller), Ross Rocklynne (for his memories of Charles R. Tanner), Alex Schomburg (for his memories of Gernsback from sixty-five years ago written in the most immaculate handwriting I have ever seen), Thomas Starzl (for details about his grandfather, R. F. Starzl), Henry Steeger (for memories about his early publishing experiences), and Richard P. Tooker (for memories from one of the longest careers in pulp fiction).

I cannot end, though, without again registering my thanks to Robert A. W. Lowndes. He maintained a faith in this project right from the start, even though at times it seemed to have faded away. Despite having originally completed his share of the work in 1985, he has been willing to revise it to fit in to my own whims, as my own section belatedly took shape. He also painstakingly read through my section in minute detail, offering much-welcome advice and criticism, and bringing a polish to it that I could not have achieved alone. Whilst we may have worked on our sections individually, the final product is a true collaboration of minds and intentions. I'm only too sorry that Bob died before the book finally appeared in print.

It's difficult to live with a project for so long, and not be prejudiced about the end result. Whilst it has been a pleasure to bring together so many memories and facts and weave them into a considered history, there was a greater pleasure in the contact that it brought me with so many wonderful people who helped shape the early days of science fiction; to be able to share their memories and to relive with them those amazing days of seventy years ago, was a real treasure and is what makes the pain and tiredness of research and writing all worth while.

Too many writers and editors from the Gernsback days have been unjustly neglected, or unfairly criticized. Now, I hope, Robert A. W. Lowndes and I have provided the grounds for a fair consideration of their efforts, and a true reconstruction of the development of science fiction. It's the closest to time travel you'll ever get. I hope you enjoy the trip.

Much has happened since I wrote those words twelve years ago. Sadly, Ted Dikty died in 1991 and the plans for the all-illustrated edition that he wanted collapsed. The project was taken on by Robert Reginald of Borgo Press and, after several years, he managed to get the book as far as the proof stage. However, after I had read and corrected the proofs and provided the index, Reginald decided to close down the operations of Borgo Press for personal reasons and *The Gernsback Days* was homeless again. Soon after Robert Lowndes died and I was very saddened that he was not able to see the final product to which he contributed to much. Soon after Charles Hornig also died.

During that period I was delighted to make contact with Patrick Merchant, the grandson of Gernsback, who was keen to revive interest in his grandfather's work. Amongst other activities he has established a Gernsback website at <www.twd.net/ird/forecast/index.html>.

Eventually this book was rescued by John Betancourt of Wildside Press. It meant I had to proof read the book again and provide a new index, but that was no bad thing as in the intervening years new research has brought further facts to light. I'm glad though that, even in the light of the remarkable volume *Science Fiction: The Gernsback Years* by Everett and Richard Bleiler, which clearly covers the same territory as this book, no one else during that time has duplicated what Lowndes and I intended here. This book still stands as the first thorough study and history of Gernsback's contribution to science fiction.

I shall say no more, but to bow my head to absent friends, especially all those who helped me with this project but who tragically did not live long enough to see its publication. This book now takes us beyond the realms of memory.

—Mike Ashley
Walderslade, England
May 2002

PART ONE

THE GERNSBACK DAYS

by

MIKE ASHLEY

1.

LUXEMBURG

Hugo Gernsbacher—to give Gernsback his filial name—was born in Luxemburg City on the night of Saturday, August 16, 1884. He was the third son born to Moritz and Bertha Gernsbacher who had moved to Luxemburg the previous year, on New Year's Day, 1883. This made Gernsback a Luxemburger by birth, though by descent he and his family were German Jews. The name Gernsbacher means "from Gernsbach," a village just four miles to the east of Baden-Baden in southern Germany. Moritz had been born at Buhl near Baden-Baden on November 8, 1845 whilst his wife, Bertha Durlacher, who was a native of Kippenheim, had been born on January 23, 1851.

Baden was a rich part of Germany and Moritz had become a prosperous wine merchant. His first son, Saly (later better known as Sidney) was born on May 17, 1876 and a second son, Eugene, on December 11, 1877. Moritz was also caring for his nephew, Willy, who had been born in 1871, so the infant Hugo grew up with a trio of elder boys.

It is believed that Moritz had moved to Luxemburg to take advantage of the tax and wine-duty concessions granted to the Duchy under the German free trade network, the Zollverein. These concessions, which also covered the Grandy Duchy of Baden were expanding through the rest of the German *landen* but their benefits were countered there by other tariffs and reforms being implemented by Bismarck. There was also continuing religious and political unrest, especially with the rapid rise of socialism in the new German Empire so Moritz would have found it financially and socially to his advantage to move to the independent Grand Duchy of Luxemburg. Moreover, since the Treaty of London in 1867, Luxemburg had been declared a neutral territory thus making it a safer haven generally to the Gernsbachers.

The move would certainly have been financially rewarding. The family were sufficiently wealthy for young Hugo to be educated by private tutors. The only problem was that the infant remained stubbornly bald. Moritz traveled throughout Europe with Hugo seeking some medication to encourage the hair's growth. Eventually the hair started to grow of its own accord when Hugo reached the age of five.

A blow hit the family when Eugene died on May 14, 1891 aged thirteen. Although nearly seven years older than Hugo he was the closest to him in age and the child, still only six, must have missed his elder brother profoundly. The eldest son, Saly, was now fifteen and old enough to help his father in the wine business, so Hugo was left to his own devices.

The thrills of discovery began on Hugo's eighth birthday, in 1892, when his father's superintendent, Jean Pierre Gögen, gave Hugo a Leclanche wet battery, a piece of wire and an electric bell. Hugo learned how to hook them up and the resultant delight when the bell rang seemed to convince him that here was a subject worthy of investigation. He purchased battery-actuated telephones and light bulbs from Paris and shortly set about electrifying the new home to which the Gernsbacher's had moved in September 1891. With this achieved he undertook other jobs in the area so that by the time he was twelve he had already undertaken a number of local contracts.

The Gernsbachers lived next door to a Carmelite convent and the mother superior was happy for young Hugo to install a set of electrical call bells and intercoms in the building. By the time the equipment was ready to install Hugo had passed his thirteenth birthday and having entered puberty he was barred from the convent. The mother superior had to seek special dispensation from the Pope to allow Hugo to carry out the work.

Such was Hugo's youthful precocity that he was soon earning his own finances without his father's help. The profundity of riches had its inevitable effects on the boy who, with little regard for the scarcity of money, was drawn to gambling at the poker tables in Luxemburg's Grand Cafe where he invariably lost to his elders. Nevertheless Hugo usually recovered his costs with a new contract so that at an early age Hugo had acquired little respect for money. As with any one born to riches, he acquired an "easy-come, easy-go" attitude, which would have been almost in-bred, to the extent that he probably had little concept that others could not also acquire or earn finances as easily as he. In later years he admitted that he had long believed that "nothing could be easier than becoming a millionaire many times over."[1] It was an attitude that we shall return to again and which, as we shall see, not only strongly influenced his life, but also the attitude of others to him.

As his electrical contracting work grew, another influence entered his life. In 1894 he read about Perceval Lowell and his belief that there was life on Mars.[2] This idea fascinated him and it drew him to other such speculative fiction, especially the works of Jules Verne and H. G. Wells, plus the American dime novels by "Noname"—Luis Senarens. He became a voracious reader of the as yet unnamed field of science fiction and of boys' adventure stories. He greatly enjoyed the writings of Mark Twain. He wrote stories of his own, with no eye to having them published, but solely to express his innermost ideas and feelings. With no brother or school friends of his own age with whom to share his adventurous thoughts, writing was the only means of escape for his wild imaginings, but it also meant there was little control over it. By the time he was seventeen he had completed a novel entitled *Ein Pechvogel*. It remains unpublished to this day. It's not science fiction (though it does include an interesting episode using solar energy to roast coffee), but a humorous tale of a hapless youth whose best efforts usually lead him into trouble. That Gernsback had persisted with this story through sixty-thousand words demonstrates that he had a firm desire to write.[3]

At that time, however, he did not pursue the hobby. Instead, the combination of an exuberant imagination and a strong fascination for science had produced the writer's counterpart—an inventor. An example of his resourceful mind was recalled in an editorial he wrote for the *Electrical Experimenter* where he was exhorting his readers to learn about practical science, as it might help them in their everyday lives. He cited an incident that happened to him as a boy, when, one winter's day, he went into an unoccupied cellar some distance from the house. The wind blew the cellar door shut, locking him in. The only other exit was an open window barred with stout iron rods through which he could not squeeze, but which allowed the icy sub-zero wind to blow through. With his parents away and the caretaker off for the night, Hugo was faced with the prospect of freezing to death unless he acted swiftly.

The cellar was empty save for a few wooden crates. He had no tools or matches with him, only a portable light with two dry-cell batteries which he had brought along to light his way. So what did he do? Gernsback explains:

> [I] unravelled the stranded electric cord and extracted a single thin copper strand an inch long. With this [I] short-circuited the dry cells. The wire became white hot. A piece of paper was touched to it which burst into flame; a broken piece of crate wood was ignited by the flame and a fire soon roared. A burning crate set the cellar door on fire, and in ten minutes the adventure had come to a close.[4]

His scientific awareness had probably saved his life—though he didn't go on to explain how the fire was put out.

Whilst his education continued—first at the Limpertsberg Industrial School, then at a boarding school in Brussels to improve his languages (he became proficient in French, German and English), and finally at the Technikum in Bingen, Germany, where he studied mathematics and electrical engineering from 1900-1903—Hugo would tinker with new ideas and concepts in his spare time. He succeeded in inventing what he regarded as "the most powerful dry cell battery in the world,"[5] which produced a current of 375 amps capable of melting a piece of metal as thick as a pencil. He sought patents in both France and Germany without success and believing that the future for young men of science was not in Europe but in the United States, he turned his sights westward.

Hugo completed his studies at Bingen in the summer of 1903. On August 3rd of that year his father died at the age of 57. There was now less to keep Hugo in Luxemburg, with Saly and Willy running the wine business. So, Hugo borrowed $100 from the family fortune, purchased a first-class ticket on the liner *Pennsylvania* sailing from Hamburg to Hoboken, and in February 1904 arrived in New York to seek his fortune. The future was his.

His background and upbringing in Luxemburg had given him a strong streak of independence, a scant regard for money, a fertile and inventive imagination, mechanical and technical skills and a determination to succeed.

2.

TELIMCO

Gernsback was so positive about his success, when he arrived in New York, that he spent twenty of his hundred dollars on a silk hat, as a top priority. He secured lodgings on West 14th Street and proceeded to set about marketing his battery. He rapidly learned, however, that although his layer battery could produce more power than other batteries it would also cost ten times as much to produce. Nothing daunted, he took a job with a storage-battery manufacturer and developed a cheaper, lighter and stronger battery case than hitherto available. Unfortunately he did not sufficiently test it for resistance to corrosion and consequently, as the newly sold batteries started to leak, they were returned by dealers.

His youthful "easy-come, easy-go" attitude, however, buoyed him along. According to Sam Moskowitz,[1] Gernsback now sold his services to William Roche as head of research in the production of dry cell batteries. Due to a misunderstanding, though, Gernsback was fired after only a few hours in the belief that he was spying on behalf of a rival firm. Never discouraged, Gernsback formed the GeeCee Dry Battery Company in partnership with an acquaintance and established a lucrative contract selling the batteries to the Packard Motor Car Company. Despite the apparent success of the venture, the flow of money was tight until Gernsback discovered that his partner was intercepting the checks.

Others might wilt in the face of this adversity, but it strengthened Gernsback's resolve. He recovered the money from his partner's millionaire father and invested it in a new business, manufacturing and supplying batteries to a distributing company for motor-car equipment. It operated from out of West 3rd Street. This venture was successful for a couple of years until the depression of 1907 led to the loss of a contract with Packard's and Gernsback's company had to be dissolved.

One might think Gernsback would have had little time for any other activities whilst trying to establish his battery business, but in fact this was only one string in his bow. Before emigrating to New York he had been working on a small portable radio transmitter-and-receiving outfit but it was taking some while to perfect and make marketable. Once in New York, he found that many of the radio parts were not available so, in partnership with fellow-boarder, telegraph operator Lewis Coggeshall, he established The Electro Importing Company to import and distribute scientific equipment from Europe, especially Germany.

With the necessary equipment to hand, Gernsback was able to work upon his portable radio set. He made a breakthrough in 1905 with a new interrupter for the induction coil. He wrote a short piece about this for the *Scientific American* and it appeared under the title "New Interrupter" in its issue for July 29, 1905 with the by-line "Huck" Gernsback. He had adopted the name Huck because of his fondness for Mark Twain's Huckleberry Finn stories. This was Gernsback's first appearance in print, a few weeks short of his twenty-first birthday. It demonstrated Gernsback's drive to publicise his activities and to promote scientific advances. This was not just the path to his future, but also the method by which he became a local celebrity, with his activities frequently reported in the New York press.

His first big opportunity came a few months later. He had now perfected his portable home radio, calling it the "Telimco" wireless telegraph—a name devised from the initials of The Electro Importing Company. Inclusion of the equipment in Gernsback's own company catalogue brought little response, so an advertisement was placed in the *Scientific American* for January 13, 1906, and the corresponding issue of *Youth's Companion*, selling the item for $7.50. This brought in a flood of orders from major department stores, including Gimbel's and Macy's, and from F.A.O. Schwarz, the country's largest toy shop. There were, though, some sceptical readers, one of whom was incredulous that a radio transmitter, which normally costs fifty-thousand dollars to build, could be marketed for $7.50. He sent a copy of the advertisement to New York's Mayor Gaynor, and shortly a policeman arrived at Gernsback's premises, at 32 Park Place. A demonstration was necessary but the officer, who could perceive nothing fraudulent, was still unconvinced. "I still think yez are fakers," he was reported as saying. "Your ad here sez it is a wire*less* set, so what are all dem here wires for?"[2]

Gernsback remembered the incident fifty years later when he gave an address to a joint meeting of the Michigan Institute of Radio Engineers and the American Radio Relay League at the Henry Ford Museum in Dearborn, Michigan where a replica of the original set is now on display. But he recalled it as more than just an amusing anecdote. It had made a powerful impression on him.

> It rankled me that there could be such ignorance in regard to science and I vowed to change the situation if I could. A few years later, in 1908, I turned publisher and brought out the world's first radio magazine, *Modern Electrics*, to teach the young generation science, radio and what was ahead for them. I've been at it ever since.[3]

Whoever that nameless sceptic was who alerted Mayor Gaynor to Gernsback's activities, he should be thanked. He created a turning point—or a "Jonbar hinge," in Jack Williamson's terminology—not just in Gernsback's life, but in the history of scientific development, and in fantastic literature. For it set Gernsback along the road of popularising science which led, in turn, to the birth of science fiction.

But that was still a few years away. In the meantime with the success of his portable home radio Gernsback was able to expand his premises, importing and supplying radio parts at his Electro Importing Company in Park Place and manufacturing and selling electrical toys at a separate establishment in Warren Street. It meant that when the GeeCee Battery company failed in 1907 he had more than enough to occupy himself. Indeed his offices expanded rapidly moving to West Broadway in 1908 and to Fulton Street in 1910 where his factory employed sixty workmen. If he was not a millionaire by then, he was certainly rich, living expensively in New York, dining at Delmonico's and seeing Victor Herbert musicals. He must have been a man of standing and charisma almost from the start to establish himself so rapidly in a foreign land, and this must have reflected upon his social life. He courted the ladies and, in 1906, he married Rose Harvey. In 1909, Gernsback was granted American citizenship. By 1911 he was established as a successful entrepreneur on the New York scene, and the next chapter in his life and in the dawn of science fiction was about to unfold.

3

MODERN ELECTRICS

When the Electro Importing Company had been founded in 1905 Gernsback had issued a catalogue of his products. This developed into the first radio catalogue in history and gave Gernsback experience of the publishing world. Once he became enthused by the zeal of converting the masses to the wonders of science he decided to issue a regular magazine. It was called *Modern Electrics* and the first issue, dated April 1908, went on sale in the last week in March. It was published by Modern Electrics Publications, a subsidiary of the E.I. Co., and was edited at the offices at 87 Warren Street though, with the expansion of the firm, the second and subsequent issues were edited from new offices at 84 West Broadway.

Although printed on quality stock, the first issue was a relatively modest publication, measuring 6 x 9.5 inches with thirty-six pages and selling for ten cents. The cover design by Lewis Coggeshall, depicting advances in science, remained standard on the first twelve issues, although the deep red cover was converted to yellow from the second.

Its lead article was "Wireless Telegraphy" by William Maver, Jr. Maver (1851-1928) was an accomplished electrical engineer and a noted scientific writer of the day having written one of the first articles about television, "Seeing by Electricity" (*Cassier's Magazine*, October 1906). Gernsback contributed two about his main areas of interest. One was "How to Make a 'Dry' Storage Battery from a 'Wet' One"; the other, "The Talking Gloves," under the transparent alias of M. G. Hugo, was linked to one of his novelty toys.

Of most significance in this first issue is Gernsback's editorial which established the basics for what would remain Gernsback's publishing practices. For a start the editorial is entitled "To Our Friends," where he pays thanks to his supporters. These supporters were the advance subscribers. Gernsback reported:

> It is uncommon and we believe it to be the first case on record that a new magazine starts out with an actual *paid-up* subscription of several thousand copies. This subscription was obtained solely by writing letters to persons whom we felt sure would believe in us sufficiently to order their subscription in advance for a magazine of which they had never heard, nor thought of.[1]

As we shall encounter with later publications, Gernsback had sounded out his potential readership first, seeking not only advance subscriptions but information on what they wanted. He had worked on the magazine for at least a year having satisfied himself that there was no equivalent periodical in the field. It was aimed primarily at the hobbyist—"the amateur electrician and electrical experimenter,"[2] as Gernsback referred to them; in other words the practician rather than theoretician. This is an interesting distinction because one might feel, from Gernsback's subsequent promotion of science fiction, that he would have marketed his publication to the creative rather than practical mind. But Gernsback's own research would have established that there was a much greater market amongst the practitioner who was anxious to find the latest news on his hobby, than from the theoretical scientist—there is never so much fervor than that of a newly converted amateur fan. Moreover, Gernsback could provide the vision in the magazine himself. It was the practitioner who would carry it out. Gernsback was keen to educate, and the most attentive pupil is the one who can reach out for his own success and grasp it. Just as we shall see later in the science-fiction world, Gernsback attracted the fan, anxious to achieve something in the world of scientific advance.

From the start Gernsback began to offer prizes for submissions. Initially it was for photographs of laboratories and experimental workshops. The best photograph received each month would be awarded a prize of three dollars [a fair sum, the equal of $60 today]. A similar contest was announced for amateur wireless stations. The contest was a standard part of Gernsback's publishing tactics and one that he would milk at every opportunity.

Finally, although Gernsback did not specify the age range at which *Modern Electrics* was aimed—and to some extent it was aimed at everybody— it was evident from the phrases used throughout that he was encouraging the young in particular. Throughout the editorial and elsewhere in the issue, Gernsback referred to "our young experimenters" or "many young men," and made a specific reference to a group of four boys in Massachusetts who had established their own wireless communication network. From the evidence of his mailing list and of visitors to his premises it must have been clear that the most ardent enthusiasts were the young, eager to learn what marvels the new sciences were bringing, whereas the old were perhaps a little too set in their ways. By encouraging the young, Gernsback was more likely to reap results.

Additionally, *Modern Electrics* carried a feature which appeared in all Gernsback's later magazines, a question and answer column, which covered all topics "pertaining to the electrical arts." There were plenty of news fillers and humorous space fillers, including one signed by Gernsback's alias, "Fips," a name which later expanded into "Mohammed Ulysses Fips," the Office Boy, which allowed Gernsback to indulge in his delectation for humorous or spoof items. It gave Gernsback a cover for disguising some of his more "impossible" predictions, primarily because there were many who thought Gernsback a crank and it was easier to put over a radical idea in a humorous way. "Fips" would always be somewhere during the next sixty years!

There was one item not in the issue that might otherwise have made headlines. Gernsback refers to a promised article on "The Telefot" *[sic]*, which had not been completed due to illness. The article was never published and we are not told whom the author was. It would be over a year before Gernsback's own contribution to television literature appeared.

Modern Electrics was an instant success. The first issue of 8,000 copies sold out, as did the second issue of 10,000 copies. Circulation rose from 18,000 in the first year, to 30,000 after two years and 52,000 by the third. Gernsback was soon consorting with the big names. He was delighted to receive a letter of well-wishes from Thomas Edison, whilst the second issue carried a feature by no less than Guglielmo Marconi on "Wireless Telegraph Oddities."

The success may have been Gernsback's own, but he was assisted by a number of colleagues who would stay with him through the years. In addition to his original partner, Lewis Coggeshall, there were two mainstays: Harold Winfield Secor, a twenty-year-old radio enthusiast, who worked for the E.I. Company, and Austin C. Lescarboura, only seventeen, but who had been appointed as Office Manager of E.I. in 1908. Secor became the magazine's Associate Editor and Lescarboura his assistant. Both wrote extensively for the magazine, Lescarboura more frequently under the alias of A. C. Austin. It is difficult to know how many other pen names were used between the three but it is evident that initially Gernsback, Secor, and Lescarboura provided most of the copy.

The detailed contents of *Modern Electrics* do not concern us greatly in this history, but there are three aspects which are worth more than a passing reference.

The first relates to Gernsback's own speculative articles. Gernsback's greatest skill was in taking the merest crumb of an idea and developing it into a multi-dimensional concept. One of his first was "Harnessing the Ocean," in the December 1908 issue, where he considers the potential of harnessing tidal power. In that same issue he brought his speculative talents into line with his delight for humorous spoofs by introducing a new feature called "The Wireless Screech" run by the pseudonymous alter-ego, "Fips." The first column included "Wireless on Saturn," with Gernsback broadening his reader's horizons beyond that of the Earth. By the February 1909 issue the column had expanded to a page and a half with "Wireless on Mars" introducing some inventive ideas on matter transmission for "conveying food through the ether."

Perhaps the most significant of Gernsback's early articles appeared in the December 1909 issue: "Television and the Telephot." Gernsback explained in simple terms the principle of television and put forward his own contribution on how television might be realized. He called his own technique the "light-relay," but he considered the device "too complicated for general use," so he did not patent it. This method, though, was more akin to the way television works now than the scanning-disc system which John Logie Baird promoted and which caused him to be recognized as the inventor of television.

The real origins of television and the true nature of its inventor is wrapped within a complicated web of scientific development. Gernsback's role in this development, and more significantly its popularization, has hitherto been understated. As we shall see in chapter sixteen, he played a considerable role in the promotion of television. It is unfortunate, therefore, that we have to dispell one myth. Gernsback has been attributed with coining the word "television" or at least introducing it to the American readership. He himself rightly denied this. So far as I know, the concept of television was first used by the extraordinary French writer and illustrator Albert Robida (1848-1926), who even coined the abbreviation "le télé"! His books are a catalogue of inventions and predictions. His ideas of television and the videophone first appeared in his fifty-issue part-work *Le vingtième siècle* which was published during 1882, and Gernsback was almost certainly familiar with this in his youth. Nevertheless the word "television" was not well known to American readers, although it had been used in one of Gernsback's news items in the November 1909 *Modern Electrics* where he reports on developments in Germany by Professor Ruhmer to develop television based on the principle of the selenium cell. But Gernsback was not the first to introduce it to American readers. To my knowledge, the first time the word "television" appeared in an American publication was in a piece entitled "Problem of Tele-Vision" by Max Dieckmann reprinted in the September 19, 1908 issue of the *Scientific American Supplement*, three months ahead of Gernsback's otherwise historic article. What Gernsback did was to promote the term television, and it is quite probable that through his own constant use of the word in *Modern Electrics* and his subsequent publications that it became the accepted name.

The second area of significance at this time was in Gernsback's work to protect the wireless amateur. It began with the establishment of the Wireless Association of America in January 1909. Gernsback was championing the amateur, and the concept behind the W.A.O.A. was to provide a cohesion to the many thousand of small wireless clubs that had become established across America. "The greatest aim of the Wireless Association of America," Gernsback reported, "is to bring young experimenters together—not in clubs, but in practical work."[3] It was a form of galvanizing the scientific youth of America and uniting them in a common goal. (It is against this perspective that we see the formation of the Science Fiction League in 1934 as a natural development.) It was all part of Gernsback's desire to provoke the young into exploring the possibilities of science and primarily the fun and practicality of wireless. The Association struck a responsive chord. Over 3,200 applications for membership were received during the first month. It had some 10,000 members by October 1910. There were no membership dues. A membership button was mailed to all applicants, and *Modern Electrics* was treated as the association's official organ. Gernsback can not be accused of trying to make a "quick buck" out of the wireless amateur. On the contrary, it must have caused him and the company considerable expense in both time and money, but it was no doubt seen as an investment in encouraging the wider promotion of wireless. The Association had a Board of Directors with Dr. Lee De Forest as President; John S. Stone, Vice President; William Maver, Jr., Secretary, and Hugo Gernsback, Chairman and Business Manager.

In addition to its organizational intentions, the Association provided a formidable platform of strength to tackle the political issues that were arising related to wireless broadcasting. During the years leading up to the formation of the W.A.O.A., the papers had reported regularly on radio amateurs who through their pranks and jokes had caused considerable confusion to the authorities and to government and commercial stations by broadcasting on shared wavelengths. In effect the prankster had become sufficient a nuisance that the Government was considering either licensing the wireless amateurs or banning them altogether. It became Gernsback's crusade to defend the amateur. He publicly attacked proposals to legislate against the wireless amateur starting with the Roberts Bill, introduced at the end of 1909. Roberts proposed that a wireless telegraph board be created which would regulate and control, by license, all wireless stations. Gernsback declared his opposition to the Bill and published a short but revealing announcement about the W.A.O.A.:

> The Wireless Association of America was founded solely to advance wireless. IT IS NOT A MONEY MAKING

ORGANIZATION. Congress threatens to pass a law to license all wireless stations. The W.A.O.A. already has over 3,000 members—the largest wireless organization in the world. When the time for action arrives, the thousands of members will exert a powerful pressure to oppose the "wireless license" bill. This is *one* of the purposes of the W.A.O.A. There are more.[4]

It reads almost like a threat, but demonstrates that Gernsback had a considerable weight behind him, through the power of the organization, to act as a lobby for amending legislative proposals. It was, after all, in Gernsback's interest, since his fortune and future were deeply entwined with the fate of the wireless amateur.

The Roberts Bill foundered, but other senators promptly brought forth their proposals. To each in turn Gernsback added his opposition. Reporting on the situation, Gernsback observed: "*Modern Electrics* was the only publication that opposed wireless legislation in Washington during 1910, and the fact that no bills have been passed, nor will be passed, at least not for a year to come, must be credited solely to the efforts of *Modern Electrics*."[5]

Bills continued to be introduced, few of which had any merit in Gernsback's eyes, until the appearance of the Alexander Wireless Bill which was laid before the House of Representatives on December 11, 1911. Gernsback felt that this Bill had possibilities and would work with only some slight amendment. To this end Gernsback made his own proposals which were laid down in his editorial in the February 1912 *Modern Electrics* and in a follow-on article, "Limited Wave Lengths," in the March issue. The proposals were straightforward:

> There should be a bill passed restraining the amateur from using too much power, say, anything above 1 kw. The wavelength of the amateur wireless station should also be regulated in order that only wavelengths from a few meters up to 200 could be used. Wavelengths of from 200 to 1000 meters, the amateurs should not be allowed to use, but they could use any wavelength above 1000. If this is done all interference with Government, as well as commercial stations, will be done away with . . .[6]

These proposals were incorporated almost without change in America's first radio law, the Wireless Act of 1912, which came into force on November 17th 1912. Gernsback received scant credit for his labors at the time, yet there is little doubt that Gernsback could rightly claim to be the Guardian Angel of Amateur Radio in America, as he literally saved the wireless amateur from extinction.

The third area of significance in *Modern Electrics* is of such importance that it requires a chapter to itself. It was, quite simply, the birth of scientific fiction.

4.

RALPH 124C 41+

One could be excused for thinking that Gernsback had enough to keep himself occupied with the business of running the Electro-Importing Company, organizing the Wireless Association of America, publishing and editing *Modern Electrics*, and continuing to experiment and invent in all fields of scientific endeavor, let alone the more mundane world of being a husband and father. Yet, throughout all this period, he continued to write. Not only did he contribute his articles and columns to *Modern Electrics*, he wrote a booklet on the *Wireless Telephone*, which his company published in June 1910; he assembled a volume on *How to Make Wireless Instruments*, with contributions by twenty wireless experts, which was issued in April 1910; and he compiled a large collection of wireless telegraph and telephone diagrams for the wireless experimenter, *Wireless Hook-Ups*, which was published in June 1911. In addition, Gernsback announced in the January 1911 *Modern Electrics* that he had secured the American rights to the landmark German volume, *Der Praktische Elektriker* (or *The Practical Electrician*) by Professor Weiler of the University of Esslingen. This book ran to over 700 pages and Gernsback stated that he would "personally . . . translate the entire book." He added: "Inasmuch as the book is quite large, it will take in all probability, from one to one-and-a-half years' time to finish the entire work . . ."[1]

Somehow, during all of this intense activity, Gernsback found time to write his pioneer work of science fiction, *Ralph 124C 41+*. According to Sam Moskowitz, Gernsback found himself a few pages short of material for the April 1911 issue of *Modern Electrics* and so dashed off the first installment of what was to become a twelve-part serial. This may be the circumstances as related to Moskowitz by Gernsback, but it is unlikely he wrote the first episode on the spur of the moment. If proof were necessary it was that the story was not only mentioned on the cover, it was specifically illustrated there, the first time one of the magazine's contents had been so depicted. Since all previous covers had been based on a standard design it would have taken time for a new cover to have been conceived, illustrated and processed, and in all likelihood the story, or certainly the first episode, must have been planned some time ahead. Furthermore the scientific content and detail in the first episode, indeed in all of the installments, were such that it is unlikely, though not impossible, that Gernsback wrote it on impulse. It is far more likely that the story had been in Gernsback's mind for some while, and that he took the opportunity to write the first installment at the earliest occasion in order to express some ideas that had been prevalent in his mind. As final proof against its spontanaiety, the first installment is preceded by a statement to the effect that "this story . . . will run serially during the coming year. . . ." This demonstrates that the story was already planned as a serial of some length and not a spur of the moment impulse.

The introductory statement is interesting for another feature. In addition to advising the reader that the purpose of the story is to give "as accurate a prophecy of the future as is consistent with the present marvellous growth of science . . ." it adds that "the author wishes to call especial attention to the fact that while there may be extremely strange and improbable devices and scenes in this narrative, they are not at all impossible, or outside the reach of science."

This is almost identical to the wording Gernsback would use later in his blurbs to stories in *Amazing Stories*. Indeed, in his editorial, "Fiction versus Facts" in the July 1926 *Amazing* (an editorial of such importance that I shall return to it later), Gernsback states that ". . . we try to impress our friends with the fact that whatever is printed in *Amazing Stories* is not necessarily pure fiction, but could or can be fact." He added that, ". . . our editorial policy is built upon this structure and will be so continued indefinitely."

The "structure," or policy, is so simple that it can be easily overlooked, but to be science fiction a story had to be scientifically possible either now—if someone set his mind to it—or at some stage in the future. *Ralph 124C 41+* was written on exactly that premise, which justified its inclusion in *Modern Electrics*. It was there, in other words, to inspire the hobbyist into visualizing the application of scientific possibilities, and to work as a further goad to scientific achievement.

The story was really an excuse for a parade of inventions, and the fertility of Gernsback's mind, in this respect, was nothing less than awesome. Set in the year 2660, the opening episode is rather brief, and merely depicts an incident in a day of Ralph 124C 41+, one of only ten super-scientists in the world, hence the "+." Ralph is talking on the telephot to a man called Edward—the scene portrayed on the cover—when the conversation is interrupted by a cross-line from an attractive girl calling from Switzerland. This girl is Alice 212B 423 who is talking in French, so Ralph adjusts his receiver's language rectifier. Upon discovering whom she is talking to, Alice asks for Ralph's autograph, which he sends to her via the teleautograph attached to his telephot.

That is the sum total of the first episode. As a story it is nothing, but as a portrayal of the potential of the wireless telephone and the telephot, it was considerable. Much of Gernsback's recent writings had been on that subject and there can be little doubt that *Ralph 124C 41+* was a natural outgrowth of Gernsback's desires to become even more daring in his speculations on the possibilities of wireless. In an article the predictions might have been ridiculed, but dressed as a story, they could be seen as harmless entertainment. It was Gernsback's belief that the story would not just be entertaining but educational and better still inspiring. If by presenting a scientific possibility he could inspire someone to seek to invent it, then he would have achieved his prime purpose, which was to educate and stimulate.

In subsequent episodes Gernsback built on the story-line, but developed even more strongly the scope of his vision of scientific advance. In part two, for instance, we learn that Alice is stranded in Switzerland in a storm. Suddenly an avalanche starts which threatens her home. Ralph directs her to make some amendments to her radio mast and he then beams a surge of electrical power from New York to Switzerland which melts the avalanche.

In episode three we get a glimpse of New York, the sky a-buzz with aeroflyers and air liners. Ralph's house was a "round tower, six hundred and fifty feet high and thirty feet in diameter, built entirely of crystal glass-bricks and steelonium."[2] The top of the tower housed Ralph's research laboratory. There's even a brief character study of Ralph, as, with some introspection, we learn that he was just a tool to advance science and was not a free man. We also learn that there is still crime in New York in 2660, and that people smoke and enjoy "little vices." The news of Ralph's exploit in saving Alice has spread across the world and people are clamoring to congratulate him. The walls in his transmission room are covered with telephot-screens by which the public have direct access to him. After his ovation, Ralph relaxes with a microfiched edition of the *New York News* projected on a screen. He then writes a lecture by means of his "menograph" or mind writer, which reads his thought waves and transcribes them on tape. Finally Ralph goes to bed and is connected to the "hypnobioscope," a machine which will transmit impulses direct to the brain whilst asleep. In this instance the machine is loaded with a film-tape of the *Odyssey* which enables Ralph to dream those adventures. The "hypnobioscope" was one of Gernsback's patented inventions, and one he was most proud of. It was subsequently developed into the "learn-while-you-sleep" process whereby students are played educational tapes in their sleep. In 1923 Gernsback was delighted to learn from Chief Radioman J. A. Phinney of the U.S. Naval Training School in Pensacola, Florida, as to how he had applied Gernsback's principles in teaching his students morse code in their sleep. Students learned faster and more accurately by this method than by any other.

Every episode of *Ralph 124C 41+* was illustrated on the cover. Initially the artist was not credited though the style suggests it was George Westcott who had produced some of the earlier stylized covers. These early covers simply depicted an invention or a scene from the story and had none of that spark of wonder that symbolized so many later science-fiction covers. One cover, portraying Alice 212B 423 was signed by E. R. Weadon, who may also have drawn the picture of Ralph on the November 1911 issue, but these lacked much in both the artistic and visionary context. Later covers, signed by Thomas N. Wrenn, did have some vestige of vision about them.

There is little point in dwelling in detail on every episode of *Ralph 124C 41+*, since each only reinforces Gernsback's intent to educate and stimulate. The story is primarily and deliberately a sequence of inventions threaded into a narrative. The human element was necessarily incidental because, for the purpose of inspiring the readers it was irrelevant. It served only to move the story along. Gernsback did introduce a romantic plot as Ralph falls in love with Alice who is kidnapped by a fellow Earthman only to be captured in turn by a Martian. Ralph rescues her but finds her dead, and brings her back to life with another of his inventions.

The most remarkable element in *Ralph* was Gernsback's prediction of radar. It occurs in the issue for December 1911, where Ralph's spaceflyer is pursuing the Martian kidnappers. Not only does he describe its operation in detail, he provides a diagram which shows accurately how it would work. The word radar did not come into existence until 1935 when Robert Watson-Watt perfected the method of tracking an airplane by the reflection of short-waves. It was radar that helped Britain win the Battle of Britain in 1941 by detecting the approach of the enemy aircraft. For his invention of radar Watson-Watt was knighted, and no credit passed to Gernsback. Gernsback's prediction was eventually shown to Watson-Watt and thereafter he always maintained

Gernsback was the true inventor of radar.

The readership's reaction to *Ralph* was encouraging. They had obviously enjoyed the speculative nature of the entertainment and found it more palatable than some of the more serious articles. Gernsback consequently encouraged others to contribute similar extrapolative features. The first to respond was Jacque Morgan[3]. I have been unable to find out much about Morgan. He had contributed some nonfiction pieces to *Modern Electrics*, and their style and subject matter suggest a young man with an inventor's zeal. Certainly that zeal was evident in his light-hearted stories which formed a series called "The Scientific Adventures of Mr. Fosdick." They began in the October 1912 issue with "The Feline Light and Power Company is Organized." Here we are introduced to the small-town misguided inventor Jason Quincy Fosdick, tinsmith, key-fitter, and scissors-grinder. All of Fosdick's previous inventions had misfired, though they had proved of some value: a corkscrew had become a hairpin, a pump had become a churn and a curling iron found better service as a nutcracker. In this episode Fosdick considers the potential of static electricity and sets up a plant whereby electricity is generated by a room full of fighting cats. Unfortunately when Fosdick and his partner come to discharge the electricity they find themselves charged with millions of volts and are only saved from death by being placed on insulated stools. The story was written in a humorous style, which helped to convey to readers details about static electricity and the dangers of experimentation in a digestible and informative way. The remaining four stories in the series were in the same vein.

The Mr. Fosdick stories were more competently written than Gernsback's *Ralph 124C 41+*, and were consequently more readable. There is an interesting distinction between the stories. Even though both concentrated on inventions and were clearly designed to inform and educate, Gernsback's was aimed far more at stimulating and inspiring. Morgan's, on the other hand, could almost be viewed as warning people from dabbling in something beyond their experience and understanding. The Fosdick stories were set in the present day of 1912 and considered a feasible invention based on current scientific knowledge. As such they were not in the same vein of science fiction as *Ralph 124C 41+*. They were not speculative. They were, in fact, typical of a long line of stories about inventions that had been evident in the popular magazines for many years.

When one considers the evolution of scientific fiction, as distinct from the utopia story or the lost race adventure, it is closely linked with the experimenter and an adventure related to a new invention. Many of Jules Verne's novels, for example, were linked directly to new inventions such as the submarine *Nautilus* in *Twenty Thousand Leagues Under the Seas* (1873) and the flying machine *Albatross* in *Robur the Conqueror* (1886). Likewise, the American Jules Verne, Luis P. Senarens, had been writing a long series of dime novels featuring the boy inventor Frank Reade, Jr. since 1879. Within ten years the invention theme in dime novels had become so dominant and well known that it was parodied in a comic story "Bulger Boom, the Inventor" by Peter Pad (1889). The turn of the century brought a host of humorous prognostications about the coming years. In Britain the best known of these were by cartoonist William Heath Robinson (1872-1944), who in scores of popular magazines illustrated spoof inventions, the majority intended as labor-saving devices. In America the pulp magazine *Argosy* featured a couple of such series. Humorist Edgar Franklin contributed stories about eccentric inventor Hawkins, usually dealing with varieties of transport, starting with "The Hawkins Horse-Brake" (May 1903), whilst Howard R. Garis began a shorter series about Professor Jonkins and his creations starting with "Professor Jonkins' Cannibal Plant" (August 1905).

Verne wrote two shorter pieces which may seem direct precursors to what Gernsback was now publishing. "In the Year 2889" (1889) was a catalogue of inventions in America a millennium hence, and was not unlike the fifth episode of *Ralph 124C 41+* where Ralph takes Alice on a sight-seeing tour of New York in 2660 AD. An earlier tale, "Dr. Ox's Experiment" (1872), was an example of the humorous invention story where everything goes wrong, as in Morgan's stories of Mr Fosdick. In Verne's story Dr. Ox sets out to provide street lighting for the town of Quiquendone in Flanders with his newly developed oxyhydric gas, but he feeds pure oxygen into the town instead. As everyone breathes it they become overexcited and trouble follows.

All of this establishes a firm pedigree for the type of fiction Gernsback was publishing. It was not his own creation. Indeed, the wonder of science was being perceived everywhere and Gernsback was starting to mine what was a prosperous vein. The difference in Gernsback's case, though, was that whereas Verne, Senarens, Franklin, and Garis had written solely to entertain, and in Robinson's case ridicule, Gernsback was endeavoring primarily to educate and to stimulate potential inventors into creative action. It was a distinction that also lead to a dilemma as scientific fiction evolved in Gernsback's magazines. If the entertainment value was paramount, then any educational element was secondary and there was a need for the story to be well written and well plotted. If the educational value was uppermost then the writing and characterization could take second place. We shall see how this dilemma affected the future of Gernsback's science fiction.

Gernsback's publishing activities had grown rapidly during 1910. The expansion of the circulation of *Modern Electrics* brought with it greater scope for advertisers with their crucial income to the magazine, and Gernsback found himself increasingly tied up with the advertising department. In August 1911 he took on Orland J. Ridenour as Business Manager in the newly incorporated Modern Publishing Company. Ridenour also became Vice-President and Treasurer of the Company. The first noticeable effect of Ridenour's presence was the expansion of advertising in the magazine to the extent that Gernsback found himself subsequently having to defend its presence as the magazine's major means of financial support. Readers, nevertheless, still objected on the basis that advertising was taking up valuable space. By April 1912 the magazine had increased from 64 to 112 pages of which forty were devoted to advertising.

Just what happened then is uncertain. It could be that Gernsback and Ridenour disagreed over the way to manage the magazine, or that Gernsback wanted to develop the publication in a new direction. Whatever the circumstances, Gernsback sold the magazine to the publisher of *Electrician and Mechanic*, with which it merged under the title *Modern Electrics and Mechanics*.

It continued for another two years with Austin Lescarboura as editor, but the magazine thereafter concentrated on the basics of the new technologies with fewer speculative or extrapolative articles. It underwent a rapid succession of title changes before merging with *Popular Science Monthly* in April 1915. Gernsback retained a connection with the company, but had no further direct dealings with the magazine.

Gernsback's last issue was dated March 1913. Within six weeks, by April 15th, Gernsback had produced a new magazine, *The Electrical Experimenter*. As he had demonstrated before, and would again, his resilience in building on one situation to develop something bigger and better was formidable and no matter what the adversity, Gernsback would surmount it.

5.

THE ELECTRICAL EXPERIMENTER

The Electrical Experimenter was a bold change from *Modern Electrics*. In a larger format, 11 x 8.5 inches, the magazine was on quality stock suitable to take photogravure illustrations. Launched in May 1913, the first few issues were a slim sixteen pages compared to *Modern Electrics'* one hundred and twelve, but sold for only five cents, ten cents less than *Modern Electrics*. The magazine boldly declared "This journal accepts no advertisements," which must have drastically cut the magazine's revenue. With the reduction in cover price also to consider, this suggests the extent to which *The Electrical Experimenter* must have been subsidized by the evidently prosperous Electro-Importing Company.

Gernsback was assisted in the editorship of the magazine by H. Winfield Secor, who was as prolific an essayist as Gernsback. In addition to his articles he had a series of booklets published by Gernsback, starting with *Construction of Induction Coils and Transformers* (Modern Electrics, 1910). Later solo books included *How and Why of Radio Apparatus* (Experimenter, 1920), *Loud-Talkers, How to Build Them* (Experimenter, 1923), and *How to Make It* (Experimenter, 1926), all based on articles previously published in Gernsback's magazines.

Sidney Gernsback had also now joined the team, having recently emmigrated from Luxemburg. He was Secretary of the Electro-Importing Company and rapidly became a regular contributor to *The Electrical Experimenter*. This raises an interesting question as to the extent to which Sidney had shared his younger brother's interests during their youth in Luxemburg. Certainly it would seem that had he concentrated solely on the wine business he would have had little time to study science in the way Hugo had, assuming he had the inclination. Yet from the first issue of *The Electrical Experimenter* Sidney Gernsback was contributing a regular column detailing an "Experimental Electricity Course" written in conjunction with Secor. This series was published as a 160-page book by Gernsback's Experimenter Publishing Company in 1916 as *Experimental Electricity Course in 20 Lessons*. Also with Secor and Lescarboura, Sidney Gernsback compiled a series on *Wireless Course in 20 Lessons* published in book form by the Electro Importing Company in 1915. Sidney's detailed technical knowledge was shown without collaborative support in *1001 Formulas: The Laboratory Handbook for the Experimenter* (Experimenter, 1920), and the definitive pioneering *Radio Encyclopedia* (Experimenter, 1927). Hugo was clearly not the only member of the Gernsback family favored with an interest in radio, and considering their background and their business acumen it is only reasonable to presume that once reunited the Gernsbacks became a formidable entrepreneurial team.

The Electrical Experimenter, despite being more attractive than *Modern Electrics* and generally more readable, was nevertheless similar in content and style. Apart from the articles, there was a question and answer column, a "How-to-Make-It" department, and features on amateur enthusiasts' developments. The magazine initially concentrated on developments in radio, almost to the exclusion of all else. When fiction first appeared in its pages it was almost incidental. The "How-To-Make-It" department offered prizes "for the most useful, practical, and original ideas" submitted on how "to accomplish new things with old apparatus or old material." The first prize of $5 in the June 1914 issue went to Thomas Benson who described how to set up a range of electrical equipment in order to play a trick on his sister's undesirable boyfriend. The piece was written in the guise of a story, "Mysterious Night," and introduced a character who became a regular feature of *The Electrical Experimenter* for the next few years, The Wireless Wizard, or Wiz. The story was not by any stretch of the imagination science fiction. It merely presented a clever gimmick in fictional form, complete with wiring diagrams and concluding explanation of "how it was done." It was painfully tailored to the magazine's readership. In its conclusion Benson even refers to having bought all the equipment from the Electro-Importing Company! Despite their regularity, the Wireless Wiz stories never rose above the level of "instructional," but are clear evidence of the soil in which science fiction would gradually germinate.

It was at this time, in 1914, that Gernsback first employed the talents of the thirty-year-old Austrian-born technical artist and cartoonist Frank R. Paul. Paul's initial work was to illustrate the technical detail in articles, and it was undistinguished. It would be a few years before his abilities at portraying futuristic technology came to the fore.

The Electrical Experimenter took a couple of years to find its feet but by 1915 it had started to expand. Gernsback, probably under pressure from his older brother, relinquished his stand against including advertisements. In March 1915 the magazine doubled in size to 32 pages with a corresponding price increase to ten cents. This was followed rapidly by another size increase to 48 pages in June 1915.

Up until now publishing had been a sideline of Gernsback's main activities, which centred on his Electro-Importing Company. A feature article about the business was published in the January 1915 *Electrical Experimenter* with photographs showing Hugo Gernsback at work in his fifth-floor special research laboratory, and Sidney Gernsback and H. Winfield Secor at work on the second floor general testing and research laboratory. The staff then working for Gernsback included Sales Engineer Milton Hymes, and Manufacturing Superintendent E. L. Hackett. The Manufacturing Division of the company had expanded in recent years and was now making practically all its own radio instruments.

With the expansion of the publishing side of the business, a subsidiary, the Experimenter Publishing Company, was established in 1915, with Hugo Gernsback as President, Sidney as Treasurer, and Milton Hymes as Secretary. Hymes, who was only 26, handled the business and advertising side of the magazine. His tenure at Experimenter was cut tragically short when he was killed in an accident on the Pennsylvania Railroad in February 1917. His office remained vacant for a couple of years until R. W. deMott was appointed as Secretary and Business Manager in 1919.

By mid-1915 *The Electrical Experimenter* was broadening its coverage beyond the confines of radio, and an increasing emphasis was being given to the wider aspects of scientific experimentation. With this expansion,

Gernsback reintroduced the scientific story, starting with another series of his own: "Baron Munchhausen's New Scientific Adventures," which began in the May 1915 issue. From here on there would scarcely be an issue of the magazine which did not contain a scientific story or speculative article.

Unlike *Ralph 124C 41+*, which was written seriously, the new Munchhausen series was a spoof, written with Gernsback's delight for humor, some of which is slightly amusing today. The opening episode, sub-titled "I Make a Wireless Acquaintance" is still strongly radio orientated. The narrator, I. M. Alier, relates some tall tales of his own, such as how he had broadcast to himself all the way round the world (until someone pointed out it was cheaper just to talk to yourself), and how he had invented a wireless mousetrap. He then settles down by the fire with his headphones and picks up signals from someone claiming to be the original Baron Munchhausen, who is now on the Moon. Munchhausen proves his existence by a light show on the Moon clearly visible from Earth. He then explains how he had survived after his apparent death in 1797 by having been embalmed while still alive. He reawoke in 1907, when the embalming fluid weakened. Munchhausen promises to reveal on the next night how he came to be on the Moon.

The second episode, "How Munchhausen and the Allies Took Berlin," starts with a long digression on Munchhausen's adventures between 1907 and 1915, in particular his involvement in the European War. Gernsback's own loyalties were at test here. Despite his naturalization in 1909, and his birth in Luxemburg, he was still a German by descent, and German loyalties are often strong. However Gernsback, perhaps feeling he might have to prove himself, delivers a long anti-Prussian diatribe. Munchhausen joins the French in battle against the Prussians, only in typical Munchhausen fashion, the French end up taking Berlin and the Germans taking Paris. Humiliated by this experience Munchhausen seeks to leave Earth. He perfects a gravity insulator, or ether-neutralizer, by passing a high voltage current through a netting made of *marconium* wires. With the current on, the *marconium* neutralizes the ether above and below itself and thus serves as a barrier to gravity. Munchhausen builds a strong steel globe, sixty feet in diameter, which he coats with his *marconium* netting, and by alternating the current above and below, he controls the ship and directs it from Earth to the Moon. Gernsback's *marconium* is a variant on H. G. Wells's cavorite in *The First Men in the Moon*, as is the reference to the first radio contact from the Moon to Earth. The influence of Wells on Gernsback is as strong here as it was in *Ralph 124C 41+*.

The covers of the May and June issues must have caught the eye of many a newsstand browser. Both were illustrated by Thomas Wrenn. The May cover showed Munchhausen on the moon, seated before his radio apparatus, with a striking image of Earth in the background against the infinity of space. Wrenn's earlier covers for *Modern Electrics* had been serious but minor attempts to capture that sense of wonder that science fiction evoked. With the full color covers of *The Electrical Experimenter* and a greater opportunity to be bold, Wrenn was able to produce some exciting scenes. June's cover depicted Munchhausen's space globe, the *Interstellar*, hovering over the lunar surface with the globe of the Earth clearly visible. These weren't the first covers on magazines to portray scenes from science-fiction stories, but they were amongst the first aimed specifically at attracting the "experimenter," or the scientific hobbyist, rather than aimed at the reader seeking escapist adventure. As such Wrenn should be better known as one of the pioneer SF artists.

The Munchhausen serial continued through thirteen installments concluding in the February 1917 issue. (The final installment, promised for the February 1918 issue, never did materialize, which suggests that either Gernsback or his readers had lost interest in the serial.) The remainder of the story concentrates on Mars where Munchhausen next visits, and there are detailed descriptions of Martian life and history, but concentrating on their scientific achievements. Despite the series title there are no "adventures." The entire narrative becomes a tour of Martian wonders taking in how they plan and build their cities, how the canals are constructed, how the atmosphere is safeguarded, plus learning the Martian telepathic means of communication and viewing the rest of the solar system through super-telescopes. At the end of the narrative Alier loses contact with Munchhausen as Mars drifts further away from Earth in its orbit.

"Baron Munchhausen's New Scientific Adventures" is tame today, and in the light of our more sophisticated reading is naive and at times, even boring. The light vein of humor that illuminates the early chapters flags as Gernsback warms to his subject and descriptions become lengthier lectures on science. But this is viewing the work from the wrong angle. Gernsback's purpose in writing it, just as with *Ralph 124C 41+* was to educate and stimulate, and secondarily to entertain.

If it were possible to imagine reading this story seventy years ago, as one of a readership of experimenters, there is little doubt that the story must have inspired. The editorials often referred to letters from readers who were always trying something new, and Gernsback constantly urged them on. His editorial in the May 1916 issue, for instance, responded to requests from potential inventors on "What to Invent." It seems remarkable that anyone should ask, as it suggests there were experimenters falling over themselves to invent something but not knowing what. This highlights the difference between the scientist and the experimenter and thus the difference in the readership of Gernsback's magazines and, say, *Nature*. The scientist undertaking research in a particular area may work toward his goal in establishing scientific principles which may in turn lead to an invention either as a by-product or an end result of that research. Gernsback's "experimenter," on the other hand, was Mr. Anybody; he may be a banker, driver, gardener or cook who, in his spare time, tinkered with radio or other gadgets. He may have lacked the imagination of a scientist, but he didn't lack the drive or enthusiasm. Gernsback had inspired a generation of hobbyists into seeking to achieve, only they didn't know what. They needed to turn to Gernsback for advice and guidance.

And Gernsback never had any shortage of that. Time and again he could turn his mind to the prospects of what inventions were needed. In his May 1916 editorial, for instance, he provided a number of suggestions including a new form of wire insulation, a muffler for the telephone, casings for storage batteries and, most interestingly, "tele-music," which he suggested as music played over the telephone for all to hear, but which in his description is a more accurate prediction of radio music. His fertile mind suggested more inventions in his February 1917 editorial ranging from air coolers to insect destroyers, electric toys to telephone bell softeners. He stated that following his initial list he had been "besieged by would-be inventors from all over the world...."

All of this was designed to stimulate the imagination and inspire the inventor. There was one further way. To try to get the inventor to foresee the inventions needed himself, and what better way than to induce him to write stories postulating the use of such inventions. "Can you write a snappy, short story, having some scientific fact for a main theme?" Gernsback wrote in the June 1915 issue.

The invitation was there, and the environment was much more appropriate than in *Modern Electrics*. Gernsback had expanded *The Electrical Experimenter* to become a crucible for fertile minds. Unlike other scientific and technical magazines where the prime purpose was to inform, Gernsback wanted his magazine to inspire. The desire to predict inventions had come from the readers themselves, because they wanted to know how to be useful and how to make money and a name for themselves. Gernsback held up people like Edison, Tesla, and Lee De Forest as prime examples of men who had been amateur experimenters but who were now household names and had changed the world through their inventions. It was all part of the American Dream, for the individual to make good. It appealed especially to immigrants, like Gernsback himself, who had come to America to make their name in a country where initiative was welcomed and encouraged, not stifled as in Europe.

It was in this climate that the real seeds of science fiction were sown.

6.

THE DAWN OF SCIENTIFIC FICTION

At this point I think there is need for a slight diversion. We have reached that time in our history when Gernsback was encouraging readers to submit scientific stories. He only defined those stories briefly as "having some scientific fact for a main theme" which suggests stories about known science, rather than some projection of future science or future inventions. But we have seen that the suggestion arose in a climate of readers wanting ideas for inventions and the stories were consequently intended as vehicles to describe, perceive or encourage some invention that at that time did not exist or to put some existing invention to a new use.

This was a new approach to fiction because it was using fiction to educate and inspire, rather than for its prime purpose as entertainment. This made Gernsback's approach to scientific fiction different from any hitherto. Sam Moskowitz has called Gernsback "the Father of Science Fiction" and, in as much as Gernsback popularized the genre, that soubriquet is correct. But Gernsback, here, in 1915, was endeavoring to encourage a new purpose for a form of fiction which already existed. Although it had yet to be called "science fiction" in the popular sense (and I shall come to the earlier use of that term by William Wilson later in this book), the style of ultra-imaginative fiction had been around for a long time. I do not intend to provide a pre-history of science fiction in this book—there are plenty of other such histories listed in the bibliography at the end of this volume. However, it is pertinent to set Gernsback's innovation in context and consider what other forms of science fiction were available to readers at this time.

In thinking of the early days of science fiction one thinks immediately of Jules Verne and H. G. Wells, certainly the most influential pioneers and arguably the most important. Verne had died only ten years earlier, in March 1905, so was still a recent author. Most of his works had been published in the United States, both in the popular magazines and in book form. *20,000 Leagues Under the Sea*, for instance, perhaps his best known work, had been published in Boston in 1873, *From the Earth to the Moon* in New York in 1874, and *Journey to the Center of the Earth* in Boston in the same year. Some of them were out of print by 1915, but the dedicated reader could have found second-hand copies without too much trouble.

H. G. Wells was still alive in 1915; indeed he was only in his late forties, though the bulk of his production of scientific fiction was in the past. His fiction was more readily available in book form than Verne's. In fact, in order to protect copyright, the first editions of a number of Wells's books had been in America rather than in Britain. *The Time Machine* had been published in New York by Henry Holt in 1895, *The Island of Doctor Moreau* by Stone & Kimball in 1896, *The War of the Worlds* by Harper in 1898 and *The First Men in the Moon* by Bowen-Merrill in Indianapolis in 1901. His short stories were also available in book form, most notably *Thirty Strange Stories* from Edward Arnold in New York in 1897 and *Tales of Space and Time* from Harper & Bros. in 1899. Wells was kept more or less regularly in print and his books would certainly have been available through the public library system to interested readers and those who could not afford the hardcover prices.

The fiction of Wells and Verne placed the emphasis upon science, and were thus squarely in the Gernsbackian court. In many of them the possibilities of a new invention were explored and its benefits, or more often dangers, were placed in the context of a believable adventure. These adventures were at one time called "romances," a term in use since the Middle Ages to describe tales of knight errantry or remarkable experiences. It is only in this century that the term "romance" has become inextricably linked with love stories. The stories by Wells and Verne were scientific romances in the true sense of scientific adventures, and this formed the main body of scientific fiction prior to Gernsback.

Almost as popular as the scientific romance, perhaps at times exceeding it, was the lost race story, popularized by H. Rider Haggard in *King Solomon's Mines* (which had seen an American edition in 1886) and *She* (1887). These are best considered as "explorers' tales." Whereas Wells and Verne concentrated on the possibilities of science and the unknown worlds of the future, the explorer's tale concentrates on unveiling the unknown in the world about us. (Verne, of course, also helped popularize the explorer's tale with his memorable *Around the World in Eighty Days*.) The Victorian age had seen a high point in colonization and discovery, especially in the exploitation of wealth in the minerals found in remote, previously unexplored areas of the world. The public interest aroused by the search for David Livingstone by Henry Stanley in 1871 had never really abated, and there was a ready fascination for knowledge about the mysteries of our globe. The most recent event to capture the public imagination had been the race by Roald Amundsen and Robert Scott to reach the South Pole in 1912, ending in the tragic deaths of Scott's entire party.

These two main themes—scientific achievement and global exploration—formed the two poles of scientific fiction. The former could be linked directly to the Gernsbackian world of invention, though the latter held its own special fascination. For all that it might weave the supernatural or the fantastic into its plot, there was always the potential for discovering a scientifically advanced lost race living in an utopian environment. There thus remained the prospect of a marriage between the two fields.

One of the best known explorer's tales of the period was Sir Arthur Conan Doyle's *The Lost World*, published in 1912. It was the first of Doyle's popular series about Professor Challenger who lead an expedition to discover a prehistoric world surviving on a plateau in South America. Probably even better known and more influential was *Tarzan of the Apes* by Edgar Rice Burroughs, first published in book form by A. C. McClurg in Chicago in 1914. Burroughs's story, which postulated a race of semi-intelligent apes in Africa, inspired many imitations, mostly about feral jungle children, but it brings us to the world of pulp magazines (which, at this time, were more easily accessible to the general reader and certainly cheaper than hardcover books). The pulp magazine was the equivalent of television in the early years of this century. It provided cheap and varied entertainment though with a remarkably high level of quality (although this would deteriorate in later years into formula stories with stereotyped plots). Since Gernsback's inventors were seeking their inspiration through Gernsback's own magazines, it's reasonable to assume they might also have sought further thrills through other magazines rather than through books.

Burroughs's *Tarzan of the Apes* had first appeared in the October 1912 issue of *All-Story Magazine*, one of a number of pulps published by the Frank A. Munsey Corporation. It was Munsey who had pioneered the pulp magazine when he converted his original children's magazine, *The Golden Argosy*, first to an adult adventure magazine, called *The Argosy*, in 1888, and then from glossy to pulp paper in 1896. Both the lost race story and the scientific romance played an increasingly important role in the success of *Argosy*, and its main companion magazines, *Munsey's*, *All-Story Magazine* (launched in 1905), *The Scrap Book* (launched in 1906), and *The Cavalier* (issued in 1908).

There were pulp magazines from other publishers, most significantly *The Popular Magazine*, which appeared in 1903, *The Blue Book* (which appeared as *The Monthly Story Magazine* in 1905 before assuming its later title in 1907), and *Adventure* in 1910. All of these would carry a share of science fiction and fantasy, but it was the Munsey magazines that provided the greatest number of stories and established the names of the leading writers. Even before Burroughs there had been several writers producing scientific fiction for Munsey. One of the earliest was William Wallace Cook (1867-1933), who wrote at least eight works of scientific fiction between 1903 and 1912, starting with *A Round Trip to the Year 2000*, serialized in *Argosy*. This time-travel adventure depicted the labor force of the year 2000 consisting almost entirely of robots, to which Cook gave the Oz-like name of Muglugs. Cook's works suffered a little from his dime-novel background, although he was always a fund of ideas. Perhaps his most Gernsbackian work was *The Eighth Wonder*, serialized in *Argosy* during 1906/07, wherein a scientist, robbed of his inventions by the world's oil trusts, sets out to corner all of the electricity in the world. He builds giant electromagnets, which achieve their purpose but shift the Earth on its axis.

Cook's successor as chief writer of scientific fiction in the pulps was George Allan England (1877-1936). He had been writing short scientific stories since 1905, but did not hit his stride until he graduated to novels with *The House of Transmutation* (*The Scrap Book*, 1909), about an attempt to transform a gorilla into a man. Next came *The Elixir of Hate*, serialized in *Cavalier* in 1911, about the search for the elixir of life, which was followed by England's masterpiece, *Darkness and Dawn* (*Cavalier*, 1912; book form, 1914). *Darkness and Dawn*, and its sequels *Beyond the Great Oblivion* and *The Afterglow*, which appeared in *The Cavalier* during 1913, were classics of early science fiction. Earth is shattered by a catastrophe. Engineer Allan Stern and his secretary lie in suspended animation in the ruins of New York for almost a thousand years. Upon recovering they set out to explore and eventually rebuild the ruined world.

At the same time as England was establishing one facet of science fiction, Edgar Rice Burroughs was promoting his worlds of adventure. Apart from the Tarzan stories, Burroughs was delivering a series of adventures about John Carter on Mars which had started with *Under the Moons of Mars* in the February 1912 *All-Story* (published in book form as *A Princess of Mars* in 1917). Burroughs followed this with *The Gods of Mars* (*All-Story*, 1913) and

The Warlord of Mars (*All-Story*, 1913/14) before starting a new series set in the world of Pellucidar and featuring the adventures of David Innes in *At the Earth's Core* (*All-Story*, 1914). Burroughs included a remarkable amount of scientific projection in his stories, though for the most part he concentrated on the adventures of his heroes, who were always somewhat larger than life, and their encounters with beautiful princesses. Burroughs had not pioneered this type of story. That credit (if credit it is) must go to Gustavus W. Pope, who began a series of "Romances of the Planets" with *Journey to Mars* (1894) and *Journey to Venus* (1895). But who today remembers Pope? It was Burroughs, with his vivacious and exciting adventures, who popularized the concept. And it was Burroughs and England, in the wake of Verne and Wells, who really popularized the scientific romance in the pages of the pulp magazines.

By 1915, the time when Gernsback was encouraging scientific stories in *The Electrical Experimenter*, the scientific romance was increasing in popularity in the pulps. Between then and 1920 there would be a blossoming of such stories. Scarcely an issue of *Argosy* or *All-Story* appeared without there being at least one scientific or lost race story or installment of a serial, and a number of new writers began to establish themselves. The earliest to follow in the footsteps of England and Burroughs were Victor Rousseau, Perley Poore Sheehan, Charles B. Stilson and John U. Giesy, soon to be joined by Austin Hall, Philip M. Fisher, Homer Eon Flint, and, as we reach the pinnacle, Abraham Merritt, Ray Cummings, and Murray Leinster.

The depth of science in these stories was frequently shallow, and there was seldom any attempt to rationalize the scientific *motif*. Today, many of these stories might be considered fantasies, although much of today's so-called science fiction is frequently as fantastic. The stories were written purely as escapist entertainment, with no attempt to educate or inspire. Nevertheless, they did alert the reading public to the wonders beyond their everyday world, and began to create an awareness of the effects of the scientific revolution upon their future.

1915 was, thus, a pivotal moment in the history of science fiction. Gernsback was such a devotee of the field that he is unlikely to have overlooked what was happening in the pulp magazines, and it is quite possible that he sensed in 1915 a growing popular demand for that type of story. It certainly suited his purpose in promoting scientific achievement and was thus an ideal vein to tap. Interestingly, 1915 was a turning point for another reason. On October 5th of that year, Street & Smith launched the first popular specialist fiction pulp, *Detective Story Magazine*. There had been two earlier specialist pulps, *The Railroad Man's Magazine* issued in 1906, and *The Ocean*, concentrating on sea stories, launched in 1907, but both of these were ahead of their time and neither created a *genre*. By 1915 the chemistry was right and the popularity of detective fiction allowed Street & Smith to issue their ground-breaking magazine.

So 1915 brought with it an increasing public appreciation both for scientific stories in the pulps and for the specialist pulp. In that year it is quite possible that had either Frank Munsey or Street & Smith launched a pulp devoted to the scientific romance it would have succeeded admirably, and the history of science fiction would have been different. But they did not, and it would be another ten years before the first all-science-fiction magazine was issued in America by Hugo Gernsback. Ironically, back in Sweden, Otto Witt, who had studied at Bingen at the same time as Gernsback, launched his own magazine of speculative science called *Hugin*. The first issue was dated April 1916 and it ran for eighty-two issues until December 1920. *Hugin* had more parallels with Gernsback's *Electrical Experimenter* than with the Munsey pulps, for it concentrated on studies and forecasts about the possibilities of science. Although it was little known outside of Sweden it is a further indication that by 1915/16 the world seemed to be ready to welcome a new world and the wonders that science would bring.

What was so special about 1915?

It is easy to speculate that because the world was in the grip of a World War people were turning to scientific fiction as a message of hope. This may have been true in part, as the prospect of future wonders must have been a solace to some. But in 1915 it was only Europe that was at War. The United States had remained defiantly in isolation and would not be pulled into the war until April 1917. Admittedly many Americans were European immigrants or first generation Americans and would have had relatives in Europe, so there would have been some sympathy to the European distress.

In fact there was a measurable drop in the popularity of scientific fiction in Europe, because of the proximity to the horrors of War. America, on the other hand, removed in its splendid isolation, became a crucible of thought for the expansion of science, but emphasising the escapist qualities of the scientific romance, not the apocalyptic terrors.

In short, the War had a consequential effect on the change in direction of scientific fiction and not a direct one on its popularity. There was a much stronger accumulative influence, and that was the rising tide of scientific achievement in the previous few decades. Men were increasingly drawn from the rural environment into the towns to work in industry where, since the 1890s, there had been a rapid expansion. One has only to consider the following list of major advancements in science in the previous forty years, well within a man's lifetime, to see the impact that science was having upon the individual, not just in the day-to-day comforts it was providing, and in the new avenues of work it was opening up, but in the widening of public awareness to the possibilities of science.

1871   Darwin considers human evolution in *The Descent of Man*.
1873   First cable cars in service in San Francisco.
1876   The carburettor invented by Gottlieb Daimler.
1876   Microphone invented by Alexander Graham Bell.
1876   Telephone invented by Alexander Graham Bell with the first exchange at Boston, Mass., in 1878.
1878   The gramophone invented by Thomas Edison.
1879   The electric lamp invented by Edison, with the first public demonstration at Menlo Park, NJ, December 20, 1879.
1882   First skyscraper completed: Home Insurance Building, Chicago.
1884   Invention of linotype by Otto Mergenthaler which revolutionized printing.
1885   The petrol-driven car invented by Karl Benz in Germany. Patented on January 26, 1886.

1887 First pneumatic tires for bicycles developed by John Dunlop. Adapted for motor cars by the Michelin brothers in 1895.

1888 The AC electric motor developed by Nikola Tesla.

1888 Photographic film invented by John Carbutt and developed by George Eastman for Kodak.

1889 Edison invented motion pictures.

1895 First public showing of a cinema film, by the Lumiere brothers in Paris, December 28.

1895 Radio telegraphy developed by Ernest Rutherford at Cambridge in England.

1895 The X-Ray discovered by Wilhelm Rontgen at the University of Wurzberg in Germany.

1897 The first subatomic particle, the electron, detected by J.J. Thomson.

1898 First seagoing submarine perfected by Simon Lake.

1900 First dirigible balloon flight by Ferdinand von Zeppelin.

1901 Marconi transmitted radio message across the Atlantic from Cornwall to Newfoundland on December 12.

1903 First flight in a heavier-than-air machine by the Wright brothers at Kitty Hawk, NC, on December 17.

1905 Einstein's theory of special relativity published.

1906 Earliest radio broadcast of speech and music, by Reginald Fessenden in Massachusetts.

1907 Bakelite invented by Leo Baekeland (though not patented until 1909), a major breakthrough in the plastics industry.

1907 First electric washing machine developed and marketed in Chicago.

1907 Concept of time as a fourth dimension proposed by Hermann Minkowski.

1908 Assembly-line mass production introduced by Henry Ford.

1909 Robert Peary reaches the North Pole.

1911 Roald Amundsen reaches the South Pole.

1913 Stainless steel developed by Harry Brearley at Sheffield, England.

1914 Quick-frozen food production pioneered by Clarence Birdseye.

1914 The armed tank invented by Sir Ernest Swinton in England, and first tested in September 1915.

The list could be much longer, but it is sufficient to show the enormous advances made in science in the four decades before 1915. As today, with the advances in the computer industry, so in 1915 many realized they were living in an age of scientific achievement, and it captured their imagination. It brought with it a fascination for what was to come, and the inevitable interest in scientific fiction was born.

Gernsback responded to that demand, but not by providing the fiction by regular pulp writers. Instead he encouraged the man in the street, the everyday hobbyist, the amateur experimenter, to write scientific fiction. It was these people who could be the new Edisons, Bells, Teslas, and Marconis of the world. In their fiction they could envisage a future that they might in turn create. Gernsback wasn't out to merely entertain, as were the pulp merchants. Gernsback was there to inspire a new world, and to encourage his readership to have a part in creating it.

The readers of *The Electrical Experimenter* could not only read about the future, they could build it.

7.

SCIENTIFIC FICTION IN CONFLICT

The British writer and historian of science fiction, Brian W. Aldiss, has commented that "science fiction is no more written for scientists than ghost stories are written for ghosts."[1] He's right, of course, provided one is considering the general concept of science fiction. But let's restrict ourselves to the development of science fiction in Gernsback's magazines. Most of the science fiction published elsewhere was fiction first, with a strong fantastic element and a smattering of science. But Gernsback was putting the emphasis strongly on the scientific values. The reason was because he wanted the stories he published to be read by scientists and inventors, most especially by the amateur scientist and inventor whom Gernsback regarded as his main market. The science fiction he wrote and encouraged others to write was produced solely for them. Hence Gernsback's science fiction *was* written for scientists, and this is a distinction that is necessary to bear in mind when watching the growth and development of science fiction over the next few years.

Gernsback stated his case for scientific fiction and the extrapolative article in his editorial for the April 1916 *Electrical Experimenter*, which is worth quoting at length:

> We are asked not infrequently why *The Electrical Experimenter* lends so much space to the exploitation of the future, or in other words, why we make so much of things which as yet exist but in imagination. We admit that such is the case and furthermore we believe that more matter of this kind is printed in our pages than in any other kindred publication. The reason should be obvious. The electrical art and its allied branches are but a comparatively new and unexploited science. An immense number of discoveries and inventions remain to be made, each succeeding day broadening our vision and showing how little we really do know as yet. Every new discovery immediately leads to hundreds of other inventions and each one of them opens up new fields. There seems to be no end or let up; indeed, there cannot be such an end in a world where everything is infinite. We will never reach a period where everything will be known, where nothing is left to be discovered, nothing further to be invented! Progress in science is as infinite as time, it is inconceivable how either could stop.
>
> Some well-meaning people with a shrunken horizon may disagree with us here, and to them we would like to quote the case of one of our government patent officials living in Washington one hundred years ago. This worthy individual left the patent service as he was certain that almost everything of importance had been invented. He felt equally certain that on account of this deplorable state of affairs the Patent Office would shortly be forced to

close its doors forever! Since that time almost one million patents have been issued! The telegraph, the telephone, the phonograph, the electric light, electric trains, the storage battery, the X-ray, wireless telegraphy, radium and scores of other inventions of the first magnitude have been made. And each succeeding year brings new wonders.

We are fully aware of the fact that some of the imaginary articles which we publish are wildly extravagant—now. But are we so sure that they will be extravagant fifty years from now? It is never safe in these days of rapid progress to call any one thing impossible or even improbable. The telephone would have been considered ridiculous fifty years ago, while the aeroplane, prophesied and predicted for generations, was declared a total impossibility by men of science as late as fifteen years ago. Some even published long scientific dissertations proving beyond doubt that such a machine could not possibly be made to remain aloft in the air. Jules Verne, who forty-six years ago in his "20,000 Leagues Under the Sea," imagined the submarine down to its very battery for propelling it under water, was ridiculed and called a dreamer in his day. Nevertheless, the aeroplane as well as the submarine are very much in evidence these days.

Of course, we could publish nothing but facts, nothing but experiments. This would be a very simple as well as easy matter and much less costly. Our self-imposed, infinitely harder task, however, has helped to make this journal what it is today: the most widely read and circulated electrical publication on earth. And all this within three short years. It is no easy matter to think out new things of the future and illustrating them adequately by means of expensive wash drawings or three-color cover illustrations. Indeed, there is nothing more difficult connected with the publication. But if we succeed—and we think we sometimes do— in firing some experimenter's imagination to work in a new direction, due directly to our imaginary illustrations, then indeed we feel amply repaid for our toil.

A world without imagination is a poor place to live in. No real electrical experimenter, worthy of the name, will ever amount to much if he has no imagination. He must be visionary to a certain extent, he must be able to look into the future and if he wants fame he must anticipate the human wants. It was precisely this quality which made Edison—a master of imagination—famous.

Imagination more than anything else makes the world go round. If we succeed in speeding it up ever so little our mission has been fulfilled. There can be no progress where imagination is lacking.[2]

The case for scientific fiction was stated. It was to stimulate the imagination and to speed up the progression of new inventions, and thus make a better world. Nothing more, nothing less. The extent to which Gernsback was successful is difficult to measure, at least at this early stage, but we will later see the cumulative effect of his actions. Before that, though, let's consider the nature of what he was publishing.

I am unsure as to why Jacque Morgan did not continue to write his Mr. Fosdick stories for Gernsback. They were as ideally suited to *The Electrical Experimenter* as they had been to *Modern Electrics*. But Morgan did not reappear. Although Thomas Benson was a regular contributor, his Wireless Wiz stories, as we have seen, were nothing more than instructional novelties, with no speculative elements.

The first writer to respond to Gernsback's plea for scientific stories with imagination was George F. Stratton. Stratton was in his sixties, having been born in 1852. He was an experienced writer of scientific articles for a variety of technical and boys' magazines and edited *The Electric Magazine*. He had written one earlier science story, "The Mystery of the Ventura Converter Station," published in the December 1913 *Modern Electrics*, the only story to appear there after Gernsback sold it. Stratton may not have realized the extent to which he was a pioneer, for moreso than either Morgan or Benson previously, he set out to write genuine speculative scientific fiction.

His first story for Gernsback was "Omegon" which appeared in the September 1915 issue while Gernsback's own *Baron Munchhausen's New Scientific Adventures* was still being serialized. It was the start of a series about millionaire entrepreneur Ned Cawthorne. Inspired by the conflict in Europe, "Omegon" is set in the near future at the time when a Sino-Japanese alliance declares war on the United States. Incapacitated by an injury in a polo match and thus unable to serve in the War, Ned Cawthorne learns from one of his mechanics of plans for a submarine which will disable ships with no loss of life, but the short-sighted Government will not back its development. Cawthorne invests some of his fortune in the project and before long five miniature submarines are completed. Cawthorne explains the principle of the submarine to Government officials. The small submarines move under a battleship and switch on powerful electromagnets so that each sub' can attach itself firmly to the ship's base. Special guns aimed directly upwards then inject clouds of ether into the ship, putting the crew to sleep. The Government officials remain sceptical, so Cawthorne's workforce man the machines themselves. As the enemy fleet approaches, Cawthorne's men go into action. They succeed in immobilizing the ships and capturing the enemy.

The story, rather like Gernsback's, was written in a juvenile, boys'-adventure style, and lacked literary skill. But that was neither here nor there. The import was that Stratton had selected a few basic scientific principles, and woven them into a stirring topical story. The intent of the story was obvious. In his introductory blurb, Gernsback asked, if a foreign power declared war on America, "Would American genius prevail? Would our inventors rise to the occasion?" What better time to inspire inventors than when the nation's safety and security are at stake.

The concepts in the story had required little imagination, since they had appeared in earlier issues of the magazine, where both submarines and electromagnets featured regularly. The imagination had come in weaving them together in a story which showed the benefits of applying scientific and inventive skills. All of Gernsback's principles are contained in this story: the solo inventor whose genius is initially ignored by government but who triumphs in the end; the entrepreneur who has made millions from investing in inventors and experimenters; the chance for further financial reward from developing the invention; plus simple scientific principles which, when combined, create something original and valuable. The message was blatant: the time was ripe for inventors to achieve fame and fortune.

The next episode in Ned Cawthorne's career appeared in the following issue. Entitled "The Gravitation Nullifier," Stratton was now firmly into the territory of speculation. Not that anti-gravitation techniques were new to fiction—quite the contrary. They had been used as a means of space travel for years in fiction, most recently by Gernsback himself in his Munchhausen narrative. But Stratton was speculating about another use for such an invention, in this case causing total havoc and chaos on enemy lines. An aeroplane, equipped with the device, would fly over the enemy who would be helplessly raised into the air, along with their weapons. Again Cawthorne finances the development of an invention ignored by government, which turns the tide of battle and defeats the enemy with no loss of life. In a scene that would become stock in Gernsbackian science fiction, Cawthorne explains the nature of the invention to the army generals:

> Four years ago . . . Mr. Farrow showed clearly that the law of gravitation is influenced by the Hertzian waves, and that they, in turn, could be influenced by electricity. I need not take up time to go into the technicalities of it all, but experimentation, right to the limit, has resulted in an apparatus—a condensing generator—which, if so handled as to throw an electric zone around anything that has weight, will eliminate that weight or, more properly, will nullify the gravitation . . .[3]

Here was the standard scientific lecture which would so mar the science-fiction narrative in later years. Stratton was following the model established by Gernsback, which was a series of descriptions of scientific achievements, linked by a fictional framework. In this story Stratton has taken that one extra step in projecting a new scientific achievement rather than building on an existing one, and it thus makes "The Gravitation Nullifier" the first true piece of science fiction published by Gernsback written by someone other than himself. Stratton was an ideal Gernsback writer, and reflected Gernsback's views exactly. When, in the story, the general is sceptical about the invention and declares that it's "beyond the realms of possibility," Cawthorne simply replies:

> Edison says that the limits of the possibilities of science are not yet in sight. What we have done seems impossible because it has never been demonstrated.[4]

This sentiment, which Gernsback often repeated in his editorials, later emerged as the slogan for *Amazing Stories*: "Extravagant Fiction Today . . . Cold Fact Tomorrow."

Cawthorne's scientific endeavors against the enemy continued in "The Poniatowski Ray" (January 1916). Death rays would later become standard in science fiction, but Stratton here was venturing into new territory. His description of the appearance of the ray (as distinct from how it was generated or its effect) is so close to that of the laser beam as to qualify as prophetic:

> Instantly a tiny ray of light, so nearly as blue as the sky as to be barely discernible, shot from the tube, and from the aero fleet a mile away and nearly a mile above the earth, came lightning flashes of flame with terrific crashes, drowning out the continuous rattle of the rapid-fire gun. Cawthorne swung the tube across the sky with some little deviation in the elevation and that ray . . . fired every bomb, every gun and every holstered revolver among them. The gasoline tanks went as instantly, wrecking the aeroplanes.[5]

Gernsback described the ray in his blurb:

> Briefly considered, the Poniatowski Ray may be visualized to consist of a powerful ionized stream of electrons which can be shot forth from a proper directing orifice or tube, in a practically parallel stream, vibrating at millions of cycles a second and capable of detonating any kind of explosive, no matter how well it is protected by external casings. The latest scientific theories advanced endeavor to prove that there really is no solid matter existent, but that what we term matter is made up of electrons electrically related or bonded to each other under certain conditions which obtain in nature. If the key to this situation is discovered, as for instance is exemplified in the Poniatowski Ray, then indeed the war of the future will be a catastrophous world-wide event unbelievable and we might almost say unimaginable.[6]

The next Cawthorne episode took a different emphasis. In "The Shirikari Tentacle" (February 1916) the Japanese had developed an American invention (which the US Government had again failed to back) that sends out a stream of electric current to the metallic hulls of ships and submarines and thus electrocutes anyone who is not shielded. Stratton misses the opportunity of having Cawthorne try to procure an opposing weapon and thus turning this into a scientific problem story, but merely has the original American inventor incapacitate the generator and escape from the enemy ship.

Stratton's stories typified what Gernsback wanted to achieve in publishing fiction in his magazines. They carried more effectively the same message he was writing in his editorials and articles. They were typical of a long line of war-inspired stories, though the bulk of those previously written, such as H. G. Wells's *The War in the Air* (1908), had considered a future war, rather than a current one. Stratton's stories contained little that hadn't previously been conjectured in earlier, better written stories. One had only to turn to Wells's *The World Set Free* (1913) for the concept of the atomic bomb, and to Conan Doyle's "Danger" (*Strand Magazine*, July 1914) for a more realistic story about submarine warfare. Stratton, however, might not have read Wells and Doyle. His concepts are more likely to have come from what he had read in *The Electrical Experimenter*. For instance, Gernsback's editorial in the July

1915 issue, "The Obsolete Submarine," talked about how the submarine's electrical power may be neutralized, and how they may be detected in the future by echo-location, a device which was not invented until 1919.

Gernsback took a leaf from Stratton's writings in his editorial "Uncle Sam and the Inventor," which appeared in the same issue as "Omegon." Gernsback berated the Government for not recognizing the talents or activities of the nation's inventors, but congratulated the Secretary of War on the foresight in establishing a Naval Advisory Board to consider proposals for new inventions to help the war effort. Gernsback quoted the Secretary in his statement that "One scientist very probably may do more for the United States than any admiral or general could do."[7] This supported Gernsback's fundamental purpose in establishing *The Electrical Experimenter*, and gave impetus to Gernsback's ethos in encouraging scientific initiative and achievement. An increasing number of speculative articles appeared in the magazine, such as "Warfare of the Future" (November 1915), an anonymous illustrative feature probably written by Gernsback and "The Mystery of Gravitation" (May 1916) by H. Winfield Secor, which inspired a super-scientific cover by Vincent Lynch depicting an anti-gravitation ray lifting a battleship out of the sea.

Submarine warfare remained one of the major items of contention in the First World War. American anger had been aroused by the German sinking of the *Lusitania* in May 1915 with the loss of 1200 lives, including many Americans. The Germans temporarily ceased the submarine attacks, but they were resumed in February 1917, reaching their peak in April that year when 196 British ships were lost. With American protests ignored, the United States entered the War on April 6.

It's no little surprise, then, to find that submarines feature so prominently in the articles and stories in *The Electrical Experimenter*. A new writer, Charles Magee Adams appeared in the May 1917 issue with "Eddy Currents." The enemy fleet has found a method of defense against submarine torpedoes, though this is not described. Inventor Billy Parker, an electrical engineer, has perfected two new inventions now installed as a trial upon an American submarine heading out to confront the enemy. The first invention is a form of radar, called a "feeler," which detects anything metallic within its range. A feeler has also been adapted to send out a powerful electrical current which will melt anything metallic. Again the inventor triumphs. Adams was a better writer than Stratton, though the story still shows an imbalance of enthusiasm and exuberance over ability.

The American entry into the War introduced a censorship on articles which might have relayed sensitive scientific data to the enemy. The type of prognosticative articles and stories that Gernsback wanted to publish were thus limited. Adams's next story, for instance, veered away from the war theme. "Joe's Experiment" (June 1917), announced as "an electrical tale," concerns a blind boy who learns all about a new hydro-electric project being built near his backwoods home. The project is imperilled by the delayed delivery of transformers, and young Joe comes up with a new way of lowering the voltage from the power lines. As a result he saves the project, and is promised the best scientific education money can buy. Again the moral is clear: scientific knowledge will secure your future.

A number of other "electrical tales" appeared, such as "'Ham' Jones—Scientist" by Harlan Eveleth (July 1917) and "The Radio Bomb" by Adams (August 1917), but the true scientific story was temporarily silenced. Gernsback and Secor did squeeze in an occasional speculative article, particularly on submarine warfare, such as "Blinding the Submarine" (August 1917) by Gernsback and "Locating the Submarine by Radio" by Secor, and there were many articles on war technology. But for a while the real power went out of Gernsback's drive to release imaginative talent within the magazine. Apart from one quite remarkable example there was little fiction of any significance published in *The Electrical Experimenter* until the end of the War.

The one exception was a quantum step forward in the type of scientific fiction Gernsback had been publishing. Hitherto the stories had been fairly restrained, taking but one invention and projecting its future potential. However in "At War with the Invisible," the co-authors R. and G. Winthrop, stood back from the here and now and made a major projection of future events. Whilst the story clearly shows the influence of H. G. Wells's *The War of the Worlds*, it was also directly inspired by the War. The Winthrops substituted Mars for Germany, and considered the consequences of a War of the Planets, engulfing the entire solar systen. The story is narrated by a former war correspondent looking back at the War from a further future when there was a universal brotherhood of peace. He recalls the year 2011, when the Martians, who were blockaded by the allies, unleashed a new force upon the solar system. By means unknown the Martians destroy first Philadelphia, then Ramillon the capital of Mercury, and then London. They issue an ultimatum that New York will be destroyed next unless the planets submit to Martian domination. Before this outbreak of disasters, the narrator was in Paris with Ava, the beautiful daughter of the Venusian President, reporting on a meeting of the War Commission. With the news of the destruction of Philadelphia he hurries back home in his special plane, flying across the Atlantic in a night, to inspect the remnants of Philadelphia, now almost covered by an inland sea. He subsequently witnesses the destruction of London. Only then does he realize how the Martians might be achieving their deadly purpose. He recalls that Ava wears a bracelet of invisible bells. It had been a gift from an inventor who was later killed in an accident. Their true nature is now perceived by the narrator, who realizes that the bells were constructed out of a series of perfect mirrors that reflected light completely with no diffusion, making it impossible for light to penetrate. The bells were thus invisible. The narrator conjectures that the Martians had achieved the same results and that their space ship was rendered invisible by these perfect mirrors. The narrator seeks the help of his scientist friend Professor Firmin. Ava's bells are rendered visible by viewing them under helium rays, in much the same manner as with X-Rays. Firmin now perfects a device to project helium rays on a scale that will detect any attack by the Martians. The machine is a success. The Martian invaders are destroyed and Earth saved.

"At War with the Invisible" suffers from unskilled writing, but remains a remarkable catalogue of inventions. Though not on Gernsback's scale, the Winthrops nevertheless perceived a future, more than a century hence, of universal harmony and a scientific utopia. Transatlantic flight and interplanetary travel are commonplace and there are such everyday objects as private planes and pocket phones.

The Winthrops had written the first piece of integrated speculative scientific fiction for Gernsback. At around 7200 words, it was also the longest story Gernsback had published until that time (excluding his own) and was serialized in two episodes, in the March and April 1918 issues. The second episode was illustrated on the cover by Vincent Lynch, showing the destruction of the Martian ship, looking not unlike a flying saucer. Finally, and of some historical significance, it was the first story illustrated by Frank R. Paul, who provided introductory illustrations to each episode, both depicting Ava. They were typical of the illustrations with which Paul would later be seen in *Amazing Stories*. As all too often, his portrayal of the female form was not exactly flattering!

The Electrical Experimenter carried no letter column at this time, so it is not possible to judge the reader reaction to the Winthrops serial. This is unfortunate as it was the most overt piece of scientific fiction published up till that time. It is not possible to measure its effect by the quantity of scientific fiction subsequently published, as this remained lamentably scarce. Apart from Gernsback's "The Magnetic Storm" (August 1918), no other pertinent scientific stories appeared for another year. Although the tide of War had turned, the armistice was not signed until November 11, 1918. Censorship still applied and thus Gernsback was not able to describe in detail in his story the means whereby Germany's electrical power is neutralized. Nevertheless he still spent two full columns in a spoof conversation with Nikola Tesla about how, in 1898, the current produced by Tesla's great electric oscillator had burned out dynamo armatures thirteen miles away. The same principle could now be used, with much greater power, to burn out all existing German electrical machines. Gernsback reported that Tesla read the original proofs to this story and supported the facts. As a story, though, "The Magnetic Storm" is not on a par with "At War with the Invisible."

Elsewhere in *The Electrical Experimenter*, Gernsback was expanding his coverage of scientific achievement and imaginative invention. With the May 1918 issue, he began an irregular series on "Coming Inventions," starting with "Television and the Telephot." It was followed in May 1919 with "The Thought Recorder," which provided the first cover illustration by Howard Brown, who would later establish himself as a noted science-fiction artist. The general coverage of *The Electrical Experimenter* was expanding. From the original concentration on electrical developments, especially wireless achievements, it was now covering the whole spectrum of scientific growth and exploration. Nikola Tesla wrote a series about his own inventions, Isabel Lewis of the US Naval Observatory provided a series on Popular Astronomy, and there were articles on the wonders of nature, the sub-atomic world and the imaginative thrills of the cinema.

It was a deliberate move. With the end of the War the nation was attempting to return to normal, and with industry relieved from a concentration on munitions, there was an expansion in production, as well as in publishing. Gernsback's market research was revealing that more readers were turning to *The Electrical Experimenter* for its coverage of science generally rather than for its specific articles on experimentation. As a further move to appeal to this market Gernsback added a sub-title to the magazine, "Science and Invention." Increasingly Gernsback felt that the magazine's title was too limiting. Before making too sudden a change, though, Gernsback planned his strategy.

His energies were first invested in establishing a new magazine. With *The Electrical Experimenter* moving toward general science and away from wireless coverage, Gernsback introduced a new publication aimed at the amateur radio enthusiast. Called *Radio Amateur News*, its first issue, dated July 1919, was published on June 25. Amateur radio had been stifled during the War with government restrictions. Gernsback began to champion the cause again, just as he had in the days of *Modern Electrics*, and *Radio Amateur News* became an active forum for all radio men. Once more Gernsback was aiming at the practitioner. He saw as his readers both those who were interested in radio broadcasting and reception, and those who were becoming radio dealers. As commercial radio started to grow in the 1920s, there was a rapid growth in jobs in the radio industry, in building, designing, selling and repairing radios. As Gernsback became attuned to this market he shortened the magazine's name to *Radio News* from its July 1920 issue.

Radio News was more of a technical magazine than *The Electrical Experimenter*, and as a rule it contained less speculative articles, though Gernsback could not help slotting in occasional references. His editorial in the February 1920 issue discussed at length the subject of "Interplanetarian Wireless" and the possibility of receiving messages from space. He also encouraged the publication of "radio stories." Very few of these are remotely identifiable as science fiction, the majority fitting into the Thomas Benson "Wireless Wiz" category—in fact it will come as little surprise to find that Benson was a regular contributor of both stories and articles. The majority of stories merely cited new uses for existing inventions, which was fine as far as Gernsback intended, because his aim was to inspire creativity, but the authors lacked any vision. A typical example is "When the Lights Grew Dim" by Robert W. Allen in the March 1920 issue. Radio messages are received, purportedly from Mars, threatening to destroy government wireless stations unless quantities of radium are made available. Science fiction? No. Our alert radio "ham" discovers that the messages are being broadcast locally, a block away, because he noticed that when the message was broadcast, his lights dimmed.

Radio News rapidly established itself, with its circulation rising to 100,000 in the first year. Initially assisted in the editorial work by Pierre Boucheron, Gernsback handed over editorship to Robert Lecault from the January 1921 issue. With *Radio News* settled, Gernsback turned his attentions back to *The Electrical Experimenter*. With this magazine now aimed at the general reader its title was a misnomer. "Your average experimenter wants more than experiments," Gernsback admitted. "He wants to know the latest in science, the newest invention, the latest developments in the realm of human endeavor."[8] Although the magazine was responding to this demand it was not reflected in the title, and so with the August 1920 issue the sub-title and main title were switched and *The Electrical Experimenter* became *Science and Invention*. In his editorial in the first new issue, Gernsback took the scientific establishment to task.

. . . it is the public that popularizes science, not our scientists. Just at present . . . educational scientific films are all the rage and the public clamors for more and heartily applauds them. But our *real* scientists are as backward as in Galileo's times. The public applauds and instantly believes in anything new that is scientific, whereas the true scientist scoffs and jeers . . . It matters little that Jules Verne or Nikola Tesla are a hundred years ahead of the times—the scientists scoff and laugh unbelievingly. But happily, the great public today appreciates the "fantastic dreamer," because it knows from experience that these "fantastic dreams" have a habit of coming true on the morrow.[9]

This is an interesting editorial in seeing how Gernsback was thinking. Firstly, he was distinguishing between the scientist and the visionary, and maintaining that most scientists were not visionaries. There were some, like Tesla, who ranked with Verne (a non-scientist) as "fantastic dreamers"—the nearest Gernsback had yet come to suggest visionaries, and thereby writers of speculative scientific fiction. There is little doubt that in converting *The Electrical Experimenter* to *Science and Invention* Gernsback was not just endeavoring to appeal to a wider and more general audience (and thereby boost circulation—his aim was to increase from 200,000 to 500,000), but he was making *Science and Invention* a forum for exploring the future possibilities of science. Secondly, Gernsback was appealing to the individual who, through his or her own scientific endeavors, could achieve what the scientific establishment, apparently blinded by its own superior knowledge, was failing to do, namely to be creative and visionary. Gernsback was now appealing specifically to the visionary and he or she was as likely to be amongst the general readership as amongst the scientific. This meant that any scientific fiction that Gernsback now published was no longer directed at the scientist, but at the general public. In just five years, albeit years of global conflict, Gernsback's perception of the scientist had changed, though not his perception of the inventor, who was almost always the solitary amateur and enthusiast and the person most responsive to change. Now Brian Aldiss's quote was coming true. Science fiction was not being written for scientists any more; it should now be by visionaries for visionaries.

Finally, Gernsback's editorial reveals that he believed that the public were clamoring for scientific achievement, whilst the scientific establishment remained cautious and reserved. Yet just how much was this the case? How ready were the public to accept the next stage of scientific advance? Having just experienced a World War, albeit on the periphery in America, the public had been witness to the death-dealing achievements of science—the submarine, the tank, aerial bombing, gas warfare. Before the war, science had been seen as a possible panacea, working towards a utopian existence with the invention of labor-saving devices, providing employment and generally improving the quality of life. Following the War the public were entitled to be sceptical. For all the good that was in science there was an equal evil.

It was a rift that would be reflected increasingly as scientific fiction developed. But whereas Gernsback's ideal was for the fiction to be technophilic, there were those who used fiction as a warning against the uncontrolled advance of science. And to see that parallel development we need to return to the pulps.

8.

THE PULP PERSPECTIVE

As we have seen, the War years brought a development in the type of scientific fiction Gernsback was publishing, though he had attracted only a few writers willing to give it a try. Of those only George F. Stratton was already known as a technical writer, and only R. and G. Winthrop made any effort to produce radical new fiction. Stratton and Adams concentrated on potential developments of existing inventions, and Thomas Benson produced simple radio novelties. The stories were all, basically, gadget stories.

The scientific fiction being published in the pulp magazines couldn't have been more different. The writers and editors were not interested in the potential of science for its own sake, but merely as a means to an end. That end was entertainment, usually a fantastic adventure with a smattering of science used only as a springboard.

Take, for instance, the effects of the submarine war. Whereas Gernsback's authors used it as an excuse to imagine new combative inventions and weaponry, and to laud the triumph of the inventor, the pulpsters used it simply as an opening for adventure. We can cite two novels by Edgar Rice Burroughs as examples. In *Beyond Thirty* (*All-Around Magazine*, February 1916), Burroughs depicts a future, two centuries hence, where the Americas have been cut off from Europe by submarine blockades and mines. A plane makes it across the Atlantic to discover that Europe has reverted to savagery, and that Abyssinia and China rule the world between them. In *The Land That Time Forgot* (*Blue Book*, August 1918) a British tug captures a German submarine, and the two are forced to land on a remote Pacific island which contains a wide diversity of animals from the evolutionary scale. Likewise in Francis Stevens's "The Nightmare" (*All-Story Weekly*, April 14, 1917) the sinking of the *Lusitania* was chosen as the springboard for adventure. A man who is sleeping on the ship wakes to find himself in the Pacific Ocean instead of the Atlantic, near an island full of weird and dangerous animals.

Fantastic adventures aside, the pulps were publishing scientific stories that were not only better written and more entertaining than those in Gernsback's magazines, but occasionally contained more scientific speculation. Perhaps the most extravagant was *The Cosmic Courtship* by Julian Hawthorne, serialized in *All-Story Weekly* (November 24-December 15, 1917). Although Hawthorne was more mystically than scientifically minded, he introduced a number of scientific elements into this interplanetary romance of the year 2001. The world is free of pollution, with industrial plants now constructed underground. Individuals have complete freedom, with their own personal anti-gravity belts as transport. The heroine finds that her spirit is transported to Saturn, and from here on the story sinks into an occult adventure, but the opening scenes would have interested any Gernsbackian devotee. Also on the cosmic scale was "The Planeteer" by Homer Eon Flint (*All-Story*, March 9, 1918). Here Earth is shifted from its orbit by the gravitational effect of an errant planetoid, and moves into orbit near Jupiter. Although the science in these stories is highly questionable, the imaginative powers are superb. Yet although they would have appealed to Gernsback, they were over the top for his need to inspire his readers into creative invention.

More down to Earth were the works of British-born Victor Rousseau. Influenced by both H. G. Wells and the world in conflict, Rousseau wrote two novels that highlighted the perils of scientific advance. In *The Messiah of the Cylinder* (*Everybody's Magazine*, June-September 1917), the protagonist is placed in suspended animation, reviving in 2017 to find a world dominated by socialism and science. He seeks to overthrow the Marxist state and restore democracy. One of the morals in the novel is that scientific advance must be contained and not given free rein. There was a similar message in *The Draft of Eternity* (*All-Story*, June 1-22, 1918), where through the use of marijuana two doctors transport themselves a thousand years hence to discover an America which has degenerated into savagery, and the surviving whites are enslaved by an Oriental race.

These stories, a slim selection of the many published in the pulps during the war years, serve to highlight the difference between them and Gernsback's fiction. Gernsback's stories were only fiction by design, their real purpose being to inspire and educate. As stories they were non-starters, and only R. and G. Winthrop's "At War with the Invisible" made any attempt to be entertaining. The pulp stories, though, were written as entertainment first and foremost, with a few containing a moral message, about the dangers of science, as a secondary motive. Nevertheless, the thrills of scientific possibilities still enthralled the readers of the pulps provided they were woven into stories of high adventure and excitement. Up until 1918, and for some while beyond, the pulps favored the fantastic adventure rather than the scientific, and the works of Edgar Rice Burroughs and Abraham Merritt, especially the latter's "The Moon Pool" (*All-Story*, June 22, 1918) and its sequel, were typical.

1919 saw a concentration of talent in the pulps for fantastic and scientific adventures. It marked the debut of Ray Cummings with "The Girl in the Golden Atom" (*All-Story*, March 15, 1919), the first of his many adventures into sub-atomic worlds. It also saw Murray Leinster's conversion to science fiction with "The Runaway Skyscraper" (*Argosy*, February 22, 1919), and it saw a range of ultra-imaginative stories from Max Brand, Tod Robbins, Austin Hall, Philip M. Fisher, Homer Eon Flint, J. U. Giesy, and Garrett Smith.

It was also the year that saw the first magazine aimed at publishing fantastic and off-trail stories. This was *The Thrill Book*, issued as a semi-monthly magazine on March 1, 1919 by Street & Smith. It lasted only sixteen issues, until October 15, 1919. It published mostly adventure stories and some weird fantasies, but did include a few scientific stories. Two were by Murray Leinster, both scientific-menace stories. In "A Thousand Degrees Below Zero" (July 15, 1919) an evil scientist tries to take over the world by freezing it. In "The Silver Menace" (September 1-15, 1919) a rapidly multiplying organism from the sea soon clogs the oceans and threatens to cover the land. Again there was a message of caution about science and the evil it might bring. The only other story of note, now regarded as a classic, was *The Heads of Cerberus* by Francis Stevens (August 15-October 15, 1919). Three protagonists, through the release of a special drug, are whisked ahead in time to Philadelphia in the year 2118, where life is severely regimented. Once again it showed concern at scientific advance.

The Thrill Book had been the brain-child of the ever-alert Henry William Ralston, Street & Smith's Business Manager. Ralston had noted the growing popularity of the fantastic and futuristic adventure story in both his own and his rivals' magazines. To edit the magazine he brought in Harold Hersey, then an untried pulp editor, who had previously turned his hand to editing small circulation literary magazines and writing the occasional fanciful story and much greater quantities of verse. Between them, Ralston and Hersey determined to put together a magazine of off-trail, bizarre and fantastic adventures, to all intents the first science-fiction magazine. But between theory and practice, ideals slipped. Hersey was too quick to get the project published, and although he began to make contact with a number of talented writers as well as having access to the back-files of Street & Smith's magazines, he failed to tap the vein he needed and all too soon settled for a compromise of a magazine of thrilling adventures, rather than pseudo-scientific ones. It would be fourteen years before Street & Smith would again enter the fields of science fiction, but that time they would get the formula right, and with remarkable effect.

Perhaps the most scientific story published in 1919 was *The Flying Legion* by George Allan England, serialized in *All-Story Weekly* from November 15 to December 20. The center-piece of the novel is an advanced aircraft, the *Eagle of the Sky*, which is part-plane, part-airship, part-helicopter. The craft is captured by "The Master," a millionaire scientist, who uses it to steal treasures from Mecca which he offers in exchange for other treasures. The story has pace and adventure, and is solid escapism.

The volume of scientific adventures in the pulps, especially in *Argosy* and *All-Story* continued into 1920, and the pace only slightly slackened when the two magazines were combined with their issues for July 24, 1920. There was no doubt as to the popularity of this type of fiction, a popularity that one might expect to be reflected in Gernsback's magazines.

Yet during 1919, the most dramatic year for scientific adventures in the pulps, Gernsback's *The Electrical Experimenter* published only a couple of weak, gadget stories that are not memorable as scientific fiction. It's quite possible that most of the technicians and scientists who wrote for Gernsback regarded it as belittling to write fiction, and had no talent or inclination to produce it. In a speech given at the Tenth World Science Fiction Convention in Chicago in August 1952, Gernsback recalled of this period that writers "thought it beneath their dignity" to write science fiction. "Most authors approached on the subject agreed to do a few stories, provided I did not use their real names."[1] The extent to which the fictional offerings in *The Electrical Experimenter* are pseudonymous is difficult to say today, but possibly some of the names do mask scientists of the period. This matter became more pertinent when Gernsback launched *Amazing Stories* in 1926.

In order to expand science fiction in *The Electrical Experimenter* Gernsback needed to attract the professional fiction writer, such as those writing for the pulps. There was an obstacle here, though. Writers valued the relationship they had with the pulps, especially with editor Bob Davis at *All-Story*, and did not feel inclined to jeopardize that market for one that did not pay as well. Gernsback had an odd system of payment to his contributors. Unless an author was under contract to Gernsback (and no pulpster with any sense would tie himself to one market), the occasional contributor was paid at rates equivalent to prizes depending upon the originality of his contribution. The top prize was $100 but it could range down to as little as $5. Writers could expect at least $30 to $40 for stories of around two to three thousand words from their pulp markets. Whilst payment for originality was a good yardstick to encourage inventive minds, it was no basis upon which to write fiction for a living. Moreover, most of the pulp scientific fiction were adventures with anti-science messages, and there were few writers producing pro-science stories.

It would require some effort from Gernsback to remedy the situation. The conversion of *The Electrical Experimenter* to *Science and Invention* was a definite step in that direction, and it is interesting to note that the change came just at the same time that *Argosy* and *All-Story* were combined. Addicts of the scientific adventure now had one less magazine to buy, and quite possibly they would turn their attentions to another title. Although at the time Gernsback could not have known about the moves at Munsey, it was an opportunity he could not overlook. He must already have had the pulp market in mind, for the covers of *Science and Invention* took on the pulp action image. The August issue, for instance, had an eye-catching cover by Howard Brown depicting two deep-sea divers fighting a shark. Although it was illustrating a non-speculative article by Gernsback on "Electrocuting Sharks," it projected the image of deep sea adventure and thrills.

The August issue also included an article by Charles I. Horne, Ph.D., "Jules Verne, the World's Greatest Prophet." Horne was Professor at the College of the City of New York and had edited the only complete English edition of *The Works of Jules Verne* (New York, 1911). He used the article to highlight the inventions that Verne had foreseen in his books, and to urge inventors to do their best to create others that Verne had imagined. There was a follow-up article, published anonymously but probably written by Gernsback, "An American Jules Verne," giving a profile of Lu Senarens, the writer of many dime novel scientific adventures for boys. Senarens admitted a certain embarrassment at the "wild impossible dreams of his younger writing days," but also conceded that "truth is indeed stranger than fiction. I believe anything is possible now."[2]

Gernsback was certainly preparing *Science and Invention* as a vehicle for prophetic fiction, and he started to publish two stories per issue. His main problem was that he did not yet have sufficient writers capable of producing such daring new concepts. What was developing both in *Radio News* and in the former *Electrical Experimenter* was the scientific mystery story. Writers were getting more fun from setting simple problems that could be solved scientifically than from trying to speculate about new inventions or forecast the future. Since there was also a wide public popularity for the detective story, the scientific detective emerged in Gernsback's pages.

One of Gernsback's writers who started to corner this field was Charles S. Wolfe. Wolfe had been a contributor for a number of years, but it was not until the March 1920 *Electrical Experimenter* that he hit his stride. In "Whispering Ether," a safecracker, trying to steal Professor Proctor's explosives formula, is caught in the act by Proctor who has also invented a thought-reading machine. It's a short, effective story, marred as fiction only by the necessary explanation of how the device works. The story was a precursor to Wolfe's "The Educated Harpoon" (April 1920), which introduced scientific detective Joe Fenner, a student, wireless telegraph enthusiast, and experimenter. From time to time the police consult him on technical matters. In this case a man has been stabbed in a room, but no weapon remains, and there was no way anyone could have entered the room without being seen. Fenner deduces that he was stabbed by a bayonet fixed to the nose of a remote-controlled model airplane.

The scientific investigations of Joe Fenner became a regular feature in *The Electrical Experimenter/Science and Invention* over the next year. Though in each case the device used for the murder was only one step ahead of existing technology, the stories were undoubtedly scientific fiction but were borderline speculative fiction. Other writers contributed similar gadget stories, but there were few who would let their imagination run full rein. There were the occasional exceptions. In "The Golden Vapor" (Febraury 1920), E. H. Johnson wrote a surprisingly readable story, despite its lengthy asides into technical lectures. Dr. Grieg invents a matter-transmitter after many years of experimentation. He eventually perfects his machine in such a way that he is able to extract gold from a bank vault and replace it with iron. Because of the slow, restrained way in which it is written, with the Doctor's final triumph, the story is one of the most effective Gernsback had published up till that time. It is not too surprising that a magazine with a wide readership of radio enthusiasts should show an interest in matter transmission, as this regularly featured in the stories from now on. Another example was "The Transformation of Professor Schmitz" by George R. Wells (*Science and Invention*, September 1921). In this story two students assist the Professor in transmitting himself, after he has demonstrated several successful transmissions of a cat, dog, canary and various inanimate objects. With the transmission of the Professor, though, something goes wrong and he never materializes.

Some of the stories became more adventurous. In "The Deflecting Wave" (*Science and Invention*, June 1921), Herbert L. Moulton tells of a remote-controlled airship freight service across the Atlantic in 1927, and how a "pirate" finds means of capturing the unmanned ships. What could have been a dull story is made interesting by the activities of the story's hero who is sent out to find what has happened to the missing airships.

One writer, however, rapidly began to dominate *Science and Invention*, Clement Fezandié. Fezandié was of French-American origin and had been born in New York in 1865. He had worked in the antiseptic business of the Declat Manufacturing Company from which he had retired in March 1919, spending the next few years travelling. Gernsback recalled that Fezandié wrote for fun only, returning all of the checks he was sent in payment for his stories.[3] He had written a science-fiction novel as early as 1898 called *Through the Earth* (Century, 1898) which was serialized in much abbreviated form in the young readers' *St. Nicholas's Magazine*. This novel concerned the construction of a tube through Earth from America to Australia, and the subsequent journey through the tunnel. The story was written with a certain technological bravado, and it's still readable today.

Fezandié first appeared in *The Electrical Experimenter* in the July 1920 issue with "My Message to Mars." This was an ideal Gernsback story, or rather lecture in the theory of interplanetary communication. The narrator tells how he contacts a Martian by radio and then elaborately explains how he teaches the Martian our numbers, formulae and alphabet. It reads more like an article on numbers by Isaac Asimov than a story though some token love interest in thrown in at the end by way of humor. The approach, though, was typical of all of Fezandié's stories.

His regular contributions began in the May 1921 *Science and Invention* with the first of his long-running series of "Doctor Hackensaw's Secrets." Like "My Message to Mars," the episodes hardly qualify as stories, but rather a series of discourses, just as you might imagine Fezandié lecturing. In the first, "The Secret of Artificial Reproduction," Dr. Hackensaw (we never learn much about him) is visited by Silas Rockett, a newspaper reporter, for an interview about his latest discovery. Hackensaw then proceeds to tell the reporter all the known facts about artificial reproduction, the processes of artificial insemination and genetic engineering, and then unveils some of his marvels, such as a half-dog/half-cat, perfect trick ponies, and a baby girl incubated inside the womb of a cow. The story concentrates solely on the possibilities generated by Hackensaw's inventions with total disregard for the human or humane consequences. The emphasis is on scientific advance, initially for profit, and secondarily for the various industrial or social advantages that might arise. In the second lecture, "The Secret of the Atom" (July 1921), Rockett again interviews Hackensaw, this time about his super-microscope which magnifies down to the atomic level. One of the consequences, Hackensaw points out, is that all microbes can be identified, and thereby cures for all known afflictions, including cancer, may be solved.

The series continued in the same vein for month after month, with Hackensaw's discourses on suspended animation (October 1921), invisibility (May 1922), robots (June 1922)—called the "tel-automaton" by Fezandié, television (October 1922), and the secret of life (July 1922). Seldom was there any action, although in a three-part sub-series, rather imitating Gernsback's own adventures of Baron Munchhausen, Hackensaw takes a trip to the moon (September-November 1923). There were also trips in time, to the year 2025 (December 1922) and then 3000 (January 1925), a journey "Around the World in Eighty Hours" (June 1924), and into sub-microscopic worlds (October 1924). There were forty stories in the series in *Science and Invention*, culminating in the only real adventure Hackensaw has, a four-part serial *Journey to the Center of the Earth* (June-September 1925).

Writing in 1961, Gernsback called Fezandié a "titan of science fiction."[4] That is hard to grasp by today's definition of science fiction, but we have to remember that Gernsback was talking about his own definition. These stories more than any others in *Science and Invention* epitomized Gernsback's model for scientific fiction. They extrapolated from existing known science to suggest future inventions and what they might achieve; and all for the sole purpose of stimulating the everyday man, who had a penchant for experimenting and tinkering with gadgets, into creating that future. To the man who could make that startling invention might come fame and fortune. Needless to say, in this environment there was no point in over-stimulation, since although the inventor might dream, he might only progress a stage at a time. Thus the stories were simply looking one step ahead of today, and not taking that cosmic leap into a bold new world.

Once in a while Gernsback did like to over-stimulate, to really pump the imagination. Perhaps his own best example was an article in the February 1922 *Science and Invention*, "10,000 Years Hence." Howard Brown provided a stunning illustration of floating health cities kept aloft in the upper atmosphere by power rays drawing their energy from the sun. Gernsback described how these cities could be directed to move around the Earth, a concept one might believe inspired two later noted works of science fiction, Edmond Hamilton's "Cities in the Air" (1929) and James Blish's *Earthman, Come Home* (1955), if it wasn't that neither author knew of it. Gernsback also postulated how individuals would have personal power packs enabling them to jet through the atmosphere propelled by power rays derived from electro-energy converted from static energy in the atmosphere.

Gernsback posed these more dramatic concepts clearly in the hope of inspiring writers to take that one extra leap of the imagination. Where his own writers could not provide the material, he chose to reprint two stories by H. G. Wells. "The New Accelerator" *(Science and Invention,* February 1923) is a straightforward invention story telling of a drug that speeds up the taker's metabolism so that to his perception time slows down. "The Star" (March 1923) is on a more cosmic scale, as Earth is threatened by an errant star but is saved when the star is eclipsed by our own Moon. Whilst most of Gernsback's writers could have attempted something along the lines of "The New Accelerator," although with moderately less success, a story such as "The Star" would not have entered their minds, because it was not a gadget story. It was a story of cosmic consequences.

Gernsback's use of these two stories and his own highly speculative articles suggest that he was trying to achieve more in *Science and Invention* than simply inspire readers into creating new inventions, although that was (and to a large extent always remained) his basic premise. He can only have been using them to provoke a response from readers as to their own feelings in having such stories in their magazine. He was probably already seriously considering the possibility of issuing a separate scientific-fiction magazine, but needed to know reader reaction and writer response. Further activities that year were also having an effect, which would make 1923 even more significant than 1919 in the evolution of science fiction.

9.

TESTING THE MARKET

Past histories of science fiction have given little regard to the period between 1919 and 1923 even though, as we have seen, there was much activity both in the pulps and in Gernsback's publishing world. Before exploring this development further, let's first pause to consider the foundation Gernsback was establishing for himself in his own business dealings.

By the early twenties, Gernsback was a successful businessman. The artist, Alex Schomburg, who first met him in 1925, remembered him as "... striking. People would turn round and look at him when he walked down the street. He dressed in a very European style ... One day there was a knock on my door and when I opened it, there stood Hugo Gernsback. He was wearing a grey homburg hat, white spats, a monocle and a cape over his coat."[1] In his personal life Gernsback had divorced from his first wife, and in October 1921 he had married Dorothy Kantrowitz. He already had two children from his first marriage, Madelon and Harvey, and there would be two more from the second, Bertina and Jocelyn.

He was still running the Electro-Importing Company, which was now manufacturing as well as importing electrical parts for the flourishing radio and electrical business. He was expanding his business concerns, establishing the Consrad Company for further radio work, and the Germott Company for various publishing and book trade dealings. His two magazines, *Science and Invention* and *Radio News*, had circulations of around 200,000 and 150,000 respectively. In 1921, on the same day as his wedding, he launched a third magazine: *Practical Electrics*. This was a rehash of the original *The Electrical Experimenter*, but with the conversion of that magazine to the more general *Science and Invention* he now needed a new vehicle to cover the basics of experimentation on electrical subjects. This didn't stop him including a stimulus in the first issue with his own article on "Fifty Years Hence," projecting a view of New York in 1971, with electric cars, individually powered roller skates, roof-top gardens and long-distance subways.

With these three magazines Gernsback needed additional editorial help. He brought in the veteran Thomas O'Conor Sloane as associate editor on *Practical Electrics*. Sloane had been born in 1851, and was thus seventy when he entered Gernsback's publishing business. He had been a former Professor of Natural Sciences at Seton Hall College in South Orange, New Jersey, but since 1884 had concentrated on technical and scientific books, of which he had written fourteen: his latest, *Rapid Arithmetic*, was just going to press. Others had included *Home Experiments in Science* (1888), *Electricity Simplified* (1891), *How to Become a Successful Electrician* (1894), and *The Electrician's Handy Book* (1905). He had been on the editorial staff of several magazines, including *Scientific American* and *Youth's Companion*, and so had probably been aware of Gernsback's scientific endeavors since 1905. His first article for Gernsback, "Liquid Air," appeared in the September 1920 *Science and Invention* and he became a regular contributor thereafter. He was a natural for editing *Practical Electrics* for, despite his age, he had an alert and experienced mind, and was solid and reliable. He was also down-to-earth with little, if any vision, but that did not matter too much in *Practical Electrics*.

Sloane also assisted Harold Secor in editing *Science and Invention*. Further assistance came from Joseph H. Kraus (1898-1967), a remarkable behind-the-scenes man, who seemed to be something of a jack-of-all-trades. We will encounter Kraus many times during this history, as a scientist, radio enthusiast, public notary, music conductor, and magazine editor. Just where and when Kraus acquired all these skills, I know not, but he was clearly a man of much value. He was also a prolific writer of articles. His first for Gernsback, on radio couplers, had been in the January 1919 *Electrical Experimenter*, but he did not become a regular contributor until he began a series of articles on, of all things, "The Amateur Magician," starting in the December 1919 issue.

Gernsback had now gathered about him all of the people, bar C. A. Brandt, with whom he would move forward into the age of science fiction, though I doubt it had been planned that way. Almost as a symbolic gesture to wireless, the foundation of his wealth and the love of his life, he issued a book, *Radio for All* (1922), which rapidly became the bible for amateur radio enthusiasts. It explained not only how everyone could have his own radio transmitter and receiver, but how radio would soon establish itself on a commercial basis with everyone receiving radio broadcasts from private and public stations. In fact Gernsback would soon be planning his own broadcasting station, which we cover in the next chapter.

The expansion of Gernsback's business also required a move to new premises. The laboratories at Fulton Street remained for the Electro Importing Company, but the Experimenter Publishing Company moved to new offices at 53 Park Place in January 1923.

In the meantime, science fiction was continuing to make itself prominent in the world about Gernsback. The combined *Argosy All-Story Weekly* had been publishing not only stirring scientific romances but stories of a more serious scientific nature. The scientific romance had probably now peaked. J. U. Giesy appeared with the last of his Jason Croft series of adventures set on a planet orbiting Sirius, *Jason, Son of Jason* (April 16-May 21, 1921), though Edgar Rice Burroughs continued his series about John Carter's adventures on Mars in *The Chessmen of Mars* (February 18-April 1, 1922). The more serious stories included Murray Leinster's tale of a far future Earth, "The Red Dust" (April 2, 1921), and Ray Cummings's "The Gravity Professor" (May 7, 1921). Whilst hybrid scientific romances included the legendary *The Blind Spot* by Austin Hall and Homer Eon Flint (May 14-June 18, 1921), and Flint's solo voyages to the stars Capella and Arcturus in "The Devolutionist" and "The Emancipatrix" (July 23 and September 3, 1921).

By 1923 *Argosy* was overstocked with such items and was turning lesser material away. *Argosy* was also giving greater emphasis to the western story and scientific fiction was temporarily out of favor. Authors who had previously relied on the dual markets of *Argosy* and *All-Story* now found themselves limited. It either meant they had to write non-scientific stories, or find another market. One possibility that emerged early in 1923 was a new pulp called *Weird Tales*. This was published in Chicago by Jacob Henneberger, who had had some success with a students' magazine called *College Humor*, and who was now expanding his own publishing empire. With the popularity of the detective story, Henneberger had issued a semi-monthly *Detective Tales*, first issue dated October 1, 1922. As editor he had appointed detective-fiction writer Edwin Baird. Since Henneberger was a fan of the work of Edgar Allan Poe, in the fields of both detective fiction and horror fiction, he brought out *Weird Tales* as a companion title. Published as a monthly, the first issue was dated March 1923. Baird edited both titles, but because he was not a great fan of horror fiction, the stories, written by many of the same writers as in *Detective Tales*, lacked imagination or originality. The magazine did publish some scientific fiction along the theme of the monstrosity-in-the-laboratory, such as Anthony M. Rud's "Ooze" in the first issue.

The two best known names from the pulps to appear in *Weird Tales* in its first year were Francis Stevens and Austin Hall, both with stories that had probably been rejected from *Argosy*. Stevens's story, "Sunfire" (July/August-September 1923) was a fantastic adventure set on a South American island where the "sunfire," a giant diamond, is worshipped by a tribe of Indians who make human sacrifices to it and its guardian, a monstrous centipede. This was not the usual Gernsbackian fare for *Science and Invention*. Hall's *People of the Comet* (September-October 1923) was more appropriate as it concerns a race of superbeings who enter our own atom-sized universe from a greater macrocosm.

Weird Tales in its first year was by and large uninspiring, though it did start to establish a number of new authors, amongst them Otis Adelbert Kline and H. P. Lovecraft.

Writers looking for new scientific-fiction markets outside *Argosy*, and aiming at more localized markets than *Weird Tales* in Chicago, turned their sights to *Science and Invention*. Although its payment rates seemed unreliable, it had a good circulation and was respectable. Gernsback's first opportunity came with George Allan England, at one time second only to Burroughs as the most popular writer of scientific romances in the pulps. England's "The Thing from—Outside," was probably a rejection from one of the main fiction pulps. England may have submitted it to Gernsback on the off-chance, but it is more likely to have been in response to an enquiry from Gernsback. The story was unlike anything Gernsback had previously published, bringing in both a higher literary quality and a strong story-line, not just a discourse on inventions. In "The Thing from—Outside" a party of three men and two women, lost in the frozen wastes of northern Canada, find themselves harrassed by an unseen intelligence. There is no attempt to identify the menace, although one of the party conjectures about the theories of Charles Fort and the possibility that there are remote parts of Earth where the original "owners" still live. The story probably owes its genesis to Fort's books, though there may be some influence from Algernon Blackwood's "The Wendigo," and it may in turn have contributed to John W. Campbell's classic "Who Goes There?" Nowhere is there the hint of an invention, or a scientist's soliloquy on the potential of science. Instead the story is pure entertainment with a helping of that "sense of wonder" that would later epitomise good science fiction.

In one jolt, George Allan England had done more to promote scientific fiction in *Science and Invention* than almost anyone previously. Coming hot on the reprint of the two stories by H. G. Wells, it almost suggests a strategy, and bearing in mind what was to follow, it either proves that Gernsback was planning a major expansion of his scientific stories, or sudden good fortune pushed him in that direction. For straight after the England story, Gernsback was able to boast a new serial by no less than Ray Cummings, certainly the hottest writer of scientific fiction in the pulps, and rated close behind Burroughs and Merritt on popularity in fantastic fiction. The story was "Around the Universe" and it ran in *Science and Invention* in six parts from July to December 1923. It was one of Cummings's stories about Tubby, a little man whose wishes come true. The series had been running for three years in *All-Story* and *Argosy*, which suggests this story was also written for them. One night, in discussion with others about the nature of Space, Tubby wishes he knew all about Space and could see what was out there. He is promptly visited by a Professor with the delightful name of Sir Isaac Swift DeFoe Wells-Verne. The Professor shows Tubby his space-flier and promptly they are off on a tour of the Universe. The whole story is a fun robinsonade, again with that "sense of wonder," and not too many scientific lectures in between. On arrival on Venus, Tubby meets and falls in love with the beautiful Ameena. He learns of plans by the Mercutians and Martians to attack Earth. Setting out to foil the plot, the three of them first visit Jupiter and the outer planets and then journey to the very edge of the Universe, which is the inner sphere of an Atom (shades of Dyson Spheres). The party then return to the solar system to outwit the enemy. At the end Tubby and Ameena marry. It's a quaint, naïve story, its science outdated, but for its time it was a remarkable space adventure, and would certainly have widened the eyes of any susceptible readers, especially the young.

Cummings was a scoop for Gernsback. Gernsback was probably already acquainted with him through the pulps, but he may have been introduced via T. O'Conor Sloane. Sloane's son had married the daughter of the inventor Thomas A. Edison, and Cummings, up until the time he turned to full-time writing, was working at Edison's phonograph factory. Cummings was rapidly becoming the most prolific writer of scientific stories in the pulps, with almost twenty to his credit in his first four years. The first, "The Girl in the Golden Atom," had been a great success and had been followed by a novel-length sequel, *The People of the Golden Atom* (*All-Story Weekly*, January 24-February 28, 1920). The two had been published as *The Girl in the Golden Atom* in hardcover in 1923 by Harper in New York, an event of some significance at a time when so little science fiction from the pulps saw book publication. To be able to boast Cummings when *Argosy* was publishing proportionately less scientific fiction, would have helped boost *Science and Invention*'s circulation, and was good news for devotees of scientific fiction.

Gernsback still needed to raise the profile of scientific fiction in *Science and Invention* if he was serious about it. He had made a step in that direction with the December 1922 issue. There he had asked one of his staff artists to devise a cover which showed a set of separate magazine covers for each of the nine departments represented in the magazine. These were "Newest Inventions," "How to Make It," "Radio," "Wrinkles, Recipes and Formulas," "Popular Astronomy," "Latest Patents," "Chemistry," "Motor Hints," and "Scientific Fiction." In producing it, the artist had created the first specific science-fiction magazine cover in history.

But the major event came eight months later. July 25, 1923 was the publication date of the August issue of *Science and Invention*. The cover, by Howard Brown, was a remarkable painting of an upside-down space-suited man in outer space surrounded by stars and planets. The cover bore the title of the story illustrated, "The Man from the Atom" as well as the bold caption: **SCIENTIFIC FICTION NUMBER**.

The table of contents was set out as usual. Disappointingly there was no section highlighted "Scientific Fiction," nor was any special attention drawn to it in Gernsback's editorial which was on "Predicting Future Inventions." This continued to promote Gernsback's belief that inventors have to be prophets in their own way in imagining future inventions.

The issue contained all the same features and regular articles readers had come to expect, but instead of the usual one or two stories, there was a total of six. The readers would have expected the second episode of Ray Cummings's "Around the Universe" and the nineteenth of Clement Fezandié's Doctor Hackensaw stories, "The Secret of the Super Telescope." The rest were a bonus. The cover story, "The Man from the Atom" was by new writer G. Peyton Wertenbaker. That mouthful disguised a young man, only sixteen years old, who came from a distinguished family of writers. The idea behind the story, that of sub- and supra-atomic worlds, was already becoming hackneyed, having been used by Cummings, Hall, and Fezandié. But in Wertenbaker's case he wrote a story full of feeling and emotion. It remains powerful today. Professor Martyn is trying to build an atomic energy motor, but by chance creates a machine that will make its wearer either double or halve in size *ad infinitum*. He gets his friend Kirby to try it. Kirby doubles in size so rapidly that soon he outgrows the Earth, and finds himself growing through the Universe until he enters a macro-universe. Wishing to return to Earth he reverses the process only to realize that with time relative to mass, the sun and Earth have grown old and died in moments and Kirby finds himself alone, isolated on an alien planet around a remote star, trillions of years in the future. The story, for all its fabricated science, emanates a feeling of despair that is tangible, and makes one yearn with Kirby. Only "The Star" by Wells and "The Thing from—Outside" by England had previously stirred any emotions. All the other stories were coldly scientific and logical. "The Man from the Atom" remains one of the best stories Gernsback ever published.

The other stories in the issue were on a par with Gernsback's usual offerings. "Advanced Chemistry" by Jack G. Huekels was a humorous story about a professor who invents a serum capable of bringing the dead back to life. All goes well until the Professor dies and a stranger administers the serum wrongly, with electrifying results. The story is slight and the science minimal. "The Electric Duel" by Gernsback is nothing more than a short squib describing a duel between two men with electrified poles. They stand on an insulated board and the first to touch the earth will be electrocuted. The "it was all a dream" ending only weakens what was already a trite piece. The final story, "Vanishing Movies" by Teddy J. Holman, hardly qualifies as science fiction. It is a reasonable scientific mystery story, about a movie-house where the picture projected on the screen vanishes when the cinema is full. Unfortunately the caption beneath Paul's illustration reveals the solution before you've even started the story.

The scientific fiction took up scarcely one-eighth of the whole issue. In wordage terms this was less than might be found in equivalent issues of the pulps. For instance, the April 23, 1921 issue of *Argosy All-Story Weekly* had contained the stories "Moon Madness" by Ray Cummings, "Madam Tsetse" by George Allan England, plus an episode of J. U. Giesy's serial *Jason, Son of Jason*, all of which amounted to about one-fifth of that issue. In quality of content the issue of *Argosy* was also better value for money, as only Wertenbaker's "The Man from the Atom" and Cummings's serial were of any entertainment value in *Science and Invention*. But in promotional terms, in what Gernsback was doing for the marketing and image of scientific fiction, the August 1923 *Science and Invention* was a landmark. It drew the magazine publishers' attentions to the fact that scientific fiction, already known to be popular amongst its readers, had a sales potential of its own.

There is not much overt evidence of the success of Gernsback's special scientific-fiction issue. The letter column contained a few polite letters commenting upon the enjoyment of the stories generally in the magazine, rather than specifically in that issue. But that is not too surprising. Gernsback preferred to publish letters that raised queries of scientific interest or challenged the scientific articles. He was not that interested in reader adulation.

By Gernsback's own actions, though, it was clear that there was much readership demand for more scientific fiction. According to Sam Moskowitz, in 1924, Gernsback issued 25,000 circulars soliciting subscriptions for a new magazine of such stories, to be called *Scientifiction*. The response was lukewarm. Moskowitz has speculated this was because readers were predominantly collectors and therefore not keen on receiving mailed copies that might be damaged or delayed. That may have been part of the reason, but it is equally likely that potential readers would rather see the magazine first, than invest money in advance in a project that might not materialize. Moreover, this was the heyday of the pulp magazine with the newsstands brimming with titles. Most readers could pick and choose and would see no reason for subscribing. Which brings us to what is probably the main reason. Gernsback would have sent his circular to his own subscribers, readers who had a special interest in *Science and Invention*, and probably also *Radio News* and *Practical Electrics*. The type of person most likely to *subscribe* to a technical magazine is the more mature, established man who could either afford hobbies of an electrical or radio nature, or who was in the electrical business. These may have appreciated the scientific stories as interesting novelties, but not to the extent of subscribing to a magazine devoted to them. After all, the August 1923 issue had not contained much fiction of note, and although one or two stories per issue was pleasing, an issue full of them may have been overegging the omelette. The type of person more likely to respond to a magazine of scientific stories, especially of the pulp-adventure type rather than of speculative science, was the young person, interested in imaginative adventures. These youngsters were unlikely to be subscribers. They would either read their father's copies, or buy them from the newsstands when the money was available. So it is no surprise that Gernsback had a mild response to his circular. It was aimed at the wrong readership.

What Gernsback did not know, but which may have otherwise prompted him into action, was that someone else was considering launching a magazine of pseudo-science stories. At about the same time that Gernsback was issuing his circular, *Weird Tales* was in all kinds of financial difficulties and had suspended publication with the May/June/July 1924 issue. The publisher Jacob Henneberger was endeavoring to obtain financial backing, but until then the future of *Weird Tales* was in the balance. Farnsworth Wright, whom Henneberger would finally select as *Weird Tales*'s new editor, was also looking for finances to launch his own magazine, *Strange Tales*, which would concentrate on pseudo-scientific stories plus a balance of the weird and fantastic. In the event, Henneberger found his finances by selling the profitable companion to *Weird Tales*, now called *Real Detective Tales*, and reinvesting that money in *Weird Tales*. Wright took up his duties as editor and forsook his interests in launching a pseudo-science magazine. Instead *Weird Tales* now published many science-fiction stories, especially those by J. Schlossel and Edmond Hamilton, and probably took on the identity of Wright's aborted *Strange Tales*. Nevertheless, had Gernsback known of Wright's intentions, he might have launched *Scientifiction* in 1924.

Gernsback did try one other measure to check the popularity of science fiction. He arranged the hardcover publication of his novel *Ralph 124C 41+*. It was issued by the Stratford Publishing Company in Boston in 1925 in an edition of 5,000 copies and sold for $2.15. I do not know the number of copies sold, but even though it was not reprinted, sales may have been sufficient to have indicated to Gernsback that there was a high interest in science fiction. But before he took that next step, Gernsback had other interests in hand.

10.

THROUGH THE ETHER

Although Gernsback had raised the profile of scientific fiction in *Science and Invention* and had floated the concept of an all science-fiction magazine, he was still not getting the response he might have wished from his readers and potential writers. Gernsback had almost certainly tied both Ray Cummings and Clement Fezandié to contracts, as they appeared regularly each issue. When Cummings's *Around the Universe* finished in the December 1923 issue it was promptly followed by a new, nine-part serial, *The Man on the Meteor* which ran from January to September 1924. This was, to a large degree, more of the same, as it explored life and adventures on a meteor as it sped through the universe.

There was now a noticeable absence of short fiction in *Science and Invention*. Only one stand-alone story appeared there in the next four years, and that was "The Infinite Vision" by Charles C. Winn in the issue for May 1924. This told of the construction of a super-telescope which reveals the rocks on the Moon and cities on Mars, but is then destroyed in a storm, as if Nature was seeking its revenge. It contained nothing that hadn't already been told by Dr. Hackensaw in Fezandié's "The Secret of the Super-Telescope" in the August 1923 issue, and indeed may have been suggested by that story.

The short fiction had now shifted to *Practical Electrics*. This magazine still had a low circulation, and it is suggestive of the sales potential of scientific fiction that Gernsback should include it in that magazine in a hope to boost sales. In the February 1924 issue, Gernsback announced that:

> Responding to a general demand from our readers . . . we are publishing the first of a series of fiction stories of an electrical nature. We will have in future issue *[sic]*, fiction stories of this kind which, of course, will be along electrical lines. Any one of our readers, who has an inclination for writing, should submit a story to us. We are paying good rates for stories, particularly if the electrical element is kept in the foreground. Of course, the stories must have some literary value.[1]

Few of the stories had any "literary value," but they were high on original ideas, even though Gernsback had not asked for a speculative element. The first author to appear was George F. Stratton, now seventy-one years old, but still capable of looking forward. He provided two invention stories, "Sam Graves' Electric Mind Revealer" and, for the March issue, "Sam Graves' Gravity Nullifier." The latter showed that Stratton's originality was perhaps limited, since the stories read like the post-war adventures of Ned Cawthorne. The other stories, were still essentially gadget stories of the type formerly seen in *Science and Invention*, though the concepts received a more mature treatment and the stories were thus more entertaining. "Premonition" by J. Kay London (April 1924), for example, whilst essentially the story of a murderer's revenge upon a witness (by creating a room bathed in harmful X-rays), also explored the intuitive or scientific nature of premonitions. Perhaps the best, and certainly the most intriguing, is "The Man Who Saw Beyond" by James Pevey (May 1924). An inventor, John Palmer, summons two doctors to his house to act as helpers and witnesses. He has perfected a ray which will disassociate the atoms in his body and thereby free his soul. A further ray reassociates the body after a given period. Palmer's experiment is a success, but what he has witnessed in the world beyond is too vast to allow him to remain on Earth, and he frees his soul again, this time destroying his invention.

Radio News continued to run its share of short radio stories, but these were seldom of a speculative nature, and in fact rarely took themselves seriously. 1924 and 1925 were dominated by two series of humorous stories. The first by Ellis Parker Butler—a famous name guaranteed to give status to the magazine—ran to sixteen spoof radio invention stories in much the same format as his own famous "Pigs Is Pigs." The second was by Robert Francis Smith, whose tales cleverly lampooned noted books or plays, with such titles as "The Wail of the Lonesome Shrine," "A Midsummer Night's Scheme," "Gentlemen Prefer Broadcasts," and "He Bloops to Conquer." Only one story published in the whole of *Radio News*'s history really qualifies as science fiction and that was an adaptation of a silent movie. "The Radio King," serialized in the November and December 1922 issues, had been adapted by George Bronson Howard from the movie serial by Robert Dillon. Government official Bradley Dane and scientist John Leydon team up to combat the mad scientist Marnee, "Wizard of the Electrons" who, with his Russian and Chinese communist accomplices, threatens to take over the world. Throughout the serial is an impressive array of inventions including a radio which can receive broadcasts from out of the past.

Gernsback was now giving emphasis in his serious science fiction to the novel-length work. There were probably two reasons for this. One, the sound commercial sense that a serial sustained readers from issue to issue and thus maintained and maybe even increased circulation. The second was that the novels allowed a greater development of scientific ideas rather than concentrate on one single invention or theory. There was possibly a third reason, and that was that he was more likely to attract the professional writers who would be more interested in the accumulated payment for a serial than for one-off short stories.

When Cummings's *The Man on the Meteor* concluded, Gernsback ran a new serial, *The Living Death* by John Martin Leahy (*Science and Invention*, October 1924-June 1925). This may have been a reject from *Argosy* or *Weird Tales* (where Leahy had had a vampire novel, *Draconda*, serialized from the November 1923 to the May/July 1924 issues). Leahy may have been a regular reader of *Science and Invention*: a later story by him, in fact his best known, "In Amundsen's Tent" (*Weird Tales*, January 1928), bears comparison with England's "The Thing from Outside." Gernsback was enthusiastic about *The Living Death*. In announcing it he said:

> This without a doubt is one of the most powerful and at the same time gripping scientific stories that we have published so far. There will not be a single installment that does not hold your undivided attention. Not only has Mr. Leahy written a tremen-

dous story, but the scientific data which he presents is such as to set everyone thinking. This story ranks with the best of Jules Verne.[2]

Praise indeed. Leahy's novel was on a par with the scientific romances in *Argosy*. It tells of an expedition to the Antarctic to explore a sub-tropical land surrounded by mountains sighted on an earlier expedition. Here the explorers discover a variety of unknown wild-life, including savage bear-men, plus the body of a young girl encased in ice. The novel ends with the girl brought back to life, and with much to reveal about the previous life in this land.

The reader reaction to "The Living Death" was good, with many highlighting it as the best Gernsback had published. A definite core of science-fiction readers were becoming apparent. One such correspondent was Donovan Helmuth of Cleveland, Ohio, whose letter appeared in the August 1925 issue. He declared he was an "enthusiast of pseudo-scientific fiction" and showed a tendency of later science-fiction fans for keeping details of their favorite fiction by submitting a list of all the stories he knew that were set on the Moon.

Leahy's serial was followed by a new Cummings novel, *Tarrano the Conqueror* (July 1925 to August 1926). Tarrano is another evil scientist intent on taking over not just the world but the solar system. His plans against the Earth and Venus are eventually thwarted by Jac Hallen and Princess Maida of Venus. This novel was straight pulp adventure of the type for which Cummings had become renowned. There was little real science in it, though it projected vividly both space travel and an elixir of immortality. Again it was received enthusiastically.

Over in *Practical Electrics* Gernsback was making a further move. The magazine's circulation remained low, around the fifty thousand mark, and Gernsback sought to recover the market he had originally gained with *The Electrical Experimenter*. Although the policy of *Practical Electrics* did not alter, he felt a title change was necessary, so with the November 1924 issue it was retitled *The Experimenter*, with the attention of appealing to all experimenters. Moreover, because of the preference of serials over short fiction, Gernsback began serialization in *The Experimenter* of Victor MacClure's *The Ark of the Covenant*. This had been published in Britain earlier that year as *Ultimatum*, and under its variant title in New York by Harper. Gernsback must have purchased the serial rights from Harper, which shows that by 1924 he was actively seeking new scientific fiction as opposed to relying purely on submissions. This novel, long regarded as a classic, tells of a mysterious airship, *The Ark of the Covenant*, which demands an end to War otherwise it will use sleep gas on all cities. The Master of the airship turns out to be a noted scientist, David Torrance, who had disappeared twenty years earlier following an accident with radioactive material. Torrance had established a base on a remote South American plateau where he continued his experiments, and discovered the sleep gas Aithon and a mysterious D-1 Ray.

Although Gernsback was still not publishing as much in the way of scientific adventures as either *Argosy* or *Weird Tales*, he had certainly increased his quota of material, and the emphasis now was more on inspiration than education. Gernsback had come to realize with the popularity of scientific fiction, that it continued to act as a stimulus even if it was primarily entertaining rather than coldly instructive. His own coterie of scientific writers may have had the talents to describe new inventions in the manner of Fezandié's Dr. Hackensaw, but they could seldom write entertaining and enjoyable fiction. For that Gernsback had to lower his scientific values in order to widen his market to attract the writers capable of both entertaining and stimulating.

However, despite being the main market for Ray Cummings, *Science and Invention* still did not have sufficient profile to attract new writers. If it had, the history of science fiction may have been significantly different. For instance, Edward E. Smith, destined to become the greatest name in the early days of magazine science fiction, had been working on his novel, *The Skylark of Space*, since 1915, and submitting it to magazines since 1920. He had sent it to *Argosy* in 1922, which was just the wrong time as science fiction was out of favor then, and it was rejected as being "too far out," a strange comment for a magazine that had published the most way-out fiction of the last ten years. Smith continued to send it to magazines and as regularly received rejections. He clearly never considered *Science and Invention* as a market for his novel, yet its cosmic scientific concepts would certainly have attracted Gernsback as it did when he eventually saw it six years later. Likewise, Edmond Hamilton, who had been a fan of science fiction in *Argosy* and *All-Story* since 1920, failed to regard *Science and Invention* for his stories when he started to write in 1924. His first submissions were to *Weird Tales*, where new editor Farnsworth Wright bought Hamilton's first science-fiction novella "Across Space" (*Weird Tales*, September-November 1926). In this Martians are surviving underground on Easter Island and have made a device which will draw Mars closer to Earth to allow the expanding population to migrate across.

Perhaps the greatest blow was the loss of the first of the Radio Man series by Ralph Milne Farley. Farley was the pen name for Roger Sherman Hoar, a thirty-seven-year old lawyer and engineer. A former state senator, Hoar was an ideal Gernsback writer and inventor. When running for the Wisconsin State Senate in 1910 his Republican opponents characterized him as "rattle-brained, consumed by wild-eyed visionary schemes." Enlisted in the War in 1918, he had risen from an artillery man to captain and had invented a device for aiming big guns by the stars, a system that formed the basis for the science of ballistics. He could almost have been one of the ignored inventors that Ned Cawthorne financed.

In 1923 Hoar completed a novel about Myles Cabot, a Boston inventor, who inadvertently invents a matter transmitter and broadcasts himself to Venus. There he has the standard Burroughsian adventures and ends up marrying the beautiful princess. As such, *The Radio Man*, was standard fare and today is regarded as pulp hack work. At the time, though, Hoar had taken a vital step forward. In Burroughs's Martian novels the means whereby John Carter ventures from Earth to Mars is never properly explained. It still smacks of the occult and astral trips. In *The Radio Man*, Hoar had found a scientific means of projecting Cabot to Venus. At a time when radio was all the rage, Hoar had brought the science into the scientific romance!

It seemed almost an insult that Hoar should not consider submitting *The Radio Man* to *Science and Invention*. The magazine had, after all, already published a number of stories involving matter transmission, most recently (and not surprisingly) one of Fezandié's Dr. Hackensaw stories, "The Secret of

Electrical Transmission" (September 1922). Moreover Hugo Gernsback was almost Mr. Radio himself, having been one of radio's most avid and vocal supporters for twenty years. Yet Hoar by-passed Gernsback—he may not even have known of his magazines—and submitted the story to *Argosy* where science fiction was now back in favor. Not only was it published, as a four-part serial from June 28, 1924, under the title "The Radio Man," it was boldly declared on the cover as "A Scientific Adventure." That issue's editorial was given over to promoting the story where it emphasized that Farley was a scientist and that everything in the story was scientifically accurate. It seems *Argosy* was playing Gernsback at his own game.

If there was any message in this it was that the scientific adventure was now a major market force. Gernsback could not claim the credit for this. If anything it had been marketed in *Argosy* and *All-Story* and the credit should go to *All-Story* editor Robert H. Davis and to his authors, especially Edgar Rice Burroughs and Abraham Merritt. But, and it's a big but, these stories, which had been termed scientific romances, had actually laid little emphasis on the science, and were much better termed fantastic adventures. What Gernsback had done had shown that there was a market interested in these stories as much for their scientific accuracy as for their fantastic adventures, and that a new breed of writer was emerging who was scientifically based and capable of weaving accurate science into their stories, and moreover speculating on the possibilities of that science and projecting prophecies of the future. This new breed included Ray Cummings, Murray Leinster, and Ralph Milne Farley.

The time was certainly ripe in the 1924/25 period to issue an all scientific fiction magazine. It is perhaps surprising that the Munsey Corporation did not do so, although this was a time of change for them. They had just launched their first specialist magazine, *Flynn's*, in the detective fiction field. The first issue was dated September 20, 1924 and it appeared as a weekly. Robert H. Davis was its editor, and his time was taken up with establishing this new magazine. Otherwise he would have been the most likely candidate to edit a new scientific fiction magazine, perhaps the only choice. Moreover, Frank Munsey died on December 22, 1925, and it may not have seemed opportune or appropriate to invest in a new publishing gamble just at that time.

Street and Smith, the other venerable pulp publisher, might have gambled but, following the failure of *The Thrill Book*, was probably biding its time. Certainly the editors there were watching market trends but were more likely waiting for someone else to make the first move. Most other publishers, such as the Ridgway Company which issued *Everybody's* and *Adventure*, and the Blue Book Company with *Blue Book*, though they published scientific fiction, would not have seen it as a worthy investment.

The only other publisher likely to have experimented was Bernarr Macfadden. Macfadden was the publisher of *Physical Culture*, which he had launched back in March 1899, though the basis of his publishing success was *True Story*, which appeared in May 1919. He was a self-confessed enthusiast of science fiction, but his personal interests in a better world lay more in the physical developments of the human body, in health, nutrition and social reform than in scientific achievement. According to the researches of Sam Moskowitz, Macfadden had been promoting science fiction for longer than Gernsback—the

earliest story he had published had been "My Bride from the Other World" by
E. C. Atkins in the June 1904 *Physical Culture*. The most significant piece of
fiction that he published was *Children of "Kultur"* by Milo Hastings (*True
Story*, June-November 1919), subsequently published in book form as *The City
of Endless Night* (Dodd, Mead, 1920). Set in the twenty-second century, it portrays a German dominated industrial Europe, with Germany's fortunes resting
on their control of a special ore called protium which is a valuable source of pro-
tein, enabling the Germans to become a super race.[3]

The financial success that *True Story* brought Macfadden had allowed
him to dabble with new magazines and it is, perhaps, surprising that he did
not issue a science-fiction magazine in the early twenties. He had issued a
specialist mystery magazine in 1922 which grew out of his exposé magazine
Midnight and was called *Midnight Mystery Stories*. He was also soon to issue
a very specialist supernatural magazine, *Ghost Stories*, with the first issue
dated June 1926.

The fact remains, though, that no publisher brought out a science-fiction
magazine in 1924 or 1925, despite the apparent timeliness. As for Hugo
Gernsback, he may have been deterred by the lack of response to his earlier
circular, and required further evidence before committing himself. He did,
also, have other things on his mind. Apart from having launched two other
magazines, *Motor Camper and Tourist* in June 1924, and *Radio Review* in
May 1925, he was heavily involved in turning himself into "The Radio Man,"
and transmitting himself through the ether.

Gernsback and the staff of the Experimenter Publishing Company had
established their own radio station, WRNY. Its studios were based at the top
of the Roosevelt Hotel at the junction of 45th Street and Vanderbilt Avenue in
New York City. After its test transmissions the first official broadcast was on
Friday, June 12, 1925, on 258.5 meters. All of Gernsback's editorial staff were
involved with the station. Gernsback himself gave a talk every Monday evening—he often experimented with his editorials first over the air. H. Winfield
Secor spoke every Tuesday night on a wide variety of modern inventions and
on the development of aircraft. A. P. Peck spoke regularly on radio-related
matters, whilst the ever-versatile Joseph Kraus delivered talks on perpetual
motion, spiritualism, medicine, in fact just about any subject, and in addition
he conducted the Radio News Orchestra! The station dealt with more than
just scientific matters. There were talks about art and culture and broadcasts
by musicians and singers. Gernsback had gathered about him a strong crew
to run the station. The Chief Engineer and Director was James V. Maresca,
who would go on to establish himself at the RKO Studios in Hollywood when
sound hit the movies. The Station Manager was Gilson Willetts, and the Program Director was initially David Reed, though he was soon succeeded by
Charles D. Isaacson, a noted organizer of shows and concerts. Isaacson was of
a similar mind to Gernsback in that he intended to make WRNY both educational and entertaining. The general program format, according to Isaacson,
was as follows:

> If you tune in on WRNY Monday, you will always find popular
> dance music, folk songs and national music of the world. Always
> on Monday there will be poetry and painting and history and ge-

ography and travel, but Tuesday, on the other hand, will be a
night for light opera and orchestral concerts, and just a word or so
on architecture. If you are of a studious turn of mind, you will
soon learn that always on Tuesday you can find lectures on law
and history—and so it will go on through the week. Wednesday
will be dedicated to songs, fiction, history and sculpture, and
Thursday the more popular music with certain concert features.
Friday will always be known as grand opera and band concert
night, and the night of unusual novelties.[4]

Station WRNY rapidly became successful. It was noted for its ingenuity
and flair, especially for its novelty nights and amateur talent programs. In
emphasising science, art and culture it had satisfactorily blended entertainment and education, in much the same way as Gernsback had mastered it in
Science and Invention.

With WRNY on the air, it was now time for Gernsback to look again at
his proposal for the new magazine *Scientifiction.* Gernsback was still unsure
of the title. He didn't want one that suggested a magazine that was dour and
clinical. He had learned that the readers enjoyed the escapist and sensational
qualities of scientifiction, and that therefore he needed a name that epito-
mised the qualities of both entertainment and instruction. That was not easy.

One of Gernsback's friends was Louis H. Silberkleit, who worked for a
distribution company which handled Gernsback's magazines. Silberkleit also
liked science fiction and would in turn become a publisher of it in 1939. In
1926 the title he suggested to Gernsback was *Future Fiction.* That did not
convey to Gernsback sufficiently the escapist qualities of the fiction.
Silberkleit always liked the title and when he issued his own SF magazines in
1939, he called one *Future Fiction.*

In the end Gernsback held a contest. He reported on this in the September 1926 issue of the new magazine, but I have been unable to find where this
competition took place. It was presumably in the pages of *Science and Invention* but may have been a loose-leaf flyer within the magazine, as I can trace
no such printed entry. Apparently the response resulted in a list of two hundred suggestions, but none could improve upon the name that Gernsback had
himself selected—*Amazing Stories.* It might not have sounded instructional
or educational, but it was certainly sensational. The first science-fiction magazine was ready to be born.

11.

AMAZING STORIES

Although Gernsback put at least two years' worth of thought into his new magazine, he may not have given it much planning. There were no advance notices in any of his other publications, which suggests that it was a relatively sudden decision. On the other hand, this was Gernsback's first all-fiction magazine, a radical departure from his previous ventures and one that required time to consider the advertising, content, design and format of the magazine, let alone the marketing and distribution. Yet, as we have seen before, when Gernsback sold *Modern Electrics* and launched *The Electrical Experimenter* within a few weeks, Gernsback was prone to act upon impulse, and his organization was clearly tailored to respond accordingly.

The likely course in Gernsback's case was to cease publication of *The Experimenter*, and to use that paper, printing time, editorial time and distribution network for the new magazine. Circulation on *The Experimenter* had still not risen above the fifty thousand level and it was almost certainly losing money. The decision was therefore made to merge *The Experimenter* with *Science and Invention* which had, after all, been its godparent. The last issue of *The Experimenter*, dated February 1926, was issued on January 20. The first issue of *Amazing Stories*, dated April 1926, went out seven weeks later, on Wednesday, March 10.

Gernsback's initial problem would have been what to include in the magazine. He would have had a number of new manuscripts in hand for *Science and Invention* and *Radio News*, but in not using those he clearly had doubts about their appropriateness for *Amazing*. Having already wrestled with his conscience over a title and favored *Amazing Stories* to *Scientifiction*, it was evident that he wanted to use the more escapist, adventurous stories in *Amazing* and keep the scientific whimsies for the technical magazines. This was clear from his editorial.

In his famous definition of "scientifiction" he said, "a charming romance intermingled with scientific fact and prophetic vision." It was the romance— the story, that is—that came first. Later in the editorial he compounded the point. "Not only do these amazing tales make tremendously interesting reading—they are also always instructive." Again, the entertainment value went first, not the scientific lecture. Indeed, Gernsback clearly did not want the lecture type of story, as he went on to say, ". . . the best of these modern writers of scientifiction have the knack of imparting knowledge, and even inspiration, without once making us aware that we are being taught."[1]

In this Gernsback was virtually saying goodbye to the former writers for *Science and Invention* unless they could combine their scientific discourses with exciting adventures. But he did not have much in the way of exciting adventures to hand. He did have a stockpile of Dr. Hackensaw stories. Interestingly, he had not run any of these since the last episode of "A Journey to the Center of the Earth" had appeared in the September 1925 *Science and Invention*, and he was clearly unsure about their value in *Amazing*. He even expressed these doubts in a boxed notice at the end of the first issue of *Amazing*:

Those who read the famous Dr. Hackensaw's Secrets in *Science and Invention* magazine, may be interested to know that we have on hand a great many of Dr. Hackensaw's manuscripts which have never been published hitherto. Before printing these in *Amazing Stories*, however, we would like to have an expression from our readers as to just how they feel about these stories, and whether they would like to have more of them.[2]

This was quite a turnabout for Gernsback. Despite the popularity of the scientific stories in *Science and Invention*, and the Dr. Hackensaw stories in particular, Gernsback had not even considered using one in the initial issue of *Amazing Stories*, even though he had a "great many" to hand. He was not even using them in *Science and Invention*. There is a clear suggestion that Gernsback was pandering to a particular market, the *Argosy* market, which wanted escapist scientific adventures, and it was only with some reluctance that he would include his scientific discourses.

For advice on the selection of stories, Gernsback had turned to C. A. Brandt, a forty-seven-year-old German-born research chemist, who possessed one of the largest libraries of fantastic fiction in America. Gernsback had been referred to him by a second-hand bookdealer. Although not credited in the magazine at the outset, Brandt became first reader and consultant editor and was probably responsible for the initial selection of most of the magazine's contents: Gernsback always had the final say. T. O'Conor Sloane, who was billed initially as Managing Editor, and as Associate Editor from the second issue, performed the main tasks in assembling each issue and readying it for press. He is unlikely to have had much say in the choice of stories, though there is no doubt that as he became acquainted with scientific fiction he would have ventured an opinion. Assisting Sloane in general proof-reading, correspondence and administrative tasks was a young secretary, Miriam Bourne.

Since Gernsback was defining "scientifiction" as "the Jules Verne, H. G. Wells, and Edgar Allan Poe type of story," it was reasonable to include works by these three, as examples in the first issue. Through his contacts with Charles Horne, the editor and translator of Jules Verne in America, Gernsback had made exclusive arrangements with the copyright holders to reprint Verne's work. It was Verne who opened the first issue, with the first episode of his novel, *Off On a Comet, or Hector Servadec*. If any proof were needed that Gernsback was abandoning scientific accuracy in favor of adventure, this was it, as *Hector Servadec* was arguably one of Verne's least scientifically plausible novels. Gernsback admits so in his introductory blurb: ". . . the author here abandons his usual scrupulously scientific attitude and gives his fancy freer rein." After summarizing the novel's plot, Gernsback says, "These events all belong to the realm of fairyland."[3] *Hector Servadec* had much in common with Ray Cummings's *Around the Universe* and *The Man on the Meteor*, which had proved popular in *Science and Invention*, as fascinating odysseys around the solar system, which happened to contain some scientific instruction.

The H. G. Wells selection was "The New Accelerator," already tested in *Science and Invention*, and in many ways the ideal Gernsback story. It not only describes a new invention—a drug that speeds up the taker's perceptions—but fits it into a "charming" story. Wells was, of course, the master at this, and it is not surprising that Gernsback selected a story by Wells for each of the first twenty-nine issues.

The Poe selection was "The Facts in the Case of M. Valdemar." Although today regarded as a horror story, it does have a scientific base: the possibility that a hypnotised mind may stay alive after the body has died. It is a testament to Poe's talent that this story, which was eighty years old, could still stand as an example of scientific fiction in 1926.

To fill the rest of the issue Gernsback chose three further reprints. It was almost certainly less expensive to do this, and the cost element was always important when assembling a new magazine, but that was probably not Gernsback's prime motive. I suspect he had no other choice. I am sure that in his sudden determination to launch *Amazing Stories*, he had no new manuscripts to hand, apart from those for *Science and Invention* and *Radio News* which were inappropriate. It is pertinent to note that the two stories Gernsback selected from *Science and Invention* for reprinting were also the most effective he had used, "The Man from the Atom" by Wertenbaker and "The Thing from—Outside" by England. Moreover, England's name was well known to the readers of the pulps, most of whom were unlikely to have seen this story when it had first appeared. For his final selection Gernsback chose a story from *All-Story Weekly* for December 13, 1919, "The Man Who Saved the Earth" by Austin Hall, another popular pulp writer. Here Martians invade Earth for its water.

It's interesting that although the average age of the six stories in this first issue was twenty-eight years, and therefore pre-twentieth century, the concepts contained in them all were still relevant, and they were all entertaining. There was nothing in them sufficiently dated to detract from the value of the story. In this sense, Gernsback probably got his selection right. We shall see, though, as science fiction rapidly developed over the next few years, not only would these stories appear dated, but stories of only one or two years vintage!

In addition to the story content, there was the presentation. Firstly, Gernsback had opted to publish *Amazing Stories* in the same format as *Science and Invention* and *Radio News*, which was the imperial octavo size: 11 x 8 inches. This may not have been by choice. *The Experimenter* was also this size, and Gernsback's printers were geared to this order. Since the larger size also gave the magazine a greater profile on the stalls, there seemed little reason to change it to the smaller standard pulp format of *Argosy*, 10 x 7 inches. Moreover other magazines, such as *Everybody's* and *True Story* were using the larger format to great success. If anything Gernsback went out of his way to exaggerate the format by using thicker paper. In a later editorial, Gernsback reflected:

> When we originally brought out *Amazing Stories*, we thought it necessary to hand you a big package for the money. Hence the bulky paper, which was made specially for our requirements. Such a paper had never been made before. Now it is known as *Amazing Stories* Bulky Weave.[4]

The approach may have been necessary because *Amazing* was selling for twenty-five cents at a time when most pulps were either ten or fifteen cents. Gernsback's idea was to make *Amazing* look big value for money, and in this he certainly succeeded.

Secondly, Gernsback chose as his cover artist and premier story illustrator, Frank R. Paul. Since 1918 Paul had been illustrating the majority of the stories in *Science and Invention* and *Radio News* and he seemed to be the obvious choice to illustrate the magazine. Paul had only painted one cover for Gernsback before, the August 1924 *Science and Invention* for Gernsback's feature "Evolution on Mars." Gernsback had a number of cover artists, and the mainstay regular was Howard V. Brown. Brown was a skilled cover artist, and ironically he would put that talent to good effect eight years later on the covers of the Street and Smith *Astounding Stories*. Gernsback had also just started to use Alex Schomburg, and Schomburg did submit some paintings to Gernsback for consideration. Gernsback, however, was satisfied with Paul's work, and it would be thirteen years before Schomburg's first science-fiction cover painting appeared, on *Startling Stories*.[5]

Paul remained the exclusive cover artist on *Amazing*. Although his human figures often lacked realism, especially his females, he more than made up for this in imaginative concept. His work, perhaps even more than the fiction, captured that "sense of wonder" that was so necessary in early science fiction, and thus conveyed the message that Gernsback desired—the thrilling possibilities that science could bring. Perhaps the first cover, showing Verne's adventurers ice-skating on a moon of Saturn, had less than that desired effect, but what so captured the public on all of Paul's paintings, was the vivid use of colors. The combination of brash reds and yellows plus an outlandish scientific scene was guaranteed to attract the eyes browsing over the newsstands. As we shall see later there was often disagreement amongst the readers about the extent to which Paul's covers lowered the tone of the magazine and gave it a juvenile quality, but there was no denying that they caught the public's eye and drew attention to the magazine, and that was always the first rule of cover art. After that the contents took over.

Paul was not the exclusive interior artist. Modern recollections of *Amazing* would have one believe Paul illustrated it from cover to cover, and although he was certainly the most prolific artist, there were others whom Gernsback was testing. Most of these, and they are today just names such as F. S. Hynd and Martin Gambee, lacked the visionary qualities in projecting a futuristic or fantastic image. Ray Wardell, who had also illustrated some of the stories in *Science and Invention* was capable but basically unimaginative. An overlooked talent was J. M. de Aragon, who apart from providing a number of effective gothic illustrations for stories also produced a one-off drawing of a monster, unimaginatively captioned "A Remarkable Drawing" in the June 1927 issue. Aragon could not capture that sense of wonder which made Paul's drawings so effective, but he could create a sense of the bizarre and foreboding which made his work the most atmospheric in the magazine. Alas he was used all too seldom, although appropriately he was assigned to illustrate H. P. Lovecraft's "The Colour Out of Space." A later artist was R. E. Lawlor, who began to appear from the May 1928 issue. His woodcut-style images had an otherworldliness about them but were otherwise lifeless, and he was technically unskilled.

Within a week of the first issue being published, Gernsback was "deluged with an avalanche of letters of approval and constructive criticism from practically every section of the country . . ."[6] The first correspondent of record was George W. Anderson of Fairmount, West Virginia, who suggested that all scientific facts included in the stories be highlighted in italics. Michael H. Kay, who must have written his letter whilst he was still reading the first issue, mentioned that his wife was anxious for him to finish it so that she could read it. Gernsback was pleased to report that "Most of our correspondents seemed to heave a great sigh of relief in at last finding a literature that appeals to the imagination, rather than carrying a sensational appeal to the emotions. It is that which justifies our new venture . . ."[7]

The correspondents in fact raised a number of issues, and these we shall look at in some detail in a later chapter. Paramount amongst them was the quality of the fiction, and the image of the magazine. There was also a demand for the magazine to appear weekly, or at least twice monthly. A reader vote brought in an astonishing response rate (if the figures reported in the September 1926 issue are to be believed) with 498 voting to keep the magazine monthly, and 32,644 to switch to twice monthly. In all probability the last "4" was printed twice in error, but even so that was a very high response, and a 1:6 vote in favor of increased publication.

This signalled to Gernsback that he was on the right track. But he was aware he still had some way to go. The initial print run was 100,000, and this was increased to 150,000 after a few months. Sales continued to rise, but Gernsback reported in the August 1927 issue that the magazine was not yet on a paying basis and needed to attract at least twenty to thirty pages of advertising. He further reported in the October 1927 issue that out of the gross print run of 150,000 there were only 5,250 subscribers. This should not have been surprising. Gernsback was learning that readers preferred to purchase their magazines from the newsstands, than await with trepidation, their delivery in the mail. The former not only had a safety factor about it, but there was a pleasure in looking over the newsstand displays with all the myriad exciting covers, and discovering the latest issue of your magazine. It is not easy to ascertain the exact paid circulation of *Amazing*. At that time a publisher might expect to sell at least 90% of his circulation at the newsstands rather than by subscription. In Gernsback's case, though, the newsstand sale might have been higher, especially, as he soon discovered, when many of his readers were youngsters more likely to buy on sight than by subscription. Also a new magazine is less likely to attract subscribers until its future is more assured. There is always the fear that money will be paid up front and the magazine will cease publication. If then we conjecture that the 5,250 represented a 5% proportion of total paid circulation, then the overall figure would be 105,000. This represents 70% of the total print run, which is a reasonably average figure. Also, since the first issue reportedly sold out, which is why Gernsback increased his print run, it's safe to assume that initial circulation was around the 100,000 mark[8]. Whether it paid its way or not (a subject we shall return to) it was a good circulation for a new magazine.

With one exception the May issue was also all-reprint, with an average age even older than the first issue—forty-five years. This was because in addition to the conclusion of Verne's *Off On a Comet*, there was a new Verne serial, *A Trip to the Center of the Earth*—arguably one of his best. Wells and Poe were again present. Wells with one of his most intriguing stories, "The Crystal Egg," where a device found in an antique shop turns out to be a viewer to Mars. Poe's item, "A Mesmeric Revelation," was not as effective as his story in the first issue. From his *Science and Invention* vaults Gernsback selected Charles C. Winn's "The Infinite Vision," the last short story to have been published there. It wasn't any better second time round, and paled in comparison to the Wells story with which it had far-viewing in common.

That left one story, and a welcome one. It was a sequel to "The Man from the Atom" by G. Peyton Wertenbaker, which had not previously been published in *Science and Invention*. I don't know if Wertenbaker had already written it with *Science and Invention* in mind or whether Gernsback requested it when planning *Amazing*. Whichever, it was the first new story to appear in *Amazing*. Although still only nineteen, Wertenbaker introduced some startling new concepts into this story which has generally been overlooked in histories of science fiction. In the first episode Kirby had become isolated on a distant planet millennia in the future. In the sequel he befriends the local inhabitants, especially a girl called Vinda, and learns from them that time passes through endless cycles. It would be possible for him to return to a new Earth which was reliving the cycle he had formerly lived through. Eventually he succeeds, but finds this Earth slightly different, with the United States a Monarchy instead of a Republic. Eventually he regrets having left Vinda behind and chooses to leave Earth for a final time. This story introduced the concept of alternate realities, albeit in the guise of future rather than parallel worlds, long before it became a standard theme in science fiction. The sequel did not quite match the atmosphere of the first story, but it still showed what an emerging talent Wertenbaker had.

With the June 1926 issue *Amazing* started to show a greater variety in its selection of reprints. Although Gernsback had assured readers that *Amazing* was not a reprint magazine and that arrangements had been made to publish stories from Europe as well as America, there was still only minimal evidence of new stories. *Amazing* had about a three month lead-time, so that even allowing authors to have rushed in their stories upon seeing *Amazing* first on March 10, it is unlikely that any could have appeared before the July issue, released on June 10. In fact there were only sixteen new stories in *Amazing*'s first year, out of sixty-nine published, a quarter of the total number, and certainly less than that in wordage. Gernsback was clearly still having problems attracting new fiction—how he solved this we shall see in the next chapter.

Unfortunately, though the reprints in the June issue were from a variety of sources, they were variable in quality. From his own archives Gernsback had selected "Whispering Ether" by Charles S. Wolfe and Jacque Morgan's humorous invention story "Mr. Fosdick Invents the Seidlitzmobile." There was another humorous invention piece, "An Experiment in Gyro-Hats" by Ellis Parker Butler. As Butler was a regular contributor to *Radio News*, he may have drawn this story to Gernsback's attention. It had appeared originally in the June 1910 issue of *Hampton's Magazine*, an unlikely source for Gernsback to be familiar with. However it may be that Brandt was aware of the original source, which only emphasizes the scale of Brandt's personal collection. When Gernsback introduced Brandt as Literary Editor in the July 1926 issue, he commented that "...there is not a work of [scientifiction] that has appeared during the last fifty years with which Mr. Brandt is not fully conversant." With these credentials it is a shame that Brandt was not selecting better reprints, as the Morgan and Butler stories, whilst they may have been fun invention stories, were painfully thin on escapism and entertainment. In addition, as there had been a favorable response to continuing Clement Fezandié's Dr. Hackensaw series, a new one appeared, "Some Minor Inventions." This was no more than a catalogue of new gadgets, and, if anything, was worse than the reprints. It seemed that despite his initial intent, Gernsback was slipping back into his old editorial habits.

There was some good news with the reprinting of Murray Leinster's "The Runaway Skyscraper" from *Argosy*. There was also a reprinting of Otis Adelbert Kline's "The Malignant Entity" from *Weird Tales*, an interesting source, showing that Gernsback was not averse to the "monster-in-the-laboratory" theme. Although standard pulp fare, Kline's story had more zest than Fezandié's, Morgan's or Butler's. Also present was Wells's "The Star," which had been reprinted in *Science and Invention* three years earlier. The average age of the reprints had dropped to just under twenty years.

There was one other story in this issue: the first new story to be recommended by Brandt, and so probably the first acceptable manuscript submitted to *Amazing*. It was "The Coming of the Ice" by G. Peyton Wertenbaker, who was continuing to develop his talent. The story, which considers the implications of immortality, had the same mood of isolation and loneliness found in his first. When, in 1981, Forrest Ackerman asked members of First Fandom to vote on the stories published in 1926, "The Coming of the Ice" was voted as the best short story of the year.

Wertenbaker was the first genuine science-fiction talent that Gernsback had discovered. Gernsback could not really lay claim to discovering George F. Stratton or Clement Fezandié, and in either case whilst these writers had the technical knowledge they lacked the vision necessary to put over science fictional concepts effectively. The Winthrops might have developed into good writers but, unless they produced anything else pseudonymously, they did not appear again in the magazines. Wertenbaker, on the other hand, sold six effective science-fiction tales before he became a noted regional writer on the south-west.

Wertenbaker had strong views on what should constitute good science fiction. In a long letter to Gernsback, probably the same one with which he submitted "The Coming of the Ice," Wertenbaker made some eloquent statements on the nature of science fiction:

> Scientifiction is a branch of literature which requires more intelligence and even more aesthetic sense than is possessed by the sex-type reading public. It is designed to reach those qualities of the mind which are aroused only by things vast, things cataclysmic, and things unfathomably strange. It is designed to reach

that portion of the imagination which grasps with its eager, feeble talons after the unknown. It should be an influence greater than the influence of any literature I know upon the restless ambition of man for further conquests, further understandings. Literature of the past and the present has made the mystery of man and his world more clear to us, and for that reason it has been less beautiful, for beauty lies only in the things that are mysterious. Beauty is a groping of the emotions towards realization of things which may be unknown only to the intellect. Scientifiction goes out into the remote vistas of the universe, where there is still mystery and so still beauty. For that reason scientifiction seems to me to be the true literature of the future.

Wertenbaker then added a word of warning:

The danger that may lie before *Amazing Stories* is that of becoming too scientific and not sufficiently literary. It is yet too early to be sure, but not too early for a warning to be issued amicably and frankly.[9]

Gernsback probably hardly needed reminding of his dilemma. This had been the same as the quandary between the titles *Scientifiction* or *Amazing Stories*. In fact, although Gernsback had taken the bold step and launched *Amazing Stories* to a clearly enthusiastic readership, he still did not really know what image to project for the magazine or where the stories were going to come from. He needed to do some thinking and planning.

12.

WHERE HAS ALL THE TALENT GONE?

In his editorial in the May 1926 *Amazing* Gernsback said: "There is only one thing that troubles us now: we have more good stories to publish than we have space in which to publish them." He listed some of the arrangements he had been making. Firstly there had been a fair demand for Fezandié's remaining Dr. Hackensaw stories. There had been requests for work by Edgar Rice Burroughs, and Gernsback was pursuing this. Gernsback also cited two recent German works to which he had bought publication rights: *Die Macht der Drei* (*The Might of the Three*), which he called "one of the greatest—and perhaps *the* greatest—recent scientifiction story," and *Feuer am Nordpol* (*The North Pole Fire*). He then went on to mention *Station X* by G. McLeod Winsor, *The Messiah of the Cylinder* by Victor Rousseau, and *The War in the Air* by H. G. Wells. These three novels were all reprints.

When we come to look at the publication record, though, we find precious few of these brought to print. Although Gernsback claimed he had "many" Dr. Hackensaw manuscripts in stock, he only printed two of them, "The Secret of the Invisible Girl" in the July 1926 issue being the last. Neither did they resurface in *Science and Invention*. Since it would have been irrational to state he had many in stock if he hadn't, we are left with the conclusion that the stories were no longer appropriate and that Hackensaw had run out of favor.

G. McLeod Winsor's *Station X* was reprinted as a three-part serial from the July to September 1926 issues. Likewise, the promise of Edgar Rice Burroughs was kept. Not only did Gernsback reprint the novel *The Land That Time Forgot* in the February to April 1927 issues, he also sought to acquire a new work from Burroughs, which we shall come to in due course.

The two German works he cited were never published. Since he was so enthusiastic about *The Might of the Three*, I cannot believe he would have dropped it by choice, and can only presume that the negotiations he was so firm about had fallen through. Perhaps that was also the case with the novels by Rousseau and Wells, as neither of those appeared. In the case of Wells, the correspondence between him and Gernsback survives, and this in part clarifies the circumstances. Gernsback had agreed rights with Wells's American agent William Chapman in Chicago to reprint the novel for $100. When Wells learnt of this, he pursued the matter and notified Gernsback that Chapman was not authorized to act on his behalf in selling subsidiary rights. The permission for reprinting *The War in the Air* was thus withdrawn. When Gernsback approached Wells again in May 1928 for permission to reprint this novel, Wells requested a reprint fee equal to $1000, which may explain why the $100 had not been acceptable. This may not have been the case with the other novels, but it's certainly suggestive that although Gernsback was going through what he believed to be the right channels, it was not always plain sailing.

If some of the works that Gernsback was enthusiastic about were denied him, there were others that he was able to use. His choice was especially strong in the novel-length works. He acquired three works by Garrett P.

Serviss, a noted science-popularizer of his day. The shorter version of *The Moon Metal* was run complete in the July 1926 issue, whilst *A Columbus of Space* was serialized from August to October 1926, followed immediately by *The Second Deluge* from November 1926 to February 1927. The last of these is still regarded as a classic and reads passably today. At the time it was hugely popular.

Gernsback did acquire the serialization rights to several of H. G. Wells's novels purchased through his authorized American agent Paul Reynolds. Wells's work was always of good quality, and well accepted by the readers. They included *The Island of Dr. Moreau* (October-November 1926), *The First Men in the Moon* (December 1926-February 1927), and *The War of the Worlds* (August-September 1927). Further Jules Verne novels were used, but these already seemed dated against the more recent work Gernsback was reprinting. Nevertheless, some readers thought that Verne was a new writer and encouraged him to contribute more!

Such was the profusion of novels suitable for reprinting that *Amazing* soon became overwhelmed with them. The October 1926 issue contained four serials and only one short story. One of these was a new serial, the first to be published in the magazine. It was *Beyond the Pole* by A. Hyatt Verrill. In introducing the story Gernsback claimed it as "one of the best scientifiction works of the modern school that we have lately seen. It is easily the best scientifiction story of this year." It was certainly a departure from the type of new material Gernsback was seeing. Although it is a "lost race" story of a lobster-like civilization on Earth, it is a quaint depiction, lacking the fanciful elements of the pulp fantastic adventure but written with a conviction and authenticity one might expect from a learned explorer, archeologist, and anthropologist. Verrill, who was now fifty-five, had for nearly forty years explored Central and South America and had become an expert on the local tribes. Apart from writing many books about his travels, he also wrote a series of boys' adventure books, so he was already an established author by the time he made his first sale to Gernsback. Though Gernsback cannot claim him as a discovery, he had not previously written adult science fiction and was certainly the second major new talent to appear in *Amazing Stories* in its first year.

There was only one other, and that was Miles J. Breuer, a doctor from Lincoln, Nebraska. He was thirty-seven when he debuted in the January 1927 *Amazing* with "The Man with the Strange Head," a twist-in-the-tail story about the secret of a restless man. Breuer would become a regular and popular contributor and produce some early classics of science fiction.

Three names in the first year was not a high score. In fact since Wertenbaker had sold to Gernsback in 1923 and Verrill was already a published author, it's fair to say that Breuer was Gernsback's only genuine discovery in 1926.

There were a few other new authors, but most did not appear again. These included M. H. Hasta, Dr. Albert B. Stuart, Alexander Snyder, Samuel M. Sargent, Jr., and Augusto Bissiri. Both Sargent and Snyder appeared once more in *Amazing*, and Snyder had earlier appeared in *Weird Tales*. Hasta, I have always felt, may have been a pseudonym, but no evidence has come to light on his identity.

There were pseudonymous writers in *Amazing*. Gernsback later recalled that authors were only willing to contribute to *Science and Invention* if they were allowed to use pen names. He then went on to say that that attitude changed when he launched *Amazing Stories*. He suggests that scientists no longer insisted upon pseudonymity.[1] In fact the opposite seems to be the case. There is not much evidence of the use of pseudonyms before 1926, but afterwards they became regular.

The first obvious one was "Kaw," whose story "The Time Eliminator" appeared in the December 1926 issue. This rather staid story has all the hallmarks of being written by a scientist rather than a writer—it is a fairly straightforward description of an invention and its uses. The writer may well have been acquainted with *Radio News*, as the invention, a device for picking up images from the past, is similar to that described in "The Radio King." Kaw was presumably, though not necessarily, someone's initials. There had been a writer, Kenneth Warner, who had a story, "Power By Radio" in the September 1921 *Radio News*. Interestingly, there was also a Kaw story in the November 1926 *Ghost Stories*, "Through a Haunted Loud Speaker," about receiving voices of the dead via radio. All three of these stories have a common thread to them, so Kaw may have been Kenneth Warner, though it's far from proven. Curiously, there was an illustrator who used the initials KAW on his drawings in *Science Wonder Stories* in 1929. He first appeared illustrating Ed Earl Repp's "The Stellar Missile" in the November 1929 issue. The drawing, which is coarse and brash, clearly displays the initials KAW, although it is credited to Winter. Winter's work appeared in a few more issues, and also in *Air Wonder Stories*, but not after May 1930. This artist was not the same as Lumen Winter who started to appear in *Wonder Stories* from November 1933. Whether this KAW was simply a coincidence of initials, or a brush-name influenced by the earlier pseudonym, or was genuinely the same person, I don't know.

A later pseudonym was Marius, who appeared with two stories in *Amazing*: "Vandals from the Moon" (July 1928) and "The Sixth Glacier" (January-February 1929). The researches of Sam Moskowitz discovered that Marius was a free-lance writer called Steve Benedict who wrote for several magazines under pseudonyms. He may even have had another in *Amazing Stories*, though this is not known. He had one other science-fiction story in *Astounding* in 1953. Interestingly, there was a writer called Marius Logan who had four stories in *Radio News* in the 1925/26 period. These radio stories don't bear much comparison to the Marius stories, but the coincidence of names gives some pause for thought.

I won't dwell on these pseudonyms, other than to make the point that, despite Gernsback's recollection, writers were using them in *Amazing* when maybe they hadn't previously. I will just mention one further curiosity. A new name in the February 1927 *Amazing* was W. Alexander with "New Stomachs for Old." Alexander became an occasional contributor over the next couple of years, with one stray story appearing in 1934. Almost all of the stories concern organ or limb transplants. They are written in such a way as to suggest their author is a medical man, or at least has medical knowledge. In the letter column in the June 1927 *Amazing*, following a letter from Miles J. Breuer, the editor (probably Sloane) commented, "Dr. Breuer is well-known to our readers from his most interesting story entitled 'New Stomachs for Old'."[2] This could have been a simple mistake though, despite his age, Sloane was meticulous. The statement was not refuted in later issues, and it's hard to believe Breuer had not read it. However the January 1929 issue contained a letter from Breuer taking exception to Alexander's story "The Ananias Gland": "No one (including Mr. Alexander) who is not a biologist, can grasp how excruciatingly absurd the transplantation of stomachs and glands and hearts looks in a story."[3] Today, when organ transplants are taken for granted, Breuer's comment seems naïve. Despite his apparent sincerity, the whole letter has a tongue-in-cheek quality about it—it even starts off as a story! Was Breuer denying that he was Alexander by attacking his stories, or was he trying to disguise the fact?

As we have seen, Gernsback continued to have problems attracting and keeping new writers in the first year of *Amazing Stories*. The writers either did not see *Amazing* as a viable market, or did not want to be identified with it in case it jeopardized their scientific standing. Gernsback had no shortage of reprint material, but there was a danger in being considered predominantly a reprint magazine, especially with a literature supposed to be as forward-looking as science fiction. Without new talent or new visions the magazine would rapidly stagnate.

He could import stories from Europe which would be new for American readers and not as dated as some of the other reprints. He had already done this in the July 1926 issue with Curt Siodmak's "The Eggs from Lake Tanganyika," translated from a German magazine. Siodmak later emigrated to America and became a noted screenwriter in the movie industry, with his brother Robert. He was the author of the science-fiction mystery classic *Donovan's Brain* (1942). He wrote other works of science fiction in the Gernsback period, but did not appear again in the SF magazines until after the Second World War. Gernsback also printed "The Malignant Flower" (September 1927), by the pseudonymous German writer "Anthos," and "The Paradise of the Ice Wilderness" (October 1927) by the Norwegian Jul. Regis.

He could have encouraged new stories from the authors he was reprinting. One of the best was Capt. H. G. Bishop with "On the Martian Way" in the February 1927 issue. This is a remarkably advanced story for its time as it takes interplanetary travel for granted and tells of an incident on an Earth-Mars passenger trip. It was far more authentic than many of Gernsback's gadget stories, or the pulps' super-science stories. The researches of Sam Moskowitz have revealed that Bishop (1874-1934), a distinguished army officer who was awarded the French Legion of Honor, had been writing scientific stories since at least as early as 1907 for the *New Broadway Magazine*. He was the type of writer Gernsback needed to attract: one with writing ability and an interest in the potential of science, but not necessarily a regular reader of Gernsback's technical magazines. Unfortunately Bishop never sold another story to Gernsback.

And where were the big names from *Argosy*? Gernsback had received no new submissions from Murray Leinster or Ralph Milne Farley. He did have a new novel from Ray Cummings, *Into the Fourth Dimension*, but Gernsback chose to serialize that in *Science and Invention* (September 1926-May 1927). It may be that as Gernsback had already made arrangements to reprint sufficient novels in *Amazing* he could not have fitted Cummings's work in in the near future. Moreover there was probably still a significant proportion of the readership of *Science and Invention* who wanted to keep the fiction content and Gernsback needed to consider them. Whatever the circumstances, Cummings's next scientific work, *Explorers into Infinity*, was serialized in *Weird Tales* (April-June 1927) and was probably submitted there directly after a rejection from *Argosy*.

Gernsback needed to do something to attract new writers, and his plan was to fall back on what had been so reliable in past issues of his magazines when trying to attract reader involvement. He set a competition.

The cover of the December 1926 issue, which went on sale on November 10, boldly announced: "$500.00 for the most Amazing Story written around this picture." The picture, by Paul, displayed a globe in the sky above an alien pillared city. From the globe hung two long poles around which a force-field seemed to operate. Just below these poles is a liner in mid-air. In the foreground, sitting on cliffs overlooking a waterfall and watching the scene, is a group of red humanoids, naked except for a fanned headdress. In his editorial, Gernsback gave the background details to the contest:

> Since the first appearance of *Amazing Stories*, we have received a great many manuscripts for publication in our magazine. We wish to state at this point that at present the magazine is not in the market for full length novels, because the editors have a great many on hand that await publication. They do, however, want short stories under 10,000 words ... Furthermore, we receive an increasing number of letters, asking if we are in the market for short stories, and to these we wish to reply in the affirmative. We can not get too many real short scientifiction stories. To encourage this, we are starting a rather unique contest this month. We have composed on our front cover a picture which illustrates a story to be written by our readers. We are frank to say that we haven't the slightest idea what the picture is supposed to show. The editors' ideas pertaining to the real solution—if one there be—based upon the picture, are necessarily vague.[4]

Readers had to submit a story which fully explained the picture in less than 10,000 words. All stories "must be of the scientifiction type and must contain correct scientific facts to make it appear plausible and within the realm of present-day knowledge of science." The entries had to be in by noon, January 5, 1927, allowing just eight weeks. There would be three cash prizes: first $250, second $150 and third $100.

Gernsback commented upon the results in the June 1927 issue, and he rated the contest a success. Some 360 manuscripts had been received, out of which the editors selected three prize-winners and four honorable mentions.

1. "The Visitation" by Cyril G. Wates of Edmonton, Alberta, Canada.
2. "The Electronic Wall" by George R. Fox of Three Oaks, Michigan.
3. "The Fate of the Poseidonia" by Mrs. F. C. Harris of Lakewood, Ohio.

4. "The Ether Ship of Oltor" by S. Maxwell Coder of Philadelphia, Pennsylvania.
5. "The Voice from the Inner World" by A. Hyatt Verrill of New York City.
6. "The Lost Continent" by Cecil B. White of Victoria, British Columbia, Canada.
7. "The Gravitomobile" by D. B. McRae of San Bernardino, California.

All seven stories were subsequently printed in *Amazing*. There was one story which failed to receive a mention but which also later saw print. Otis Adelbert Kline had submitted an entry, "The Log of the Lauritania." This story was later revised, retitled "The Bird People," and sold to *Weird Tales*, where it appeared in the January 1930 issue.

It was good to see the geographical spread of the entrants, with Canada, not at this time noted for its imaginative writers, featuring twice. Gernsback concluded his round-up of the contest results by saying: "We are certain that you will hear more from the prize-winning authors. All of them have the makings of future scientifiction writers."[5]

That is, of course, what Gernsback wanted: to establish a coterie of short story writers. We cannot tell how many of the unsuccessful entrants made subsequent sales. Of those in the list, Fox, Coder, and McRae never appeared in the science-fiction magazines again. Verrill was already selling to Gernsback and would remain a regular writer of SF for the next ten years. The winner, Cyril G. Wates, sold three more stories to Gernsback and Sloane, but none of them is memorable although, as Lowndes identifies in his survey, "Gold Dust and Star Dust" (*Amazing Stories*, September 1929) contains a remarkable prediction.

Mrs. F. C. Harris was better known as Clare Winger Harris. She had already made one earlier sale, "A Runaway World" to *Weird Tales* (July 1926), but now went on to become a Gernsback regular and one of his most popular writers. Miles J. Breuer rated her "The Miracle of the Lily" (November 1928) as the best story published in *Amazing* up to that date. She later went on to collaborate with Breuer on the fascinating "A Baby on Neptune" (December 1929). She was the first regular female writer of science fiction in the specialist magazines, though Francis Stevens had preceded her in the general pulps. Gernsback commented about her: ". . . as a rule, women do not make good scientifiction writers, because their education and general tendencies on scientific matters are usually limited."[6] This may today seem a sexist comment, but it was almost certainly a clinical observation of the day. As it happened Gernsback would encourage women writers as much as men, and a number would establish themselves in his magazines.

Finally, Cecil B. White wrote two other stories for Gernsback, both sequels to this first sale. White is an example of a pseudonymous scientist. He was really William H. Christie, a thirty-year-old British-born astronomer then at the Dominion Observatory in British Columbia, but who shortly moved on to the Mount Wilson Observatory near Los Angeles. He published a number of astronomical papers during the thirties, and sold articles on astronomy to *Science and Invention* under his real name, but no more science fiction. He remained a noted astronomer and died in 1955.

Whilst the full benefits of the competition were being assessed, Gernsback tried another ploy to attract writers. There was one sure-fire way both to satisfy his readers and to demonstrate that *Amazing* was the equal of the general pulps as a market for new stories by the pulp writers, and that was to present a new story by the greatest fantastic-adventure writer of them all, Edgar Rice Burroughs. Gernsback's readers had asked for Burroughs from the start, and Gernsback had already reprinted *The Land That Time Forgot*. In April 1927 Gernsback wrote to Burroughs seeking new material. Burroughs response was to offer a new Martian novel, then titled *Vad Varo of Barsoom*. This had already been rejected by three magazines, including *Argosy*, with one editor calling certain aspects of the story, probably those related to the transplant of human organs, "repellent." It was, of course, ideal for Gernsback. But there was a snag. Burroughs had requested payment of $1250, which was in the order of two cents a word. Gernsback responded that this price was too high for *Amazing* in its current stage of development, but he proposed a solution. He would publish the novel in a single *Annual*, and, if successful, he would pay the asking price. Burroughs accepted the proposal.

Gernsback had first given thought to the *Annual* in January 1927. In his March editorial he mentioned, "It is our aim to get out a book with at least 150 pages during the coming year."[7] It's probable that the original idea was for a Yearbook made up totally of reprints from *Amazing* but including one novel not previously reprinted in the magazine, which was Abraham Merritt's *The Face in the Abyss*. This Yearbook may have retailed at twenty-five cents. Gernsback now considered incorporating the Burroughs novel as well and doubling the price of the magazine. Thus, in July 1927 appeared the *Amazing Stories Annual* with a gaudy Frank R. Paul cover which boasted Burroughs's name in letters almost bigger than the magazine's title, plus the novel's new title, *Master Mind of Mars*. The *Annual* was a solid 128-pages and cost fifty cents, but its 100,000 copy print-run sold out. The Burroughs novel was the only new material. The rest of the *Annual* contained all reprints, serving as a sampler of the type of fiction available in the monthly magazine. Readers thus attracted by the Burroughs novel might then be lured to check out *Amazing* on a more regular basis.

By the end of the first year Gernsback expressed satisfaction with the development of *Amazing*. ". . . it is safe to say that the magazine has definitely arrived," he wrote in his editorial to the August 1927 issue. He confirmed that the magazine was not yet on a paying basis and would not be until it was carrying twenty or thirty pages of advertising. "The expense of publishing and distributing the magazine and placing it on some 30,000 newsstands throughout the country is enormous."[8] Gernsback was in favor of encouraging growth through subscription, and he asked readers to return a printed form to *Amazing* giving the names of two friends who would be sent free back issues of *Amazing* in an attempt to encourage new readers and, hopefully, new subscribers. This tack was tried not just in *Amazing* but in a range of magazines, but its success, or otherwise, is not recorded. The paid circulation of *Amazing*, however, is known. In a letter to H. G. Wells, dated May 5, 1927, Gernsback stated: "We may add that the magazine is making progress, and we are now printing 150,000 gross per month, with the net figures around 90,000 at present. In another year the magazine should be on a paying basis, but at the present time a great deal of money is being spent to build up a market for scientifiction."[9]

In catering for that market Gernsback had had to make some adjustments to his original concept of scientifiction. The stories he was now publishing in *Amazing* were already a step removed from those fledgling items published in *Science and Invention*, and, in some cases, that step was considerable. The first serial to start in the second year of *Amazing*, was Abraham Merritt's classic novel *The Moon Pool*. But was this science fiction? Within a year, was Gernsback already redefining the field?

13.

SCIENTIFICTION OR FAIRY TALE?: THE IMAGE DILEMMA

For fifty years after its publication, *The Moon Pool* was one of the most popular works of fantastic fiction. As with almost all of the other works of Abraham Merritt it acquired a near legendary status, and its very name still conjures a frisson of pleasure in the memories of those who had the opportunity to read it in those magical days of the pulps. The original story of "The Moon Pool" had appeared in *All-Story Weekly* for June 22, 1918. It met with such success that Merritt wrote a novel-length sequel, *The Conquest of the Moon Pool* (*All-Story*, February 15-March 22, 1919). Merritt then revised the text and the two stories were published in book-form by Putnam in November 1919 as *The Moon Pool*. It was this hardcover version that Gernsback purchased for reprinting in *Amazing*.

"Heeding the requests of hundreds of readers, we have made arrangements for the publication of 'The Moon Pool'," Gernsback wrote in his introductory blurb. "This classic is, without doubt, one of the outstanding works of scientifiction today. For sheer imagination, astounding situations, extraordinary science, which has no parallel in all scientifiction, this story easily ranks first. When Mr. Merritt wrote this story he had to invent an entirely new and incredibly amazing science, which is neither electricity nor light nor anything you have ever thought or dreamt of."[1]

The Moon Pool is an exotic adventure set in the remote islands of the Pacific, with all the mystery and fascination of the Indiana Jones movies. It tells of the discovery of a radioactive pool in the Caroline Islands which marks the entrance to the ruins of an ancient civilization. A coded design on the rock wall allows the explorers to summon a beautiful girl, the handmaiden to the Shining One, who explains how they may further use the coded device to enter the rocks and travel deep down to earth-heart. There they encounter a breathtaking scene—the Veil of the Shining One:

> At first all that I could see was space—a space filled with the same coruscating effulgence that pulsed about me. I glanced upward, obeying that instinctive impulse of earth folk that bids them seek within the sky for sources of light. There was no sky— at least no sky such as we know—all was a sparkling nebulosity rising into infinite distances as the azure above the day-world seems to fill all the heavens—through it ran pulsing waves and flashing javelin rays that were like shining shadows of the aurora echoes, octaves lower, of those brilliant arpeggios and chords that play about the poles. My eyes fell beneath its splendor; I stared outward.
>
> Miles away, gigantic luminous cliffs sprang sheer from the limits of a lake whose waters were of milky opalescence. It was from these cliffs that the spangled radiance came, shimmering

out from all their lustrous surfaces. To left and to right, as far as the eye could see, they stretched—and they vanished in the auroral nebulosity on high!

"Look at that!" exclaimed Larry. I followed his pointing finger. On the face of the shining wall, stretched between two colossal columns, hung an incredible veil; prismatic, gleaming with all the colors of the spectrum. It was like a web of rainbows woven by the fingers of the daughters of the Jinn.[2]

It is some further time before they witness the Shining One itself:

> Only for a moment did that which we had called the Dweller and which these named the Shining One, pause. It swept up the ramp to the daïs, rested there, slowly turning, plumes and spirals lacing and unlacing, throbbing, pulsing. Now its nucleus grew plainer, stronger—human in a fashion, and all inhuman; neither man nor woman; neither god nor devil; subtly partaking of all. Nor could I doubt that whatever it was, within that shining nucleus was something sentient; something that had will and energy, and in some awful, supernormal fashion—intelligence![3]

The Moon Pool continues in this vein, with wondrous descriptions and adventures delivered in what has become termed as Merritt's "purple prose," but which was really the enthusiasm of a vivid imagination, hampered by the limitations of a terrestrial language.

Although acceding to readers' requests, and despite his laudatory blurb, Gernsback clearly had some reservations about the story. In his editorial he considered the basis of the Shining One:

> In the story by Mr. A. Merritt in the current issue, the author had hit upon a most extraordinary invention, which as you will find, he calls "The Shining One." Here is really a new thought, because "The Shining One" is neither a human being, nor a god, nor is it electricity, or light, yet it is possessed of some intelligence. Very strange and fascinating, and most exciting. At first thought you might feel that a story of this kind, while highly interesting, really should be classed with fairy tales. You will, however, soon discover your error, because, after all, the thing is not really impossible. While "The Shining One" may never become a reality, it is conceivable that such an entity might come into existence at some future time, when we know more about science in general and . . . more about rays and radio-activity.

Gernsback went on to say:

> The thought that intelligence dwells only in an animal or an insect seems ludicrous. What guarantee have we that reasoning and intelligence could not be well found in entirely different surroundings? It is not inconceivable that an intelligence could be in

a gas, in a liquid, or even in a solid. All this probably sounds foolish to most of us but, after all, our intelligence is really rather feeble and many things cannot be comprehended or understood by
us at all.[4]

All this suggests that Gernsback needed to make a case to justify his
publication of *The Moon Pool*, despite the overwhelming demand by readers.
Moreover, despite the welcome it received, Gernsback forever had reservations about its inclusion. Years later he confessed to Sam Moskowitz doubts
about his judgment in reprinting the story because of its lack of science. Today, though we might generally classify *The Moon Pool* as a fantastic adventure, I believe most critics would place it on the science fiction side rather
than fantasy, though some might term it "science fantasy" as a compromise.
In his study of science fiction, *The World Beyond the Hill*, Alexei Panshin
writes:

> *The Moon Pool* forces us to ask ourselves whether there is any
> meaningful difference between the transcendent beings of tradi-
> tional fantasy and the new transcendent beings imagined in sci-
> entific fiction—or whether the two in essence might not be the
> same.[5]

Panshin highlights Gernsback's dilemma. From our so-called sophisticated high-tech 1990s it is easy to look back on these early works of scientific
fiction and think of them as fantastic imaginings, but at that time the writers
were grasping new concepts which opened up an infinity of possibilities. The
world was still only a generation from the gaslit Victorian era, and had already had to witness the tragedy of a world war fought with the horrors that
science could create. In that rapid scientific revolution, the future might contain anything that man could imagine.

This was the very concept that Gernsback was trying to encourage
through his use of science fiction, but in *The Moon Pool* it had gone several
stages too far. If we recall the reasons Gernsback introduced scientific fiction
into his magazines, it had been to inspire and stimulate the amateur inventor
into creating new scientific devices and thereby build a new scientific world.
The story as a vehicle was a means to capture the imagination, but it was education leading to inspiration first, and entertainment second.

When he broadened his publication of science fiction from *Science and
Invention* into *Amazing Stories* he was shifting from education to entertainment, but it was an uneasy balance; Gernsback was still finding his way. Increasingly the type of story that he wanted to publish—the basic invention
story—was not what most readers wanted to read or that most writers were
capable of writing. The readers wanted the fantastic scientific adventure. In
the interests of commerciality, and in promoting the new field of scientific fiction, Gernsback had settled for that, but he did not want to forsake the basic
values of the scientific possibilites of the stories he published. Otherwise, if
what he put forward was impossible, then inventors could not be stimulated
but more probably deluded. There had to be a limit to what he could publish.
Beyond that was fairy tale. Despite what he wrote, Gernsback's conscience

told him that *The Moon Pool* was more fairy tale. Yet there is a scientific rationale to the story. The ancient god Taithu explains how the Shining One was created from an energy source, and later developed an intelligence of its own.

In fact there is more science in *The Moon Pool* than in some other stories that Gernsback would publish. A typical example is "The Voyage to Kemptonia" by E. M. Scott (*Amazing Stories*, October 1928), which postulated a number of natural miniature satellites orbitting the Earth at a distance of about thirty miles. The author gives a detailed description of the orbit and size of the largest. The first problem, though, is why no one else has seen this satellite, or the others, through telescopes, when they're the size Scott says they are. All of Scott's orbit calculations are also wrong and Gernsback or Sloane should have spotted this or had them checked by Secor or advisor Donald H. Menzel. Then the description of Kemptonia itself as a living world is pure fantasy. Gernsback later admitted that he was prepared to allow the occasional scientific error if it helped stimulate the reader, but this was probably more an admission that he had overlooked an error than encouraged it.

Despite the radical nature of his beliefs, Gernsback was rooted in science, but he was also a visionary wanting to look beyond the next stage of scientific achievement into the far future. For Gernsback, in his first year of launching *Amazing Stories* this dilemma caused some mental anguish. How far could he go in abandoning his scientific principles?

We can see evidence of this dilemma in his editorials and the blurbs he wrote for a variety of stories, and in some of the repercussions in the reader department. Gernsback outlined the issue in his editorial in the July 1926 *Amazing*:

> A few letters have come to the Editor's desk from some readers who wish to know what prompts us to so frequently preface our stories in our introductory remarks with the statement that this or that scientific plot is not impossible, but quite probable. These readers seem to have the idea that we try to impress our friends with the fact that whatever is printed in *Amazing Stories* is not necessarily pure fiction, but could or can be fact. That impression is quite correct. We DO wish to do so, and have tried to do so ever since we started *Amazing Stories*. As a matter of fact our entire editorial policy is built upon this structure and will be so continued indefinitely. The reason is quite simple. The human mind, not only of today, but of ten thousand years ago, is and was so constituted that being merged into the present it can see neither the past nor the future clearly. If only five hundred years ago (or little more than ten generations), which is not a long time as human progress goes, anyone had come along with a story wherein radio telephone, steamships, airplanes, electricity, painless surgery, the phonograph, and a few other modern marvels were described, he would probably have been promptly flung into a dungeon.[6]

In fact Edmond Hamilton would use exactly that premise in "The Man Who Saw the Future" (*Amazing Stories*, October 1930) about an apothecary who is brought from the past to the present. Upon his return he tells of the wonders he has seen and is promptly sentenced to death as a sorcerer.

Gernsback went on to say:

> It is most unwise in this age to declare anything impossible, because you may never be sure but that even while you are talking it has already become a reality . . .
>
> There are few stories published in this magazine that can be called downright impossible. As a matter of fact in selecting our stories we always consider their possibility. We reject stories often on the ground that, in our opinion, the plot or action is not in keeping with science as we know it today. For instance, when we see a plot wherein the hero is turned into a tree, later on into a stone, and then again back to himself, we do not consider this science, but, rather a fairy tale, and such stories have no place in *Amazing Stories*.[7]

Gernsback must have forgotten having written this statement, or soon radically altered his beliefs, for only three years later, in the first issue of his magazine *Science Wonder Stories*, he published "The Marble Virgin" by Kennie McDowd, wherein a statue is brought to life. He was taken to task for this story, and challenged on its scientific credibility. Gernsback's response was: "It is undoubtedly uncanny but who can say that it is a thing which will never come to pass."[8]

The "who can say" response was a cop-out, and one that Gernsback was starting to use with some frequency. He rapidly accepted that in the interests of entertainment, authors were allowed a certain stretching of the truth with scientific possibilities. In fact, he started to use this to his advantage. Firstly, in order to confirm that scientific truths were contained in the stories, he introduced a "What Do You Know?" column from the July 1927 issue with questions derived from the stories. Secondly, he started running stories with deliberate, or sometimes accidental errors, and challenged readers to spot them. The first of these was "The Astounding Discoveries of Doctor Mentiroso" by A. Hyatt Verrill (November 1927) which was an exercise in time logic. Verrill provided an answer in the next issue. The error in "Ten Million Miles Sunward" by Geoffrey Hewelcke (March 1928), was probably unintentional, but Gernsback set up a challenge to readers to spot the mistake and in the next issue ran an article by Professor William Luyten of Harvard College Observatory explaining the error. It meant that whilst Gernsback may have compromised his scientific values, he encouraged readers to learn from such variations from veracity.

He was rewarded in his beliefs because the commercialisation of scientific fiction brought the field to a wider readership, and its stimulation inspired readers to study the sciences. This was evidenced by the many letters Gernsback received on the subject. Typical was one from Californian electrical engineer, Harold A. Lower. Lower had previously sold one story to *Amazing*, "Rice's Ray" (January 1928). (It had been mistakenly attributed to Harold Martin, the narrator.) Lower was then aged thirty-three. He wrote in to Gernsback and, in a letter published in the February 1929 issue, commented that it had been through *Amazing* that he had been inspired to study astronomy. This had in turn led him to develop a business constructing telescopes.

By the end of *Amazing's* first year Gernsback had reconciled himself to publishing what was primarily a good story first, with scientific values second. As a consequence the quality of new science fiction in *Amazing* began to improve. Some of it still may not have had high literary values, even by contemporary pulp standards, but the stories were generally much better than the type Gernsback had published in *Science and Invention*.

A strong example of this change, perhaps even more pronounced than *The Moon Pool*, was the appearance, in the September 1927 issue, of that stalwart of *Weird Tales*, H. P. Lovecraft, with "The Colour Out of Space." This story, amongst Lovecraft's best, might be science fiction on the surface, but deep down it contained much wider cosmic concepts. In fact it did not qualify as science fiction at all by Gernsback's original definitions. Yet he immediately saw its value as fiction. "Here is a totally different story that we can highly recommend to you," he said in his blurb. "We could wax rhapsodical in our praise, as the story is one of the finest pieces of literature it has been our good fortune to read. The theme is original, and yet fantastic enough to make it rise head and shoulders above many contemporary scientifiction stories."[8] This story received an honorable mention in Edward J. O'Brien's *Best American Short Stories for 1928*, the first story from *Amazing* to receive that distinction in so prestigeous a series.

Gernsback's original scientific story, the gadget story, once typified by Jacque Morgan and Clement Fezandié, began to fade away. The last of these were Henry Hugh Simmons's stories of "Hicks' Inventions with a Kick," which had started with the "Automatic Self-Serving Dining Table" in the April 1927 issue. Two more appeared that year with one final one, "The Perambulating Home" in the August 1928 issue. Interestingly that was the same issue which saw the first episode of *The Skylark of Space* by Edward Elmer Smith, as well as the first Anthony (later "Buck") Rogers story, "Armageddon—2419 AD," by Philip Francis Nowlan, which would firmly mark the dawn of the new age of adventure in *Amazing*.

This change in direction of *Amazing* was also being foreseen by the readers and more conscientious writers. For *Amazing* to grow and survive it had to move to a more literary position away from scientific lectures. Miles J. Breuer summed it up in a letter published in the July 1928 issue, which echoed the sentiments G. Peyton Wertenbaker had made two years earlier. He argued that the general opinion of the stories was that they lacked a modern literary quality, to which he added: "I don't care how much science you put in, if the stories conform to modern literary standards the above criticisms will not occur. Let your stories have plot and unity of impression and the general reader will like them, in spite of the science . . . Which is the better purpose for your magazine: to provide light entertainment for the scientific people; or to carry the message of science to the vast masses who prefer to read fiction?"[10]

Gernsback's answer summed up his views:

> Our stories . . . are written to popularize science. Our efforts
> have led to the publication and production of a quantity of good

literature seasoned with science—perhaps too far-fetched in the latter aspect. This last is a dangerous admission, however, for no one knows how far science will develop in the future. the last sixty years have seen the world revolutionized by the developments of science. The younger readers, we believe, will live through another generation of almost miracles, and they seem especially to enjoy these stories. We are, of course, always on the look-out for "literary scientific fiction."[10]

The changes in *Amazing* might have been a shift from the scientific lecture to the adventure story, but not necessarily with a corresponding growth in literary values. Although it was a change in intent, it was a confirmation of the image that the title and cover art already suggested. It was what had been feared by many of the scientific purists who came to *Amazing* from *Science and Invention*. The stories might be educational and contain strong scientific principles but they were packaged in such a way as to suggest a more puerile content. This may not in itself have been a bad thing. Gernsback could see no problems in attracting young readers as these were more impressionable to the wonders of science and more likely to be stimulated into scientific achievement. Gernsback became quite proud of the many young readers who wrote in to the magazine. He devoted the editorial of the October 1927 issue to a consideration of "Amazing Youth" and printed a photograph of Robert Smith of New York, aged seven, possibly the youngest reader of *Amazing*. Gernsback commented:

> This is gratifying, for if we can make the youngsters think, we feel that we are accomplishing our mission, and that the future of the magazine, and, to a degree, the future of progress through the younger generation, is in excellent hands.[12]

A few months later Gernsback received a letter from E. E. Twiggens of Le Mars, Iowa, who at 97 claimed to be *Amazing's* oldest reader. Twiggens was a remarkable man. He had enjoyed the work of Jules Verne, having read it when it first appeared, but he regarded it now as dated and requested that no more be reprinted. He had apparently always been a reader of scientific fiction, adding that "it has been during my lifetime that many of the great scientific fictionists have done their work. When I was a boy, long before the Civil War, I traveled 300 miles on horseback to see a 'flying machine' that a mechanic was building at Troy, New York. He had been getting 'funny writeups' in all the papers in the country for his crazy notion, and his delight was pathetic when I actually expressed confidence that some day men might fly. I helped him with the machine for some weeks, but we were never able to get it off the ground. It was finally wrecked in a gust of wind."[13]

Such was the appeal of science fiction, to all ages. Nevertheless, the purists still believed the name and cover art were demeaning science fiction and that it was necessary to raise standards. It was one of the reasons that scientists were reluctant to contribute to the magazine other than pseudonymously. Yet Gernsback seemed blind to the situation. In his 1952 Worldcon speech, Gernsback made an interesting remark. ". . . after I had brought into life the world's first science-fiction magazine . . . in 1926, suddenly Science

Fiction became respectable."[14] This must have come as a surprise to Gernsback's many critics. Both Damon Knight in *In Search of Wonder* (1967) and James Blish in his pseudonymous *More Issues at Hand* (1970) refer to how Gernsback's actions had forced science fiction "into the ghetto," with the consequence that it had lost all respectability, and standards had dropped alarmingly.

The irony is that both are true. Before science fiction was categorized, it had been a standard part of the output of many leading writers, and there is no doubt that the works of Jules Verne and H. G. Wells were highly respected. However the scientific romance in the pulp magazines had little equivalent respect. It had an ardent following, in fact the same ones who supported *Amazing Stories*, but the more serious publishers were disdainful of it. By this token it had already lost its respectability, perhaps most strongly at the hands of Edgar Rice Burroughs. Yet critics do not blame Burroughs, or his editor Bob Davis, for the loss of respect for science fiction. By 1926 the pulps had lost much of their own interest in science fiction, in favor of general adventure fiction, especially westerns and detective stories (both of which had already been "ghettoized" by other publishers with the same effects as happened to science fiction). When Gernsback made a success of publishing science fiction on its own, other publishers sat up and took notice. Science fiction began to reappear in the pulps, and publishers considered issuing their own magazines.

The distinction is clear. Science fiction had gained respectability amongst publishers, but not necessarily amongst writers, and not always amongst readers. Many complained that they felt embarrassed buying the magazine at the newsstand because of Paul's lurid covers. Others claimed that their parents did not allow them to read such "trash."

Two good examples of readers' reactions to the image of *Amazing Stories* both appeared in the October 1928 issue. The first was from pioneer fan Ray Palmer, who supported Paul's covers one hundred percent, but added:

> Several months ago I had the opportunity to induce a friend to read AMAZING STORIES but he was forced to discontinue it by reason of his parents dislike of the cover illustrations. He thought it was "trash."[15]

The other came from the recently married Mrs. L. Silberberg, who would soon debut in science fiction under her maiden name, Leslie F. Stone. Her mother had encouraged her to develop her imagination, so there had been no parental restrictions here. It was Miss Stone who had reservations about the magazine's image:

> Lots of people have commented upon the illustrations of Mr. Paul, and most of them seem to agree that his drawings are quite vivid and most often in keeping with the stories, but I do wish your covers were not quite so lurid. In the first place, your readers do not need these over brilliant covers to recognize their favorite magazine and, on the other hand, strangers would more often hesitate in picking up a magazine so amazingly bound. He could expect nothing but trash in a magazine so glaringly cov-

ered.

I always do feel a little sheepish when I carry my new issue of AMAZING STORIES through the lobby of a hotel, and I have been told that others suffer in the same manner as I do under a barrage of eyes, as they try to sneak unnoticed with that blatant pictorial atrocity under their arm. And were we to have a vote then I know that almost every reader of AMAZING STORIES would agree with me fully. Please, please tone Mr. Paul down.[16]

Gernsback was not deaf to their appeals, but for sound publishing reasons he was unsure what to do. Several readers suggested that the magazine be retitled *Scientifiction*, which had been Gernsback's own idea back in 1924. Now, though, he felt that that name would not have sufficient attraction on the market. However, he was willing to try an experiment. In the April 1928 *Amazing* he suggested a new competition for a symbol or design to represent the concept of scientifiction. He offered a first prize of $100 plus a range of smaller cash prizes, up to ten in all. He also had Frank R. Paul produce his own design and this was displayed on the cover. It depicted a giant eye, meant to signify the mind's eye, in which were shown many of the images of science fiction. Although this was a symbolic cover, it was still pictorial and, if you pardon the pun, eye-catching.

When the results were published in the September 1928 issue, Paul drew a further cover showing the winning design. In fact Paul embellished the rather basic design of A. A. Kaufman, the winner, but the result, a pen on a cog writing the word "Scientifiction" moving between fact and theory, still looked overly mechanical. Gernsback reported the effect the cover had on that issue's sales in the April 1929 "Discussions." First he gave some additional background:

> For a long time, the battle regarding our somewhat lurid covers has been waxing hot and heavy. One faction contends that a more dignified cover will be better for the magazine, while the other, and equally strong faction maintains that the present covers are acceptable to them and, as a matter of fact, first attracted them to become readers of the magazine.

Gernsback then went on to remind readers of the September 1928 cover and the extent he had gone to to make it as dignified, "tame and unsensational" as possible. He then discussed the effect on sales.

> . . . sad to relate, from a selling standpoint, it proved a huge disappointment. The number preceding it, i.e. the August issue, sold 14 percent better. The next issue, the October issue, sold almost 16% better. This, however, is only part of the story, because for the September issue, we put out an average of 20 per cent more copies than of the other months to make a real test and satisfy ourselves whether there was anything in the dignified cover idea or not.

The result . . . proved conclusively that the public at large is not attracted by a dignified or more or less meaningless design, but on the other hand IS attracted to the newsstand by the more lurid designs, which may not be aesthetic but which, after all, sell more magazines.[17]

Gernsback then discussed alternatives but emphasized, in conclusion, that "until *Amazing Stories* reaches a net circulation of some 300,000 copies, which at the present time does not seem likely for some months, at least, it will be necessary to continue with the present colorful designs."

It was a blow to those who wanted to see *Amazing* presented as a serious magazine, but the evidence was strongly in favor of the image that the lurid covers gave in the sales to the public. By giving those figures in percentages Gernsback disguises his true sales figures, but by good fortune a promotional advertisement in the August 1928 issue stated that although the print run was still 150,000 sales were seldom in excess of 125,000.[18] If we take those figures as the maximum, and translate the above percentages into circulation, we have the following:

August 1928:	Printed 150,000	Sold 123,000
September 1928:	Printed 180,000	Sold 108,000
October 1928:	Printed 150,000	Sold 125,000

In other words, the unsensational cover resulted not just in a direct drop in sales of 17,000 copies against the norm, but a rise in the number of unsold copies from 25,000 to 72,000, an increase of nearly 300%! No publisher would ignore those figures. If, by producing a specialist magazine, Gernsback found that he had to produce lurid covers in order to maintain sales, a direct consequence of which was that science fiction became tarred with the juvenile, sensationalistic image, then that was the public's choice. Throughout his years of publishing *Science and Invention* and *Amazing* he had made the point over and over about the seriousness of science fiction, and its strength in educating and inspiring the hobbyist experimenter. But if in order to reach that readership he had to pander to the public's requirements in how they selected their reading matter, then Gernsback had no choice but to follow that path.

The direct effect of that was that science fiction began to attract a different type of reader and writer, both of whom had entertainment at the fore of their intentions, not education. Whether Gernsback liked it or not, now that he had opened science fiction up to the public, it was becoming their baby, not his, and it was taking on an identity and character of its own.

14.

THE GROWTH OF SCIENTIFICTION

So far we have concentrated on the development scientific fiction underwent in its transfer from *Science and Invention* to *Amazing Stories*. 1927 was a year of self-exploration, with science fiction feeling its way, seeking its parameters, and trying to understand its own identity. It was just like a newborn baby, with Gernsback as parent trying to do the best for the infant, but realising there was a big wide world out there only too anxious to have its own way with the child. In another analogy, *Amazing Stories* was like a young sapling getting its roots into the earth, and 1927 saw it finding rich soil in which to establish itself. It could now start to grow and look toward bearing fruit, and in turn bringing forth seed. It was 1928 that would see this fructification in a way unforeseen by even Gernsback's prophetic vision.

The first development was a new companion magazine to *Amazing Stories*. From the start readers had clamored for *Amazing* to be semi-monthly, but Gernsback could find no practical way to achieve this. The Experimenter Publishing Company was a small concern compared to the major pulp firms who were geared to rapid production. Experimenter already had enough magazines produced on the regular monthly cycle. In addition to *Science and Invention, Radio News, Motor Camper and Tourist, Radio Review*, and now *Amazing*, the Gernsbacks had been launching other new magazines. The first had been *Money Making*, issued in October 1926 and edited by Sidney Gernsback under the Consrad subsidiary. This magazine subsequently merged with *Spare Time Money Making* which had been issued in February 1927. Two new radio magazines were issued as an aid to listeners to Experimenter's station WRNY: *Radio Listeners Guide and Call Book*, in November 1926, and *Radio Program Weekly* in March 1927. Though this last-named was a weekly magazine it was a simple booklet of radio program listings issued locally. In June 1927 Gernsback took a bold step and issued the first magazine devoted to television. Gernsback's developments in this field will be considered in the next chapter.

Gernsback did experiment with a weekly magazine called *French Humor*. It ran for sixty-three numbers from July 16, 1927 to September 29, 1928, changing its name to *Tidbits* with the July 7, 1928 issue. It was edited by Valentine Erskine, and contained little American material, relying instead on translations from the French magazines *Le Pele-mele, Parisiana, Le Journal amusant, Ruy Blas, L'Humor, Le Sourire* and *Sans-gene*. Although this magazine has little to do with the development of science fiction, it does show that Gernsback was now established in the publishing industry and looking to find further areas of interest. He had always had a sense of humor, as evidenced by his "Fips quips" and the many humorous invention stories he published. He had also noted the growth of "titillating" men's magazines in the shape of *Snappy Stories, The Parisienne*, and *Paris Nights*. *French Humor* was a slim magazine, and more easily edited and illustrated than *Amazing Stories*, but it was still a major logistical exercise to publish and distribute the magazine much beyond the environs of New York.

Following the success of *Amazing Stories Annual*, Gernsback could see the value in issuing a big companion to *Amazing* containing one or two novel-length works plus a few supporting short stories, on a quarterly basis. The first readers new about this was on December 5, 1927 in an announcement published in the January 1928 *Amazing*:

> The idea of publishing *Amazing Stories* twice a month has been abandoned for the time being as being uneconomical and impractical, for a number of publishing reasons. Several months ago the experiment of an *Amazing Stories Annual* was made and has proven more or less satisfactory. It is therefore proposed by the publishers that they will get out at more or less frequent intervals, a 50c *Amazing Stories* Supplement rather than an *Annual*, to be sold on the newsstands. Only a relatively small class of readers would buy *Amazing Stories* twice a month, so those who wish to buy additional scientifiction literature will have their wish gratified by the supplement.[1]

More detailed news was given in the editorial to the February 1928 *Amazing* published on January 5. Gernsback confirmed the demand for further scientifiction and and stated that there would be an *Amazing Stories Quarterly* to be published on the 20th of January, April, July and October.

> In make up it will be similar to the *Annual*. It will sell for 50c, but will contain a great deal more material than is to be found in the regular issues of *Amazing Stories*. As a matter of fact, it will contain twice as much matter, and will be profusely illustrated. In the *Quarterly*, we will have a good chance to catch up on our full-length novels, of which we have a great many excellent ones on hand, but which, due to the time element, we cannot publish quickly enough in *Amazing Stories*.[2]

The first issue of *Amazing Stories Quarterly*, dated Winter 1928, appeared two weeks later on Friday, January 20, 1928, allowing fans a bumper offering for the weekend. Paul's cover depicted a scene from H. G. Wells's novel *When the Sleeper Wakes*. A request to purchase this story had been issued to Wells in May 1927, with the intention of serializing it in *Amazing*. It showed that despite the accumulation of manuscripts, Gernsback still felt a need to use reprints. Indeed, the first issue also reprinted E. H. Johnson's "The Golden Vapor" from *The Electrical Experimenter*. The other four stories were new including a short novel, *The Moon of Doom*, by Earl L. Bell. Bell was a native of Augusta, Georgia, and had previously sold a short story, "Doctor DeBruce," to *Weird Tales* (February 1924). The sale of this novel to Gernsback made him a local celebrity with his name in the newspaper. He did not further his talents, as he sold only two more stories though one of those, "The Young Old Man" (*Amazing Stories*, September 1929) is a powerful piece about immortality.

Some of the stories announced for the first issue were not present, amongst them a new story by Homer Eon Flint, "The Nth Man." Most readers may not have known that Flint had died under mysterious circumstances on March 27, 1924 at the age of 35. His body was found under an automobile, impaled by the rear axle. The car had belonged to a gangster who claimed Flint had taken the car by force and driven away alone. The full facts never became known, but one of the field's more imaginative talents was lost. Flint's death, two years before the birth of *Amazing Stories*, meant that he never knew of the growth in a field that he had helped to popularize, and in which he would almost certainly have been one of the leading stars. "The Nth Man" had been purchased by the Munsey Company on March 26, 1920, but had remained unpublished until Munsey's subsidiary rights agency sold the story to Gernsback in November 1927. It appeared in the Spring issue of the *Quarterly*. By and large it received an unfavorable response, as the prospect of a giant man was considered unscientific. "When Mr. Pendleton reached a weight of a few hundred tons, how was he able to obtain his supply of chemicals for sustaining the glandular stimulus causing his prodigious growth," wrote one reader.[3] Clearly the readership of *Amazing* was more critical in respect of a story pertaining to be scientific than those by other pulp writers that were primarily fantastic adventures.

The *Quarterly*, like the monthly, was an immediate success, and during 1928 both magazines grew and prospered. There had been a fifty per cent increase in the amount of science fiction published, but more than that, with the rapid reduction in the amount of stories reprinted, there was a growth in the market for new stories, especially novels. A simple story count (excluding *Science and Invention*) shows that in 1927 Gernsback published a total of 5 novels and 67 stories, whilst in 1928 he published 13 novels and 72 stories. In 1927 all 5 of those novels were reprints. In 1928 there were still 5 reprints, but 8 were new. Of the short stories in 1927, 45 were new, increasing to 67 in 1928. The number of reprinted short stories had dropped to 5 from 22, and they became the exception after the August 1928 issue.

1928 thus saw a rapid expansion in new stories allowing a growth in new talent. During 1926 only one author had debuted in *Amazing*: Miles J. Breuer. Other important writers making a mark in *Amazing* were G. Peyton Wertenbaker from *Science & Invention*, A. Hyatt Verrill, and Clare Winger Harris from the competition. 1927 had seen a steady increase in the new recruits.

First came Bob Olsen in the June 1927 issue. Olsen was in many ways a typical Gernsback writer. He loved gadget stories, but wrote them with a sense of humor and some character. He had been born in 1884, the son of a Norwegian goldsmith who had emigrated to America in 1880. His full name was Alfred Johannes Olsen, but he was always known as Bob. He delighted in scholarly pursuits and, after graduating from Brown University, in Providence, R.I., became a high school teacher. In 1915 he turned to the world of advertising, first as a copywriter, but later becoming vice-president of one of the largest advertising agencies in Los Angeles. He had a fascination for the fourth dimension and began a series on fourth-dimensional inventions, starting with "The Four-Dimensional Roller-Press." He soon became a regular contributor, and had over twenty stories published during the Gernsback period, but almost nothing thereafter.

The September 1927 issue saw Otis Adelbert Kline's first new sale to Gernsback, "The Radio Ghost," a title guaranteed to attract Gernsback's attention. It was only science fiction by Gernsback's narrow definition. It dealt with an apparently haunted house where, it transpires, the contents were moved by remote control. Ideal Gernsback material. Kline, born in Chicago on July 1, 1891, had undertaken a succession of jobs before turning to writing. He had been a compositor and pressman in the print trade, an advertising manager for a newspaper, a traveling salesman and a fairly successful song writer. He also wrote scenarios for the early film industry, something he had in common with Homer Eon Flint. His first story sale had been "The Thing of a Thousand Shapes" serialized in the first two issues of *Weird Tales*. He sold to a variety of markets, not exclusively fantastic or science fiction, though he is probably known best for his Burroughs-imitation novels in *Argosy* starting with *The Planet of Peril* (July 20 to August 24, 1929). Although Kline had over forty fantasy or SF stories in the pulps during the Gernsback period, he sold only one more story directly to Gernsback, a novel written with his brother Allen, *The Secret Kingdom* (*Amazing Stories*, October to December 1929). He established his own literary agency in 1936, which he pursued till his death in 1946. Kline was an example of the type of popular writer Gernsback would have been wise to attract, but who sold to more lucrative and attractive markets.

The next new writer was Francis Flagg. Flagg was the pseudonym of Henry George Weiss (1898-1946). He took the pseudonym in memory of his brother, Francis Flagg Weiss, who had died in painful circumstances in 1922. Henry Weiss had a weak constitution and had been privately educated at the family home in Nova Scotia. He later moved to California for his health, studied at the University, and turned to poetry and fiction. His first sale was "The Machine Man of Ardathia" in the November 1927 *Amazing*. Perhaps not too surprisingly, it shows a physically emaciated human from the far future whose brain has evolved to a size too big for the body to support and who now relies wholly on machines for its bodily activities. Flagg was a talented writer, his poetical imagery shining through the occasional clumsy notions. He sold over twenty stories to the magazines in this period.

The last new talent Gernsback published in 1927, would also be one of the biggest, though he was an author who had already established a reputation for his science fiction in *Weird Tales*—Edmond Hamilton. Hamilton was one of the most prolific and popular writers of science fiction and fantasy during this period, with over eighty published stories. He had been born in Youngstown, Ohio on October 21, 1904, the son of a newspaper cartoonist. He started trying to sell stories to *Weird Tales* in 1924, and eventually succeeded with "Across Space" (September-November 1926) about a Martian invasion of Earth. Published earlier was "The Monster-God of Mamurth" (August 1926) about an invisible spider-like monster in a remote desert ruins. Hamilton then worked his way through all the known themes of science fiction. "The Metal Giants" (December 1926) introduced a mighty atom-powered robot; "The Atomic Conquerors" (February 1927) told of a war between the sub-atomic world and the macro-universe; "Evolution Island" (March 1927) has a ray speed up evolution bringing forth intelligent plants; "The Moon Menace" (September 1927) has the moon-men invade Earth; and *The Time Raider* (October 1927-January 1928) has a man bring together an army of warriors from various moments of history. All of this before Gernsback published him in the January 1928 *Amazing* with "The Comet Doom." It was stories like "The Comet Doom," but more significantly *Crashing Suns* (*Weird Tales*, August-September 1928), that gave birth to the sub-genre of "space opera," which Hamilton almost created single-handedly. It would grow out of all proportion in the later pulps, especially the early issues of *Astounding Stories of Super-Science*, and is probably responsible more for the later poor reputation of science fiction than anything Gernsback published. We shall explore this area later. Hamilton's early stories had similar plots with one man saving the world against astronomical odds. The culmination of these stories was *The Universe Wreckers* (*Amazing*, May-July 1930), which earned Hamilton the nickname of the World-Wrecker. It took him years to live it down, if he ever did. It did not stop him remaining one of the most popular writers of science fiction for almost fifty years to his death in 1977. His works are a useful barometer of the state of science fiction over the years and, consequently, we will return to him frequently in this history.

"The Comet Doom" was held by Gernsback for some time until purchased. On August 29, 1927 Miriam Bourne wrote apologizing for the delay, due to the summer holidays. As first reader she short-listed the story from the slush pile and passed it to Gernsback for final judgment. Gernsback responded on September 3, and his letter reveals the extent to which he was involved with the stories:

> I personally liked this story very much, but took the liberty to make the changes as per attached copy . . . You will notice that I elaborated, somewhat, on the brain operation, to make it more scientifically correct, as in your original you had some omissions on which we should have been picked up very quickly by our more scientifically inclined readers.

The story was eventually purchased on September 28, 1927 for $30.

During 1927 there was a lack of urgency given to manuscripts submitted to *Amazing*. Gernsback insisted upon vetting all material purchased for his magazines, of which there were now ten, and although each of these had their own editors and sub-editors, there were still insufficient staff to cope with the advice and help to new writers. Because in later years John W. Campbell earned a reputation at *Astounding* for the scale of encouragement he gave to writers, other editors have been compared unfavorably to him, especially Gernsback, who has been given a reputation of providing no help at all. In fact, as we shall see, this was not the case. It was only the lack of staff time in the early days that precluded any significant help. This was a factor that would keep writers away from Gernsback in favor of more encouraging markets. Hamilton retained *Weird Tales* as his prime market, and only sold sparingly to Gernsback over the next few years. It was not until David Lasser came on the scene that the proper encouragement new writers needed was made available.

The February 1928 issue introduced David H. Keller, a writer who would rival Hamilton for popularity in the magazines during this period. He also sold over eighty stories to the science-fiction magazines, but whereas Hamilton was in his early twenties, and a college drop-out, who had previously earned his living on the railroad, Keller was a qualified doctor in his late forties, working at that time as Assistant Superintendent of the Louisiana State Mental Hospital. Keller was not interested in the wild super-science of the far future or deep space, but in the social implications of scientific developments. He probably appealed to a different age range than Hamilton, and though his writing was at times almost as poor, the visualization of his concepts was sharp and ingenious. He was one of the most inventive of Gernsback's discoveries.

Keller's first sale was "The Revolt of the Pedestrians" which was the first social satire Gernsback published. It considered a future where the reliance by humanity on automobiles had caused it to physically weaken and for legs to atrophy. Only the occasional throwback pedestrian appeared. "They are not like us," commented an automobolist in the story, "in fact some say they are not human beings at all." James Gunn, who selected the story as representative of the evolution of science fiction in his series-anthology *The Road to Science Fiction* (1979), wrote that it "exhibits some sophisticated techniques surprising for its time: the calm acceptance of change, the casual division of humanity into automobolists and pedestrians, and the emergence of satire from the story itself."[4]

Keller and Gernsback were to become friends and Gernsback would subsequently employ Keller as editor on his medical magazines. However, it can be shown how easy it might have been for Keller and Gernsback never to have become acquainted, and thus a considerable talent lost to the science-fiction field, due to the image *Amazing* was originally projecting. In an unpublished memoir, "The Folly of Writing," Keller looked back on the circumstances around the sale of this first story.

> In June 1925 I wrote in longhand a tale which I titled "The Revolt of the Pedestrians." I made a typed copy which I bound in the Bookseller volume, a collection of tales which represented fond hopes and vain anticipations but up to this time had brought no financial reward. My family were now tired of my spending so many hours for my own pleasure. The wife bought a copy of a new magazine, *Amazing Stories*, owned and edited by Hugo Gernsback. She insisted that my tales were as good as those in the magazine and asked me to send one to Gernsback. At that time *Amazing Stories* was printing the old tales of Jules Verne . . . and only occasionally printed one by an American author. I had little hope of selling a story to this magazine but to please the wife I typed and sent to New York, on the 27 of February, a copy of "The Revolt of the Pedestrians." Receiving no reply I wrote a letter of inquiry on May 12, 1927 and a second one on June 6. Finally on October 2, 1927 I received a letter from the Editorial Department stating that my story had been accepted and would be published either in the January or February number in 1928. . . . Looking back on that period I have wondered whether Gernsback, when he first read the manuscript, realized that it would introduce a

new style of science fiction.[5]

This tells us two things. It reiterates the problem of getting a response from Gernsback. But more importantly it showed a reluctance by Keller to submit a story because *Amazing* had the image of being predominantly a reprint magazine. Lovecraft had the same disparaging feelings about it. When, at last, he sold "The Colour Out of Space" to Gernsback, he wrote to Frank Belknap Long, saying:

> Oh, by the way, *Amazing Stories* lived up to its name by amazing me almost into unconsciousness . . . they took "The Colour Out of Space"! No spoofing—I enclose their card to prove it. If they pay respectably, I ought to get a decent little check out of this, for the manuscript ran to thirty-two pages; but perhaps they're so used to free reprints that they haven't formed the paying habit.[6]

Fortunately, by 1928, *Amazing* was rapidly ridding itself of the reprint image, but one wonders how many other potential writers that had deterred. Lovecraft would soon learn that the Gernsbacks hadn't quite "formed the paying habit," but we shall return to that in a few chapters hence.

In Keller's memoirs, he had one other admission to make about his first sale which is pertinent to record here:

> At that time I was the Assistant Superintendent of a State Hospital and was not convinced that it was the proper thing for me to write and actually sell stories for pulp magazines. So I went to all the bookstores in Alexandria and bought all the copies of the February 1928 issue. Thus for a while I kept the secret from even my closest friends.[7]

Again, the image of *Amazing Stories* had become a deterrant to the very professional Gernsback was hoping to attract.

March 1928's issue brought forth another new talent, one that might have become prodigious if fate had been kinder. Charles Cloukey was fifteen when his first story, "Sub-Satellite" appeared. It was a clever story for one so young, about a man who fires a bullet at another on the moon but misses. The bullet orbits the moon and strikes the man in the back! Cloukey's was a precocious talent. He was recorded as one of the most brilliant students ever to attend Lansdowne High School, Pennsylvania, making a straight A grade for each of his four years there. In 1930 he entered the Thomas Edison Competition at Orange, New Jersey, and came seventh. He entered Haverford College in 1931 where he won first honors as a freshman in the intelligence test. Dr Rufus Jones of the College described Cloukey as a "rare and unusual person of extraordinary brilliance."[8] He was studying to be a chemical engineer when he was struck down by typhoid fever and died in September 1931, aged eighteen. During those years of study he sold nine stories to the science-fiction magazines, including a novel which was published posthumously. Several were concerned with the fascination of time paradoxes. Had Cloukey lived and continued to write science fiction he might have become one of the major talents of the thirties and beyond.

No new talent emerged in the April 1928 *Amazing*, but May's issue introduced us to Fletcher Pratt. Pratt (1897-1956), the son of a farmer, was, early in his life, a librarian and a prizefighter, before settling to become a reporter and book editor, and eventually a full-time writer. His early works were often collaborations with friends, most notably Irvin Lester, with whom he appeared on his first sale, "The Octopus Cycle." Pratt's rapid emergence in the thirties as a writer of serious historical books, and his subsequent collaboration with L. Sprague de Camp on a series of humorous fantasies for *Unknown*, has given Pratt a reputation as a respectable writer unsullied by the early pulps. By and large his science-fiction work for Gernsback has been forgotten, even though he sold him twelve stories, plus a number of translations of European novels. His stories were amongst the best written in the science-fiction magazines and should be better remembered than they are.

Hardly a month passed without some new talent appearing. The Spring 1928 *Quarterly* introduced J. Schlossel with his interplanetary extravaganza "The Second Swarm." Schlossel (1902-77) is not remembered today, though he was a pioneer of space opera, writing some highly imaginative material. His early sales were to *Weird Tales* where he had debuted with "Invaders from Outside" in January 1925. His story-telling skills were weak, but Schlossel showed tremendous inventiveness in his adventures, with intergalactic wars and invasions on an immense scale. His shorter works showed a vision that was advanced for its day. In "A Message from Space" (*Weird Tales*, March 1926) a man builds a television receiving-set and receives messages from a distant planet orbitting a double sun. Schlossel may well have received his inspiration for this from Gernsback's articles and editorials in *Science and Invention* and *Radio News* where he encouraged the idea of interplanetary communication. To my mind Schlossel's most inventive story is "To the Moon by Proxy" (*Amazing*, October 1928) wherein a crippled scientist sends a robot to the moon in his stead and monitors the progress by television. This was the first story ever to consider sending an unmanned probe to the moon and watching the results on television, and Schlossel should have full credit.

Harl Vincent was the next talent to appear with "The Golden Girl of Munan" in the June 1928 *Amazing*. The title suggests to me all that was poor about the growing image of science fiction. Vincent (1893-1968) was the pseudonym of mechanical engineer Harold Vincent Schoepflin. He became a prolific and popular pulpster with fifty-five stories in the magazines of this period. He seldom had original plots, but often had clever ideas. His best work did not start to appear until he began to sell to *Astounding* in 1934.

The July 1928 Amazing offered no new writers apart from the pseudonymous Marius, but helped to confirm the talents of Cloukey and Olsen. It also contained a novelty item, showing the extent to which Gernsback was prepared to be experimental, and that was a play, called "Just Around the Corner" by Raymond Knight. This was not the first time Gernsback had published plays. Erald Schivo had written three for *Radio News* in 1922, but it was a bold move for a popular fiction magazine.

With August 1928 we come to a significant turning point in our history. More precisely, it was July 5, 1928 when that issue appeared, or even more precisely June 10, when the issue went to press. I have already refered to some of the reasons in earlier chapters, but there is no harm in bringing them all together. For a start the August issue was the last sequential issue to contain a reprint, "The Moth" by H. G. Wells, and also the last with a straightforward "gadget" story, "The Perambulating Home" by Henry Hugh Simmons. It was thus an end of two chapters—the old invention story from *Science and Invention* and the need to bolster the contents with reprints. By either coincidence or design, the concurrent issue of *Science and Invention* was the last to contain any fiction, the final episode of A. Merritt's revised *The Metal Emperor*. Curiously Gernsback never reprinted this in his magazines, even though it was the preferred version by Merritt of his *The Metal Monster*. Perhaps Gernsback was precluded by contract. In short, we can therefore point at the August 1928 issue as being the final chapter of Gernsback's *Science and Invention* days of scientific fiction.

In its place came the super-science extravaganza, and the August issue contained two memorable examples of this: Edward Elmer Smith's *The Skylark of Space* and Philip Francis Nowlan's "Armageddon—2419 A.D." In one issue Gernsback shed his old coat and donned a new one of many colors and dimensions. Goodbye scientific fiction, welcome super-science stories.

E. E. "Doc" Smith didn't write much in *The Skylark of Space* that Hamilton and Schlossel hadn't used in their *Weird Tales* extravaganzas, or that Homer Eon Flint hadn't tried in *All-Story* and *Argosy*. But it seems the fates had only now decreed that the time was right. Remember, Smith had been trying to sell this story for seven years. And if further confirmation is needed, it was also in the August 1928 issue of *Weird Tales* that Edmond Hamilton's galaxy-bursting serial, *Crashing Suns*, started.

What Smith did in *The Skylark of Space* was redefine the horizons of science fiction in all its terms. Gone was any chance to think of science fiction in the parochial way of Gernsback's original gadget stories. The "what if" hypothesis Gernsback had originally challenged his readers with had first brought forth only a new use for a radio, or at best, two new uses for a radio. Now, little more than ten years later, writers were considering new uses for the suns and planets and the basic energy sources of our universe. Other authors had been pushing the boundaries toward this moment, but never quite so convincingly. When Smith did it, the science-fiction world stood openmouthed with eyes-a-poppin', and the universe was never the same again. The novel has all the qualities of archetypal space opera. Super-scientist Richard Seaton discovers atomic energy, builds his own spaceship, and sets off to explore the universe pursued by the villainous but equally super-scientific Blackie DuQuesne.

Smith's own image does not live up to his larger-than-life fiction. A quiet, small man, the son of a whaler, he was born in Wisconsin in 1890 and grew up in Washington and Idaho. He subsequently qualified as a chemist, and spent much of his working life in the food industry. But in the world of science fiction, Smith's name will for ever be synonymous with super-science fiction, and expanding the limits of man's imagination.

Philip Francis Nowlan was two years older than Smith. He was a financial reporter on the *Philadelphia Public Ledger* and had become increasingly bored with the business world. Whereas Smith pushed back the frontiers of space, Nowlan confined himself to Earth, but stretched the frontiers of future science. He took a modern American, Anthony Rogers, five centuries into the future where America is dominated by a superscientific Mongol race, the Airlords of Han. Rogers joins forces with a guerilla faction, and attacks the enemy by using their own amazing weapons.

This story was seen by John F. Dille, president of the National Newspaper Syndicate, who convinced Nowlan to convert it into a comic strip with Nowlan writing the continuity and illustrations by Dick Calkins. Nowlan reluctantly agreed and *Buck Rogers in the 25th Century* was syndicated in scores of newspapers starting on January 7, 1929. Nowlan's own direct sequel, "The Airlords of Han" appeared in the March 1929 *Amazing Stories* published on February 5. Throughout the thirties the Buck Rogers adventures typified science fiction. He also featured on the radio and in films. The Buck Rogers stories, even in their comic strip incarnation, were still basically Gernsbackian SF, depicting the marvels of a future age, and thus orientated children on the future possibilities of science. It seems almost certain that without *Amazing Stories* there would have been no Buck Rogers, and who knows what would have taken its place in the hearts and souls of countless children. In the space of a few short years, Gernsback's young sapling had started to multiply. Buck Rogers was the first fruit.

The torrent of talent continued with two more names appearing in the Summer issue of *Amazing Stories Quarterly*: Stanton A. Coblentz and R. F. Starzl. Coblentz (1896-1982) was already a published author. He had written poetry whilst still at college, and a book of verse, *The Thinker and Other Poems*, had appeared in 1923. He was writing regularly for the newspapers and a nonfiction study, *The Decline of Man*, had been published in 1925. He turned to science fiction as a vehicle to convey his feelings about mankind and society and, like Keller, realized its potential for satire. Coblentz had written his first novel, *The Sunken World*, about the discovery of Atlantis, before he knew of the science-fiction magazines. The other publishers of the day were too conservative to consider the book. Then Coblentz read about *Amazing Stories* and delivered the manuscript to Miriam Bourne by hand. About three weeks later he was asked if he could reduce the ninety-thousand word story by a third. Coblentz refused, but shortly afterwards they wrote again saying they now had more space and would like to use the story. This must have placed its submission around October 1927 when thoughts on the new *Quarterly* were still crystalizing. Coblentz thereafter became a regular contributor. He was a good writer and his stories were always readable though he was later overcome by the pulp style, forsaking the more lyrical qualities of his better work.

Rome F. Starzl (1899-1976) was a life-long newspaperman. His father was owner of the LeMars, Iowa *Globe-Post*. Starzl worked first as a reporter, becoming a partner in 1934, and from 1940 sole owner and publisher until a fire destroyed the printing plant in 1968. He had a talent with words and a gift for smart ideas that made him one of the more readable writers of the period. He had twenty-four stories published in the brief six years of his SF career until the pressure of newspaper work stopped his output. His first appearance, "Out of the Sub-Universe," built upon the idea that Wertenbaker had used in "The Man from the Atom," though it also satirised the concept perpetrated by Ray Cummings in his endless Golden Atom series. In Starzl's story a couple descend into a sub-atomic world. The scientist who has arranged the experiment awaits their return but is greeted instead, after only fifteen minutes of his own time, by the return of the hundreds of descendants of the first couple.

Three other new names from 1928 are worth highlighting. Of these, Jack Williamson must stand as Gernsback's most durable discovery, able to produce fiction as pertinent to the nineties as his early work was to the twenties. Williamson's discovery of science fiction and its effect upon him is perhaps typical of many young men of his period. John Stewart Williamson had been born in Bisbee in what was still Arizona Territory, on April 29, 1908. He came from a long line of frontier families. The family regularly shifted between Texas and Mexico before eventually settling in New Mexico in 1915. In the outback young Jack was not particularly conscious of the progress of science, though his imagination was stirred when he read exciting stories in *Youth's Companion* and *American Boy*. A radio-ham friend drew Williamson's attention to *Amazing Stories* with the November 1926 issue. Subsequently Williamson acquired a free copy of the March 1927 issue through a promotional ad in *Pathfinder* and with his sister's help, he raised the money for a subscription. He was soon writing letters of comment to "Discussions," the first appearing in the October 1927 issue. It was prompted by the revelation in Gernsback's editorial that *Amazing* was not yet paying its way. Williamson wrote:

> I am alarmed to find that *Amazing Stories* is not yet on a paying basis. I feel that this magazine fills a real need. I believe that it will increase the public interest in scientific topics, develop our country's scientific imagination, and increase the well-known American power of invention.[9]

He was also soon attempting science-fiction stories of his own. His first attempt, "The Silent Man," was a scientific murder story. It was submitted on June 14, 1927, along with Williamson's request that "I should be deeply grateful for any suggestions you might be so kind as to make. I should like to know if this manuscript shows any promise for its writer in the field of scientifiction." This was when *Amazing* was becoming swamped with manuscripts and there was no time for a response, just rejection slips. Williamson persisted. He even sold a couple of jokes to *French Humor*. He responded to a request for letters about scientifiction, the best of which would be awarded fifty dollars and published as a prize-winning editorial. Williamson was rewarded by winning the first of the regular quarterly contests and his editorial, "Scientifiction, Searchlight of Science" was published in the Fall 1928 *Quarterly*. It was a good analogy: the idea that scientifiction went ahead of science like a searchlight beam, seeking out the way. It showed the optimism that was held in the twenties, even after the War, that science would create a new world, and that science fiction was building the pathway there.

Less than three weeks later Williamson saw his first story in print, "The Metal Man" in the December 1928 *Amazing Stories*. It was introduced by Gernsback with the praise that, "Not since we published 'The Moon Pool' has such a story as this been published by us." "The Metal Man" had, indeed, been modeled on Merritt's work, and Merritt would remain a strong influence on Williamson for some years. Williamson also began to develop a maturity of style much beyond his years which, when linked with his exotic vision, made him one of the most impressive new writers in Gernsback's firmament.

The second writer of note was Captain S. P. Meek. His first sale had been a nonfiction piece about "Taming Poachers" to Clayton's *Field & Stream* (September 1928). His first science fiction, "The Murgatroyd Experiment," appeared in the Winter 1929 *Amazing Stories Quarterly*. Meek (1894-1972) was a chemist in the U.S. Army, and for a while was one of the most regular contributors to the pulps, with some forty stories, though he also wrote children's books and animal stories. He could always be relied on for an original idea, and his writing was often capable, though it deteriorated as the pulp formula took hold.

The final writer worth mentioning amongst Gernsback's roll call of talent is Wallace G. West. West (1900-1980) was a lawyer and public relations man from Kentucky who had sold his first piece—a gadget story at that—to *Sea Stories* in 1926. He then began to sell to *Weird Tales* with "Loup-Garou" (October 1927), a standard werewolf story, progressing to science fiction with "The Incubator Man" (October 1928). His next story, "The Last Man," was sent first to *Amazing Stories* in the belief that the magazine might pay more than *Weird Tales*. Weeks passed with no response, and, after several further letters of enquiry, West wrote a final letter, withdrawing the story and saying he would be submitting it to *Weird Tales*. Farnsworth Wright bought the story and scheduled it for the February 1929 issue, which would be published on February 1. On January 5, 1929 Wright saw the story in the February 1929 *Amazing Stories* and cabled West, who was on his honeymoon, to find out what was happening. Wright was able to stop publication of the story in *Weird Tales* at a cost of $300. West took legal action against Gernsback, only to learn that the Experimenter Publishing Company was now in receivership. We shall return to the story of Experimenter's bankruptcy later.

In the space of less than two years *Amazing* had revolutionized the pace of science fiction. Gernsback had launched the careers of a dozen new writers, the majority of whom would shape science fiction over the next few years. In addition he had become a major market for a half-dozen writers who had previously sold to *Weird Tales* or *Argosy*. But it was at a price. Within that two years science fiction had metamorphosed from the "invention catalog" type to encompass both the super-science and the exotic adventure. In fact it was a genuine bonding of the pulp pseudo-science story and the techno-visionary tale in Gernsback's magazines. The appeal of science fiction remained with both the professional and the amateur, but the image was now much more closely associated with the latter. This was inevitable. Gernsback's market had always been the hobbyist and experimenter. He had had problems in encouraging them to write scientific fiction, certainly of the visionary kind, but with *Amazing* he was now attracting regular writers as well as newspapermen and reporters acquainted with the use of language and style. The hobbyists became the most vocal readership, not the professional, and, this resulted in the birth of science-fiction fandom.

15.

THE BIRTH OF FANDOM

Gernsback should not have been too surprised when he launched *Amazing Stories* to find a receptive readership of fans awaiting the magazine. After all, he had deliberately aimed his earlier magazines, especially *The Electrical Experimenter*, at the amateur hobbyist and the radio "ham," because their enthusiasm was so responsive, and because he had hoped they might be stimulated into helping to create tomorrow's world.

Perhaps because of the dull response given to his 1924 circular, he had believed the scientifiction hobbyist existed only in limited numbers. Yet within a few weeks of launching *Amazing Stories*, Gernsback found himself inundated by mail from what he called "scientifiction fans—who seem to be pretty well orientated in this sort of literature." He wrote about them in his June 1926 editorial, "The Lure of Scientifiction":

> From the suggestions for reprints that are coming in, these "fans" seem to have a hobby all their own of hunting up scientifiction stories, not only in English, but in many other languages. There is not a day, now, that passes, but we get from a dozen to fifty suggestions as to stories of which, frankly, we have no record, although we have a list of some 600 or 700 scientifiction stories. Some of these fans are constantly visiting the book stories with the express purpose of buying new or old scientifiction tales, and they even go to the trouble of advertising for some volumes that have long ago gone out of print.[1]

At this stage Gernsback was talking primarily about collectors. Book collectors have existed for centuries, avidly pursuing their particular brand of bibliophilia. It is not surprising that amongst them would be those who delighted in the fantastic tale.

What these collectors lacked was any form of organization. The desire to read is often linked with the desire to write, and both amateur writers' circles and amateur journalist associations had been around for a century or more. The latter became more organized in 1876 with the formation of the National Amateur Press Association followed twenty years later by the United Amateur Press Association. Both organizations published their own amateur magazines, concentrating usually on literary criticism and poetry, with little place for fantasy or science fiction.

It was into this circle that H. P. Lovecraft was invited in 1914, and he soon became a leading contributor to the amateur journals. Initially this consisted of poetry and essays, but he finally began to contribute fiction with "The Alchemist" in *The United Amateur* for November 1916. His main encourager was W. Paul Cook (1880-1948), a printer from Athol, Massachusetts, and a leading light in amateur journalism. Cook published fifteen issues of an amateur magazine called *The Vagrant* which ran from 1918 to 1927 and which, because of the Lovecraftian contributions, is highly collected today. Although an amateur publication, it was not a fan magazine, and was certainly not inspired by either science fiction or fantasy. Cook's later magazine, *The Recluse* (1927), which saw only one issue, had a heavier bias to fantasy, containing work by Clark Ashton Smith, Donald Wandrei, H. Warner Munn, Frank Belknap Long, and Samuel Loveman, as well as Lovecraft's long essay on *Supernatural Horror in Literature*, and might be classified as the first amateur fantasy magazine.

Because, through Lovecraft, these writers had also been attracted to *Weird Tales*, one might argue that there was a form of organized fandom of the *Weird Tales* school prior to 1927, but this primarily revolved around Lovecraft's own circle of friends kept together by his prodigious letter writing. It was certainly not dedicated to the promotion of weird fiction, or the study of the supernatural or the occult in any form. As such it may only be classified as a group of fellow devotees and admirers and not as a proper form of fandom.

Science fiction is a narrower form of fantastic literature and consequently, at the time, had a limited circle of followers. As a result they were almost certainly isolated. It was unlikely, even in a big city, to know of another "kid on the block" who read science fiction. It made science-fiction devotees appear to be loners, when in fact they were only too keen to get to know kindred spirits who did not regard them as cranks.

It was long believed that the earliest attempt at organizing science-fiction fans had been in England. This was the Science Fiction Club run by Paul Enever of Hayes in Middlesex. He wrote about it much later in *Wonder Stories*:

> This society was formed back in 1927, before any science-fiction had reached England, other than Wells, Verne and a few contemporary "dreamers." On very rare occasions there would come into the possession of the club, a tattered copy of one of the existing American magazines, and such an event was always celebrated with high glee in the club meetings.[2]

Enever went on to refer to the club's "perpetual instability" However, it was later revealed that Enever had been perpetrating a hoax. The society had not been formed until 1932 and lasted only till 1934, making no mark on the development of fandom. Walter Gillings, the real father of British science-fiction magazines, encountered it only once with an enquiry about how to publish a journal which might keep the club together. Apparently it had a fanzine called *Fantasia* which lasted for only three issues during 1933 but never graduated to the status of a formal journal.

In America, isolation was the common state of the science-fiction fan. Jack Williamson echoed the thoughts of many when he wrote in his first published letter in *Amazing Stories*:

> Few of my friends will read *Amazing Stories*. They say that they do not want to be amazed—that it is a cheap magazine—that such intellectual acrobatics are unhealthy—that the stories are too fantastic. While I admit that there is some justification, it is mostly blind prejudice.[3]

They needed a forum to unite them. That came when Gernsback started the "Discussions" letter column from the January 1927 *Amazing*. Initially he published only the correspondent's home town but, from the January 1928 issue, he began to publish their address as well, and this enabled fans to contact fellows anywhere in the world. It was by this means that Jack Williamson contacted Miles J. Breuer, which led to their collaborations. It also started fandom on the road to organization.

Most of the early letters in "Discussions" were devoted to comments on the stories or on their scientific principles. There arose lengthy debates on the possibilities of space travel and time travel, on sub-atomic worlds, giantism, and especially the fourth dimension. There must have been more written about Einstein's Theory of Relativity in the letters in *Amazing Stories* than in the rest of the nation's scientific journals. At times, the letter column was more interesting than the rest of the issue!

It is certainly a valuable source of letters from writers in the early stages of their careers, or before they turned to writing. Names in "Discussions" in *Amazing Stories*, whilst under Gernsback's control, who sold professionally include Miles J. Breuer, Frank Brueckel, Stuart J. Byrne, A. Bertram Chandler, Sophie Wenzel Ellis, Richard V. Happel, Clare Winger Harris, P. Schuyler Miller, Raymond A. Palmer, Mearle Prout, Jerome Siegel, Leslie F. Stone, E. D. Skinner, David M. Speaker, Robert A. Wait, Cecil B. White, and Jack Williamson. Whilst leading names in the fan world who appeared in "Discussions" in *Amazing*'s first three years include Clifton Amsbury, Walter Dennis, Robert Eades, Allen Glasser, Ronald E. Graham, and Clifford Kornoelje (better known under his alias Jack Darrow).

"Discussions" also gave some idea of the circulation of the magazine. Although the data is more appropriate to identifying the locale of responsive fans, it nevertheless is some guide to the extent of the magazine's distribution. There were 469 letters published in *Amazing* and the *Quarterly* during Gernsback's tenure. Of these, fifty came from outside the United States. Canada inevitably led the way with twenty-eight letters, and England with ten, but there were also letters from Australia, Brazil, Hawaii, Ireland, New Zealand, the Philippines, South Africa, China, and India. The international status of science fiction would continue throughout the Gernsback period, as we shall see in later chapters.

As regards the United States, forty-one of the then forty-eight States were represented. New York, not surprisingly, was most prominent, with 71 of the 419 letters, California was next with 51, Illinois with 31, Pennsylvania 25, Ohio 22, New Jersey 19, Michigan and Texas each 16, Massachusetts 14, and Missouri and Washington with 12 each. The only States not represented were Alabama, Delaware, Idaho, Mississippi, New Hampshire, South Carolina, and Utah, which may have either indicated the lassitude of their readers, or the vicissitudes of the distribution system. Certainly all of these States had readers represented in the magazines before much longer.

The early attempts at organization were based on the further pursuit of science, not the study of science fiction. The first suggestion for a club came from John Mackay of Jersey City, New Jersey. Writing in the August 1927 *Amazing* he stated that a group of young men were planning to form a Science

Club with the purpose of scientific discussion and experimentation. This must have been music to Gernsback's ears. His belief that science fiction would stimulate and inspire was coming true. Mackay was hoping that if enough people could join the Club the fees would enable them to afford a laboratory for their experiments. He sought a response from men in the New Jersey area aged between eighteen and twenty-three.

It brought a swift response from Holger Lindgren in Olympia, Washington, who felt that such a Club should not be limited to one city or state. He believed that "it would be a wiser thing if an International Science Club was formed, and all interested in science, from 18 to 25 years of age could join. (Yes, it would have to be correspondence)."[4] This suggestion received the total backing of Gernsback who offered to make *Amazing Stories* the official organ of the Club, provided there was a sufficient response and members were prepared to pay a small fee.

Donald L. Campbell of Chicago proposed, in the November 1927 *Amazing*, that the lower age limit be reduced from eighteen, as he himself was fifteen, and he believed that there were plenty of young readers who would want to join. Again Gernsback agreed.

More ideas came in. J. C. McAlister of Yellow Grass, Canada, hoped there would be a special feature in *Amazing* on the activities of the Club, and Wilbur S. Jones of Little Rock, Arkansas, suggested that the Club have local chapters for discussion and experimentation. Jack Williamson proposed that experiments as suggested by readers could be conducted in members' laboratories on a rota basis. George A. Wines of Seneca, Michigan, stated that he had organized such a club in 1914 for the local high school boys called the American Order of Science. Its activities sounded like something out of Gernsback's *Electrical Experimenter*, since they had, amongst other things, built a local broadcasting station, and an electric gun which they had presented to the government when War broke out. Wines wanted to extend this organization on a national scale.

The May 1928 issue contained two letters (one from Lindgren again) suggesting that Gernsback act as the co-ordinator on the Science Club and appoint a committee to set up a constitution. Gernsback was reticent, probably because of the limitation on his time, and certainly no one else in his employ had the time to devote to this. It was not like the situation six years later when Gernsback had the energetic Charles Hornig on his payroll ambitious to organize the Science Fiction League. In 1928 Gernsback wanted someone else to take the initiative and form the Club.

Soon the more active readers took the initiative. In the March 1929 issue, George Lasky of New York City asked for readers to write to him about getting the Science Club on its feet. A number did, most notably Walter Dennis and Sidney Gerson of Chicago, who reported on progress in the Summer 1929 *Amazing Stories Quarterly*. Between them Lasky was going to write to all correspondents in *Amazing* in the New York area, and Dennis and Gerson were going to do the same for the Chicago area. Dennis now became the driving force. Through his correspondence he began to learn of small local clubs in existence, most of which had been created during 1928. The earliest was probably the Eastbay Club in Oakland, California, which had been formed by Aubrey MacDermott, Clifton Amsbury, Louis Smith, and Lester Anderson in

June 1928. Dennis had formed his own Pickwick Club in Chicago with Sidney Gerson and Paul McDermott, and there were other small gatherings in Atlanta, Oklahoma City, and New York.

It was Dennis who decided something should be done to bring these together. He contacted Raymond A. Palmer, then living in Milwaukee, and the two arranged to meet at Palmer's home. This was sometime early in 1929, though Dennis cannot now recall the date. It was at that meeting that Palmer and Dennis conceived the name of the Science Correspondence Club. Implementation of the Club from then on was handled by Dennis, Gerson, and Paul McDermott, since Palmer had no resources to handle volumes of mail, printing of membership cards and stationery.

One of the charter members was A. B. Maloire of Centralia, Washington, who had been one of the first to appear in "Discussions" in the January 1927 *Amazing*. He was the first to alert readers to the newly formed Science Correspondence Club in the August 1929 *Science Wonder Stories*. Since his letter referred to the June 1929 issue, published on May 3, we can presume that the Club had been formed some time in March or April 1929. It was the first national organization of its kind created by science-fiction fans for the furtherance of science. Maloire's letter revealed one of the consequences of becoming an active fan which has plagued fans ever since:

> ... unfortunately I have no time to read all [the stories] as corresponding with members of the recently created Science Correspondence Club has taken up much of my time. Up to date we have a membership of twenty-five enthusiastic science-fiction fans all anxious to devour every bit of science fiction that they can grab. Later we may ask a little space in some corner of your magazine to report our progress. At present we are voting for officers.[5]

The Science Correspondence Club was the birth of organized fandom. Even though its formation had been designed for "the furtherance of science and its dissemination among the laymen of the world and the final betterment of humanity,"[6] the members soon found they had a greater interest in discussing the latest developments in science fiction, and though the two went hand in hand for some years, it was clear that fandom was starting to organize itself for the promotion and glorification of science fiction.

Gernsback's original desire that science fiction would educate and stimulate men in the further exploration of science, had worked to begin with, but had now turned in on itself. Science fiction had become a cause in itself, and fandom was preparing itself for the battles ahead. Yet fandom could have had no idea what was going to happen next, even as it was getting organized. Before we look at that, though, let's not forget how Gernsback was looking at his own vision of the future.

16.

TELEVISIONARY DAYS

Television had been a standard device in Gernsback's fiction since *Ralph 124C 41+*, and he had so regularly promoted it in his magazines that it must have seemed old hat to many, when at last the earliest transmissions began. I shall not attempt to trace the origins and development of television, which seems to have had as many inventors as it now has stations, but I plan to concentrate on Gernsback's role in that development. Suffice it to say that the two main role-players in the birth of television were John Logie Baird and Vladimir Zworykin. Baird (1888-1946) had been a Scottish businessman until ill-health forced him to retire and he pursued the possibilities of the mechanical transmission of television. His first public demonstration showing detailed human faces was given before the Royal Institution in London on January 27, 1926. Vladimir Zworykin (1889-1982) had been born in Russia and emigrated to America after the Revolution, becoming an American citizen in 1924. He pursued the electronic transmission of vision by exploring the possibilities of the cathode-ray tube as originally suggested by A. Campbell-Swinton in 1908. He found a way of scanning the electron beams in the cathode ray tube by a variable magnetic field and patented this idea in 1928.

Gernsback and his team had been following these developments. H. Winfield Secor described Campbell-Swinton's experiments in "Television, or the Projection of Pictures Over a Wire" for the August 1915 *Electrical Experimenter*. Nevertheless, when Gernsback wrote up his own concept of television for "Television and the Telephot" (*The Electrical Experimenter*, May-June 1918) he considered that the Campbell-Swinton method was too clumsy and impractical. He opted for the mechanical method, which Baird would later pursue, as the better of the two.

Inevitably, once Gernsback had launched his radio station WRNY in 1925, he also considered the possibility of transmitting televised images. In the June 1927 *Science and Invention*, Secor reported on the successful trial televised transmission of a speech by Herbert Hoover in Washington on April 7, by a scanning disc device perfected by engineers at the Bell Telephone Laboratories. Further development of this televisor was pursued by Theodore Nakken and John Geloso of the Pilot Electric Manufacturing Company assisted by the technical staff of Gernsback's *Radio News*. Gernsback threw himself into the science of television. He brought out a new magazine, *Television*, dated Summer 1927. It was probably released in August, but certainly before there had been any regular television transmissions and before most people were aware of television. A second issue appeared on July 16, 1928. By that time the *New York Times* were reporting Gernsback's plans:

> We plan first to put on the air a glimpse of each of our performers just before they step before the microphone. The station announcer, asking the performer to stand before the televisor, will say before the microphone that Mr. So-and-so is being televised. After a short interval, the microphone will be switched to

the transmitting apparatus, cutting out the televisor, and Mr. So-and-so will step before the microphone to be heard instead of seen.[1]

The equipment built by the Pilot Electric Manufacturing Company was installed in the transmitting house of WRNY at Coytseville, New Jersey on August 12, 1928. An experimental receiver was placed about a quarter of a mile away and images were successfully transmitted. A public demonstration was then given at Philosophy Hall in New York University on August 21. The results were reported in the *New York Times* the next day:

> Reception of television images transmitted over the regular broadcast wavelength of WRNY was demonstrated last night . . . before a group of radio engineers, scientists and newspaper men. It was estimated that about 500 persons passed before the televisor receiver and saw the received image of a face as it moved before the televisor transmitter of the station at Coytesville, N.J., atop the Palisades across from 181st Street. The broadcast image was that of Mrs. John Geloso, wife of the engineer who perfected the apparatus. Mrs. Geloso closed her eyes, opened and closed her mouth and moved from side to side. The images were about one and one-half inches square, but were magnified by a lens to twice that size. The demonstration was characterized by Hugo Gernsback, owner of WRNY, as the first successful accomplishment of its kind over broadcast waves from a transmitter in New York . . . In an address Mr. Gernsback said television was still in a crude state, fit only for the amateur who wished to experiment. "In six months we may have television for the public," he said, "but so far we have not got it."[2]

Gernsback inaugurated a regular daily television broadcast along the same lines. It was the first in New York, but not the first in America; Station WGY in Schenectady had started three months earlier, whilst Station WOR in Newark had broadcast a puppet play, "The Spirit of Television," on the same day as Gernsback's demonstration.

Nevertheless, Gernsback was more successful at promoting his scheme and, although he remained cautious about the short-term future of television, he nevertheless attracted much attention to his station, especially amongst advertisers who wanted to know the potential of the medium. It would be a further eight years before the first national broadcast of television, and the first regular transmission of television programs began in England with the BBC on November 2, 1936. That transmission used both the Baird mechanical system and the Marconi-EMI electronic system operating on Zworykin's principles. Baird's system was so inferior that it was soon dropped and the electronic system continued, which is the one we use today. Gernsback had predicted this, even though he had originally pursued the mechanical method:

The ideal television receiver of the future will have no moving parts at all. There will be no motor, or if there is, there won't be a large disc such as we have now. What we probably will have is some sort of cathode tube, in which a weightless electron beam will rotate in an induced magnetic field. It will be much easier to keep a device such as this in synchronism, and there is no doubt that the built-up picture thus produced at the receiving end will be far superior to what we have today.[3]

Gernsback did not have the opportunity to develop his television broadcasts along the lines that he had wished. Within six months of his inaugural broadcast, Station WRNY was in the hands of official receivers. If Gernsback's scientific practices had made him a notable public figure, his business practices had incurred the wrath of many influential people. If he could have foreseen his own future as well as he had television's, he might have acted sooner, but he did not. In February 1929 Gernsback's world and along with it the world of science fiction was about to change.

17.

FINANCIALLY EMBARRASSED

If there is one issue that clings closest to the memory of Hugo Gernsback it is that he was very bad at paying his authors. There are two main sources quoted. The second, and more damning, came from Donald A. Wollheim in 1935, when Gernsback earned the reputation of "payment upon lawsuit," and we shall be considering that later. The earlier came from H. P. Lovecraft, who gave Gernsback the soubriquet "Hugo the Rat"[1] in his letters, a title that has stuck amongst the wide circle of Lovecraft devotees. It is also considered that because of his poor payment practices, Gernsback left his company open to be sued into bankruptcy in 1929, which is how he lost control of *Amazing Stories*.

To pursue these two issues we need to start earlier than the bankruptcy proceedings in February 1929, in fact that is where we shall conclude. We can start even before the publication of *Amazing Stories*.

I have already referred to Gernsback's strange practice in *Science and Invention* of awarding cash prizes for articles. Over the first fifteen years of his publishing he had established four methods of paying for the items he used. Firstly, he had his own staff writers such as H. Winfield Secor, T. O'Conor Sloane, and Joseph H. Kraus, who were in his employ and paid a regular salary. After these, his preferred option was to place a writer under contract, which would then be a standard fee for each piece of work. The fee varied, depending upon the writer, but this approach was used for most of his regular columnists, notably Joseph Dunninger, Isabel M. Lewis, and Donald H. Menzel. He probably had this arrangement with Clement Fezandié, even though Fezandié returned the checks. In both these cases he was dealing with "professionals." On rare occasions he wanted to acquire *ad hoc* items from other professionals, and these he paid for at his standard rates. He tried to keep these simple. Rather than pay a wordage rate, he paid within a wordage band. For short items (length not defined) he would pay up to $50 depending on the merit of the writer. When Gernsback sought to encourage the contribution of stories to *Practical Electrics* in 1924, he specifically cited a fixed payment of $50 for stories of up to 4,000 words.

Finally, he liked to encourage submissions from the amateur, the long-suffering experimenter. To these Gernsback offered cash prizes totalling $1000 each month. The prize was awarded based on the originality of the concept or idea promoted in the article, the judges being the magazine's editorial staff. There was a first prize of $100, two prizes of $50, ten of $25, five of $20, ten of $15, twenty of $10, ten of $5, twenty of $2 and ten of $1, though this varied depending upon the number and length of submissions used each month. The range, of course, was considerable. It meant that an average article of about 2,500 words winning the first prize received a wordage rate of four cents a word—a very good rate at that time. However, if it only received the $1 prize then it was equal to 1/25th of a cent a word. But remember the prize was basically for an "idea" which need only be written up in a few hundred words. Gernsback was clever. Amateur experimenters would be more than satisfied, he reckoned, to be treated as prize-winners and their names highlighted each issue, even when it was for a token dollar, than anonymously receive a wordage rate, and he was probably right. He encouraged his readers to become reporters and he issued a *"Science and Invention* Correspondent Reporter's Identification" card of which over 20,000 had been handed out free by 1925. This worked just like any other press card, allowing the holder access to scientific establishments, industrial plants, movie studios and business houses. Readers clamored for these and would have regarded them as a perquisite more valuable than the lower prize rates.

On top of this Gernsback was always awarding other prizes. For instance, from 1923 on Gernsback was offering $11,000 in prizes for irrefutable proof of spiritualism and psychic phenomena, plus another $5000 for a working perpetual motion machine. Neither of these prizes was ever awarded, despite regular claims. One claimant who believed he had invented a perpetual motion machine sued Gernsback for non-payment of the prize, but Gernsback wrote a long article establishing how this machine was not eligible.

However one looks at it, Gernsback's payment rates were not that bad. Whether or not he paid promptly, I cannot be sure. The only evidence I have is from the private files of Donald H. Menzel, which makes no reference to any delayed payments. Gernsback almost certainly paid upon publication.

Although Gernsback did not continue these practices to the same extent in *Amazing Stories*, he would have retained the same attitude to his contributors. Looking at his four methods, we can soon see that he had no one on his staff capable of producing science fiction, so that option was excluded. His next choice, if he could find sufficient worthy writers, was to place them under contract. The flat rates here depended upon the writer, and we shall explore those shortly. He did not like to negotiate *ad hoc* rates, and there is little evidence that this ever arose other than in the case of Edgar Rice Burroughs, and to some extent H. G. Wells. Considering the stature of these writers the need is perhaps not surprising. As for the prizes, whilst not offered in such abundance, the December 1926 cover contest and subsequent competitions maintained that option whenever encouragement was needed.

Now let's consider the evidence. The most telling is that which emerges from the surviving correspondence between Gernsback and H. G. Wells. Gernsback had already purchased reprint rights to "The Star," "The New Accelerator" and "The Crystal Egg" for $50 each from Wells's agent, William Chapman, in 1923. It appears he did not seek permission to use these stories again in the first few issues of *Amazing*, so although the original payment rate was reasonable, the subsequent use for no extra charge halved the wordage rate to an average six-tenths of a cent for the three stories. Gernsback wrote to Wells on April 8, 1926, sending him a copy of the first issue of *Amazing* and asking "what price you would wish us to pay you in connection with the serial rights to your stories which are of the scientific fiction type." Wells quoted his usual price of $100 per story. Gernsback responded with a letter that is worth reproducing at length:

> We notice that you request $100.00 per story, which price is satisfactory providing it means the full length story as, for instance, *The War of the Worlds* . . . but we do not presume that you would wish this amount for small, short stories, for which we

have never paid more than $25 or $50 apiece. *Amazing Stories* is a new magazine, facing an uphill fight for recognition by the reading public, and there can be no question about your interest in a magazine of this kind, which is the first to come out with scientifiction. It really deserves your best cooperation to help put this publication on its feet. As soon as the magazine gets going we shall be in the market for original stories from you, and shall then be able to pay you real prices for your work.

Unless we hear from you to the contrary, we shall presume that the arrangement whereby we shall reprint your stories in our publication at the rate of $100.00 apiece for the long ones and $50.00 apiece for the short ones is satisfactory to you, and we may proceed on this basis without further negotiation.[2]

Gernsback subsequently regarded this letter as the basis for all his dealings with Wells. It shows a certain presumptiousness and arrogance to expect Wells to cooperate to make *Amazing* a success. In all likelihood Wells cared very little about the magazine. Wells was adamant that each story must be the subject of separate negotiation, not a standard fee. What is amazing is that Wells accepted the terms of $50 and $100. $50 for the reprint of a short story may not be too bad, depending upon its length. For instance, "The Plattner Story," at 7,600 words equates to about two-thirds of a cent a word, whereas "The Flowering of the Strange Orchid," at only 2,700 words, equates to 1.85¢ a word. Both of these are still fair rates for reprints. However, for a novel, the rate is absurd. Take *The War of the Worlds*, which Gernsback cited. This is just over 60,000 words, so that $100 equates to only one-sixth of a cent a word.

Yet Wells accepted this rate for a number of novels. That this was a standard offer by Gernsback is supported by Irwin Porges's evidence in his biography of Edgar Rice Burroughs, *The Man Who Created Tarzan*, where he cites that Gernsback paid only $100 for the reprint serial rights of *The Land That Time Forgot*. Since this novel runs to just over 100,000 words, it equated to a rate of one-eleventh of a cent a word, the lowest rate I can find anywhere. However, remember that Gernsback was not primarily reimbursing on a wordage rate, but on a fixed scale, and in his eyes $100 for a novel was the rate.

There is some evidence to suggest that Wells had mistaken dollars for pounds sterling. Wells certainly became increasingly frustrated with Gernsback, whose staff failed to secure approval in advance of reprinting a story, but went ahead and paid $50 after the event. In a letter dated May 4, 1928 from his secretary and daughter-in-law, Marjorie Wells, Wells's reprint rates for selected items are set out clearly. For novels they are £200 and for short stories £20. At this time the exchange rate was equal to about five dollars to the pound, so that £20 equated to $100, and £200 to $1000. This would have made Wells's reprint rate for novels about one cent a word, a realistic sum.

Gernsback, not surprisingly, was horrified. He left it to the patriarchal T. O'Conor Sloane who wrote to Wells on June 11, 1928:

> . . . the prices you now quote for rights to reprint stories be-
> comes entirely prohibitive. We believe we have shown in the past,
> that you had a rather nice income from our source, but at the
> prices now quoted, we are afraid we will have to do without these
> stories for a long time to come.

Wells was nonplussed. He simply noted: "File. No reduction. No reply."

Despite this, *Amazing* continued to reprint Wells's stories without permission at the old rates. As Wells continued to receive complimentary copies
he knew of the reprints and was able to pursue recovery of the money, but the
situation became increasingly acrimonious. Gernsback paid only $100 for *The
Invisible Man* (less than one-fifth of a cent a word), but Wells insisted on $250
for "The Story of the Days to Come" (almost four-fifths of a cent a word), and
the full $100 for the short story "The Moth," which was equal to a lucrative
2.8¢ a word.

By this time Miriam Bourne was pursuing Wells in the vain hope that he
was mistakenly quoting pounds instead of dollars. In response to Bourne's letter of August 27, 1928, Wells noted: "Tell her she is correct in supposing the
sum to have been 200 pounds sterling and not dollars for *The World Set Free*."
There was no way Gernsback could afford that fee and apart from one further
short story, he stopped reprinting Wells all together.

This is a revealing episode. It shows that Gernsback was initially open
and honest about his negotiations, pursuing what he believed to be a fair rate
even though, at the extreme, it was an insult. Nevertheless, at the outset
Wells undeniably agreed, and it was almost two years before he discovered his
error. In that time Gernsback and his staff had already taken it as a matter of
course that these stories could be used at the agreed fee without further reference to Wells, even though he had stipulated that each story should be negotiated separately. The presumption, in fact, was probably not Gernsback's but
that of his staff, most likely Sloane himself, who seemed to be of the belief that
Wells was making a good living out of these reprints.

However, the final irony of all this is that if you total up the wordage of
Wells's stories, which is 464,000, and divide that into the total paid, which is
$2150, we find an average wordage rate of .46¢. This is sufficiently close to
Amazing's basic flat rate of half-a-cent a word as to make no difference, and
for reprint stories it was a low but not wholly unreasonable rate. Nevertheless, we can see that by their uncompromising attitude, Gernsback and his
staff in the end alienated Wells and lost all opportunity to reprint further stories.

The only other details I have for reprinted story-rates support the low
figures. In reprinting the stories by Murray Leinster, Gernsback dealt directly with Leinster's agent, Robert T. Hardy. Gernsback paid $45 for the re-
print of "The Red Dust." Since this runs to 23,000 words, it equates to one-
fifth of a cent a word. This was the same as the fee paid to *Argosy* for the use of
"The Nth Man" by Homer Eon Flint, which was $75 for 40,000 words, or again
one-fifth of a cent a word. Two other facts are relevant here. Firstly, the
money for Leinster's story was received by Hardy on September 28, 1926, ten
weeks *before* publication. No doubt Leinster's agent had insisted, but
Gernsback had still paid up demonstrating that he would pay upon contract

and not upon publication if circumstances dictated.

The other fact relates to the stories reprinted from the Munsey magazines. Munsey usually purchased all rights to their stories unless the authors, like Leinster, negotiated to retain certain rights. As a consequence although Gernsback was making payments to the Munsey subsidiary rights company, Services for Authors, the authors themselves, despite the company name, received no payments at all. The evidence for this is all too clear in a letter dated April 15, 1926 sent by A. B. Gaunt, the Assistant Treasurer of the Munsey Company to Garrett P. Serviss:

> We have received your note advising that the Experimenter Publishing Company of New York had asked your permission to republish four of your stories and requesting us to release to you the serial rights which we hold to these stories. We very greatly regret that it is impossible for us to do this. Your request is only one of numerous requests of this kind which we have received from authors for the release to them of various rights which they had sold us and which, perhaps, for one reason or another, had enhanced in value subsequent to the sale. We cannot go back and re-open transactions that were closed on a perfectly fair and equitable basis. To do so would open a door that from a business point of view should not be opened; it would establish a precedent from which we could never extricate ourselves and which, in the end, would lead to untold confusion. For these reasons we have made it our policy, in fairness to all concerned, to refuse requests of this nature, and in line with that policy we are unable to release to you the serial rights in question.[3]

In other words: hard luck, Serviss; whatever money Munsey gets, Munsey keeps. This was, in fact, a standard practice, and shows that unless authors, or their agents, were on their guard, most publishers would seek to acquire their very souls. Gernsback employed the same practice when buying stories. In a letter dated November 28, 1928 to Edmond Hamilton, in purchasing "Locked Worlds," he stated that:

> It is understood, of course, all stories accepted for publication in *Amazing Stories* or *Amazing Stories Quarterly* take with it all publishing rights, which include newspaper, reprint, translations, moving picture, publication in foreign periodicals, etc.

Remember that at this time science-fiction stories were seldom reprinted, thus few authors would have given a second thought to any subsidiary rights. What many did not know was the extent to which these stories were sold overseas, often for lucrative fees for the publisher, and nothing for the author. But this did not make Gernsback any better or any worse than the other publishers.

Where Gernsback can be compared is on his rates for new stories in comparison to other publishers, in particular his two main rivals, *Weird Tales* and *Argosy*.

Let's go back to Murray Leinster. Leinster had already established such a reputation in *Argosy* for his science fiction that Gernsback was keen to acquire new stories from him. Gernsback learned from Leinster's agent that he had a new short novel, *The Strange People.* In a letter dated January 10, 1927, Gernsback expressed a desire to see it and he also requested a sequel to "The Mad Planet" and "The Red Dust." In fact he suggested that Leinster provide up to six such stories a year. Nowhere in the letter is there any reference to money. Hardy forwarded the request to Leinster at the same time responding to Gernsback regarding fees. "The chances are they won't pay enough to make it worth your while," was his general feeling. A week passed and Hardy wrote again. Gernsback responded on January 25, 1927:

> Regarding the Murray Leinster stories, *Amazing Stories* Magazine is not as yet on a paying basis, as you may well imagine. We are trying to create a market for fiction of this kind, but so far the magazine has not paid, and until it does we have to buy material as low as we possibly can. At this time we would rather not make an offer, but would much rather have the offer come from Mr. Leinster himself.

Clearly Gernsback felt that if he quoted his standard half-a-cent a word, there would be no response from Hardy at all. Better to see what might come his way. Hardy's consequential letter to Leinster is revealing:

> Do you want to suggest a price? I don't know whether it would pay you to undertake to write this for two cents a word, if payment was on acceptance. I am not sure it would, as he probably wouldn't order them in advance, and if you didn't sell them to him you might find some difficulty in disposing of the stories elsewhere. Don't you think you could put your time in to better advantage?

Firstly, it seems as if Hardy was citing even two cents a word as a low rate, and clearly Leinster had been getting more than this in the major markets. As a result Hardy was of the view that writing scientifiction for such a low-paying market was a potential waste of time and would have preferred that Leinster wrote something more profitable. He reiterated this in a letter a few days later to Leinster:

> How much are you willing to write that *Amazing Stories* stuff for—the minimum? There is no use of telling them two cents a word, as I feel pretty sure they won't pay it. We might get a cent a word out of them, but of course you would be doing the story at your own risk.

Hardy was doing a good job at deterring Leinster and it worked. Instead he tried to peddle the two Burl stories to book publishers, without success, which emphasizes the lack of any major markets for "freak stories," as Hardy came to call them. With the lack of any firm quote from Gernsback, Hardy submitted *The Strange People* to *Weird Tales*, where it must have sold for at least one cent a word, otherwise Hardy would not have accepted the terms. It was serialized there from March to May 1928. Because of his caution, Gernsback lost one of the field's leading writers, which would not help either his or the magazine's reputation.

He had the same attitude with Edgar Rice Burroughs. Burroughs had responded to Gernsback's enquiry about available material with the offer of his novel *Vad Varo of Barsoom*. This eventually became *The Master Mind of Mars* in *Amazing Stories Annual*. Burroughs asked $1250 for the story. Gernsback responded that "at the present stage of *Amazing Stories*' development we would not be justified in paying the amount you ask . . ." Nevertheless Gernsback was already considering the *Annual* at that stage and agreed to meet Burroughs's price if the *Annual* was successful. The *Annual* was a success, but Gernsback did not immediately pay up. After Burroughs's insistence, Gernsback offered trade acceptances (a form of credit against bills of exchange) in lieu of payment. These totalled $1266, so Burroughs was paid in full, but he was not happy with the deal. When Gernsback subsequently enquired about the availability of the second serial rights to the short novel *Beyond Thirty*, Burroughs asked for $800. Gernsback could not meet this price, and Burroughs refused to negotiate.[4]

I can cite a number of prices paid by other pulps for stories, most of the evidence coming from the files of Sam Moskowitz. For instance, take Edmond Hamilton's "The Atomic Conquerors" (*Weird Tales*, February 1927). Farnsworth Wright paid him $98 for all serial rights. The story was 9,800 words, so this was a straight cent-a-word. Compare this to the $30 Gernsback paid Hamilton for the 15,000 word "The Comet Doom," only one-fifth of a cent a word. It's hard to believe Hamilton would accept that unless the story had already been rejected by *Weird Tales*. Sam Moskowitz has stated that *Weird Tales* never rejected another Hamilton story after his first, but I would question that in respect of "The Comet Doom." *Amazing*'s letter to Hamilton, written by Miriam Bourne and dated September 28, 1927, contains an interesting paragraph:

> *Amazing Stories*, being still in its infant stage, our rates per story are hardly based on the story's merit—rather on the extent of our budget for the year. Our rates for short stories just now range from $15 to $30 per story . . . We hope you will help us launch *Amazing Stories* into the large field which it deserves, by giving us good short stories at our present rates, until we can afford to pay more.

That reads like a standard letter that Bourne had been churning out for some while. It's difficult to see how, after nearly eighteen months, she can still talk about "launching" *Amazing*. H. P. Lovecraft, who had sold them "The Colour Out of Space" only a few months earlier, probably received much the same letter, only then the rates were even lower. He was paid $25 for the 12,000 word novelette, again equal to one-fifth of a cent a word. Compare this to the $165 Lovecraft received from *Weird Tales* for the 11,200-word "The Call of Cthulhu," which was 1.5 cents-a-word, over seven times Gernsback's offer. No wonder Lovecraft called him "Hugo the rat."

Wright also paid 1.5 cents a word to Abraham Merritt for "The Woman of the Wood" (*Weird Tales*, August 1926). At that time *Argosy* was paying Merritt their regular rate of one-cent a word, which he'd received from his first story, "Through the Dragon Glass," back in 1917. It's unfortunate that we do not know the rate Gernsback paid for the revised version of Merritt's *The Metal Monster*, which was run as *The Metal Emperor* in *Science and Invention*. Merritt was not desperate for money and would not have pushed like Burroughs, so Gernsback may well have managed to pay less than one cent a word. It would be interesting to know.

Because of his high-handed attitude and a reluctance to pay, Gernsback managed to alienate Wells, Burroughs, Leinster, and subsequently Lovecraft. He did not alienate Merritt, who was willing to write a sequel to *The Face in the Abyss* for Gernsback until he found that a contractual obligation negated that opportunity. Nevertheless, Gernsback's track record for sustaining writer response was generally poor.

There was a better arrangement in respect of the contest winners. Gernsback had liked this approach in his earlier magazines and used it fruitfully again here. The three prize-winners all received respectable sums. "The Visitation" was a long story, 19,000 words, but the $250 first prize equated to 1.3¢ a word to Cyril Wates. George Fox received $150 as the second prize for "The Electronic Wall." As it was a much shorter story at 9700 words, it equated to 1.55¢ a word—a higher rate than was paid Burroughs! Clare Winger Harris, in third place, received $100 for "The Fate of the *Poseidonia*," which was equal to 1.21¢ a word.

A less remunerative arrangement, but better than the *ad hoc* arrangement, was to write under contract. When David H. Keller submitted "The Revolt of the Pedestrians," Gernsback offered him a contract for twelve stories a year at $40 a story. When Keller hesitated Gernsback increased the offer to $60. Since ". . . Pedestrians" was a long story, around 11,000 words, the original offer would have meant a little over one-third of a cent a word, better than Hamilton received, but still not high. The revised rate averaged out at just over half-a-cent a word, still low, but good by *Amazing*'s standards. As Keller signed this contract it meant he was assured $60 even for stories of a shorter length, hence "Unlocking the Past," at only 5,200 words, came out at 1.15¢ a word. Clearly it was better to sign a contract with Gernsback.

Hamilton didn't, and his next sale, "Locked Worlds," was bought for only $100. At 26,000 words that was less than two-fifths of a cent a word. E. E. Smith probably fared the worst. The 90,000 words of *The Skylark of Space* was bought for $125, or one-seventh of a cent a word. Sloane's original offer had been $75, which was an horrendous one-twelfth of a cent a word! Finally, when Jack Williamson sold his first story, "The Metal Man," he received $25. This must have been the new rate for short stories, upped from the earlier quote to Hamilton of $15. As the story was only 4,500 words long, this equated to half-a-cent a word. Williamson did not receive payment until mid-January 1929, two months after the story was published.

If you total all of the monies paid for new stories and divide it by the wordage it equates to .53¢ a word. If you add the Wells stories to this, then for the grand total of 980,690 words for which I have purchase details, the total payment was $4876, or almost exactly half-a-cent a word. This suggests that Sloane and Bourne could vary their rates within an overall annual budget based on an average of a half-cent a word. Gernsback's market reports were thus in theory correct, even if in practice subject to a fair degree of variation.

Gernsback's argument that *Amazing* was not yet on a paying basis was constant throughout 1926 and 1927, and much of 1928. Yet with the circulation figures in excess of 100,000, it had a greater circulation than *Weird Tales* and was in a position that *All-Story* had been in only a few years earlier. Now combined with *Argosy*, by 1928 *Argosy* had a circulation of around 250,000 and was thus attracting better paying advertisers.

100,000 was a good circulation for a specialist pulp. A new magazine might not at first break even because of the initial investment in launching the magazine. In Gernsback's case this was minimal. *Amazing Stories* had merely superseded *The Experimenter* and there should have been no additional setting up costs. Printing costs were always high, but these would have been shared with *Science and Invention*, *Radio News*, and the other magazines. In the July 1926 editorial Gernsback does refer to the improvements in the magazine's paper and binding. The new binding machine had cost $30,000, producing bound copies at 2,500 an hour. But again this cost (if it was Gernsback's and not his printer's) would have been spread over several magazines and probably, as a capital cost, on loan over several years. For *Amazing* not to be on a paying basis suggests there were some heavy overheads at Experimenter.

It's not hard to work out what these were. We've already seen Gernsback establishing his radio station with limited advertising support, which must have been heavily subsidized by his publishing enterprises. By 1928 he had expanded into television, and the cost of that development must have been high. This did not stop the company moving into plush new offices on Fifth Avenue in March 1927, and Gernsback himself living in an expensive apartment on Riverside Drive. The best image of Gernsback was given by David H. Keller in his unpublished memoir, "The Folly of Writing":

> Late in 1928 I visited Gernsback in New York. He was living in luxury at that time and was publishing four magazines for which he was offered a million dollars. He was the President of the company and his brother Sidney was the Treasurer. Each drew a salary of one hundred thousand dollars a year. Gernsback made an effort to dazzle the country doctor from the South and took me to the roof garden of the Astor Hotel for lunch. He told me the price of everything we ate and praised the iced coffee which cost eighty-five cents a glass.

One fact that came to light during the subsequent bankruptcy proceedings was the salary the Gernsbacks were drawing as directors from the Experimenter Company. Hugo's aggregated to $54,340 a year and Sidney's to $39,000. Whilst individually these are less than the $100,000 Keller remembered, in total they are not far short, and it may be this that Keller was recalling. Alternatively, Gernsback probably had income from other business concerns which may have been substantial.

Either way, Gernsback lived rich, and poured the remaining profits of the magazines into his other scientific enterprises. He was probably generous to those in his favor. Why else would H. Winfield Secor, for example, have stayed with him for so long? He remained in Gernsback's employ for most of forty years. But for the aspiring authors: they were lucky to receive whatever was available.

In business circles, Gernsback was already making enemies. In 1927, Lewis Landes, President of radio station WGL, had formed the WRNY Broadcasting Corporation as an additional outlet for some of the commercial contracts of the International Broadcasting Corporation. Gernsback was approached to lease his own station WRNY to Landes for ten years at $12,000 a year. A dispute arose, however, over the status of the agreement. Landes and his attorney, James F. O'Neill, maintained that a written contract existed. Gernsback, on the other hand, stated that "No papers of any kind have ever been signed by the owners of WRNY, nor have any agreements been made, either verbally or in writing." The dispute was reported in the *New York Times* for August 18, 1927, but there was no follow-up on the case. It was probably settled out of court, but I do not know the basis.

The Gernsbacks continued to make enemies simply by not paying creditors. Because Gernsback was ploughing the company's income primarily into their radio and television enterprises other creditors had to wait their turn. The authors soon began to suffer, including those under contract. A. Hyatt Verrill, responding to an enquiry from Forrest J Ackerman in 1932, related his circumstances:

> I stopped writing for *Amazing Stories* because I found it next to impossible to collect my money from them. I was under a contract to supply a certain number of words per month for which they were to pay a stipulated sum on a certain date each month, but they never could stick to their contract. I never collected a single payment on time, and when it got so that they ran several months behind, and I had a tip they were on the verge of bankruptcy and changing hands, I quit.[5]

*   *   *

On their own, authors had little influence—or so they probably felt at the time—but companies had more power. As unpaid bills piled up, the two largest creditors—the Art Color Printing Company (Gernsback's printers) and Bulkly, Dunton & Company (the paper suppliers)—took action. First, some time in 1928, they installed an employee of the printing company, Ernest Macklin, into the offices of Experimenter to help sort out the companies' debts. This proved a long process and debts were still not being paid. In the end, unsatisfied with the procedure, the companies arranged with their lawyers for them to institute individual suits against Experimenter for payment of overdue bills. Under the law of the day, the National Bankruptcy Act of 1896, if the total number of creditors of a company exceeded twelve, three had to combine to file involuntary bankruptcy. Art Color and Bulkly, Dunton achieved this by assigning some of the debts to three representatives of their lawyers. The action was filed on Wednesday, February 20, 1929. It was reported in the *New York Times* the next day:

RADIO NEWS PUBLISHER IN HANDS OF RECEIVER
Gernsback's Concern is Called Insolvent
WRNY Not Affected, Counsel Says.

An involuntary petition in bankruptcy was filed yesterday in the United States District Court against the Experimenter Publishing Company of 230 Fifth Avenue, according to Walter Ernst of McManus, Ernst & Ernst, attorneys for the petitioners. The Experimenter Publishing Company publishes Science and Invention, Radio News, Amazing Stories and other magazines, and also operates radio station WRNY, New York. Mr. Ernst said the broadcasting station would not be involved in the proceedings, and that the petition was filed only against the publishers.

Liabilities are estimated at $600,000 and assets at $182,000. Federal Judge Mack appointed the Irving Trust Company receiver in bankruptcy under a $100 bond. The attorneys filed the papers for Daniel A. Walters, Marie E. Bachmann and Robert Halpern, claiming $2030, $2094 and $2095 respectively.

When questioned regarding the bankruptcy petition Hugo Gernsback, President of the Experimenter Publishing Company, said: "Plans are being formulated to reorganize and continue publication as heretofore. I am authorized to say this by the receiver."

Mr. Ernst said further for himself and for Joseph M. Herzberg, attorney for Mr. Gernsback, that station WRNY would continue operations, and that the publications of the company would be carried on under the temporary receivership of the Irving Trust Company.

This was the start of the famous, or more properly infamous, Gernsback bankruptcy proceedings. I do not want to dwell too much on the case. Those interested in a detailed insight should read Tom Perry's "Experiment in Bankruptcy" and Sam Moskowitz's "Amazing Encounter" (cited in the Bibliography). It is those two articles, plus the reports in the *New York Times* that I have relied on for most of the summary presented here.

Irving Trust's first action was to put up over $50,000 of its own money in regaining confidence in the Experimenter Company. With this money it was able to pay employees and keep activities going thereby maintaining good faith with the advertisers and the trade. The first creditors meeting was held on February 23. There it was also agreed that in order to secure the continued confidence in the company it was "necessary to improve the executive personnel"—in other words, the Board of Directors. The Gernsbacks and Secretary Irving Manheimer had to go. As employees, Secor, Sloane, Kraus, Brandt, and Bourne remained with the magazines, whilst Arthur H. Lynch was brought in as editor-in-chief. Lynch was a radio expert and had been a regular contributor to *Science and Invention* and *Radio News*, before becoming editor of *Radio Broadcast* for Doubleday, Doran. His role was primarily to serve as acting publisher with principal interest in *Radio News*. He would have had no interest in science fiction. Brandt and Sloane continued to serve as editors for *Amazing*.

Having secured confidence in Experimenter and settled the company's affairs, Irving Trust then requested bids for the sale of the company as a going concern. Irving Trust had shown considerable initiative here in recognizing that Experimenter was only in trouble because of poor financial management, chiefly because of Gernsback's insistence in running his radio/television station—his major interest—at a loss. Rather than wind up the company, Irving Trust had refloated it.

A number of bids were received with only two of any significance. These were from publishers B. A. MacKinnon and Bernarr Macfadden, both for $250,000, with MacKinnon's bid the better because of his payment terms. The bids were subsequently modified and Macfadden later withdrew. Another bid of $60,000 was submitted for the two radio stations alone by lawyer Chester Cuthell on behalf of his client, the Curtiss Aeroplane and Motor Company.

The bids were put to a meeting of the creditors on April 3, 1929 and, with subsequent modifications, accepted. The final outcome was that the publishing company was sold to B. A. MacKinnon for $336,000, with the radio stations passing to the Curtiss Company for $100,000. Station WRNY remained a commercial local station, but the short-wave station W2XAL, which Gernsback had used for beaming broadcasts to South America, was to serve the twenty-five airports and flying schools of the Curtiss Flying Service.

Many of the creditors eventually received payment in full, including those who wrote under contract—which allowed them the strength as a secured creditor—in preference to those submitting stories on spec. The most remarkable case, though, is that of Wallace West. I have already recounted the problem over the publication of West's "The Last Man" in *Amazing* after West had placed the story with *Weird Tales*. West sued Gernsback for payment for the story, but Experimenter went into receivership. West, who seemed to know more law than his attorney, filed a lien as first claim on the assets under the workman's compensation law. He had received no formal acceptance and had no idea what he would have been paid, but under the law he was entitled to demand the highest rate he had ever received. West had been paid 3 cents a-word for some nonfiction material, and so he claimed $300 for the 10,000 word story—and was paid in full! He was able to pay *Weird Tales* $100 towards its losses, pay his attorney, and keep $100, which is probably still three times what he would have received had Gernsback paid his normal rates.[6]

By their initiative and skill Irving Trust had saved the Experimenter Company and with it *Amazing Stories*. Even had it failed, though, the future of science fiction was assured. In effect the Gernsbacks abandoned the company the moment the bankruptcy suit was filed in order to pursue their new activities. After February 20, they had ten days in which to submit a statement of their assets and liabilities and thus proving their liquidity. They did not do so, and the company was judged bankrupt on March 6, 1929.

On February 23, 1929, the day the creditors ousted the Gernsbacks from the management of the company, Hugo sent a *pro forma* letter to his authors saying:

The manuscript you sent to me to read is still in my possession. I now intend to bring out a new and better magazine, and if you still desire to have me accept your manuscript for publishing, I will do so and pay you for same at regular space rates upon publication.

We've seen before how resilient Gernsback was. No matter what adversity arose he could bounce back, usually bigger and better than before. To him, almost overnight, another chapter had closed, but a new one was opening, and for science fiction this was the biggest and boldest chapter yet. The Age of Wonder was about to begin.

18.

THE BIRTH OF WONDER

The last issue of *Amazing Stories* over which Gernsback had any direct influence was that for April 1929. It had been published on March 5, but was ready for the printer by February 10, ten days before the bankruptcy proceedings began. It is interesting for the inclusion of "The Revolt of the Atoms" by V. Orlovsky. This story is remarkable for its prediction of the devastation caused by the release of atomic energy and even hints at the nuclear winter. It's also interesting as probably being the first Russian science-fiction story to be translated for the American magazines, having originated in the March 1927 issue of *Mir priklyuchenniv*, a magazine of science and adventure. It reveals the extent of Gernsback's overseas deals, as a number of items from *Science and Invention* also appeared in the Russian magazine.

Although Gernsback would have been responsible for accepting the stories in the May 1929 issue, his name no longer appeared in the magazine. The editorial, written by Sloane, was almost disloyal to his former employer:

> The change in editorial management, which this magazine has recently experienced, will result in a great improvement. The editorial policies will suffer no change except in the direction of effecting progressive improvements.[1]

What improvements did Sloane mean? He could not have meant better stories, since although Gernsback had always had the final say on acceptance, the main selection process had been through Brandt and Sloane. Perhaps Sloane meant that they now had a freer hand in the selection of stories, though readers may not have felt this would necessarily have led to an improvement. Elsewhere in that same editorial, in commenting upon the popularity of interplanetary stories, Sloane remarked that ". . . it appears an impossible achievement. . . ." Unlike the constant urgings of Gernsback, who regarded interplanetary travel as only a matter of time, Sloane, with his scientific training firmly rooted in the days of gaslight, believed it impossible. This hardly seemed to be an attitude that would inject a sense of wonder or stimulate the spirit.

I suspect that Sloane's reference to improvements meant that with the improved financial management the company was promised, Experimenter could pay better rates more promptly and might consequently attract more writers, possibly even better writers. This is confirmed by a revealing letter that Miriam Bourne sent to Edmond Hamilton on March 2, 1929:

> Perhaps you have heard by this time, that the Experimenter Publishing Company has gone into the hands of a Receiver. However, that does not mean that *Amazing Stories* or *Amazing Stories Quarterly* are going to suspend publication, or in any way change their editorial policy, unless the change is a definite improvement both for the writers who have been with us since we

started, and for our readers.

It might be particularly reassuring to state that the entire management has changed. The Irving Trust Company, supported by a strong group of creditors, have assumed full responsibility for the further success of *Amazing Stories*, so that there is every reason to hope that *Amazing Stories* will, with the help of its authors, be a bigger and better publication in the future.

Whereas in the past authors have been underpaid, and payments delayed over extended periods, we are now in a position to say that—if we cannot yet pay what we might think a story is worth—at least we can increase our rates immediately, and can assure prompt payment for all manuscripts published. A more prompt decision on manuscripts submitted for publication is also assured.

With promises like that it is not surprising that Sloane was able to confirm in his editorial that:

It is a pleasure to us to be able to state that some of our better known authors, such as Dr. David H. Keller, Dr. Miles J. Breuer, Harl Vincent, Stanton A. Coblentz, Clare Winger Harris, Edmond Hamilton, Dr. Edward B. *[sic]* Smith, author of "The Skylark of Space" who promises us a sequel soon, Frederick Arthur Hodge . . . Earl L. Bell, and others—are going to stand by *Amazing Stories* and will continue as contributors to the Monthly and Quarterly. And their efforts, because of the various improvements we have already been able to institute, will, we feel sure, exceed anything they have done in the past.

The phrase "stand by *Amazing*" is interesting. On the surface it suggests that these authors were still willing to write for the magazines even though, with Experimenter in receivership, the future might be bleak. But it also suggests that Sloane knew of Gernsback's plans to bring out a new magazine. Apart from Gernsback's *pro forma* letter of February 23, a further letter, dated March 5, had been sent to various authors. Edmond Hamilton received a copy, just three days after the letter from Miriam Bourne. Gernsback's letter was sent out under the letterhead of Gernsback Publications, Inc. at 96-98 Park Place. It stated:

On February 20th, the Experimenter Publishing Company, who as you know are the publishers of *Amazing Stories*, was forced into involuntary bankruptcy. What will happen to the old company, no one knows. In the meanwhile, we intend to bring out a new and better magazine of the scientifiction type and this letter is written merely to apprise you of the fact that we would like to see your manuscripts along scientifiction lines, if you care to submit them to us for consideration here. We will give you a quick decision and pay a good price upon publication.

Gernsback did not say what "a good price" was. The very next day, Hamilton received a letter dated March 6 from Miriam Bourne at *Amazing*, on paper still showing Gernsback as President of the Company, offering to buy Hamilton's story "The Universe Wreckers," then only in outline form. "We are, at least until we get our finances straightened out, paying a half-cent per word for stories which we publish," Miriam explained. "Although this is far from an enormous rate, it is almost twice what we have been paying, and we hope to do better soon."

Whether or not Hamilton was "standing by" *Amazing*, there was certainly no harm in enquiring into Gernsback's new magazine. Other writers did the same, amongst them Neil R. Jones. Jones had yet to sell a story, but he had written enquiring of Gernsback on February 13, at *Amazing*. Gernsback had replied to him on February 19, the day before the bankruptcy proceedings, on his personal notepaper. This letter ran:

> I have your favor of the 13th with which you enclosed a synopsis of a story you have written, and shall be pleased to have you submit the story in full. Please address it to me personally, in order that it will come to my desk first.

Why would Gernsback have written that letter personally, and made such a request, if he had not already had some inkling that the bankruptcy proceedings were afoot. Since Ernest Macklin was in his offices he may well have given some indication, albeit unintentionally, that something was about to happen and Gernsback was therefore already making plans to corner new manuscripts. The letter of February 23 also went to Jones and he replied to Gernsback on March 10. In his response Gernsback confirmed that the new magazine would be "a scientifiction one" and added, "I will pay as high as a half a cent a word on any story that may be accepted."

At this stage, therefore, both Gernsback and *Amazing* were still only promising up to half-a-cent a word on new stories. Since the future of *Amazing* must still have been in some doubt, and since dealings with Gernsback in the past had also had their doubtful aspects, writers did not have much to choose between them. They might just as well appreciate the potential growth in the market and submit to both publishers.

March and April were intense months for Hugo and Sidney Gernsback. Not only were they endeavoring to launch three new magazines, they also had to contend with the bankruptcy proceedings, culminating in a hearing before the official referee, Peter B. Olney, on April 17. Before that date, though, plans for the new fiction magazine, *Science Wonder Stories*, had been finalized. In a letter dated March 11, to Edmond Hamilton, Gernsback stated that, "We are now planning to get our new magazine out within the next thirty days, or even sooner." That suggested an early April publication date, which would have been within six weeks of the original file for bankruptcy. By anyone's standards, even Gernsback's, that is taking determination too far. In the event there were delays, but a circular announcing the new magazine eventually went out. It is undated, but was probably written in March. The earliest date I can attach to it is April 2, the date of a letter sent to Neil R. Jones enclosing the circular, but it was almost certainly mailed to others earlier than that, as it does not give the title of the new magazine, whilst the letter to Jones does.

The circular was simply announcing publicly that a new magazine was imminent. It requested charter subscriptions at $1.50 for one year, $2.40 for two years, and $3.25 for three years. It also asked readers what they would like to see in the new magazine and to give suggestions for a title.

By early April the first issue had been assembled and was ready for the printer, where it was delivered by April 10 or so. It was officially issued on Friday, May 3, 1929, less than ten weeks after the original bankruptcy order. As if that was not achievement enough, four weeks later, on June 5, a new radio magazine, *Radio-Craft*, appeared, and a week after that a second fiction magazine, *Air Wonder Stories*. And there was promise of more.

Its rapid appearance naturally raises a number of questions. Firstly, since Gernsback's profits were tied up in the Experimenter Company, where did he get the capital to establish three new magazines and two new publishing companies? Secondly, how was he able to solicit for new subscriptions? Thirdly, from where did he get the stories to fill the magazines? And finally, since his employees remained with *Amazing Stories*, where did his new staff come from?

The first point to remember is that the Experimenter Company was not the only company with which Gernsback was associated. The company had started out as a subsidiary of the Electro-Importing Company and was not separately incorporated until March 10, 1926, at the time of the issue of *Amazing Stories*. The Electro-Importing Company continued at 233 Fulton Street, and was not itself involved in the bankruptcy proceedings. In addition, Gernsback had established in 1921 the Radio Speciality Company at 98 Park Place (the offices now used for the Stellar Publishing and Techni-Craft Publishing companies). This was a family company, with his wife, Dorothy, the secretary and her sister, Harriet Kantrowitz, the treasurer.

The profits from these companies along with Gernsback's own personal wealth would have been more than sufficient for Gernsback to obtain credit from his bank to finance his new companies. Since his bank was the Irving Trust Company, they would also have known of his activities. In addition, Gernsback had a working relationship with a Chicago advertising agency. The original firm was called Finucan and McClure in Cass Street, and Michael Finucan was one of the majority shareholders in the original Experimenter Publishing Company. When Gernsback launched his new publishing companies he retained the services of L. F. McClure, who would have secured for Gernsback much needed advertising revenue in the crucial early stages of the magazines' development.

A further source of income was advance subscriptions, which brings us to our second question. Here Gernsback was treading on dangerous territory, because the likeliest way for him to be able to solicit subscriptions was from his magazine mailing list and that formed part of the assets of Experimenter. To use it was equal to diverting assets, which was illegal under the Bankruptcy Act. This was raised at the bankruptcy hearing on April 17, 1929, and reported in the *New York Times* the next day under the headline "Gernsbacks Deny Diverting Assets." Hugo Gernsback was asked specifically about the circular he had sent to potential subscribers and whether he had used the subscription lists for *Radio News* and *Amazing Stories*. Gernsback was adamant. "Certainly not. We were most anxious not to do that; we were advised by counsel not to do that and we did not do it because being subscribers to one magazine they certainly would not subscribe to another." That belief is naïve, because throughout the circular Gernsback refers to *Amazing Stories* and says his new magazine will be "infinitely better than *Amazing Stories*." The letter was clearly aimed at readers of *Amazing*; who else could Gernsback have written to? However he did not have to use the current subscription list. He could have used an old one. Or, equally valid, he could have taken addresses from the letters written to *Amazing*. The letters would not form part of the assets, and these would include letters from readers who were not subscribers. Although it cannot be proven either way, and although the subscription list was a more likely source for Gernsback's new mailing list, it shows there was an alternative approach.

Whatever he did, according to Gernsback he received around eight thousand advance subscriptions. The bulk of these were for one year, but others were for two or three, so Gernsback certainly received a minimum of $10,000, and more likely around $12-$15,000, for *Science Wonder Stories* alone. Add to this further advance subscriptions for *Radio-Craft* and *Air Wonder Stories*, and Gernsback probably had somewhere in the region of $40,000 up front. That demonstrates the degree of interest there was in science fiction by 1929, compared to the apparent apathy five years earlier when Gernsback had tried to solicit subscriptions for his proposed *Scientifiction*, and even compared to the 5,250 subscribers to *Amazing* after its first year in 1927. At the time of subscribing, readers could not have known that *Amazing* would continue in publication. By subscribing to Gernsback's new magazine, readers were assured the continued pleasure of their unique form of literature.

As to the third question of where Gernsback obtained the stories for his new magazines, we have already seen that he was writing to authors requesting new stories as early as March 2. We've also seen he had despatched a proforma letter as early as February 23 to authors whose manuscripts were already in his possession. These should not be mistaken for stories already purchased for *Amazing*. It is difficult to know, in *Amazing*'s case, when a story was officially purchased, as letters were not always promptly despatched advising authors of the potential sale. These were probably manuscripts passed by Brandt and Sloane and which Gernsback had at home for final assent. As they had been submitted to *Amazing* they should have been treated as *Amazing*'s property but legally, at this stage, Experimenter had no such title to them. In his letter of February 23, which was quoted at the end of the last chapter, Gernsback did give the writer the option of having the manuscript returned to him, but as that was tantamount to a rejection, I can hardly believe any writer would say yes, especially since *Amazing*'s future, at that time, would have seemed bleak. Gernsback also put pressure on the writers by concluding, "Please advise me at once, as I desire to close all pending matters at the earliest possible moment." I believe Gernsback had no problem at all in obtaining manuscripts.

That leaves us with the fourth point: new staff. Since the staff at Experimenter now stood a chance of receiving a regular wage, at least while Irving Trust were looking after the company, it was unlikely they would leave to follow Gernsback in his new venture. Only one did at the time: Charles P. Mason. He had joined Gernsback as Associate Editor at *Radio News* during 1928 and took up a similar position at *Radio-Craft*. Frank R. Paul also joined him as Art Director, but Paul was a free-lance artist, not directly in Gernsback's employ, and thus able to work for both magazines.

Beyond these, Gernsback had to seek a new team of editorial staff. It was not too difficult to find technical writers with sufficient editorial ability to work on *Radio-Craft,* and he employed R. D. Washburne as technical editor. But it was harder to find anyone with a working knowledge of science fiction and Gernsback considered whether any of his writers might wish to edit the new magazine. He asked Stanton A. Coblentz. Coblentz was not keen on the idea. In an interview in 1979 he reflected: "I figured that I aimed to be a writer and not an editor. If I tied myself down to looking over manuscripts and trying to drum up subscribers, I wouldn't get very far with my writing, so I regretfully declined."[2]

So Gernsback advertized in the *New York Times,* and one of the applicants was a twenty-seven-year-old son of Russian Jewish immigrants, David Lasser. He had graduated from M.I.T. in 1924 with a degree in engineering and business administration. He worked for a while as an engineer, an insurance agent and a technical writer for the New York Edison Company. Lasser believes it was the degree that impressed the Gernsbacks and they hired him on a wage of $65 a week, a very reasonable sum. It was a good choice. Here was someone young, with vision and a command of the language. Although Lasser knew next to nothing about science fiction or editing, he had strong views about what a good story should be, and how scientific ideas should be promoted. He took science fiction to heart and, during the period of his involvement with science fiction, 1929 to 1933, he was without a doubt the best of the magazine editors. It is almost entirely due to Lasser that science fiction continued to develop and not stagnate during the years of the Depression. Science fiction's Golden Age really began with him.[3]

19.

ENTER SCIENCE FICTION

Experimenter's creditors should be thanked for bringing the bankruptcy charges. Without them, *Amazing Stories* and the *Quarterly* may have remained the only science-fiction magazines. The rapidly growing success of the *Buck Rogers* strip syndicated through the newspapers may have seen an increase in comic strip science fiction, but there may not have been any need to exploit that growth in the pulps. In fact the opposite may have happened. If Gernsback had continued to invest heavily in his radio and television enterprises, *Amazing* may have suffered financially itself. The world's first science-fiction magazines may have lingered on into 1930, but may then have died alone, and what an example that would have been.

Instead, a remarkable thing happened. Within a year of the bankruptcy suit, instead of two magazines there would be seven! Science fiction took off in 1929 at the start of a boom that has had its ups and downs in the ensuing years, but has never failed. Moreover, the term science fiction itself, came into being. And it was all because of the bankruptcy.

Once Gernsback was ousted by Experimenter, he set about establishing a new company and clearly made a fundamental decision. Hitherto his prime interest had been in the development of radio, and he still had business interests there. But the promotional aspect of that work was no longer necessary. Radio was established and it was big business. Gernsback did not have the capital to establish a new radio station, so he did not have the same motives for continuing to exploit the radio market. Instead he established *Radio-Craft* to cater for the servicing side of the industry. It was aimed chiefly at the radio craftsman and later issues bore the banner, "for the Professional-Serviceman-Radiotrician." There was no need to inspire the readers into the further development of radio. Gernsback was here interested in the nuts-and-bolts of radio, and not so much in the radio fan. Consequently, *Radio-Craft* carried no fiction and only the occasional speculative article by Gernsback on the future of radio.

Gernsback was also interested in establishing a new magazine to parallel his old *Science and Invention*, but if he was to develop that he would have needed more capital up front, and there was a limit to what he could achieve. He continued to pursue this aim, and eventually took over an existing Chicago magazine, *Illustrated Science and Mechanics*, and reissued it as *Everyday Mechanics* with the July 1930 number. This later developed into *Everyday Science and Mechanics*.

Whilst at Experimenter, Gernsback had been planning a new magazine to exploit the rapidly growing aviation business. Aeroplanes had been considered toys for the rich until the Great War, when the rapid growth in their development had shown their true potential. Charles Lindbergh's non-stop flight across the Atlantic in May 1927 had captured the public's imagination and aeronautics had come of age. The magazine, *Aero Mechanics*, was well into production by the time of the bankruptcy suit, and must have been a further drain upon Experimenter's resources. Nevertheless, to their credit,

Irving Trust continued with it, and *Aero Mechanics* was issued as a fifty-cent quarterly in Summer 1929, edited by Augustus Post, one of the great aviation pioneers.

With that magazine launched, it was too soon for Gernsback to pursue the same market with his new company. He now had little option but to alter his priorities. He probably did so willingly because Gernsback enjoyed pandering to the dedicated fan. With the days of the pioneer radio enthusiast and inventor in the past, Gernsback could achieve more by inspiring the young readers and science enthusiasts who had responded so vociferously to *Amazing Stories*. It was natural for him to invest in science fiction for his own future.

It was important, though, that the emphasis was still on *SCIENCE*. Gernsback still wished to educate and stimulate within a framework of thrills and entertainment. Moreover, because his interest in aviation had been nipped in the bud at Experimenter, he could satisfy that urge by looking to the future of aviation. Hence, when his two new magazines were named, they became *Science Wonder Stories* and *Air Wonder Stories*.

His editorials for the new magazines both made the same point, that in *Air Wonder* perhaps more positively: "We must instruct while we entertain. For the future of aviation springs from the imagination! And by translating the imagination into actuality, the evolution of aviation will be hastened."[1] Gernsback had not really altered his views over the last ten years. The fiction was there to further the cause of science. He was also aware that the desire for thrills and adventures had led to some weak attention to scientific detail by some of the writers. Writing in *Science Wonder*'s editorial, Gernsback said, "There has been altogether too much pseudo-science fiction of a questionable quality in the past. Over-enthusiastic authors with little scientific training have rushed into print and unconsciously misled the reader by the distortion of scientific facts to achieve results that are clearly impossible."[2] Gernsback did not admit that as editor he had allowed such distortions into print. Instead he now used it to his advantage by proclaiming that for the new magazines he had established a Board of Associate Science Editors. Their purpose was to serve as "an authority . . . who would pass upon the scientific correctness of such stories . . ." and thus ". . . be of the greatest aid in mapping the future course of science fiction."[3] The same point was made in *Air Wonder Stories* which had a board of aeronautical advisors. Their duties were to "carefully scrutinize all manuscripts in *AWS* before they are printed, with the object to prevent gross scientific-aviation misinformation from reaching our readers."[4]

The precise role these scientists took is unclear. Certainly two of them, David H. Keller and Donald H. Menzel, recall being sent stories in manuscript and knew that Gernsback acted upon their comments. Others amongst them had comments published in the letter columns to the magazines, so there is little reason to doubt that they were consulted, but the extent to which they mapped "the future course of science fiction" is open to doubt. It is unlikely that Elmer G. Campbell, for instance, one of the associate editors for botany, was sent stories in advance. In a letter published in the September 1929 *Air Wonder* he commented:

I have received your magazine and am tremendously interested in the stories. I have one boy of sixteen years of age and
when *Science Wonder Stories* and *Air Wonder Stories* come, about
a dozen boys of the neighborhood gather in. And such interest I
have never seen. So far as I have been able to judge in my own
rush of affairs I think your magazines are great. If you desire I
will write more fully about them when I can find time.

Whilst this was encouraging for Gernsback it is clear that Campbell was
not commenting on stories in advance, but that Gernsback was seeking his
advice in retrospect. Professor William Bevan of Iowa State College wrote in a
similar vein in the same issue, also correcting a point of scientific principal in
an earlier issue.

Nevertheless, their names on the magazine masthead were impressive
and no doubt encouraged parents to allow their children to read the magazine, which was probably Gernsback's main aim. Amongst them were some
interesting characters, pioneer scientists whose names are now largely forgotten. Since some of them may have influenced writers or readers, it is worth
spending a little time in looking at them, and three in particular.

In *Science Wonder* the names were grouped by the respective sciences,
and the list grew in subsequent issues. In total there were eighteen, with a
further five in *Air Wonder*. The best known to readers of the magazines was
David H. Keller, listed as the advisor for medicine. Keller (1880-1966) was no
simple country practitioner, though. Having served in a state mental institution he was one of the pioneers in the practice of psychology and psychoanaly-
sis. In the spring of 1928 he had taken up new employment as Assistant
Superintendent at the Western State Hospital in Bolivar, Tennessee, but
work there was unsatisfactory and he left within the year. At the same time
he had contracted with Hugo Gernsback to provide a ready supply of medical
articles for his new magazine, *Your Body*, which Sidney Gernsback edited and
which first appeared in April 1928 as a fifty-cent quarterly. When he left
Western State in February 1929, Keller became a full-time writer for six
months until he became Assistant Superintendent of the Pennhurst State
School for mental defectives. Keller's science fiction is covered in detail in
Lowndes's section. He usually focussed on the more human side of scientific
development. As a consequence his work was often more realistic, if less exciting, than that of his contemporaries.

Donald H. Menzel (1901-1976) was also a friend of science fiction, and a
great patron of science. In 1929 he was Assistant Astronomer of Lick Observatory at the University of California, but in 1932 he moved to Harvard University as Assistant Professor of Astronomy and eventually became Director
of Harvard College Observatory in 1954. He was a prolific writer of science articles, doing his best to popularize astronomy in the general magazines. He
edited *The Telescope* between 1937 and 1941, and took over after Willy Ley's
death as science columnist in *Galaxy* in 1969. It was Hugo Gernsback who
had first encouraged Menzel to write. He wrote to him while he was studying
for his Ph.D. at Harvard and asked him to contribute to *Science and Invention*. His first piece was "Measuring the Heat from the Planets" (May 1923),
and he went on to write over fifty pieces for that magazine alone, many of

them under pseudonyms. In 1924 Gernsback offered Menzel an assistant editorship on *Science and Invention* at a salary twice what he was then receiving as an instructor at the University of Iowa. In a private letter in 1970, Menzel commented, "I owed a great deal to Hugo for his encouragement and the financial assistance in my youth, when I was so badly underpaid as an astronomer."[5] That's good to note, after so many complaints by others about Gernsback's miserliness. In 1970, in gratitude to Gernsback, Menzel succeeded in getting a crater on the moon named after him. It's a big crater, thirty miles in diameter, at 36° S, 99° E.

Gernsback probably recognized in Menzel a similar spirit. Menzel was keen to write speculative articles of a radical nature. These included "Can We Visit the Planets?" as Don Home in *Science and Invention* for February 1924, "Can We Signal Mars?" as Charles T. Dahama (March 1924), "The End of the World" (June 1924), "The Mystery of Atomic Energy" (May 1925), and a series on "Space, Time and Relativity" (March to August 1929). It's surprising he didn't turn his hand to writing scientific fiction for Gernsback, but apart from a short piece in *Weird Tales*, "The Machine from Outside" as Don Howard (May-June-July 1924), Menzel wrote no fiction until Gernsback launched *Science-Fiction Plus* in 1953, to which he contributed "The Other Side of Zero" (March 1953). Nevertheless, Menzel was often a source of ideas to Gernsback, and the two probably worked well together in promoting new concepts in Gernsback's magazines.

Frank E. Austin (1873-1964) is listed as science adviser on electricity. I doubt if he could have had much to say on the subject in the pages of Gernsback's magazines, though he clearly read them as he enquired about the accuracy of the Fitzgerald Contraction equation used in February 1930 "Science Questions and Answers" column. Austin was Professor of Electrical Engineering at Dartmouth College, but was also a pioneer in another area. Although unheralded, Austin was involved in the development of X-rays, paralleling Röntgen's work. Along with two colleagues, Austin took the first human X-ray photograph on February 3, 1896. After Austin had retired from teaching, the stock market crash of 1929 wiped out his savings. He thereupon turned his hobby into a business and set about marketing ant houses. These were wooden-frames, eighteen inches square, holding two panes of glass about an inch or two apart. He filled the space between the glass with sand, earth and sawdust, plus a handful of ants, and let nature do the rest. He later developed these for bees and crickets. They are still around today and are both fascinating and educational. Austin used to sell between four or five hundred a month. He had long held a fascination for ants, and, as we shall see, so did writers of science fiction. Austin may well have indirectly provided valuable advice on these stories.

There was another scientist amongst the advisers who also had a special interest in ants. William M. Wheeler (1865-1937), Professor of Entomology at Harvard University's Bussey Institute, wrote a number of books on insects starting with *Ants: Their Structure, Development and Behavior* (1910), and including *Social Life Among the Insects* (1923) and *The Social Insects: Their Origin and Evolution* (1928). His works were likely consulted by the many writers who used ants as subjects in their science fiction.

The most eminent name on the roster was that of Dr. Lee De Forest (1873-1961). De Forest is known as the father of radio, primarily because of his invention of the triode, which allowed the development of the radio tube. He had been a regular contributor to Gernsback's *Science and Invention* and Gernsback counted him amongst his friends. He later wrote an introduction to a 1950 reprinting of Gernsback's *Ralph 124C 41+* where he said of Gernsback: "He is gifted with a mind eternally alert, trained from childhood to observe and think. His unbridled imagination has ever fed on the facts of science and technology which his habit of omniverous reading has been continually storing within his brain."[6]

The above gives some idea of the range of scientists with whom Gernsback was in contact and who had an interest in the visionary side of science.

This emphasis on scientific accuracy brought with it one other direct consequence. Hitherto Gernsback had called the stories he published, scientifiction, a neologism he had coined by simply contracting his earlier phrase, scientific fiction. Having left Experimenter, though, he felt obliged to coin a new term. The one he chose was "science fiction." This was not for the sake of originality. Reader Lester Anderson was curious why Gernsback had stopped using the word scientifiction. He wrote to the magazine, asking: "Is that word copyrighted? If it is, it shouldn't be. Anybody ought to be able to use it." Gernsback's response was, "The word scientifiction is a trade symbol."[7]

That is most revealing. You will recall that Gernsback had set a contest for readers to devise a symbol for scientifiction and this was now used on the magazine's cover and on the letters. The phrase "scientifiction" had therefore become an integral part of *Amazing*'s image and, probably under legal advice, Gernsback believed he had no right to use it. Certainly he would not have wanted to promote its use in his new magazine being assembled just at the time of the bankruptcy hearings, so it was in his interest to devise a new term. With the emphasis on "science," the new name came naturally. Exactly when Gernsback switched from the old to the new is difficult to determine, but it can certainly be narrowed to a two-week period. His letter to Neil R. Jones on March 18, 1929, rejected "The Electrical Man" on the grounds that "it has not enough **scientifiction** matter for our new magazine." Two weeks later, on April 2, writing again to Jones, seeking new material, Gernsback wrote: "I hope you will be good enough to let me have the first refusal on all of your **science-fiction** manuscripts."

At this same time Gernsback mailed out his circular to readers seeking submissions in a $50 competition for the best letter on "What Science Fiction Means To Me." As a result, in the first issue of *Science Wonder Stories*, not only did Gernsback use the term throughout the magazine, but so did his correspondents. The winner was B. S. Moore from South Carolina, who has not gone down in SF history. But interestingly the two honorable mentions were from Jack Williamson and E. E. Smith, who were thus the first two authors to use the phrase science fiction.

Actually, the phrase had appeared earlier in *Amazing Stories*, as far back as the January 1927 issue. The editorial response to Ralph Campbell's letter objecting to the reprinting of Jules Verne was to remind Campbell that "Jules Verne was a sort of Shakespeare in science fiction."[8] This may have been written by T. O'Conor Sloane, and Gernsback may have been totally unaware of its usage. The phrase does not appear to have been repeated.

In 1975, antiquarian bookdealer John Eggeling chanced upon a volume entitled *A Little Earnest Book Upon a Great Old Subject* by William Wilson, published in 1851. In the course of this book, which contained Wilson's thoughts on the subject of poetry, Wilson used the phrase "science-fiction" in describing R. H. Horne's work "The Poor Artist; or, Seven Eye-sights and One Object." This is the first known use of the phrase "science-fiction," and its loss to the world for over a century is sufficient evidence that Gernsback had not himself encountered it when he coined the phrase anew. The work that it was describing is scarcely science fiction, even by Gernsback's definition. It deals with six creatures—a bee, ant, spider, perch, robin, and cat—all of whom describe an object to an artist, but in six different ways. When the artist investigates, the object turns out to be a gold coin. Yet Wilson's definition of science-fiction, "a charming and naïve mixture of poetic and imagination and scientific fact" is so akin to Gernsback's original definition of scientifiction, "a charming romance intermingled with scientific fact and prophetic vision," to indicate that both authors had the same concept in mind. Nevertheless it was not until Gernsback concocted the term in 1929, because of the bankruptcy proceedings, that the field was effectively named. I'm sure William Wilson would have favored the results.

20

SCIENCE AND IMAGE

Outwardly, both *Science Wonder Stories* and *Air Wonder Stories* were similar to *Amazing Stories* in appearance. They were the same large format, with lurid covers by Frank R. Paul and a comfortable thickness which highlighted them on the stands. Inwardly, the magazines were also similar, though Gernsback added a new feature. Each story included a sketch of the author by staff artist Walter Blythe, based on photographs submitted by the authors. In general they were good likenesses, although some authors claimed they were not. In the absence of many photographs of authors of the day, these are now of historical importance.

To emphasize the informative aspects of the magazines, Gernsback instituted two new columns: "Science News of the Month" in *Science Wonder* and "Aviation News of the Month" in *Air Wonder*. He continued the feature of questions based on scientific facts in the stories, which he had introduced in *Amazing*. A few issues later he began a column in each magazine where readers could raise their own questions on science or aviation for the staff or board of advisors to answer.

With all this emphasis on science one might expect the science in the stories to be impeccable but, from the start, Gernsback published some real howlers, probably in his haste to compile the first issue. We have already mentioned Kennie McDowd's "The Marble Virgin," where, by meddling with the atomic structure of a stone statue, a scientist brings it to life, complete with arteries, brain, heart and other internal organs. Gernsback went so far as to say in his introduction, "Improbable as the accompanying story may sound, at first, it is certainly based upon excellent facts and some such thing may actually come about during the next few hundred years."[1] The readers did not think so and the letter column was so full of criticism that McDowd was driven to defend his story in the August issue. His detailed explanation is no more convincing than the story, and his offer to write a sequel based on equally sound scientific facts was not taken up.

Criticism was also levied at James P. Marshall, whose "Warriors of Space" was also in the first issue. This was a sequel to "The World in the Balance," published in the April 16, 1927 issue of *Argosy*, but contained rather more super-science. Earth is invaded and war breaks out in the solar system with the end result that Saturn is shifted from its orbit and plunges into the sun. The story had probably been rejected by *Argosy* and was not written with Gernsback's astute readership in mind. Readers were uncertain whether Saturn could be shifted from its orbit in the first place, let alone without dire effects upon the other planets. Marshall defended his story rather more convincingly than McDowd.

This demonstrates that the readers of Gernsback's magazines were keen for the science to be accurate and for the stories to treat scientific principles seriously. Gernsback started to pay more attention to detail. It may have been because he no longer had Sloane as a filter for scientific accuracy, or perhaps he wanted to be seen to be encouraging authors and thus lure them to his magazines away from *Amazing*, or as likely that with less pressure from his other business activities he could now give science fiction the attention it needed. Whatever the reason, Gernsback became more active in his dealings with authors and in suggesting ideas for stories.

The most obvious, because its origins were described in *Science Wonder Stories*, was *The Human Termites* by David H. Keller, serialized in the issues from September to November 1929. In an introduction Keller recounts how he visited Gernsback in April 1929 and, after dinner, the conversation turned to the ideas behind stories. Keller recalled how much of the discourse in "Stenographer's Hands" (*Amazing Stories Quarterly*, Fall 1928) had stemmed from an earlier meeting with Gernsback. Keller continued, "The hard thing is to get a new idea." Gernsback pondered for a moment and then fetched a book from his library. It was *The Life of the White Ant* by Maurice Maeterlinck, which had just been translated by Alfred Sutor and published in America by Dodd, Mead. Gernsback had only recently read it, and a review in the forthcoming August 1929 *Science Wonder* stated: "For any student . . . this little volume should prove stimulating." Gernsback handed the book to Keller. "You take this book with you and read it. There is a big story in it." Maeterlinck had theorized that termites may be controlled by a central intelligence. Gernsback extrapolated that all life may be that way, which might explain why people in different parts of the world have the same idea simultaneously. Keller read the book on the train back to Stroudsburg, and conceived the plot of the story en route. It was written "at white heat" over the next two weeks. By May 11, Keller had submitted a one and only draft which needed some editing at Stellar's offices, probably by David Lasser. When published it brought forth a torrent of letters, many in favor, but almost as many against. It was probably one of the most controversial stories that Gernsback published.

Gernsback's other involvements with stories were less overt. He was attracted to Edmond Hamilton's *Cities of the Air* (serialized in *Air Wonder Stories*, November-December 1929 as *Cities in the Air*) because it drew upon the same idea Gernsback had used in his article "10,000 Years Hence" in *Science and Invention*. Although the story was accepted, Gernsback felt obliged to offer some advice on the science, "as in its present shape it will not pass muster with our Science Editors who comprise our Editorial Board." It's not clear whether Gernsback was using this as an excuse, or was serious, but the rest of his letter to Hamilton highlighted scientific errors in the story and suggested corrections. For example:

> One of the things that we cannot pass, is the speed of one thousand miles an hour of these Air Cities. This is an impossibility. Take the Woolworth Building, for instance; this building has been designed to withstand a wind velocity of no more than 150 miles. It is doubtless [sic] that any structure put up by man could stand a wind velocity of more than 200 miles.[2]

Whilst a keen observation at the time, it suggests a near-sightedness in Gernsback's normally far-sighted vision by presuming that a technology capable of designing aerial cities could not also design them capable of withstanding the greater wind velocities likely to be encountered.

A few days later Gernsback rejected Lloyd A. Eshbach's "The Valley of Titans," but with detailed reasons why, and requesting a revision. The story dealt with a valley isolated from the rest of the world where creatures had remained in suspended evolution, like Doyle's *The Lost World*. Gernsback considered that:

> As we conceive your theme, that possibly because these prehistoric men and animals lived in an unchanged environment they have not developed as their brethren, who were forced to move from place to place. In other words, a static environment produces a condition of static evolution. What you should do is to write this into your story making it pretty evident what your idea is, and have the hero engaged in exciting adventures with these people. As it is now, your story is too much that of an observer and it fails to catch the reader's interest.[3]

Looking back on this, Eshbach remarked that "It was a most encouraging rejection. I was making progress. I still have a copy of that original version—and nothing good can be said about it. I'm really surprised that Gernsback saw any signs of promise in its pages."[4] When Eshbach completed the rewrite he submitted it to *Amazing* rather than to Gernsback, in the hope of receiving better payment. When *Amazing* took too long to reply, Eshbach submitted a new story to Gernsback, "The Man with the Silver Disc," because, money aside, Gernsback's response had been encouraging.

Gernsback issued a detailed two-page "Suggestions to Authors" which formed the basis for an article, "Hugo Gernsback Tells," in the April 1930 *Writer's Digest*. The guidelines set down the basis for science fiction:

> Let it be understood in the first place, that a science-fiction story must be an exposition of a scientific theme and it must be also a story. As an exposition of a scientific theme, it must be reasonable and logical and must be based upon known scientific principles. You have a perfect right to use your imagination as you will in developing the principles, but the fundamental scientific theory must be correct. As a story, it must be interesting. Even though you are making a description of some dry scientific apparatus, invention or principle, you should never bore your reader by making your description dry or uninteresting. A really good writer arranges descriptions so that they will always be interesting.

There followed a lengthy offering of advice in order to make the story more interesting and readable:

> In the first place, you are writing science fiction. A love element in your story should be there because it belongs there. Do not drag a love element in by the hair. If it has no place in your story, keep it out . . . Of course, if you can weave into your story a love element and make the action of the story depend on that, so

much the better, but do not feel that it *must* be there.

About 95% of the stories that are submitted to us deal with some old wizened Professor who makes a remarkable discovery which he says will revolutionize human life. He constructs his machine and is killed or badly damaged and everybody is no much the wiser. This is what I call a "factory-made" story, or a "pot-boiler." That is the kind of story that will reflect credit on neither you nor us . . . It is a mistake to imagine that all inventors are old Professors living in some hut miles from civilization. Many of our great modern discoveries were made by well-dressed, well-fed and prosperous looking gentlemen, drawing large salaries from industrial corporations. So there is no standard inventor type . . .

Don't think that a lecture in the form of conversation is necessarily a science-fiction story. A story must contain adventure, something must happen to people and things, and what happens must be interesting enough to hold the attention of the reader.

Throughout the guidelines, Gernsback was counselling against the very type of "gadget" story with which he is so typically identified. This may have been the trait of his fiction ten or even five years earlier, but Gernsback had recognized that science fiction was rapidly evolving. It was taking on a new identity and had to be treated seriously. The most revealing paragraph in the essay shows how Gernsback was every bit as aware of the need to make science fiction real as Campbell was ten years later:

One of the greatest points of interest in a story, especially an imaginative story, is that the story has verisimilitude. In other words, that it has "life-likeness," that it ring with truth. If you are writing a story of a trip to another planet, try to put yourself in the position of the characters, not only in traveling to the planet, but also of their feelings and experiences on arriving there. If the planet you describe is just like our own earth and if the people are just the same, speak the same and act the same, your story will certainly not carry the same element of truth as if you made the people part of their environment.

Gernsback wanted the characters to be real, not stereotyped or two-dimensional. He wanted the situations to be realistic and exciting. He wanted all the things one would expect of science fiction, and most of the things he is accused of not developing in his writers.

There is one passage in the *Writer's Digest* article which does not appear in the guidelines, but is fundamental to Gernsback's belief in the future of science fiction:

Remember that the main reason why the reader buys a magazine is to be entertained and, therefore, it should be the first duty of a writer to entertain. A science-fiction story should not be a scientific lecture, thinly clothed in conversation and characters. It should be a real adventure story, with a scientific background. But the story should always come first. For if a story is not well written, well founded in incidents, and exciting enough to keep the interest of a reader, the scientific point that the writer wishes to make will be lost, for no one will read the story.[5]

He added to this:

> Remember always that you are writing to a public that is not nearly so scientifically minded as you are, and in your role of educator you must talk down to their level.

In his conclusion to the article he brought all his thoughts together in one concise paragraph.

> The dual purpose of science fiction is to entertain and to educate. But if you make your educational material so uninteresting that few care to read it, then you have failed entirely in both of your purposes. To sum up: In all your stories be human and write about human beings and for human beings.[6]

Gernsback could not have said it more plainly. He was certainly not in the market for the type of stories he used to publish in *Science and Invention*. Though the end result was the same—to inspire and educate—it had to be as a by-product of entertainment, not of lecturing, and the stories had to contain action, adventure and realism. That is not so different to what we expect from our science fiction today, though we also expect it to be well-written, a point that Gernsback makes but does not emphasize elsewhere in his essay. Also we would not expect it to be written down to a basic level.

Both the guidelines and the article are credited to Hugo Gernsback, and the style suggests that Gernsback was the writer. I suspect, though, that David Lasser had a hand in the composition of the guidelines. They may even have been written at his instigation. When interviewed by Eric Davin in 1986, David Lasser had a number of memories, albeit vague, about his days at Stellar almost sixty years earlier: "I said to Gernsback that if we wanted to compete with *Amazing* we had to lift the quality of the stories. We needed more imagination in the stories, we needed a sound scientific basis and, since these were appealing mainly to young people, there should also be a socially useful theme to inspire the readers. Gernsback agreed with this, so I was given a free hand." Lasser also made the observation that "if the story itself wasn't any good, then the science part was useless," which is the same sentiment as in Gernsback's article.

It seems certain that Gernsback was anxious to establish his magazines as the field leaders. After all, this new and relatively untested field, was already supporting two magazines, amounting to sixteen issues a year. Gernsback was now about to almost triple that, with twelve issues each of *Science Wonder Stories* and *Air Wonder Stories* plus, from September 1929, a new *Science Wonder Quarterly*. He was also contemplating an *Air Wonder Quarterly*, which never materialized, and a *Scientific Detective Monthly*, which did. How could he be sure the market could support so much material? He had the drive and tenacity to succeed, and he had faith in his readers and writers. He was probably also of the belief that *Amazing*'s days were numbered and that it was only a matter of time before he was again the sole purveyor of science fiction.

So, as 1929 progressed, Gernsback continued to pile on the pressure. Inevitably he introduced a cover-story competition. The November 1929 *Science Wonder* offered prizes totalling $300 in gold for the best story under 1500 words written around Paul's cover. The first prize, of $150 thus equated to a rate of ten cents a word! Who could ignore that? Every one of the finalists— seven in all—were writers who either established themselves at the time, or subsequently pursued writing careers. The winner was Charles R. Tanner, with "The Color of Space." Tanner (1896-1974) sold one further story to Gernsback, but then appeared in the pages of *Amazing* with his Tumithak series, set on a far future Earth ravaged by years of domination by the Shelks of Venus, with mankind at last emerging from the Dark Ages.

Second prize went to John R. Pierce for "The Relics from the Earth." Pierce (1910-2002) was then a student at the California Institute of Technology and had already been vociferous in his comments about *Amazing* since 1927. He sold several more stories to the magazines, but later established himself as a writer of popular science articles. He went on to become a leading electronics engineer in the field of telecommunications and satellite communications, and is known as the father of Telstar. Pierce is one of many examples of leading scientists who were initially inspired in their studies by Gernsback's science-fiction magazines.

The other finalists were Frank J. Brueckel, Jr., Harold A. Lower, Bob Olsen, Victor A. Endersby, and Arthur G. Stangland. All except Endersby had made previous sales to Gernsback. Stangland went on to become a regular in *Wonder Stories*. Endersby, a civil engineer, had fewer sales, but he could always be counted on for an original story. He was prominent in the letter columns where his strong opinions led to lively and entertaining conflict. One hopeful who was not a finalist was Ross Rocklin, then sixteen years old. It would be another five years and a name change to Ross Rocklynne, before he would start to sell regularly and establish a major reputation in the field.

There was a similar cover-story competition for longer stories in the February 1930 *Air Wonder Stories*. This brought in over five hundred manuscripts. The winner was P. Schuyler Miller with "The Red Plague." Miller (1912-1974) had already appeared in the letter column of *Amazing Stories* and had sold a story to Sloane, "Through the Vibrations," which would not appear for a further ten months. He became a regular contributor to both *Wonder* and *Amazing* in the early thirties, and to *Astounding* in the late thirties, but is frequently overlooked in assessments of writers of this period, even though he was one of the more original and talented. He was also an early active fan, though he is better remembered as the book critic and reviewer for *Astounding* (later *Analog*) where he ran his own column from 1950 to 1974.

Other successful entrants were Clyde F. Beck (1912-85), Lowell Howard Morrow, and J. Harvey Haggard. Beck's story was his only professional sale during this period, though he remained an active fan throughout the thirties, together with his brother Claire. Morrow had already sold several stories to

Gernsback, starting with "Islands in the Air" in the first issue of *Air Wonder*. Ironically, his third-place story, "A Rescue in Space," was his last sale to Gernsback, though he had a story which *Amazing* held for three years before publishing. Haggard (1913-2001) had sold a few poems under the alias "The Planet Prince," starting with "My Little Martian Sweetheart" in the November 1929 *Science Wonder*. His fourth-placed story, "Faster Than Light," was his first fiction. He became a regular contributor to the pulps during the thirties, his stories being competent but unremarkable.

The contest winners were not the only new writers Gernsback was attracting. In fact his track record for 1929 was every bit as commendable as that for 1928. One of the first was Leslie F. Stone, whose "Men with Wings," which was probably one of the manuscripts submitted to *Amazing* that Gernsback took with him, appeared in the first issue of *Air Wonder Stories*. She was the next major female writer to contribute to science fiction after Clare Winger Harris. Her stories throughout the thirties were consistently inventive and challenging.

One name closely associated with the thirties style of science fiction was Ed Earl Repp (1901-1979). Richard A. Lupoff called him "the ultimate example of the hack pulp writer," and there were many in the thirties who condemned his work. Yet he remained popular, with some readers proclaiming him their favorite writer. He first appeared in *Science Wonder* with the serial *The Radium Pool* (August-September 1929). Clearly inspired by Merritt's *The Moon Pool*, Repp's novel has long remained a favorite with science-fiction fans, who regard it with a certain awed fascination. Repp had been a newspaper reporter and movie publicity man before he followed the suggestions of Edgar Rice Burroughs and Zane Grey and turned to fiction. These two mentors influenced him highly and there are those who have said his stories read like outer space westerns. In later years Repp wrote many westerns, including stories for *The Lone Ranger* television series, but it is only for his science fiction that he is remembered today.

The other newcomer in the August 1929 *Science Wonder* was Drury D. Sharp. Sharp (1880-1960) was not a Gernsback discovery. He wrote for several pulp adventure magazines and had first appeared in the April 1929 *Weird Tales* with a lost-race story, "The Goddess of the Painted Priests." He was a capable writer, which meant that even when his scientific accuracy was questionable, the story was still entertaining. His opener, "The Eternal Man" is readable today, and has the same mood of melancholy as generated by Wertenbaker's "The Coming of the Ice," emphasising the isolation of immortality.

Gernsback's next discovery was Henrik Dahl Juve (1899-1990), an electrical engineer of Norwegian descent. Juve wrote only eight stories for Gernsback, starting with "The Silent Destroyer" (*Air Wonder*, August 1929), a story of future warfare and a catalog of Gernsbackian-like inventions. Juve is attributed as being the first writer to describe the laser-beam in his fiction though, as we have seen, George F. Stratton's Poniatowski ray was a similar device. Nevertheless, Juve's application of the beam as a tool rather than as a weapon is much closer to today's reality. Juve should also be remembered as the first to describe the instantly developed photograph, though his description of its use is more as a photocopier than a polaroid camera. As Juve's writing developed he moved away from the scientifically-based story to the scientific adventure, bringing in stronger elements of realism. It was a shift that came about predominantly through coaxing by Gernsback and Lasser in their letters and guidelines, resulting from reader pressure.

Two other writers of note debuted in 1929. Raymond Z. Gallun (1911-1994) had a double debut with "The Space Dwellers" in the November 1929 *Science Wonder Stories* and "The Crystal Ray" in the concurrent *Air Wonder*. Both stories were submitted to *Amazing* early in 1929, and were amongst the manuscripts Gernsback had at home. When Gernsback wrote to Gallun about them, Gallun mentioned having submitted them to *Amazing*, so Gernsback felt duty bound to return them. (In truth he should have handed them back to *Amazing*.) Gallun promptly resubmitted them to Gernsback at his home address and Gernsback accepted them! Gallun's recollection of these events[7] is useful in demonstrating how Gernsback continued to tread the trail of honesty by the narrowest of legal divides.

After months of trying, Neil R. Jones sold his first story, "The Death's Head Meteor" (*Air Wonder*, January 1930). Jones (1909-1988) was a zealous young man whose enthusiasm was way ahead of his writing abilities. His stories bristle with ideas and frequently survive on their breathless exuberance and imaginative qualities. He tended to take Gernsback's and Lasser's advice too personally. This resulted in Jones's best known work appearing in *Amazing*. On December 12, 1929 Gernsback returned Jones's "The Jameson Satellite" with the following explanation:

> After reading over your manuscript, "The Jameson Satellite," carefully, and remembering your note that you mean the story as preliminary to a much longer story, to be entitled "After Forty Million Years," we thought that the best thing to do was to advise you to take the essential details from "The Jameson Satellite" and use that as a prologue to your main story.
>
> "The Jameson Satellite," as it is now, really does not contain enough of an idea for it to stand alone, and we think if you show briefly in the prologue how the Satellite came into being that you could then go on to your real story and work out quite an interesting theme. Anyway, we would be very glad to see the story when it is finished.

Gernsback was offering sound advice. Jones accordingly rewrote the story, but was by then dissatisfied with the payment for "The Electrical Man," which had been rejected by Gernsback for insufficient science for *Science Wonder Stories* but had subsequently been accepted for *Scientific Detective Monthly*. He sent the revised "Jameson Satellite" to *Amazing* where it finally saw print in the July 1931 issue. The story tells of Professor Jameson, who arranges for his body to be buried in Earth orbit. Millennia later it was discovered by a friendly race of aliens, the Zóromes, who had transferred their own brains into robot bodies, making them almost immortal. They revive Jameson and transfer his brain to a metal body, and he accompanies them on their space travels. The story was instantly hailed as a classic by the readers, and led to a long series of sequels. Rumor had it during the mid-thirties that this series sustained *Amazing's* circulation and kept it alive. What might it have done for *Wonder Stories* had Gernsback published it? Although it was his poor payment that alienated Jones, it was Gernsback's own helpful advice that initially lost the story!

During 1929, therefore, despite the upheaval of the Experimenter receivership, Gernsback managed to promote and encourage new science-fiction writers, adding another dozen regulars to the score of names he had established at *Amazing*. In this same period only one major new name appeared in *Amazing*, John W. Campbell, Jr., with "When the Atoms Failed" (January 1930). Although arguably the most important new author of the period, one has to remember that technically, Campbell was also a Gernsback discovery. He had submitted a story, "Invaders from the Infinite," early in 1929, and it had been accepted. Months passed without its appearance and, during the summer, Campbell visited *Amazing's* offices to enquire of its publication. Sloane admitted that the story had been lost. In the light of the events of February 1929, it's possible that this story had been amongst those in Gernsback's possession. As time passed Gernsback may have discovered that he had some manuscripts which he no longer needed and which he should rightly have either returned to the authors or handed back to *Amazing*. He may have taken either course and the manuscript was lost in the mail, or any number of actions might have ensued. Whatever, it is not too surprising that manuscripts were mislaid at this time.

Campbell's "When the Atoms Failed" is interesting for its prediction of the computer, though that name is not used. The machine is primarily a super-calculator, but it reasons with scientific logic, and through its development its inventor discovers the secret of atomic energy.

Although Gernsback was attracting new writers, he was still not luring the established pulpsters from *Argosy*. Even Ray Cummings, who had sold to him earlier, was now selling regularly to *Argosy*, as were Murray Leinster, Ralph Milne Farley, Otis Adelbert Kline, and Abraham Merritt. Gernsback's magazines were not pulps in the accepted sense, but despite Gernsback's attempts to give them a veneer of scientific respectability, their brash covers, slack payment, and sub-literary content were giving them a poor reputation.

This is best exemplified by comments made by George Allan England. England had helped establish the success of science fiction in the Munsey magazines, and though he had not written much in recent years he was still a strong devotee of the field. When Gernsback had reprinted "The Thing from— Outside" in *Amazing's* first issue, England had responded favorably. Writing to Gernsback on June 4, 1926, he stated:

> I cannot thank you too cordially for the opportunity you gave me to say something in approval of your plan to print scientific fiction. This is supposed to be the Age of Science, and the more widely scientific ideas are spread, the better. Fiction is certainly one of the most effective methods of disseminating scientific ideas.
>
> The world is too much given over to silly, meaningless and licentious fiction. The type of stories you propose to print can do much to combat this evil tendency.[8]

England then went into much discussion about the ignorance of science as testified by the notorious Scopes trial of 1925 wherein John Scopes, a biology teacher, was charged with blasphemy by religious fundamentalists for teaching evolution. England strongly advocated the teaching of evolution, and concluded his letter by saying:

> By all means, Mr. Gernsback, publish all the scientific fiction you can, especially with bearing on evolution. The clergy can dominate educational systems, but they cannot control magazines. If the people cannot be reached through the schools, they can through the magazines. Your work is of the utmost importance.

Three years later, Gernsback was seeking to reprint England's serial *The Flying Legion*, and while he was negotiating terms with Munsey's Service for Authors, he sent a copy of *Air Wonder Stories* to England. England wrote to R. H. Titherington at the Munsey Agency on October 25, 1929, in rather less than glowing terms:

> I have received a letter from a Mr. H. Gernsback, running rather a 10th-rate magazine, saying that he has bought the reprint rights to my "Flying Legion." This is the first I have heard of the transaction. It is bad enough to have the story butchered by reappearing in such a medium, but apparently not even the salve of a few dollars is to be applied to my bleeding wounds.

Clearly *Air Wonder* did not strike the same responsive chord as had *Amazing Stories* a mere three years earlier. The paradox here is that the image of the magazine was now closer to that of *Argosy* with its scientific adventure stories, than ever the early *Amazing*s had been, but in England's perceptions the publication of a science-fiction magazine seems to have sunk from work of "utmost importance" to a medium of "butchery," and tenth-rate at that.

It is also unfortunate that England's ire should be taken out on Gernsback and not on Munsey's agency. Gernsback had paid a reasonable $535 for the reprint rights to *The Flying Legion*, which is about a half-cent a word, and all of that money was retained by the Munsey Corporation.

The final irony is that over the next twelve months the quality of science fiction was going to sink even lower, and not by any of Gernsback's doing, but by that of a pulp publisher, the firm of William Clayton. The pulp world was becoming aware of the popularity of science fiction and Gernsback was about to lose control of his creation.

21.

SCIENCE FICTION TAKES HOLD

The expansion of science-fiction publishing in 1929 could not have gone unnoticed by Gernsback's fellow publishers, who were increasingly seeking to specialize and tap a rich vein of commercial popularity. The twenties had marked the rise of the detective and western pulps. These continued to hold their popularity, but the sudden upsurge in science-fiction magazines and their apparent sustainable sales may have been an indication that a change was imminent.

This growth had been entirely the work of Gernsback. As 1929 progressed he continued to dominate the field. I am sure that when he started *Science Wonder* and *Air Wonder* he believed that *Amazing Stories* and its *Quarterly* would not long survive the bankruptcy proceedings. In order that his backers and distributors, and especially his advertisers, were assured that science fiction sold well, and that it was not poor sales at *Amazing* that had made Experimenter bankrupt, Gernsback had to rapidly re-establish the field. He announced plans for the first issue of *Science Wonder Quarterly* as early as June 3, 1929, in the July issue of *Science Wonder Stories*. It was published on September 15, 1929 with a bold gold cover, an experiment Gernsback had used on *Science and Invention*. It had the same policy as *Amazing Stories Quarterly*—to present full length novels—though there was a decided bias towards interplanetary stories.

Once that magazine was released, Gernsback was considering a fourth. He sent a letter to his regular writers on October 8, 1929 stating that he was getting an increasing demand "for detective or criminal mystery stories with a good *scientific* background." He cited as an example the Craig Kennedy stories of Arthur B. Reeve, where science was employed in the solution of the crimes, and the Philo Vance stories of S. S. Van Dine. The Vance stories were at that time enormously popular. *The Canary Murder Case* (1927) had broken all modern publishing records in America for detective fiction. Gernsback wanted some of that success, linked with his constant theme for the advancement of science. The science of forensics was in its infancy, but the police were increasingly using scientific analysis in their detective work. The criminal was also resorting more to scientific methods in the planning and execution of his crimes.

As this was another opportunity for the furtherance of science, it was an inevitable cause for Gernsback to champion. He had already published a number of scientific detective stories in *Science and Invention* and *Amazing Stories* and they were clearly popular. Now Gernsback actively sought such stories, leading to the launch of *Scientific Detective Monthly*. The first issue, dated January 1930, was released on December 15, 1929. It was not published under the Stellar imprint, but by Techni-Craft, which had Joseph Herzberg, Gernsback's attorney, as its Vice-President.

In his opening editorial, Gernsback gave his view that the advancement of science would eventually eradicate crime. He believed that criminals should receive scientific treatment to divert their criminal tendencies along constructive lines. Until that day, though, he anticipated that both the police and the criminal would use more scientific methods in their approaches to crime, and hoped that the magazine would contain stories developing these ideas.

The magazine's masthead displayed a typical Gernsbackian catalog of experts such as Edwin Cooley, Professor of Criminology at Fordham University, New York and Henry A. Higgins of the Department of Criminology at the Massachusetts Prison Association. Others of Gernsback's staff or contributing editors gained fanciful titles. C. P. Mason became Scientific Criminologist and Dr. Alfred Gradenwitz, who had been a contributing correspondent to *Science and Invention* for ten years, was listed as Correspondent-Inspector Detective! The man who assisted Gernsback in the main editorial duties was Hector G. Grey, who served as managing editor. Grey was knowledgeable about detective fiction, but his impact on the magazine seems to have been minimal, and may have been predominantly in an advisory capacity on selecting reprints.

The magazine was something of an anomaly. Gernsback was bringing together some of the noted scientific detective stories of the past and printing them alongside attempts by fledgling science-fiction writers at scientific crime and detection. The result was a curious hybrid that was only partly successful. The first issue was probably well received. Not only did it offer the first serial publication of S. S. Van Dine's Philo Vance novel *The Bishop Murder Case*, which had been a bestseller in hardcover earlier that year, but it also published a new Craig Kennedy story by Arthur B. Reeve, "The Mystery of the Bulawayo Diamond." Craig Kennedy epitomized "the Scientific Detective." His adventures had been appearing for twenty years, since "The Case of Helen Bond" (*Cosmopolitan*, December 1910), and had proved exceptionally popular. Kennedy was a criminologist and consulting detective, an American Sherlock Holmes, who solved crimes by scientific analysis. The heyday of Craig Kennedy, and to a large degree scientific detective stories, had passed, but a new Kennedy story was probably still strong enough to capture the public eye.

Gernsback used most of his standard features in the magazine. There was a letter column, "The Readers' Verdict," from the first issue, a detective contest, book reviews and the latest news on science and crime.

There is some dispute over whether *Scientific Detective Monthly* should be classified as a science-fiction magazine. The bulk of its contents are not science fiction by today's definition, since they concentrate on new uses for existing inventions, or contain only a slight extrapolation in scientific invention. In fact they were typical of the "gadget" stories Gernsback had featured in *Science and Invention* ten years earlier. They were aiming to achieve exactly the same purpose as those stories, which was to promote the science of detection. The magazine, therefore, was properly in the Gernsbackian mold, and more closely related to his original desire for scientific fiction than the latest super-science in *Science Wonder*. There may even have been a belief that with science fiction taking on a more stupendous life of its own, there was a need for the simpler stories of scientific achievement for the experimenters and gadgeteers.

With *Scientific Detective Monthly* launched, Gernsback continued to expand his empire. A month after he originally commissioned stories for that magazine, he asked Lasser to write to the regular authors seeking more interplanetary stories. In the course of this letter, dated November 16, 1929, Lasser noted that they were "also considering an *Air Wonder Quarterly*, and for that we would be interested in looking over some novel-length stories in which the 'air wonder' element was prominent, and which were also interplanetarian." The *Air Wonder Quarterly* idea must have been strongly considered at that time, because Lasser also mentioned it in his editorial response to a letter from Warren Fitzgerald published in the January 1930 *Air Wonder Stories*. The fact that it never materialized must have indicated that, shortly after November 1929, there came a noticeable change in Gernsback's fortune that would make him pull in the reins and reconsider the direction of his publications. The obvious factor might be the Wall Street Crash of October 24, 1929, where billions of dollars in stocks and shares were obliterated in a single day. However, although the stock market crash ultimately had a major effect on all publishers as America sank into the Depression, its immediate effect was less noticeable. It was initially only paper profits that had vanished, not liquid cash, and business and industry, though jolted, carried on much as before. It was some months before the effects of the Crash would start to bite.

Gernsback, in fact, was going from strength to strength. In addition to his magazines he began to publish the *Science Fiction Series*, a set of booklets each containing twenty-four pages, measuring six inches by eight and offered at a bargain price. The first batch of six were released in October 1929, and a second series of six were released the following spring. Each book contained either a novelette or two short stories, and carried a handsome black-and-white cover by Frank R. Paul. The first in the series was *The Girl from Mars* by Jack Williamson and Miles J. Breuer. This was yet another of the manuscripts Gernsback had had at home when Experimenter went bankrupt, but he offered the authors a much better price for it than they would previously have received—a full one-cent a word—and they were paid promptly.

This series was a clever ploy. The total wordage for the first set was around 40,000, less than half that of a standard magazine issue, yet they were selling for a total of fifty cents, twice the cost of the monthly. Nevertheless the element of choice, plus the psychological belief that you were getting six whole books for just fifty cents meant that the idea prospered. This was not the first time Gernsback had tried it. Just one year earlier, as part of a subscription drive and market research project, Gernsback had offered a similar booklet free to new subscribers to *Amazing*. This was *The Vanguard of Venus* by Landell Bartlett, which has since become a scarce collector's item, although the story's of questionable quality.

All this activity in the space of nine months since the Experimenter bankruptcy was not missed by other publishers. The first to respond was William Clayton, who had established his publishing empire with the saucy magazine *Snappy Stories*, launched in 1912. These outwardly titillating but inwardly mild stories began to pale by 1919, the devotees of that field looking for something raunchier. Clayton moved on to adventure fiction. With his head editor, Harold Hersey, who joined him in 1919 after editing *The Thrill Book* for Street & Smith, Clayton launched *Ranch Romances* which united the two popular fields of love stories and the wild west, and brought Clayton further fortune. Clayton published other popular western magazines, especially *Cowboy Stories*, but his other big success came in the detective story field with *Clues*. First issued in 1926, this became one of the detective field's big magazines, alongside *Black Mask* and *Detective Fiction Weekly*. Like all other publishers, Clayton had his failures as well as his successes, but generally he had a thriving empire. He was a popular publisher with authors as he paid at least two cents a word on acceptance, not on publication.

Despite having a wide variety of adventure magazines Clayton had not entered either the weird or science-fiction fields. Sometime in 1928 Harold Hersey discussed the possibility with Clayton, which suggests the influence *Amazing Stories* was having even then, but Clayton exercised caution. Soon after, Hersey left Clayton to work as Supervising Editor at Macfadden Publications, and he was replaced by Harry Bates. Sometime in September 1929, Clayton asked Bates to work up a prospectus for a new magazine of period-history to be called *Torchlights of History*. Bates rebelled against the idea but knowing he'd have to come up with something better, considered an alternative. He recalled the garish covers of *Amazing Stories* and was not a fan of Gernsback's SF. "What awful stuff," he later called it. "Cluttered with trivia! Packed with puerilities. Written by unimaginables!"[1] But he gave thought as to whether there was a market for a well-written magazine along the lines of the "science-monster" type.

Bates considered a number of possible titles. His preferred choice was *Tomorrow*, but he believed that too mild and indefinite and rather highbrow. He also considered the title *Science Fiction*, which shows the impact Gernsback's new term was having, but believed that would give an image of orthodox stories dealing with known science. So he opted for *Astounding Stories*, a title close enough to *Amazing* to attract its readers, but with sufficient power to suggest excitement and adventure. In fact Bates went further with a substitute for "science fiction" by expanding the title to *Astounding Stories . . . of Super-Science*.

Clayton bought the idea and Bates got the go-ahead. His first problem was to find stories. He did not want the scientific stuffiness of most of Gernsback's writers, but apart from others writing for Munsey or *Weird Tales*, science-fiction writers were in short supply. Bates had three choices. To lure the Munsey writers over to Clayton, to work with those of Gernsback's writers most capable of producing the scientific adventures Bates wanted, or to tempt Clayton's western and crime writers to try their hand at super-science. With little over a month to get the magazine ready for the printer, Bates had no choice but to try all three.

This is where Clayton's popularity as a publisher came into play. His high rates and prompt payment meant that writers were keen to write for him. When the word went out, the manuscripts came in. Through Douglas Dold, a former Clayton editor who remained involved in a consulting capacity, Bates acquired manuscripts from Murray Leinster and Victor Rousseau. Leinster was probably the most capable writer of science fiction of the day, but Gernsback had never been able to tempt him to write for his magazines. Clayton secured him from the first issue of *Astounding*. Along with them came Ray Cummings, arguably the most popular regular writer of science fiction for the Munsey pulps. Cummings had written for Gernsback during the lean years at *Argosy* when scientific romances were out of favor, but he soon went back to them when their popularity returned. As for Victor Rousseau, he supplied *Astounding*'s first serial, *The Beetle Horde*.

Leinster's story, "Tanks," was written in his usual smooth style. It was a fairly mundane story of a future war between the United States and the Yellow Empire, but gave a veneer of quality to the magazine. Cummings's and Rousseau's stories were more in line with *Astounding*'s fast-action super-science image. Rousseau's serial dealt with a race of man-sized beetles under the control of a mad scientist who planned to release them on an unsuspecting world. The science was negligible, yet I feel Gernsback might still have bought it had it been submitted to him. Cummings's story, "Phantoms of Reality," used a theme popular at the time, namely that there are other worlds about us separated by a different range of vibrations and thus invisible to us unless we tune in to those vibrations. Needless to say Cummings's heroes do just that.

Those three names alone would have been sufficient to secure good sales for *Astounding*'s first issue, and almost certainly raised Gernsback's envy. Also in that issue was S. P. Meek, who is often remembered as a Gernsback writer, but who at that point had only sold him one story. He was more a Clayton writer as he was selling to Clayton's *Field and Stream* and went on to establish far more of a reputation in *Astounding*, and to a lesser extent in *Amazing*, than he ever did in Gernsback's magazines. The remaining writers for the first issue all came from Clayton's stable. M. L. Staley I know nothing about. C. V. Tench was a regular writer of detective and adventure stories for the pulps. Anthony Pelcher also made sales to other pulp magazines, and by coincidence had a letter published in the concurrent issue of *Science Wonder Stories*, which showed his keen interest in the possibilities of space travel.

Astounding's covers were the work of Hans Wessolowski, a German-born artist who emigrated to the United States in 1914 at the age of twenty. He illustrated many magazines but had neither read nor seen any science fiction before he was asked to provide his first cover for the September 1929 *Amazing Stories*. Though he had no vision for future technology, he had a particular talent for monsters, and some of his work presaged the bug-eyed monsters of later pulps. His covers were all colorful and eye-catching, and frequently better executed than Paul's. A few years later Gernsback approached Wesso to see if he would undertake some cover work, but Wesso refused because Gernsback could not meet his price.

Astounding's first few issues boasted other leading names: Charles Willard Diffin, Hugh B. Cave, Sewell Peaslee Wright, and Arthur J. Burks, all popular contributors to other pulps. Their science may have been highly questionable, but the stories were action-packed entertainment and proved popular from the start. In addition to these popular pulpsters a number of Gernsback's discoveries began to appear in *Astounding*, amongst them Harl Vincent, Lilith Lorraine, R. F. Starzl, Edmond Hamilton, and Miles J. Breuer.

The significance of *Astounding*'s appearance was underlined by the publication of a market report on "The Pseudo-Scientific Field" by R. Jere Black, Jr. in the May 1930 *Author & Journalist*. Black prefaced his report by saying that:

> With the recent appearance of *Astounding Stories* . . . and its two-cent-a-word rate, a field hitherto comparatively little known, and rather unprofitable for the general fiction writer, now assumes a new and more enticing aspect. This is the field of pseudo-scientific fiction, and, from all indications, it is one which will repay investigation by the aspiring author. For scientific fiction or, as it is sometimes called, scientifiction, has come to stay. The demand for it has been growing steadily, and apparently the saturation point is far from reached. In addition to the five monthlies now exclusively devoted to tales of this type, there are numbers of general fiction magazines—such as *Argosy, Blue Book* and even that Holy Grail of writers, the *Post*—which are running them more and more frequently.[2]

Gernsback now had serious opposition. Not only could Clayton leach away his best authors with promise of more money promptly, but *Astounding* sold for five cents less than any of Gernsback's monthlies. Since Clayton had a respectable publishing network, *Astounding* could potentially reach a wider readership than Gernsback's magazines. There was little possibility that *Astounding* might falter in the same way *Amazing* might have done under Gernsback's pressure. Indeed, it was Gernsback who was saturating the field, and thus Gernsback was likely to be the first affected when readers started to become selective. Moreover Black's report revealed that Harold Hersey was planning his own magazine, *Astonishing Stories*, as a market for "all types of fantastic and pseudo-scientific fiction."

Contrary to R. Jere Black's belief, the saturation point might have been nearer than he believed. This was clearly stated by reader George Gatter in his letter published in the May 1930 *Scientific Detective Monthly*.

> All of your magazines have been successful so far, but if you publish any more you are likely to lose some of your followers, including myself. Not that I object to paying for them, but three monthlies and a quarterly (and your former publication and a quarterly) are more than enough reading for anyone whose time is limited, and I am four monthlies and two quarterlies behind now. When you start specializing in one type of story they are bound to become somewhat similar in plot and lose interest.[3]

As Gatter highlighted, it was not the cost that was becoming prohibitive, it was the amount of science fiction being published. With the appearance of *Astounding* there was a potential sixty-eight issues a year which amounted to one every five days. If you included *Weird Tales* in this it became eighty a year, and allowing for the issues of *Argosy* containing science fiction (of which there were twenty in 1930) there was a grand total of one hundred issues, or an average read of two per week. It doesn't take long to realize that those who were working and could thus afford these one hundred issues (a total of $25.60) would not have the time to read them, and those with the time to read them were probably not working and so could not afford them. Something had to give, and the only room for somewhere to go was Gernsback.

Gernsback's reactions in 1930, therefore, were a response to market forces, not to the Depression. It was the simple fact of survival of the fittest. And the measure that now dictated the pace was not within Gernsback's control. Whereas hitherto he had always dictated the trend and controlled the dice, now he had to consider the effect of external forces.

The first indication came in his dealings with *Air Wonder Stories*. David Lasser had already written to regular contributors on November 16, 1929 advising them that they were extending the scope of *Air Wonder* to include interplanetary stories. "Such a story . . . might cover the building of a space ship and the aeronautical problems encountered." The authors did not readily respond and, with the appearance of *Astounding*, another reminder went out over Gernsback's signature in a letter dated January 23, 1930. This "friendly message of advice" started by admonishing writers for creating the impression that the scope of stories in *Air Wonder* was limited to three subjects:

1. Stories about air bandits of the future;
2. Stories about men who want to control the world for some reason or another;
3. Stories of aerial warfare (principally the yellow race against the white).

He then continued:

> It is unfortunate that this impression has arisen, because there is nothing so detrimental to the standing of a new magazine such as ours, with such a broad policy as we have, than to have our readers feel that our stories are only "Wild West stories of the future."

Gernsback then cited Otto Willi Gail's *Shot into Infinity* and R. H. Roman's "The Moon Conquerors" from *Science Wonder Quarterly* as examples of "aviation stories of the future." He added:

> Man is not simply concerned with predatory things. His desire to create rather than to destroy, his passion for peaceful exploration and discovering new lands and new things are properly themes for aviation stories of the future, and yet they have been used by other authors very seldom.

On February 19, 1930 Gernsback sent out another long and personal letter to his regular contributors. The advice in this letter borrowed from his article "Hugo Gernsback Tells," cited in the previous chapter, and emphasized the need for story and characterization instead of scientific lecturing. Now Gernsback began to emphasize action as essential to the stories. In a letter dated February 25, 1930 to Edmond Hamilton, Gernsback wrote:

> Please note . . . that we are besieged by our readers to incorpo-

rate more action in our stories. Will you please bear this in mind when writing future stories. We feel that if you put a little more incident in your stories, and make them move a little faster, that they will make quite a "hit" with our readers.

It was clear that Gernsback was moving even further away from the scientific story to which he had given birth. *Astounding* had taken on the pulp image of science fiction previously projected by *Argosy*, and though this was not entirely what Gernsback's readers wanted, there were enough of them, plus many others, who favored the *Astounding* approach.

With *Air Wonder*'s image becoming a problem, and with its contents becoming closer to *Science Wonder*'s, there was little point in running the two magazines. Nevertheless the decision to stop *Air Wonder* must have been sudden. In the letter column in its last issue, dated May 1930, David Lasser responded to urgings from Jack Darrow and Forrest Ackerman about *Air Wonder Quarterly* by saying: "As for *Air Wonder Quarterly*, we shall get this when we are mechanically able to do so. The publishing of four magazines with the large circulation of *Air Wonder*, is in itself, a stupendous task, necessitating an organization not always appreciated by the actual reader."4 The general tone used throughout the editorial responses in the letter column was that *Air Wonder* was continuing. Moreover a contest launched in the February 1930 issue seeking a slogan for *Air Wonder* and offering $100 in gold, was still running in the May issue, which reminded readers of the rules and that the winner would be announced in the July 1930 issue of *Air Wonder Stories*.

However in the place of Gernsback's usual editorial to the May issue was a simple but bold announcement stating that *Air Wonder Stories* will be combined with *Science Wonder Stories* effective with the next issue. In the past Gernsback had always applied reasoned arguments in his editorials for any changes to magazines, just as he had done in the last issue of *The Experimenter*, but here there was none. This suggests that his normal editorial was replaced at the very last minute with this notice.

We know when the May issue of *Air Wonder* went to press because of a letter David Lasser wrote to Edmond Hamilton asking where his latest story was in the hope they could still schedule it for the May issue. "We are just about ready to make up our schedule," Lasser wrote, "and if you could write me at once and let me know whether you will have anything ready I may be able to reserve some space for it in the magazine." This letter was dated March 11, 1930. Hamilton submitted "The Men from the Meteor," though he was unsatisfied with it and felt it needed further work. Lasser returned it on March 17, saying that if the story was resubmitted within the next two weeks he would schedule it for the June *Air Wonder*. At this stage there is no mention of the magazine merger.

The May *Science Wonder Stories* was published on April 3, 1930, and though this contained an announcement about its change of name, there was no reference to a merger with *Air Wonder*. All the indications were that *Air Wonder* would continue its separate existence. The final proofs for the May *Science Wonder* would have been passed a week before its publication, or around March 27, which suggests the decision to merge *Air Wonder* had not been made then. The proofs for the final issue of *Air Wonder* were probably checked in the week of April 1, 1930 and it seems likely that the decision was made then, probably on impulse.

The last time Gernsback made such an instant decision was when he was launching a new magazine urgently and wanted a slot into which to fit it. Sure enough, the same situation had arisen. In that same month Gernsback launched his new magazine *Aviation Mechanics*. This was a bi-monthly magazine, with the first issue released on May 15, 1930. With Gernsback's aeronautical desires filled by this new magazine, and the need for an additional slot for *Everyday Mechanics*, *Air Wonder* could be dropped.

Air Wonder's demise was not a reflection of its unpopularity or its circulation. There is good reason to believe the magazine could have continued for the foreseeable future, despite the short-term problem of obtaining good manuscripts. It was dropped more for technical and self-indulgent reasons. But it was also sound logic. *Air* and *Science Wonder* were becoming similar in content and there was much sense in merging them. What it did not do is suddenly boost *Wonder*'s circulation. Gernsback stated that the majority of readers read both magazines with perhaps no more than a thousand at *Air Wonder* who were added to *Wonder*'s subscription list.

More significant than the demise of *Air Wonder* was the change of name of *Science Wonder* to *Wonder Stories*. For seasoned followers of Gernsback the announcement in the May 1930 issue must have seemed like sacrilege. Gernsback wanted the magazine to reach a wider readership. He explained:

> It has been felt for some time that the word "Science" has tended to retard the progress of the magazine, because many people had the impression that it is a sort of scientific periodical rather than a fiction magazine.[5]

This must have been a bitter pill for Gernsback to swallow. His whole reason for creating a field for science fiction had been to promote science. Now the very reference to it was retarding the magazine. Science fiction was becoming a Frankenstein's monster over which Gernsback was losing control. The child had turned upon the parent. In truth the content and policy of *Wonder Stories* remained largely unchanged, but the image that the magazine was now projecting reflected more that of *Astounding Stories*.

As if one name change was not sufficient, "science" was also banned from *Scientific Detective Monthly*. With the same June 1930 issue, this was retitled *Amazing Detective Tales*, and David Lasser was put in charge. Likewise, with its Summer 1930 issue *Science Wonder Quarterly* became *Wonder Stories Quarterly*.

The name change to *Amazing Detective Tales* did not help this hybrid magazine. From the outset it was destined to have limited appeal, because detective-story fans would regard it as a science-fiction magazine, and vice versa. Moreover the science-fiction fans would have been disappointed to find stories which, in their eyes, were already old-fashioned and lacked a sense of wonder and were far from the adventurous super-science image that science fiction was now projecting. The magazine was basically too specialized, and too late. This time, however, Gernsback did not choose to simply cease publication, although, as ever, his decision was impromptu. The contents of the November 1930 *Amazing Detective Tales*, due on October 15, were still announced in the November *Wonder Stories* published on October 3, so the decision must have been made around October 1. This time Gernsback put the magazine up for sale. The December 1930 *Author & Journalist* announced that the title had been purchased by Fiction Publishers, run by Wallace Bamber. The magazine was relaunched as *Amazing Detective Stories*, probably in January or February 1931, though only five more issues are known, folding in August 1931. This new incarnation was an orthodox detective magazine complete with an Edgar Wallace serial, *The Feathered Serpent*.

Before the sale, though, Gernsback had intended one further change for *Amazing Detective Tales*, a change he was also planning for *Wonder Stories*, and that was a shift from the large size to standard pulp size. This was probably another sudden decision because once again the news took the form of an announcement in the October 1930 *Wonder Stories*:

> This action was taken after an extensive survey conducted among a large number of readers to discover which size they preferred. We found that 87.5 per cent voted for the more convenient size. The reasons for the preference were chiefly that the new size is handier and the magazine can be carried more easily, read in a crowd, and slipped into a coat pocket.[6]

There is no reference to the fact that the new-size *Wonder Stories* closely resembled *Astounding Stories*. *Astounding* had been a standard pulp from the start, and its impact upon Gernsback was only too clear. He increased the action and adventure in his stories and toned down the science; he eradicated the reference to science in the magazines' titles so that they were more closely associated with *Astounding*; and finally he took the ultimate step and switched to the pulp size.

From the start, *Amazing Stories* and later *Science Wonder* had stood aloof from the pulps in their large format. Association with the bigger circulation magazines also published in that size gave *Amazing* and *Wonder* a measure of superiority. *Astounding*, on the other hand, looked every inch a sensationalistic pulp. But the readers had responded to that image and Gernsback, ever responsive to the market, had taken note. There were those fans who welcomed the change, but there were others who felt Gernsback had sold his soul to the devil. Science fiction was no longer a speciality for the elite. Now it was mass-produced pabulum for the unscientific, untrained plebs. For those who felt that the period starting in May 1929 had heralded in a golden age for science fiction, the sparkle had gone. From October 1930 on, science fiction would never be the same.

Which raises the question, what had science fiction become?

22.

SONS OF SUPER SCIENCE

As we have seen, when Gernsback launched *Amazing Stories* in 1926 there had been three types of science fiction appearing in the magazines. The general pulps preferred the scientific romance, usually represented by the explorers' tale, the lost-race form of fantastic adventure with mystical science elements as typified by Abraham Merritt and Edgar Rice Burroughs. *Weird Tales* favored the monster-in-the-laboratory type of weird-science story, concentrating on the monstrous aberrations that science might produce. Then there was Gernsback's specific form of scientific fiction concentrating on new inventions, known colloquially as the "gadget" story.

Outside of the magazines there was a fourth type of science fiction which was the utopia story. Whilst its history parallels science fiction to some extent, these stories were predominantly concerned with political and social utopias and often took the form of lost-world stories, as in the grandfather of them all, Thomas More's *Utopia* (1516). The political utopia story had a separate existence for centuries, and only gradually merged with the scientific utopia when utopias were projected into the future rather than elsewhere on Earth. The scientific utopia story is largely a projection of Gernsback's "gadget" story, where the future world is depicted as a paradise built upon the wonders that science could achieve.

Prior to 1926 the interplanetary story was seldom scientific and was largely an extension of the explorers' tale as established by Jules Verne. As the unknown areas of our Earth were explored the need to seek new locales for fanciful adventures forced writers' imaginations either within Earth, under the sea or into space. Trips into space were frequently spirit or astral journeys, such as that by John Carter to Mars in Edgar Rice Burroughs's novels. Anti-gravity was the favored means of space travel when pseudo-science was introduced to these stories.

By 1928, however, the universe had become the stage for super-science extravaganzas. Whilst these had been developing in the writings of Homer Eon Flint and Ray Cummings in the general pulps, they were given a more scientific base by Edward E. Smith and Edmond Hamilton in *Amazing Stories* and *Weird Tales*. Along with the extrapolation of super-science into the future, in Philip Nowlan's "Armageddon—2419 A.D.," science fiction in Gernsback's magazines shifted more toward the fantastic adventure of the general pulps, but brought with it a strong scientific base.

The appearance of *Astounding* in 1930 completed this process. Now the action adventure of the general pulps had become the dominant form, but bolstered by a stronger application of pseudo-science than in the pre-1926 stories. The science was not as sound as Gernsback wanted for his own magazines, but it was evident. However one of Gernsback's original desires— that readers would be educated through science fiction—had now taken a back seat to the rôle of science fiction as entertainment. What remained was the ability of science fiction to inspire and stimulate, both in terms of scientific attainment and in terms of the urge to write science fiction. Both of these issues are considered in the next couple of chapters.

It is important to pause at this stage, and consider this super-science phase of science fiction. For phase it was. We shall see that by 1932/33, a new type of science fiction would emerge, with the super-science of the first *Astounding* era passing as a brief but significant transition. It is fortunate that Gernsback's article "Hugo Gernsback Tells" and R. Jere Black's market report "The Pseudo-Scientific Field" appeared within a month of each other in April and May 1930,[1] as it gives us a focal point for the science-fiction tale at the moment of this transition.

Gernsback's article included an extract from his editorial policy at Stellar. This was almost identical to the policy reissued for contributors to *Wonder Stories* a few months later, so clearly represented Gernsback's needs during 1930. In this statement Gernsback listed the types of stories he desired. They fell into ten categories.

(1) Interplanetarian.
(2) Stories of atomic disintegration, radium or other stories dealing with chemistry.
(3) Stories of biology and medicine.
(4) Stories of future warfare.
(5) Descriptions of the world of the future; ultra-modern cities, etc.
(6) Stories of insect life.
(7) Stories of the future evolution of man. This is a field that has been practically untouched. There is no doubt that in the future man will evolve physically as well as mentally. He may have a large skull and a small body, long hands and short feet, etc. His mental processes in a highly complex civilization may also be very much different from what they now are, as well as his ideals and aspirations.
(8) Exploration into unknown lands, in the deep sea and within the earth.
(9) Scientific detective stories of the Craig Kennedy type.
(10) New uses for radio and television.

In his later *Wonder Stories* statement, Gernsback dropped one of these categories. Curiously it was not the scientific detective story, but the stories of future warfare. Perhaps with the preponderance of these in *Astounding* Gernsback wished to disassociate himself from the field, though in fact he continued to publish them regularly. More likely, he wished to promote the positive aspects of science, not the negative horrors of war.

Gernsback's ten categories are not mutually exclusive. The tales of evolution that he was now strongly promoting would fit into the division for stories of biology and medicine, both of which also suggest the story of mutant creatures. This is where the giant insect story might fit although Gernsback referred generally to stories of insect life, because of the number of stories based on the wonders of the natural world, especially bees and ants. The interplanetary tale headed the list, not too surprisingly, but the explorers' tale of unknown lands was also included, even though these share the same origin. Gernsback's own gadget story remains in the guise of the "new uses for radio and television" and to some extent in his scientific-detective tale. We may, in fact, group Gernsback's editorial wants into the following six categories:

(1)   Interplanetarian and explorers' tales.
(2)   Stories of atomic power.
(3)   Biology, medicine and evolution.
(4)   The world of the future.
(5)   New inventions.
(6)   The wonders of the natural world.

This grouping has only a partial similarity to that given in Black's article. Black, who claimed to have read all the science-fiction magazines since 1926, based his categories "upon the announced preferences of the readers of the various magazines and also upon my own tabulations of the relative quantity of each kind published." Unlike Gernsback's list, therefore, which was a statement of editorial wants, Black's was a list of readers preferences and stories published. He tabulated four categories:

(1)   The Interplanetary Tale.
(2)   The Tale of the Future.
(3)   The Giant Insect Tale.
(4)   The Fourth Dimension Tale.

The first two, and to a degree the third, are common to Gernsback's listing. Strangely, Gernsback either overlooked or ignored the fourth category, even though tales of the fourth dimension had been appearing in his magazines since 1927. Initially, though, these concentrated on the fourth dimension as a mathematical concept, which allowed traveling through time, or as some form of hyper-space allowing direct access between two points otherwise unconnected in three dimensions. What had started to emerge more strongly from 1928 onwards was the concept of the fourth dimension as another world. In effect the fourth dimension had become a sub-category of the interplanetary or explorers' tale.

Curiously, Black does not list the invention story, which was how Gernsback's originated, though he does refer to them in a mopping up paragraph toward the end of his article where he says:

> Nor must we overlook the minor motifs. Super-radio inventions; gravity nullifiers; mechanical robots who turn human, escape from their creators, and perpetrate a reign of terror; men with wings; the elixir of perpetual life invented, stolen, and recovered; strange discoveries on our own planet; transmutation of base metals into gold; bodies made invisible . . .

Black's four categories are the four most popular, hence we must deduce that Gernsback's invention stories had been relegated to the "also-rans" by 1930. Whilst the fantastic-adventure tale continued in the form of the explorers' tale, and whilst the giant-insect story was having its peculiar though short-lived heyday, science fiction by 1930 was synonymous with the interplanetary story and the tale of the future.

Black wrote in rather disparaging tones about the interplanetary tale. Firstly he stressed that the main intention is to get the hero to another planet quickly, so that the details of the means of space travel are "rather meager." Black then describes the general approach once the planet is reached:

> Once there, the writer can let his imagination run riot, restricted only by certain earth-bound tabus. While there does not absolutely have to be a girl, there generally is—one who either accompanied the scientist hero (properly chaperoned, of course) from the earth, or a maiden of the moon, a Neptune niftie, Jupiter Juno or what have you? Then there must be a battle with the inhabitants of the visited planet, almost invariably equipped with death rays, in which combat of course the hero is triumphant, foiling their attempts to steal his space car or the girl, and, finally, after many fantastic adventures, returning to earth together with his sweetheart and some rare unearthly spoils. In other words, it is the conventional wish-fulfillment plot so dear to all magazines, except that this variety takes place beneath strange skies, and consequently the writer can unleash his imagination in depicting the forms of life, the cities, and the customs of other worlds.

Black then refers to the sister story of the interplanetary, which is the alien invasion story, where monsters from the moon or Venus or Mars are intent on taking over the earth because their own world is dying or lacks some essentials. The theme after that is much the same as the interplanetary with a battle and a triumphant hero.

Black points out that the world of the future also has similarities. After a none too specific means of traveling to the future ("either a 'time traveling machine' or some 'obscure' drug"), our hero reaches a future world. "From then on, same formula as in the interplanetary theme. Beautiful heroine, savage time-dwellers, battles with weapons of the future, triumph of scientist, ending with safe return to present time." Since the giant insect theme can also be boiled down to "hero versus alien," Black deduces that the pseudo-science field is actually very shallow. Pick a strange locale, a monster or villain, super-scientific weapons, a hero, a heroine, and mix accordingly.

This is certainly not the field Gernsback had set out to establish, but it was one that had mutated, following a mating with the fantastic adventure of the pulps. There was little doubt that from Gernsback's original ideals, and from the earlier pulps literary pretensions, science fiction had rapidly degenerated into formula hero versus aliens/villains in a weird locale. This had not been Gernsback's fault. It had come about primarily by reader demand, essentially because the market science fiction was now attracting was the younger reader who did not want to read lengthy scientific extrapolations but wanted simple wondrous action and adventure.

The natural result of the popularity of the interplanetary action story was what became termed "space opera," though this phrase was not itself coined until Bob Tucker used it in the January 1941 issue of his fan magazine, *Le Zombie*. The origins of space opera can easily be seen in the pages of *All-Story* and *Argosy*, and its founding fathers include Homer Eon Flint, Ray Cummings, and Edmond Hamilton. Hamilton, in fact, for all that he later developed into a talented and capable writer, is probably more guilty than most of creating the hack formula for space-opera fiction, chiefly in *Weird Tales*, where his Interstellar Patrol series continued apace during 1930. These were straight action stories strong on imagination and visionary power but with little regard for scientific accuracy, characterization or dialogue.

At the same time, another series, featuring the characters Arcot, Wade and Morey, was being established in *Amazing Stories* and the *Quarterly* by John W. Campbell, Jr. Although Campbell's stories had some scientific grounding in their super-science they were still space opera extravaganzas on a cosmic scale. The first story in the series, "Piracy Preferred" (*Amazing Stories* June 1930) shows how they developed from the basic premise of space piracy, which was a regular feature in the magazines at this time. Each story developed on a grander scale reaching a peak in the novels *Islands of Space* (*Amazing Stories Quarterly*, Spring 1931) and *Invaders from the Infinite* (*Amazing Stories Quarterly*, Spring-Summer 1932).

In the meantime E. E. Smith, who had first made super-science popular in *The Skylark of Space*, had provided the even better and ecstatically received sequel *Skylark Three* (*Amazing Stories*, August-October 1930). This was followed by the slightly more moderate, solar-system confined, *Spacehounds of IPC* (*Amazing Stories*, July-September 1931).

In both their works, Campbell and Smith tried to introduce bold new scientific concepts amongst the action-packed adventure. Smith, for instance, proposed the ion-drive as a means of space-ship propulsion, whilst Campbell suggested the harnessing of emotions as a weapon in space conflict. Not all such writers were as advanced. The nadir of space opera appeared in *Astounding* in the shape of the Hawk Carse adventures, written pseudonymously by Harry Bates and Desmond Hall. The first story in the series, "Hawk Carse," appeared in the November 1931 *Astounding*, whilst the last (apart from an abortive reprise in 1942), "The Passing of Ku Sui" was a year later in the November 1932 issue. Despite its popularity at the time, the Hawk Carse stories so epitomized all that was bad about interplanetary fiction, that nothing of the kind could follow it. To produce any type of interplanetary story after 1932 writers had to take an intelligent new approach to the theme.

The science fiction in *Astounding* during 1930-1932 had few redeeming qualities, and what there was has been captured in wonderfully self-indulgent style in Arthur C. Clarke's science-fictional autobiography, *Astounding Days*. To my mind there was only one story of lasting quality in the Clayton *Astounding* and that was "The Power and the Glory" by Charles W. Diffin (July 1930), a profound short statement on the need to keep the key to atomic energy a secret for the salvation of the Earth. Diffin was a good writer, with eight stories and three serials in the Clayton *Astounding*. He was older than the majority of other contributors to *Astounding* and generally brought a more mature outlook to his fiction, though he still revelled in the fun and frolics of scientific adventures as exemplified by his Dark Moon series.

Astounding, because of its wider circulation and distribution, rapidly established its own image for science fiction, and though the quality of fiction in *Wonder Stories* and *Amazing Stories* was better, these magazines became tarred with the same brush. In fact, the stories in *Wonder* and *Amazing* were by no means as poor as in *Astounding*, which highlights an interesting feature generally overlooked. Although *Astounding* paid more, and regularly, it was nothing but a commercial venture, and published fiction in line with a popular formula. Neither *Wonder* nor *Amazing* tried to be formula. They obviously wanted to be popular, to ensure a wide circulation, but did not cater to commercial factors as much as *Astounding*. As a consequence both magazines were open to more original, bold ideas. The problem at *Amazing* was that Sloane held on to manuscripts for so long that few of these stories saw the light of day in the 1930/31 period. Authors started to put *Amazing* at the bottom of their list because it only paid on publication and that timing was unpredictable. *Wonder Stories* also paid on publication, but at least the stories usually appeared within six months after acceptance.

As a consequence it was *Wonder* that frequently published the better, more original stories of this period, and there is no better evidence for this than in the work of Clark Ashton Smith.

Smith (1893-1961), ironically, was not a fan of science fiction, and yet he became one of the most regular contributors to *Wonder Stories*. He liked to write about weird and wonderful worlds with an exotic vocabulary which brought color and atmosphere to the most alien terrains. Although Smith had written some short non-fantastic adventure stories in his teens, he had concentrated on poetry until returning to fiction in 1928 with "The Ninth Skeleton" in *Weird Tales*. *Weird Tales* remained his major market, but he branched into science fiction when he decided to earn a living from writing and needed to expand his markets. His first sale to Gernsback had been "Murder in the Fourth Dimension" in the October 1930 *Amazing Detective Tales*, though a later sale, "Marooned in Andromeda" appeared a week earlier in the October 1930 *Wonder Stories*. Smith had started this story in January 1930. He told Lovecraft: "I am beginning 'Marooned in Andromeda', which will be a wild tale about some mutineers on a space flier who are put off without weapons or provisions on an alien world. The idea will form an excellent peg for a lot of fantasy, horror, grotesquery and satire."[2] Lasser was apparently enthusiastic in his acceptance of "Marooned in Andromeda." Smith told Lovecraft of his response: ". . . They want me to do a series about the same crew of characters (Capt. Volmar, etc.) and their adventures on different planets, saying that they would use a novelette of this type every other month."[3]

David Lasser had an eye for quality writing regardless of scientific content. He was attracted to Smith's work and encouraged him with an idea for a time travel story. He wrote to Smith on November 19, 1930:

> I believe that you have the ability to portray local color, so that you could show not only the difference in the physical surroundings and the mode of life of our descendents, but also in their different habits of thought. It is quite possible for a man going into the future, to find an entirely different set of moral and social ideas, as is illustrated very well in Shaw's "Back to Methu-

selah." He would find these people absorbed in entirely different ideas, and he would be truly lost as he would be among people of a different race.

I have in mind a story in which no use is made of the old hackneyed, outworn plots. There need not be any rescues of fair maidens of the future, but instead I believe you could work out a stirring drama in which our twentieth century hero is a part.

Lasser finished by saying that he wanted "to work as closely with you in this as possible, and offer as much assistance as I can to help you to produce a corking good story." Lasser was certainly keen to develop Smith as a writer of science fiction, and Smith was happy to respond. Although he preferred to work on his own ideas, he developed Lasser's suggestion into the story "An Adventure in Futurity" (*Wonder*, April 1931). Although some of the glamor of language is evident, the story is unlike Smith's normal fare, being something of a robinsonade of the year 15,000, depicting future scientific marvels, and considering the prospect of trade between Earth, Mars and Venus at a time when the aliens were hostile. Smith had completed the story in January 1931 and commented to H. P. Lovecraft at the time that he regarded it as "an awful piece of junk."[4]

Smith was better when left to his own devices. Rather than be restricted by the limitations of Earth, Smith preferred the unbounded wonders of beyond. He still did not regard science fiction as his main market, but, as he remarked in a letter to August Derleth in April 1931: "Through financial necessity I have written nothing lately but scientifiction." Smith had tried two stories, neither of which had amounted to much. Lasser rejected "The Red World of Polaris" on the basis that the first part was too descriptive with insufficient action. Lasser evidently believed Smith needed coaxing as an author to control his imaginative skills and work them into an action-orientated story.

Smith eventually started a new Volmar story, "A Captivity in Serpens," commenting to Lovecraft that "I'll give them their action this time!!!" He informed Derleth of the story's sale. "The Gernsback outfit has taken a long novelette which will appear in an early issue under the title 'The Amazing Planet'. God knows why. They seem to have a mania for changing titles." In buying the story, Lasser had written to Smith on March 27, 1931 adding, "We were quite pleased with the story and believe it strikes the proper note for effective interplanetary atmosphere. We will be happy to receive more stories of the adventures of your explorers, showing their contact with other strange forms of life and other civilization."

Smith was not keen to pursue this. He had found "A Captivity in Serpens" hard to complete and preferred to write his more fantastic stories. A clear division was forming. Smith was of the opinion that he was writing hack work, junk written to order, whilst Lasser was perceiving a talented and imaginative writer whom he was developing.

Smith completed a story of his own, "The City of [the] Singing Flame," which Lasser rushed into print in the July 1931 *Wonder Stories*. This story has some of the atmosphere of Merritt's work, and was instantly recognized by readers as a classic. A sequel, "Beyond the Singing Flame" (November

1931) was written on demand. Smith now found that he could use the fantastic imagery he so enjoyed in his science-fiction stories to the satisfaction of both Lasser and himself. Since no one else could write like Smith, there is no doubt that he was the most original writer appearing in *Wonder Stories* in the 1930/32 period. His work, probably more than any others, helped sustain a different image for *Wonder Stories* during the excess of super-science in *Astounding*.

A few other writers were also developing new styles. Amongst them was no less than Edmond Hamilton himself. Since Hamilton was the first to explore the space opera theme, he must also have been amongst the first to tire of it. He took note of Gernsback's comment in his policy statement that there were too few stories about the evolution of man, and promptly wrote "The Man Who Evolved" (*Wonder Stories*, April 1931). It explored the accelerated evolution of a human subject which eventually reverted to protoplasmic slime. Never one to waste an idea, Hamilton used it again in "Devolution," though this manuscript hung around at *Amazing* for some years before appearing in the December 1936 issue.

Generally, though, the fiction was becoming uninspiring. 1930 had seen the science-fiction field a cauldron of activity. Most of that activity was positive in the growth of awareness of science fiction, and (as we shall see in the next chapter) the emergence of a strong science-fiction fandom. But retrospectively it was essentially a disappointing year, because the quality of science fiction was changing. Gernsback had set standards which he had never really been able to keep, simply because there were not the number of talented writer/inventors about. The pulps were unable to even set a standard, other than rip-roaring action and super-science, as there were not enough writer/visionaries about. Science fiction was being created by amateurs. Some may have been professional writers, but they had no knowledge of the field, or, more significantly, no awareness of the purpose of science fiction originally planned by Gernsback.

A new science fiction was emerging which was not Gernsback's original intention. It might still have inspired the youth, but only into starry-eyed action and adventure, not into scientific achievement. This was evident not just from the way that science-fiction fandom was already shifting from the pursuit of science to the pursuit of science fiction, but in the critical letters being published in the magazines.

The views of readers were best summarized in a letter from W. E. Wilson of Naches, Washington, published in the April 1931 *Wonder Stories*.

> Sometimes I think that the field of science fiction has been worked out like a rich pocket of gold. Like the western thrillers, they all seem to be copies of one original good story. Then someone comes along with fireworks in the form of a new idea and I get all enthused again . . . Still, I have noticed a tendency toward cheap sensationalism in the last year in science fiction. Not only "our" mag but others have helped develop a taste for shrieking damsels always helplessly in the power of a sneering villain—and superheroic tireless heroes who can make all sorts of blunders and live, and never do much of anything until fifty minutes past

the eleventh hour when they suddenly become masters of all sorts of science, language, etc. Too melodramatic by far.[5]

Lasser's response was defensive but astute:

> We agree that science fiction is not perfect—it is too young, too struggling, too new. It is now cutting its teeth so to speak, learning by experience, and getting the wisdom of the world to grow up into the strong, healthy being it is sure to become.[6]

To encourage writers to try something new David Lasser issued a long and detailed letter on May 11, 1931. Key extracts are copied below.

> Mr. Gernsback, the Publisher, has always maintained that science fiction evolves, like any other form of literature; and that the evolution of science fiction is perhaps a bit more rapid because it is such a young art, and has not yet reached a mature form. When Mr. Gernsback started his first science-fiction magazine, which was the pioneer in this country, he found it necessary to have stories probe very deeply into science, and to keep them quite technical. Since publishing WONDER STORIES, however, it has been found that our readers do not wish such heavy doses of science, but they want the human element—human conflicts and dramas—stressed more and more.
>
> WONDER STORIES and WONDER STORIES QUARTERLY are now being read by an expanding class of readers in all walks of life. the majority of readers are neither scientists nor technicians, and they insist upon only enough science to give them the scientific basis of the story and its setting.
>
> In other words, science fiction should deal *realistically* with the effect upon people, individually and in groups, of a scientific invention or discovery. The flow of the story should be reasonable, although dramatic; the situation should be convincing, the atmosphere conveyed vividly and the characters should really be human. In other words, allow yourself one fundamental assumption—that a certain machine or discovery is possible—and then show what would be its logical and dramatic consequences upon the world; also, what would be the effect upon the group of characters that you pick to carry your theme. The "modern" science story should not try to be a world-sweeping epic. It should rather try to portray *intensively* some particular phase of our future civilization.
>
> Once you have made your assumption, everything from that point on should follow logically and convincingly, and as realistically as in our present-day realistic literature. I do not mean by this that stories should not be stimulating to the imagination. In fact they *should* take us to far-off places and times, and allow us to see vividly what an infinity of possible worlds there are. But we must, on the other hand, prevent science fiction from becoming

mere fairy tales.

Summing up, we intend to strike a balance in our editorial policy between the excessively scientific story and the "wild-west science" stories (in which the hero conquers a great army of impossible monsters or indulges in other absurdities—where one paragraph follows another with childish hair-raising escapades, and where the hero always comes out on top). We are getting away from hackneyed plots and dime-novel melodrama. We want stories aimed at the great mass of readers, old and young, who delight in exercising their imagination and joy of adventure in these "possible worlds," but who do not want their reason and sense of the fitness of things outraged.

While we leave the usual wide latitude to the author, in his choice of subject, we are not inclined to look with favor on the hackneyed type of bug-and-insect stories, or the stereotyped huge-monster story.

In one swoop Lasser outlawed the space-opera story, the giant-insect story, and the hero-versus-monster story—almost everything published by *Astounding* and much that *Wonder Stories* was finding itself receiving from the growing generation of science-fiction writers. Lasser referred to this as their "new policy," not to be confused with the New Policy that Charles Hornig would launch a little over two years later.

Gernsback's comment about the rapid evolution of science fiction was correct. In the generations prior to 1926, science fiction had scarcely evolved at all because there was no stimulating force. Apart from references to modern science, there was little to distinguish between the science-fiction story of 1925 and that of 1825, which was why Gernsback was able to reprint so many old stories. Now, within the space of six years, science fiction had undergone two phases, and was about to enter a third.

The full impact of *Wonder*'s new policy would not become noticeable until 1932. Before then, let us see what impact science fiction was having upon its readers and devotees.

23.

THE VOICE OF FANDOM

With the bankruptcy of the Experimenter Publishing Company, those science-fiction fans who were aware of the situation, must have been apprehensive about the future of science fiction. They must have been relieved when in March 1929 they received a circular from Gernsback announcing plans for his new magazines. This time Gernsback was appealing directly to the science-fiction fans. Individually they must have felt a surge of importance. Gernsback was asking them to advise on the policy for his new magazines and to suggest a name. Here the fans were intimately involved with the creation of *their* publication. Gernsback was doing no more than he had done when he launched *Modern Electrics* in 1908. Then he had canvassed subscribers to his radio catalog and his electrical mail-order business on what they wanted in a radio magazine. He merely repeated the exercise, but this time to a more avid and vocal body of people. Science-fiction fans had an enthusiasm for their favorite form of reading unlike any other genre devotees, and of course their response to Gernsback's requests was overwhelming.

Gernsback also encouraged readers to voice their opinions on science fiction, offering a $50 first prize to the best letter on "What Science Fiction Means To Me." But he then went further. In launching *Science Wonder Quarterly* on September 15, 1929, he appealed to the active science-fiction fan. He announced a $500 competition on "What I Have Done to Spread Science Fiction." The object of the competition was "to convert others to the cause of science fiction." Elsewhere in the editorial, with an evangelical zeal, Gernsback explained that cause:

> In publishing a number of science-fiction magazines, the editors feel that they have a great mission to perform; their mission being to get the great mass of readers, not only to think what the world in the future is likely to become, but also to become better versed in things scientific. But it is impossible for us to succeed in our mission unless our science-fiction readers preach the gospel of science fiction, wherever and whenever they have a chance to do so.[1]

The contest ran for three issues, with a first prize of $100, $50 as second prize and $20 for third in each issue. The winner of the first prize in the Winter 1930 issue was deservedly Walter Dennis for his pioneer work in organizing the Science Correspondence Club. Second and third prizes went to Victor Szanton and Julius Unger respectively.

The Spring 1930 *Science Wonder Quarterly* brought forth the next batch of winners. The first prize went to Raymond A. Palmer for his activities in helping develop the Science Correspondence Club, whilst the third prize went to Allen Glasser for work in developing the New York fan organization The Scienceers. Glasser was probably the leading fan correspondent of the day, having appeared regularly in the magazine letter columns since the June

1927 *Amazing* where he used his real full name of Aaron L. Glasser. Glasser, like Dennis, had used the addresses available in *Amazing* and *Science Wonder* to contact fellow New Yorkers to form an association devoted to the furtherance of science and the study of science fiction. It was officially formed in December 1929, and an earlier announcement had appeared in the April 1930 *Air Wonder Stories*. "Anyone over sixteen, regardless of race, creed, sex, or color, is eligible to membership, provided he or she is in sympathy with the purpose of the club."[2] The Scienceers proposed to hold regular weekly meetings in New York which thus limited its membership to the New York area. For some years Glasser was an active force in science-fiction fandom, and also sold science fiction and detective stories professionally, before his ignominious departure from the field in 1933 under the shadow of plagiarism.

The second prize was given special attention by Gernsback. This was the suggestion by Conrad H. Ruppert for a Science Fiction Week. Ruppert was writing to all newspapers urging them to print an editorial about science fiction. Gernsback adopted the idea and promoted a Science Fiction Week for the period March 31 to April 7, 1930. During this week readers were urged to promote science fiction in their area. To help them Gernsback offered free stickers to be posted in places of prominence. No doubt a number of fans played their part in this, and there were apparently thousands of requests for stickers, more than Gernsback could cope with, but nothing more was heard about the success or failure of the Science Fiction Week until four years later when Joseph Dockweiler (who became better known as Dirk Wylie) asked in a letter to *Wonder Stories*. The response, probably from Hornig, stated: "Science Fiction Week did not seem to go over so well when we sponsored it in 1930. Why must science-fiction fans set a week aside each year to spread the 'gospel' anyway? The enthusiastic fan will boost it every day in the year, whenever he is given the opportunity."[3]

Perhaps some evidence of the failure of Science Fiction Week came from the lack of response in the letters to *Wonder Stories*, in particular the third and final part of the contest. Gernsback had encouraged fans who had contributed to Science Fiction Week to enter the competition, but there was little evidence of this. The second and third prizes went to Frank B. Eason and Robert Konikow for their activities in the Science Correspondence Club. First prize, interestingly, went to the writer Ralph Milne Farley, which showed that whilst he did not contribute to *Wonder Stories* he did, at least, read it. Farley received first prize for his activities in promoting science fiction amongst such noted personalities as Senator Frederick Gillett and the explorer Admiral Richard Byrd. During Science Fiction Week Farley gave lectures to the local South Milwaukee High and Junior High schools on science fiction.

Regardless of any effect Science Fiction Week might have had, or of Gernsback's promotion of science fiction, it was clear that science-fiction fever was spreading. The magazines' letter columns contained frequent references to new science-fiction clubs, most of them becoming either chapters of the Science Correspondence Club or branches of the Scienceers. There was also a Scientific Fiction Library Association formed in New York City. Since most of these clubs was organized for devotees aged sixteen and over, a Boys' Scientifiction Club was formed in October 1930 to promote scientific interest among boys between the ages of ten and fifteen, to encourage the reading of science fiction and scientific works, and to create a bond of friendship among them. The President of this Club was destined to become the world's most famous science-fiction fan, Forrest J Ackerman. Ackerman's first letter to the magazines had been published in that same first issue of *Science Wonder Quarterly* announcing the "What I Have Done to Spread Science Fiction" competition, and though Ackerman did not feature in the contest, there is no doubt that he has done more to promote science fiction throughout the world than anyone else since. Other members of the Boys' Scientifiction Club were Linus Hogenmiller, the Vice President, and Frank Sipos, the Secretary-Treasurer.

When the announcement of the Club was made in the December 1930 *Wonder Stories*, Ackerman was promptly contacted by Walter Dennis of the Science Correspondence Club seeking an affiliation. The S.C.C. was now becoming truly national, and Dennis worked constantly in the promotion and organization of science-fiction fandom. His role in the creation of fandom has never been properly recognized, but he was the first to organize American fandom on a national scale, indeed on an international scale, with members in Europe, India, Australia, South Africa and New Zealand. In producing the Club's official magazine, called *Comet* for its first issue, dated May 1930, Dennis was also responsible for editing the first science-fiction fanzine. Dennis (1911-) was only active in fandom for the period 1928 to 1934, but it was an intense activity that started a revolution. He collaborated with P. Schuyler Miller on a couple of stories, one of which, "The Duel on the Asteroid" was published in the January 1932 *Wonder Stories* as by P. Schuyler Miller and Dennis McDermott. He has retained an interest in the field, though, ever since. There is also the possibility that Dennis's profile became the model for Superman, but more of that later.

Comet went through a few dull title changes before settling on *Cosmology* under the editorship of Arthur Gowing (until July/August 1931), and then Clifton Amsbury and Aubrey MacDermott until its final, seventeenth issue in 1933. The initial scientific bias of the magazine soon began to shift to discussions about the latest science fiction, with new stories and articles by leading writers such as P. Schuyler Miller, Jack Williamson, and Miles J. Breuer, all of whom had become members of the S.C.C. By January 1931 the Club had metamorphosed into the International Scientific Association and later still the International Scientific Society. It finally ceased in 1933, due primarily to the biting effects of the Depression, which made correspondence clubs an expensive luxury, and strengthened the need for local science-fiction societies. By then the S.C.C., thanks to Walter Dennis, had served its purpose. Science-fiction fandom had found its voice, and that soon became a chorus which has echoed down the decades.

The production of science-fiction fanzines soon followed in the wake of *Comet*. The New York Scienceers produced their official clubzine, *The Planet* under the editorship of Allen Glasser. This lasted for six monthly issues from July to December 1930, and consisted mostly of reviews and analysis of science-fiction stories, books and films. Richard Leary's Bay State Science Club in Boston produced three issues of *The Asteroid* starting in July 1930, and Forrest Ackerman and Jim Nicholson produced four issues of *The Meteor* for the Boys' Scientifiction Club, starting in February 1931.

These early fanzines were all club organs, but it was from them that the opportunity for an independent fan magazine emerged. There was now a recognizable core of active fans, which included Raymond A. Palmer, Mort Weisinger, Julius Schwartz, Allen Glasser, Forrest J Ackerman, and Conrad H. Ruppert. Their efforts would eventually produce the first independent fanzine, *The Time Traveller*, which was issued in January 1932 with Glasser as editor. This and its successors become the first major force in science-fiction fandom and, as we shall see, began to exert its own influence on the future of the field.

Another influence that the voice of science fiction seemed to be exerting was on the movie industry, and the growth in science-fiction films. The development of the cinema has many parallels with that of the growth of science fiction, too many to be adequately discussed here. It was sufficient to show that film makers, in their desire to attract people to the cinema, were always delighted to experiment with special effects and larger-than-life dramas, and science fiction allowed plenty of scope for that. Gernsback had been fascinated by the potential of the cinema for years, and had been regularly reporting on developments in filming in *The Electrical Experimenter* since 1915. The first film which Gernsback actively promoted was Harry Hoyt's *The Lost World* (1925), with its effective use of stop-motion animation for the dinosaurs created by Willis O'Brien. During the twenties the main development of the science-fiction film had been in Europe, with such classics as *Metropolis* (1926) and *Die Frau im Mond* (1929), both directed by Fritz Lang.

The introduction of sound to the movies in 1929 opened up the cinema and one of the consequences was that the first major science-fiction talkie was also a musical, *Just Imagine* (1930). Directed and co-written by David Butler, this was a total Gernsbackian film and might even have been derived from a reading of *Ralph 124C 41+*. A man from 1930 is killed by lightning, but revives in New York in 1980 where everyone is known by numbers, not names. The film concentrates on some of the mechanical marvels of the future, and even involves a flight to Mars, but the plot was thin. When reviewed in *Wonder Stories* it was "cordially recommended," with the hope that "the Fox Company can be induced to try a more serious story in which the more serious and tragic aspects of future existence can be shown."[4]

Fans echoed that view, and hoped that the new media could produce some serious science-fiction films. The first to take up the cudgel was Allen Glasser. His letter in the July 1931 *Wonder Stories* is revealing:

> The indifference of movie makers to science fiction is probably due to a mistaken idea on their part that the public does not care for science fiction. Perhaps if a sufficient number of readers of *Wonder Stories* wrote to various film companies asking for more science-fantasy pictures, their request would be heeded. Some time ago I sent a letter along that line to Carl Laemmie, President of Universal Pictures, suggesting that a good talkie might be made from Mrs. Shelley's "Frankenstein," a widely-known story of the science-fiction type. Now I understand that Universal will

do "Frankenstein" in a few months. Here's hoping it will be followed by more of the same kind.[5]

Had Glasser been the catalyst that got Hollywood interested in science-
fiction films? It is unlikely that Glasser was the sole promoter of *Frankenstein*
as a film. It was picked up by Universal following the success of *Dracula*
(1931) and these two became the cornerstone of the SF-horror films of the
thirties (and for thirty years after). But it may be that Glasser's appeal had
tipped the scales in its favor.

Glasser's promotional activities were soon joined by those of Forrest J
Ackerman, who rapidly became the science-fiction voice of Hollywood.
Ackerman began to feed ideas for films to the film companies, as well as reporting back to the magazines on developments in the industry. "Our
compaign for more science-fiction motion pictures is resulting in huge success," he proudly reported in the November 1931 *Wonder Stories*.[6] That same
issue included a cut-out petition for readers to sign which *Wonder Stories*
would consolidate and send to Hollywood to show the demand for science-fiction films. Many readers responded, though not the tens of thousands Lasser
had expected, but it may have been sufficient to advise Hollywood that there
was a highly receptive market for science fiction. The voice of fandom was
starting to be heard.

24.

PER ARDUA AD ASTRA

Paralleling the emergence of science-fiction fandom was the birth of the American Interplanetary Society, another Gernsback off-shoot.

It was, perhaps, inevitable that the interplanetary story would become the most popular form of science fiction, appealing to the pioneering spirit of so many American immigrants. A large proportion of the writers attracted to science fiction were either direct immigrants or first-generation Americans imbued with the frontier spirit which had driven them to settle in the New World. It was not a coincidence that the space opera was first called "wild-west science," because writers were merely translating that same spirit to the frontiers of space. Some of these writers and readers were determined to put thoughts into actions. The force behind Gernsback's initiative in launching a science-fiction magazine had been to inspire readers into creativity. The quickest and most blatant success came with the American Interplanetary Society.

In finding that the interplanetary story was what most readers wanted, Gernsback was quick to respond, making space stories prominent in his new magazines. Keen to instruct, and not just entertain, Gernsback had translated, for the July, August and September 1929 issues of *Science Wonder Stories*, "The Problems of Space Flying" by Hermann Noordung, which had been published in Berlin the previous year. This was an astonishingly accurate and detailed consideration of the problems associated with man living in space. Noordung's book expanded upon the pioneering work of Hermann Oberth whose *Die Rakete zu den Planetenräumen [The Rocket Into Interplanetary Space]*, published in Munich in 1923, was the first mathematical treatise on space travel. It was Oberth who devised the phrase space station, which was readily adopted by Gernsback's readers.

This was not a new approach by Gernsback. He had long promoted interest in space travel in his technical magazines. As early as the February 1920 *The Electrical Experimenter* he had published an article on "The Goddard Moon Rocket" which looked at the work of the American rocket pioneer Robert H. Goddard (1882-1945). In an editorial in the following issue Gernsback went on record as saying that whilst "theoretically the scheme of firing a rocket to the moon is feasible, practically, we are much afraid it is not."[1] Gernsback explains his unusually negative attitude by describing the problems of calculating the rocket's trajectory and ensuring that it follows that route, considering all the external and unpredictable factors.

It was Oberth's book that considered these problems and provided answers. This gave Gernsback a positive stance to take, and the pages of *Science and Invention* began to include regular articles and news items on advances in rocketry. The most significant was "Can We Fly to the Planets?" (June 1927) an anonymous article translated from a German paper by Dr. Alfred Gradenwitz, which looked at the development of rocketry up to that date and considered all of the possibilities for a cosmic flier. It was illustrated by Ray

Wardell, depicting re-entry to Earth in a capsule by parachute, exactly as happened forty years later.

The concentration of these articles in *Science and Invention* missed the readership most attuned to the wonders of space travel. When Gernsback lost control of the Experimenter Company he had no technical magazine in which to print those which were already being translated, so he switched the studies on rocketry and life in space to his science-fiction magazines. He found a readership ready to act. Once again we have the bankruptcy proceedings to thank, this time for the furtherance of the study of interplanetary travel in America.

Gernsback's magazine contained a wealth of inspirational material. This was most noticeable in *Science Wonder Quarterly*, which published several leading European space novels written in authentic detail, not in the sensationalistic mood of the pulps. The first had been *The Shot into Infinity* by Otto Willi Gail (Fall 1929), published in Germany in 1925. This novel described the step-rocket exactly as it came to be used. It was also a gripping novel of a rescue mission into space to save an earlier astronaut. The mathematics and technology described, based on Oberth's work, were lessons to all readers about the real science of space travel. From this time on the rocket became the only logical method of space travel and all former means, such as gravity-nullifiers or ether ships, faded into obscurity. Gernsback also published Gail's sequel, *The Stone from the Moon* (Spring 1930), two pieces by the purportedly French author R. H. Romans, "The Moon Conquerors" (Winter 1930) and "The War of the Planets" (Summer 1930), plus Otfrid von Hanstein's "Between the Earth and the Moon" (Fall 1930). These later works, whilst not as scientifically accurate as Gail's, were written in an authentic structured style, not flavored with the pulp formula, and constituted a powerful body of work. Some of the credit must go to their translator, Francis M. Currier, who was able to give a passable rendition into English of what was a technological minefield.

Currier also translated for Gernsback a German article by Dr. Theodor Wolff entitled "Can Man Free Himself from Gravity?" (*Science Wonder*, February 1930). Wolff not only discounted all forms of anti-gravity devices but he calculated that man would not be able to escape Earth's gravity, giving an upper limit of four hundred kilometers. (This was an opinion shared by T. O'Conor Sloane at *Amazing* till the end of his life.) Gernsback made the article the basis of a symposium, inviting comments from his Board of Scientific Advisors, as well as Robert H. Goddard. Goddard refuted Wolff's claim, maintaining that by utilizing the step-rocket principle, which he had first suggested in 1916, rockets could attain the velocity necessary to leave Earth. The other contributors agreed, with reservations.

Any publicity by Gernsback was upstaged on March 13, 1930, when it was announced that Clyde Tombaugh of Lowell Observatory had detected a new planet in the solar system, Pluto. There had been speculation about the existence of a trans-Neptunian planet ever since the discovery of Neptune in 1846, but no one had expected it to be so tiny or so remote. Once it was announced it captured the public imagination and Pluto stories began to be submitted to Gernsback's offices. The first two accepted were published almost simultaneously: "The Emperor of the Stars" by Nathan Schachner and Arthur Leo Zagat (*Wonder Stories*, April 1931) and *Into Plutonian Depths* by Stanton

Coblentz (*Wonder Stories Quarterly*, Spring 1931).

With all of this activity and development it was inevitable that something would happen, and in the same way as science-fiction fandom was becoming organized, so were the interplanetarianists. The man who took the initiative was David Lasser. On the evening of Friday, April 4, 1930 he brought together a group of like-minded writers in the apartment of G. Edward Pendray on West 22nd Street, New York City. The others present included Lasser's Associate Editor, C. P. Mason; copy editor, Adolph L. Fierst; writers Laurence Manning, Fletcher Pratt, Nathan Schachner, and William Lemkin, and fan Warren Fitzgerald, who was a member of the Scienceers. Lasser was elected President; Pendray, Vice-President; Mason, Secretary; Manning, Treasurer, and Pratt, Librarian.

As Secretary, Mason wrote a letter, published in the June 1930 *Wonder Stories*, announcing the formation of the Society:

> I wish to inform you of the formation of the first organization in America whose sole purpose is the promotion of Interplanetary travel—I refer to the *American Interplanetary Society*. Quoting its constitution, the objects are: "the promotion and interest in and experimentation toward interplanetary expeditions and travel; the mutual enlightenment of its members bearing on the astronomical, physical and other problems pertinent to man's ultimate conquest of space; the stimulation, by expenditure of funds and otherwise, of American scientists toward a solution of the problems which at present bar the way toward travel among the planets; the collection, correlation and dissemination of facts, information, articles, books, pamphlets and other literature bearing on interplanetary travel and subjects relating thereto; the establishment of a library containing such literature for the information of members, scientists and others to whom the privilege may be granted by the society; the raising of funds for research, experimentation, and such other activities as the Society may from time to time deem necessary or valuable in connection with the general aim of hastening the day when interplanetary travel shall become a reality."[2]

Although the constitution was doubtless a group effort its final wording was probably by Schachner, who was a professional lawyer. Mason's letter went on to emphasize the need for a strong national society for the encouragement of experiments and creating public interest and enthusiasm. Lasser's editorial comment to the letter was:

> We cannot speak too highly of the efforts of this society to popularize and promote the idea of interplanetary traveling. There is no doubt but that the United States at present lags far behind the European nations in its interest and activity. this is chiefly due to the skeptical *[sic]* belief of the American public, and its newspapers, that interplanetary traveling is another wild chimera of someone's disordered imagination.[3]

Lasser was right that America lagged behind Europe. Although America could boast an earlier Rocket Society, created in 1918 by Dr. Matho Mietk-Liuba, its work seemed to be far more theoretical than experimental, and had little impact on the progress of rocketry. In Europe, however, scientists and engineers were far more active. The Austrian chemist Franz von Hoefft had founded the Society for High Altitude Exploration in 1926. In 1928 the Russians, under Professor Nikolai Rynin, organized the Society for Interplanetary Travel. But by far the most influential and important was the German Rocket Society, originally called the Society for Space Ship Travel, founded on July 5, 1927.

The impetus for the German Rocket Society had come from Austrian rocket engineer Max Valier, who contacted Willy Ley with the proposal that a society be formed to raise funds to support the experiments of Hermann Oberth. Ley (1906-1969), who would become one of the driving forces in the space program, and a noted popularizer of science, helped create the Society, which voted in Johannes Winkler as its inaugural President. Hermann Oberth and Wernher von Braun, though not charter members, soon joined. It published a regular monthly newsletter, *Die Rakete*, and, under Ley's editorial hand the Society assembled a volume of articles entitled *Die Moglichkeit der Weltramfahrt* [*The Possibility of Space Travel*] (1928). This in turn attracted the attention of German film-maker Fritz Lang, who had already directed the classic *Metropolis* (1926), and inspired him to work on a new science-fiction film, *The Girl in the Moon* (1929).

Several American enthusiasts joined the German Rocket Society, amongst them R. F. Starzl. It was through him that Willy Ley was introduced to science-fiction magazines and fandom. He sent Ley copies of *Science Wonder Quarterly* and the I.S.A.'s *Cosmology*. The latter printed the first of Ley's contributions to an American magazine. Ley became a regular reader of Gernsback's magazines and had his first letter published in the September 1930 *Wonder Stories*, providing information about the German Rocket Society and his forthcoming talk about science fiction.

The German Rocket Society, thus, had an auspicious start, and gave the new American Interplanetary Society much to strive for. In its first year the Society had limited funds, and did little but publish its regular *Bulletin of the American Interplanetary Society*, launched in June 1930. This was later retitled *Astronautics*, by which it is still known today. Members were active in their writing, lecturing and experimentation. Pendray was the leading experimenter, resigning his Presidency in 1932 to concentrate on practical work. It was not until November 1932 that he had his first test rocket, and not until May 14, 1933 that he demonstrated his first rocket flight, which reached a height of 250 feet.

Lasser was the main writer. Not only did he deliver a variety of lectures, many of which were published in the *Bulletin* and in magazines such as *Nature* and *Scientific American*, but he also wrote the first English-language book on the possibility of interplanetary travel, *The Conquest of Space*. No American publisher would consider the book, so Lasser, Pendray, and Schachner financed the cost of publication themselves, around $12,000. It was published under the imprint of Penguin Press in September 1931, and distributed by Gernsback's Popular Book Corporation. It was dedicated to Max Valier, "the First to Give His life For the Conquest of Space." Valier had been killed on May 17, 1930 in an explosion while testing liquid oxygen as a rocket propellant. Lasser had reprinted Valier's short story, "A Daring Trip to Mars," in the July 1931 *Wonder Stories*. He might have chosen a better phrasing of words when referring to Valier's death by explosion as "a great blow to the rocket pioneers"!

As managing editor of *Wonder Stories* and *Wonder Stories Quarterly*, Lasser was in an ideal role to help promote interest in space travel. The *Quarterly* took on a policy of publishing predominantly interplanetary stories, declaring so on the cover. In the Spring 1931 issue Lasser launched an "Interplanetary Plot Contest." The idea was for readers to submit the plot for a story which would be given to a writer to develop. Seven prizes were on offer, totalling $110 in all, with a first of $50. The winners were announced in the Summer 1931 issue, published on July 1, from several thousand submissions. All of the winners had good ideas. The first prize went to William Thurmond of Victoria, Texas, who conceived the idea of a *Marie Celeste* in space. The idea was passed to Ray Cummings, who wrote "The Derelict of Space" (Fall 1931). The second prize, which went to E. M. Johnston of Collingwood, Ontario, resulted in "The Planet Entity" by Clark Ashton Smith (Fall 1931). The outline was originally called "The Martian." Smith received the idea on July 15 with the request from Lasser that he submit a story of around 15,000 words by the end of the month. That did not give Smith much time. He remarked on it in a letter to H. P. Lovecraft. "The plot . . . was pretty good, so the job wasn't so disagreeable as it sounds. I had to write and retype the whole yarn—about 16,000 words—in a little more than a week, so that it could reach N.Y. by the end of July. I hope it will pass muster—it ought to be a pretty fair scientifictional opus."[4]

Only two of the contest winners are remembered today. The third prize went to Allen Glasser for an idea developed into "The Martian" by A. Rowley Hilliard (Winter 1932). Moskowitz later reported that the idea had been suggested by Mortimer Weisinger and thus stolen by Glasser. It was the first of a series of incidents that led to fandom's ostracism of Glasser, who was one of its founding fathers.

The seventh prize of only $2.50, went to John B. Michel of Brooklyn for an idea worked up by Raymond Z. Gallun as "The Menace from Mercury" (Summer 1932). Michel (1917-1968) was only fourteen when he submitted his entry, and it would be a few more years before he would emerge with his fellow fans in opposition to Gernsback's Science Fiction League.

The plot contest was deemed a success and Lasser made it a regular feature, with a $10 prize for the best plot idea submitted each quarter. Only three further winners were announced, though, and only one of those, Edward Morris, had his idea published.

1930 was a significant year in the history and development of science fiction. Firstly it saw a major growth in the popularity of the field with the success of *Astounding Stories* bringing with it a consequential degeneration of quality in the fiction. Secondly it saw the birth of science-fiction fanzines with the consolidation of fandom. Thirdly it saw an active involvement in the aggrandizement of science-fiction movies. And fourthly it saw the creation of the

American Interplanetary Society as a focal point for the promotion of rocket development and space exploration. These four factors coming together in one year are not a coincidence, but a natural consequence of Gernsback's actions in developing the field of scientific fiction. They may have happened of their own accord at different times in other ways had Gernsback not taken his initiative, but it is unlikely they would have happened so soon or so positively.

Moreover, if the Depression started by the stock-market crash of 1929, had not begun to make its impact on the American economy by 1931, there is little doubt that even greater glories would have happened. As it is the future of science fiction now entered the balance, and the scales had no favorites.

25.

WONDER ANEW

Despite the Depression, Gernsback had continued to expand his publishing empire during 1930. The merger of *Air Wonder* with *Science Wonder* and the sale of *Amazing Detective Tales* were inevitable transactions as Gernsback dewrinkled his operations. The same kind of changes were going on in his technical publications. *Radio Craft* and the new *Short-Wave Craft*, launched in the summer of 1930, prospered but *Aviation Mechanics* was suspended after its issue for July/August 1931. In its place came *Television News* with a first issue dated March/April 1931, published on February 15.

Television News was a return to the Gernsback of old. Whereas *Radio Craft* and *Everyday Mechanics* had been aimed at the craftsman and operative, *Television News* turned its attention back to the experimenter. Gernsback urged the experimenter to dabble in the potential of television, just as he had in respect of radio in the days of *Modern Electrics* and *The Electrical Experimenter*. Some of the pioneer verve returned to Gernsback's editorials.

There is a possibility that, having launched his new science-fiction magazines, and finding them selling respectably, Gernsback's interests returned to his first love of experimentation. With radio being fully operational and commercialized by 1930, his attention naturally switched to television. He had been robbed of his radio and television station in 1929, and though there was no sign that he was planning to set up another, it did not stop him experimenting.

The bankruptcy proceedings had not made Gernsback change his ways. He continued to live richly, and indulge in his scientific delights. For instance, in his first editorial for *Television News*, called "The Television Art," Gernsback relates how he sat in his apartment in January 1931 with not one, but three television receivers. These may have been donated by a supplier for promotion in *Television News*, but they may have been an example of his profligacy.

Gernsback now had four publishing companies. The parent was Gernsback Publications, the holding company with no direct magazines of its own. The Stellar Publishing Corporation issued *Wonder Stories* and *Wonder Stories Quarterly*, a total of sixteen issues a year. The Techni-Craft Publishing Corporation issued *Radio-Craft*, with twelve issues a year. The Popular Book Corporation published the two bi-monthlies, *Television News* and *Short-Wave Craft*, a further twelve issues a year. *Everyday Mechanics* was published by its own imprint in Chicago, as a separate operation.

Gernsback was assisted on most of his technical magazines by H. Winfield Secor, who had returned to Gernsback's employ in September 1930, when the Experimenter Publishing Company was finally dissolved and a new company, Radio-Science Publications, established. Both *Science and Invention* and *Amazing Stories* were now published under that imprint with Sloane continuing to edit *Amazing* and Joseph H. Kraus editing *Science and Invention*. Radio-Science was, at that time, still in the ownership of B. A.

Mackinnon and H. K. Fly, but they sold out early in 1931 to W. Z. Shafer, who took over the company. He re-established it in August 1931 as Teck Publications, a subsidiary of Macfadden Publications. At that point there was a shake-up in the company. *Your Body*, a magazine which Gernsback had launched in 1928, was discontinued. This should have been no surprise, because *Your Body* had been a direct rival to Macfadden's *Physical Culture*. *Science and Invention* was sold to the Chicago publisher of *Popular Mechanics* and merged with that magazine. Teck now published only *Amazing Stories* and *Radio News*, out of Gernsback's original magazines, the latter being their main money spinner. They also published two other genre pulps, *Complete Detective Novel Magazine* and *Wild West Stories*.

It is worth remembering that these events took place in the summer of 1931, culminating in the take-over of *Amazing* by Bernarr Macfadden with the Teck Publishing Company in August of that year. It was also that summer, on August 19 to be precise, that a letter went out from the Stellar Publishing Company, over David Lasser's name, stating the following:

> It is with a great deal of regret that we inform you that WONDER STORIES will cease publication with its October issue. Financial conditions have compelled us to discontinue the magazine. We hope to put out another science-fiction magazine next Spring, at which time further information will be sent to all our former readers.[1]

Gernsback was noted for acting on impulse, and this may have been a sudden decision on that day to cut his losses in the light of some financial difficulties. However, the letter is odd in that it is only the monthly that is referred to, not the *Quarterly*, and it is more likely that the *Quarterly* would have been the first to be discontinued. Moreover when the October 1931 issue did appear, far from there being any announcement of its demise, the editorial was given over to an announcement of its expansion! Gernsback promised that the next issue would revert to the former large size, in response to requests from many readers who had "argued that a magazine of such educational value as ours should not be placed on a par with the pulp magazines of a more sensational type."

The October issue was published on September 3, 1931, just two weeks after Gernsback's notice went out. Since the final proofs for that issue would have been returned to the printer at least ten days earlier, or around August 24, it means that Gernsback had changed his mind from discontinuing *Wonder Stories* within a week.

There is no doubt that Gernsback had started to experience financial problems with his magazines during the summer of 1931, for a number of authors were becoming incensed at their delayed payments. But he must also have made a deal which ensured him an injection of funds. He clearly made some financial recovery. There are clues in several letters issued in early September. One, a *pro forma*, endeavoring to establish contracts with ten writers for the exclusive use of their work on a regular payment basis, was mailed on September 5. On September 8, a letter to Lloyd Eshbach in relation to payment for stories, commented that "We are now working under a much better plan, and you will get your money much quicker than ever before." Gernsback was making a credible effort to pay his authors. His cash flow had improved by September and he was endeavoring to catch up on payments. Jack Williamson, whose "Through the Purple Cloud" had been published in the May 1931 *Wonder Stories*, was paid $40 on September 14. The $40 was a straight half-cent a word for this 8,000 word story. The same letter containing the check promised that Williamson's "Twelve Hours to Live," published in the August issue, would be paid in the following week, although it was eventually paid on October 21. On October 13, Neil R. Jones was paid $60 for "The Asteroid of Death," which had been published just six weeks earlier in the Fall 1931 *Quarterly*. That same author's "Spacewrecked on Venus" in the Winter 1932 *Quarterly* was paid for on February 12, again just six weeks later.

Where had Gernsback's money come from? My own belief is that it was linked with a new distribution deal arranged through Gernsback's printer Kable. With *Science and Invention* no longer on the scene, Gernsback had an opportunity to plug that gap and launch his own magazine in the same mould. He thus revamped *Everyday Mechanics* and relaunched it as *Everyday Science and Mechanics* in October 1931. For this purpose Gernsback had established a new company, the Publishing Company of America at 100 Park Place, New York, in offices adjacent to Stellar Publishing. The success of the old *Science and Invention* under Gernsback had been well known, and a distributor and advertisers would feel secure in investing in such a venture.

Moreover, Gernsback was able to point at the success of science fiction, then riding high. Not only were *Astounding*, *Amazing*, and *Wonder Stories* all measurably successful, other publishers were entering the field. Harold Hersey had established his own Good Story Magazine Company and one of his new titles, formerly announced as *Astonishing Stories*, was *Miracle Science and Fantasy Stories*. It was as much a hybrid as its title suggested. It contained fiction that echoed both the super-science of *Astounding* and the fantastic adventure of *Argosy*. There was no attempt at any rationalistic science. It was all intended as good honest fun. *Miracle* only saw two issues, dated April-May and June-July 1931. Its disappearance was not because it sold poorly, or because of the Depression. According to Hersey it was the illness of its editor and artist, Elliott Dold[2], which caused the magazine to be set aside, and it was never revived. Knowing Hersey's fortunes with his own publications, its life would have been short-lived anyway. Its existence, though only a blip on the world-line of science fiction, nevertheless attests to the popularity and commercial viability of the field in 1931.

There were other developments. William Clayton launched *Strange Tales* as a companion to *Astounding Stories* in August 1931, with the first issue dated September. It was published bi-monthly, and the was closest rival that *Weird Tales* had for off-trail stories. It secured some fine stories, which with Wesso's striking covers, made it an attractive and collectible magazine, but it published little in the way of science fiction. The closest was Jack Williamson's tale of trans-dimensional invasion, "Wolves of Darkness" (January 1932). Also in the summer of 1931 the Shade Publishing Company in Philadelphia launched an occult-adventure magazine, *Mind Magic*. This was some way distant from Gernsback's realm of science fiction, but was further proof that the public were ready for off-trail and bizarre stories, and in distributors' and advertisers' minds, it was all one and the same thing—"crazy stuff."

Gernsback would have been able to point to all of this as grounds for the advantage of investing in the profitable fields of science fiction and science promotion. Kable would have known of Gernsback's past dealings and reputation and no doubt tied Gernsback to a tight contract ensuring that the various parties concerned first call on the finances. Gernsback would have been happy with that deal. Provided that his main creditors were paid, he would worry about the rest when the time came.

But the extent to which Gernsback ever intended to cease publication of *Wonder Stories* is still far from clear. On September 28, 1931, he wrote a personal letter to Forrest Ackerman on his own letterhead, not company paper. Within this long letter, Gernsback asked a favor of Ackerman:

> For some time, there has been a low-down snake-in-the-grass who, for some reasons of his own, has tried to harm us by writing letters, one of which you got, that WONDER STORIES is being discontinued. The favor I am asking you is to send me that letter which, with a number of others that this party wrote, is going to be used in some Court proceedings. Of course, I know that you don't believe these rumors, and when you see the November issue which is out next week, you will know what a damnable lie it was.

Gernsback went on to say that *Wonder Stories* is "financially in better shape today than any of my other magazines ever were before."

What do we make of this? Had someone played a trick on Gernsback, or was Gernsback regretting his action and trying to cover it up? The only known copy of Gernsback's notice was in the possession of Sam Moskowitz. It is a carbon copy, not an original, which in itself is unusual. Moskowitz's own researches have failed to find any further evidence that Gernsback had planned to discontinue the magazine. Indeed, Gernsback himself, for whom Moskowitz worked in 1953, had no recollection of it. If someone had played a trick, was it connected to the final Macfadden takeover of *Amazing*, or was that coincidental? I do not know if any court proceedings were taken, or against whom. Gernsback's letter to Ackerman is ambiguous as to whether or not he knew the individual involved. Whoever it was had to have access both to Stellar's letterheads and the subscription list. There is also the question as to whether letters had gone to subscribers to Gernsback's other magazines, for it is more likely that a third party may have had a grudge against Gernsback personally, or one of his leading magazines, than against *Wonder Stories* alone. Over the years memories have faded and papers destroyed, and the mystery may never be fully resolved. Whatever the circumstances, *Wonder Stories* did not die with the October 1931 issue. It was born anew.

The November 1931 issue was imposing and delivered what it promised. Paul's cover portrayed the crystalline menace of "Tetrahedra of Space" by P. Schuyler Miller. Inside readers discovered that the magazine was now printed on good quality stock, not pulp paper. This, combined with the larger format and trimmed edges, raised *Wonder* out of the pulp category into that of the quality magazine. It contained marginally more advertising, not sufficient to support the magazine, but enough to show that advertisers were taking interest.

More importantly, the quality of the fiction was high. In addition to Miller's story was the popular sequel "Beyond the Singing Flame" by Clark Ashton Smith, and "The Superman of Dr. Jukes" by Francis Flagg. (The latter, incidentally, had been entitled "Man Plus" by Flagg, forty years before Frederik Pohl used the title. It had been changed, for no good reason, by Lasser.) Nowhere was there any hint of space opera. The final episode of Nathan Schachner and Arthur Leo Zagat's serial, *Exiles of the Moon*, was as much a political statement as an interplanetary adventure, showing the plight of the Workers against the Aristocracy.

There was also promise of much to come. In a half-page spread Gernsback announced upcoming stories. Amongst them was a new serial, *The Time Stream* by John Taine. Taine was the pseudonym of noted mathematician and author Eric Temple Bell. Bell (1883-1960) was Scottish by birth, but had emigrated to the United States in 1902, where he eventually became Professor of Mathematics at the California Institute of Technology in 1927. He had been writing scientific and fantastic adventures since the publication of *The Purple Sapphire* by Dutton in 1924. Taine's name was linked with quality, since he had always been published in hardcover and was not a regular contributor to the pulps. Gernsback had probably long sought to publish Taine, and must have been chagrined when he lost Taine's first work for the magazines, *White Lily*, to the Winter 1930 *Amazing Stories Quarterly*, with another novel, *Seeds of Life* in the Fall 1931 *Quarterly*. *The Time Stream*, which was serialized in the December 1931 to March 1932 *Wonder Stories*, has long been considered Taine's best novel. It is far from sensationalistic, and is one of the first novels to consider the mathematical implications of time.

The December issue also contained the first story by Clifford D. Simak, "The World of the Red Sun." Simak would later become one of the prime movers in the reshaping of science fiction under John W. Campbell, Jr. The issue also marked the fictional debuts of Arthur K. Barnes and Robert Arthur. Lasser's search for new talent was starting to bear fruit.

Another bold promise was that Frank R. Paul would now be the exclusive artist in *Wonder Stories*. Paul was still held in much esteem by science-fiction fans for the imaginative qualities of his work.

There was no doubt that Gernsback was making *Wonder Stories* the premier science-fiction magazine. With the rebirth of *Everyday Mechanics* as *Everyday Science and Mechanics* Gernsback had a solid double bill, just as he had once had with *Amazing* and *Science and Invention*. The word "*Everyday*" in the title was played down so that from a distance it read simply *Science and Mechanics* and could easily have been mistaken for the old title. Many of the departments from *Science and Invention* reappeared, along with Gernsback's prophetic articles. The December issue, for instance, had *three*: "Super-Cities 50 Years Hence," "The Glass Skyscraper," and "The Solar Space Mirror—a Titanic Peace Weapon." The first three issues were edited by Clyde Fitch, but the fourth brought back Joseph H. Kraus, who remained editor thereafter. With Kraus and Secor back in the camp, it was just like old times. Gernsback was ready to fight again.

26.

ROMANTICISM VERSUS REALISM

By 1932 many science-fiction fans were growing tired of action-packed super-science. Although it continued with the Hawk Carse stories in *Astounding* and occasionally erupted elsewhere, science fiction was now taking stock of itself, and writers were attempting something new. Interestingly *Astounding* had dropped the *"of Super-Science"* subtitle with the February 1931 issue, though it would briefly restore it with the January 1933 issue.

The driving force for the new approach in science fiction was David Lasser. His long letter of May 11, 1931, quoted in chapter 22, had pushed for realism in science fiction, with greater emphasis on the human aspects of scientific development. One particular phrase in his letter had sought to close the door on the space opera epic: "The modern science story should not try to be a world-sweeping epic. It should rather try to portray intensively some particular phase of our future civilization." The reaction to realism was already becoming apparent in *Wonder Stories* which had not succumbed to the space opera epic on the scale of the other magazines. For example, take reader Floyd Swiggett's, views on the January 1931 issue:

> The quality of your stories maintains a high level, and I particularly approve of "The Outpost on the Moon." "The Soulless Entity," besides introducing an idea which I believe is new, was well written and is that kind of story that is not soon forgotten. However, "The Satellite of Doom" takes the prize in the last issue, largely because of the realistic way in which his characters talk and act."[1]

Realism and characterization are what readers wanted. They also wanted their imaginations stretched and their sense of wonder appeased, but it had to be in a realistic framework. There was one immediate problem. Introducing the element of human drama on an individual basis brought with it the matter of love and romance, and worse still, sex! Right from the birth of *Amazing Stories*, readers had urged that the science fiction be kept clean, without descending into sexual titillation. Others wanted action and adventure, and did not want it slowed down by love interest.

By 1931 readers were clearly split on the issue. In the February 1931 issue, Donald Hendrixson of Cincinnatti, Ohio raised the matter of scientific sexual education and asked why science-fiction writers did not address this issue. "Sexual education without a sensual influence is what is needed." The editorial response wholly concurred, pointing to the Russian approach in making divorce easier, to allow individuals to select their right mates, resolve any sexual problems "and then devote their energies to more important matters." Lasser made the point that our western world was unhealthily obsessed with sex, due to our own repression and inhibition, and that the sooner this repression was released and overcome the better. "However," he added, "it is quite difficult to put much emphasis on the deeper relations between the sexes in a science-fiction story. The story then becomes too psychological."[2]

This brought forth a range of responses not least a long and considered one from the always erudite and often controversial Victor Endersby. He concluded his letter by saying:

> Scientific fiction has its faults and much of it is as yet painfully crude, but it remains almost the last island of decency in the midst of the sewer literature of today. If you can do nothing else than keep it so, you will have rendered a service to the race by taking men's minds off their curse and obsession. Love stories by all means, where the author has sufficient talent to blend their love motive with the scientific theme, artistically and homogenously. But love is not lust and cannot exist in the unrestrained presence of the latter, even though in reading most contemporary literature, it is sadly evident that the words are synonymous to the authors.[3]

Needless to say, it was a subject that had to be handled carefully, and the howls of protest were predictable following publication in the Winter 1931 *Wonder Stories Quarterly* of "The Scarlet Planet" by Don Mark Lemon. In this novel, intended as a satirical spoof on society, spacemen land on a planet inhabited by thousands of scantily clad girls, some of whom are vampires and were-snakes. The men, needless to say, enjoy themselves. Many readers found the whole idea disgusting and it was clear that sex was best treated with caution at this stage in science fiction's development. One writer, Thomas S. Gardner, succeeded in satirising the subject in what is a rather poignant story, "The Last Woman" (April 1932). Here we find that men have evolved beyond the need to breed and that the last surviving woman is a museum exhibit. The one man who falls in love with her is regarded as a throwback, an atavist, and the two are destroyed.

The idea of female-dominated utopias also emerged under Lasser's editorship. Lasser's growing socialist beliefs became evident in the type of fiction he was selecting, and he willingly explored not just the equality of women, but their supremacy. Lilith Lorraine made her magazine debut with the exploration of a female-dominated society, "Into the 28th Century" (*Science Wonder Quarterly*, Winter 1930). The story is little more than a sociological history of eight centuries since the twentieth, showing how women came to exert a greater hold over world power. Once in control, they established a society of euality and chivalry. Another lady writer, M. F. Rupert, contributed a similar story, "Via the Hewitt Ray" (*Science Wonder Quarterly*, Spring 1930), where a daughter, seeking her lost inventor-father, finds a matriarchial fourth-dimensional world. Here the women have slaughtered all of the men save a few of high intelligence for breeding purposes, and some handsome men for sexual gratification.

Not only women writers explored matriarchal worlds. Richard Vaughan, in "The Woman from Space" (*Wonder Stories Quarterly*, Spring 1932), considered a planet where the men had all but destroyed themselves in an unrelenting world war. The women become super-scientists and establish a utopia on their world. They show concern for their neighboring planets and, when they plan to shift their planet from the dark cold wastes of the outer solar system to the relative warmth of the asteroid belt, they first seek contact with the other planets to ensure their safety.

Another subject for caution was religion. Gernsback and Lasser were sufficiently enlightened to publish anything that inspired and stimulated thought and creativity, but with religion they had to tread even more carefully than with sex. Religious fundamentalists were strong in their views and this influenced the actions of printers, distributors and advertisers. The only advice Gernsback had ever heeded from his distributors was to steer clear of religious issues. Nevertheless, he believed his readers would have mature scientific minds not cluttered with religious hang-ups. He had long supported the theory of evolution, even though this was occasionally challenged by his readers. A long debate started in the letter columns when reader Curtis Taylor of Utica, N.Y., took issue over Ray Myers's story "Into the Subconscious" (*Science Wonder*, October 1929) where, through racial memory, a man recalls his existences as more primitive life forms. Taylor was incensed that the Biblical story of creation should be treated as a myth. "Many stories like this and I am sure you will be deserted by a large circle of readers." Lasser stood his ground. He began a lengthy response in which he supported evolution with the comment, "It does not come within the province of *Science Wonder Stories* to argue either for or against religious issues in any phase. But when it comes to evolution, this is a question of science and, as such, it becomes our duty to discuss it in the light of the latest knowledge." He then proceeded to soundly denounce anti-evolutionists, concluding with ". . . the time will come when the anti-evolutionist will be relegated to the class of those individuals who still insist that the earth stands still and that the sun revolves around it."[4]

Several readers protested about Taylor's beliefs, not least Allen Glasser, who went beyond the issue of evolution, calling the Bible ". . . no more sacred than a cook-book, and far less useful. It is full of myths and contradictions—not to mention obscenities. Its sole value is to reveal the ignorance of its writers—and to provide a living for the clergy. Otherwise it's a dead loss."[5] Lasser was not happy with emotional and unreasoned attacks on the Bible.

> The Bible is not by any means a dead loss. The King James version is one of the greatest pieces of English literature, and it has been the model for many of our greatest prose writers. While we do not accept the statements in the Book of Genesis, we prize the Bible for its great literary value and for the profound psychological truth of many of its assertions. It happens far too often in our present era of religious skepticism *[sic]* that we are apt to sweep aside everything relating to the past and to look upon only what is new, modern and scientifically proved as being of any value. Therefore it has become quite fashionable to speak contemptuously of the Bible. While most scientists assert that the Bible is not a scientific textbook of geology or biological evolution—those who are broadminded and free from puritanship recognized that it is a monumental work of inestimable moral, historical and literary value.[6]

Some readers who took science fiction to heart soon found themselves taking on new forms of religious thought. Edsel Newton, who would write seven stories for Gernsback during this period, had first been disgusted by science fiction but it then took on a fatal attraction. Writing in the December 1930 *Wonder Stories*, Newton made the point that, "The more I read such stories . . . the more I realize that while we read to be entertained we might also read to think, and to dream and to create. Personally, I have built up a religious belief—or rather I have approached a sort of probability—by reading science fiction and delving into the mysteries of science through as many of its branches as time will permit."[7] Lasser agreed strongly. "By understanding the physical universe," he commented, "one can really find a meaning in it and from that meaning he can find a religion."

This brought in another wave of letters including one from an ordained minister, Roy T. Johnson, of Harviell, Missouri.

> Religion has dreamed of a Utopia where there is no evil, no criminals and all is good and holy. It is only through science that this can come about. Religion has dreamed of the resurrection of the dead, but science through the use of adrenalin has actually brought dead persons back to life. True they were only dead a few minutes, but it is a good beginning.[8]

Johnson felt that there was no conflict between science and religion and that the one would always benefit the other. However, George R. Kirkpatrick of Piermont, New York, was not so sure. He believed that if science could establish that there was no God, then religion would crumble.

Occasional semi-religious stories appeared in the magazines. "The Voice in the Void" by Clifford D. Simak (*Wonder Stories Quarterly*, Spring 1932), for instance, challenged basic concepts with its discovery of a sacred tomb on Mars said to contain the remains of the Messiah. It transpires the bones were those of an early explorer from Earth. This was soon followed by "The Venus Adventure" by John Beynon Harris (*Wonder Stories*, May 1932), which showed how a space pioneer with puritanical religious beliefs had a degenerative affect upon the previously pure natives of Venus. That these two stories were published in 1932 and by a new generation of writers is in itself revealing, and part proof that the old school of super science was being swept away. Lasser's introductory blurb to Harris's novelette hammers home the point:

> Mr. Harris, whose "Worlds to Barter" provoked such a storm of controversy, gives us now what he calls "realism in interplanetary travel." This is no ordinary interplanetary story; it is a human and gripping adventure of explorations into a new world with a surprising series of developments.[9]

Sex, socialism, and religion aside, it was interplanetary realism that Lasser was striving for, and which was emerging in *Wonder Stories* and the *Quarterly* more noticeably than in any other publication. Instead of stories featuring the adventures of daring space heroes intent on obliterating alien races in their pursuit of fame and fortune, writers began to consider what the effect would be upon the explorers themselves as they faced new worlds and environments. In this area a handful of writers made giant strides in 1932.

There had already been signs in 1931. "The Conquest of Gola" (*Wonder Stories*, April 1931) by Leslie F. Stone looked at the invasion of another planet from the viewpoint of the natives and told how they repulsed the invaders by simple and effective means. "The Red Spot of Jupiter" (July 1931) is an interesting hybrid between space opera and the emerging realism. It was written by P. Schuyler Miller with some assistance from Walter L. Dennis and published under the alias Dennis McDermott. It has as its lead protagonist not a hero but a devious villain called Gulliver, with no redeeming qualities who is exiled by the Martians on Jupiter. By his own strength and determination he overcomes the perils of Jupiter and escapes.

Miller and Dennis, with the encouragement of Lasser, saw the possibilities of developing the character of Gulliver, and in the next in the series, "The Duel on the Asteroid" (January 1932) there is an effort to humanize him. The plot is still basic space opera—straightforward cops-and-robbers in space—but Miller and Dennis were working at making the characters develop the plot. Miller was working on the third story in the series, "The Hell Moon," and Dennis on the fourth, "The Metal-Men of Mercury," but neither were completed. If they had been, the series may have developed into something memorable.

Miller did, however, continue to shape his form of science fiction. He made a profound statement in "The Forgotten Man of Space" (*Wonder Stories*, May 1933) about an explorer, Cramer, who survives on Mars for twenty Earth years, befriending the local rabbit-like inhabitants and living amongst them. When more Earthmen come to exploit the rich minerals, Cramer kills himself and them rather than endanger his alien friends. It was a remarkable story of human sacrifice and, to my mind, more important than Miller's "The Titan" which, hitherto, has been held up as an example of a forward-thinking story, too advanced for the magazines of the day. To be sure "The Titan," which was written during 1932, considered an advanced but decadent Martian civilization from the viewpoint of the Martians. It was rejected by the magazines apparently because of passages about the sexual relations between the female aristocracy and the male worker-slaves.

We have already seen how Edmond Hamilton was adapting his fiction to take account of Lasser's new demands. He had heeded Gernsback's editorial dicta with stories like "The Man Who Saw the Future" (in *Amazing Stories*) and "The Man Who Evolved," but his first significant change came with "A Conquest of Two Worlds" (*Wonder Stories*, February 1932). Lasser had previously rejected this story, then titled "An Interplanetary Renegade" and asked for revisions, putting in more realism and strengthening the characters. Hamilton complied. The theme was again one of greed. "Suppose," Lasser poses in his blurb, "the selfish exploitation of other planets was being accomplished by greedy exploiters, and to conquer those worlds meant the decimation of its harmless population, would you aid in that process?"[10] Hamilton developed exactly the same theme Miller later used. In his story, Mart Halkett becomes so disgusted at man's thoughtless killing of the friendly Jovians that he rebels against man. "I've come to love these Jovians," Halkett explains, "so mild and child-like, so trustful to anyone friendly. It just seemed that somebody ought to stand up for them." Lasser so liked the story that he suggested a sequel showing the truth of Halkett's prediction that Mars and Jupiter would be overrun by greedy exploiters. Hamilton sent back a proposal which Lasser thought better than the original. Lasser urged for Hamilton to develop the parallels in man's original corruption of the American Indian by European settlers. Hamilton hesitated to write the story because of a delay in payments for earlier stories and in the end it was never completed.

Some authors were slow in adapting. Neil R. Jones, for instance, continued to submit stories of space piracy and planetary invasion. In rejecting "Swordsmen of Saturn," in a letter dated February 24, 1932, Lasser remarked: "We find that our readers are becoming tired of merely fantastic adventures and bloodshed and are insisting that our stories be more reasonable and more plausible." In fact Jones never sold another story to Gernsback's magazines, despite many attempts.

Others were more ready to adapt. Leslie F. Stone returned with another realistic story, questioning the need for man to explore other worlds. In "The Hell Planet" (June 1932) her explorers venture to the planet Vulcan, which was at one time believed to circle the sun within the orbit of Mercury. Miss Stone portrays man's greed and desire to explore and exploit as symptoms of man as victim, and that the lure of exploration is no different than pigs being led to slaughter. Henrik Dahl Juve took the same approach in what would be his last story, "In Martian Depths" (September 1932) where pioneers on Mars find the planet unfriendly and hostile, and several explorers die before they manage to leave.

This theme was developed further by Laurence Manning. In "The Voyage of the *Asteroid*" (*Wonder Stories Quarterly*, Summer 1932) he depicted a realistic (for the period) expedition to Venus. In his blurb, David Lasser hammered home the point of realism versus romanticism: ". . . assuming it were possible to go to Venus or Mars, what could one do there? Would there be the Venusian or Martian princess just waiting to marry our hero and bestow unlimited wealth upon him, or might our explorers meet dangers, terrors, discomforts so great that all attempts at exploration would completely fail and our explorers would be glad to get back to earth with their skins?"[11] In the sequel, "The Wreck of the *Asteroid*" (*Wonder Stories*, December 1932-February 1933), the adventure becomes even more grim. On an expedition to Mars, the *Asteroid* crashes and the crew have to fight for their survival in a hostile environment.

One other writer was doing his part to portray the realistic probabilities of space exploration. Frank K. Kelly was only sixteen when he had sold his first story, "The Light Bender," to David Lasser for the June 1931 *Wonder Stories*. His early stories show his lack of developed writing skills, but he soon made up for this in the depth of his imagination in portraying the bleakness of space. In each successive story, starting with "Exiles of Mars" (Summer 1932), through "The Crisis with Mars" (Fall 1932) to "The Moon Tragedy" (October 1933), Kelly emphasized the perils of exploration and the unknown. Throughout this phase he had the full encouragement of David Lasser who had found in Kelly a writer of emerging talent which he could mould and develop. If Kelly had not been lured into other fields of endeavor, but had stayed in science fiction, he would have been ideal for the world John W. Campbell was trying to create, and would probably have become one of the major names in science fiction.

1932 was a key transitional year in science fiction. The challenges Lasser and Gernsback were posing their authors were having their effect on the field. Even *Astounding* sat up and took notice. Though Harry Bates was still a believer in pulp action, he realized that the stories needed more realism and genuine science. A letter to that effect, though without going over the top, went from Bates to several writers in August 1932. "Henceforth two-thirds of the material we buy for ASTOUNDING STORIES will have emphasis equally on story values and scientific content. The remaining third will be the sort of stories we have used in the past."

For good, realistic science fiction, *Wonder Stories* led the field in 1932. Not all readers agreed, because not all readers were ready to accept the new approach. Julius Schwartz, one of the field's leading fans, wrote a long rebuking letter to *Wonder Stories*, which was published in the April 1933 issue. He accused the editors of buying stories from inexperienced authors on the cheap rather than paying higher rates to the bigger named authors of the past. "I'd rather not see a science-fiction magazine on the market if it's continually going to give us the paltry, puerile and putrid stuff that it is publishing today," Schwartz wrote. "Where are your ace authors of former years: Dr. David H. Keller, Harl Vincent, Bob Olsen, Miles J. Breuer, Gawain Edwards and some of the others?"[12] Lasser's response was that many of the leading authors had run out of ideas and were unable to adapt to the new developments in science fiction and ended up writing trash. "The thing to do is to help develop the younger men who have talent and originality."

That is exactly what Lasser was doing. However, Lasser was so keen to develop science fiction that he sometimes went too far in his dealings with writers, just as Campbell would six years later. In fact he alienated two of the magazine's most popular writers: David H. Keller and Clark Ashton Smith. With Keller, Lasser developed the concept of "The Time Projector," a machine that could extrapolate the future from existing known facts. He fed the idea plus three thousand words of notes to Keller, who wrote the novel, but Lasser, unsatisfied with the result, drastically revised it for publication in the July and August 1931 *Wonder Stories*. "I did not recognize the poor thing," Keller remarked in an interview two years later. "Lasser had amputated some of my best chapters. That is never going to happen to any more of my brain children."[13] As for Smith, he had submitted the manuscript of "The Dweller in the Gulf" to Lasser only to have it returned for revisions, bringing in more "scientific motivation." The story was basically an interplanetary horror tale, and Smith was not pleased at having to introduce a scientific rationale. But he complied and the story was accepted. When it was published, it had not only been retitled as "The Dweller in Martian Depths" (*Wonder Stories*, March 1933), but the gruesome ending had been toned down by Lasser, apparently at Gernsback's request. As far as Smith was concerned the main element in the story, "the atmosphere of mystery and horror," had been ruined. "It is very doubtful if I shall publish anything more in *Wonder Stories*," Smith remarked in a letter to Robert H. Barlow, in February 1933, and he submitted nothing more, though two earlier manuscripts were subsequently published.

Lasser also frustrated the developing writer Raymond Z. Gallun. Gallun had submitted the manuscript for the story "The Revolt of the Star Men" which portrayed a unique form of interstellar life based, not on carbon, but a radioactive element at that time unknown but high in the periodic table. These life-forms created their own inner heat, and did not need food or oxygen for their survival. As a means of transport, these creatures had harnessed another life-form in the shape of a flat disc with claws at the edges and a mouth for eating minerals on the underside. These creatures also had a radioactive base and were able to use this energy as a propulsion force. Whilst Lasser was able to accept the initial premise, either he, or Gernsback, objected to the disc-shaped life-forms and they were converted to machines, which ruined the basic concept of the story, as the Star Men were supposed to be a primitive life-form with no technology capable of manufacturing such discs! Gallun was annoyed. "The way I figured it," he later rationalized, "Gernsback was so hung up on the great inventive wizardry of the human race that he couldn't realize that Nature is a superior competitor to Man."[14] As a consequence Lasser lost Gallun, who rapidly became one of the major names in science fiction in the thirties.

These incidents aside, Lasser was working well at developing authors. He was achieving marked success with Edmond Hamilton, Henrik Dahl Juve, Frank K. Kelly, Leslie F. Stone, A. Rowley Hilliard, P. Schuyler Miller, and others. He was also, single-handedly, establishing science-fiction as a serious vehicle to consider social, sexual and religious topics. Had that development been allowed to continue in *Wonder Stories*, the magazine would have benefited tremendously. But the grip of the depression was making itself felt, and the harvest of riches for which Lasser was sowing the seeds would not be reaped by him, but by another.

27.

SCIENCE-FICTION DEPRESSION

By the end of 1932 science fiction could no longer escape the Depression. It was not only having an effect on the publishers, writers and magazines, but also on the purpose and content of science fiction. We'll consider both in this chapter, and first concentrate on the direct effect upon the field.

Gernsback's first setback came in December 1931, only three months after his new financial deal had refloated *Wonder Stories* and allowed the expansion of *Everyday Science and Mechanics*. According to Samuel Schiff in Stellar's accounting department, in apologies for non-payment he mailed to authors in February, "our bank closed in the early part of December and our funds were tied up. The State Banking Department advises us that a dividend will probably be declared during the month of March, at which time we will be pleased to remit to you for the amount due."

The main effect at this stage was that Gernsback delayed paying his authors. A number remember it plainly. When Eric Leif Davin interviewed Raymond Z. Gallun in 1986, he asked him when his financial troubles with Gernsback began. Gallun recalled, "It began early in 1932 with 'Revolt of the Star Men'."[1] That story was published in the Winter 1932 *Quarterly*. Gernsback had already made payments for some stories in that issue during February, so clearly his cash-flow problems began that month. Jack Williamson has the same recollection in connection with "Red Slag of Mars," the story he had based on the idea submitted by Laurence Schwartzman in the plot contest. This was published in the Spring 1932 *Quarterly* but, as Williamson recalls, "his checks had quit coming."[2] Clark Ashton Smith wasn't paid for his collaboration in the plot-idea competition, and his contribution, "The Planet Entity" had been published in the Fall 1931 *Quarterly*.

Gernsback had sufficient credit with his printer and distributor, though, for the magazines to continue appearing.

Others had greater problems. On April 28, 1932, William Clayton instructed Harry Bates to shift publication of *Astounding Stories* from a monthly to bi-monthly schedule, and to drop payment rates from two cents on acceptance to one cent on publication. *Astounding* had, by then, just started to make a profit and Bates was hoping this state of affairs would be temporary. A letter was sent to their regular writers which included, in part, the following. "I am hoping and expecting . . . that this will result in our skipping one or two of the profitless summer and early fall issues, and that thereafter our normal monthly schedule will be resumed: this, however, is in the lap of the gods, and is all bound up with conditions throughout the country in general and those in the hapless publishing business in particular."

In fact it was more Clayton's problem than the nation's. When Robert A. W. Lowndes met Harry Bates in the fifties, he learned the background details. Clayton had been in joint partnership with his printer, with an agreement that either one could buy out the other. In 1932, Clayton was urged by his accountant to buy the printer out. It was a foolish thing to do at that time, but Clayton's greed got the better of him. A price was fixed with the printer payable in four installments, with a first installment of $150,000. When the final installment was due Clayton was short by some $25,000. Another of Clayton's employees, Ed Zoty, whom Lowndes met in the sixties, speculated that this was because Clayton had been betting on the horses and was temporarily embarrassed.

Under the law, the failure to make that payment would force Clayton into bankruptcy. Trying to fend off the final blow, Clayton began to stop publication of his magazines. The instruction to stop *Astounding* was issued on October 27, 1932 with effect from the January 1933 issue. A month later, realizing he had enough material for a further issue which might bring in some more revenue, Clayton asked Bates to put out one final *Astounding*, the March 1933 issue.

Meanwhile other problems were emerging. In mid 1932 the Eastern Distributing Corporation, which distributed many of the independent pulps, went bankrupt. In writing to his authors Gernsback remarked that this resulted in the loss of "a vast sum of money." This was probably so. The distributors often paid cash over three months in arrears, allowing for the time lapse between the issue being despatched to them from the printer, the magazine coming off sale, and the accounts received by the distributor from the dealers. If we take *Wonder Stories* alone, and assume a monthly sale of 75,000 copies this would cover 225,000 copies. If the mark-up to distributor and dealer were 40%, then Gernsback was losing 60% of 225,000 copies at 25 cents each, or $33,750. This would be equal to ten times that today, and Gernsback may have lost that for each of his monthly magazines.

Other publishers suffered, some less financially viable than Gernsback, but they survived. An interesting case in point was Popular Publications, run by Henry Steeger. Steeger, fresh from college, had established the company in 1930, with a capital of $20,000. The company had hardly begun to make a profit when it was hit by the Eastern Distributing bankruptcy. By good fortune, however, in November 1931, Steeger had launched a new magazine, *Dime Detective*. The detective pulp was taking over the supremacy of the western in the 1930s, and Steeger had established a pulp with a new policy, that of the weird menace. With the magazine selling for only ten cents, and promising bizarre detective stories, it captured an audience, and sales rocketed. Steeger added other "Dime" titles to his line, including the notorious *Dime Mystery*, and he was soon able to re-establish his empire, which became one of the biggest in the pulps. Ten years later he would buy out the Munsey chain of pulps.

So it was possible to make a success in the pulps during the Depression. Street and Smith were another example. This long-established firm had started a new revolution in pulp magazines in April 1931 when they launched *The Shadow*. This was the first of the hero pulps, and was later followed by *Doc Savage* and Popular's own *The Spider*. All of these sold for ten cents each, and had circulations in the hundreds of thousands.

Gernsback did not have an equivalent market to build upon. His most successful title was *Radio-Craft*, which kept him buoyant during this period, but which did not give an opportunity for expansion. Clearly Gernsback had to recognize the new restrictions of the market. With the Fall 1932 *Quarterly*, issued on September 15, he cut the size from 144 pages to 96, and the cover price from 50 to 25 cents. Likewise the November 1932 *Wonder Stories* dropped in price from 25 to 15 cents, and the page count dropped from 96 to 64. Although this made *Wonder* the cheapest of the science-fiction pulps, it was also the smallest.

The price may have sustained *Wonder*'s circulation, but is unlikely to have increased it, and there would have been a net reduction in the magazine's income. The cover price for the *Quarterly* was certainly too high at a time when a quarter of the male population of the United States was out of work. The last issue appeared on December 15, 1932, dated Winter 1933. This issue promised another, to appear on March 15, but it never did. Instead Gernsback added the pages to the monthly and increased its size back to 96 pages from the April 1933 issue. He also took the gamble to restore the price to 25 cents. There was probably a sound reason for doing this. By April, Gernsback knew that *Astounding* had seen its last issue. *Astounding* sold for 20 cents. He probably anticipated that readers of that magazine might now turn to *Wonder*, for although they doubtless shared a common core of readers, there were likely to be a fair number more that had not read *Wonder* previously.

The winter of 1932 saw the turning point in the Depression, with the introduction of Roosevelt's New Deal taking more care of the welfare needs of the workers. Those publishers that survived 1932, by and large, continued. William Clayton did not. Unable to raise the funds for the final payment, he went bankrupt. He fought through into 1933 in an attempt to recover his publishing empire, and nearly succeeded, but the odds were too high. He ended his days, which were not many more, as a traveling liquor salesman. His magazines were put up for auction, and the title to a number, including *Clues* and *Astounding*, were bought by businessman T. R. Foley (later the partner with William Delaney in publishing *Weird Tales* from 1938 on), who then sold them in August 1933 to the highly successful Street & Smith company. Bates did not go with the title, although another of Clayton's editors, F. Orlin Tremaine, did. The new *Astounding Stories* was relaunched in September 1933. As we shall see, it was to make history.

Amazing Stories managed to survive, and publish some good stories, though it lacked the sparkle and vivacity of *Wonder*. This was mostly due to Sloane's pedestrian editing. Now approaching eighty-two, he was remarkably bright for his age, but could not take science fiction seriously. His scientific attainment was back at the dawn of electricity, and he sought to thrill his readers with editorials on the light bulb. As a cost-cutting exercise he selected a number of reprints, which he probably regarded as excellent fiction, but which were by then extremely dated, and only tenuously science fiction. The best of them was Fitz-James O'Brien's "The Diamond Lens" in the October 1933 issue. The worst was Edward Everett Hale's "The Good Natured Pendulum" (May 1933), which is about schoolboys meddling with a clock! *Amazing Stories* was kept alive chiefly by the Professor Jameson stories by Neil R. Jones, and some lingering contributions by David H. Keller, Bob Olsen, and P. Schuyler Miller.

Somehow *Amazing Stories Quarterly* staggered through 1933, though with fewer issues. The final two issues, dated Winter 1933 and Fall 1934, contained mostly reprints. Thereafter it just faded away.[3] To all intents the magazine died with the Spring/Summer 1933 issue released in January.

With the field virtually to himself, Gernsback could have made a killing in 1933. David Lasser had developed a number of new authors, and other popular writers at *Astounding* must have been looking for any market, even Gernsback's. Although Gernsback was tight for cash, had he invested it in developing *Wonder Stories* and in paying good rates, he could have scooped the field. But he did not.

Instead he did two things: one bizarre, the other a life saver. The bizarre move was to launch *Technocracy Review*. Because of that magazine's close link with the Depression and science fiction, I shall return to that in a moment. The other move was to set up a new company, Science Publications, and launch *Sexology*.

Sexology was probably another impulse move by Gernsback, though it may have had a long gestation period. Gernsback had long had an interest in the scientific education of sex and health culture. He had published a successful book on the subject, *Your Body*, in October 1926, which he then converted to a regular magazine, resulting in the rivalry with Bernarr Macfadden. More recently, through his newly established Norley Book Company, he had issued a number of similar books. There was the *Anatomical Manual*, which boasted twelve full-page color plates and fifty photographs of all organs and parts of the body, male and female! He also published a limited edition of Dr. William J. Robinson's *Sex, Love and Morality*, which, "because of its unusual frankness" sold only by subscription.

There is no doubt that these books sold well, and Gernsback knew that here was a potential market. Despite the Depression, the professional man, who was still in employ, would be more interested in, and more readily able to buy, a magazine about sexual problems, than the escapism of *Wonder Stories*. Gernsback issued *Sexology* in June 1933. So quickly had the magazine been assembled that it had no table of contents, and a spurious editor—Maxwell Vidaver, M.D. Its editorial stated the reason for *Sexology*:

> At the present time there exists no magazine in the United States on sex hygiene and sex education. It is a curious commentary upon our times that where there is an abundance of obscene literature published in the United States today, there is not a single magazine, outside of professional medical magazines, of a strictly serious and scientific nature, devoted to this subject. There is so much mis-information on sex matters today, there is so much sickness and unhappiness directly traceable to ignorance in sex information, that the publishers feel that SEXOLOGY, a serious magazine, will do a tremendous amount of good to correct such mis-information and help make the world a better place to live in.

Gernsback emphasized that the magazine would be strictly on the educational and scientific level. "If you expect to find smut in this magazine you had better not buy it," he rebuked. "You will not find it in its pages." It was a bold move to issue such a magazine, and perhaps unsure of its acceptance,

Gernsback chose not to have his name printed on the cover—the only example of this with his magazines.

Gernsback now had another crusade. If he could not cure the world's ills by the promotion of scientific achievement, he could help do it through sex education. He had struck a gold-mine. *Sexology*, in its handy pocket-size, instantly caught on, and shifted to a monthly schedule from its planned quarterly, with the second issue. With the third issue, David H. Keller was brought in as editor, and he remained so till 1938. He also edited the new companion magazines that Gernsback launched in the wake of *Sexology's* success: *Popular Medicine* from September 1934 and *Facts of Life* from January 1938. This kept Keller from writing much fiction in the mid- and late thirties, but it sustained Gernsback as a publisher. With the success of *Sexology* and the strength of *Radio-Craft*, which remained a popular magazine, Gernsback was able to weather the Depression and beyond.

Technocracy Review was another matter entirely, and an odd experiment on Gernsback's part. The field of technocracy came to life during the Depression although it had been founded as early as 1920. Its basic tenet was that there should be a scientific review of the administration of the whole of the nation's resources. It had grown naturally out of the aftermath of the First World War when, with increasing use of technology in industry, it was felt that technical experts should have a greater hand in advising on the nation's administration and economy. Technocracy had taken a back seat during the relatively prosperous twenties, but it gathered pace during the Depression in 1932, with the formation of the Committee on Technocracy, and took the nation by storm. With the economic upheaval, the technocrats, dominated by Howard Scott, were advocating an end to the capitalist system, and a rise in social, even communal, control.

Gernsback saw nothing in technocracy that had not already been proposed in science fiction, but he did see in the subject an opportunity to promote science fiction. He gave over his editorial in the March 1933 *Wonder Stories* to a study of "Wonders of Technocracy":

> Now that the world has suddenly become Technocracy-minded, the average reader of *Wonder Stories* will probably look on the furor as rather strange. So far as the aims and aspirations of Technocracy are concerned, they are nothing new to science fiction. When the Technocrats tell us that our economic system is all wrong, and is obsolete, an anticipation of this can be found in the writer's book "Ralph 124C 41+" (written in 1911) under the chapter "No More Money." When Technocracy tells us that we will shortly have to adopt a four-hour working day for five days a week, that is not news to science-fiction readers either. Hundreds of stories have treated on this point. Indeed, there is very little that Technocracy offers that has not been anticipated in stories from H. G. Wells down to last month's issue of WONDER STORIES. Every reader of science fiction has lived in the future so long, that he is probably amused that the rest of the country has found a new plaything in Technocracy.
>
> Everything that the machine age has to offer, many of the

possibilities arising from the reign of the machine, have been anticipated by authors of science fiction for many years. Indeed, it would be most interesting to take every statement made now by spokesmen of Technocracy and check up on some of the past science fiction stories. I am certain that practically all the statements now made can easily be found in the writings of our authors.

And that, of course, shows vividly that the great mission of science fiction is becoming more recognized, day by day. This is the triumph of our readers over those who scorned science fiction. If science fiction can make serious people sit up and take notice, and THINK about the future of humanity it will have accomplished a tremendous good.[4]

Gernsback was especially concerned that the unemployed would be blaming technology for their predicament rather than welcoming the fact that the new machine age should increase productivity and thereby expand the nation's wealth and ultimately improve the situation of the workers, by allowing them more money and leisure time. He had discussed the subject at length in an earlier editorial "Wonders of the Machine Age" which, though it does not use the word technocracy, is nevertheless a technocratic essay. In this important article Gernsback decried the scaremongers who pointed at the machine as the cause of the nation's ills. Instead he maintained that the machine was the solution to the problem. He blamed *people* for the Depression, not machines, saying that, "I have always felt that the present depression is purely psychological rather than physical . . ."[5] Gernsback had written the editorial because of the increasing number of stories he was receiving (and rejecting) wherein the machine is portrayed as a "Frankenstein monster," and where humanity rises in revolt and destroys all machines, reverting to a pre-industrial golden age.

Although Gernsback rejected these stories, their existence emphasizes how much science fiction was a reflection of the age. The origins of science fiction were rooted in the industrial revolution of the previous century, and a growing awareness of science. As the dark age of industry took hold science fiction became increasingly bleak and eventually authors had rebelled, attempting to portray fantastic golden ages. The main advocates of this type of fiction had been socialists themselves: Edward Bellamy in the United States and William Morris in England. Bellamy (1850-1898) made his forecasts in the ground-breaking *Looking Backward, 2000-1887* (1888). He projected a totalitarian state where science had been harnessed and a true social utopia achieved. Morris (1834-1896) rebelled totally against the machine state, and in *News from Nowhere* (1890) portrayed a peaceful, idealized pseudo-medieval world, where man had reverted to manual crafts. It was Morris's rebellion that caused him to write a number of pseudo-historical fantasies, resulting in the birth of modern fantasy fiction.

The same thing began to happen in America in 1931 with the birth of the sub-genre of sword and sorcery. This was predominant in the pages of *Weird Tales* and its chief pioneer was Robert E. Howard (1906-1936). Unlike Morris, Howard was not a socialist, and he was not driven by the same reformist zeal.

He had a fascination for both the Celtic Age and pre-history and had woven one or both of these into his fiction since his first story, "Spear and Fang" (*Weird Tales*, July 1925). He developed this in his stories about primeval heroes King Kull and Bran Mak Morn, culminating in the mighty barbarian, Conan of Cimmeria, starting in "The Phoenix on the Sword" (December 1932). One of the reasons for the popularity of these stories was the nation's rebellion against the machine age and a desire to revert to the frontier simplicity, pitting man against nature.

Gernsback would have none of it. His whole world was based upon technological advance, and this was the basis of science fiction. "Without it there could be no science fiction," he concluded in his July 1931 editorial. However, in order for science fiction to redeem itself, it had to give thought to the beneficial effects of the machine upon man. The truth is that, despite what Gernsback believed, science-fiction writers had given little thought to the social consequences of technological advance. They had concentrated on the invention and the wonders of super science, and only a few writers, like David H. Keller, had given any thought to the effects this might have on society and the individual.

By 1932 the tide could not be stemmed. David Lasser had already urged writers to bring realism into their fiction. They had applied this to space travel but now, with the economic pressures, they started to apply it to the rest of science fiction. Some of the motivation came from the European novels that Gernsback was importing. His prime reason had been economical, since he could acquire these novels more cheaply than from American writers (though he still had problems paying the translators). Of special significance was *The Death of Iron* by S. S. Held serialized in *Wonder Stories* from September to December 1932, which shows the upheaval that follows once iron starts to oxidise and crumble.[6]

The pulp author who took the social change closest to heart was Nathan Schachner (1895-1955). We have already seen the prime role Schachner had taken in the American Interplanetary Society and the popularization of space travel. A pioneer in chemical warfare, he became a lawyer in 1919 and turned to free-lance writing in 1933, subsequently producing several authoritative works on America's political forefathers. In his science fiction, Schachner explored many of the consequences of social reform and technocracy. This had started in his novel *Exiles of the Moon* (*Wonder Stories*, September-November 1931), his last collaboration with Arthur Leo Zagat, wherein an Aristocracy, made up of just five families, control the rest of the world's enslaved workers. One of the working class, Garry Parker, a rocket pilot, is in love with Naomi, a daughter of the Aristocracy. For disobeying an order Parker is banished to a remote part of Earth. By his cunning he escapes, steals a rocket liner and flees to the moon with other exiled workers. There they discover a mineral which absorbs oxygen and they return with it to Earth to bargain with the Aristocrats. The Aristocrats will not enter into a bargain, so the Workers rebel. Needless to say they are victorious, and are granted equality with the Aristocrats. This opened up an opportunity for all Workers to destroy their oppressors, but Garry Parker stopped them. His admonition is a lecture in socialism:

"Equal, I say." The word pealed round the world. "Equal, not superior. For a Society founded on the proposition that any man is by even the shade of a hair the superior of another, that one man, by so much as the paring of a nail is entitled to more of privilege, of opportunity, than another, cannot long survive."[7]

Parker's speech continues, concluding with the statement that the Aristocrats were needed as much as the Workers to build a new world:

". . . For hundreds upon hundreds of years they have learned the vast and intricate science of government, of organization. Today that vast and necessary knowledge is theirs, and theirs alone. We need them, and they need us. Together, we can, we shall, work for a better, a fairer, a happier world."[8]

This sermon was a statement about technocracy, about the need to wed the knowledge of government, technology and society. It was a statement against the policy of President Hoover, who opposed federal assistance to the unemployed. When Hoover was trounced in the presidential election that brought Franklin Roosevelt to power, the nation took on a new optimism, and this was immediately reflected in Schachner's fiction. "The Time Express" (December 1932) portrays an apparently idyllic future in the year 4800 where mankind has reverted to manual labor. As one of the leaders of the day comments to the time travelers: "You represent an early stage of the Machine Age that ultimately caused the almost complete degeneracy of the race. It was only through the mighty effort of a few that mankind survived and continued to evolve. The curse of machinery has been eradicated, yet there are misguided ones among us who still long for the slothful ease that only the slavish machines could grant them."[9] In fact, as Schachner reveals, the world is far from utopian, as the manual labor requires people to work all of their lives, with little opportunity for leisure or relaxation. Needless to say there is a revolution, aided by the time travelers, whereby the plans for power machinery are made available.

In "The Robot Technocrat" (March 1933), Schachner pulled out all of the stops. It is set in the year 1954, when America has sunk into chaos, but remains the last vestige of hope in a world that had become overrun by dictators. Hugh Corbin is the leader of the Reconstructionists, trying to rebuild society. His beliefs are clear:

"If only the factions could see things clearly. We must rebuild the machines that the masses destroyed in their blind rage against overproduction. We must repair the wreckage of twenty years, and then *co-operate!* See to it that every man, woman and child in the country gets a fair share of the machine's products. The machine was not to blame, only we who handled it. But that presupposes statesmen, and the party leaders are just ambitious self-seekers, ready to sacrifice the people to their lust for power. We need a new deal; a new vision; possibly a new plan."[10]

The new plan comes from an invention of Russian scientist Anton Kalmikoff—a giant computer which can predict the future from a series of political, scientific and socio-economic factors. (This is the same concept David Lasser had proposed in "The Time Projector," and Lasser may have also suggested it to Schachner.) Its prediction based on the anarchic America of 1954 is for civil war, pestilence, invasion and the end of civilization. The future predicted in the hands of the Nationalist Leader, Adolph Hiller, is a total dictatorship and a reign of terror. By eliminating the futures of the various leaders one by one, the computer shows that Corbin's Reconstructionist future is the only viable proposal.

In this story Schachner converted the policies of the technocrats to the science of mathematics and prediction and wrote the first true technocratic science fiction story. He followed it with a short series called "The Revolt of the Scientists" (April-June 1933) which, though unconnected to "The Robot Technocrat," considered the plans of technocracy if put into action. It starts in the near future—1937—and follows the activities of the Council of the Technocrats, an organization of world famous scientists who are attempting to remodel the world. They initially triumph by taking over control of the liquor and oil industries, but it soon transpires that scientists alone cannot run big business. The government retaliates but finds it cannot outwit the scientists. After three years a compromise is reached and government is changed to allow a technocratic division, with a thousand of the country's greatest engineers, scientists, technicians and economists put in control of industry.

Schachner generally supported technocracy in his stories, because it favored a scientific solution to problems, but he also recognized that there needed to be a balance kept of all skills. There was no simple answer to the nation's problems, but rebelling against science rather than utilizing its knowledge was not the answer.

Other writers considered these same consequences. Edmond Hamilton, in "The Island of Unreason" (May 1933), shows what happens when rebels against society are imprisoned on an island with no form of government and no technology. Living in this primitive state is rough, but Hamilton shows how the rational, scientific mind can triumph.

In his stories about "The Man Who Awoke," Laurence Manning also depicted the possibilities of social evolution related to scientific achievement. The series, which ran for five stories from the March to August 1933 issues of Wonder Stories, was the first in the pulps to depict a sequential future history based on existing and projected trends. The first episode allowed Manning his commentary upon the social problems of the thirties. Norman Winters goes into suspended animation and awakes in the pastoral pleasantness of the year 5000. In this age, metals were carefully conserved, farming was unknown. Everything was provided by trees, including food, housing, clothing and fuel, and each colony was ruled by a Forester. The Foresters measure civilization from two thousand years earlier, when the Great Revolution overthrew the Wasters "and True Economics lifted her torch to guide the world on its upward path." The Wasters were the governments of the twentieth century. A Forester explains to Winters his views of the Wasters:

"Fossil plants were ruthlessly burned in furnaces to provide heat, petroleum was consumed by the million barrels, cheap metal cars were built and thrown away to rust after a few years' use, men crowded into ill-ventilated villages of a million inhabitants . . . That was the age of race-fights where whole countrysides raised mobs and gave them explosives and poisons and sent them to destroy other mobs."

The Forester adds:

". . . But for what should we thank the humans of three thousand years ago? For exhausting the coal supplies of the world? For leaving us no petroleum for our chemical factories? For destroying the forests on whole mountain ranges and letting the soil erode in the valleys? Shall we thank them, perhaps, for the Sahara or the Gobi deserts?"[11]

Manning was forecasting not just an economical revolution, but the Green revolution. Along with earlier anti-exploitation stories by Hamilton and Miller, there was the start of ecological science fiction in *Wonder Stories*. Manning (1899-1972), a nurseryman and former lieutenant in the Royal Canadian Air Force, was, with Lasser and Schachner, a leading member of the American Interplanetary Society. By the start of 1933 Schachner had taken over as President, Manning was Treasurer and Lasser, the founder and former President, was editor of the journal *Astronautics*. It must be more than a coincidence that these same people should be the most vocal in *Wonder Stories* about socio-economic reform.

Lasser was, in fact, becoming more involved in the rights of the unemployed. Where he lived, in Greenwich Village, the majority of the Italian residents were out of work. Lasser felt a responsibility to help, so he formed a group to represent them at City Hall. By 1933 he was more involved with the unemployed than with the Interplanetary Society, and had become a member of the Socialist Party. As he recalled in an interview in 1986: "The country was really in terrible shape. I felt that this was the important question of the moment and space would have to wait."[12]

It was inevitable, therefore, that Lasser would work closely with his writer colleagues to help promote social reform in science fiction. It was also inevitable that he would edit a magazine like *Technocracy Review*. The magazine may have been issued at Lasser's request, though he later no longer recalled how it came about. The first issue, dated February 1933, was launched on January 5. In his editorial Gernsback stated that he was keeping an open mind on the subject of technocracy and the magazine would show no bias, but allow all views to be expressed. Gernsback contributed his own views on "The Machine and the Depression," reiterating his July 1931 *Wonder Stories*'s editorial. There were articles on "Technocracy and Communism" and "Technocracy and the Unemployed," plus a symposium on the movement toward technocracy from a handful of scientists and economists. It only ran for two issues when, according to Moskowitz, Gernsback dropped it, "made uncomfortable by the company he was keeping."[13] The Technocrats, under Howard

Scott, were certainly radical, encouraging revolution, and Gernsback was probably fearing a Communist infiltration.

Lasser found his involvement with the unemployed becoming total. His local group grew into a city-wide organization and would evolve, by 1935, into a national concern, the Workers Alliance. Lasser found less time to edit *Wonder Stories*. In the end, according to Lasser, Gernsback summoned him into his office and said, "If you like working with the unemployed so much, I suggest you go and join them." Lasser was fired.

The change would probably have come anyway. Lasser was as dedicated to his fight for the unemployed as he had been to his revolution in science fiction. If he had spent another year or two as an editor, there is little doubt that he would have revolutionized the field. In the space of less than two years, once he had got to grips with science fiction in May 1931, Lasser had turned the field on its head, and a more mature, reflective, and realistic field had emerged. Alas, just at the time when he could have built upon that reform, he left.

Gernsback probably had other motives for sacking Lasser. He had needed the necessary capital to launch *Sexology*, and *Wonder Stories* was losing money. He sought to reduce whatever overheads he could. Lasser was drawing a salary of around $70 a week, a good wage at that time. By sacking him, Gernsback could employ someone at much less cost. His eventual choice was Charles D. Hornig, a sixteen-year-old fan who had just started publishing the magazine *The Fantasy Fan*. Gernsback employed him in August 1933 at $20 a week, thus saving $2600 a year. We'll look more closely at Hornig's sudden rise to fame in the next chapter.

Gernsback now had a year's backlog of payments to authors, many of whom were threatening him with legal action. Some, who had signed contracts, were belatedly receiving payment. *Wonder Stories* contained around 75,000 words of fiction each issue. If Gernsback had not paid for stories as a rule since February 1932, then a year's backlog was around 900,000 words which, at half-a-cent a word, was $4500. Even the accumulation of salary saved by the sacking of David Lasser was not enough to pay for that.

The irony was that in Gernsback's other companies, particularly the Popular Book Corporation, Techni-Craft, and now Science Publications, Gernsback was making a profit which, had he wished, he could have used as the basis of a loan to support Stellar. But he chose not to. Instead he took the easy way out and dissolved the Stellar Publishing Corporation. At this stage his liabilities had probably exceeded his assets, so in effect he went into voluntary liquidation. It was an arrangement almost certainly supported by his printers and suppliers, who through their contractual arrangements with Gernsback had probably already been paid prior to the liquidation. The only ones who lost out were the authors, who had to wait to see what they might receive at the end of the line, which was likely to be nothing. In fact, many authors would not have known about the arrangement. Gernsback continued publication of *Wonder Stories*, but with a new company, Continental Publications. The full details of the arrangement may now never be known, but they also involved Sidney Gernsback moving to Chicago, where he was in charge of the business affairs of the various Gernsback enterprises in that region. He stayed in Chicago until his death in February 1953 at the age of 76.

All these events took place in the summer of 1933. *Wonder Stories* missed two issues, combining the July/August and the September/October numbers, because sales were traditionally low in the summer (*Amazing Stories* did the same with the August/September 1933 issue). With no issue to assemble for July, it was safe to sack Lasser then, and allow some weeks to appoint a successor. Lasser had purchased sufficient stories for at least two more issues so there was no rush. It also allowed a month for Gernsback to dissolve Stellar and launch Continental. Since by that time the sales of the first issue of *Sexology* were coming in, by late August 1933 Gernsback must have been feeling relatively smug. He'd survived the Depression, cut his running costs, reduced his overheads, written off past debts, and launched a successful new magazine.

He had one further change to make. Despite the popularity of the larger-size *Wonder Stories* with the readers, sales had not improved, and Gernsback claimed he had invested a lot of money in the change from pulp to large format. From the November 1933 issue of *Wonder Stories*, the first under the editorship of Charles D. Hornig, Gernsback converted the magazine back to the smaller pulp size. That issue appeared on the stands on October 1, 1933. One month earlier, *Amazing Stories* had also taken the plunge and converted to the pulp format. And ten days earlier had seen the reappearance of *Astounding Stories*. Here was another of those Jonbar hinges whereupon the future of science fiction pivoted. A new world was about to dawn.

28.

AMATEUR PRESSURE

By 1932 science fiction fans had become not only vociferous in the letter columns of the magazines (which were far bigger and contained a greater variety of discussion than in any other pulps), but also more active. The Depression was a catalyst in bringing fan groups physically together, rather than through correspondence, and to share costs in their own activities. The early fan-club organs were giving way to more general-circulation magazines. Some of these found their readers from addresses available in the magazines. Dan McPhail, for instance, who began his handwritten *Science Fiction News* in June 1931, mailed it at first to all correspondents in the magazines with an Oklahoma address. After three issues he acquired a typewriter and produced carbon-copy issues which rapidly grew in size. He kept the magazine going for five years and thirty-six issues, the final few being printed as the official organ of the Oklahoma Scientifiction Association, which had grown up around it. It was the first regular science fiction news magazine.

Oklahoma is a long way from New York, and members of the highly active New York fandom, the Scienceers, were keen to produce their own publications. When The Scienceers, as an organization, withered, a group of fans decided to publish a magazine to take its place. The fans were Julius Schwartz, Mort Weisinger, and Allan Glasser, and the magazine was *The Time Traveller*. Its first issue appeared in January 1932 and it was the first proper fan magazine. At the outset it was mimeographed and only six pages long, and lacked for quality. When Bob Olsen received his copy he wrote to Forrest Ackerman saying: "The copy that reached me was not only executed in a very untidy fashion but in some parts was absolutely undecipherable. You can hardly expect a person to pay even a small sum of money for a publication, portions of which can't even be read."[1] The third issue was printed, and it was this appearance that catapulted the magazine from the underworld of fandom, into the ranks of quality small press.

The man who provided the printing facilities was Conrad H. Ruppert (1912-1997), a native of Brooklyn, who had been a fan of science fiction since he first encountered *Science and Invention* in 1922. He had even become one of Gernsback's reporters for the magazine. It was Ruppert who had been responsible for suggesting the idea of a Science Fiction Week in 1930, which was the first promotional fan activity, and he had also urged Gernsback to continue to print fan addresses in *Science Wonder Stories* to enable fan contact. Ruppert, like Walter Dennis, should be recognized as one of the crucial pioneer active fans.

In 1932 Ruppert, who was working in his father's bakery, bought a small hand press. In later years he became a professional printer, but at this time he started to produce booklets as a hobby. He offered his services to Glasser to print *The Time Traveller* with effect from the March 1932 issue. The magazine was transformed, and given an aura of respectability that would never have been achieved with ordinary hektograph or mimeograph methods. Ruppert's efforts are often overlooked in the shadow of the work done by other early fans, but it was Ruppert who gave the magazine the gloss of professionalism, and it was that which made publishers take notice of the science fiction fraternity and which encouraged writers to contribute free to the magazines, joining in the fun and family atmosphere.

The Time Traveller met with much success, but there was trouble in the camp. Glasser and Weisinger had fallen out over the plot contest in Wonder Stories Quarterly, where Glasser had taken credit in submitting Weisinger's idea for "The Martian," eventually written up, to much acclaim, by A. Rowley Hilliard. Glasser was already making a number of professional sales, not just to the science fiction magazines, but to Illustrated Detective, Mind Magic, and Amazing's companion, Complete Detective Novel Magazine. There were rumors that Glasser was plagiarizing these stories, and this was in part confirmed when a story Glasser had earlier sold to Amazing Stories eventually appeared in the August/September 1933 issue. It was seen to be an almost direct copy of "The Heat Wave" by Marion Ryan and Robert Ord from the April 1929 Munsey's Magazine.

By then Glasser and Weisinger had already split, but not before Conrad Ruppert and Julius Schwartz had set up their own Solar Publications, and issued a twenty-page booklet of Glasser's story The Cavemen of Venus. This was the first specialist science-fiction small-press publication. It was well received by readers, went rapidly out of print, and is now a collectors' item amongst those few who know of its existence. Ruppert and Schwartz followed it with The Price of Peace by Mort Weisinger. Weisinger was able to sell this neatly printed story to Amazing, where it appeared in the November 1933 issue, starting Weisinger's professional career.

With Glasser ostracized, Schwartz, Ruppert and Weisinger joined forces with another Brooklynite, Morris Ingher and Forrest Ackerman from Los Angeles, to bring out a new magazine, Science Fiction Digest. This first appeared in September 1932, with Ingher as editor, and kept up a regular monthly schedule for the next four years, missing only a couple of issues in early 1935. Ruppert took over as editor from April 1933 and he was succeeded by Schwartz from June 1934. It was retitled Fantasy Magazine in January 1934. Science Fiction Digest, like The Time Traveller, was a mixture of news, articles, and interviews. It became the unofficial trade journal of the science-fiction scene, and was such a reliable cornerstone of news and information during the dark days of the Depression that it gave some semblance of order and continuity for the dedicated fans whilst all else around seemed bleak. Although its circulation was only a few hundred, and thus unavailable to the majority of readers of science fiction, it served as a bond for those of the inner core, many of whom later emerged as leading lights in the science-fiction field.

One inevitable consequence of these publications was the desire for fans to vote on their favorite stories. Glasser conducted a poll in The Time Traveller for the best science fiction of 1932, and Edmond Hamilton won with "A Conquest of Two Worlds." Raymond Palmer then sought to formalize the process and initiated the Jules Verne Prize for the best science fiction of 1933. The concept never really blossomed, but Palmer announced in the February 1934 Fantasy Magazine that the winner was "The Island of Unreason," again by Edmond Hamilton.

Although *Science Fiction Digest* carried fiction, that was not its main feature. Palmer, however, sought to remedy that by instigating a novelty in the form of a round-robin story to be published as a supplement. The story had the overall title of *Cosmos* and ran for seventeen chapters, from July 1933 to January 1935. Palmer provided the outline, which was rather old-hat space opera, and then reached agreement with sixteen other authors to write the series. The authors joined in for the fun of it, interested to see how their chapters fitted in with that preceding, and what problems they could set for others to solve. Since Palmer had set out the framework, the authors worked in advance on their sections before seeing the earlier chapters. Francis Flagg, for instance, had already plotted his chapter before he saw the opening chapter from Ralph Milne Farley. He put his thoughts in a letter to Ackerman:

> A swell beginning, I think, tho on general principles I dislike emperors and princes as heroes of stories. You will note I never use them in that sense . . . However, Farley has done a good opening chapter; it will test the rest of us to live up to it. Mine isn't even written yet, tho plotted out somewhat. But I've two months to do it in. I'm looking forward to seeing Keller's chapter. He CAN write and should give us something original. Farley's will be a hard chapter to best for science, tho.[2]

The full line-up of writers in *Cosmos* was awesome. In addition to Farley, Keller and Flagg, were Arthur J. Burks, Bob Olsen, John W. Campbell, Otis Adelbert Kline and E. Hoffmann Price, Abner J. Gelula, A. Merritt, J. Harvey Haggard, E. E. Smith, P. Schuyler Miller, Lloyd A. Eshbach, Eando Binder, and Edmond Hamilton. They were all top names in the pulps, but to be able to bring together both Merritt and Smith in one serial was a bonanza for all fans. *Cosmos* is far from great science fiction, and has to be read in the manner in which it was written. Most of the chapters can stand on their own and Merritt's in particular, "The Last Poet and the Robots" (April 1934), which was voted the most popular, is a gem of a story. It is some measure of the affinity that existed between science-fiction devotees that writers were willing to spend time and contribute stories free of charge to the fan press while, at the same time, they were instigating legal proceedings against Hugo Gernsback for recovery of unpaid fees for stories. It is the clear distinction between work done for fun and that for profit.

Although science fiction continued to appear in *Science Fiction Digest* its emphasis was always on nonfiction, and it cannot be thought of as a science-fiction magazine. But moves were also afoot in the fan field to launch an amateur magazine consisting wholly of stories. The first plans in this direction had been explored by Carl Swanson, a bookdealer in Washburn, North Dakota. In December 1931 he circulated a number of writers with a proposal to issue a magazine of weird-science fiction to be called *Galaxy*. Swanson was after new fiction if he could acquire it, but otherwise sought the option of reprinting stories. Swanson was unable to raise the necessary finances, however, and by May 1932 had dropped the idea.

Swanson had struck up correspondence with a fan from Cleveland, Ohio, called Jerome Siegel. Siegel had been a long time fan. His first letter had appeared in *Amazing Stories* in August 1929 where he urged a further cover contest so that he and his friends could enter. His friends' names, John Riebel and Bernard Kantor, were almost certainly his own pseudonyms, because Siegel was soon submitting letters to the magazines under both his own name and that of Bernard J. Kenton. In 1930 a story, "Miracles on Antares," was accepted by *Amazing*, but Sloane, with his constant backlog of stories, never used it and it was returned to Siegel in 1935.

Also in 1930, although the date is uncertain, Siegel produced a typewritten magazine called *Cosmic Stories*. The magazine, circulated only in the Cleveland area, consisted of a handful of copies, but in addition to one of Siegel's own stories, it contained a new story by local author Clare Winger Harris, and one from fan Walter Dennis. *Cosmic Stories* was arguably, therefore, the first amateur science-fiction magazine, even though its circulation may not have reached double figures.

When Siegel and Swanson struck up correspondence, the two decided to publish some small booklets. Siegel issued his own *Guests of the Earth* under the alias of Hugh Langley, whilst Swanson put together a copy of Edmond Hamilton's *The Metal Giants*, which had been made available to him for *Galaxy*. Both of these, issued in 1932, were rather poor mimeographed copies which paled in comparison to Ruppert's printed magazines.

Siegel now issued a new magazine called simply *Science Fiction* co-edited with a local artist, Joseph Schuster. Its first number was issued in October 1932, but was poorly duplicated, and consisted entirely of Siegel's own pseudonymous stories. Nevertheless Siegel began to attract submissions from leadings fans and authors including Raymond Palmer, David H. Keller, and again Clare Winger Harris. The magazine ran for five issues; the last two, undated, appearing in early and mid-1933. They were unremarkable other than for being the first regular issues of an amateur science-fiction magazine. Siegel's fiction was poor and more imitative of the super-science of the 1928-1930 period, than the mature fiction emerging in 1932. It is not too surprising, therefore, to find that when Siegel and Schuster combined their talent to produce a comic strip adventure they should devise the character of Superman. The character had grown from one of Siegel's stories, "The Reign of the Superman," in the January 1933 *Science Fiction*, but it changed significantly as Siegel and Schuster devised the concept of Superman incognito as Clark Kent, selflessly working to right the world's ills. The character was a creation of the Depression, when Siegel wished he had superpowers to make the world a better place. Although the whole character and strip were created in 1933, it was not until 1938 that the two were able to sell it to the forerunner of the DC Comics company, where Superman debuted in the June 1938 *Action Comics*. The popularity of the character resulted in him getting his own magazine, *Superman*, issued in May 1939. By one of those interesting twists of fate, the later editors of *Superman* included Mort Weisinger, from 1941, and Julius Schwartz, from 1943.[3]

Had Siegel been able to use the printing facitilites of Conrad Ruppert, *Science Fiction* might have made more impact than it did. Ruppert, though, was already using all of his spare time printing New York-based magazines and booklets. On top of *Science Fiction Digest*, he had taken on the American Interplanetary Society's *Astronautics*, and had arranged with Charles D.

Hornig to print his new magazine *The Fantasy Fan*. He had also formed the company ARRA Printers with colleague Donald Alexander, and under this imprint he issued two special booklets. The first was a reprint of A. Merritt's *Thru the Dragon Glass* [sic], which is now a much sought-after collectors' item. The other was *Wolf Hollow Bubbles*, one of David H. Keller's Taine of San Francisco stories, intended as the first in a projected Scientific Detective Series, though no other titles appeared.

Ruppert was not the only printer in the amateur science-fiction field. William L. Crawford, a dedicated fan in Everett, Pennsylvania, had been striving to issue a small-press magazine called *Unusual Stories*. Throughout 1933 he was plagued with problems from his local cheap printer. In the end he bought a second-hand printing press himself, though that left him without any money to acquire type. With the help of Lloyd Eshbach, Crawford issued a flyer promoting the forthcoming *Unusual Stories*. The flyer, issued in November 1933, is especially important for the announcement, apparently written by Eshbach, which gives the view of the science-fiction field at that time. Under the sub-heading, "Literary Science Fiction and Fantasy Tales," it stated:

> It has been said that science fiction as an art is undergoing a period of slow and painful evolution, from which it will eventually emerge as the literature of tomorrow. Though this is undoubtedly true, it has long been our conviction that science fiction should have a definite place in the literature of today. It does not occupy that position now, we believe, because of the restrictions placed upon it by short-sighted editors and publishers. They use only those tales which follow certain stereotyped forms. They avoid the "off-trail" story because it violates one or another of their editorial taboos—with the result that science fiction has been sinking into the mire of the commonplace. We believe that discriminating readers of science and fantasy fiction will welcome stories of a truly unusual nature, stories which have cast off the shackles of precedence to brave the dangers of originality. We believe that you, as a fantasy fan, are ready to lend your whole-hearted support to a periodical which will publish only "different stories."

That same plea has been used in all subsequent revolutions in the field, especially with Harlan Ellison's *Dangerous Visions* in 1967. In Crawford's case, the announcement took as its starting point David Lasser's letter of May 1931, which also argued the case for new stories. Eshbach had received a copy of that letter and it is that to which he alludes in his first sentence. He is not entirely fair to Lasser, who had tried to break down taboos, few of which were editorial in nature, but were imposed by printers and distributors who would not handle what they considered "risky" material.

It meant, though, that Crawford was now able to bring into print some of those stories. The flyer for *Unusual* gave a tantalizing glimpse of one, printing just the first page of P. Schuyler Miller's "The Titan." Crawford also announced that he had secured stories from Ralph Milne Farley, Stanton A. Coblentz, Miles J. Breuer, H. P. Lovecraft, Clark Ashton Smith, David H.

Keller, Victor Endersby, Richard Tooker, Amelia Reynolds Long, Lowell Howard Morrow, and many others. Unfortunately, the response to the flyer was only mild, and Crawford was still unable to raise the cash to complete printing the first issue. It was with a determined effort in order to satisfy those few subscribers that Crawford distributed an "advance issue" of *Unusual Stories* in March 1934. It ran to only twenty-two pages and contained a complete story by Cyril G. Wates, "When the Waker Sleeps," plus the first part of Richard Tooker's story, "Tharda, Queen of Vampires."

Crawford had been endeavoring to secure newsstand distribution for *Unusual Stories* but learned from his flyer the difficulty of this. He also knew he needed to learn more himself about printing. He therefore decided to issue a small booklet by subscription only, containing weird and fantasy fiction. The result was *Marvel Tales* issued in May 1934. It contained three weird stories by Lovecraft, Keller, and August Derleth, and one science-fiction story, "The Man with the Hour Glass" by Eshbach. It was moderately well printed but rather amateurishly illustrated. It had a circulation of only a few hundred copies, but Crawford received enough encouragement and further subscriptions to produce a second and third issue. Most of the contents were the type you would expect to see in *Weird Tales*, though some may have been rejected because of Farnsworth Wright's editorial whims. The third issue, dated Winter 1934, is important because it saw Robert Bloch's first appearance in print with a simple ghost story, "Lilies." That same issue saw the first episode of Miller's "The Titan."

The next issue, dated March/April 1935, brought into print Clifford Simak's "The Creator," a story which has since passed into legend because of its treatment of the taboo subject of God. At about that same time Crawford managed to get *Unusual Stories* back into production. Eventually that saw two issues and *Marvel Tales* five issues before Crawford was forced to stop publication due to financial problems. The fifth and final issue of *Marvel Tales* had made newsstand distribution, and Crawford is to be admired for his effort and determination against overwhelming odds during such difficult times. His magazines had made their case. There was room, and a readership, for the weird, off-trail story, with a more literate style, that could be incorporated into the science-fiction story.

All of this had not gone unnoticed by Charles D. Hornig. I've mentioned Hornig several times already, but not in detail. This chapter comes full circle with Hornig and gives us a springboard into the next, so it's time I introduced him properly.

Charles Derwin Hornig was born in Jersey City on May 25, 1916. He was thrilled by science-fiction movies, especially *The Golem* and *Metropolis*. One day in 1930, realizing he'd seen all the films, he spent his precious quarter on a magazine that caught his eye, the September 1930 issue of *Amazing Stories*. Hornig was hooked. He acquired back issues from a variety of sources, including Carl Swanson's mail-order business and it was Swanson who alerted Hornig to the appearance of *The Time Traveller*. Through that Hornig encountered fandom, attended meetings of the Scienceers, and thus met Conrad Ruppert. The urge to publish is irresistible in any active fan, and Hornig was not immune. In the spring of 1933 he began to contact the leading writers of the day who again happily donated rejects. Ruppert agreed to print 250 copies of the first issue for ten dollars. Hornig assembled *The Fantasy Fan* and mailed out the first issue in late July 1933 (dated September). He sent a copy to Gernsback, but never expected what happened next. He received a telegram from Gernsback asking him call in on him. Hornig did not know that Lasser had just been sacked. Gernsback was looking for a new editor. Something in the presentation of *The Fantasy Fan* had suggested a mature and serious mind. Gernsback was a little taken aback to discover Hornig was only seventeen, but he was prepared to hire him. It is worth pausing to consider, if Hornig had produced a mimeographed magazine like *Science Fiction*, whether Gernsback would have taken a second look at it. Ruppert's printing enhanced the appearance of the magazine and was almost certainly the cause of Gernsback's attention.

Although Hornig started to work for Gernsback on August 7, 1933, he continued to publish *The Fantasy Fan* and remained active in fandom. The first issue had been oriented toward science fiction, but thereafter, recognizing a potential conflict of loyalties in his new professional role, Hornig shifted the emphasis of *The Fantasy Fan* from science fiction to weird and fantasy fiction. Although only sixteen pages per issue, *The Fantasy Fan* maintained a regular monthly schedule through to its last issue in February 1935, and sustained a high quality of fiction, with contributions by H. P. Lovecraft, Robert E. Howard, Clark Ashton Smith, August Derleth, Duane Rimel, Eando Binder, and David H. Keller. It was the last high spot of the small press movement of the early 1930s. By 1935 Ruppert was having to devote more of his time to printing professionally and could not produce the fan magazines. William Crawford helped for a while, but by then the momentum was lost. A much wider world of fandom was emerging; but more on that later.

29.

THE YEAR OF THE GREAT CHANGE

Long time fan and bookdealer Robert A. Madle dubbed 1934 "Science Fiction's Greatest Year,"[1] and I'm inclined to agree with him. There may have been years when better stories were published, and there may have been years when there were events of such significance that they altered the course of science-fiction history. Everyone will have their own candidates for those. But I can't think of another year wherein so much happened that was so good and so exciting, which made everything that came before it seem like a rehearsal. If in the earlier years Gernsback, Sloane, Bates, and Lasser had been loading the cannon, in 1934 it didn't just fire, it exploded, and the fragments took a long time to settle.

Before exploring 1934, which is going to take three chapters, let's see how we get there. By October 1933 the three monthly magazines had put on their new suits of armour and were ready for battle. *Astounding Stories* had just been relaunched by Street & Smith from their venerable, but increasingly antiquated and cluttered offices on Seventh Avenue, with F. Orlin Tremaine as editor. Tremaine (1899-1956), although only 34, was already an experienced hand. He had edited *True Story* for Bernarr Macfadden and *The Smart Set* for William Randolph Hearst, and had been a senior editor for William Clayton since 1926. He came across to Street & Smith as incumbent editor of *Clues* and *Cowboy Stories*, and inherited two more: *Astounding Stories* and *Top-Notch*. As his assistant, Tremaine employed Desmond Hall, who had for a while assisted Harry Bates, and had also co-written the notorious Hawk Carse series.

Amazing Stories was still edited by the venerable T. O'Conor Sloane, now aproaching his eighty-second birthday. Teck's offices on West 39th Street were even more claustrophobic than Street & Smith's. Sloane was assisted by a secretary, Florence Bothner, and by C. A. Brandt, who, after a brief few months working for Gernsback as Literary Editor, had returned as first reader and book reviewer.

Wonder Stories still came from Gernsback's offices on Park Place, though in May 1934, they would move to less auspicious rooms in Hudson Street. The offices were rather dark and a little damp, and the atmosphere was overwhelmed by the cigars of Joseph Kraus and the pipe of C. P. Mason. It was into these surroundings that seventeen-year-old Charles D. Hornig took up his rôle as editor from the November 1933 issue.

All three magazines were now in pulp format. *Amazing* and *Wonder* each cost 25 cents, whilst *Astounding* was 20 cents. *Wonder* had only 128 pages, however, and a fair quota of that was the letter column and departments. Both *Amazing* and *Astounding* ran to 144 pages, and *Astounding* would increase to 160 from March 1934. It was not difficult to assess which provided the value for money in terms of quantity. In terms of quality, however, there was a different standard.

The October and November 1933 issues of *Astounding* gave no hint of what was to come, and fans were generally disappointed. They contained an odd mixture of obscure science fiction and weird stories. Since the manuscripts for *Strange Tales* had been returned to their authors, it suggests that Street & Smith, who had purchased the rights to *Strange Tales*, had acquired stories for a relaunch and then changed their minds, and used those stories up in *Astounding*.

Hornig's first two issues of *Wonder Stories* had a little more to offer. Some of these stories may have been purchased by David Lasser, though to my mind "The End of Tyme" by A. Fedor and Henry Hasse, a spoof involving a time traveler turning up in the editorial offices of a science-fiction magazine, is a typical Hornig acquisition, as it reeks of fan humor. "The Tomb from Beyond" by Carl Jacobi was probably also a Hornig purchase, as it was more weird than scientific (it had already been rejected by both *Weird Tales* and *Strange Tales* and Jacobi totally rewrote it before submitting it to *Wonder Stories*). These were both in the November 1933 issue which contained two other stories. "The Man with the X-Ray Eyes" was a novel idea from Edmond Hamilton, who throughout 1932 and 1933 had made a regular effort to be original. "The Call of the Mech-Men" was the start of Laurence Manning's Stranger Club series, a run of five explorers' tales, written in Manning's enjoyable style, and still read well today.

The November and December issues of *Amazing Stories* contained little of merit except for Mort Weisinger's "The Price of Peace" and Frank Kelly's "Into the Meteorite Orbit." Neil R. Jones's "Time's Mausoleum" was another of his Professor Jameson stories, and of interest because Jones set out his own canvas of future history, which he explored in many of his later stories. Sloane was still bolstering his wordage with such ancient tales as "The Watch's Soul" by Jules Verne and "Mellonta Tauta" by Edgar Allan Poe. As 1933 drew to a close, *Wonder Stories* undoubtedly led the field.

The first sign of change came in the December 1933 *Astounding*. The previous issue had declared with a remarkable lack of restraint, that the next issue would contain "a story that will awaken more controversy than any story ever published in a science-fiction magazine." The story was "Ancestral Voices" by Nat Schachner. The story isn't, in fact, that remarkable and aroused little controversy. It deals with a question discussed in science-fiction circles for years—what happens if you go back in time and kill your own ancestor? Schachner answered it by suggesting that if you go back far enough, in this case to the fifth century, and kill a Hun, you wipe out the bulk of today's population, regardless of race! It was the race issue that made the story controversial, especially in the light of the anti-semitic, pure-Aryan stock frenzy being whipped up in Europe by Adolf Hitler.

Tremaine gave this story the tag of "thought variant," meaning a new twist on an old idea. It is pertinent that Schachner should be the writer whom fate chose to launch this concept, because Schachner had been the one closest to responding to Lasser's demands for new fiction in *Wonder*. I have wondered whether Schachner wrote the story for *Wonder*, but shifted it to Tremaine when Lasser left *Wonder*. It was between Lasser's departure and Hornig's appointment that Street & Smith relaunched *Astounding*, and with the promise of a more reliable market, Schachner, now writing full-time, was almost bound to switch allegiance. In fact Schachner never again appeared in *Wonder Stories* but he became an *Astounding* regular. Was this the first casualty of Gernsback's change of editors? Might science-fiction history have changed had *Wonder* published "Ancestral Voices"?

It is also interesting to see that Tremaine was pushing for a new treatment of science fiction. Although he had not edited *Astounding* when at Clayton, he would have been aware of the magazine at editorial meetings, and doubtless discussed it with Bates. He was probably no fan of the super-science extravaganza, but was clearly a fan of the off-trail story. His plan, therefore, was to publish a variant of the weird-science story that *Weird Tales* was noted for, but with a sense of wonder rather than of fear, and with more quality writing. It is unlikely that Tremaine had seen the flyer for *Unusual Stories* at the time he announced his "thought variant" concept; indeed he may never have seen it. But his desire for something new echoed the wishes expressed by Crawford and Eshbach. It is also probable that he was guided in this new field by Desmond Hall who had a wider knowledge of science fiction, and did seem comfortable with the super-science epics. (In fact, so taken was Tremaine with the off-trail scientific story that he introduced it into *Top-Notch*. That magazine had regularly tried to emulate *Adventure* and *Popular*, its cover formerly boasting "Top-Notch Western, Detective and Sports Stories." But from late 1933 on it began to feature a regular science-fiction or fantastic-adventure story each issue, by authors including R. F. Starzl, C. T. Stoneham, Nelson S. Bond, Charles Willard Diffin, and Ralph Milne Farley.)

Charles Hornig had almost certainly seen Crawford's flyer, and he had his own response. The January 1934 *Wonder Stories*, published on December 1, 1933, contained a special notice on "Our New Policy." Hornig announced that he was outlawing old-fashioned stories with time-worn plots and insisting upon "good, logical and accurate science." He emphasized the word "NEW" throughout: "NEW plots; NEW theories; NEW action; NEW characterizations." He ended by saying: "*Wonder Stories* is attempting a RADICAL REVOLUTION in science-fiction, and we hope that 1934 will be set down as the year of the GREAT CHANGE in scientific literature!"[2] How right he was.

The stage was now set in both *Astounding* and *Wonder* for that revolution. There was less likelihood in *Amazing*, although the magazine had announced E. E. Smith's *Triplanetary* as forthcoming, and launched into this four-part serial with its January 1934 issue. *Triplanetary* had been the novel planned to start in the March 1933 *Astounding*, but as that had been the magazine's last issue, Bates had returned the novel to Smith. Apart from *Triplanetary*, and the Professor Jameson stories by Neil R. Jones, there was little else of significance published in *Amazing* in 1934 (or for the remainder of the thirties for that matter), and it would have to wait another twenty-five years before it again exerted a beneficial influence upon the science-fiction field.

The battle for supremacy in 1934 was between *Astounding* and *Wonder*—in effect between Goliath and David—although in this case the latter had no divine assistance. *Astounding* had Tremaine as an experienced editor with the weight of Street & Smith's name and resources, and was able to pay at least one cent a word on acceptance. Hornig was totally unexperienced, and had no financial backing or resources from Gernsback's publications. Authors were lucky if they were paid at all. Hornig's only advantage was his enthusiasm, his innocence, and his contacts with the fan field. He might also hope for a little luck.

To a large extent, though, it was no contest. Once Tremaine and Hall had stated their case, the writers began to flock to them. Just consider the following, which are but a few of the stories published by *Astounding* in the first six months of 1934.

"Colossus," by Donald Wandrei. Although this utilized the already dated concept of a macro-universe, Wandrei powered the story with a poetic sweep of cosmic wonder that was positively breath-taking. It left most readers awestruck, and the story was, and still is, acclaimed a classic.

"Redmask of the Outlands," by Nat Schachner. Another of his carefully considered sociological projections which may either have been written with Lasser in mind, or written as a consequence of Lasser's guidance.

Rebirth, **by Thomas Calvert McClary**. A short novel wherein a scientist, with technocratic urgings, pleas for the end of war and hatred. As no one responds he eradicates all memory from mankind, so that they have to learn everything over again. This was a bold concept which haunted readers of the magazine for months to come.

"Born of the Sun," by Jack Williamson. A wild idea that all of the planets are but eggs of the parent sun. Williamson wrote it with such boldness that he got away with it.

"The Man Who Stopped the Dust," by John Russell Fearn. Fearn later earned a reputation as a hack writer and has been much maligned, but his thought variants for *Astounding* all contained bold, original ideas. The first looked at the possibility of eradicating dust by destroying the electrons within the dust molecules, which had bizarre consequences.

"A Matter of Size," by Harry Bates. The idea of a shrinking man was not new, but Bates treated it with considerably originality and proved that he was a capable writer.

The Legion of Space, **by Jack Williamson**. The first full-length novel serialized in *Astounding*. Although it's a wham-bang of a space opera, Williamson had injected some character and purpose into this adventure, unlike earlier extravaganzas. It's still an enjoyable romp when read today.

"Sidewise in Time," by Murray Leinster. Another classic, and the first detailed consideration of alternate realities.

"Crater 17, Near Tycho," by Frank K. Kelly. One of Kelly's thoughtful, downbeat stories on the perils of space exploration.

"The Blinding Shadows," by Donald Wandrei. A compelling story in which a scientist's experiment lets loose within our own world the three-dimensional shadows of a fourth-dimensional being.

These are just ten of the best stories published in *Astounding* in the first half of 1934. Compare *Wonder*:

"Evolution Satellite," by J. Harvey Haggard. One of the first items Hornig purchased. Evolution is caused by a force emanating from a satellite of Uranus, with the rate of evolution varying in proportion to the distance from the source. Life on the satellite goes through a cycle of evolution during each creature's own lifetime!

The Exile of the Skies, **by Richard Vaughan.** This was the first serial of the year and was a much-loved space opera written with compassion and style. Vaughan had only written one previous story, and wrote nothing subsequently. This story of a tour through the solar system by a super-scientist banished from Earth, is still fondly remembered by old-timers, though it has never been published in book form.

"The Man from Ariel," by Donald A. Wollheim. Wollheim's first story and a touching tale of a dying alien visitor.

"Today's Yesterday," by Russell Blaiklock [published under the alias Rice Ray]. Time is seen as a series of waves with yesterday and tomorrow on the previous and next crest of the wave.

"The Spore Doom," by Eando Binder. A forecast of chemical warfare with the creation of a fungus that destroys crops, mutates and then absorbs the oxygen from the atmosphere, forcing mankind into air-tight underground cities.

"The Sublime Vigil," by Chester D. Cuthbert. Gernsback later selected this as his favorite story from *Wonder Stories*. It is totally original, and is essentially a character study of a man who has lost his loved one to a strange cosmic force, and awaits its return so that he might join her. Gernsback said of it that, "the author wove into [the idea] a remarkable tapestry of emotion which depicts a cold, scientific notion with rare humanity."

"The Literary Corkscrew," by David H. Keller. A clever psychological tale of a man who has varying bouts of creativity.

"The Last Planet," by R. F. Starzl. The last survivors on Earth build a mighty spaceship to take them to a new world. With a little more thought Starzl could have made this the first story on the generation starship theme, but it had to wait a few more years before Don Wilcox did that in "The Voyage That Lasted 600 Years" (*Amazing Stories*, October 1940).

Unlike *Astounding*, where one was spoiled for choice in picking new concepts, they were harder to find in *Wonder*, and the above list just about exhausts them. The problem was that even when these authors hit upon a new idea they still tended to deliver it in a traditional way. Whereas at *Astounding* the writers were bringing a new treatment to science fiction, at *Wonder* they were merely dressing old plots in new clothes. The majority of stories that Hornig was publishing, despite his editorial hype, were still traditional.

There had been a retread of Wells's *The Invisible Man* in Abner J. Gelula's "The Vengeance of a Scientist," a grand Merritesque adventure in Jack Williamson's "Xandulu" set in a sub-Saharan lost city, giant insects in "The Land of Mighty Insects" by A. C. Stimson, a rerun of Conan Doyle's *The Poison Belt* in "The Green Cloud from Space" by Eando Binder, and sub-microscopic worlds in "Into the Infinitesimal" by Kaye Raymond.

There was still a sense of fun and adventure about *Wonder Stories*, but the one thing it lacked was "wonder," whereas *Astounding* certainly did "astound." It was there one looked for breathtaking concepts and thrills. Each issue of *Astounding* was now approached with trembling anticipation, whilst each new *Wonder* was approached rather like an old pal for a friendly chat. Whereas *Astounding* was attracting new concepts in fiction, *Wonder* was not. Hornig was keen to attract new writers and concepts, especially once *Astounding* revealed its strength of opposition. He hammered his point home in an article on "Novelty—The Essential of Science Fiction" in the July 1934 *Author & Journalist*. He highlighted the development of science fiction over the last few years, emphasising its evolutionary nature. He instructed authors to keep the novelty factor at the forefront of their minds in producing fiction. "Their plots must be based on something that has never been used before in a story, preferably a plausible scientific theory that attempts to explain some mystery which scientists cannot solve at the present time." He cited the works by Haggard, Cuthbert, Blaiklock, and Binder, mentioned above, as examples of new ideas.

Although Hornig was having some success, he was also starting to alienate writers already biased against *Wonder* due to the lack of payment for stories, by chiding them for a lack of originality. Yet some of them were turning in original stories, only for Hornig to reject them. In December 1933 Edmond Hamilton sent him a new story called "Colonists of Mars," which looked at the hardships of space colonization. As we have seen, at that time Hamilton was one of the most popular writers for the magazine, now noted for his original ideas. Hornig rejected this story on the grounds that it did not live up to his new policy. Yet Hornig liked the story. "[I] found it exceptionally well-written and vividly portrayed. Your ability to compose such a human story shows that you have an insight of human nature and the tale is very convincing. Although it is perhaps the best story written on the horrors of interplanetary travel as they would affect the voyagers, the idea has been used before. The fact that space travel would be no picnic is not new to science-fiction. Your story, while an elaboration of this idea, does not really introduce anything new . . ."[3]

That is how to cut off your nose to spite your face. Hornig lost a gem. The story was rejected by the other magazines as well. It certainly did not fit into *Astounding*'s sense of cosmic wonder, and was "too horrible" for *Amazing*, but it was ideal for *Wonder*, and there is no doubt that Lasser would have pounced on it. As it is, the story languished in a trunk for nearly twenty years before being brushed off, retitled, and published in the December 1952 *Thrilling Wonder Stories* as "What's It Like Out There?" It was hailed at that time as a remarkable breakthrough in fiction. What would it have done for *Wonder* in 1934?

Luckily, Hornig did recognize one masterpiece when it came his way: "A

Martian Odyssey" by Stanley G. Weinbaum, published in the July 1934 issue. This story has a status in fiction that has raised it to the level of legend. There is no denying that the story is a landmark, and is certainly one of the most enjoyable stories from the Gernsback period. But comments that it was the only story of lasting merit published in the pre-Campbell period is stretching adulation too far. We have already mentioned many stories of lasting merit, and some of much greater originality than Weinbaum's classic. What Weinbaum brought to science fiction was a mature and stylish treatment of character, with humor, inventiveness and imagination. He portrayed creatures ideally adapted to their environment and thus expanded the horizons of the bizarre. Yet the basic plot of "A Martian Odyssey" is little more than a travelogue, another explorer's tale; but it was so polished and alive, compared to the bulk of mediocrity that Hornig was publishing that the readers went into raptures over it, claiming the story as the best ever published in *Wonder Stories*.

Weinbaum (1902-1935) was a tonic for science fiction. His was the talent that was needed to take science fiction forward along the road of realism that Lasser had been promoting, and that writers like Hamilton, Miller, Kelly, and Schachner had been developing, but a realism injected with a good dose of humor, and an eye for something original. Lasser would probably have worked wonders with Weinbaum. Hornig, on the other hand, could not see past his concept of novelty, and made his standards too exacting. To meet reader demands, Hornig acquired a sequel to "A Martian Odyssey" called "The Valley of Dreams" (November 1934), but when Weinbaum submitted his next story, "Flight on Titan," Hornig rejected it on the grounds that it was too like its predecessors, and thus lacked novelty! Weinbaum consequently sold the story to *Astounding*, which became his main market thereafter. *Wonder* lost its greatest asset. It only published four more stories by Weinbaum, none on a par with his *Astounding* stories.

"A Martian Odyssey," therefore, might be one of the greatest stories of early magazine science fiction, but it was not typical of what *Wonder* was publishing. As we enter the second half of 1934 the number of original, and in particular, *memorable* stories in *Wonder Stories* was limited.

"The Living Galaxy," by Laurence Manning. Probably the most original, depicting a galaxy as a single sentient entity.

"The Man from Beyond," by John Beynon Harris. Interesting treatment of a man stranded on Venus in a state of suspended animation until he is revived millennia hence by the newly evolved Venusians.

"Dawn to Dusk," by Eando Binder. Consideration of the whole state of man's evolution, with time travel to the distant future and the world of the last man.

And that's about it. There were a few other stories struggling to use original ideas but their impact was lost in hackneyed treatment. There were others that were well written but unoriginal. There were some, like "Dimensional Fate" by A. L. Burkholder, "The Final Struggle" by Francesco Bivona, and "House of Monstrosities" by Edsel Newton, that should never have been published due to a lack of originality and writing ability.

Compare *Astounding*. Here I need only list the titles because the majority of these stories are known instantly, and even if they aren't they are covered in Lowndes's survey:

The Skylark of Valeron, by Edward E. Smith.
"The Living Equation," by Nat Schachner.
"Inflexure," by Clyde Crane Campbell.
"The Bright Illusion," by C. L. Moore.
"The Mole Pirate," by Murray Leinster.
"Twilight," by Don A. Stuart [John W. Campbell, Jr].
The Mightiest Machine, by John W. Campbell, Jr.
"The Irrelevant," by Karl van Campen [John W. Campbell, Jr].
"Atomic Power," by Don A. Stuart [John W. Campbell, Jr].
"Colossus Eternal," by Donald Wandrei.
"Old Faithful," by Raymond Z. Gallun.

And that list isn't even trying. The irony here is that, apart from "The Irrelevant," not one of them contains a new idea. All had been developed in
Wonder Stories and even earlier in *Amazing*. But what these stories do
achieve is to bring the idea alive by a bold new treatment. Both Smith's latest
Skylark adventure and Campbell's *The Mightiest Machine* were cosmic space
operas, but with the characters and events treated realistically. "Twilight,"
one of the best-known stories from this period, is only another dying Earth
story, a theme used so often before by writers from Wertenbaker to Binder,
but it was unveiled against a three-dimensional tapestry of time. "Old Faithful" is another story on the theme of sacrifice, like those previously written by
Hamilton and Miller, but with a depth of poignancy not previously explored.
Every story Tremaine bought could equally have been written for *Wonder*
based on the development of concepts that Lasser was promoting. The realism
he wanted was now emerging, but the writers had forsaken *Wonder* for *Astounding*. The reason was simple. Not only were they paid for their efforts, at
Astounding they were appreciated as writers and encouraged. At *Wonder*
they were not paid and were chided for a lack of originality.

This reaction to *Astounding* can be exemplified by the attitude of E. E.
Smith. During 1933 he had grown increasingly more dismayed with the science-fiction field. After Clayton's *Astounding* had folded and Bates had returned *Triplanetary*, Smith had submitted it to *Wonder Stories*, where it was
rejected as lacking originality. It was then submitted to *Amazing*, where it
was accepted, but Sloane ignored Smith's subsequent letters, and Smith was
tempted to withdraw *Triplanetary* and await the hopeful re-emergence of *Astounding*. In the end he left *Triplanetary* at *Amazing* and spent the winter of
1933/34 working on *The Skylark of Valeron*. By the time he had typed out the
third draft he felt it was poorer than he had hoped, and was discouraged. He
explained the circumstances to Forrest Ackerman:

> I wrote Desmond Hall, telling him all about it, and suggesting
> that he should read the rough draft and wade into it himself with
> a green pencil. I marked the places I thought particularly poor
> and told him what I intended to do about them. He replied that

that was a keen idea and I sent him the draft, with due apologies for its messiness, and asking him for a quick reading because of the jittery state I was in.

He gave me the quick service, all right—the fastest I ever had from an editor. I more than half expected a flat rejection, and the best I hoped for was a chance to rewrite the whole thing—so you may well imagine that I just about passed out when he accepted the ROUGH DRAFT, saying that it was perfect the way it was and that he didn't want a word changed anywhere![4]

What *Astounding* gave their authors was a quick service, and confidence in their works.

As Charles Hornig had predicted, 1934 was "the year of the great change," but it wasn't the change he'd bargained for. *Wonder* which, since 1929, had been the leading science-fiction magazine, was now in second place, and not a close second, but way behind the leader, and there was no catching up.

1934 was significant for another reason. It saw the first English language science-fiction magazine outside the American continent, and though it was a poor example, it was a sign of the expansion of science-fiction fever.

30.

OTHER WORLDS

So far this survey has covered Gernsback's role in the development of science fiction on American soil only. We should not forget that Gernsback often selected material from European writers to print, or reprint, in his magazines. Whilst the science-fiction magazine was now established as an American phenomenon, science fiction had global potential, and was essentially more European in its development, than American.

That a science-fiction magazine emerged at all on the American continent was due entirely to Gernsback's drive and tenacity. One might well question why one had not appeared earlier in Europe. Early claimants as pioneer science-fiction magazines can be no more seriously considered than Gernsback's own *Science and Invention* or Munsey's *All-Story*. The Swedish *Hugin* (1916-1920) carried a combination of scientific news, speculation and analysis. The Russian *Mir prikliuchenii* (1910-1930) was an adventure magazine with a sprinkling of science stories, some translated from Gernsback's publications. The German *Der Luftpirat* (1908-1913), better known under the title of its hero-villain, Kapitan Mors, was a series of short dime novels like Luis Senarens's Frank Reade series, whilst the later German title, *Der Orchideengarten* (1919-1921) was more interested in fantasy and the weird than scientific fiction. Only *Hugin* came any where near the Gernsback ideal of promoting scientific advance but this magazine, edited, published and almost entirely written by engineer Otto Witt (1875-1923), seems to have had little influence within Sweden, let alone beyond its borders. It was not until 1934 that a genuine science-fiction magazine appeared outside the United States. Unfortunately this title, *Scoops*, is more of an embarrassment than a major step forward, and its appearance is indicative of the treatment accorded science fiction outside North America.

The following for science fiction in Europe suffered after the First World War when the public, with its front-line involvement, had been repulsed at the carnage science could wreak. The leading pre-War European writer of science fiction, H. G. Wells, had more or less abandoned the form by the twenties. The chief development of Gernsbackian-style science fiction, with its emphasis on scientific gadgetry, was in Germany, where a number of writers, some closely allied to the German Rocket Society, were producing memorable work. We have already mentioned Otto Willi Gail whose *The Shot into Infinity* (1925) and *The Stone from the Moon* (1926) were seminal works of space travel, and were reprinted with much acclaim in *Science Wonder Quarterly*. There was also Curt Siodmak, whose "The Eggs from Lake Tanganyika" had been reprinted in the fourth issue of *Amazing Stories*, who produced the highly Gernsbackian novel *F.P.1 Does Not Reply* (1931) about mid-ocean air platforms and a transatlantic tunnel. Curiously Gernsback did not reprint this in his magazines. Gernsback did reprint a number of the novels by Otfrid von Hanstein, who looked every inch the solid Prussian, and who wrote a number of novels about the creation of super scientific utopias on Earth, such as *The Emperor of the Sahara* (1922) and *Elektropolis* (1927). All of these works reflect the extent to which Germany was at the forefront of scientific advance in the twenties, but with increasing Nazi domination in the thirties, the scientists and creative artists began to leave. Siodmak entered England in 1931, working in the cinema, and eventually arrived in the United States in 1937. Willy Ley also emigrated to the States, via England, in 1935.

By the early thirties the initiative in developing a positive approach to science fiction was back on British shores. In the mainstream of literature the two major successors to H. G. Wells were S. Fowler Wright and Olaf Stapledon. Stapledon would become the more influential of the two, though he did not start developing his philosophical form of science fiction until 1930 with *Last and First Men*. Wright wrote more in the vein of Wells, but with the style of some of the better American pulpsters, (especially George Allan England), whose work *The Amphibians* (1924), and its expansion *The World Below* (1929), closely resembles.

The British magazine scene was different to the American. There was not such a rift between the prestigeous slick magazines and the pulps. Britain had a wide range of popular magazines following in the wake of the successful *Strand Magazine* developed by George Newnes in 1891. These included such imitations as *Pearson's*, *Pall Mall*, *The Windsor*, *The Idler*, and *The Royal*. The British pulp magazines, such as *The Grand*, *The Novel*, *The Storyteller*, and *The Red Magazine* were only an extension of the popular slicks, but were generally all-fiction. They lacked the glossy illustrations and photographs and were generally less attractive, but still published the same regular writers. In fact they were seldom referred to as pulps, though they were printed on the same low-quality newspaper stock.

After the War these magazines rarely published science fiction. When they did, it usually took the form of either humorous tales, spoofing the potential of science, or chilling tales of scientific horrors. There was an emphasis on the fear of discovery of atomic energy, most writers believing it would lead to untold horror. Typical was Michael Storm's "The World Crisis" (*Red Magazine*, December 1930), where a Russian mad scientist develops atomic energy and threatens the world.

Although Britain was rich in fiction magazines, it was some time before any specialist titles were developed. They began to emerge in the twenties, to some extent driven by the volume of pulp genre-fiction available through the sale of subsidiary rights by American publishers' or authors' agents. The prime mover in Britain was Walter Hutchinson (1887-1950), who launched *Adventure-Story Magazine* in September 1922 and *Mystery-Story Magazine* in February 1923. The period also saw a growth in women's magazines, especially romance titles. But magazine publishers were chary at experimenting with anything so revolutionary as a magazine of science-fiction stories. Whilst British magazines frequently reprinted adventure, mystery and love stories from American pulps (and vice versa) it was a rare moment for a science-fiction story to be reprinted, and I know of none from a Gernsback publication to appear in an adult fiction magazine. However, some did appear in the boys' adventure magazine *Chums*, which is the level at which science fiction was pitched in Britain.

Chums was a typical example of the "ripping yarns"-school of upper-class boys' magazine, originally typified by *The Boys' Own Paper*. It delivered a regular diet of stirring stories of piracy, jungle adventure, air battles, foreign legion and all-round derring-do. Jules Verne's adventure stories had fitted into this category—indeed they had been written primarily for younger readers—and had featured regularly in *The Boys' Own Paper*, but science fiction in the shape of the space opera was not part of the standard fare in boys' magazines at this time. *Chums*, more than its fellow magazines, was receptive to the occasional space adventure. One of its regular contributors was Hector Hawton, who wrote wrote several science-fiction stories for *Chums* under the name John Sylvester. These included a serial, *The Master of the World*, which began in the May 1930 issue.[1] It tells of inventor Max Carnac, and his combined submarine-flying machine *The Black Hawk*, who becomes a modern-day aerial Robin Hood. The story bears an immediate comparison with Verne's own *Master of the World*, which had seen a British edition from Sampson Low in 1914; but a detailed consideration of the story shows a more direct comparison with George Allan England's *The Flying Legion*, which had not had a British printing. It had, however, only just been reprinted in Gernsback's *Air Wonder Stories* (January-April 1930), and Hawton could have taken the concept from there, merged it with Verne's story, to produce his own version. Stories had a short lead-in time at *Chums*, and it was perfectly possible for Hawton to have read the early episodes of England's serial and write his novel in readiness for the weekly edition of *Chums*, where his first installment was set in type in the middle of April. It may even have been the editor of *Chums* who suggested the idea. Copies of Gernsback's magazines were available in *Chums*'s editorial offices as Gernsback seems to have come to a short-term arrangement with Amalgamated Press over reprints. J. P. Marshall's "Warriors of Space," from the June 1929 *Science Wonder Stories*, was reprinted in the December 1929 *Chums* (as by S. P. Marshall). Two other stories, "Beyond the Aurora" by Ed Earl Repp and "The Second Shell" by Jack Williamson, both from the November 1929 *Air Wonder Stories*, later surfaced in the May 1931 *Chums*.

Whatever Gernsback's arrangements with Amalgamated Press, his impact on *Chums* and its writers was limited. The most important influence that Gernsback's magazines had in Britain at this time, was to encourage contributions from British writers. With few British markets, they had to turn to America for publication. One of the first was George C. Wallis, a printer and cinema manager, who had been writing science fiction and fantasy for the major British magazines since 1896, but was now finding his markets diminishing unless he wrote for the boys' magazines. Through a Canadian cousin, Bruce Wallis, who had himself been selling to *Weird Tales* and *Argosy*, George began to sell stories to a number of markets, including *Amazing Stories* with *The World at Bay* (November-December 1928).

The real British invasion began in 1931. First in print was Benson Herbert with "The World Without" (*Wonder Stories*, February 1931). A radio technician who for some years had been writing poetry and science essays, Herbert developed a fascination for psychic research and regarded his science fiction as a natural part of that interest. He remained actively involved in psychic research until his death in 1991. He was followed by John Beynon Harris, who had earlier won a contest in *Air Wonder Stories* for the magazine's slogan, though his winning entry, "Future Flying Fiction," was never used because the magazine ceased publication. Harris's first story, "Worlds to Barter" (*Wonder Stories*, May 1931), challenged some of the concepts of time travel, and many of his later stories brought fresh views to standard ideas. Harris would later become popular under his pseudonym John Wyndham. Next came J. M. Walsh, better known for his mystery stories, though he preferred writing super-scientific space operas when opportunity allowed. The first, *Vandals of the Void*, was published in hardcover in London by Hamilton's in 1931, and ran in the Summer 1931 *Wonder Stories Quarterly*.

Walsh was Australian by birth, and Australia would later produce some good science-fiction writers. As a curious aside, one of the most prolific, R. Coutts Armour, who wrote under the pen names of Coutts Brisbane and Reid Whitley, appeared regularly in the British pulps but never in the American. The best-known Australian writer to surface in the Gernsback magazines was Alan Connell, who sold four stories to Charles Hornig during 1935.

Other British writers were Ralph Stranger, Festus Pragnell, John Edwards, Philip E. Cleator (founder of the British Interplanetary Society), W. P. Cockroft, Harry O. Dickinson, and the most prolific of them all, John Russell Fearn. Fearn aside, only Pragnell, a policeman who had retired early through ill-health, made any impact upon the science-fiction scene.

In July 1932, during the brief heyday of Lasser's new story policy at *Wonder Stories*, Hugo Gernsback undertook a European tour. It was not a science-fiction tour but one aimed at "making an intensive study of radio and television conditions." He wrote about the trip in the October 1932 *Radio-Craft*, where he deduced that Europe was technologically five years behind America. This aside, the presence of Gernsback outside of the United States gave the British a chance to hear directly from "the world's greatest prophet" as he was dubbed in the *Daily Express*. The reporter gave Gernsback a high profile in America. "What Mr. Gernsback says in the line of scientific prophecy 'goes' in America," he wrote. "This slim-built, dark-featured, middle-aged man, who has made science a best-seller, foretold the wonders of wireless telegraphy some years before it actually happened. There has scarcely been an advance in science which Mr. Gernsback, through his publications, has not outlined before it took place."[2] Reported under the headline "One Day We Shall Visit Mars," the article went on to list Gernsback's predictions of passenger-carrying rocket trips to the Moon, Mars, and Venus within fifty years, and television probes sent in advance to the planets. He also predicted it would be quicker to fly from London to New York than to get across London by public transport, and in that he was right!

I don't know whether, during his visit, Gernsback met the British author and engineer, I. O. Evans, but Evans had developed a fascination for science fiction and the future of science, and in 1933 produced what must have been an inspirational book for youngsters of the day: *The World of Tomorrow*. Subtitled *A Junior Book of Forecasts*, this volume, bound in "translucent rhodoid," considered many predictions in areas such as communications, transport, food and clothing, the weather, health, industry, government, war and peace, human evolution, and, of course, space travel. It was liberally illustrated with film stills and pictures from various magazines, including *Amazing Stories*. Evans projected the same missionary zeal in his text where he encouraged his young readers to work with a common aim toward building a new and better world.

One fan who certainly regretted missing Hugo Gernsback was journalist Walter Gillings. "Had I known that he was only ten miles away, there is no doubt I would have waylaid the prophetic genius, pleading with him to take me home with him to the Land of Science Fiction, or at least to appoint me editor of a British edition of *Wonder Stories*. The hope would almost certainly have been in vain; yet the meeting, if it had taken place, might well have changed the course of British SF—whether for better or worse we can only speculate."[3]

Gillings was the prime mover and organizer for science fiction in Britain, and was the genuine father of British magazine science fiction. His first success did not come until 1937, though, with the publication of *Tales of Wonder*, which drew heavily upon Gernsback's magazines for its reprinted material. Despite Gillings's persistence, in the early to mid-thirties, the prospect for science fiction in Britain was bleak, and it is hard to believe a Gillings-Gernsback meeting could have made matters much better. Although the revamped weekly slick magazine *The Passing Show* began to feature an occasional science-fiction serial or story (which was a surprising development as *The Passing Show* was an upper-class society magazine), publishers generally regarded science fiction as stories for boys. So when the publishing firm of C. Arthur Pearson decided to experiment with a science-fiction adventure magazine, they launched one aimed directly at the boys-fiction market. It was called *Scoops* and appeared as a weekly tabloid starting with the February 10, 1934 issue.

In charge as managing editor was Haydn Dimmock, editor of *The Scout*. He brought in a tribe of boys' adventure-fiction writers to churn out the kind of juvenile science fiction that Gernsback and Lasser abhorred, but which had been prevalent in the American magazines in 1930-1931. Gernsback's observation that Europe was five years behind America on radio matters, was equally appropriate to science fiction.

Scoops projected a lower-quality image than did *Chums* or *The Boys' Own Paper*, which in itself suggested the level at which the British would accept science fiction, and though it was fun for youngsters, it was an embarrassment for the older reader who might have felt it necessary to support *Scoops* in the hope it would develop into a serious magazine. The main guard of British writers and devotees, amongst them Walter Gillings, John Russell Fearn, P. E. Cleator, Maurice Hugi, and W. P. Cockroft, exhorted Dimmock and his team to treat science fiction seriously. Dimmock admitted he had not realized that there was an adult audience for this type of fiction, and by May 1934 started to give *Scoops* a face-lift. Where originally most of the stories had appeared anonymously, apart from a serial by Professor A. M. Low, they began to carry the names of their contributors, amongst them Fearn, Hugi, and Cockroft, whilst Cleator provided a series of articles, "To the Planets." The face-lift was minimal, however, and the general quality of the fiction remained puerile. *Scoops* had no real opportunity to develop into a serious magazine. The sales began to diminish and the magazine was discontinued with its twentieth issue, dated June 23, 1934. Dimmock reported to Gillings that "demand was not sufficient to give us confidence for the future."[4]

Thus Britain's first experiment with a science-fiction magazine had proved a failure, and that gave the message to other publishers that it was not a field for investment. This, despite the fact that Gernsback was recognizing a high level of interest in *Wonder Stories* from British readers, and even made the letter column of the August 1935 issue an all-British affair. But *Scoops*'s failure had given a clear message. Charles Hornig commented upon it in response to a letter from James Dudley of Nottingham, England, in the April 1936 *Wonder Stories*. Dudley believed a British edition of *Wonder Stories* would sell well. Hornig's response referred to the *Scoops* failure and remarked: "This proved to us and other British publishers that your country is not yet prepared to support a professional science-fiction magazine enough to make it pay for itself."[5]

It set back the development of a serious British science-fiction magazine for a further three years until Gernsbackian science fiction triumphed in the hands of Walter Gillings and *Tales of Wonder*. But that is another decade and another story. 1934 had at least demonstrated that science fiction had a following in Britain, but it needed to get its act in order first. In the meantime, in the United States, that's just what Gernsback and fandom were doing.

31.

UNITED WE STAND

Gernsback had always admired the hobbyist. That was the reason behind *Modern Electrics* in 1908, and *The Electrical Experimenter* in 1913. His formation of the Wireless Association of America in 1909 and the Radio League of America in 1916 had been ways of harnessing that dedicated energy partly as a means to promote his magazines, but primarily as a means of achievement. Gernsback could not abide wasted time and energy. If that energy could be tapped and channeled, it could become creative. His latest moves in that direction had been to form a Short Wave League of Radio Hams in his magazine *Short Wave Craft*. As a parallel to that Gernsback suggested that Hornig start a Science Fiction League for the growing army of fans.

There was a preliminary announcement of the League's creation in the April 1934 *Wonder Stories*. It stated that the League was being formed to "coordinate all who are interested in science fiction, into one comprehensive international group. . . . It is to be hoped that this new League will in due time become the parent organization of innumerable local science-fiction clubs throughout the world."[1]

Advance copies of that editorial were mailed to selected writers and fans on February 5 seeking their approval to be made Honorary Members. Gernsback emphasized in this letter that "No financial outlay of any kind is expected of you as the League is purely a membership organization, without dues or fees of any kind. It is simply a good will movement to further the science-fiction movement all over the world." Eight writers responded and these became the first honorary members and executive directors of the League. They were Forrest J Ackerman, Eando Binder, Jack Darrow, Edmond Hamilton, David H. Keller, P. Schuyler Miller, Clark Ashton Smith, and R. F. Starzl.

Gernsback was able to display their names at the heading to his editorial in the May *Wonder Stories*, which gave full details of the League. Here Gernsback compared the rise in science-fiction fandom to the early days of radio:

> The movement is akin to the state of amateur radio before broadcasting appeared: the radio amateur movement was then confined to a few thousand earnest young men who pursued the new art as a hobby. the great public did not come into radio until broadcasting arrived in the early twenties. A similar condition prevails in Science Fiction today. The movement still has not reached the great public, but efforts are made by all Science Fiction enthusiasts to spread its vogue from year to year. The motion pictures have already been converted, if only partially, to Science Fiction, and a number of excellent films on Science Fiction have been presented to the public at large. Much remains to be done . . .[2]

Gernsback went on to talk about the educational qualities of science fiction. He declared that it was time that the public were turned from "meaningless detective and love trash to the elevating and imaginary literature of Science Fiction." It was incumbent upon the League members to spread the gospel throughout the world.

Elsewhere were stated the purposes of the League, which were slightly different to those already announced. It was not solely to organize fandom, but to "continually broaden the scope and to popularize the art of Science Fiction." Gernsback elaborated how this could be done:

> By word of mouth in the school and classroom, by getting new readers to read Science Fiction magazines, by inducing motion-picture corporations to run Science Fiction films, by getting newspapers to publish Science Fiction stories, by getting broadcast stations to broadcast Science Fiction, etc.[3]

This was not dissimilar to the promotional campaign Gernsback had advocated in 1930 as part of the Science Fiction Week suggested by Conrad Ruppert. Gernsback was now recognizing, though, that the movement needed to be fostered as an encouragement to the study of science fiction rather than of science directly, which was how he had originally envisaged the fan movement in the early stirrings of 1929.

The League offered to members a lapel button, emblematic letterheads, envelopes and seals, plus a free membership certificate. It encouraged the formation of local chapters with gatherings of three or more local members of the League.

The response was immediate, with hundreds of fans clamoring to join. Frederik Pohl remembers that he sent off his application form immediately, but was still member number 490. It must have caused a lot of work for Hornig and his secretary in getting the League organized and operational. A new department was opened in the magazine, which reported on the developments of the League and the activities of its members.

As a special gift, the first ten members were offered a copy of an original manuscript from David H. Keller. They had to write to Keller for it, but that was a thrill in itself. I wonder where those manuscripts are now. The lucky fan who succeeded in becoming Member Number One, was George Gordon Clark from Brooklyn, and he received from Keller a copy of his manuscript of "The Pent House." Clark hadn't been especially active before now, and had not even had a letter published in any of the magazines, but his pioneer membership made him a celebrity, and he set about organizing what became the first local chapter of the League in Brooklyn. It was officially granted chapter status on October 15, 1934, and the first of the League's eventual thirty-six official chapters (there were many not officially inaugurated, plus some post-Gernsback entrants) was born.

The Science Fiction League was a major event in fandom, and important in what it did for the devotees of science fiction, several of whom would later graduate to professional status. In his autobiography, Frederik Pohl makes the point that "it got us out of the closet and into Fandom."[4] It started fans meeting each other, organizing and achieving things. David A. Kyle (Member #359), in his Fan Guest of Honor speech at the 41st World Science Fiction

Convention, made the stronger point that the creation of fandom gave the fans a "Sense of Mission." It gave them a purpose in life. It is worth remembering that many fans were loners. They were seldom life's *wunderkind*, but were more likely the spotty kids on the beach that the bully kicked sand over. Science fiction was their world of escape, but they had no one to share their enthusiasm with. Correspondence through the magazine letter columns had helped ameliorate their isolation, but it was not until the League positively promoted the formation of local clubs that fans started to unite and progress. Alone they would have languished, but united they became a formidable force. The fan magazines had only united them in spirit. Gernsback united them in body.

The League Department in *Wonder Stories* became a bustle with news and activity. There were a couple of quizzes originally aimed at giving readers Degrees in Science Fiction if they attained a certain pass mark. The questions were easy for any one acquainted with the science-fiction magazines though some, like "The title of the first famous science-fiction story is: (1) Ralph 124C 41+ (2) Skylark of Space (3) The Moon Pool (4) Frankenstein" were to a large degree subjective and there are grounds for all four qualifying, or indeed none of them. Other questions, like the true or false one "Very few stories have appeared in which mad scientists have conquered the world." were just plain silly. Fans Forrest Ackerman, William Dellenback, and Lewis Torrance tied in first place with a score of 97%. Some of the well-known names in the list were Milton A. Rothman and Julius Schwartz, both with 95%, Robert W. Lowndes with 94%, Donald A. Wollheim and Thomas S. Gardner with 93%, and Raymond A. Palmer with a surprisingly low 88%.

What was more interesting in the results were the responses to the questions of favorite authors and stories. The top three favorite authors were, in order, David H. Keller, A. Merritt, and John W. Campbell. Curiously, Edmond Hamilton didn't receive a single vote. Merritt's *The Moon Pool* was voted as favorite story, with Smith's *The Skylark of Space* and Vaughan's "Exile of the Skies" joint runners-up.

There is sufficient activity recorded about the League and related events to fill a book. Most of it is not relevant here, though it is of interest to note the birth of science-fiction bibliography from the League. Fans were avid collectors and indexers, and various efforts had been made over the years to compile an exhaustive index to all science-fiction stories, but these always seemed doomed to failure. In the May 1935 column, P. Schuyler Miller, argued the need for a complete and accurate science-fiction bibliography. Miller's wish was for a checklist to issues of old magazines featuring science fiction as a helpful guide to know what old issues to acquire. He was not advocating a book index because, at that stage, science fiction was not regularly published in bookform (although there was more of it about than most people suspected). A response to Miller's request came in promptly from J. O. Bailey of Chapel Hill, North Carolina, stating that he had been working on such a bibliography for years and hoped that League members would not pre-empt him. The League requested fans to help him complete the work. In the end, having reached 5,000 titles, Bailey abandoned the project as too big. His records passed to A. Langley Searles who doggedly worked on the project. The sudden awareness of his activities prompted E. F. Bleiler into completing his own

Checklist of Fantastic Literature (Shasta, 1948). In the meantime Bailey had converted his data and knowledge into a critical analysis of the evolution of science fiction in *Pilgrims through Space and Time* (Argus, 1947) the first such book about the field. Although neither project owed much to the Science Fiction League there is a sense that their roots belong there.

League members promoted science fiction in newspapers, magazines and the cinema, and the full effect of the League is probably immeasurable, though it would be fascinating to assess. Interestingly much of the work settled on a few individuals who now had a sense of purpose working with the moral support of others. Few of the local chapters amounted to much, the majority being just a group of three or four fans who huddled together once in a while and talked shop. A number produced their own club magazines. The earliest was the *Brooklyn Reporter* from George Clark, launched on February 25, 1935. It only lasted five issues, but gave the earliest editorial responsibilities to the fifteen-year-old Frederik Pohl.

By the end of 1935 there had been a split in the Brooklyn Chapter, and Harold Kirshenblit formed the East New York Chapter issuing his own magazine, *Arcturus* in December 1935. Fairly soon this chapter became the dominant force in New York fandom and the Brooklyn Chapter collapsed.

The only other chapters of significance were those in Chicago, under William Dellenback, Philadelphia, under Milton A. Rothman, and Los Angeles, under E. C. Reynolds. The last named, later reconstituted as the Los Angeles Science Fiction Society (LASFS), continues to meet today, after nearly seventy years.

The first overseas chapter was in Leeds, England, run by Douglas Mayer. In rapid succession came Belfast, Nuneaton, Glasgow, and, furthest afield, Sydney, Australia, under Wallace Osland. There were individual members from many countries, of whom the most active was Andrew Lenard in Budapest, Hungary, who had long and interesting letters in almost every issue.

Frederik Pohl has said that if Gernsback had not created the Science Fiction League it would have been necessary for someone else to. The time for it was right, and it galvanized fans into cohesive action. Having done that, and set the machine going, its continued existence served only to oil the wheels. Fans liked to read about their activities in *Wonder Stories*, but many of them would have continued to do it anyway.

But the League also became a public forum in which to attack Gernsback. The first sign of this appeared in the September 1935 issue with a notice that on June 12, three members had been expelled for having "done all within their power . . . to disrepute the League, *Wonder Stories* and the Gernsback outfit by spreading gross untruths and libelous slander to other science-fiction fans and authors." The three fans were Donald A. Wollheim, John B. Michel, and William S. Sykora.

The grounds for this rebellion were two-fold. The prime mover was Wollheim (1914-1990). He had sold two stories to *Wonder Stories* and had been paid for neither. He teamed up with two other unpaid writers, Chester Cuthbert and W. Varick Nevins III, and employed a lawyer to pursue the debt. They were successful. Thereafter Wollheim believed that Gernsback bore a grudge against him. This was unlikely. As we shall see in the next chapter, Wollheim was far from the first to sue Gernsback for non-payment, and certainly not the last. The problem with Wollheim was that he made such a noise about it, spreading the news everywhere, and inciting people against Gernsback. He disrupted a meeting of the Brooklyn Chapter of the League, almost causing its demise, and then made waves in other New York chapters. Hornig was highly embarrassed at one of these sessions, and the expulsion was inevitable. Wollheim did not mind, as it was further publicity for his grievance. Michel was similarly aggrieved, as he had never received his prize money for the plot idea contest from several years before. Sykora, though, had a different resentment.

Sykora (1913-), a tool designer at the Westinghouse X-Ray Company, was a genuine Gernsback science-hobbyist, a purist, who felt that science fiction was for the furtherance of science. He conducted a number of experiments and created a stir on September 22, 1935 when he launched a rocket with a payload of letters. The rocket only rose a few feet and exploded, injuring a young boy nearby. In 1934, Sykora had been instrumental in organizing, or more properly reorganizing, the International Cosmos Science Club, along similar lines to Dennis's Science Correspondence Club. Sykora, helped later by Michel, Pohl, and Wollheim, edited the club's magazine, *The International Observer*. Sykora publicized his experiments, especially his earlier rocket activities, at various meetings of the League's New York chapters, and tried to drum up membership for the ICSC. Hornig could not agree to this, believing that the League was capable of achieving anything the ICSC could do. This led to open hostility. Sykora was not in favor of the League's promotion of science fiction in favor of science experimentation and did not believe that the two organizations shared a common goal.

Looking back over fifty years we can see that at the time this turmoil was little more than a storm in a very large teacup. But I suspect that Gernsback became rather resentful of the way fans were starting to treat him. To his mind the backlash of vehemence from the growing numbers led by Wollheim was tantamount to disloyalty. All Gernsback was trying to do was provide a forum for the furtherance of science fiction. I doubt he would concede the argument that, by not paying authors, he had brought this trouble upon himself. The two issues should not be related. Gernsback had paid Wollheim upon suit, and that should have been an end of it.

Wollheim, perhaps wilfully, but I suspect unknowingly, was probably adding a final nail in the coffin on *Wonder Stories*. If Gernsback had not already grown disillusioned with the field, he very soon would.

32.

DIVIDED WE FALL

When Gernsback's name surfaces in conversation today it is almost always linked with his failure to pay authors. That comment is also almost always linked with the name of Donald Wollheim, who made the most fuss about it. As we have seen through this history, though, Gernsback was always a lousy paymaster, but he usually paid when he could. When he couldn't he made sure that he satisfied the essential parties—the printer, paper supplier, distributor—and the authors had to sing for their supper. I suspect he had a deep-down belief that many authors were writing science fiction out of love, and therefore their prime desires, to explore an interesting concept and see their work in print, were satisfied. Any payment was a bonus. Real writers—those who wrote for a living—did not write science fiction, so Gernsback did not have to worry about them.

In this, of course, Gernsback was misguided, but half right. There were those writers who stopped writing for Gernsback once he stopped paying, but there were others, like Hamilton, Manning, Keller, Binder, and, for a while, Clark Ashton Smith, who continued to submit stories after the checks stopped coming. A number of these were now selling through the auspices of Julius Schwartz and Mort Weisinger's new literary agency, the Solar Sales Service. Schwartz recalls that he conducted his business solely with Hornig and that he "never had any trouble collecting checks for stories accepted."[1] Schwartz must have been able to pull certain strings, because by this time even Frank R. Paul was having trouble collecting payment. His family recall that the checks received from Gernsback either bounced, or were pre-dated.

In many cases the writers probably did not worry too much, despite the Depression. 1933 had been a difficult year, because there were only *Amazing* and *Wonder* publishing science fiction. Gernsback didn't pay, and Sloane only paid on publication, which could be years away. This drove many writers away from the field. Some (like Juve and Simak) just stopped writing. Others (like Hamilton and Schachner) turned to the more lucrative fields of detective fiction, and only wrote science fiction when the urge took them. When *Astounding* returned to the fold and paid reliably, authors used that as their main science-fiction market. Any story rejected from that could as easily go to *Amazing* or *Wonder*, since a story may just as well be in print and unpaid for, as lying in a drawer.

Wollheim's objection came from a natural resentment to Gernsback's practices. Perhaps he took it personally. Had he sold his first story to some other publisher, he might have found the same problem, as Gernsback was not the only one who failed to pay authors promptly, though most usually paid up in the end. Many of the small independent publishers in 1933 and 1934 were finding it difficult to meet their debts, and they frequently dissolved one company and started another in order to limit their liabilities. Even *Weird Tales* was having problems. Jack Williamson recalls it was paying Edmond Hamilton $25 a month on a debt of $700.[2]

Hornig must have taken the brunt of the complaints, and he remained steadfastly loyal to Gernsback. On October 9, 1933, only two months after his employment as editor, he wrote to Forrest Ackerman defending Gernsback's payment practice:

> If our company actually owes you money . . . you will get paid—don't worry. You claim that *Wonder* is your favorite mag—O.K. Suppose they paid every author promptly during the past year—that would have been possible (maybe!)—*but*, there would not be any more *Wonder Stories* . . . So, although stalling some of their authors for a while is not a good policy, they have saved the magazine from going under by holding them off until good times return (as they are returning now). Do you realize what this means? It means that Gernsback actually forsaked his good name and reputation, although temporarily, in order to save *Wonder Stories*—and that goes for *Everyday Science and Mechanics*. That was really a sacrifice. Other editors have rather let their pubs fail, taking from thousands of people part of the joy of their life, because their character was too weak to permit them to sacrifice their name for a few months. But times have taken a sudden turn and *Wonder* will soon have all their authors paid in full and will be back on her feet again!

I doubt if Gernsback's honorable sacrifice would have convinced Wollheim, but it was an interesting argument. Gernsback did not have a good name or reputation, as he had been a notoriously bad payer since at least 1927, as we have seen with the Burroughs and Lovecraft incidents. But the argument about the dilemma between paying authors or keeping the magazine going was a real one and one that, in the final analysis, most writers would support. Some, though, were past waiting. On February 10, 1934 Jack Williamson gave Gernsback an ultimatum that unless he paid the $334 now long overdue, Williamson would seek legal advice. Getting only Gernsback's customary holding letter, Williamson employed the attorney of the American Fiction Guild and started to receive small but regular monthly installments.

Gernsback's finances must have improved slightly in early 1934, because he started to expand his publishing activities again. Some of this must have been due to the success of *Sexology*, but the Depression was also gradually releasing its grip and money markets were starting to rise. Cash was gradually becoming unfrozen. Gernsback's first idea was to issue a *Wonder Stories Annual*, to contain reprints from early issues, selling for fifty cents. New readers unable to acquire back issues welcomed the suggestion, but most of the active readers were avid collectors and resented the idea. It was dropped.

Gernsback then considered the possibility of issuing general adventure magazines, not related to science fiction. In July 1934 he issued two dummy titles, which have been identified by Sam Moskowitz. One was *Buccaneer Stories* and the other *Exploration Tales*. Both reprinted a single science-fiction story from *Wonder Stories*. Gernsback then set up a new company, Adventure Publications, with Margaret H. Jacobsen as editor, and launched the two magazines under new titles. *Pirate Stories* appeared first, dated November 1934, and *High-Seas Adventures* followed the next month. Both were bimonthly and alternated until the June 1935 issue of *High-Seas Adventures*. Thereafter it was merged with *Pirate Stories*, which saw two more issues. Both magazines were something of an aberration in Gernsback's publishing line because, apart from *French Humor*, which had been a self-indulgent pandering to Gernsback's sense of humor, they were the only magazines Gernsback published with the sole purpose of entertaining, not educating. They proved marginally popular, but lacked a clear editorial policy. With *Pirate Stories*, readers were expecting traditional stories of piracy and buccaneering on the high seas. But *Pirate* tried to include all types of piracy, including air piracy, and even encouraged writers to submit stories of space piracy—the very type of fiction outlawed at *Wonder* as being hackneyed. Readers did not want modern stories, and certainly not gangster stories, which is what was appearing. Nevertheless, I suspect that the magazines were more popular than their short life suggests, and that their failure was due to Gernsback's financial difficulties in the summer of 1935. But more of that later.

All this suggests that in the spring of 1934 Gernsback saw his finances improving. On March 10 of that year Hornig wrote slyly to Clark Ashton Smith on *Fantasy Fan*-headed paper advising Smith that it was now timely to pursue his debts. Hornig remarked that *Wonder* was "paying much better now than before." Smith must have tried and failed, but encouraged by Hornig's advice, he approached Ione Weber, a New York attorney who had some measure of success in extracting money from Gernsback for her clients, amongst them Raymond Z. Gallun. According to Gallun, Weber had succeeded in holding Gernsback to a payment of $15 a week against a debt of around $200, a schedule he apparently maintained.

When Weber took on Smith's case, Gernsback owed him $741, perhaps the greatest owed to any author. Ione Weber cautioned Smith that she was "not optimistic as to how soon collection can be made. The last few months I have been having more than the usual difficulty in collecting from them." She explained further. "Gernsback himself told me that these magazines were not paying but made an arrangement with me by which he would pay my other author clients at stated intervals. However, this promise was not kept."[3]

Smith's total credit went back as far as "The Planet Entity" published in the Fall 1931 *Quarterly*. All of the stories had been published under the former Stellar Publishing imprint, the last being "Visitors from Mlok" in the May 1933 *Wonder*. Since Stellar had been dissolved and Continental Publications created, Smith's claim must have been limited. Yet Gernsback honored it, and from July 1934 started to pay a minimum of $50 a month (sometimes as high as $80) until the debt was cleared. At one point Smith was the only author being paid. In a letter dated March 15, 1935 Weber commented that she had not had a check for any other author for months.

It was during 1934 that the number of legal claims against Gernsback reached their peak, and fueled Wollheim's argument in the articles he was writing and actions he was taking. Yet we find, on October 5, 1934, Hornig writing to Lloyd Eshbach with the same optimism that he had to Ackerman a year before. In addition to the story about Gernsback's sacrifice of name and reputation, Hornig added the following:

> I can assure you that Mr. Gernsback had, and still has, intention of paying for everything published and I have some good news along that line. Mr. Scheff, our comptroller, knows more about the financial conditions of the business than anyone else in the company, and when he makes a prediction, it never fails to come out as he says. A couple of months ago he predicted to me that WONDER STORIES would be paying promptly upon publication again before next summer, and just last week he told me that in just about THREE MONTHS it would be doing this—and paying for past debts at a rapid rate.

But it did not happen. Soon after Hornig's outburst of optimism something happened that forced *Wonder Stories* into a decline.

33.

THE FINAL DAYS

1935 must have opened with a certain degree of optimism, if Scheff's predictions were valid. Gernsback was publishing two successful magazines, *Sexology* and *Radio-Craft*, plus two slightly less successful, *Everyday Science and Mechanics* and *Short-Wave Craft*. He had launched the initially well-received *Pirate Stories* and *High-Seas Adventures*, and his one main problem, *Wonder Stories* was, according to Scheff, crawling out of the red, perhaps as a consequence of the Science Fiction League. His other business concerns were also running relatively smoothly. He had started another book company called Gernpark, which issued such volumes as *How to Collect Stamps* and the "rollicking humorous," *The Perfect Bartending Host at Home.*

He was looking to expand further. In October 1934 he had registered a dummy issue of *True Supernatural Stories*. This is a tempting collector's item, as it contained two stories by Clark Ashton Smith and one by H. P. Lovecraft, all selected from Hornig's *The Fantasy Fan*. Gernsback was still planning this magazine eight months later. He explained his intentions in a revealing letter to Jack Williamson on May 24, 1935:

> We are getting out a new magazine very shortly in which the supernatural will be featured. Please note that this is not a ghost story magazine but it will feature *true* supernatural experiences, either sent in by our readers or occurrences which are printed in the daily press and for which there is not a ready answer. Such subjects as telepathy, psychic powers, occurrences in nature which seem supernatural and for which there is no explanation today, will be dramatized in this magazine, similar to what *True Story* Magazine does with love stories.

Gernsback went on to emphasize the scientific side of the supernatural. He wanted to concentrate on stories for which there seemed no ready explanation, but for which there might be one some day, "such as carrier pigeons, dogs and cats finding their way home. . . ."

The astonishing part of the letter is where Gernsback promises to "pay on acceptance" and not on publication. Could any of his authors believe that? There is no record that Williamson responded, and he was probably wise to treat Gernsback with caution. In the event he would have wasted his time as the magazine never appeared. Since Gernsback opened his letter by saying the magazine would be out "very shortly," we can only assume that Gernsback again acted on impulse.

Let's consider the sequence of dates. We have seen in the past how Gernsback often played ducks and drakes with his magazines, dropping one to make space for another. At the start of May he had decided to combine *High-Seas Adventures* with *Pirate Stories*. This left a gap in the printer's June schedule for the now abandoned August *High-Seas*, and it is likely that Gernsback considered launching *True Supernatural Stories* on July 1, with an August cover date. It never appeared. Instead, the last number of *Pirate Stories* was issued.

What prompted Gernsback to change his mind and drop both *True Supernatural* and *Pirate*? Who can say what thoughts went through Gernsback's mind during the summer of 1935. But he took one positive action, which probably decided the future of his company. In June he decided to launch a further health magazine, *Popular Medicine*, trading on the success of *Sexology*. The first issue, in exactly the same format as *Sexology*, was published on August 15, 1935 with a September cover date.

In June, therefore, Gernsback made a conscious decision not to pursue the pulp market, even though only a few weeks before he had considered expanding in that area. By 1935 the specialist pulp magazine market was expanding rapidly. In addition to the always popular detective stories, westerns, and air adventures, the main successes were arising in the hero character pulps, such as *The Shadow* and *Doc Savage*, and in the new range of weird menace and terror pulps spawned from the success of *Dime Mystery*, such as *Terror Tales* and *Horror Stories*. Gernsback could well believe that there was a future in this area, but he chose not to. I don't know why, but I suspect that Gernsback felt uncomfortable with the fiction pulps. Gernsback's publishing empire had grown from his reliance on promoting science and educating his readers, and perhaps at last he realized this was where he needed to concentrate. The pulp fiction field had caused him no end of financial worries. He was much better cutting his losses, reducing his staff, and consolidating his publications. With Secor, Kraus, Mason, and Keller he could continue quite happily and successfully with his technical magazines. Why complicate it?

But out of dedication to the field he loved, and that he had helped to create, he decided to have one last go at making *Wonder Stories* work. He had led the field before; perhaps he could again.

His first need was to rebuild *Wonder*'s circulation. It had clearly been dropping during 1933 and 1934. In the July 1934 Science Fiction League column, Hornig referred to the magazine's 75,000 readers. That figure may or may not refer to paid circulation. It is customary, certainly in advertising promotion, to count two or three readers per issue. This might suggest, therefore, that the paid circulation was as low as 25,000. This is supported by a statement Gernsback made in the April 1936 issue. Here Gernsback commented that when he launched *Amazing Stories* he had no trouble maintaining a circulation of 100,000. "Today, all the science-fiction magazines combined hardly reach this figure."[1] In his editorial in the same issue he mentioned that most pulps sell 80,000 copies tops, whereas most science-fiction pulps were less than 50,000. It's hard to believe that *Astounding* was selling less than 50,000 copies, but if Gernsback believed it was, that leaves *Amazing* and *Wonder* sharing the other 50,000.

In order to boost circulation, Gernsback dropped his cover price back to 15 cents. This made him the cheapest science-fiction magazine on the market, especially as he did not reduce the number of pages. This was a dramatic move, for it meant that he had to increase his circulation to 42,000 just to equal the income at the old price. Where were those readers going to come from? There were now such a variety of specialist pulps on the market that

Gernsback was unlikely to attract too many readers not already acquainted with science fiction. In addition, he probably shared a fair-size core of readers with *Amazing* and *Astounding*. So the only possible extra readers he could attract were from *Astounding*. And *Wonder* was no competition. During 1934 Gernsback had probably attracted all the regular readers he was going to with his Science Fiction League. To attract more from *Astounding* he would have to be delivering the same quality of fiction and writers, and he just did not have them.

During 1935 and early 1936 *Wonder Stories* published a few interesting stories by David H. Keller, Lilith Lorraine, and Edmond Hamilton. The best were those by Laurence Manning, with the oddly curious "The Prophetic Voice" and the fascinating serial *World of the Mist*, plus the last of the Stranger Club series, "Seeds from Space." There was a good serial by Stanton A. Coblentz, *In Caverns Below*, considered by many to be his best. There were some humorous gadget stories by Weinbaum, though not a patch on his pieces in *Astounding*. There were a few interesting speculative pieces, such as Raymond A. Palmer's "Three from the Test-Tube" which looked at test-tube babies, and "The Duplicate" by Alan Connell, which presaged cloning. There were some novelties, such as "The Mystery of the -/-" by W. Varick Nevins III, the complex time travel narrative "The Branches of Time" by David R. Daniels, and the distinctly mystical "Dream's End" by Alan Connell. But outside these, there was little else of merit. At times Gernsback was scraping the barrel. He published a mystery serial, *The Waltz of Death* by P. B. Maxon, which had been a runner-up in a competition run by *Liberty* magazine (a magazine, incidentally, published by Bernarr Macfadden). He even brought the multi-talented Joseph H. Kraus into the ranks of science-fiction writers with the totally boring "Phantom Monsters," about a diver who goes so deep that the pressure affects his eyes causing them to enlarge everything.

There was nothing here that could hold a candle to the powerhouse fiction Tremaine was publishing. *Astounding* had closed 1934 with a plan to go semi-monthly, and was promising greater things ahead. Two writers dominated the year: Stanley G. Weinbaum, with his wonderful travelogues of alien worlds and cultures, and John W. Campbell, Jr., writing mostly under the Don A. Stuart alias, and producing such poignant, humanistic stories as "Blindness" and the classic "Night." Other gems of the year included "Proxima Centauri" by Murray Leinster, "Prowler of the Wastelands" by Harl Vincent, "Set Your Course by the Stars" by Eando Binder, "Alas, All Thinking" by Harry Bates, "The Son of Old Faithful" and "Derelict" by Raymond Z. Gallun, "Islands of the Sun" by Jack Williamson, and the beautiful "Greater Glories" by C. L. Moore.

What also captured people's attention at the newsstands were the powerfully evocative covers by Howard V. Brown. These were so much more exciting than the relatively staid and artistically flat works by Frank R. Paul on *Wonder*. It is ironic that Gernsback had used Brown's work fifteen years earlier, but had chosen to use Paul as his main staff artist over either Brown or Schomburg. Gernsback also used Paul as his chief interior artist, although in 1934 and 1935 he started to use the talents of Lumen Winter and the youthful Charles Schneeman. Tremaine was using the impressive skills of Elliot Dold, who could create very imaginative and thrilling scenes, and also Mark

Marchioni, who had illustrated *Wonder* in the early thirties. By mid-1935 Tremaine was also using Schneeman.

In fact by mid-1935 Tremaine had attracted and held just about every good talent in science fiction, and was starting to develop the new writers. His first discoveries were Horace L. Gold (writing as Clyde Crane Campbell) and Ross Rocklynne. The rest of his science fiction was provided primarily by writers whom Gernsback had discovered and Lasser had nurtured, and secondarily by skilled fantasists from the other pulps, especially *Weird Tales*, who had either avoided Gernsback completely or sold to him when unavoidable.

When cornered, Gernsback resorted to his one surviving weapon—the cover-story contest. The prizes reflected the times. Gone was the big money; in fact the prizes were not even announced on the cover, but in total they only came to $68, with a first prize of $25. This was for a short-short story of between 1,000 and 1,500 words written round what was, frankly, one of Paul's worst covers. Gernsback never revealed how many entries he received, though he had on all previous occasions, which suggests they were limited. The winner was R. D. Parkinson with "The Rays from the Asteroid," though neither this, nor the two runners-up, were worth reading. The level of entry was obviously poor though it included a fifth-placed item from the normally inventive Thomas S. Gardner, "Cosmic Tragedy." This was eventually published in the March 1941 issue of *Comet*, edited, ironically, by Tremaine. It also included an entry from John B. Michel, "The Room and the Picture," which, considering his antipathy toward Gernsback, suggests a certain januformity on Michel's part.

Gernsback was on a losing streak. Again acting on impulse, he combined the November and December 1935 issues, published on October 1, with no explanation of why. At this stage that was a desperation measure. It only happens when costs exceed revenue, because it means instead of reducing his income, he was actually limiting his expenditure. The editorial banter still pushed the "New Policy." In the February 1936 issue (published on December 1, 1935), Hornig revealed that some authors had stated they enjoyed writing for *Wonder Stories* more than any other magazine because the audience was more appreciative and that the new policy had inspired them to greater things. The latter point may be true, though Tremaine's thought variant policy was working far better. The former certainly was a point, because the letter column in *Wonder* was more extensive and more exuberant than in *Astounding*. However, if you look closely at Hornig's statement, you'll see that he prefaces it by saying that "more than one author" had made this comment, which suggests there may only have been two, and I suspect that they were Manning and Keller, since they were the only authors regularly in Gernsback's offices.

Despite the slipped schedule, *Wonder*'s masthead still recorded the magazine as monthly, until it changed to bi-monthly with the April 1936 issue. That issue also contained two grave announcements. The first was an obituary for Stanley G. Weinbaum, who had died of cancer on December 13, 1935, aged 33. Weinbaum had planned a third Tweel story for *Wonder* but had not been able to complete it. The notice concluded by saying "We can truly state that the death of Mr. Weinbaum is the greatest blow science-fiction has ever received, and his work will never be forgotten."[2] That was certainly true on the last count, and may well be right on the first.

The second announcement proposed a new plan to his readers. Gernsback bemoaned the wastage of the magazine-distribution system where less than half the magazines distributed were sold, and the remainder passed for waste either being repulped or going into the second-hand market. Indeed, some dealers deliberately returned the covers as proof of non-sale and sold off the coverless copies for more cash than by selling the magazine direct. Gernsback wanted to bypass the distribution system. He appreciated that not everyone had the funds to subscribe in advance to the magazine. Moreover readers preferred to browse at newsstands rather than subscribe, especially since they might change allegiance to other magazines.

Gernsback's proposal was that readers could return a pre-paid notice in the magazine which would entitle them to a copy of the next issue of the magazine. This would be mailed direct with a return envelope and a bill for the 15 cents. Gernsback vowed faith and trust in his readers to honor the bill. He concluded his plan by stating, "I know that you will not fail me in this great experiment."

Oh yes they did. For it to have worked, Gernsback would have needed to see a good response within the next two weeks, before the June issue was ready for distribution. The April issue had been published on February 1. On February 7 we find Hornig writing to Edmond Hamilton, asking him to resubmit "Colonists of Mars," as he thought the time was now right to publish it, so at that stage forward plans were still in motion. The June issue was despatched to the printers and set up in type complete with editorial blurbs and artwork. This must have happened around mid-February.

But the lack of response from readers was evident. Gernsback must already have been considering an offer to buy *Wonder Stories*, and now acted on impulse. In the week beginning February 17, 1936 Gernsback came to an agreement with Ned Pines of Standard Magazines, and with effect from February 21 the magazine was sold. Almost ten years to the day from the moment Gernsback had brought the science-fiction magazine into the world, the toddler had deserted him, and found new, stronger parents. That is not to say that Gernsback had not been a kindly father. He had done all that he thought was best for his infant. If anything he had been over-protective, giving the child a strict upbringing, although allowing it to learn a little for itself. But when the child looked for financial support, it was not there. The child grew lean and hungry, and lonely. The moment it could fend for itself, it was away. The fans now owned science fiction, and they had appointed its new foster parent at *Astounding*. Gernsback had no part in that new world.

34.

AFTERMATH

News of the sale soon hit the fan world. Julius Schwartz, writing in his capacity as a literary agent rather than a fanzine publisher, wrote to Lloyd Eshbach with details on February 28, 1936:

> Biggest news of the year is that Standard Magazines (where Mort works) has bought *Wonder Stories* and will publish the magazine henceforth, with a one cent a word on acceptance rate. So now you've got to write. They'll change their policy, and will probably concentrate on the action science-fiction yarn. Cummings sort of stuff (who'll appear in the first issue, by the way). They're considering Weinbaum's "Circle of Zero" for the first issue too. They've asked Merritt and Burroughs for yarns. Wesso will probably do cover as well as the inside illustrations.

"Mort" was Mort Weisinger, Schwartz's old partner in his agency and fan activities, who had gone to work at Standard Magazines a year earlier under the editorial direction of Leo Margulies. Standard had been in business since 1931, shortly after Ned Pines had graduated from Columbia University at the age of 26. He began with two titles, *Thrilling Love Stories* and *Thrilling Detective*, a two-pronged attack on the two most popular fields. The titles were followed by *Thrilling Adventures, Thrilling Western,* and *Thrilling Mystery*, so it was no surprise when they took over *Wonder* that it would re-emerge as *Thrilling Wonder Stories*.

Apart from continuing the volume numbering and the Science Fiction League, *Thrilling Wonder* was to all intents a new magazine. Hornig did not remain as editor, so he was clearly not part of the deal. He was not needed. Weisinger was their resident science-fiction expert and he could handle the magazine. He had more editorial acumen than Hornig, though it was Margulies who determined the magazine's editorial policy. Margulies (1900-1975) had started work as an office boy assisting Bob Davis at the Munsey Corporation. He then served in various short editorial stints before joining Ned Pines's team in establishing Standard. By 1936 he was one of the highest paid editors in the pulp field. He had little experience of science fiction, though he grew to like it, but knew how to tailor it to a readership. It was clear that science-fiction readers fell into two groups, with some overlap. There were those who preferred the more mature, thoughtful stories, and Tremaine had captured those at *Astounding*. The other, and bigger market, were the young readers who liked action and thrills. It was those that Margulies aimed *Thrilling Wonder* at. Relaunched in June 1936, with an August cover date, *Thrilling Wonder* looked like a reincarnation of the Clayton *Astounding*. It had a strong contents list, with stories by Ray Cummings, Eando Binder, Stanley G. Weinbaum, Arthur Leo Zagat, Paul Ernst, A. Merritt, Otis Adelbert Kline, and Weisinger himself. There was also a comic-strip called "Zarnak," drawn by Max Plaisted. This recognized the increased growth in popularity of the comic strip, which would soon emerge in its own comic-book world with *Action Comics* in June 1938.

Weisinger rejected all the stories that Hornig had planned to run in *Wonder*, even though they were set in type. As a consequence the fourth-placed story in the cover contest, "The Malign Intelligence" by Morris Miller, was not published. Nor were other promised stories. It's possible to make-up that missing June issue of *Wonder Stories* from Hornig's forthcoming announcements. In addition to Miller's story, it was likely to have contained "Beyond the Limit" by Eando Binder, "Golden Nemesis" the first story by David A. Kyle, "The Jester of Xenonia" by Philip Jacques Bartel, "The Other Side," the sequel to "The Man with the Four-Dimensional Eyes" by Leslie F. Stone, "Into the Darkness" by Ross Rocklynne, "Black World" by Paul K. Chapple, "Another Chance" by William F. Temple, which would have been his first magazine appearance, and *Maze of Creation*, a three-part sequel to "World of the Mist," by Laurence Manning. Kyle's, Rocklynne's, and Temple's stories appeared subsequently,[1] but the others, unless retitled, have vanished into those lost issues of another reality.

Gernsback may have missed his science-fiction magazine, but he was probably relieved at ridding himself of a financial headache. He had plenty to keep himself occupied. He carried on as he always had. With a gap in the schedules, he started a new magazine, *Woman's Digest*. The same month he renamed *Popular Medicine* as *Your Body*, a title with more reader appeal, and one he had used eight years earlier. People could be excused for thinking Gernsback was on a sex kick, because in January 1937 he brought out a further magazine, *Facts of Life*. David H. Keller was expected to edit these, but it reached a point with the new title where Keller felt he was being taken advantage of. Gernsback was not paying him for the articles he was using, and Keller brought in his son-in-law, an attorney, to pursue the debt. Gernsback paid up, but Keller stopped working for him. With his departure, *Facts of Life* and *Your Body* were dropped.

1937 continued to see Gernsback's publications chopping and changing. *Woman's Digest* metamorphosed into the more prim and proper *Milady*, but that only lasted until September 1937. *Everyday Science and Mechanics* was retitled *Science and Mechanics* whilst *Short-Wave Craft* became *Short Wave and Television*. In July, Gernsback started a magazine with a title that many might feel summed him up, *Gadgets*. Surprisingly, it lasted only five months. Another magazine, *New Ideas for Everybody*, was as ephemeral, from October 1937 to January 1938. Two new magazines took their place, *Know Yourself* and *Your Dreams*, but both were short-lived. *Foto-Craft* came and went during 1939. *Short Wave and Television* was retitled *Radio and Television* in May 1939. All of which demonstrates that Gernsback was even more impulsive and erratic after the sale of *Wonder Stories* than he was before, trying out any new market, bolstered by the constant good sales of *Radio-Craft* and *Sexology*.

In 1940, Gernsback re-entered the world of science fiction. He had noticed the success of the science-fiction comics. *Action Comics* had had a runaway success with Siegel and Schuster's character, Superman, from its first issue in June 1938. Within a year the character had its own comic, *Superman*, and rapidly super-heroes became as successful in the comics as they had been in the pulps. *Marvel Mystery Comics*, with their covers by Frank R. Paul and

Alex Schomburg, began in November 1939; Batman, who had first appeared in the May 1939 *Detective Comics*, received his own comic in Summer 1940, whilst Street and Smith issued *Shadow Comics* in March 1940 and *Doc Savage Comics* in May 1940. Gernsback, ever-protective of his science-fiction offspring may have been perturbed at the unscientific bases of these characters. In an attempt to purify the medium, he launched *Superworld Comics* in April 1940. Gernsback treated the comic-book field in the way that he had his science-fiction magazines: to educate and inform. His editorial, the same in the first two issues, was addressed "To Parents and School Teachers," and promised that "No superhuman feats impossible of accomplishment are ever printed." Its instructive purpose was emphasized throughout. He also incorporated a "How Smart Are You?" science questionnaire based on the stories. Evidently neither the children nor their parents found Gernsback's comic, which was written by Charles Hornig and drawn by Frank R. Paul, as exciting as the other comic-books. It ran for only three bi-monthly issues. By 1940 it was clear that Gernsback was no longer in touch with the field.

Gernsback's last short-lived pre-War experiment was *Flight*, which flew from 1940 to 1941. *Radio and Television* saw its last issue in September 1941. That left Gernsback with his two leading magazines, *Sexology* and *Radio-Craft*, and these sustained him through the War years and to the end of his days. *Radio-Craft* was retitled *Radio Electronics* in October 1948. *Sexology* was briefly retitled *Together* in the seventies, and eventually folded in 1978, leaving *Radio-Electronics* the only surviving Gernsback magazine, still going after seventy years. No matter what one may say about Hugo Gernsback or his publishing activities, the fact remains that his company is one of the few to have survived from the pulp days, and for all his whims and financial practices, he remained a success.

He dabbled one final time in the science-fiction magazine field when he issued *Science-Fiction Plus* in 1953. It contained some good stories, but lasted only seven issues, and its whole mood showed that Gernsback had not developed his thoughts about the purpose and nature of science fiction one iota since 1936. In the intervening period, science fiction had advanced dramatically under John W. Campbell, who took over as editor of *Astounding* in 1937. When the world entered the atomic age in 1945, science fiction grew up and even *Thrilling Wonder Stories* and its six-year-old companion, *Startling Stories*, took on a maturity that should have impressed Gernsback. But Gernsback steadfastly refused to recognize many of the stories that were being published as science fiction, classifying them as fairy tales.

The writers who brought science fiction through the Second World War and developed it into today's modern force, had all been introduced to science fiction by Gernsback's magazines. These included not only the best of the early generation, who had sold directly to Gernsback, and who adapted to John W. Campbell's needs at *Astounding*—such as E. E. Smith, Jack Williamson, Clifford D. Simak, and P. Schuyler Miller—but also those readers and early active fans who had responded directly to the fascination of Gernsback's message and developed into the next generation of writers. Amongst these were Ray Bradbury, Isaac Asimov, Frederik Pohl, Cyril M. Kornbluth, Robert A. Heinlein, James Blish, Theodore Sturgeon, A. E. van Vogt, Henry Kuttner, Lester del Rey, and Damon Knight. Without Gernsback's initiatives there would not have been a first or a second generation.

The fandom that Gernsback had helped to organize flourished after *Wonder's* passing and in 1939 ran the First World Science Fiction Convention. Gernsback was honored at the 1953 World Science Fiction Convention when the annual science-fiction achievement awards were nicknamed Hugos in his honor. Yet when he came to review Isaac Asimov's first anthology of *The Hugo Winners* (Doubleday, 1962), he only recognized one of the stories as science fiction.

Gernsback was very protective of his phrase "science fiction," and thought it too often misused. He was outraged in 1956 when he heard a piece of music entitled "Science Fiction," because to him it was a tuneless cacophony. A similar incident occurred the following year when *Playboy* published George Langelaan's story "The Fly." The story was run under the one-word label, "fiction." Shortly after its appearance *Playboy's* executive editor, Ray Russell, received from Gernsback a tearsheet of the first page of "The Fly" with the "fiction" label amended in red ink to read emphatically "SCIENCE fiction." Gernsback believed that the genre should be properly promoted.

Gernsback continued to keep his hand in the business of speculative science. Apart from regular articles in *Radio-Electronics*, he also issued an annual *Forecast* during the 1950s which highlighted predictions he had made in the pulps and looked ahead to future developments. Throughout his life Gernsback kept his sense of humor. His April Fool essays appeared annually in *Radio-Electronics* and a number were posthumously assembled as *The Collected Works of Mohammed Ullyses Fips* (Gernsback, 1986). He issued a spoof science-fiction magazine called *Prescience Fiction* in September 1952, which contained two spoof predictions by him, "The Electronic Baby" and "The Superperfect Crime." During 1958/59 he completed a new novel, *Ultimate World*, about alien scientists who conduct experiments upon humans. Lengthy scientific dissertations spoiled the story-line until it was edited by Sam Moskowitz for posthumous publication in 1971.

It's impossible in this summary to consider all of Gernsback's activities in the thirty years after the sale of *Wonder Stories* till his death on August 19, 1967, three days after his eighty-third birthday. These must wait for a full biography, which is long overdue, or at very least a book-length assessment of his scientific achievements and predictions.

This book set out to consider Gernsback's contribution to science fiction, and a hundred thousand words later we have reached that end. I hope that by setting out the events in their proper context and sequence, the full facts, such as they can be found, have delineated the proper picture. You will no doubt draw your own conclusions, but at least they can now be informed and not based on hearsay or biased judgment.

I found that during my research and writing of this book my admiration for Gernsback increased. He was a phenomenon. His one major weakness was also his strength, namely his hard-headed determination. His innate Prussian superiority, and the strength of will and character that developed, meant that Gernsback found it difficult to admit when he was wrong, or to concede defeat. When problems arose, they were usually blamed on other factors, when in fact they usually revolved around his own lack of financial management. That was inevitable. His father had been prosperous and Gernsback's upbringing had brought about a carefree attitude in money matters that allowed him to indulge in his own whims and fancies at the expense of other people. It was this one factor that earned him his bad reputation. I must say that, regardless of the Depression, this was a severe weakness in Gernsback and he deserved the bad press it gave him.

And yet it's that same dogged determination that made him the very man, perhaps the only man, who would persevere with promoting and developing science fiction against such odds. Consider: he launched *Amazing* when the pulps were steeped in westerns and romance, and after such a weak response to his original circular. When he was forced into bankruptcy in 1929, he went straight ahead and launched four more science-fiction magazines. Even when the Depression bit and the going got rough, he persevered, organizing fandom in the process, and developing a new generation of writers.

Gernsback was a man of remarkable foresight, and a genius at organizing enthusiasm. It was by harnessing the energies of the amateur wireless enthusiast that he promoted the radio industry in America, and he should be remembered as its leading advocate. It was by encouraging the amateur experimenter in all avenues of scientific research that he helped develop a generation of new scientists, many of whom went on to become leaders in the space and communications industries. And it was by recognizing the demands of the science-fiction enthusiasts that Gernsback popularized science fiction and made it the force that it is today.

It does not matter that Gernsback's view and definition of science fiction was limited, and that it required later editors, especially John W. Campbell at *Astounding*, Horace L. Gold at *Galaxy*, and Anthony Boucher at *Fantasy & Science Fiction* to bring science fiction into the modern world. That would have happened anyway. Gernsback's importance was that he had created the means whereby science fiction was allowed to develop, by promoting it as a vehicle for education and inspiration. Gernsback's genius was in identifying a purpose in science fiction as a means of creating tomorrow. Through all of his activities, in his technical magazines and in science fiction, Gernsback brought science to the general public, rather than to other scientists. And he sold to those people a vision that the creation of tomorrow was in their own hands. They could build the future.

That was Gernsback's genius. No one had done it before, and nobody has done it since.

PART TWO

YESTERDAY'S WORLDS
OF TOMORROW

A Personal Survey
of the Fiction
in the Gernsback Magazines

by

Robert A. W. Lowndes

FOREWORD

With a few exceptions, which I shall mention at the appropriate time, I possess all of the science fiction magazines discussed here; most were purchased when they first came out. Circumstances required my disposing of my collection more than once, but I always managed to recollect in time. The magazines never lay ignored on my shelves when I had them—I was constantly re-reading, and am still doing so. As a result, every story I discuss has been re-read within the last decade, some quite recently.

No attempt has been made to evaluate, or even list, each and every story. I shall mention all serials, however, because they were the backbone of the magazines in the Gernsback era, and I'll mention "first" stories, both by known writers on their debut in the SF magazines, and the first appearance of certain themes and concepts, in SF magazines, despite earlier appearances elsewhere. I also refer to month of publication, throughout, which is when the magazine went on sale, usually the month previous to the cover date. (No American science fiction magazine ever went on sale "in" the month you see on the cover; that date always refers to the off-sale date.) Thus the January issue of a magazine would be covered in the survey for the previous year.

Re-reading those old tales reminds me that SF was fun to read back in those days. Some stories which seemed splendid then no longer seem that way now, while others I cared little for at the time now seem better. Taking them as a whole, for what they are, it's astonishing that so many remain fun to read—and some have literary values above their entertainment level. James Blish once described those old stories, at their best, as "yesterday's world of tomorrow." I think he hit the nail squarely.

35.

GERNSBACK ALONE: 1926-1929

I was nine-and-a-half years old in March 1926, going to grammar school in Newport, Rhode Island. My father was an electrician; he had built the first radio we ever had from an instruction magazine or booklet published by Hugo Gernsback, whose name also appeared on some other magazines he bought. I'd pass by a radio and electrics store on my way to school and see a rack in its window containing the latest issue of *Science and Invention*. Then, one day, another magazine was added to the display: *Amazing Stories*, also containing the line "Hugo Gernsback, Editor."

The cover was striking indeed. Frank R. Paul's scene shows the planet Saturn looming huge in a yellowish sky, its rings seeming almost to touch two big hills of ice. We see two ships, one on top of each hill, and below is a group of fur-clad people skating on a frozen pond. But what really catches the eye is the dynamic layout of the magazine's logo. Behind a large block-letter capital "A" the other letters in the title (also block letters) diminish in size, seeming to extend into space. That is the famous "comet-tail" title that was the hallmark of the magazine.

Gernsback's name appeared on every cover throughout the period of his editorship, as did the names of three authors represented in each particular issue. There were never any story titles on the cover in the early years. The cover of the April issue declared that it contained stories by H. G. Wells, Jules Verne, and Edgar Allen (*sic*) Poe, but we have to look inside to find that the stories were, respectively, "The New Accelerator," *Off on a Comet—or, Hector Servadec*, and "The Facts in the Case of M. Valdemar."

Since the bulk of the contents of the April and May issues were reprints, I'll discuss them together.

Jules Verne's novel *Off on a Comet* opened in the April and concluded in the May issue. It relates the adventures of a group of people present on a small section of Earth that was torn away through collision with a comet. That fragment is now on a "tour" through the solar system. The story still retains much charm but is seriously marred by Verne's intensely anti-semitic portrayal of the character Isaac Hakkabut. It is not only that Hakkabut is presented as excessively unattractive; it is that everything loathsome about him is tied in to the fact of his being Jewish, in such a way as to suggest that all Jews are like that. Many years later I learned that Verne was strongly antisemitic in his personal views.

"The Man from the Atom" by G. Peyton Wertenbaker is about an experiment wherein the subject is expanded into the macrocosm. There he finds worlds and people much like those we know in our own. He also finds he cannot reverse the workings of the mechanism that brought him to the macrocosm and he is marooned. At that point the story stops with "End of Part One," which suggests it is the beginning of a serial. However, in the May issue "Part Two" is listed as a sequel and the two stories do stand by themselves. (We were not told that part two is a new story, actually the first new story to appear in the magazine.)

The pulp-style plot appears in "The Man Who Saved the Earth" by Austin Hall, who was strong on imagination, but often inept in written English. Intelligences from Mars invade Earth to steal its oceans. The Martian works are destroyed before Earth becomes oceanless, but not before Mars has received a fair share of water. The invaders make no hostile moves toward Earth's inhabitants in their venture and the story ends with the implication that future relations between the two worlds can be friendly.

"The Thing from—Outside" by George Allan England deals with the irruption of a superior intelligence in a form beyond human capacity not only to understand but to perceive, and it treats the humans it encounters the way we would treat an interesting species of insect. Poe's story deals with survival-after-death philosophy and mesmerism. It's an attempt to justify communication with the "dead" scientifically. "The Mesmeric Revelation" in the May issue is another Poe tale on the same theme.

H. G. Wells appeared in every issue of *Amazing* from the April 1926 to the August 1928 issues, and I shall not attempt to discuss every story, but shall concentrate on those for which Paul painted a cover and on the novels that appeared as serials. His short story "The Crystal Egg" inspired one of Paul's most imaginative and colorful paintings for the cover of the May issue. It depicts a scene on Mars where one of the inhabitants—a giant, butterfly-like creature—is gazing into a crystal like the one the protagonist on Earth is looking into.

A second Jules Verne serial, *A Trip to the Center of the Earth*, began in the May issue and a scene from it provided a cover to illustrate the second episode in the June issue. It depicts the explorers on a raft in an underground lake, menaced by a prehistoric saurian. This novel remains one of Verne's most lastingly enjoyable, even though our protagonists never get anywhere near the planet's center.

Reprints still dominated the June issue. There began a series of Jacque Morgan's "Scientific Adventures of Mr. Fosdick" from the 1912 issues of *Modern Electrics*. All the stories are humorous and remain enjoyable reading, albeit quaint. In "Mr. Fosdick Invents the Seidlitzmobile," we have an automobile propelled by enhanced seidlitz powders. Otis Adelbert Kline appears with "The Malignant Entity," the first tale to deal with a protoplasmic creature that gets out of hand. The theme was not new outside the SF magazines, not even in *Weird Tales* where Kline's story had first appeared. Though Kline would have new stories later in the SF magazines, he became better known for his Burroughs-style interplanetary adventures in *Argosy*.

"The Runaway Skyscraper" by Murray Leinster is a science-directed fantasy, assuming, as it does, that time travel is possible and that there is a scientific explanation for it. Reprinted from *Argosy*, it was Leinster's first attempt at what were then called "different" stories He would appear with new stories in the magazines throughout the period but he sold no new ones to Gernsback. While not a great stylist, and often given to stereotyped plots and characterizations, Leinster nonetheless wrote interesting, genuine science fiction.

The June issue was the first to contain newly-submitted stories: "The Coming of the Ice" by G. Peyton Wertenbaker and an installment of Clement Fezandié's humorous series of inventions and discoveries series, "Dr.

Hackensaw's Secrets," which had been running for some years in *Science and Invention*. Wertenbaker's story tells of a man who achieves immortality and is still alive during the last days of Earth as an inhabitable planet. Mankind has greatly evolved during the millennia and our protagonist can no longer understand them. He is treated kindly by them as an interesting primitive. It is a powerfully written, emotional story, showing Wertenbaker's youthful gifts as a writer. Fezandié's Hackensaw piece, "Some Minor Inventions," is more of an article than a story. It includes, among other things, a voice-operated typewriter that can handle eight languages.

The contents page of the July issue specifically drew the reader's attention to the fact that two of the stories were new. One is another Dr. Hackensaw episode by Fezandié, "The Secret of the Invisible Girl," this time more of a story than an article. There are two secrets: the nature of the girl's invisibility and the fact that she has to go naked because she cannot make clothing invisible. The other is "The Eggs from Lake Tanganyika" by Curt Siodmak, translated from the German. Siodmak would become well known later, but didn't appear again in the SF magazines during the Gernsback period. The eponymous eggs were those of an enormous tsetse fly, and Paul's cover shows sailors on the deck of a ship trying to bring a gun to bear upon a giant fly swooping toward them.

I was nine, going on ten, when that issue appeared, and the cover gave me nightmares. That was the first issue that I actually picked up and looked through. There was another giant-insect depicted—a death's-head moth, for Edgar Allan Poe's story of optical illusion, "The Sphinx." When I told some of my friends about that cover and those illustrations, one of them said, "You should read *Weird Tales*. They cut out your heart with a glass knife." The next time I went back to the store, I looked through the July 1926 issue of *Weird Tales*, but the magazine didn't look very interesting, in its pulp size and untrimmed edges. (At the same time, I noticed a magazine called *Ghost Stories*, and on looking it through, found it much more fascinating than *Amazing Stories* or *Weird Tales*. The trick photography by which you seemed to see real photos of ghosts was very effective. There was no way I could buy a copy and take it home, but for a couple of years I looked through every copy I could pick up, and only noticed some of the covers on *Amazing Stories*.)

Back to the July 1926 *Amazing*: Hugo Gernsback himself is present with a reprint of "The Magnetic Storm" from *The Electrical Experimenter*. This may be the only science fiction story in which Nikola Tesla appears as a character. Gernsback sent Tesla the manuscript prior to publication for approval and correction; Tesla was pleased with it. It extrapolates on Tesla's own devices for transmitting electric power, and our protagonist's invention burns out all the electrical equipment in the German army within reach of its very considerable range. Gernsback's fiction has often been criticised for being something other than it was intended to be. He wrote in a crisp, reportorial style such as you see in his editorials. His fiction was simple narrative based on scientific ideas and he never made any effort at characterization. Read for what they are—popularized scientific extrapolations—they remain entertaining.

Station X by George McLeod Winsor starts in this issue. Gernsback describes it as the greatest radio story he had ever read. The "Station X" of the novel is an isolated radio station where intelligences from both Mars and Venus have made mental contact with members of the crew. The invading minds take over, using Earthmen as pawns in their struggle against each other.

Paul's cover for the August issue shows a severed human head attached to a scientific-looking apparatus. Two men are observing it, one apparently communicating with it through a speaking tube. It illustrates "The Talking Brain" by M. H. Hasta and deals with the theme of keeping a person's brain alive. The victim had suffered permanent crippling from an accident and had been close to death when he consented to the experiment. The story is played for horror in the Poe manner and is effective—the "head" lives, but its owner is in torment, pleading for final death.

Garrett P. Serviss's novel *A Columbus of Space* starts in this issue. It's an adventure story dealing with an expedition to Venus in a spaceship controlled by interatomic energy. Serviss lacked the flamboyant imagination of Burroughs or Kline, but tells an enjoyable story nonetheless. It differs from others of the kind in its exploration of character, and it has a tragic ending.

September's cover, illustrating "In the Abyss" by H. G. Wells, shows a man in a bathysphere looking through a window at a subsea creature that is carrying a spear and appears to be intelligent. We are only told about that brief glimpse; Wells does not develop the idea. There are no new stories in the issue and of the five present, three are serials. The other complete story is "The Moon Hoax" by Richard Adams Locke. A sensation at the time it was first published (in 1835, as a true scientific report, later revealed as a hoax), it makes very slow reading today.

Two serials start in the October issue: *The Island of Dr. Moreau* by H. G. Wells and *Beyond the Pole* by A. Hyatt Verrill. The latter is not only the first appearance by an author who would become a favorite in *Amazing*, but is also the first new serial. Verrill was a learned archaeologist and anthropologist. He wrote in a leisurely style, appropriate to nineteenth-century literature: character is explored and there are long descriptions. Nothing farther from the fast-action pulp story could be imagined, but Verrill had a vivid imagination and most of his stories can be re-read with pleasure today. *Beyond the Pole*, effectively illustrated by Paul both on the cover and inside, deals with a castaway in the Antarctic area, who finds a civilization of man-size, intelligent lobster creatures that walk upright and have become land-dwellers. Theirs is a super-scientific civilization and they are friendly toward the intruder. This may be the first tale of its kind wherein such non-human creatures are pacific and have no interest in expanding their domain or exploring, let alone conquering, mankind. They are menaced by super-intelligent and highly aggressive ants and the human does his best to aid them in their struggle against the insects.

Of the five stories in this issue, four are serials and only one is complete, a new story, "Blasphemer's Plateau," by Alexander Snyder. It tells of scientific attempts to create life and much is made of the fact that all the scientists are atheists; only the narrator believes that the experiment is a blasphemy against God. It all comes to a sticky end, because the radiations produce fast-acting cancer in all the participants.

The November issue is again dominated by serials and the two complete stories are both reprints: "A Drama in the Air" by Jules Verne and "The Mad Planet" by Murray Leinster. Leinster's story is among his best, telling of a future Earth where plants and insects have grown to enormous size, while human beings have reverted to savagery. Despite the impossibility of the situation—the square-cube law makes giant insects impossible—the descriptions of insect behavior provide the type of instruction that Gernsback wanted. Here, and in other places, both Gernsback and Sloane would allow "poetic license" to override scientific plausibility of details. Verne's short story is an early balloon tale, which would not have been reprinted had it been written by someone else.

The Second Deluge by Garrett P. Serviss began in this issue. It's a first-class catastrophe tale describing Earth's passage through a watery nebula in space and Cosmo Versal's attempts to save doomed humanity. Despite the many outdated aspects, it remains vivid reading today. Paul's cover shows the final attempt to storm the Ark by those who had formerly laughed at Versal.

The December issue presents Gernsback's first cover contest. Prizes are offered for the most amazing story written around Paul's cover scene. Up in a blue sky we see an aircraft that looks like a giant gyroscope. Depending from its poles are lines carrying giant electromagnets and they have captured an ocean liner, which we see floating serenely above strange-looking buildings. On a mesa below are a group of nude humanoid beings, somewhat reddish in color, with feather-like fringes growing on their heads and extending halfway down their backs and on the backs of their arms.

New stories were not identified as such in this issue, but we can be sure about "Through the Crater's Rim" by A. Hyatt Verrill, dealing with a lost city in South America and giant carnivorous trees surrounding the approaches to the city. "The Man Higher Up" by Edwin Balmer and William B. MacHarg is the first of several stories to be reprinted about the scientific detective Luther Trant, published in 1910. The Trant stories cannot rightly be called science fiction because they all deal with devices that were known at the time. The novelty was Trant's adaptation of them for solving crimes. Thus, the stories are fiction *about* science—like Sinclair Lewis's novel *Arrowsmith*—rather than science fiction.

The final issue to appear in 1926, dated January 1927, showed a slight change in the publication date, coming forward to the fifth of the preceding month. The cover illustrated "The Man Who Could Vanish" by A. Hyatt Verrill. The story takes a humorous, but not slapstick, look at the problems of invisibility. The inventor is neither a madman nor one lusting after power and, at the end, he decides that invisibility may not be such a boon for humanity after all.

"The Red Dust" by Murray Leinster, another reprint, is a sequel to "The Mad Planet" and was his final appearance in the Gernsback *Amazing*. Making his first appearance was Miles J. Breuer who, according to Sam Moskowitz, pronounced his name "Brewer" rather than "Broyer" as I and many other readers assumed. Dr. Breuer would become a favorite and appear in all of the magazines of the period. His first story, "The Man with the Strange Head," is a short-short tale with a surprise ending, which can still be re-read without the knowledge of the ending spoiling the story. The man is decidedly not what he appears to be.

And so 1926 came to an end and *Amazing*'s first ten issues. The domination of reprints makes it difficult to see any trend developing, though the

Wertenbaker and Breuer stories show that Gernsback was eager to publish good writing and characterization presented in more contemporary styles than we find in the older stories, so long as they fulfilled his requirements for scientific plausibility. H. G. Wells's stories aside—which are still enjoyable reading today—my nominations for the best items from 1926 are *Beyond the Pole* by Verrill, "The Coming of the Ice" by Wertenbaker and "The Man with the Strange Head" by Breuer, plus Leinster's reprinted "The Mad Planet" and its sequel. To all appearances *Amazing* was a success and now the question that many readers wanted to see answered was whether the magazine would become a semi-monthly in 1927.

1927

One reader later wrote in to *Amazing* to say that as soon as he saw the cover of the February 1927 issue, showing a submarine, the *U33*, surrounded by prehistoric creatures, he bought the magazine at once. He remembered the part that the *U33* had played in *The Land That Time Forgot* by Edgar Rice Burroughs and was delighted to re-read the story. Burroughs's novel still stands as excellent science fiction speculation based, as it is, on an unusual theory of evolution. Nothing like it had appeared in the magazines before, nor would anything like it recur until we encounter the planet Lithia as described by James Blish in 1953 in *A Case of Conscience*.

The February issue also presented the first of an unconnected series of medical speculations by W. Alexander. All are light in tone. "New Stomachs for Old" is the first story about organ transplants. A rich banker pays a sturdy young laborer to exchange stomachs with him. The results are more funny than plausible, and it all winds up with a re-exchange.

Captain H. G. Bishop's "On the Martian Way" is the first spaceship story in *Amazing*, and a good one, too. It tells of a passenger liner plying between Earth and Mars and encountering a comet en route. The *Columbia* is propelled by gravity screens; rocket ships for interplanetary travel would not appear until later.

The March issue has one of Paul's best covers. We see an atomic-powered spaceship taking off from a vertical position in a mountainous country somewhere in South America. It illustrates "The Green Splotches," from a 1920 *Adventure*, by T. S. Stribling, who would later receive a Pulitzer prize for his novel, *The Store*. The ship is operated by a race of plant-like aliens who have achieved a high-technology civilization. (The "green splotches" are gouts of chlorophyll, which is their blood.) They are here to investigate Earth and bring back specimens to their home world, which is apparently Jupiter. It's a wry, ironic tale, with excellent characterization and suspense.

The April cover, by contrast, is one of Paul's worst. The scene shows several poorly-drawn people around a bed in which a young girl is lying. There are some scientific devices on a table and the girl is being subjected to a test. It illustrates "The Man in the Room," a Luther Trant story by Balmer and MacHarg. The feature story of the issue is a long novelette, "The Plague of the Living Dead" by A. Hyatt Verrill. Dr. Franham discovers that his new serum apparently imbues living creatures with indefinitely extended mortality—they grow no older. There is a volcanic eruption in the remote village where he is conducting his research and the poisonous gasses released causes the deaths of hundreds. The doctor experiments to see if his serum can revive the dead. It does, but not as he hoped. The dead return to life but without minds: they are sub-beasts, ravenous and omnivorous. and now cannot be killed.

Starting this issue is Henry Hugh Simmons's series, "Hicks's Inventions with a Kick." The first story, "The Automatic Self-Service Dining Table," sets the tone for them all. Hicks is an inventor and his inventions all seem plausible and workable. Each one, however, depends upon tons of water under high pressure and each time he demonstrates his latest idea something goes wrong and everything goes wild, ending with a flood. It's all sheer slapstick and each individual tale is amusing, but after you've read two you know what's likely to happen in the rest.

More unusual is a vignette of the future by Harry Stephen Keeler, "John Jones's Dollar." Humans have become small men with big heads and schools are conducted by two-way television. The story deals with a lecture on economics given on the "201st day of the year 3221 A.D." The instructor starts by telling that in 1921 a man named John Jones deposited a dollar in a bank with instructions that it was to remain there, compounded annually, until the time of his fortieth descendant. By the time of John Jones's fortieth descendant along the line of the oldest child of each generation, there wasn't enough money in the solar system to meet the debt! (Fortunately, the 39th descendant died childless.) It's a charming speculation, but not really plausible. Bankers can calculate, too, and have devised ways to prevent anything remotely like that happening.

The May, June and July issues of *Amazing* reprint "The Moon Pool" by A. Merritt. It had been widely acclaimed when the original novelette appeared in *All-Story Weekly* in 1918, followed by its six-part sequel, *The Conquest of the Moon Pool* in 1919. The two stories were combined as a novel in a hardcover edition published by Putnam in New York in 1919 under the title *The Moon Pool* and that is the version reprinted here. Letters published in the "Discussions" column, not only in 1927 but throughout this period, show that it was one of the two most popular serials in the Gernsback *Amazing*. Strangely, Gernsback told Sam Moskowitz in 1953 that "The Moon Pool" was the only story he regretted publishing in *Amazing*—he now felt that there wasn't enough science therein to justify his doing so.

Like many of Merritt's other novels, "The Moon Pool" is a tale of fantastic adventure in a colorful lost land amidst a forgotten people. Later science fiction critics would look down upon it as well as the author's other SF novels for the "purple" prose and often stereotyped characters. I myself was an ardent admirer of *The Moon Pool* when I first read it in the revised hardcover reprint of 1932, though I do find it harder to read today. Alas, Merritt is no longer readily available.

A truly different story in the May issue is "The Man Who Was" by Walter Burch. It's the first to deal with the scientific revival of the dead in a non-sensational manner. The subject has been convicted of murder and is to be electrocuted. His doctor and friend, who is also a scientific experimenter, believes he can restore life to the dead man. That he succeeds in doing and the man returns "from the dead" unharmed excerpt for burns that soon heal. The story then deals with the legal status of the "man who was."

The June issue presented the three prize-winning stories in the December 1926 cover contest: "The Visitation" by Cyril G. Wates, "The Electronic Wall" by Geo. R. Fox, and "The Fate of the Poseidonia" by Clare Winger Harris. It also introduced another new writer, Bob Olsen, with "The Four-Dimensional Roller Press," the first of an extended series illustrating Olsen's concept of the fourth dimension. He would become one of the most popular authors of the period. Many, though not all, of his stories are humorous.

The July issue presents the "honorable mention" stories from the December cover contest. Amongst them is "The Voice from the Inner World" by A. Hyatt Verrill, a powerful horror tale about an Amazon race of cannibals. The issue also offers the first story to deal with matter-transmission, and on the cover we see our inventor about to transmit his beloved, who is standing in a huge tube. His apparatus will dissolve her into radio waves so that she can be transmitted and then reassembled at a receiving station. The story, "Radio Mates" by Benjamin Witwer, leaves one wishing that the author had been more specific about how and where his human subject would be reassembled.

The big news in the July issue is the advertisement on the inside back cover for *Amazing Stories Annual*. No publication date is given, but it seems likely that the *Annual* went on sale in June or July. The *Annual* was a tremendous bargain. It had the same general format as the monthly, but ran to 132-pages with very little advertising. The feature novel was a new story by Edgar Rice Burroughs, *The Master Mind of Mars*. It was profusely illustrated by Paul, and his cover painting shows John Carter looking on while the red Martian prepares to transplant the brain of a wrinkled old woman into the body of a beautiful young girl.

The rest of the *Annual* consisted of reprints either from the monthly or from the Munsey pulps. Amongst them were "The People of the Pit" by Abraham Merritt, which had recently been reprinted in the March 1927 *Amazing*, and *The Face in the Abyss*, also by Merritt. Readers were told that Merritt had promised to write a sequel to *The Face in the Abyss* specifically for *Amazing* and, indeed, that was the author's intention. His sequel, "The Snake Mother," contains much more science than you usually find in the author's work. However, as Sam Moskowitz explains in his *Reflections in the Moon Pool*, Merritt had either overlooked or forgotten the small print on the payment check he signed for *The Face in the Abyss*, which obligated him to let *Argosy* have first look at any sequel, or any other stories including the same characters.

For the rest of 1927 the serials were all two-part novels, and all reprints. The first was H. G. Wells's *The War of the Worlds* (August, September), which had a very effective cover showing the formidable Martian strollers and the havoc they caused. That novel led to a prolonged debate in "Discussions" between those readers who found it high-quality literature and those who found it dull and too long.

The August issue reprinted "The Tissue-Culture King" by Julian Huxley, grandson of the famous scientist Thomas Henry Huxley, under whom H. G. Wells had studied and been inspired. The story deals with super-scientific tissue culture which produces monstrosities such as two-headed toads, human giants, dwarfs and clones. Also thrown in is a mix of hypnotism and telepathy. Yet for all that it is treated scientifically, without sensationalism or a catastrophic ending. It's a true Gernsback-type story.

A. Hyatt Verrill's "The Ultra-Elixir of Youth" deals with a potion that not only restores youth but causes the subject to revert progressively to the foetal stage and beyond—one supposes—to the individual sperm. The process, once started, proves irreversible. Cecil B. White has a peaceful Martian story, "The Retreat to Mars," wherein a Martian library is found on Earth. Translators discover that an expedition to Earth had failed because terrestrial conditions proved to have a devolutionizing effect upon successive Martian generations. The colonists returned home before the situation had developed so far as to make return impossible. The story was a "sleeper": it isn't mentioned at all in "Discussions" for the rest of 1927, then there were two approving mentions in early 1928, just before the sequel appeared. By the time I began following *Amazing* in 1930, some readers were remembering it as among the best.

"The Chemical Magnet" by Victor Thaddeus has a most original idea. The protagonist searches for something that will act like a magnet upon chemicals, and succeeds—it can draw all of the salts out of a solution, for example. Unfortunately the author cannot think of any way to develop the idea so has the inventor go too far, perfecting a magnet that draws unknown but intensely radioactive material from the bottom of the sea. "I have found the secret of life!" he cries, and his attempt to bring the substance to the surface is successful but immediately catastrophic. Of course there are no notes, so the magnet is lost.

The September cover is the first to show a man caught in the clutches of a giant carnivorous plant; the story is "The Malignant Flower" by Anthos. Dr. Breuer has a short-short story, "The Stone Cat," which proves not to be a statue but a scientifically petrified animal. "The Electric Duel" by Hugo Gernsback is a single-page account of a duel wherein the antagonists meet on a large wooden platform and wear wired caps, which saturate them with static electricity. They "fight" with long poles that have boxing gloves on their tips. The aim for each is to push the other off the platform, which will result in instant electrocution when the victim is "grounded." The tale is marred by the "only a dream" ending. Otis Adelbert Kline's "The Radio Ghost" deals with an alleged haunted house where furniture moves around and other apparent supernatural phenomena occur. But it's all done through remote control by radio.

The most remarkable story in the issue is H. P. Lovecraft's "The Colour Out of Space," which was his first appearance in a science fiction magazine. It's closer to science fiction than most of A. Merritt's science-directed fantasies and among Lovecraft's best short stories. Lovecraft himself considered it his best short piece.

The October cover shows one of Paul's fascinating spaceships, illustrating Ray Cummings's novella "Around the Universe." It's a Jules Verne-style extraordinary voyage tale which outlines for the reader what was known about the eight known planets in the solar system. It's dull reading now.

Francis Flagg was the third new author to receive a cover illustration for his first sale to *Amazing*. "The Machine Man of Ardathia," in the November issue, is also the first story to deal with the visit of a man from the far future to the present time—and a strange man it is. The "machine man" is a human evolved to the point where he is little more than a big head blending into a spindly body. He lives within a large cylinder and could not survive outside it. Flagg was a good writer but not prolific. His stories were well received and some still repay reading today.

A. Hyatt Verrill contributed "The Astounding Discoveries of Doctor Mentiroso," a dazzling display of "logic" about the fourth dimension that is really a joke upon the reader. ("Mentiroso" means "liar" and the doctor's first name, "Fenomeno," translates to "phenomenal.") The editor presented the story straight, undoubtedly chuckling as he wondered how many readers would catch the fundamental flaw in the tale. It caused much discussion in the letter columns.

The December 1927/January 1928 issues reprint Jules Verne's *Robur the Conqueror*, rather dry reading today, even though it's a great-invention/wonderful-voyage tale. Verne's early prediction that heaver-than-air craft would prevail over the lighter-than-air variety was sound, though it may not have seemed that way when the story was first published. It is marred further for today's readers by the portrayal of the black servant, Frycollin, as an amusingly ignorant and cowardly negro. (True, the "comic-relief nigger" appeared in many otherwise respectable stories published at that time, but Verne overdoes it. He was virulently White-Supremacist.)

Dr. Breuer has a short-short tale, "The Riot at Sanderac," the first to deal with the subliminal effects of sound on human behavior. A "mad Russian" produces unheard but subliminally felt sounds on an organ that rouse people to frenzy, unaware of what is happening to them.

The January 1928 issue went on sale on December 5, 1927 with a fascinating cover for "The Comet Doom," Edmond Hamilton's debut in a science fiction magazine. Hamilton had already been selling similar stories to *Weird Tales* starting with "The Monster-God of Mamurth" in the August 1926 issue. He reappeared in the September issue with a three-part serial *Across Space* about an invasion from Mars. Better, and still remembered, is "The Metal Giants" from the December 1926 issue. It tells of a semi-intelligent, giant mechanical man which runs amok, but is conquered by a similar giant-sized spiked wheel. For those who had not read story after story with the same basic plot by Hamilton in *Weird Tales*, "The Comet Doom" would go over well on its own terms. Very likely there was little overlap between the readers of the two magazines in 1927. Gernsback's blurb, praising the story, calls Hamilton a "new author."

Reprints had dominated the serials in 1927 but most of the complete stories were new and while they had not become plot-heavy as yet, they did show a more contemporary writing style: we get to the point of the story much sooner. There were still stories about great inventions which lead to catastrophe which destroys the invention, but they were fewer and more fully developed than earlier examples.

My nominations for the best stories of 1927 (aside from the Merritt and Burroughs novels) are "The Plague of the Living Dead" by Verrill, "The Retreat from Mars" by White, and "The Riot at Sanderac" by Breuer, plus, amongst the reprints, "The Green Splotches" by Stribling, and "The People of the Pit" and *The Face in the Abyss* by A. Merritt.

1928

1928 has to stand as the first big year for science fiction magazines for a number of reasons. Firstly, readers disappointed by the news in the January *Amazing* that the magazine would not go semi-monthly, were soon elated at the news of a new magazine, *Amazing Stories Quarterly*, announced in the editorial in the February issue. That went on sale on January 5, 1928 and the first issue of the *Quarterly* would follow on January 20. The second reason was the number of new writers who emerged during 1928 together with the variety of exciting new stories and ideas.

The February issue, though, was perhaps not wholly an indication of what was in store. Paul's striking cover shows a spherical spacecraft hovering near the surface of the moon with the full Earth visible on the horizon. It illustrated Gernsback's own "Baron Munchhausen's Scientific Adventures," and the same scene had appeared on a cover of *The Electrical Experimenter* when the series had first appeared in 1915. For the reprint in *Amazing*, all the artwork was redone, and the many episodes were combined so that they were only six installments. There's no plot, but the descriptions of the moon and of the wonderful Martian civilization make interesting reading still.

The new serial was Jules Verne's *The Master of the World*, the sequel to *Robur the Conqueror*, written near the end of his life. By then, Verne's faith in science as a sure means to a better world had turned sour. In the first story, an enthusiastic young Robur was eager to share his discoveries with the world, which rejected him. Now, a bitter old man, he keeps them to himself having decided that the only way to improve the world is under his own personal rule. Robur's new invention is an omnibile: a device that can not only fly in the air, but run on land, and on and under the water.

Bob Olsen continues his fourth-dimensional series with "Four Dimensional Surgery" wherein gallstones are removed without cutting the patient open. W. Alexander tells another organ transplant story, "The Fighting Heart." A coward becomes brave after exchanging hearts with a man of great courage.

The first signs of the improvements to come were with the two new authors who made their debut in this issue: Walter Kateley with "The Fourteenth Earth" and David H. Keller, M.D., with "The Revolt of the Pedestrians."

Kateley was a good example of the "reliable" author, whose stories generally pleased but were seldom memorable. Most of his tales deal with the scientific adventures of Mr. George Kingston. In the first, the narrator tells how he contacted Kingston, who had perfected a device making travel possible to other "Earths" on different frequency levels than our own. The narrator is transported to the "fourteenth Earth."

Dr. Keller made a strong impression from the first, and would appear in all the other magazines of the period except *Astounding Stories*. (Harry Bates admired his weird tales, but felt that Keller had no talent for writing science fiction; F. Orlin Tremaine liked Keller, but Keller wasn't writing much SF during the years that Tremaine edited *Astounding*. He sent Tremaine some weird tales, but *Astounding* was no longer using weird material.) Keller wrote in a simple manner which, at times, was both artistic and effective, though at other times it seemed simple-minded. All of his characters talked naturally:

you never found that form of rhetorical speech you encountered in "literary" writing—but many of them came across like cracker-barrel philosophers. The response to Keller was nearly always extreme—very few readers were indifferent. Some of his stories were highly controversial and those who disliked them wrote vitriolic comments.

His initial story was set in a future where the majority of humans had become so dependent upon automobiles that their legs had atrophied, and they can barely walk. There is a small minority of "atavistic" humans with normal legs; the "automobilist" majority are trying to exterminate them. The story tells how a scientist among the pedestrians sabotages the power lines to their vehicles and the helpless automobilists die, leaving civilization to the healthy pedestrians.

In the "Discussions" department a letter from one Schuyler Miller takes the pro side in the continuing argument about The War of the Worlds and Wells's other stories. In his later letters Miller would put an initial "P" before the Schuyler. He became well known as a thoughtful and interesting letter writer some years before he emerged as an author.

The first issue of Amazing Stories Quarterly, dated Winter 1928, featured When the Sleeper Wakes by H. G. Wells. The illustrations were reprints of the pictures from the hardcover edition then in print. Paul's cover is based on one of them and copies the feeling of the original artist effectively. The lead story is a novelette, "The Moon of Doom" by Earl L. Bell, which tells of a future where the moon draws closer to Earth, causing massive tides, but also making it possible to go from Earth to the moon in atomic-powered aircraft. Explorers find the remains of an ancient Lunar civilization—not human, but humanoid. I did get to look through this issue, and was most impressed by an illustration of a huge moon, and people standing on high cliffs to escape super tides.

"The Terrors of the Upper Air" by Frank Orndorff presented an idea new to those who had not read "The Horror of the Heights" by Arthur Conan Doyle. Orndorff's story is good in its own right, telling of monsters that live in the stratosphere.

In the March Amazing, readers were invited to see if they could spot the fundamental flaw in Geoffrey Hewelcke's "Ten Million Miles Sunward." It deals with an attempt to force Earth into an orbit closer to the sun by shifting the balance of Earth. That is done by emptying all of the water out of the Caspian Sea, a staggering engineering feat. At the end of the story an announcement tells us that in the next issue a noted scientist will explain what is wrong. The scientist turned out to be Professor W. J. Luyten, who revealed that it would require a force from outside the planet to change Earth's orbit. At the most, the method described in the story might ". . . slow down the rotation of the earth a little and make the day a few seconds longer, but would have no further effect."

A short story, "Sub-Satellite," introduced a new author, Charles Cloukey, who would become quite popular in the years to come. The sub-satellite wasn't what you might think; it was a bullet fired by one character on the moon at another. It misses its target and, there being no atmospheric friction to slow it down or sufficient gravity to change its course, the missile travels completely around the moon and strikes the man who fired it in the back!

The only reason for mentioning "Lakh-Dahl, Destroyer of Souls" by W. F. Hammond is that it was the subject of one of Paul's silliest covers. It shows the sinister mandarin training a ray upon one of his victims. We are told that the ray is constituted from "concentrated rays of isolated moonbeams or Lunacy Rays" and the subject becomes a hopeless lunatic after five minutes exposure to it. The story is a poor imitation of Fu-Manchu.

Paul's cover for the April 1928 issue is the first symbolic one on an SF magazine. We see little pictures within what looks like a giant eye and the cover has the title "Scientifiction." The editorial page announces a contest for a design that will symbolize scientifiction. There are two memorable new stories in the issue. Cecil B. White's well-written sequel to "The Retreat from Mars," "The Return of the Martians," wherein, as before, the Martians are presented as a peaceful race, and good relationships are set up between them and the Earth people. "The Miracle of the Lily" by Clare Winger Harris tells of a future where humans are in contact with Venusians, and seek their help in dealing with the insect menace on Earth. Alas, the illustration gives away the surprise ending.

Two stories in the May issue dealt with oversized, familiar forms of Earthlife. The cover shows formidable-looking and rather frightening giant octopi walking on their tentacles on dry land; the phenomenon proves to be temporary, but is impressive while it lasts. That story, "The Octopus Cycle," introduced the writing team of Irving Lester and Fletcher Pratt. The other story, "The Master Ants" by Francis Flagg, tells of a far future where enlarged, though not giant, ants are the rulers of the planet. Humanity has been reduced to a primitive state and are slaves of the ants.

A new artist, R. E. Lawlor, illustrated the conclusion of Wells's serial, *A Story of the Days to Come.* Lawlor had an interesting and individual style; most of his drawings are pleasing to the eye and some are symbolic, but he had no feeling for futuristic machinery and his people are no more natural looking than Paul's.

The second issue of *Amazing Stories Quarterly*, dated Spring, appeared on schedule on April 20. Paul's cover, illustrating "The Second Swarm" by J. Schlossel, shows a massive spaceship about to land on Earth. Schlossel had previously had interplanetary stories in *Weird Tales.* They had imaginative sweep but were essentially simple. Gernsback's policy allowed him to expand his descriptions and make the stories more scientific in texture. The "swarms" in the story refer to humanity's swarming to the stars in the far future. During the first swarm some expeditions were destroyed by hostile inhabitants of far worlds; the second swarm is a punitive expedition. An interesting sidelight is that the commander of one of the expedition's ships is a black man— but nothing is made of it. All the races of Earth now live in peace and harmony with each other.

The lead novel, *A Modern Atlantis* by Frederick Arthur Hodge, deals with an artificial island in the middle of the Atlantic. At the time it was written, such structures were considered a likely development in the future. Along with Paul's illustrations, there is a photograph of a model of such an island made by Edward Armstrong. We still have nothing like them as yet, though present-day offshore oil rigs are a step in their direction. Hodge's novel seems rather dull today.

Homer Eon Flint's last (and posthumous) appearance was in this issue with "The Nth Man." It's the story of a human giant produced artificially by glandular manipulations. He is a giant mentally as well and sets out to put the world aright. A human being that size on Earth is no more credible than giant ants.

The June cover is from "The Blue Dimension" by Francis Flagg, and, aside from a rather sappy-looking face on the scientist, is effective. The story deals with the invention of "dimensional goggles" by one Doctor Crewe, his discovery of the blue dimension, and his successful incursion into it. The cover depicts the narrator looking into a strange world through the goggles and seeing a greatly enlarged Crewe there. Unfortunately, formula plot now takes over; Crewe is unable to return and the narrator is suspected of having murdered him.

Dr. Keller's "A Biological Experiment" is the first of his many stories dealing with the sociological effects of scientific discoveries. The present one deals with synthetic babies and a society where there are no natural-born children.

The June issue is notable for the debut of Harl Vincent, who would become one of the most popular and prolific authors of the period. His scientific ideas were nearly always interesting, but his plots were generally routine and melodramatic. With the exception of two book-length novels, which appeared in later issues of the *Quarterly*, Vincent wrote only short stories and novelets. "The Golden Girl of Munan," his first story, tells of a plot against civilisation by a secret group of scientific criminals on an "unknown" island. It is divulged to the hero through his television set by a mysterious and beautiful girl. He and his older super-scientist friend follow the lead, go the Munan, and foil the villains.

The feature story in the July issue is "Vandals from the Moon" by Marius. Although clearly patterned after *The War of the Worlds*, the story has enough individual touches to make it good reading. Two shorter items are worth mentioning. "The Educated Pill" by Bob Olsen is the first story wherein super-science is applied to sports. Here it's an artificial baseball with a small motor inside which can be set to make the baseball's flight sufficiently eccentric to baffle any batsman. The other item, "Just Around the Corner" by Raymond Knight, is a short one-act play designed for production by small amateur groups. It's about a scientific plan whereby a dying man will transmit messages through a type of super-phonograph after his death. The play's effective and could be presented today.

The August 1928 issue can be nominated as the most important of the early Gernsback days. It introduced two authors who became instantly popular and had a wide influence on science fiction, although in different ways. (I was on vacation in Newport, Rhode Island, in the summer of 1928 and had access to a newsstand where all the current magazines were piled flat upon large tables. I was thus able to pick up and leaf through the August, September and October issues. That had not been possible in Stamford, Connecticut, where I lived and was attending Junior High School.)

The more important of the two stories is *The Skylark of Space* by Edward Elmer Smith, Ph.D. and Lee Hawkins Garby. The story had been written in 1915, but Hugo Gernsback was the first editor to show interest in it. It is the pioneer novel of adventure beyond the limits of the solar system in spacecraft propelled at fantastic speeds by inter-atomic energy. It proved to rival "The Moon Pool" in popularity and many were the requests for a sequel. Paul's cover, showing Richard Seaton flying around with only a strange-looking rod attached to an apparatus strapped to his back, looks quaint today, because of the outdated costumes, but it was very effective at the time.

The other story of special note was "Armageddon—2419" by Philip Francis Nowlan, wherein one Anthony Rogers went into suspended animation in the year 1927 and awoke in 2419 to find himself living in a United States occupied by the Han warlords of Mongolia. A sequel to the story appeared six months later and meanwhile Anthony Rogers became the basis of a comic strip, *Buck Rogers in the 25th Century*. In 1930, I heard a few episodes of a radio serial with the same title. I disqualify myself from comment on the comic strip because I never paid any attention to it nor to any other science-fiction comics in the period. I did, however, consider the radio serial a debasement of science fiction.

"The Head" by Joe Kleier has the same theme as "The Talking Brain" by M. H. Hasta but does more with it. The man's disembodied head is virtually immortal and we see future history through its eyes—not pleasant history. "The Perambulating Home" is the last of Henry Hugh Simmons's "Hicks's Inventions with a Kick," and to my mind the most amusing. The home can rotate to face the sun, or avoid it, but when things go wrong it starts perambulating end-over-end and winds up in the ocean as a floating house.

With "The Moth" we conclude the unbroken series of Wells's reprints that began with the first issue of *Amazing Stories*. They not only gave the magazine tone but they introduced innumerable readers to a master of the short story and to a wealth of science-fiction ideas. Some of the readers who later became writers first encountered Wells here and were inspired by him.

Two new names appear in the Summer 1928 *Amazing Stories Quarterly*. The cover shows a scene from "Out of the Sub-Universe" by R. F. Starzl. Starzl would become well-known for action-filled short stories and novelettes in all the magazines of the period. Paul's cover shows a diminutive couple standing on a metal disc within an apparatus that is reducing their size as the first experiment in visiting an electron. Starzl was the first to take note of something no one else writing "smallness" stories had considered: as the subjects grew smaller, their subjective time became faster relative to time in the scientist's laboratory. When, fifteen minutes later, the power on the machine is reversed to bring them back, it is not they who return but a swarm of their descendants; generations have passed, relative to the electron, in those fifteen minutes.

The other newcomer is Stanton A. Coblentz, who would become one of the most popular writers of the period. Most of his novels and stories were satirical and he was at his best in that vein. This first novel, *The Sunken World*, tells of a lost submarine (during the Great War) which discovers Atlantis, still in existence, under a massive dome at the bottom of the sea. The story was highly praised at the time, and I enjoyed it when I managed to get a copy of the magazine in 1932, but now it seems to be little more than a tour of a Utopia with a tragic and ironic conclusion.

Most unusual is the way in which Dr. David H. Keller's scientific detective, Taine of San Francisco, is introduced here. We have a series of four short stories, each complete in itself, under the overall title of "The Menace." The author was clearly writing with his tongue in his cheek—Taine is a burlesque of the fictional "great detective," though he is neither a fool nor a bumbler. Today those four stories would be considered racist because the menace in the series is a group of black scientists who call themselves "The Powerful Ones" and use their discoveries in an attempt to crush White Supremacy. Taine defeats them single-handedly in each story using his wits alone; he never resorts to violence.

In his editorial, Gernsback invited readers to submit editorials about science fiction, its meaning and its future, offering $50 for the best one received in time for the next issue. We shall comment on some as we encounter them.

We can't leave the month of July 1928 without looking at *Weird Tales*, because at the very same time that we saw the beginning of *The Skylark of Space* in *Amazing*, a two-part novella, *Crashing Suns* by Edmond Hamilton, started here. The story takes place 100,000 years in the future, when the human race has spread out and occupied all the planets in the solar system. An interstellar expedition sets out to deal with a runaway sun on a collision course with our system. They find that the sun has been artificially deflected and is controlled in its passage by an alien, non-humanoid race of beings. For those disturbed by the romantic "mush" in Smith's novel, Hamilton's all-male epics were welcome.

I still remember how eagerly I awaited the September *Amazing Stories*, and how disappointed I was when I saw the cover. It did not illustrate a story; on an all-white background we see a large symbol representing "scientifiction" and inside a double-page spread shows various other symbols that had been submitted in the contest. Here, for once, was a quiet, non-lurid cover, and those who had complained about "sensational" covers should have been pleased. (Perhaps they were, but sales on that issue fell off markedly from the previous one; and the next issue, with a gaudy Paul illustration, picked up sales over the August issue.)

Harl Vincent's lead-off novelette, "The Ambassador from Mars," showed that his first story had not been just a flash in the pan. In this story, the human-like Martians are presented as friendly and civilized and there is no threat of an invasion of Earth. More interesting was "The Great Steel Panic" by Irvin Lester and Fletcher Pratt, the first to deal with a disease that attacks metal.

The October cover showed a mechanical man battling a lion in an arena. It illustrated "To the Moon by Proxy" by J. Schlossel, the first story dealing with an unmanned first flight to the moon. The inventor is a cripple who could not survive the trip himself; he sends the robot and watches the proceedings via television.

Clare Winger Harris's "The Menace of Mars" is not an invasion story but about strange cosmic changes which result in shifting planetary orbits. It's the planet itself, not its inhabitants, that proves to be the menace. A different and truly amazing story is "Reprisal" by Thomas Richard Jones. It's a story *about* science, rather than SF, in that the events could have happened in

1928. An oceanologist with a grudge against England discovers the right spot beneath the sea and blocks off the Gulf Stream with a wall of cement bags just enough to change its direction. The result is that England starts to freeze and the perpetrator demands a large ransom and amnesty as a reward for taking the wall down. England pays up and the situation is restored to normal.

It was after I returned from Newport that I came across a copy of *The Open Road for Boys* in the Stamford Public Library and, with sharp twinges of guilt (after all, I was mutilating the magazine), removed the coupon from an advertisement that offered a free sample copy of *Amazing*. I'd hoped that I would receive the October issue and thus be able to read the concluding installment of *The Skylark of Space*, but what happened was much better. I received a copy of the new November issue. The cover remains one of Paul's best and most amazing. It turns out that it was also the first issue that Arthur C. Clarke saw, and he points out, in an article published in the *New York Times Book Review* (March 6, 1983), exactly why the cover is so remarkable. After noting that the scene on Ganymede itself is rather unlikely, (". . . improbable because the temperature of the Jovian satellites is around minus 150 degrees centigrade . . ."), he comments on Paul's depiction of Jupiter, which we see enormous in the sky. "But the giant planet is painted with what has proved to be such stunning accuracy that one could use this cover to make a very good case for precognition. Frank Paul has shown turbulent cloud formations, cyclonic patterns and enigmatic white structures like earth-sized amoebas that were not revealed until the *Voyager* missions over fifty years later. *How did he know?*"

The new serial was *The World at Bay* by Bruce and George C. Wallis, whose stories had been seen previously by readers of *Weird Tales*. A race of troglodytes, living within Earth, have access to radium mines and have developed a power through which they have built an airship that can rise and fall vertically. They also have a gas that produces not only instant death but shrivels the body of the victim. Thus provided, they invade the upper world. At the time, it never occurred to me to wonder how a people as primitive as they are described were capable of the sophisticated technology that such an airship would require.

W. Alexander continues his series with "The Ananias Gland." Dr. Wentworth's patient is not only a persistent but compulsive liar. He cannot tell the truth even when he wants to. The doctor is sure that the problem springs from a little known gland, which he calls the "ananias gland." He adjusts its operation whereupon the patient becomes so totally truthful that he's worse off than before. A second adjustment puts it into balance and he can now lie when necessary but is free to be truthful otherwise.

Young as I was when I first read this issue (twelve) and for all the excitement of the serial, I was most impressed by Dr. Keller's "The Psychophonic Nurse." The nurse is a robot constructed to look and sound like a black "mammy." It is acquired by the husband of a writer who wants to be relieved of the tedious trivialities required in taking care of her baby. We discover the limitations of even the best-constructed robots in the course of the story.

I didn't see the Fall 1928 issue of the *Quarterly* at the time. Paul's cover shows a huge red ant standing about eight feet tall on its hind legs. It is placing its forelegs on the shoulders of a black man who dutifully looks alarmed. It illustrates A. Hyatt Verrill's book-length novel *The World of Giant Ants*. The story combines sound entomology with a fascinating narrative—an adventure story without villains (human or insect)—and remains good reading. Many today would resent the black man, Tom's, dialect, but such is the general way that uneducated people talk the world around and Tom is not presented as inferior otherwise, but as a brave and good man.

Dr. Keller contributes one of his most famous early stories, "Stenographer's Hands." A big-business man is trying to solve the problem of stenographers' mistakes by breeding superior stenographers; a new species—*homo stenographicus*—emerges. However, there is a hidden defect in his otherwise flawless plan, and the conclusion of the story is uncomfortable, but believable. In Bob Olsen's novelette "Four Dimensional Transit," a visit to the moon is accomplished via fourth dimensional devices. It's pretty much of a "Rovers Boys" type of story, but well done.

The historical interest of this issue is the first $50 prize-winning editorial from a reader: "Scientifiction, Searchlight of Science" by Jack Williamson. It outlines the Gernsback view of science fiction and its role in literature with the usual idealistic assumptions. "Science has made hardly a single step that scientifiction has not foretold." That was an exaggeration even in 1928. The opposite view, though (that SF has played *no* part in scientific developments), would be even farther from the truth.

As the month of November drew near, and I knew that the December *Amazing*, would soon be out, the question uppermost in my mind was: how could I get a copy? Obviously I could not expect to receive another free sample. Then I had an idea. I had loaned my November copy to a friend who lived next door. So I got him a coupon like the one I'd used myself and he sent off for his free sample copy. It worked; he received the December issue and loaned it to me after he'd read it.

The cover is one of Paul's best fantastic scenes. On a greenish background we see a valley surrounded by mountains; in the distance are strange-looking pillars with glowing red lights at their tops. A red river flows diagonally down the center of the scene and we see a number of dead birds on the ground. The action consists of a man in an aviator's costume being lifted off the ground by reddish-looking filaments emanating from a huge hexagonal figure in the sky. Its face is mostly geometrical designs but there are two eyes within purple triangles at the top and bottom. The man is firing vainly at the creature with an automatic. The story illustrated is "The Metal Man," Jack Williamson's first tale. It is short, and has the feeling of A. Merritt, without too much purple writing. The protagonist gets away from the weird creature, but finds that forces in the area are turning his body to metal. The juice of some local berries provides a temporary antidote; but when that is gone, the process continues until he becomes a metal man.

Dr. Breuer offers the first of a non-connected series explaining the fourth dimension. He stated later that he wrote the series because he disagreed with Bob Olsen's ideas about the fourth dimension. This first story, "The Appendix and the Spectacles," is medical; the surgeon enters the patient's body via the fourth dimension and removes the diseased organ without touching the man's skin. There is a mildly humorous touch: the doctor discovers later that he has left his spectacles inside the patient's body and has to go back to recover them.

Another debut in this issue is "Flight to Venus" introducing Edwin K. Sloat, who would be seen frequently during the period. The story is plot-heavy in the pulp sense. A proposed flight to Venus is intended as a hoax but something goes wrong and the spaceship and its pilot really do go to Venus. Meanwhile the facts about the intended hoax have leaked out and when the spaceflyer returns, no one believes him.

"The Fifth Dimension" by Clare Winger Harris is the first story to explain the phenomenon of precognition by dimensional planes of time wherein possible events not realized in our own plane of existence, come true. The narrator tells of a morning when she has the feeling that everything she is doing is something she has done before. She sees her neighbor walking toward the garage next door and has an impulse to run out and talk to her. She decides not to. The neighbor enters the garage and a moment later there is an explosion in which the woman is seriously injured. Later, the narrator's husband plans to take a night train to an important business meeting. Again she has a feeling that it happened before and led to disaster. Her husband agrees to take the morning train instead and the next day they read of a catastrophic train wreck. The fifth dimension is described as the interlocking of the various time lines from which "hunches" or "precognition" leak across to us now and then.

We return to Venus in "The Space Bender," a light-hearted tale by Edward L. Rementer. Here our explorer encounters a feline civilization, the first to be described in SF. Unfortunately, at a crucial point, the author pulls down the curtain and passes it all off as a spoof on the reader.

December came all too soon, it seemed. I managed to scrape together an extra 25 cents and bought the January issue which had another effective cover by Paul. We see the Woolworth building being pushed over by a massive wall of ice. It illustrates the first part of *The Sixth Glacier* by Marius. The issue opens with "The War of the Planets" by Harl Vincent, a sequel to "The Golden Girl of Munan." Twenty years have passed and we find that the villains in the first story had not all perished in the destruction of Munan. They had escaped to Venus and have now returned in globular spaceships armed with super-scientific weapons that can destroy cities.

Irving Lester and Fletcher Pratt collaborated on "The Roger Bacon Formula," which proves to be the recipe for a drug that permits the user's consciousness to explore the planets. The single episode offers a fascinating glimpse of another world with a strange, almost humanoid, civilization. Thereafter an accident makes it impossible for the protagonists to manufacture any more of the drug.

And then the axe fell. My parents forbade my purchase of any further issues of *Amazing Stories*. Now and then during 1929 I managed to see some of the covers but there was no opportunity to look through the issues, let alone to read them. It was ten years before I managed to find a copy of the February issue and read the conclusion to Marius's serial!

The main trend in 1928 had been to phase out reprints. It was the publication of "The Metal Man" by Jack Williamson that gave the first hint of future developments: the SF writer who started writing after having been a reader and sometimes contributor to the letter columns.

I would nominate the following as the best stories of 1928: *The World of Giant Ants* by Verrill, "The Second Swarm" by Schlossel, "The Return of the Martians" by White, "The Miracle of the Lily" by Harris, "The Master Ants" by Flagg, *The Skylark of Space* by Smith, "The Psychophonic Nurse" by Keller, and "The Metal Man" by Williamson.

1928 had been a comfortable year in science fiction with *Amazing* and its writers getting established. There was no hint at the end of the year how crucial a change was about to happen in 1929.

WINTER/SPRING 1929

1929 has to be one of the most important years in this era of science fiction, rivalled only by 1934. At the start of 1929, there were two SF magazines, *Amazing Stories* and the *Quarterly*. By the end of the year there would be seven! None of that could have been foreseen in January.

With the February *Amazing* came another new author receiving a cover for his first published story. Paul's painting of insectoid creatures with ray guns encountering a Tyrannosaur illustrated "The Death of the Moon" by Alexander Phillips, which tells of an expedition to Earth by the inhabitants of the dying moon. Their weapons prove inadequate in the end.

"The Captured Cross-Section" by Miles J. Breuer is the second in his fourth-dimension series and raises a point no one had mentioned before. If we could go into the fourth dimension, we would still only be able to perceive it in three dimensions and would see, in Breuer's thesis, only a bewildering collection of apparent cross-sections.

The Sixth Glacier concludes without any super-scientific discovery of ways to combat the great ice, which reaches its high point and begins to recede. On my first reading, in 1939, I found that somewhat disappointing, but later re-reading convinced me that the story was better without such added fantasy. It remains powerful and well-written even if the behavior of the glacier (". . . moving with the speed of an express train . . ." in part one, and the time-scale of its recession in part two) is open to doubt.

"Phagocytes" by A. H. Johnson is the first to present white blood corpuscles as sentient creatures—the tale is told from the viewpoint of one of them. There's an embarrassing error in the presentation of the story "Mernos." It's credited as being by "Henry James," who is actually the fictional narrator. In a later issue the editor apologized and informed us that the author was really L. G. Kellenberger. Mernos is a "missing" planet in the solar system that suddenly appears. The story tells of an expedition there and the discovery of its intelligent and peaceful inhabitants.

Most memorable in the issue was the debut of Wallace West in the SF magazines (he had appeared earlier in *Weird Tales*). "The Last Man" tells of a relic in a completely feminine world and, without overdoing it, West shows why such a world would not be a utopia. West never became a really "big" name in science fiction, but his stories and novels would be enjoyed beyond the Gernsback era, right up to his death in 1980.

Three new authors debut in the Winter issue of the *Quarterly*: Aladra Septama, Captain S. P. Meek, and L. Taylor Hansen. Septama's contributions would be confined to the *Quarterly*. His first, "The Beast Men of Ceres," starts a series dealing with scientific mysteries of the future—though they are not just detective stories. They are tales of interplanetary adventure and intrigue. The "beast men" are the invisible inhabitants of Ceres, who have been kidnapping Earthwomen. However, they prove to be neither villains nor hideous creatures, and Cereans join forces with Earthmen in the next two stories in the series.

"The Murgatroyd Experiment" by Captain S. P. Meek retains its punch upon re-reading today. The "experiment" is an attempt to solve the food problem in an overpopulated world by changing human beings into plant-like creatures that obtain their sustenance from the sun. Meek's stories were all based on interesting scientific speculations; even the pulpiest of some of the later ones were more than mere variations on well-known SF themes.

The identity of the third new author, L. Taylor Hansen, still remains something of a mystery. During the thirties we learned in the fan press that the "L" stood for Louise, but later she revealed that she had merely been the agent for her brother, who had written the stories. Whatever the circumstances, "What the Sodium Lines Revealed" revealed a new author with a different approach. An astronomer accidently discovers a phenomenon involving sodium lines in a grille while he is searching the skies in the vicinity of Jupiter. It transpires that a message is being sent through those lines and the message is the story itself. It's a wild adventure involving a super-scientific though peaceful race of alien beings.

In "The Evolutionary Monstrosity" Clare Winger Harris offers an effective scientific horror story about a scientist who evolves into a hideous entity. Walter Kateley presents the charmingly impossible "The Hollister Experiment." The tale deals with the unintentional havoc caused by an artificially produced giant grasshopper. (If giant insects were possible at all, there would be no need to produce them scientifically; they'd exist where the conditions were right.)

The lead novel is the updated version of Hugo Gernsback's *Ralph 124C 41+*, which had been issued in hardcover in 1925. It is even more remarkable for its visions of scientific possibility than the original 1911 version, but the story remains the same: a simple narrative as a vehicle for speculation.

The March and April issues of the monthly *Amazing* featured a two-part serial by A. Hyatt Verrill, *Into the Green Prism*, wherein he combines his sound scientific knowledge of South American Indians and their mysterious past cultures with sheer fantasy about a form of crystal that can reduce or enlarge the size of objects. An entire village of the Manabis has been reduced to microscopic size and still exists as viewed through the green prism. At the end of the story Professor Ramon Amador, who has fallen in love with a woman in the village that he sees through the prism, makes use of the prism to reduce himself to her size. There the story ends, though the readers demonstrably wanted more, as well as some explanations for the more dubious scientific elements of the story.

Paul's cover on the March issue illustrates a scene from "The Airlords of Han" by Philip Francis Nowlan, the sequel to "Armageddon—2419," wherein the Mongols are finally bested and the Americans regain their independence. Dr. Keller's horror tale, "The Worm," aroused controversy. Read with a willingness to suspend belief, it has power, but to describe it in a few words would make it sound as absurd as many readers considered it. A short story, "The

Face of Isis" by Cyril G. Wates, describes the finding of a chemical formula that the discoverer believes to have been used in ancient Egypt in an attempt at flight between worlds. The powder derived from the formula proves effective but a mistranslation of the ancient Egyptian results in an ironic fiasco: the powder increases gravity instead of reducing it.

The blurb for April's cover story tells us that "The Revolt of the Atoms," by V. Orlovsky, is the first science fiction tale to come from Soviet Russia. Sam Moskowitz has identified its source as the March 1927 issue of *Mir priklyuchenniv*. It tells of an experiment that goes wrong and creates a world menace—a rapidly expanding atomic fireball that is becoming a miniature sun. Paul's cover shows the now-monstrous fireball hovering in the sky.

"The Terror of the Streets" by George McLeod Winsor deals with a super-scientific automobile, in effect an armored car, that can go faster than any other car then in existence. It's used to terrorize speeders.

An amusing tale of the future, "Buried Treasure" by Miles J. Breuer, contains a message in code that takes up a full page in the magazine. Overleaf is a blank page. The reader is instructed to "carefully cut out this page using a sharp penknife. Then place the page with the unprinted part up on a clean newspaper. Next procure a bottle of fine oil, such as 3-in-1 brand, and pour about one teaspoonful on the page. Take a clean wad of absorbent cotton and distribute oil all over page, making sure the entire page is covered. Wipe off surplus oil. The page is now translucent. Next, with the printed part up, place it over the key symbol on page 43. Read from the circle towards dots. Circle and each dot gives one letter. Each of fifty-six boxes on this page contains one word." Gernsback was nothing if not experimental! The treasure proves to be some cases of wine. (Remember, in 1929 Prohibition was still in effect.)

Few of those who read that April issue of *Amazing Stories* realized that it was the end of a chapter in the history of the development of the science fiction magazine.

36.

INTERLUDE: APRIL 1929

At the time I only managed to see the cover of the May *Amazing Stories* but I noticed one thing that puzzled me. Nowhere on it did I see that well-known line, "Hugo Gernsback, *Editor*." Those who purchased the issue found that all mention of Hugo Gernsback had disappeared from the magazine. On the editorial page Arthur H. Lynch is listed as Editor-in-Chief. The editorial, "Amazing Stories," is by T. O'Conor Sloane, who is still listed as Associate Editor.

I wonder how many readers at the time knew of the bankruptcy proceedings taken against Experimenter Publications and of the ousting of Gernsback from *Amazing Stories*. That story is told elsewhere in this volume so I will not dwell on it here. Instead I will note the caution with which some may have read Sloane's editorial where he stated that, "Some stories published many years ago are so distinctively good that from time to time we give reprints in our columns." And the May issue opens with the first installment of *The English at the North Pole* by Jules Verne—not an auspicious start to the new editorial aegis. The novel is a tale of high adventure, suspense and exploration in the then little-known territory of the North Pole. But upon what basis Gernsback, Sloane, or anyone else could consider it science fiction is something else. A good deal of natural science does appear in it but there is not a trace of imaginative speculation, such as we find in other of Verne's stories that can be considered science fiction.

The rest of the issue was more favorable. Stanton A. Coblentz made his first short-story appearance with "The Gas Weed," dealing with a deadly and noxious form of plant life brought to Earth by a meteor. "The Diabolical Drug" by Clare Winger Harris tells of an experiment with a synthetic drug that speeds up animal metabolism; it's a good cautionary tale. And the cover, which brought forth one of Paul's excellent lunar landscapes, "The Moon Strollers" by J. Rogers Ullrich, is concerned with the exploration of the moon in space-suits.

The Spring issue of the *Quarterly* appeared on time, April 20, 1929, and, as with the monthly companion, differed from the previous issue only in the absence of Gernsback's name from the cover and interior. The feature novel was *After 12,000 Years* by Stanton A. Coblentz. One characteristic fault of Coblentz's novels is the length of introductory chapters; it takes so long to get to the point where the story really begins. The preliminaries are where the author's occasional stodginess is most apparent. Such is the case in *After 12,000 Years*. The protagonist, in need of work, encounters a scientist who claims to have invented a survival drug—a means of reviving the dead. He submits to the drug but instead of coming back to life within the expected time, he remains in suspended animation for twelve thousand years. When he awakes he finds himself in a world where the human race has mutated in several different ways and the various factions are at war using mutated insects as weapons.

"The Cry from the Ether" by Aladra Septama is the second in his series and deals with a mysterious call for help from an unknown world; Earthmen and Cerians go to the rescue. Septama's stories all moved rather slowly and would have benefited from some cutting. In "Locked Worlds," Edmond Hamilton repeats his formula of the experimenter who contacts an alien civilization (this time an arachnid one), visits their area with some friends, and finds that they are dupes in a plan for the conquest of Earth. Frequently there is another, benign, set of creatures in the same world oppressed by the aggressive race. And just as frequently everything centers about some master-control point: if the heroes can reach it and activate the right device all will be destroyed. "The City of Eric" by Quien Sabe (Spanish for "Who Knows?") is a slow-moving tour of a utopia.

And so passed April 1929. It seemed at the time that Hugo Gernsback was out of science fiction, but few suspected what was going on behind the scenes. In later years when I was an editor at Columbia Publications I met Maurice Coyne, the company's treasurer, who was a friend of Gernsback's and had been a member of the Board of Trustees set up to handle the Experimenter Publishing Company whilst it was in receivership. He told me that he and the other members of the Board realized that Gernsback had been a victim of injustice and their idea was to find a way to return the magazines to him. However, Gernsback told them not to bother; he was already going ahead with other plans. There would be a big surprise for Gernsback followers early in May.

37.

THE FIRST SCIENCE FICTION BOOM: 1929-1930

SUMMER/FALL 1929

On May 3, 1929, two days before the June *Amazing Stories* was due, a new science-fiction title appeared on the newsstands: *Science Wonder Stories*, and just below the date and the cover price was the familiar line, "Hugo Gernsback, *Editor*." Compared to the dynamic logo of *Amazing Stories*, the one for the new magazine was tame: in a white box of approximately 5 x 3 inches, with a red border rounded at the corners, was the word SCIENCE in red, WONDER in black, slanted so that it had the full width of the box, and below that STORIES in red. Below the box was a one-inch shield informing us that it was "A Gernsback Publication." The shield would be present on all subsequent issues.

Paul's cover shows a slim, golden spacecraft with a long pointed nose, crashing into a large, globular ship, which is surrounded by a greenish haze. It is night, and we are over the sea; down at the right another globe, badly shattered, floats on the water. In the sky both to the left and right are two more globular ships at a distance and thus unharmed. It illustrated "Warriors of Space" by James P. Marshall, a sequel to "The World in the Balance," which had run in *Argosy* two years earlier, telling of an invasion from Saturn. The invaders' weapon disintegrates everything except gold. Their first, lone ship was defeated, but now they are back in force. Earth is equipped with gold-plated ships, such as we see on Paul's cover. It's a wild tale culminating in the planet Saturn being shifted from its orbit to the extent that it is drawn into the sun. Many readers questioned whether that was possible and wondered if it would not have a disastrous effect upon the other planets. In "The Reader Speaks," September 1929, Professor Samuel G. Barton of the Flower Observatory, University of Pennsylvania, states: "The annihilation of Saturn and its satellites would cause but a very slight disturbance in the solar system." There might be some temporary disturbance if, during the transportation, Saturn came close to any of the other planets, but no permanent damage.

Leading off the issue was a two-part novella, "The Reign of the Ray" by Irvin Lester and Fletcher Pratt.

> "What you see here is probably the largest vacuum tube ever built. It is the Coolidge type with modifications. I've killed a rabbit in two seconds with its emanations and set up such violent atomic disturbance in gasoline as to cause it to explode in a closed dish. Lord alone knows what else it will do. I haven't given it a thorough trial yet."
>
> Schneider's eyes bulged. "Why you might be able to set off explosives at a distance with it," he exclaimed. "Such a thing would be worth millions to any country."

And, of course, that is what happens. The story is a "future history," told in episodes from various viewpoints. There is no single protagonist but the story remains a powerful one.

The rest of the contents do not live up to the level of the Lester/Pratt serial. H. G. Wells makes his final appearance in a Gernsback magazine with "The Diamond Maker" which, though not a poor story, is not amongst his best either and was almost certainly used for window dressing. "The Marble Virgin" by Kennie McDowd was as controversial amongst the readers as the Marshall story for its scientific questionability and it certainly makes one wonder what use there was in having a board of consultants to pass judgment on the scientific principles in the stories. Part of it is sound enough in theory. If it were possible to make a device that would add or subtract electrons from any particular substance then one form of matter could be turned into another. That is what Professor Carl Huxhold's electron dissolver and cabinet does in the story. The "virgin" is a marble statue with which, like Pygmalion, its sculptor has fallen in love. Huxhold says that his apparatus can transform the statue into a living woman, and it does! There is no indication that anything need be done except to transform a *solid marble* statue into flesh and blood— and behold we have a complete, perfectly formed human female with every organ in its right place and functioning. It still takes my breath away that the story could have appeared in a magazine as dedicated to plausible science as was Gernsback's. Here was poetic license with a vengeance! Those who loved romantic stories loved "The Marble Virgin" but others more concerned with scientific plausibility roasted it heartily.

With all the action and controversy in the first *Science Wonder Stories*, the June *Amazing Stories* seemed somewhat tame by comparison. Paul's cover, illustrating "The Beetle Experiment" by Russell Hays, shows a sunrise over a meadow where a man with a shotgun confronts a giant beetle. The story itself is well executed and not over-sensational. That marked Paul's last cover for *Amazing Stories* for the remainder of this period. The only other story of much interest in the issue is Peter Brough's "Fingers of the Mist," dealing with synthetic life. *The English at the North Pole* by Jules Verne concludes in this issue and is immediately followed by its sequel, *The Desert of Ice*, which would conclude in the next issue.

Hot on the heels of Gernsback's new *Science Wonder Stories* came a further magazine, *Air Wonder Stories*. According to a promotional advertisement in *Science Wonder* the first issue, dated July 1929, appeared on June 1, though all later issues appeared on the tenth of the preceding month. Paul's cover shows an airplane landing-platform floating in the sky with one plane about to land on it while others are nearby. Below, on the ground, we see a landing field, most of which is occupied by impressive apparatus which, apparently, is what keeps the platform suspended in the air. I was a little surprised when I first saw the cover. Having seen the black-and-white reduction in *Science Wonder* I had expected a blue sky background. On the contrary the issue appeared with a red-sky background, something that appeared rather frequently on the Gernsback SF magazines and to which many readers objected. It wasn't until I became an editor in the 1940s that I came to realize the reason for it. Gernsback Publications was a small company and they couldn't afford the quality of engraving that one saw on the covers of magazines from some of the larger pulp chains. A three-plate (red, yellow, blue) rather than a four-plate (red, yellow, blue, black) process was used, and that made it difficult to reproduce various tones of color, particularly some background tones, and a real black was impossible. In addition, Gernsback wanted his covers to have a poster effect, which meant that many of them had a flat, single color for a background with no shading. Thus, whatever Paul's original background color might have been, the picture was in effect cut out and pasted onto a flat poster background. The result was effective in catching the eye, but readers who knew something about art must have thought that Paul's color sense wasn't very good, because background and foreground colors sometimes did not match very well.

The story this cover illustrated was "Islands in the Air" by new writer, Lowell Howard Morrow. It dealt with the rivalry between two inventors who have come up with the same invention, with one having stolen the other's plans. In the end the original inventor crashes his island into his rival's; both perish and the secret is lost.

The serial was a reprint of Victor MacClure's *The Ark of the Covenant*, which had been published in hardcover in 1924 and which Gernsback had previously serialized in *The Experimenter*. Gernsback considered it "the greatest air story that has yet been written," and re-reading it today I'm inclined to agree that it probably was for 1929. Where earlier novels about the future in the air were war stories, here was an air mystery, the secret of which is an attempt to stop war. The merits of the story triumph over its datedness.

"The Beacon of Airport Seven" by Harold S. Sykes tells of a successful attempt to bend light rays; when the device is trained on the beacon, airplane crashes start because the light that incoming pilots see is not where it appears to be. "The Bloodless War" by David H. Keller deals with an air-fleet under remote control and a planned onslaught that is foiled. The surprise of the issue was the debut of Leslie F. Stone, whose picture revealed that she was an attractive-looking woman. Miss Stone became a favorite rather quickly, and rightly so. "Men with Wings" is a novella about a generations-spawning secret experiment that results in a hidden civilization of winged humans. The winged men are kidnapping women all over the world—though not for the reasons you'd expect in a pulp thriller—and investigators find the hidden colony.

The July issue of *Science Wonder Stories* had a flat yellow background and illustrated the editorial "The Wonders of Gravitation" which, we are told in the squib on the contents page, "bears directly on the series starting this month, entitled 'The Problems of Space Flying'. Mr. Paul, our artist, has shown how, under certain conditions, it is possible for a single man to lift the 60,000-ton steamship *Leviathan* without straining his muscles." The cover depicts two men in naval uniform standing on the surface of a small asteroid; one of them holds the massive ship, with its complement of crew and officers, in his hand. That is certainly impressive but it gives more a feeling of a "popular science" illustration than science fiction. Indeed, the same concept had been used for a painting by George Wall on the cover of the September 1919 *Electrical Experimenter* to illustrate an article by Isabel Lewis on gravitation. The article mentioned in the squib, "The Problems of Space Flying" by Captain Hermann Noordung, A.D.M.E., was announced as a two-part serial, though it finally ran to three parts. It was a classic of its kind. Translated from the German by Francis Currier it influenced SF writers for many years to come. The article, though, was somewhat abridged, and I later learned that the missing material was responsible for some of the errors made by those who believed that they now had all of the background necessary for accurate speculation on the subject.

Also starting in this issue was a two-part serial, *The Alien Intelligence* by Jack Williamson, the first of his novellas with fantastic themes that are reminiscent of A. Merritt's work. Winfield Fowler, a young American living in Australia, receives a message from an explorer friend, Dr. Horace Austin, who has gone on an exploration of the Mountain of the Moon in the Great Victoria Desert. Austin asks Fowler to come to him, bringing various scientific equipment, "for the sake of mankind," and gives him directions, telling him to look up "Melvar of the crystal city." Fowler finds, first of all, a great metal ladder, with which to ascend to a plateau, then another one going down into the valley. The descent of the second ladder certainly brings Merritt's "The People of the Pit" to mind. In the valley, he finds a "lost" civilization, and a weird (though scientific rather than supernatural) alien menace. It comes across as first-class fantastic adventure even when read today.

The feature novelette was "The Menace from Below" by Harl Vincent which starts with the strange disappearance of an entire subway train filled with commuters. Two scientists have discovered a means of using the fourth dimension to kidnap people or transport objects. They are engaged in experiments on human beings and apes and believe they'll produce a super-race. It's more thrilling than plausible, but is fun to read. Dr. Keller's short story, "The Boneless Horror," is as much fantasy as science fiction. The "science" part deals with the indefinite prolongation of life through the use of royal jelly, something that was considered possible at the time. The rest, dealing with the destruction of two mythical empires, Mu and Gobi, is fantasy. "The Reign of the Ray" concludes with glimpses of a new civilization growing out of the war resulting from the ray. The war ended in 1936, which seemed futuristic enough in 1929.

On the cover of the July *Amazing Stories* is a scene from the concluding chapters of Verne's *The Desert of Ice* by Hugh McKay. McKay was a creditable artist but he had little feeling for science fiction. The present cover, depicting a group of polar bears being blown up amid the arctic wastes, does not even remotely suggest science fiction—not that there was a scene in the story that could be depicted as science fictional.

The lead-off story, illustrated by Paul, concludes Miles J. Breuer's four-dimensional trilogy. In *The Book of Worlds*, the scientist uses the fourth dimension as a means of looking into the future—not just one future, but various possible ones. All of them that the inventor sees are hideous and he loses his reason and destroys the machine. "The Flying Fool" is one of Dr. Keller's charming tales of the domestic problems of the ordinary man, in this case an inventor, but it cannot be called science fiction. The proposed invention might have qualified but we never know if it would work because the device is tampered with.

The one story in this issue that stands out is "Futility" by Captain S. P. Meek. Is the future fixed or fluid? it asks. If the future is fixed would it be possible to construct a machine that would produce accurate information about things to come? The predictograph, constructed by a friend of the narrator, seems to be just such a device. But it brings with it the question of whether we would be any happier or better off knowing what the future will bring if we also know it cannot be changed. One question remains in the inventor's mind: are the predictions absolutes or first-order probabilities? He proposes to test that out. He reveals to the narrator that he has less than a year to live but that he will leave his entire fortune to his friend provided he can teach him how to use the predictograph and to figure out his life span for him. The narrator thinks about it and realizes that if the machine does what it is supposed to do, and if it should reveal that he is also to die soon, having the inventor's fortune would be little consolation. If he refuses, the inventor says, he will destroy the machine. The narrator decides not to accept, which was just what the predictograph had foretold!

Paul's cover for the August *Science Wonder Stories* looks more like a detail from a story, though it illustrates Noordung's article, "The Problems of Space Flying." Two people inside a space flyer are looking out at Noordung's projected Space House, which is the main part of a station in space. Attached to it are the observatory and an engine house. In the bottom of the scene are Earth and the Moon.

A new author, Ed Earl Repp, appears with a two-part serial, *The Radium Pool*. The story tells of two old desert rats who come upon an open pool of radium salts in the desert. One sticks his fingers into it and their tips melt away, and at once he becomes a young man again. The other prospector retains his age and is unaffected. The pool, it is discovered, is part of the setup of a secret expedition to Earth by the super-scientific inhabitants of Jupiter. The story was well-received although some sharply questioned the effect of the radium pool upon the two men.

Short stories in the issue were "The Moon Beasts" by William P. Locke, a well-done portrayal of a truly alien, but not hostile, creature; "The Eternal Man," which heralded D. D. Sharp's first appearance, and "The Feminine Metamorphosis" by Dr. David H. Keller. Sharp's story was hailed at once as a minor classic: it tells of an attempt to achieve immortality, which succeeds too well. Zulerich has tried his "immortality" formula on a rat; the rat stiffens, paralyzed, at first, but regains ability to move when touched with bicarbonate of soda. So the old man takes a glass of soda in one hand to drink the moment he has swallowed his elixir—and is frozen into immobility thus. He seems to be dead. In Keller's story, Taine of San Francisco solves the secret of what seems to be a new breed of super-businessmen. It's actually an attempt by women to achieve equality with men by transforming themselves into males by special surgical operations. But they aren't satisfied with equality; they want total domination.

The August *Air Wonder Stories* presented a new author, Henrik Dahl Juve, whose early stories were on a somewhat higher level than the general run of the day. The first, "The Silent Destroyer," was also depicted on the cover, which portrayed two super aircraft shaped like long cigars, and for the first time we see "atomic" rays in action. One ship is slicing the other in two. (I've seen Paul's original. It had a gray background, which was more effective than the cobalt blue of the published painting.)

The most popular story in the issue was "The Planet's Air Master" by Edward E. Chappelow. It's a thriller about a super-scientist who has invented a telepathy ray through which he can not only read minds but can also control them. The detective hero has a metal plate in his head, a result of an accident, and so is not susceptible. Also in the issue was "Beyond Gravity" by Ed Earl Repp, which tells of a super-plane that gets caught in an updraft and is carried into the stratosphere where its propellers are useless; in effect, it's in orbit.

On the cover of the August *Amazing Stories*, McKay shows that he can draw faces very well and the rather simple scene (what appears to be a fireball hovering over the head of one figure who seems to be in a trance) is effective. But the apparatus which produces the phenomenon looks primitive indeed—there's no imagination at all in its portrayal. It illustrates "Barton's Island," a thriller by Harl Vincent. Inside it becomes apparent that the magazine is in need of illustrators who have both the feel and technique needed for science fiction art. Aside from one fairly good illustration by Paul, the art is no pleasure to look at.

The new serial is *Out of the Void* by Leslie F. Stone, which is charming but not particularly memorable, except for one point. The hero, who is one of the two-man team to try a trip to Mars (but which misses Mars and lands on an unknown planet) turns out to be a woman posing as a man. Dr. Keller's "The Eternal Professors" is another instance of heads being kept alive outside of the bodies. "The Dimension Segregator" by J. Harold Click presents new thoughts on what it might be like going into the fourth dimension. Among other things the explorers find that parts of their bodies, such as hands, are suddenly segregated; it looks as though one man's right hand has been cut off—but it hasn't; it's just there at a distance, and still in operation.

If the August *Amazing Stories* was a disappointment in respect to interior artwork, the Summer *Amazing Stories Quarterly* was even more so. While the cover shows an exciting scene from Harl Vincent's enjoyable novel *Venus Liberated*, what we see inside is best forgotten. There is an effective drawing by Austin Briggs for "The Singing Moonbeams"—a good detective story by Edward R. Sears, but not really science fiction. Briggs's other drawings are also good, but none suggest science fiction. The cover artist is unidentified but the crude ray guns that humans—Earthmen and Venusians—are training upon squid-like monsters (from which our heroes liberate the kindly Venusians) as well as the faces and figures themselves, suggest McKay.

Still interesting is "Paradox" by Charles Cloukey, blurbed as "a story of the fourth dimension and its paradoxes." Via the fourth dimension the protagonist goes into the future—Cloukey presents us with a fascinating future world—and, among other things, the protagonist learns the date of his death. His object then is to return to the present the day *after* that fatal date. It seems he has succeeded, but . . . Both "Rays and Men" by Dr. Breuer and "White Collars" by Dr. Keller, have elements of sociological interest, particularly the latter, which deals with the psychological shock that "white collar" workers undergo when they find that their services, for which they have had a lifetime of training, are now no longer of any use.

The prize-winning editorial this time is "The Future of Scientifiction" by Dr. Miles J. Breuer. In short, he believes that this "new art" has a great future, that it will become a compelling part of the general progress of humanity, and that historians will trace it all back to *Amazing Stories.*

The September *Science Wonder Stories* is graced by what came to be called Paul's mechanical chicken, because the earth-moving device used by the invaders in Frank Phillips's novelette, looks like one. It stands on two legs and its scooplike "hands" and "beak" dig up soil into a mound which is fed into the atomic-furnace that provides the power for the expedition. Those were still the days when writers imagined that in the future any kind of matter was fuel for an atomic-power device. (Frank Phillips was a pseudonym for Philip Francis Nowlan; it's just as well that his real name was not used, because "The Onslaught from Venus" is a forgettable story, far from the level of his two "Armageddon" novelettes.)

The new serial was *The Human Termites* by Dr. David H. Keller. It proved to be one of his most controversial stories; letters of praise and condemnation would come in for months afterward. The story is based upon *The Life of the White Ant* by Maurice Maeterlinck, a classic of entomology. In the first installment we meet Dr. Hans Souderman, an expert entomologist who has been studying termites all his life. He has devised a means through which he can look into a termitary without having to break into it. He also believes that the termites have a language, a way of intercommunication that can be learned and, further, that termites are planning to extend their territory over Earth—and not to the benefit of humankind. With the aid of friends he returns to Africa to try out his devices, and it is the termites who contact him through what he has already deduced as their Central Intelligence. They tell him that while he has been studying them, they have been studying him, but now his usefulness is ended. He escapes from Africa just in time as the first installment ends.

With the September issue of *Air Wonder Stories*, the clover-leaf logo was moved from dead center to a tilted position at the left. It looked more interesting that way. Paul's cover, illustrating "Flight in 1999" by Bob Olsen is, indeed, charming, and the poster-yellow background that covers the top third does not harm it. It shows the San Francisco airliner coming into a platform that is way up in the air—but not a free-flying platform. It's so high that we can see a vast expanse of land and water beneath it. People are flying up to the platform on individual, artificial wings. The story itself was considered silly even at the time. Our protagonist, knowing that the great air liners have been plagued by bandits for some time has invented a self-protection device. The bandits, a gang of masked females, make their attempt and he overcomes them with ease. The reward money enables him to prevent the mortgage on his home from being foreclosed.

Harl Vincent's "The Yellow Air Peril" is an ordinary future attempted-conquest story. It would bring some criticism upon him because the "yellow peril" is an amalgamated Eastern empire rooted in a perversion of Buddhism. Vincent was charged with misrepresenting Buddhism, which has been a peaceful, non-aggressive religion throughout its history. The main scientific interest in the story is the description of massive airships driven by wind tunnels. (Vincent was accused of slandering Buddhism by one reader, but his reply, wherein he states that he had no such intention, and had carefully noted that he was dealing with a perversion of the religion, is certainly adequate.)

"Where Gravity Ends," by Robert H. Leitfred is a short tale of an aviator who crashes on a tiny planetoid that is orbiting within Earth's atmosphere and is beginning to break up. What the story's title has to do with it remains a mystery.

The cover of the September *Amazing Stories* introduced a new artist who showed both skill and scientific imagination and who could draw people, on the whole, more believably than Paul. The only name we are given is "Wesso"—he is so credited on his interior artwork for the cover story, "The Red Peril" by Captain S. P. Meek. It would not be long before many readers were declaring him better than Paul all around.

The stories in this issue are generally forgettable except for Cyril G. Wates's offering, which contains one of the most fascinating throwaway lines of the period. At the beginning of "Gold Dust and Star Dust," a dimensional mystery tale, the detective in the case calls our narrator.

> "Can you come up to the lab immediately, Frank?" he said, after the usual trimmings.
>
> "I guess I can, if it's important, Hil," I replied. "I was planning to stay at home and watch the game between the Yanks and the Giants, but that doesn't matter."
>
> "Never mind about the game, Frank. Set your recorder and you can watch it after you get back . . ."

What kind of video-recorder did Frank have? Tape? Disc? We are not told and there's no further mention of it in the story. It's just there to give us a feeling of the future, but it's a remarkable prediction. The story itself deals with a mysterious vanishing of valuables, which proves to have a fourth-dimensional, rather than a criminal explanation.

What makes this issue memorable is the bombshell that Dr. Sloane drops in the "Discussions" department in reply to a reader's letter. "We do not personally believe in the possibility of a rocket reaching the moon." Dr. Sloane was roundly denounced for that statement though, when we look back to the state of the art of rocketry as it was in 1929 and remember the innumerable technological advances that had to be made before the feat became possible, Dr. Sloane's quiet realism becomes understandable. There would be no basic change in the situation before his death. (The uproar shows more about the insecurity of many fans, and their tendency to treat any such questioning as heresy, than about the facts in the case.)

The cover of the October *Science Wonder* shows an experiment in progress. Two figures are seated, facing each other. Each wears a strange helmet that covers his entire head and neck, and the front of each helmet has what looks like a tv screen. The operator's screen is blank but on that of the subject we see a huge lizard-like creature standing in water. Behind the experimenters are two awestricken observers and the whole picture is set on the now-familiar red background. It illustrates, "Into the Subconscious" by Ray Avery Myers, about an attempt to view the prehistoric past through the subconscious memories of the subject, memories that purportedly extend back to a time before the subject's ancestors were human. Knowing that there would be a considerable debate about the story from the readers, Gernsback published it as a contest. He offered $50 in prizes for the best letters on the story. "If you read this story carefully," he explained, "you will find that it will contain one fundamental, logical mistake, one impossibility in other words." The lizard-like creature which we see in the visiplate on the cover is about to catch and devour a frog-like creature that was the subject's remote ancestor.

In part two of *The Human Termites* the wild speculations start. The sister of Adam Fry, a member of Souderman's expedition, is captured by the termites and brought to the termitary's Central Intelligence, which is an oval slug-like thing. We learn that super-warrior termites have been developed; they are truly fearsome creatures, twenty feet long and about three feet high. One of the sailors on the ship has also been captured. After explaining to Susan Fry how the termites will extinguish the human race, the Intelligence also notes that experiments in combining some aspects of the human and termite have been in progress for some time. Some of the giant termites (not all are warriors) have human-like faces and can speak and understand a few words of English. Now the Intelligence is going to move into the body of the sailor and mate with Susan to produce a new strain of human termites. The Intelligence is not aware that Susan is armed; when it is completely within the sailor's body, Susan produces her pistol and destroys the man's brain, then escapes with the aid of one of the friendly semi-human giants.

The cover for the October *Air Wonder Stories* has a pleasing background scene of mountains and a lake and the blue sky is probably close to Paul's original tone. It illustrates Harl Vincent's "Through the Air Tunnel" and the editor explains: "Here we see how the special air car moves at the rate of one thousand miles and hour, through the artificially created vacuum in the air tunnel. By electrical means the inside of the air tunnel becomes a vacuum in which the onrushing car moves free of friction." What we actually see are a line of what look like enormous rings set on sturdy metal bases and a long, narrow car is entering one of them. But the idea is the thing. The story does not live up to the expectation; it has an all-too-familiar plot. Much better is Hendrik Dahl Juve's sequel to "The Silent Destroyer"—"The Sky Maniac," wherein we meet the menace of a scientific genius, and the way in which he is overcome is not predictable in advance.

In both the October *Science* and *Air Wonder*, a full-page advertisement announced *Science Wonder Quarterly*. The large black-and-white reproduction of the cover was most impressive. It showed the rocket-ship *Geryon* nearing the moon and several of the astronauts in space-suits floating outside the ship, connected to it by wires. The ad urges us to look out for the *gold* cover. And that is exactly what we saw on the Fall 1929 issue when it appeared. The entire cover had a gold overlay which, to my eyes, vitiated its effectiveness. (The original, which Sam Moskowitz showed me, didn't have a black background but one of deep green. Black would have been best, but the original is still more striking than the gold-dust as published.) The cover illustrates *The Shot into Infinity* by Otto Willi Gail translated from the German by Francis Currier. In Germany it had been a hardcover book and was very popular. From the time that it appeared in English, the rocket became the vehicle of choice by authors for interplanetary stories except for mavericks like Edward E. Smith and John W. Campbell, Jr., who invented inter-atomic or molecular drives. The *Geryon* is a step rocket, with fold-in wings at the nose for use in an atmosphere. It leaves Earth as a long, segmented rocket; each segment (which contains fuel) is ejected to drift in space once the fuel is used so that what is portrayed on the cover is only the nose cone. The story tells not of the first but of the second rocket flight into space on a rescue mission for the first. August Korf and his associates do find the original rocket but too late to save Natalka, the original astronaut.

Three other stories round out the issue. "The Artificial Man" by Clare Winger Harris tells of a man who has had his various limbs and organs gradually replaced so that he can almost entirely dissemble himself. "The Hidden World," a novella by Edmond Hamilton, is a wild story of invasion by intelligent flesh-creatures from within Earth. They have created a vast technology and are set to conquer the surface because their inner world is about to break up. The story combines the author's usual elements of vivid imagination and description of an alien culture and the all-too-familiar epic plot: two of the four heroes are killed; the other two capture an enemy sphere and single-handed prevent the entire fleet of spheres from coming up the single tunnel leading to the surface until the inner world breaks up and all the flesh creatures are destroyed. Exciting?—yes, indeed. Credible?—I had to pretend very hard even the first time I read it. Finally, "The Gravitational Deflector" by Harry D. Parker tells of a gravity-destroying device attached to an automobile. It works: indeed, as soon as it is turned on the car immediately shoots off from Earth's surface as a result of centrifugal force and neither the vehicle nor the inventor are seen again.

The October *Amazing Stories* has a quiet but effective cover by Wesso illustrating "The Steam God" by Walter Kateley. The story tells of a valley in the far north that is warmed by geysers to the point where it is sub-tropical. It's inhabited by humans who have attained the average height of ten feet and have a fascinating half technological, half superstition-dominated society. The protagonist saves himself by making use of the latter element. Wesso's cover and interior illustrations prove that his first appearance was not a fluke. The rest of the artwork ranges from passable to dismal. A cartoonist named Bob Deam was chosen to illustrate A. Hyatt Verrill's powerful novelette "Death from the Skies" (dealing with a bombardment of meteorites from Mars) and the new serial, *The Secret Kingdom* by Allen S. and Otis A. Kline. The latter story would have gone better in *Argosy* and may have been a reject from there. W. Alexander tells, in "One Leg Too Many," of a physician who has found a way of regrowing lost limbs in humans as crustaceans do.

Paul's cover for the November *Science Wonder Stories* was the first to portray the kind of spacecraft that would later be called a flying saucer. Most of the cover is occupied by a huge disc with a golden surface and edges and apparatus in red. From the apparatus we see four tentacle-like arms that are encasing the Woolworth building, and two rod-like projections emit green rays. At the bottom right we see part of Earth and above it, in the distance, another similar spacecraft clutches the Eiffel Tower. The background is blue, sprinkled with white dots for stars, though not in any recognizable pattern. In a large orange circle with white outlines is the announcement "$300.00 for the best short, SHORT story written around this picture. . . ." Readers were urged to study the picture carefully, for the story should account for every element depicted in the cover. Hugo Gernsback presented his own example of an SF short-short story in "The Killing Flash," written for the occasion. Though interesting, it ends with a letter purportedly from the editor, explaining that it is being rejected due to both scientific and plot defects.

A new author, who would become one of the favorites of the period, made his debut in this issue, Raymond Z. Gallun. The story, "The Space Dwellers," tells of a race of long-lived humanoids who have adapted themselves to live in space, even though they use spaceships for their explorations. Pleasant, but Gallun would improve as he continued. Ed Earl Repp's "The Stellar Missile" tells of an apparent meteorite which is actually a space-ship, filled with what appear to be the mummified remains of an alien, humanoid race.

The final installment of *The Human Termites* is the wildest of all. Our protagonists are not only battling the Central Intelligence of the termites and its fearsome mutations, but have also discovered that the various human races also have central intelligences. They make contact with that which controls the white race. It resents their awareness of it and immediately sets everyone against our heroes. The termite invasion, however, is defeated by means that are perfectly sound entomologically. The giant warriors are fed cattle infused with an intensified strain of the bubonic plague. They die a few seconds after eating the poisoned meat and, because termites eat their own dead, all are wiped out in short order. (The menace of the "human" central intelligence is allowed to drop.) In the letters department, Dr. Keller was leaned on heavily by a reader who proclaimed that the good doctor had interesting ideas, but that his stories were "rotten" and that *The Human Termites* was the worst of the lot.

The "obligatory" red background went a long way to spoil Paul's cover for "Cities in the Air" by Edmond Hamilton, which began in the November *Air Wonder Stories*. As explained inside, "Here we see the future city of New York suspended high in the air, kept aloft by cosmic rays and made mobile by the mysterious propeller tubes. The city can rise above storms and, if necessary, above clouds to escape rains and snow. In the center we see the electrostatic tower which gathers energy for the city's operation." On page 404 of the issue Gernsback reprinted a page from the February 1922 issue of *Science and Invention*. Headlined "10,000 Years Hence—A Prediction," we see somewhat similar cities. All the wonder in Hamilton's story lies in the cities themselves; the entire population of Earth lives in them, while the surface of the planet has long been deserted. We are then treated to a typical Hamilton plot: it's war between the cities of the East and West, with New York the capital of the Western cities. I must confess that I was somewhat disappointed with how little science and how much slam-bang-action there was when I first read the story in 1930.

Among the short stories in the issue were "When Space Ripped Open" by Ralph W. Wilkins, dealing with an irruption of giant insects from another dimension, and Raymond Z. Gallun's future-war story, "The Crystal Ray." The "ray" is the invention which enables the Good Guys to win the war.

Wesso's cover for the November 1929 *Amazing Stories* is one of his magic ones. It shows a beautiful city in a vast cavern, the roof of which we see at the top; at the bottom there is something that might be a tube, broken. There are no signs of life in the city. The cover illustrates "The Undersea Tube" by L. Taylor Hansen, and the story is not about the underearth city at all. That particular section of the tube connects the USA with France; there is a break-down and it is at that point that the city is seen.

A new artist, Leo Morey, illustrated Harl Vincent's "Microcosmic Bucca-neers," which is about a trip to a microcosmic universe, and followed the usual pattern of discovering two separate intelligent races, one of which is the Good Guys, and the other the Bad Guys. Our protagonists rescue the Good Guys. Wesso's double-spread laboratory illustration for "The Brain Accelerator," by Dr. Daniel Dressler, is more promising than the story. The brain accelerator elevates the intelligence of the subject—in this case a dog—but leads to a fatal fire that wipes out the experimenter and all traces of his work before anything can really be done with it.

"Cold Light" by William Lemkin, Ph.D. is something else: a light-hearted (but not farcical) tale of a scientist who perfects a cold-light method of illumination—something still beyond present-day technology—and the grad-ual acceptance of the discovery. All aspects of it couldn't be covered in the compass of a short story, but the reader's intelligence is not insulted by a cop-out at the end.

Wesso is with us again on the cover of the Fall *Amazing Stories Quar-terly*, illustrating the climactic scene in "The Other Side of the Moon" by Edmond Hamilton. Our hero has battled his way to the single crucial control of the turtle creatures' super-scientific civilization on the far side of the moon and we see chaos setting in immediately. Years later, in a short article titled (I think) "Self Plagiarism?" H. C. Koenig proved, by setting up two separate col-umns of parallels, that this story was a carbon copy of "The Hidden World." The only differences were Hamilton's well-thought-out descriptions of the two alien civilizations.

The feature novel is one of A. Hyatt Verrill's finest scientific fantasies about ancient South American civilizations still in existence in hidden sur-roundings. *The Bridge of Light* has lost nothing in the way of fantastic enter-tainment (without ludicrous action or plot devices) that it had in 1929. There is also a short story by Dr. Keller, "Euthanasia Limited," featuring Taine of San Francisco, which is par for the Taine series. The only point of interest about "When the Earth Grew Cold" by Paul H. Lovering was that some read-ers wondered if Lovering might be a pseudonym for H. P. Lovecraft. The sug-gestion was absurd; two pages would have been enough to have convinced anyone familiar with Lovecraft's work that he couldn't possibly have written it.

The cover for the December *Science Wonder Stories* was unusual in that the background is deep green—a color rarely seen on pulp magazines at that time. The scene depicted is quiet but impressive. Two figures, clad completely in something resembling brown mesh, with some kind of small tanks strapped to their backs, are seated on camp stools in the middle of the air with apparently no means of support. There is a suggestion that the chairs are on an invisible floor and we see what looks like a doctor's black bag beside one. Both figures are looking at a rather primitive city on a small mountain. The scene comes from "The Time Oscillator" by Henry F. Kirkham. The travelers first visit the past as unseen viewers, then manage to participate directly. There is a short piece of boxed copy halfway through the tale wherein the edi-tor raises the question of time-traveling and invites letters from readers discussing the pros and cons of its possibility, especially the issue of participation in past events. Many readers responded. (In fact, the argument continued for the rest of the Gernsback years. He published more time-travel stories in his magazines than in all the others combined, and many of them brought forth new arguments.)

The new serial is *The Conquerors* by Dr. Keller, one of his most effective short novels. It deals with a race of supermen (highly evolved humans) that have been inhabiting Earth, concealed from ordinary mortals, for centuries. The Conquerors are dwarf-like in size with large heads and have developed a technology, including robots, that requires little physical effort on their part to do anything. They have decided to explore the planet Venus and need a certain area of the upper world for their spacefield. The chosen area covers five of our Southern States. The Conquerors require that the entire area be evacuated and when the United States refuses proceed to make the area uninhabitable by controlling the weather. It becomes unbearably humid as well as hot; everything mildews and decays. That is simply the opening situation. The story becomes more complicated as it develops, but is neither action-centered nor over-plotted.

The cover for the December *Air Wonder Stories* shows a great rocket-driven airliner plunging through a waterspout, illustrating a scene in "Flight of the Eastern Star" by Ed Earl Repp. The liner is breaking up the waterspout to save a ship which would otherwise be engulfed by it.

Paul's illustration for the second part of Hamilton's *Cities in the Air* shows the cities of the Western Alliance in a tight ring around the Eastern cities and the battle is on. The cities bombard each other seeking to destroy the central towers which control them. We see several cities on both sides plunging in flames to the ground. In the 1950s, when I read James Blish's "Okie" stories, also dealing with flying cities, I assumed that he had been at least partly inspired by Hamilton's story and the illustrations. It turned out, however, that not only had he never read the story, but had never seen the issues either.

The December *Amazing Stories* has one of Wesso's most attractive and fantastic covers. Explorers from Earth are looking at a large pool on a far world wherein we see a massive, black many-tentacled monster which is about to engulf one of the jellyfish-like creatures in the pool. It illustrates "A Baby on Neptune" by Clare Winger Harris and Miles J. Breuer, M.D., a story of relativity in relation to time. The Earthmen have been in touch with a scientist on Neptune. On his invitation they go there for a visit but cannot find their host. They see what we see on the cover but there is no motion; it looks as though everything in the pool has been frozen solid. When they return to Earth contact with the scientist is resumed and the creature suddenly breaks off with a cry for help: a monster is about the engulf his child. The time differential is so great that they can make a return trip to Neptune and arrive in time to rescue the Neptunian "baby." The situation is similar to that in Ray Cummings's "Explorers into Infinity," where the rescuers arrive in time to save a girl months after they saw her in imminent danger. Harris and Breuer offer a more polished treatment of the incident.

"Vampires of the Desert" by A. Hyatt Verrill tells of a malignant form of plant life that sends forth free-floating blood-eating flowers. It's an effective science fiction horror tale. "The Time Deflector" by Edward Rementer is a satiric look at the future where, among other things, people rent space on their foreheads for advertising.

DECEMBER 1929

December 1929 was to prove a month full of surprises for the science fiction fan, though initially it dawned as expected with the January 1930 issue of *Science Wonder Stories*—the first I actually owned. Paul's cover has a natural-looking blue background for a summer night scene. We see a large pond at the bottom, a line of houses on the far side, and a line of hills beyond. On the bank of the pond at lower right, five men with rifles are firing at a weird object in the air that fills the picture. It seems to be mechanical yet somehow alive. There's a huge spinning white globe, the reflection of which can be seen in the water. A structure at the top, looking something like a column, ends in a box from which project four discs at the end of cable-like tentacles. The entire upper part is surrounded by a glow and the column is also spinning, but not the box. The story illustrated is "The Vapor Intelligence" by Jack Barnette and the thing we see has come to Earth via a monstrous meteorite. The thing succumbs to rifle fire and breaks up, sinking into the pond, so we do not learn too much about it except that it was potentially dangerous, since it had fed on some cattle and people in the area.

This issue marked the beginning of my regular science-fiction magazine reading. I was a very methodical reader, starting with the contents page's announcement of what was coming next month, through the stories, articles and departments in order. I loved the suspense of waiting for the next installment of a serial, but never turned to it first. After a few years, though, I would turn to the letters department as soon as I had looked through the entire issue; even then, I still read the rest of the contents in order.

"The Red Dimension" by Ed Earl Repp tells of a man who constructs helmets that allow you to look into another dimension inhabited by intelligent aliens. The aliens, aware of being spied upon, use their unknown weapons to destroy the helmet and kill its inventor. Years later, when I finally had a chance to read Francis Flagg's "The Blue Dimension" in the June 1928 *Amazing*, I realized that Repp's story was only a slight variation on Flagg's, and not as good.

The issue's lead novelette is "The Fitzgerald Contraction" by Dr. Miles J. Breuer. It tells of an expedition by a long-past Lunarian civilization wherein their interstellar vehicle approaches the speed of light. They had planned a generations-long tour of the universe and instruments were designed to give a signal when they returned to our own solar system. The signal is triggered prematurely and they find themselves back on a dead world and so they turn their attention to Earth. What had seemed only a few days to them had been over two hundred thousand years of objective time.

In the concluding installment of *The Conquerors*, expert psychologist Sir Harry Brunton convinces the super-intellectual dwarfs that he is sympathetic to their views. They accept him as one of themselves and he solves a vital problem affecting their race—one beyond their own abilities. He is thus permitted to accompany them on the Venusian expedition and he persuades them to postpone their planned destruction of most of humanity, which they call the "Middle Men," until after their return.

In "The Reader Speaks" there's an attack on "The Time Oscillator" by reader William S. Sykora who calls himself "militantly anti time travel." He would prove to be militant about other matters a few years later. The prize letters in the Fundamental Error Contest showed that many readers had spotted the flaw in Ray Myers's "Into the Subconscious." Since visions of the past came from the subject's racial memories there could not be any episode showing his death in a former life. The winner was Frank O. Everett of Quinton, New Jersey. The third prize winner was Jack Williamson.

December 5 brought a real surprise to scientifictionists: the initial issue of *Astounding Stories of Super Science*. It was the first science fiction magazine that was not founded by Hugo Gernsback, and also the first SF *pulp*—not just in format, but in its entire approach to science fiction.

I'm indebted to Sam Moskowitz for sending me a transcript of the editorial, which merits reprinting in full:

Introducing Astounding Stories

What are "astounding" stories?

Well, if you lived in Europe in 1490, and someone told you the Earth was round and moved around the sun—that would have been an "astounding" story.

Or, if you lived in 1840, and were told that some day men a thousand miles apart would be able to talk to each other through a little wire—or without any wire at all—that would have been another.

Or if, in 1900, they predicted ocean-crossing airplanes and submarines, world-girdling Zeppelins, sixty-storey buildings, radio, metal that can be made to resist gravity and float in the air—these would have been other "astounding" stories.

Today, more astounding things are going to happen. Your children—or their children—are going to take a trip to the moon. They will be able to render themselves invisible—a problem that has already been partly solved. They will be able to disintegrate their bodies in New York and reintegrate them in China—in a matter of seconds.

Astounding? Indeed, yes.

Impossible? Well—television would have been impossible, almost unthinkable, ten years ago.

Now you will see the kind of magazine that it is our pleasure to offer you beginning with this, the first number of Astounding Stories.

It is a magazine whose stories will anticipate the super-science achievements of tomorrow—whose stories will not only be strictly accurate in their science but will be vividly, dramatically and thrillingly told.

Already we have secured stories by some of the finest writers of fantasy in the world—men such as Ray Cummings, Murray

Leinster, Captain S. P. Meek, Harl Vincent, R. F. Starzl and Victor Rousseau.

So—order your next month's copy of Astounding Stories in advance.

—The Editor

"The Editor" was Harry Bates, a young man with a scientific education and an inventor in his spare time. He was editor of several magazines in the considerable pulp chain issued by William M. Clayton. On the front cover of all those magazines you saw a little blue banner proclaiming that this was "A Clayton Magazine." On the contents pages the Clayton "standard" on a magazine guaranteed:

> That the stories therein are clean, interesting, vivid; by leading writers of the day and purchased under conditions approved by the Authors' League of America;
> That such magazines are manufactured in Union Shops by American workmen;
> That each newsealer and agent is insured a fair profit;
> That an intelligent censorship guards their advertising pages.

The first paragraph of these standards was one reason why so many "name" writers sent manuscripts to *Astounding Stories*. All contributors were paid on acceptance at rates running to two-cents a word (higher for some of the biggest names). Neither Gernsback nor Sloane could compete on that score.

I do not own that first issue though I've borrowed and read it at least twice. The cover by H. W. Wessolowski (we now learned Wesso's full name) was gaudy indeed. It showed an arctic scene, a wrecked airplane, and an aviator in the costume of the day. He's attacking a giant beetle which is standing upright. Behind him is a frightened blonde dressed in animal skins. It illustrates the first part of Victor Rousseau's serial, *The Beetle Horde*, which, if one accepts giant insects as plausible, was a good thriller. Better was "Tanks," one of Murray Leinster's future-war stories, concentrating on science. "Phantoms of Reality" by Ray Cummings was somewhat similar to his novel *Into the Fourth Dimension*. "The Cave of Horror" by Captain S. P. Meek, introduced Dr. Bird and Inspector Carnes, whose adventures would appear in all three of the monthly SF magazines. There were also some weird stories, though concentrating on the weird-scientific rather than the supernatural. Overall the magazine contained some enjoyable stories, though the editorial claim that all stories were "strictly accurate in their science" was, at best, greatly exaggerated. Bates would reveal many years later that he had to rewrite a number of stories in the early issues to correct ludicrous blunders in science, or just to get some touch of science in at all!

December 10 brought the January 1930 *Air Wonder Stories*. It contained the first part of *The Flying Legion* by George Allan England, reprinted from *All-Story Weekly* in 1919. It remains a good adventure fantasy of its kind, somewhat like H. Rider Haggard's work, though containing some fanciful scientific speculation about vibrations.

The super-airship from "The Thunderer" by A. H. Johnson was shown on the cover hovering above a small lake. Two cables from the ship reach down into the water which is being decomposed by electrolysis. The "thunderer's" bid for supreme power is his threat to wipe out the Great Lakes and other fresh water lakes around the world.

Neil R. Jones made his debut in this issue with "The Death's Head Meteor," a tale of the far future, wherein an astronaut encounters a dangerous meteorite. This story marked the first use of the word "astronaut." From this issue on, *Air Wonder* ran at least one interplanetary story each month. I felt then that they didn't belong in a magazine supposedly devoted to speculations about the future of aviation but other readers were much in favor.

Also on December 10 came the January 1930 *Amazing Stories*. It had a memorable cover by Wesso illustrating John W. Campbell's debut, "When the Atoms Failed." It shows the Martian fleet landing on Earth and humanoid Martians are emerging. They're little men with big ears. The story is a super-scientific thriller, larded with long scientific explanations. The Martians are defeated and peace and amity follows the war.

Beyond the Green Prism by A. Hyatt Verrill was the new two-part serial. Dr. Sloane wrote in the blurb that this sequel will answer the questions left open at the end of *Into the Green Prism*. Well, *some* were answered, and the story retained its slow-moving charm, but we still didn't know at the end how any creatures can live when every trace of metal has been removed from their bodies, since no metal could be translated through the prism to the microscopic world.

We visit a microcosmic world again in "Fourth Dimensional Space Penetrator" by Julian Kendig via the inventor's vehicle. This time, however, there are no Good Guys vs. Bad Guys, and it's still something more than a tour of a different world, but with understandable people. Dr. Breuer has a story of giantism in "The Hungry Guinea Pig," and Dr. Keller offers another of his ironic man-vs-liberated woman tales in "Air Lines." It anticipated several, though not all, of the attitudes that would arise thirty to fifty years later. With this issue *Amazing* seems to have solved the problem of having adequate illustrators. Wesso and Morey handle most of the interior artwork, and handle it well.

A few days later we saw the second issue of *Science Wonder Quarterly*. This time the cover had a silver overlay, which reduced the effectiveness of the scene, though not as badly as the gold overlay on the first issue. A red rocket ship rests on the moon's surface with craters and mountains in the near distance. Earth is in the lunar sky to the left; to the right is a green sphere from which emanates a green ray. It's clearly a heat ray because the rocket is melting where the ray touches it. The story illustrated is *The Moon Conquerors* by R. H. Romans, a book-length novel translated from the French. It deals with a young woman's passion to explore the moon having observed it for some time through a super-telescope her father perfected. During that period of observation she discovered that there is a human civilization beneath the moon's surface and she falls in love with one of the men she sees. Of course she becomes one of the first expedition to the moon. It's a romantic story, well done, and the Lunarian history is interesting.

Short stories in the issue include "The Osmotic Theorem" by Captain S. P. Meek, dealing with an attempt to bore farther into the Earth's interior than ever before, to test a new hypothesis, and "Into the 28th Century" by Lilith Lorraine, where the time traveler encounters a utopia. I found it absorbing at the time, but I hadn't read many "utopia" stories by 1930. Now it seems rather dull and entirely improbable.

The three winners in the first "What I Have Done to Spread Science Fiction" contest were Walter Dennis, whose method was correspondence; Victor Szanton of the University of Alabama, whose method was to hammer at people—even buying them copies of the magazines; and Julius Unger, whose method was by personal contacts. Unger later became known as a dealer and small publisher in SF books and magazines. He told me that he was still in High School when that issue announcing his win appeared. Without hesitation he played hooky the next day, going directly to the Gernsback offices and collecting his prize from Gernsback in person. That issue's "The Reader Speaks" contained a highly enthusiastic letter from a young reader who long retained his youthful enthusiasm: Forrest J Ackerman.

1929's surprises were not yet finished. In each of the three Gernsback titles that came out in December was a full page advertisement announcing *Scientific Detective Monthly*. It would go on sale on the 15th of each month. Strictly speaking it was not a science fiction magazine—it was concerned with fiction about science in the fight against crime. But because so many people, then and now, think of it as a Gernsback SF title, I shall consider it here. Every issue had at least one story that was science fiction and many SF authors appeared in the magazine, but most stories were straight detective stories utilizing scientific devices.

The first issue's cover, by Jno Ruger, has a red background and showed a man being questioned while sitting in a chair rigged to include some kind of scientific apparatus that enables his emotional responses to be read on a meter. It illustrates "The Fast Watch" by Edwin Balmer and William MacHarg, another of the Luther Trant stories, some of which had been reprinted earlier in *Amazing Stories*. All but the final issue contained a Luther Trant story.

Arthur B. Reeve, creator of Craig Kennedy, was credited as Editorial Commissioner on the cover, and a Craig Kennedy story appeared in every issue. Except for "The Mystery of the Bulawayo Diamond," which he wrote especially for the first issue, all the others were reprinted from his 1912 collection *The Silent Bullet*. The first issue also reprinted S. S. Van Dine's *The Bishop Murder Case* as a three-part serial. For those who had not read it either in book form or in its first serialization in the *American Magazine*, its appearance here for a total of seventy-five cents, plus other stories, was a true bargain. But there is nothing science-fictional about it.

The one story in the issue that *was* science fiction was "The Perfect Counterfeit," a Dr. Bird adventure by S. P. Meek. The counterfeit bills are indeed perfect, except that they all have the same serial number. They had been reproduced by a matter-duplication machine—which marked its first appearance in the SF magazines.

At the beginning of 1929 there had been just two science fiction magazines and we had expected to see sixteen issues. By December 31 there were six, totalling thirty-two issues, exclusive of *Scientific Detective Monthly*. The year had also seen three trends gather pace: the increased use of new stories over reprints, Gernsback's presentation of foreign SF novels in translation, and the appearance of action-based SF without any pretence of educating the readers.

My nominations for the best novels appearing in 1929 are *The Bridge of Light* by Verrill, *The Reign of the Ray* by Lester and Pratt, the translation of *The Shot into Infinity* by Gail, and the reprint of *The Ark of the Covenant* by MacClure. Among the shorter works I'd choose "The Last Man" by West, "The Face of Isis" by Wates, "Futility" and "The Murgatroyd Experiment" by Meek, and "Men with Wings" by Leslie F. Stone.

JANUARY-APRIL 1930

In respect to the number of different titles, the first science fiction boom reached its high-water mark in December 1929, and the tide remained there for the first half of 1930 before starting to recede. There were just too many titles, and with readers starting to feel the after effects of the great stock market crash of October 1929, the ready cash was not there to sustain them all. At the time, though, no one knew just how widespread the Depression would be or how long it would last. The magazines continued to present the bold face of the future.

In describing the fiction from here on, it is more appropriate to consider the Gernsback magazines as a single unit and compare them in total against their competition.

The February and March issues of *Science Wonder Stories* featured a two-part serial, *A Rescue from Jupiter* by Gawain Edwards, a tale of the far future. Paul's illustration for part one told the story. We see a futuristic city, but only the tops of the tallest buildings—the rest is buried in sand. Atop the highest is the figure of a man, with his hand uplifted, passing a scroll to a winged man in the air. He is one of a group of human explorers from a moon of Jupiter. The scroll tells the story of how Earth became an uninhabited desert. In the conclusion, in the March issue, we learn that it was the over-use of a new means of power—a motor that splits water into its constituent parts through a catalyst—that made Earth a desert.

Francis Flagg's "The Land of the Bipos" deals with a trip to another dimension where the ruling form of life are giant birds, whilst humans serve as food. "The World of a Hundred Men" by Walter Kateley tells of the discovery of a giant meteor, which proves to be the remains of a small planetoid that had been inhabited. Records are found which, when translated, tell of the tragic history of the little world. There was a symposium on "Can Man Free Himself from Gravity?" which was also the subject of the editorial, wherein seven learned scientists, including Robert H. Goddard and Donald H. Menzel, gave their views. And there was a new competition with a prize of $100 to the reader who could submit the best slogan for *Science Wonder Stories*. Given as samples, and thus eliminated, were "The Magazine of Science Fiction" and "Science Taught Through Fiction."

The cover for the February *Air Wonder Stories* was another contest presentation with a total of $300 being offered for the best short stories written around it. The scene is non-terrestrial. A strange spaceship hovers in the blue skies of a small planet, with two moons in the distance. From two domes on the surface we see a swarm of small humanoids in space-suits from the arms of which project yellow rays. They seem to be attacking the spaceship. It was clearly an interplanetary cover and of the three complete tales in the issue, two were space stories. Only "The Vanishing Fleet" by Hendrik Dahl Juve, which completed the trilogy started with "The Silent Destroyer," and the conclusion of *The Flying Legion* are limited to this planet and to future developments in aircraft. An article, "Berlin to New York in One Hour" by Max Valier, considered the possibility of giant rocket-powered airplanes.

The February *Scientific Detective Monthly* marked the debut of Lloyd Arthur Eshbach with "The Man with the Silver Disc," which was solid science fiction. The "silver disc" is implanted in the subject's skull and receives thoughts transmitted by a controller. The purpose is to reform hardened criminals, as they will not be able to distinguish between their own thoughts and those transmitted to them. Unfortunately the first subject breaks loose after the operation, kills the inventor, and escapes. The inventor's son uses the apparatus to exact a chilling revenge on the criminal. It's a thrilling story but something of a cop-out, since we do not learn how the equipment might have worked as originally intended. Dr. David H. Keller is present with the first of a new series about Taine of San Francisco. These are all early Taine stories, and the series is launched with "A Scientific Widowhood," which was enjoyable, but not science fiction.

The lead and cover story for the March *Science Wonder* is "Before the Asteroids" by Harl Vincent. Purporting to be a translation of records found on Mars, it tells of a war between Arin (Mars) and another planet, called Voris. The war ends with an Arinian scientist developing a concentrated energy beam that destroys the other planet. Paul's cover shows the event on the screen in the Arinian's laboratory.

The four prize-winning cover-contest stories came next. The first prize went to Charles R. Tanner for "The Color of Space," and the editor reveals that Tanner was the only entrant who not only noticed but made use of Paul's intentional error in making the background of space deep blue instead of black. "Relics of Earth" by John Pierce came second. It tells of an expedition to an abandoned Earth to pick up still-standing monuments. Frank J. Brueckel, Jr. and Harold A. Lower came third and fourth with forgettable entries.

"The Insatiable Entity" by Harold S. Sykes tells of the creation of artificial life. The story is memorable only in that, unlike others to follow, the creature does not develop into a universal menace.

The cover of the March *Air Wonder Stories* announces "The Return of the Air Master" by Edward E. Chappelow, and Paul's painting shows the Master's super-aircraft, surrounded by an artificial cloud, hovering over a building. With one of his super-rays the Master has bored a hole through the roof and a tractor ray is bringing out machinery from within. The cover is spoiled by its pinkish-red background. For although I've seen that exact color in the sky at sunset or dawn many times, the scene illustrated takes place shortly after midnight!

Most memorable in the March issue is "The Space Visitors" by Edmond Hamilton, which had a Fortean flavor. Apparently from nowhere, a giant scoop descends to Earth's surface, taking enormous samples from it, including parts of small cities. We never encounter the invaders or the mother ship—they are repelled by super-science—but for once there are no brave heroes who go forth, get captured, and overcome the menace, as was Hamilton's previous trademark.

The cover of the March *Scientific Detective Monthly* illustrates "The Robot Terror" by Melbourne Huff, which is clearly science fiction. It depicts a robot menacing two humans. The robot 'is used for jewel robberies and is initially successful. The story, though, does not live up to its potential. Jack Barnette's "The Power Ray" has scientifictional aspects—the ray is intended to be a super-means of transmitting power—but the murder element turns out to have been an accident.

I still remember the unpleasant shock that I received when I took the April issue out of its wrapper. There was now a streamer at the top of the cover reading "MYSTERY-ADVENTURE-ROMANCE," and the world "SCIENCE" in the magazine's title was no longer in red but yellow on the white box background. That made it almost invisible. (I was afraid that the apparent downgrading of the word "science" would endanger parental permission to continue reading the Gernsback science-fiction magazines.) The cover itself, though, was one of Paul's best, showing sunrise over water and a pleasing-looking building on the land, while in the sky we see a figure clad in some kind of mesh and wearing an apparatus with big platform-like devices into which the user's shoes are inserted. The figure is apparently walking on air. It illustrates "An Adventure into Time" by Francis Flagg; it describes a future feminist society wherein males are a minority and subservient to the females. Not pleasant reading, but it stands as a cautionary tale about reverse discrimination—something unknown in the 1930s.

Isaac R. Nathanson made his debut in this issue with "The Falling Planetoid." The planetoid is on a collision course with Earth and the story describes the panic and the super-scientific measures to dispel the menace. I read in a fan magazine years later, that Mr. Nathanson was an ordained minister. At any rate, there was a distinct moralistic tone in his stories.

The April and May issues features *The Evening Star*, a two-part serial by Dr. David H. Keller and a sequel to *The Conquerors*. We read of the expedition to Venus and how and why the super-dwarves destroy themselves without realising what they're doing. Keller's astronomy aroused much criticism but the story itself remains readable.

The April issue contains another sequel, "The Return to Subterranea" by Harl Vincent. Subterranea is the enclave of the scientists who constituted "The Menace from Below." One of them survived the catastrophe at the end of that story and has now repented. He makes contact with his former opponents asking them to help him undo his work. That meant restoring to their human bodies the brains of those upper-worlders that had been transferred to the bodies of giant anthropoids. It was a good sequel to the original thriller.

In box copy in the issue, Hugo Gernsback announced "Science Fiction Week," to run from March 31 to April 7, 1930. Readers were urged to take all possible measures that week to promote science fiction. *Science Wonder Stories* had printed a supply of little posters (six by four inches) which readers could have for the asking. I must confess that I did not ask for any, and learned later that "Science Fiction Week" made no splash at all.

The April *Air Wonder Stories* has another red-background but here, unlike the March issue, it does not spoil the scene. It depicts a huge flying buzz-saw cutting a fighter plane in two and illustrates "The Flying Buzz-saw" by H. McKay. The idea is fascinating, but the story is marred by its "only-a-dream" ending. There are two interplanetary stories in this issue. "Through the Meteors" by Lowell Howard Morrow deals with a theme that was prevalent in Gernsback's magazines at the time: that Earth is surrounded by a meteor-curtain, and any attempt at space-flight would have to take the risk of destruction of the ship by meteors. Here, an attempted invasion of Earth by humanoid aliens is hampered by this; many of the egg-shaped ships are destroyed or damaged. Our protagonist perfects a meteor-repellant device for his spaceship and is thus able to go through the curtain safely. "Evans of the Earth Guard" by Edmond Hamilton is a future "air pirate" tale dealing with craft that operate beyond the stratosphere.

Paul's cover of the April *Scientific Detective Monthly*, illustrating the first part of Tom Curry's serial, *Rays of Death*, suggests science fiction. It shows a figure, completely enmeshed in a protective lead apparatus, about to secrete a vial of radium salts under a mattress, which will certainly not improve the health of whoever sleeps there. But the story is in no way science fiction. Likewise Edmond Hamilton's "The Invisible Master," which describes what seems to be a way of achieving invisibility. It's a fine detective story but the invisibility turns out to have been an ingenious hoax. Neither was there anything scientifictional about "A Denizen of the Underworld" by Walter Kateley, though it showed he could write a good mystery story.

The Spring 1930 *Science Wonder Quarterly*, on sale on March 15, has another fantastic space scene on the cover, showing *Astropol*, a futuristic space station. Its full effect was again spoiled by a gold overlay. *Astropol* is described in the feature novel, *The Stone from the Moon* by Otto Willi Gail, translated from the German. The sequel to *The Shot into Infinity*, it was a wild and adventurous tale, though by no means deficient in sound scientific speculation. Among the short stories the most memorable is "Via the Hewitt Ray" by M. F. Rupert, whose picture reveals that she is female. The protagonist is a young woman whose father has invented a device—the Hewitt Ray—that allows him to penetrate another dimension, which is inhabited by intelligent humans. He disappears and his daughter follows and rescues him. In the process we encounter a completely feminist society. Here, unlike the case in the matriarchy described in Flagg's "Adventure into Time," the males are entirely inferior and exist only as breeders or sterile concubines for the women's pleasure. The story opened the way to considerable reader-comment on sexual issues in the monthly magazine.

Another female writer, Clare Winger Harris, appeared with "The Ape Cycle," dealing with artificially evolved apes, programmed to be servants. As one might anticipate from the stories at this time, there is a revolt of the super-apes against their masters.

In the May *Science Wonder Stories* is an announcement that, starting next month, the word "science" would be dropped from the title completely. Gernsback had decided that its presence was more misinterpreted than understood, with many potential readers assuming that the magazine was a technical or popular science periodical, not a magazine of fiction. He assured readers that the contents of the re-named *Wonder Stories* would remain the same.

The cover story for the May issue is "The City of the Living Dead" by Laurence Manning and Fletcher Pratt—their first collaboration, and the first appearance of Manning in print. The "living dead" are people who have been wired to dream machines and spend the rest of their lives in vicarious experiences supplied by the machines. The operation cannot be reversed. The story remains powerful today, even though the theme has been explored in greater detail by later writers. So does "The Infinite Brain," John Scott Campbell's debut. It deals with an artificial brain that constructs a huge body for itself and proceeds to treat humans as inconveniences to be eliminated except for those few for whom it has some uses.

The May *Air Wonder Stories* had a new slogan on the cover, "Startling Stories of Future Aviation"—though it was not the winner of the slogan contest announced in an earlier issue. A new serial was launched, *The Bat-Men of Mars* by Wood Jackson—a straight interplanetary adventure of the *Argosy* variety. A further interplanetary story was "Women with Wings" by Leslie F. Stone, a sequel to "Men with Wings." It takes place two hundred years after the first story. Now all human males on Earth are winged. There's a crisis, because a large percentage of women (who are unwinged) die in childbirth. A winged race of females exists on Venus, however, and after various initial hostilities, the two races settle down amicably. The most unusual story in the issue, though, is "The Arctic Rescue" by Walter Kateley, which tells how surviving members of an expedition stranded in the Arctic save themselves by constructing a balloon from the carcass of an enormous whale.

Instead of an editorial in this issue there is an announcement that with the next issue *Air Wonder Stories* will be combined with *Science Wonder Stories* under the single title of *Wonder Stories*. The reader is promised that the air-wonder type of story will continue to appear.

"The Electrical Man" by Neil R. Jones, illustrated by Ruger on the cover of the May *Scientific Detective Monthly*, could pass as borderline science fiction in that it describes a means of physical protection that hasn't yet been invented. We have a suit filled with wires, powered by remote control. When the current is turned on, the user is virtually invulnerable. Bullets will not penetrate the electrical field and anyone who touches the wearer will receive a knockout shock. The cover shows what happens when an unsavory denizen of Chinatown tries to stab him: the knife is electrified and its wielder is sent to join his ancestors. The story remains basically a thriller. Edmond Hamilton is present again in the issue with a fine scientific mystery, "The Murder in the Clinic." The clinic involved was devoted to plastic surgery and was used to change the faces of criminals. That leads to the murder and the solution may have evaded many other readers than I, even though the author gave some leading hints.

As in the other Gernsback monthlies, this issue contained an announcement that with the next issue the magazine's title would change to *Amazing Detective Tales*. What with the merger of *Air* and *Science Wonder* into *Wonder Stories*, it was a sign that retrenchments were afoot and that the tide of the SF magazines was on the ebb.

Before moving on to the next period, though, let's consider the competition that Gernsback's magazines had during the first part of 1930.

Amazing Stories had one immediate advantage. Except for a generous letters department, a page of book reviews and the editorial, the entire content was fiction, with no articles, news of the month or question-and-answer features. You received more for your twenty-five cents than in either *Science Wonder* or *Air Wonder*. That alone may have made an important difference to SF lovers who were less concerned with the educational value of a magazine over its entertainment value.

The magazine's covers were not so bold as Paul's. All were the work of Leo Morey, and ran from interesting (that for March showed a submarine bursting through the bottom of the ocean into the sky of a land beneath) to excellent (May showed spacesuited figures repairing a polygon-shaped ship with Saturn and its rings in the background). Morey had a fine color sense and an appreciation of scenery. His spaceships were generally pleasing to look at if less inventive than Paul's. His futuristic machinery was not very imaginative and he could not compete with Paul at all. But his weakest point was in faces; Paul could draw an attractive face when he wasn't rushed, but Morey's were seldom more than acceptable and often very poor. And while Paul could draw an attractive-looking woman now and then, Morey's females were practically never attractive-looking.

In December 1929, I got permission from my father to use one dollar of my Christmas money to subscribe to *Science Wonder Stories*. I must confess, I lost little time exploiting that permission; I started buying *Air Wonder Stories* at once. I also found another "free-sample copy" coupon for *Amazing Stories* in one of my father's radio magazines. I cut it out and sent it in. I'd hoped, thus, to get the January issue, forgetting that the magazines were all dated ahead and that the February issue was now about to go on sale. So it was, that the issue of *Amazing Stories* I received bore Morey's first cover, illustrating "Explorers of Callisto" by Harl Vincent. The cover shows a space scene, featuring several space-suited figures on the moon, who are being menaced by a ray that ends in a flame, like a super flame-thrower. It was, and remains, a good cover, but was disappointing to me, because it couldn't match the excellence of the Wesso covers I had seen on the newsstands. The title of Vincent's story is somewhat misleading; Callisto is now being explored. Our protagonists are exploring our moon, and find the hostile Callistans there.

That issue also offered a satire, "The Ice Man" by William Withers Douglas. Here we have an ancient Roman, frozen in a scientific experiment now restored to life. He believes that he is still living in the days of Caesar and writes a report on the wonders of our world. There is a Dr. Bird story, "The Radio Robbery" by S. P. Meek, which deals with transmuting gold into copper. But what is most frustrating about the issue is that there are four "reader-cheaters." In Dr. Keller's "A 20th Century Homunculus," the great experiment comes to nothing, on its own terms. "The Man from Space" by L. Taylor Hansen, and "Lanterns of God" by Robert A. Wait are both "only-a-dream" stories; and, after a fascinating build-up, the inventor in "Vitamin Z" by Dr. William Lemkin is about to take a sample of his new vitamin when he has a heart attack, drops the tube, and dies. Needless to say, that was all the Vitamin Z there was, and all the notes were in the inventor's head.

The March issue was more impressive. It featured a new serial, *The Green Girl* by Jack Williamson, with the wonderful attention-grabbing opening sentence, "At high noon, on May 4, 1999, the sun went out!" We learn, however, from Sam Weldon, superscientist, that nothing has gone wrong with the sun itself. Some force, originating from below the sea, is interfering with the sun's light. Weldon has perfected a vehicle that can fly, run on land, sail on the sea, or act as a submarine. (One thinks of *The Master of the World* by Jules Verne, wherein the would-be master, Robur, uses just such a vehicle.) Weldon, and his friend, Melvin Dane, the narrator, descend through a point in the Pacific Ocean and, after going through a luminous red gas at its bottom, which apparently keeps the waters in place, find themselves in the skies of an inner world. It's all another of the author's Merrittesque fantasies, filled with adventure and wonder. The "green girl" is a native of the inner world, whose skin-tone is a faint green. The story remains a most enjoyable fantastic adventure, with an alien menace fully up to Merritt standards.

Two other good stories in that issue were "The Ship That Turned Aside" by G. Peyton Wertenbaker—it turned through the fourth dimension—and "The Gostak and the Doshes" by Dr. Miles J. Breuer, where a dimensional trip is used as a satire on our own civilization, concentrating on the use of meaningless slogans to arouse warlike reactions.

The April issue also had an offering of good short stories. In "The Conquest of the Earth" by Isaac R. Nathanson we have conch-like super-scientific creatures from Andromeda landing on Earth. They are neither hostile nor repulsive—Morey's cover depicts one of them very well. They have merely come to Earth to make a new home for themselves and wouldn't think of harming humans so long as humans leave them alone. (Of course, humans don't—for very sound reasons!) "Remote Control" by Walter Kateley tells of experiments in communication with animals and insects to use them to accomplish tasks which are easy for them but hard for humans. "The Metal Horde" by John W. Campbell, Jr. brings back his characters from "When the Atoms Failed" to deal with an invasion of super-intelligent machines. The sequel has both the strengths and weaknesses of the first story.

A new three-part serial opened in the May *Amazing*, *The Universe Wreckers* by Edmond Hamilton. That was the first Hamilton story I read and, despite its flaws, it has a certain excitement even today. Our sun has started to rotate faster and if that is sustained it will split and destroy all the inner planets. Earth's scientists discover that the phenomenon is caused by a force ray, apparently from Neptune. They duplicate the ray and use it to propel the polygon-shaped ship depicted on the cover, taking our four heroes to Neptune. It's an all-male-cast epic and would have been easier to read had the editor deleted ninety-nine percent of the "great"s that infest the story. Everything is "great!" and one yearns for another adjective—or no adjective at all. Readers of *Amazing* who were not too proud to purchase the May issue of *Weird Tales* would have found a companion piece to *The Universe Wreckers* in Hamilton's "The Sun People." One of his Interstellar Patrol series, it was exciting but lacked the scope of the *Amazing* serial.

Also in the May *Amazing* were "Madness of the Dust" by R. F. Starzl, about a man performing an emergency operation by following an unseen surgeon's instructions over the radio, and "The Ivy War" by David H. Keller, which tells what happens when ordinary ivy becomes carnivorous. By a coincidence, Edmond Hamilton's "The Plant Revolt" in the April *Weird Tales* also dealt with deadly plants attacking people. Keller's story remains the better.

The Winter 1930 *Amazing Stories Quarterly*, which went on sale on January 20, brought the name of John Taine into the science fiction magazines. *White Lily*, the feature novel, could have benefited from some cutting, but Taine was a master of suspense however slowly his stories moved. This tale of a crystalline life-form brought into being through a chemist's experimental errors, and which rapidly becomes a world menace, is still powerful today. Also in the issue was "The Dirigibles of Death" by A. Hyatt Verrill, about an invasion of England by dirigibles containing bloodthirsty anthropoid creatures, artificially produced. It is on my short list of the really nasty but compelling stories of the period.

The Spring *Amazing Stories Quarterly*, released on April 20, was the first issue I bought. It had an excellent cover by Morey showing the giant creatures described in Aladra Septama's "Dragons of Space." They look like mushrooms with tentacles and they can survive both in space and in a planet's atmosphere. They're also carnivorous. It is the final story in the trilogy that began with "The Beast Men of Ceres," and to my mind the best of the three. Morey's cover shows one of the creatures hovering over the sea at night and capturing a small airplane.

Airplanes were certainly under threat in this issue. One of Morey's internal illustrations to David H. Keller's "The Flying Threat" shows a private airplane being captured by a giant dragon-fly. Although another giant insect story, it is one of the better ones. The menace is restricted to only two huge eggs and it does not become a global catastrophe.

The contents of the concurrent issues of *Astounding* were less memorable. Best in the February issue were "The Thief of Time," a Dr. Bird adventure by S. P. Meek, which tells how a time machine was used to frame an innocent man, and "Creatures of the Light" by Sophie Wenzel Ellis, a clever novelette dealing with an attempt to create supermen. The issue also saw the debut of Charles Willard Diffin with "Spawn of the Stars," illustrated by Wesso on the cover, which depicts a protoplasmic alien emerging from a spaceship as two aviators look on.

The March cover was also by Wesso. Illustrating the first part of Ray Cummings's serial *Brigands of the Moon*, it shows the spaceship *Planetara* en route between Earth and the Moon. Despite the blue background and the sight of Saturn large in the background, with all its rings, it remains a magical painting. Also in the issue is another Dr. Bird story by S. P. Meek, "Cold Light." J. Fleming Gould's illustration showing human bodies shattered like glass is exceptionally good; neither Paul nor Wesso could have portrayed the scene more effectively. Sewell Peaslee Wright makes his SF debut with "From the Ocean's Depths," dealing with a fragment of humanity that returned to the sea and cannot now live on land.

In the April issue only Meek's Dr. Bird story, "The Ray of Madness," and the Cummings serial, are worthy of consideration. The May issue was better. It included Wright's sequel to his March story, "Into the Ocean Depths." Our characters aid the sea people in overcoming the menace they face. A new serial began, *Murder Madness*, by Murray Leinster. It's an excellent tale of

South American intrigue but has no SF content of note. A would-be dictator has discovered a drug that turns its victim into a homicidal maniac if the antidote is not taken within a few weeks. Only the mastermind can provide the antidote, but that contains more of the original drug, so the victim is ensnared forever. That's all the "SF" you'll find in the novel. There's a delightful off-trail story by Lillith Lorraine, "The Jovian Jest," which includes a strange celestial visitor, a message for humanity, and an ironic trick. Two humans are needed for a contact with the visitor in order to convey the message. After it's delivered the visitor releases them and departs, but has inadvertently (?) exchanged their personalities.

Outside of the science fiction pulps there was a growth of SF in other magazines. *Weird Tales*, always a reliable source for weird-scientific stories, contained a number of good items, suggesting a deliberate acknowledgement of the growing acceptance of SF. An item of special interest was "The Bird People" by Otis Adelbert Kline in the January 1930 issue. I didn't get to read this story until late in the 1930s. When I did I was struck by some descriptions that seemed very familiar. Then it came to me that I was reading a description of Paul's cover-contest painting on the December 1926 *Amazing Stories*. If any other reader noticed that at the time there was no mention of it in the letter department. Edmond Hamilton was well represented in *Weird Tales* with "The Life-Masters" (January), "The Comet Drivers" (February), "The Plant Revolt" (April), and "The Sun People" (May)—two being from his Interstellar Patrol series, the other two doom and mad-scientist tales.

Argosy also had several SF stories, including "The Man Who Was Two Men" by Ray Cummings and "The Storm That Had to be Stopped" by Murray Leinster, but the main regeneration of SF in *Argosy* would appear later in 1930.

There was no doubt that science fiction had at last become recognized as a viable genre for promotion and was now being utilized by the other pulp publishers, as would become increasingly apparent during the next year or two. That posed a problem to Gernsback in a market he had hitherto monopolized, for as the economic pressure of the Depression began to bite, he found it necessary to consolidate his stable of magazines into a tighter group. That development we shall now follow through the next few months.

38.

THE TIDE RECEDES, MAY-DECEMBER 1930

MAY-SEPTEMBER 1930

May brought the second volume of the now-retitled *Wonder Stories*. On the cover was the clover-leaf logo for *Air Wonder Stories*, very small, printed in black on a blue background. It states: "*Air Wonder Stories* combined with ..." leading to the tilted title box containing the new *Wonder Stories* logo. The cover scene itself, showing a new-type of submarine menaced by a giant octopus is not one of Paul's best.

The serial from *Air Wonder Stories*, *The Bat-Men of Mars*, continued in this issue and a new serial, *A Subterranean Adventure* by George Paul Bauer, began. The title tells it all: explorers with a depth-boring machine break into a world within the planet and find a civilization of dwarfed humans. Raymond A. Palmer made his debut with "The Time-Ray of Jandra," where the time traveler is an observer only. It was a good story but lacked imagination. Much more imaginative was Walter Kateley's "The Incredible Monstrosity," a misleading title. The "monstrosity" is a giant sphere designed to travel at tremendous speeds along a continent-spanning runway. At the climax an invading army marches down the runway and the sphere easily annihilates them. "Waves of Death" by Wesley Arnold—the token "air wonder" story—presented an interesting speculation that seemed plausible at the time: an aircraft would fall to pieces when its velocity broke the sound barrier.

Only one story in the newly retitled June *Amazing Detective Tales* might be called science fiction. In "Burning Water" by Dr. David H. Keller, Taine of San Francisco encounters a scientist who claims to have perfected atomic power and intends to conquer all nations involved in the centuries-long humiliation of his native Poland. Taine prevails in the end with the conspirators killed in a grand explosion, though there's deliberate doubt as to the cause of the explosion. Did Taine cause the atomic device to go off, or was the explosion caused by an accident in an anarchists' headquarters? S. P. Meek's Dr. Bird adventure, "The Gland Murders," comes close to science fiction: a poison extracted from the pineal glands of stranglers turns its victims into homicidal maniacs.

The cover of the July *Wonder Stories* was the first to carry a white background since Gernsback's experiment with a symbolic cover on the September 1928 *Amazing*. It depicts a futuristic airplane, without visible propellers, in the sky of an alien world; the pilot is shaking his fist at the weird life forms below. It illustrates "The Flight of the Mercury" by Charles R. Tanner, about a flight to Mars in a sealed aircraft by means of an ether propeller (though this latter device is not shown in the cover or interior illustrations). There is no violent action in the story and the explorer is unable to communicate with the inhabitants of Mars, nor they with him. Neither harms the other but the Martians keep him isolated from his ship after he lands and he finds that one night on Mars is enough. With daylight the Martians become torpid and he makes his escape.

This issue saw the first appearance of P. Schuyler Miller, with the first prize-winning entry in the February 1930 *Air Wonder Stories* cover contest. That wasn't Miller's first sale. "Through the Vibrations" had been sold earlier to *Amazing*, but had to wait many more months before publication. Another new author in this issue was Victor A. Endersby with "After 5000 Years, " wherein a present-day accident is linked with a similar occurrence in ancient Egypt. Endersby would have only a few stories published later, but all were thought-provoking and well written. Finally, "The Time Valve" by Dr. Miles J. Breuer was a sequel to "The Fitzgerald Contraction." The Lunarians travel into the far future and become king-gods to our savage descendants.

June 15 saw the Summer 1930 *Wonder Stories Quarterly*, retitled without a previous announcement. It bore the last of the gold or silver overlay covers, and this time the silver background did not harm the effectiveness of the painting. It illustrates "The Monsters of Neptune" by Hendrik Dahl Juve, a semi-humorous action story that was below the author's previous standards. The cover showed a cyclopean scaled monster bearing a massive rock with which it was battering a spaceship into junk.

Two of the stories in this issue were translations. "The War of the Planets" by R. H. Romans, from the French, was billed as a sequel to *The Moon Conquerors*, but it wasn't. It's an account of long-past Lunar history that the characters in the first story read and translated. I enjoyed the story back in 1930, but today it's rather tedious reading. "Electropolis," from the German, marked Otfried von Hanstein's first American appearance. Several of his novels would be translated for Gernsback's magazines. This one was a sequel to *The Hidden Colony* that wouldn't be serialized for another four years. It tells of a utopian, super-scientific colony in Australia and its triumph over attempts to destroy it.

"The Tower of Evil" brought the debut of Nathan Schachner and Arthur Leo Zagat, bringing super-science and devil-worship into an Eastern menace story. "The Eternal Man Revives" was D. D. Sharp's sequel to "The Eternal Man," underlining the point made in the first story somewhat more heavily. The two stories run well together.

The July *Amazing Detective Tales* contained two SF stories: "The Mind Machine" by Eugene George Key and "The Grey Shadow" by W. F. Hammond. The first takes place in the future and tells of a machine which can control thoughts. The second deals with invisibility and through it a scientist's vengeance on those who railroaded his father into prison. Also in the issue was Amelia Reynolds Long with "The Mystery of the Phantom Shot," an ingenious mystery but not SF. Miss Long is betrayed by an illustration which not only shows how the crime was done but who did it.

The cover of the August *Wonder Stories* issue returned to the standard red background with a scene showing two men in the clutches of a robot—it all struck me as much too cartoony and pulpish at the time. The cover illustrates "The Radium Master" by Jim Vanny, a less than memorable story about a power-crazed dictator. Much better was "The Martian Revenge" by Hendrik Dahl Juve, about an expedition nearly destroyed by truly alien but hitherto friendly Martians when a member of the expedition violates one of their taboos. Ed Earl Repp's "The Annihilator Comes" is an example of an unnecessary sequel. There was no need to bring in the characters and the airship from "Beyond Gravity" in this action-packed tale of a strange non-human civilization in a torrid region of the unexplored Arctic.

The issue's "The Reader Speaks" contained an interesting but positive attack on *Wonder Stories* from someone signing himself "Booth Cody." This was later revealed to be the well-known fan of the time, Allen Glasser, who would write excoriating letters to the magazines under his alias, and then join in the denunciation of Cody under his real name.

In the August *Amazing Detective Tales*, Morton Brotman's "The Phantom Killer" is SF. The killer is a robot—in fact, two robots, giving the impression of one man being in two places at once.

Mark Marchioni made his debut in the September *Wonder Stories*, illustrating the new three-part serial, *The Warlord of Venus* by Frank J. Bridge. Marchioni could draw human figures well and also had a good imagination, although his machines were more bizarre than scientific-looking. (Paul's always looked as though they could work.) As time went on and Marchioni had to work faster his human figures became more stylized and sometimes sloppy, but he did have an individual style. I re-read *The Warlord of Venus* recently, and it remains a good story even though set on a prehistoric Earth-like Venus. There's good characterization, an interesting plot, and action that is soundly motivated.

In "20,000 A.D." by Nathan Schachner and Arthur Leo Zagat, we find an interesting new development in portraying a world of the future with its robot-men and "evolved" slave humans, all ruled over by a giant brain in an enclosed sphere. An attempted revolt against the brain—the Jed—fails and the narrator barely escapes to tell the tale. There would be many other "great brain" stories to follow, but this remains one of the best.

Another new theme tells of Chicago completely enclosed within a vibrational wall that is impenetrable in either direction. Local gangsters have taken over the city and kidnapped the inventor so that he cannot disrupt the wall. "The King of the Black Bowl" by R. F. Starzl remains interesting, but there would be better "impenetrable wall of force" stories later. "A Rescue from Space" by Lowell Howard Morrow was third in the *Air Wonder Stories* contest, and on recently re-reading it I wondered if it was really better than some of the losers!

The September *Amazing Detective Tales* featured another Taine of San Francisco story by Dr. Keller, "Menacing Claws," only this was a straight tale of detection. And although "The Temple of Dust" by Eugene George Key featured the detective team from "The Mind Machine," and thus is set in the future, it contained nothing science-fictional or futuristic, and would have worked better in a contemporary 1930s setting. "The Black Cabinet" by Henry Leverage at least suggests science fiction. There is a machine which can produce television-like scenes from the near future, but it is taken over by a criminal who uses the device as a hoax, so we never learn the true reality or benefits of the machine. A similar reader-cheater was the two-part serial, *The Carewe Murder Mystery* by Ed Earl Repp. The blurb for part one read: "Did death come from the Nth dimension to strike down the eminent Dr. Carewe?" Well, the victim was working on what he called "Nth dimensional goggles," but they were tampered with and the dimensional element proves irrelevant in the end.

The cover of the October *Wonder Stories* is breathtakingly lurid and for once a flat yellow background seemed exactly right. Portrayed is a man caught in the tendrils of a giant flower and being drawn into its maw. It illustrates "Marooned in Andromeda" by Clark Ashton Smith, his first appearance in an SF magazine. He had just begun to appear in *Weird Tales* with the type of story and exotic vocabulary for which he became famous. This story is long on imagination but has a standard action plot and is written rather simply for Smith. "The Lizard Men of Buh-Lo" by Francis Flagg is a tale of another dimension and possibly the first story in which one of the characters talks about reading a story by Flagg. I suppose Flagg meant it more for verisimilitude than self-puffery but I found that it distracted from the story. J. Harvey Haggard makes his debut with the fourth-prize-winning *Air Wonder* cover-contest story, "Faster Than Light." It's a reader-cheater with an only-a-dream ending. Haggard would become a regular, and his stories were generally liked, though seldom memorable.

Perhaps the most startling content was an announcement instead of an editorial, which I found distressing at the time: with the next issue *Wonder Stories* would adopt the pulp format. There had been something grand about the large-sized issues that seemed to put them on a higher level than the lowly pulps, and I feared that a change in format would so cheapen the magazine in appearance as to deprive it of what little respectability it had—and possibly result in my being forbidden to continue buying it.

The Fall 1930 *Wonder Stories Quarterly* has a lunar scene on the cover with a blue background, for which no justification appears in the story. (I am still puzzled as to why Hugo Gernsback, of all people, sometimes approved covers showing blue skies on the moon.) It illustrates "Between Earth and Moon" from the German of Otfrid von Hanstein. The story either lost something in translation or was insensitively edited, because the opening chapters are choppy, and contain abrupt transitions that make it hard to follow. However the lunar episodes remain good reading as does the plight of the astronaut cut off from his spaceship and floating helplessly in space. "An Atomic Adventure" by William Lemkin, Ph.D. discusses the submicroscopic world through treating atoms as if they were sentient human beings. The story was the first of its kind and though overlong is well handled. "The Island of Terror" by Ransome Sutton deals with natural but horrifying freaks on a remote tropical island. There is no super-scientist behind it, but a natural result of Mendelian laws.

There were three stories in the October *Amazing Detective Tales* that could be considered science fiction. "Death in a Drop," a Professor Macklin case by Ralph W. Wilkins, tells of a poison so virulent that a single drop on the victim's skin brings immediate and painful death. "The Flower of Evil" by C. R. Sumner deals with a super-botanist who produces a plant with an odor that has powerful hypnotic qualities. "Murder in the Fourth Dimension," by Clark Ashton Smith, offers a science-fictional means of disposing of the body of one's intended victim—you abduct the subject to the fourth dimension, murder him or her, and leave the corpse there. (But you'd better be sure that you can return yourself; Smith's protagonist finds that he can't.) "Shadows of the Night" by Neil R. Jones was a prequel to "The Electrical Man," and dealt with Miller Rand's earlier efforts to aid the police, but it was straight crime action with no mystery or SF element, and a disappointment after the first story. As in *Wonder Stories* the editorial page contained a notice that with the next issue *Amazing Detective Tales* would convert to pulp size.

The Gernsback magazines contained a continual breath of wonder even though the stories were variable in quality. That same variability, but not always supported by the sense of wonder, permeated the rival magazines. The June 1930 *Amazing Stories* featured "The Non-Gravitational Vortex" by A. Hyatt Verrill, telling of an apparently natural but unknown teleporting phenomenon. The story is overlong and leaves much unexplained at the end. More memorable in the issue was John W. Campbell, Jr.'s novelette, "Piracy Preferred," which introduces the humane, super-scientific air pirate, Wade, who is finally captured by Arcot and Morey. It turns out that Wade is psychologically unbalanced, but he hasn't killed anyone, and, moreover, the gas that he used to the victims to sleep also cures cancer. He is pardoned and rehabilitated and thereafter joins Arcot and Morey in their adventures.

The July *Amazing* offers a charming satire by A. Hyatt Verrill, "A Visit to Suari," about a Martian who visits Earth in the guise of a human and is constantly puzzled by human beings' strange and illogical behaviour. "Paradox +" is Charles Cloukey's sequel to "Paradox." It carries on directly from the first story though does not resolve everything. The cover story is "The Message from Space" by David M. Speaker, telling about a struggle between two alien races somewhere in time and space. One of the two races is humanoid, though cyclopean. Morey's cover scene shows several of these single-eyed creatures fleeing from the aliens. One reader noted that the menacing creatures look like giant stuffed olives. He was right; they do!

An interesting off-trail story in the issue was "Flamingo" by Clarence Edward Heller, describing a stage drama as produced in 1950 with all the performers being robots, and with many special effects.

The Summer 1930 *Amazing Stories Quarterly* produced the most literate novel of the year: "Paradise and Iron" by Dr. Miles J. Breuer. It's about a machine-dependent colony on a remote island where the machines take over. For all its outdatedness today it remains a fine cautionary tale. Also in the issue were A. Hyatt Verrill's fascinating science fantasy, "Monsters of the Ray," dealing with ethnological secrets; John W. Campbell's space epic, "The Voice of the Void," and Aladra Septama's now very dated, slow-moving, "The Princess of Arelli"—Arelli is the Lunarian's own name for our moon. (It's another supposedly present-day story of people living on the surface of the moon, which has an adequate atmosphere and livable weather.)

The cover of the August *Amazing Stories* broke tradition by giving the title of a story. It announced the eagerly awaited sequel to *The Skylark of Space*, *Skylark III* by E. E. Smith, which was highly acclaimed, but not so universally as the first novel, simply because in the space of just two years Smith's super-science was becoming a regular feature of the SF magazines. The cover was Wesso's last for *Amazing*, and was a wonderful farewell. It shows the nose of the mighty Fenachrome battleship being sliced off by the zone of force that surrounds the *Skylark II*. There were two other stories in that issue memorable for other reasons: "World Atavism" by Edmond Hamilton wherein everyone starts to regress to a primitive state, and civilization crumbles, and "The Last War" by S. P. Meek, a sequel to "The Red Peril," and featuring what may be the first appearance of a super-weapon that eventually destroys both sides. More and more stories like those would appear, emphasizing the bleaker aspects of the future.

The September *Amazing* contained little of note. "The Passing Star" by Isaac R. Nathanson was a straightforward catastrophe tale, and Morey's cover, showing the Chrysler building being torn up by its roots and heading skyward, is quite effective. "The Troglodytes" by Fred M. Barclay, was about a strange civilization within the Earth, which has no interest in conquering the surface. "The Inferiority Complex" by Miles J. Breuer, is a psychological story rather than SF. And Harl Vincent's "Free Energy" tells of a scientist's revenge on the industrialist who ruined his father by the perpetration of a scientific hoax.

October's *Amazing* offered "The Prince of Liars," a clever tale of relativity and time-scales in various parts of the universe by L. Taylor Hansen. Otis A. Kline's "The Man from the Moon" utilized the same background as his earlier *Argosy* serial, *Maza of the Moon*, though the writing was somewhat less juvenile. The story is about a war between Lunarites and Martians that finally makes both worlds uninhabitable. The best story in the issue was "The Man Who Saw the Future," an off-trail piece by Edmond Hamilton. Scientists of our own time are experimenting with time travel and succeed in bringing a young Frenchman from the Middle ages to the present world. When they return him and he tries to tell of the wonders of the future he is accused of witchcraft, convicted, and burned at the stake.

The June 1930 *Astounding Stories of Super-Science* was the first issue of that magazine that I bought—with many feelings of guilt about purchasing a lowly pulp. I was finally persuaded by J. Fleming Gould's illustration for "Out of the Dreadful Depths" by C. D. Willard, which shows a sea monster bearing tentacles each of which has a head, eyes and mouth. The Willard story rewarded my attention, but the rest of the issue confirmed my worst fears. Wesso's cover illustrating "The Moon Master" by Charles Willard Diffin depicts a Lunar scene but with two Earthmen without spacesuits, atop a cliff rolling boulders down upon dinosaur-like creatures in the valley. We also see some greenery on which the saurians are nibbling. Evidently the moon has an atmosphere and isn't too cold. I had hoped to be able to read the final installment of Ray Cummings's *Brigands of the Moon*, but I was frustrated to find, when I took the issue home, that there was no synopsis of the first three parts. This was a practice that Bates started and which Tremaine continued, and Sloane took it up in *Amazing Stories* in 1934. I considered it unfair then, and still do.

I decided to try one more issue (July) where I was able to read the first installment of a new serial, *Earth, the Marauder* by Arthur J. Burks. Earth itself becomes a spaceship on a tour on conquest. The story is so wild and lacking anything like a scientific explanation for the fantastic events, that I was again turned off. Apart from the serial, the July issue did contain more memorable stories. "The Forgotten Planet" by Sewell Peaslee Wright introduced his popular character John Hanson of the Special Patrol. The inhabitants have developed an all-engulfing fungus, such as was described in Eshbach's "A Voice from the Ether"; Hanson manages to turn it upon the planet itself. "The Power and the Glory" by Charles Willard Diffin is the first to tell of an important discovery (atomic power), which the inventor is persuaded to destroy on the grounds that it would create more human misery than good. S. P. Meek's "Beyond the Heaviside Layer" suggests that it is an impassable barrier and an attempt to drive through it involves the ship with the formidable, non-intelligent creatures that live there. "From an Amber Block" by Tom Curry deals with an unpleasant survivor from the distant past that has been trapped in amber and still survives.

At that time my father happened to look through those two issues and was appalled. I promised not to buy any more and, truth to tell, felt no great loss. It was over a year before I reneged and began to procure back issues. I had gone back to the November 1930 issue, and sent in an order for five more back issues, when I learned that they were now charging fifty cents for 1930 issues earlier than November. So I settled for the September and October issues and did not get to the earlier ones (aside from June and July, which I still had) for many years.

There was little that is memorable in the August, September or October issues. The August cover illustrates "The Planet of Dread" by R. F. Starzl, a good adventure marred by a *deus-ex-machina* ending. The two stranded protagonists manage to struggle back to the surface of the little world Indra just at the moment that a spaceship from Earth is cruising past.

The September cover shows two men with what looks like large garden hoses from which flame, rather than water, is issuing. They're attacking huge, tentacled fish-like creatures that are wearing glass helmets filled with water. It illustrated Paul Ernst's first appearance in an SF magazine with "Marooned Under the Sea," an exciting adventure story, with reasonable science if you accept the premise. September also saw the start of a new, three-part serial by Ray Cummings: *Jetta of the Lowlands*. Earth's oceans have greatly receded and the lowlands are those areas formerly covered. On that background we have a story of international intrigue and romance that could have been set in an entirely different background without too many changes. Better was "A Problem in Communication" by Dr. Miles J. Breuer, telling of a secret, super-scientific society that plans to take over the United States through a "religion of science." It may be the first SF tale about brain-washing to appear in the magazines. The whole tone is closer to Gernsbackian SF than anything we'd seen before in *Astounding*. Predictably, many readers found it dull. The October issue had an interesting story in "An Extra Man" by Jackson Gee, about a machine that can duplicate people. Gee handled the theme in a humorous manner to which many readers objected.

Such was evidence that, as 1930 progressed, the rift was widening between the original desire for the promotion of science through SF and the commerciality of basic adventure SF. And with the conversion of *Wonder Stories* to a pulp format I was fearing the worst.

OCTOBER-DECEMBER 1930

The new *Wonder Stories* did indeed look cheap. The paper was rougher and edges untrimmed, and it no longer stood out amongst the other magazines. The "Science News of the Month" column had also gone and though that allowed more space for the stories it also signalled that Gernsback was dropping his original concepts and endeavouring to compete directly with *As-*

tounding. Moreover neither of Paul's covers on the November or December issues could compete with Morey's concurrent ones on *Amazing Stories*.

The November cover story was "The Time Annihilator" by Edgar A. Manley and Walter Thode, and dealt with a chase through time and the menace of a future Oriental mastermind's artificial creatures intended to replace humans. Although the characters manage to materialize physically in various futures they find they cannot change anything. John Scott Campbell's "The Invulnerable Scourge" is not about giant insects, but a super-insect of natural size developed by an entomologist. It has been genetically designed to be almost unkillable as well as omniverous, so when a pair escape and start breeding into millions, there is real trouble.

The Outpost on the Moon, a three-part serial by Joslyn Maxwell, started in the December issue. Two members of a privately organized Lunar expedition, after building a spaceship themselves, land on the Moon and are captured by other Earthmen, members of a secret lunar colony. Our heroes join the colony and become part of an exploring team sent to Ganymede where they find an unfriendly culture.

The cover for the January 1931 issue was more striking. It portrays an attractive woman, on her knees, trying to embrace a man in a chair. He wears a sort of helmet, there is an electronic device on his chest, and has a completely blank expression on his face. The story, "The Soulless Entity" by Anthony Pelcher, deals with an executed criminal who is brought back to life but is now no more than an animated robot with no personality. The story avoids a supernatural or horror element and is memorable. In "The Gland Men of the Island," Malcolm Afford deals with an artificial race of monster men, created through gland manipulation. The story is nothing special, but it would subsequently cause an uproar, as we shall see later. Finally D. D. Sharp's "The Satellite of Doom" may be the first story dealing with a man trapped in orbit. Some of the science was questionable but the story was effective.

The Winter 1931 *Wonder Stories Quarterly* was memorable for a number of features. Firstly the cover at last had a reasonable background for a space scene—a deep brown, which was usually as close to black as Gernsback's engravers and printers could achieve. (The printers could not always match the engravers' colors exactly.) We see one of Paul's beautifully ornate golden ships being destroyed by a meteor. It illustrates "The Mark of the Meteor" by Ray Cummings, a tale of survival after disaster.

The feature novel was *The Scarlet Planet*, by Don Mark Lemon which proved to be controversial because of its erotic (for the time) content. One reader labelled it an elaborate sex dream, which summed it up pretty well. It's very tame reading today. The issue also contained "The Man of Bronze" by A. L. Fierst, a title which had been announced for the forthcoming *Amazing Detective Tales*. That issue had never appeared, although a crime magazine, *Amazing Detective Stories*, had materialized from another publisher. Gernsback had, in fact, sold the magazine to Wallace R. Bamber. I did not know that at the time and did not miss the magazine very much. (I did glance through the first of Bamber's issues; it was a cheap-looking, straight crime-story magazine, and bore no resemblance to Gernsback's version.) "The Man of Bronze" was typical of the type of story I did not miss. The "man" is a real man electroplated so that his remains appear as a bronze statue.

"Pithecanthropus Island" by Isaac R. Nathanson takes us to another remote island where survivals from the dim past make things difficult and scary for a group of castaways.

In general there was a drop in the quality of content as well as format of the Gernsback magazines, which was not a good sign. The stories were becoming closer in tone to the pulp standards, although few could be called "pulp-formula" fiction. *Amazing* on the other hand, perhaps fortuitously oblivious of commercial rivalry, maintained a good standard.

The November cover is particularly eye-catching. It shows a huge marine creature that looks like a giant pumpkin with eyes, mouth and tongue, as well as tentacles, scooping up three men running across the beach. The story illustrated is "The Globoid Terror" by R. F. Starzl, another *deus-ex-machina* tale. It isn't about the globoid terror at all, but is a tale of interworld intrigue. The monster suddenly appears on the final page of the story and disposes of the villains who are about to make their escape. Starting in this issue was a three-part serial of a hidden civilisation in South America. *The Drums of Tapajos* by S. P. Meek remains an excellent adventure story with some clever science. "Solarite" is the second of the Arcot-Wade-Morey series by John W. Campbell, Jr. "Missionaries from the Sky" by Stanton A. Coblentz is refreshingly different. A super-scientist contacts a superior Martian civilization. They're rather monstrous in appearance, but in no way harmful. They are, in fact, rather concerned about the sad state of human affairs and offer to send missionaries to Earth to help us. At the end the scientist destroys the communications device; the Martians will not come without a specific invitation, and the inventor decides that we are better off solving our own problems. Finally, "The Cosmic Express" by Jack Williamson, dealt with a future in which people seeking adventure can make short trips to other worlds and live there briefly in dangerous surroundings.

The cover story for the Fall 1930 *Amazing Stories Quarterly* is "The Black Star Passes" by John W. Campbell, Jr., wherein Arcot, Wade and Morey are part of a struggle against invasion. The feature novel was *A Modern Prometheus* by Cyril G. Wates, dealing with a static future utopia wherein all scientific research is forbidden and an underground movement endeavours to reclaim scientific progress. "The Terrors of Arelli" marked Aladra Septama's final appearance. It is a sequel to "The Princess of Arelli," and deals with monstrous survivals from the moon's past.

The cover for the December *Amazing* illustrates "The Second Missile" by Ed Earl Repp and shows a group of aliens hovering over an unconscious man. The story was a sequel to "The Stellar Missile" from the November 1929 *Science Wonder*. The official explanation was that Repp's agent had forgotten where the first story had been published and submitted his manuscript to *Amazing*. Well, maybe, but I still suspect that *Wonder Stories* had seen it and rejected it, as it adds nothing of importance to the original story.

"The Eclipse Special" by Dr. William Lemkin is a more directly scientific tale. It deals with a stratosphere ship so co-ordinated that it can follow a solar eclipse around the world, thus giving astronomers an opportunity to make crucial observations otherwise impossible.

In "Anachronism," Charles Cloukey concludes his Paradox series. The story was illustrated by an artist named Muller, and his drawing turned out to be the most controversial published in an SF magazine of this period. The scene is straightforward—the protagonist, surprising and killing three Martians at their secret headquarters. What aroused the wrath of many readers (and the admiration of some) was the modernistic style.

The January 1931 issue features "The Prince of Space" by Jack Williamson, about a Robin Hood of the future where space cities can be found between the planets. Morey's effective cover shows a Martian scene with an ape-like creature being attacked by a spider-like being. The Prince saves the Earth from an invasion by these creatures. Morey's interior illustration of the space city also remains striking. "Via the Time Accelerator" by Frank J. Bridge depicted a far future Earth and raised one of the many time-travel paradoxes: the protagonist sees himself returning just as he was departing in his airplane/time-traveling device.

The November *Astounding Stories* started a four-part serial, *The Pirate Planet* by Charles Willard Diffin. The plot is routine: nasties from Venus kidnap two Earthmen, one an astronomer, to obtain useful knowledge for their projected mission of conquest. There is also a decent human society, forced underground by the "man-things," as the would-be invaders are called. Diffin's later novels would follow much the same formula, but show increasing imagination. Harl Vincent's "Wanderers of Space" was greatly liked at the time, and I enjoyed it, too, then. Re-reading it proved to be a mistake; but it may be the first tale to have an amoeboid or protoplasmic space-creature large enough to engulf and devour spaceships.

The December issue began the last sequence of Dr. Bird stories by S. P. Meek. From "The Sea Terror" on, all the tales would be about Dr. Bird versus the evil super-scientist Ivan Saranoff. They soon became monotonous—we knew that Saranoff would escape at the end and come back with another super-scientific device just as deadly—but I must admit that I rather liked the individual stories at the time.

Wesso's cover shows a giant ape, with one arm about a man armed with a club, another around a frightened blonde. It illustrates "The Ape-Men of Xlotli" by David R. Sparks, a story that would have been fine in *Argosy*, but try to find any science in it!

The January cover shows how well a red background can be handled when it isn't a poster effect; it also shows how well Wesso could draw human figures when he took his time. The metal "man" in the center of the picture is also well done. The painting illustrates a routine story, "The Gate to Xoran" by Hal K. Wells, which tells of a metal man disguised as a human, who comes to build a gate between Earth and Xoran, for most unfriendly purposes. S. P. Wright continues his John Hanson series with "The Dark Side of Antri." While those tales are no enduring masterpieces, they shine in the general context of the magazine. So does "The Fifth Dimension Catapult" by Murray Leinster. Leinster had his faults, but downgrading his strengths to fit a "policy" was not one of them. He would have written the story the same way had he aimed it at *Amazing, Wonder,* or *Argosy*. There is a feeling of control—the essence of professionalism—about most of his works.

Weird Tales did not have much to offer science fiction fans during these months apart from Edmond Hamilton's Interstellar Patrol story "The Cosmic Cloud" (November) and Donald Wandrei's "Something from Above" (December), which suggests an influence of Charles Fort's books, then a good source for science-directed fantasy. *Argosy*, on the other hand, printed two serials. Pre-eminent was A. Merritt's *The Snake Mother*, the long-awaited sequel to *The Face in the Abyss*, which ran in seven parts starting in the October 25, issue. It was followed by a new Ray Cummings serial, *Tama of the Light Country*. The "Light Country" is Mercury, but the story has a routine Cummings plot; however, both it and a sequel, *Tama, Princess of Mercury*, were liked at the time.

The main trend in 1930 was the formula pulp approach to science fiction in *Astounding Stories of Super Science*. In the *Wonder* group, plots became more important, and the writing was tighter. *Amazing* continued to run material in the old-fashioned way, but more of the stories have a fresh feeling than in earlier years.

My list of the year's best stories is somewhat longer, so I'll break them down by source.

From Gernsback's *Wonder* group, amongst the serials and novels, *A Rescue from Jupiter* by Gawain Edwards, *The War Lord of Venus* by Frank J. Bridge, and *The Stone from the Moon* by Otto Willi Gail. From short stories and novelettes, "An Adventure into Time" by Francis Flagg, "The City of the Living Dead" by Laurence Manning and Fletcher Pratt, "In 20,000 A.D." by Nathan Schachner and Arthur L. Zagat, "The Invulnerable Scourge" by John Scott Campbell, and "Via the Hewitt Ray" by M. F. Rupert.

From the *Amazing* group, amongst serials and novels, *The Green Girl* by Jack Williamson, *Skylark Three* by Edward E. Smith, *The Drums of Tapajos* by S. P. Meek, and *Paradise and Iron* by Miles J. Breuer. From short stories and novelettes, "The Gostak and the Doshes" by Miles J. Breuer, "Piracy Preferred" by John W. Campbell, Jr., "The Prince of Liars" by L. Taylor Hansen, and "Monsters of the Ray" by A. Hyatt Verrill.

From *Astounding* the choice is limited, with *Brigands of the Moon* by Ray Cummings the best novel, and "The Power and the Glory" by Charles Willard Diffin the best short story.

39.

THE SUPER-SCIENCE YEAR, 1931

JANUARY-APRIL 1931

The February *Wonder Stories* features "Dust of Destruction" by P. Schuyler Miller. Something is disintegrating the nitrogen in Earth's atmosphere, and the residue of it falls as a greenish dust that is inimical to all life. It's the result of a massive vacuum tube on the moon, sending forth cathode rays. The age-old Lunarian civilization seeks to prepare Earth for an invasion, changing its atmosphere to suit their needs. Paul's cover shows one of the three men who go to the moon martyring himself by plunging headfirst into the giant tube, shattering it.

Ray Cummings's "The Great Transformation" tells of an attempt to make a young ape into a human being. The results are unhappy, but in the end the creature does show a trace of un-apish, human behavior. Dr. Keller's "The Sleeping War," deals with an attempted conquest of the USA by means of a drug introduced into the water supply by the Russians. It puts the victims into a coma from which they'll never emerge unless injected with the antidote. George Beattie's "The Murders on the Moonship," originally scheduled for the November *Amazing Detective Tales*, is an effective murder mystery with a science-fictional explanation. It would have been truly baffling had not the illustration given everything away. In "A Flight into Time," Robert H. Wilson tells of a much-advanced and peaceful future. There is no action, but the story has an enduring charm. More exciting is "The World Without" by Benson Herbert, who would contribute other memorable stories. It is about a dimensional excursion. The explorers finally discover they have landed in the mouth of a gigantic creature on that other plane.

Paul's cover for March shows a robot-type machine that looks surprisingly like some of the robots that electronics hobbyists are building today. The machine is covered with glowing, needle-pointed spikes, and is attracted to a belt worn by a man who is trying to escape from it. It illustrates "The Green Torture," A. Rowley Hilliard's first story. The spikes on the machine are smeared with poison, and a scratch will be fatal. It can cross the small room in twenty seconds. The victim has to keep out of its way, though he can end the torture at any time by calling out that he is ready to talk. There's a clever, ironic ending.

A new serial, *The Return from Jupiter* by Gawain Edwards, is a sequel to *The Rescue from Jupiter*, and tells of the restoration of Earth through a super-scientific means of restoring water to the arid planet. There is also a war between the winged moon-people (originally Earthmen) and the conquest-mad native Jovians, who are also humanoid. The sequel lacks the impact of the original.

"Back to 20,000 A.D." by Schachner and Zagat is a different matter. Here the unfinished business is achieved in a way that adds to the wonder of the first story. The great brain (the Jed) is overcome in a plausible manner. Also in the issue, R. F. Starzl continues his IFP series in "The Terrors of Aryl," whilst "From Out of the Earth" by Ed Earl Repp is an effective tale of the monstrous survival of a dragon-like creature.

Schachner and Zagat lead off the April issue (on sale March 1) with "The Emperor of the Stars," which had been announced as the first story about an expedition to Pluto. Well, we do find at the opening that the two protagonists are the first exploration team sent to Pluto, but we also find that they're off course, and they never get there. Instead they go into another plane where a superscientist has preceded them and made himself "emperor" of the non-humanoid natives. The story is enjoyable, but Pluto should have been left out altogether.

More to the point is "The Man Who Evolved" by Edmond Hamilton. Paul's cover shows the scientist, who has discovered a means of accelerating his physical evolution via cosmic rays. We see him in his "evolution cabinet," bathed in cosmic rays, where he has become a small man with a large head. The story is more exciting than credible, and ends with the reduction of the subject to primal protoplasmic slime, implying that evolution is cyclical and will return all things to their beginning.

Less well remembered, but a better story, is "The Conquest of Gola" by Leslie F. Stone, dealing with an alien matriarchy and told from the viewpoint of its ruler. The contents-page blurb summarizes the story well: "Into the peaceful life of Gola came the predatory earthmen . . . sneering they looked upon the woman rulers." The Golans prevail.

Featured in the Spring *Wonder Stories Quarterly* (on sale March 15) is *Into Plutonian Depths* by Stanton A. Coblentz. It is the first story wherein the newly discovered planet is reached. It proves to be a small world, with a surface looking like our own polar regions, except for a total absence of life, even though it has a breathable atmosphere. Once we get into the depths, we realize that the author is not much concerned about the planet itself. What matters is his pointed comments upon human foibles in the bizarre Plutonian humanoids and their culture. I rated Coblentz's satire highly at first, but less so after I'd read Voltaire and Jonathan Swift.

Short stories in the *Quarterly* include "The Empire of Glass" by Frank Miloche, telling of a far-future humanity that lives in mighty glass cities. Though still human-looking, they have become dwarfed in size, and are menaced by giant insects. In "The Avenging Ray," A. Rowley Hilliard deals with a biological experiment that gets out of control and produces an especially nasty, weasel-like creature. In "The Inverted World," J. Rogers Ullrich tells of the strange effects that a substance found in a meteorite has upon human vision.

The editorial page announces a new contest. Readers are invited to submit plots for interplanetary stories to be turned over to regular authors to work up. We shall see some of the results in due course.

With the May issue, *Wonder*'s cover slogan is changed to "Adventures of Future Science." It features one of the more pleasing-looking covers for this period, showing a futuristic airliner passing through a huge, disc-shaped purple cloud. On the one side we see the blue skies and green and brown of Earth; on the other a red-skied, barren, rocky land. It illustrates "Through the Purple Cloud" by Jack Williamson, more fantasy than science fiction.

Otfrid von Hanstein's two-part serial, *Utopia Island*, begins here, and is another of that author's plausible projections of super-technology. The island and its population are to be the basis of a new scientific civilization. Of course, the human element intereferes with the utopian ideals, but the story holds up.

John Beynon Harris, who would become world-famous two decades later as John Wyndham, makes his debut with "Worlds to Barter," a new twist on time travel. The evolved inhabitants of Earth, far in the future when the planet has become almost uninhabitable because of a dying sun, invade our present to force its people to exchange worlds.

Elsewhere in the issue were "The War of the Giants," wherein Fletcher Pratt presents speculations on the evolution of tanks into massive land cruisers, and "The Cosmic Gun," by Morrison F. Colladay, which considers a new source of seemingly unlimited power.

Amazing Stories, for this same period, featured some of Morey's best covers. For February's issue he painted a lunar scene, showing spacesuited figures on the surface with their ship above them. The background is blue, but a dark blue! It illustrates "The Man Who Annexed the Moon," Bob Olsen's sequel to "Four-Dimensional Transit." The issue saw the start of George McLeod Winsor's two-part serial, *Television Hill*. It's still super-technical, because the television station described can see everywhere (no need for local apparatus) and report on everything going on in the world. The plot is a cheater, though. The apparatus uncovers a superior, hidden civilization, the members of which destroy television hill. We never know what changes in the world might otherwise have ensued from the invention.

In "The Bees from Borneo," Will H. Gray tells of a virulent new strain of bees. In "The Purple Plague," Russell Hays deals with biological warfare, whilst A. Hyatt Verrill's brief story, "The Exterminator" (which proves to be a leucocyte), is more effective than earlier, longer tales about blood cells.

The Winter *Amazing Stories Quarterly* features "The Birth of a New Republic" by Jack Williamson and Dr. Miles J. Breuer. It's a good story, but, as one reader complained, is a retelling of the break of the American colonies from England and the war that followed. Not only are elements and incidents repeated, with slight changes to allow for Lunar conditions, but many characters' names are too similar to their historical counterparts. We know at once, therefore, that Benedict will become a traitor. (In one instance, the character who is the equivalent of Benjamin Franklin is referred to as "Franklin," and neither authors nor editor caught the error.) "When the Moon Ran Wild" is a grand mixture of speculations by A. Hyatt Verrill, starting with the moon's approach to Earth and our protagonists' escape from the monstrous tides. It moves on to the discovery of a herbivorous dinosaur in the protagonists' South American refuge, and then introduces a horrible parasitic form of life that is a real menace. It's fun to read and it's clear that Verrill had fun writing it.

Morey's March cover illustrates "The Valley of Titans" by Lloyd Arthur Eshbach, and shows a giant clamp coming down from a huge airplane and grappling a smaller one below it. The story is a Merrittesque science-fantasy; Dr. Sloane, who was especially fond of Merritt, was highly pleased with it. Sloane had only accepted the story on December 5, 1930 (as Eshbach reveals in *Over My Shoulder*), so for once, that usually slow-moving editor acted quickly to get it into print. Also in the issue is "The Thing That Walked in the

Rain" by Otis Adelbert Kline—the thing proves to be a giant, artifically-produced, hydra—and Captain S. P. Meek's Dr. Bird and Operator Carnes encounter, "The Earth's Cancer," an adventure preceding the protracted duel with Ivan Saranoff running in *Astounding*.

Morey's cover for the April *Amazing* shows a warship being overwhelmed by a titanic mass of greenish, gelatin-like substance, which is "The Menace from Andromeda," as portrayed by Schachner and Zagat. A three-part serial, *Across the Void* by Leslie F. Stone, starts here, a sequel to *Out of the Void*. The villain of the first story is now the hero—he has truly repented and reformed; from arrogant ambition to rule, he has become a compassionate helper to the alien beings encountered in the sequel, and loses his life as the result. It's a far better story than *Out of the Void*, and stands on its own feet.

There is also the first of three short stories by David H. Keller dealing with the oriental super-surgeon Wing Loo. "The Ambidexter" tells of Wing Loo's vengeance on an American surgeon. It's a chilling tale, but our sympathy goes to the wronged Chinese. In "The Laughing Death" by Stephen G. Hale, an atomic-powered super-borer is used to perpetrate a vendetta, and the story ends with the Earth being split into two equal halves!

The cover to the May *Amazing* uses a red background to good, natural effect. We see humanoid creatures, wearing an apparatus on their backs, rising out of a volcano. It illustrates "The Great Catastrophe of 2974" by Woods Peters, and tells what happens when the volcano-living creatures emerge in an attempt to conquer the world outside. Paul's interior illustration for "Through the Vibrations" by P. Schuyler Miller, is one of his most magical. We see a magnificent city of Atlantis from above; two people, in what look like spacesuits, are drifting down toward it. It transpires that Atlantis did not sink beneath the waves, but was translated into another plane of vibrations, where our explorers unexpectedly encounter it.

Wing Loo reappears in "The Cerebral Library" by David H. Keller, but this time he's just a patsy for Taine of San Francisco. The surgeon was hired to remove the brains of several hundred college students, keep the brains alive, and link them together to form a permanent, living (after a fashion), data base. The same theme would be used in another way, later. Lloyd A. Eshbach's tale, "A Voice from the Ether," tells of a particularly virulent form of fungus which is used in a scheme of vengeance on a distant world (presumably Mars) but which gets out of control and destroys all animal life.

The Spring *Amazing Stories Quarterly* is an all-interplanetary issue, featuring John W. Campbell's first novel, *Islands of Space*. Arcot, Wade, and Morey, who appeared in the three earlier novelettes, are the heroes, and the story is one of interstellar exploration and war. In places the debt to E. E. Smith's Skylark stories is too obvious. As with Edmond Hamilton's epics, there is an all-male cast, and Campbell's protracted explanations may still serve as a cure for insomnia. In "Moon People of Jupiter" by Isaac R. Nathanson, Earthmen encounter a Lilliputian humanoid race when their spaceship accidently crashes through a miniature city when landing upon Ganymede. Paul's illustration is very effective. J. Schlossel makes his final appearance with "Extra-Galactic Invaders." Though it has the cosmic feel of "The Second Swarm," it had now been outdated by E. E. Smith's and John W. Campbell's novels.

With its February issue, *Astounding Stories* dropped the "of Super Science" from its titles. But that did not stop the super science in the stories. Wesso's cover illustrates "The Tentacles from Below" by Anthony Gilmore, and shows a man in a super-diving suit encountering a giant octopus that is also wearing a form of apparatus. That tale of machine-fish suffers from its routine pulp plot, but the author would become much better liked before the year was over.

Phalanxes of Atlans by F. V. W. Mason is a two-part serial, and deals with a lost civilization apparently descended from ancient Hebrew tribes, in an undiscovered, warm valley in the Arctic. Mason was one of the better pulp writers who appeared regularly in the adventure magazines. This story has a distinct *Argosy* feeling, and the author's inventions make up for the predictable plot turns. Dr. Bird, Carnes, and Saranoff continue their battle in "The Black Lamp" by S. P. Meek.

Wesso's March cover has considerable impact, even today. On a golden background, we see what appears to be a giant's head and shoulders. He is reaching out, trying to grasp three doll-sized people. The scene is from "Beyond the Vanishing Point" by Ray Cummings, one of his spinoffs from "The Girl in the Golden Atom."

There's a charming, fantastic quality about Wesso's April cover, showing two Earthmen leaping toward a group of crocodile men in a cone-shaped city on Mars. Unfortunately, "Monsters of Mars" by Edmond Hamilton, is just another variation on his routine tale about gullible terrestrial scientists victimized by cunning super-scientific aliens who want to take over our planet. This issue sees the beginning of Ray Cummings's four-part serial, *The Exile of Time*, one of his last long stories that went beyond self-repetition. We meet a strange man and a time machine that links the New York City of the near future (1935), of the eighteenth century (the Revolutionary War period) and the year 2930.

Commander John Hanson is with us in "The Ghost World" by Sewell Peaslee Wright, during the course of which small atomic bombs are tossed around like hand grenades. No one thought of radiation at that time. (But let's remember that no one thought of radiation effects when the first atomic bombs were dropped on Japan. They came as a surprise to everyone.) In "The Lake of Light," Jack Williamson tells of two explorers in the antarctic, who encounter an enclave of super-evolved crab creatures that have enslaves the humans within their realm.

Wesso's May cover has the most effective bug-eyed monster yet seen on the cover of a science fiction magazine. Bug-eyed monsters were rare in the Gernsback era; they became prevalent during the second science fiction boom in the late thirties. (Actually, "bug-eyed monster" does not mean "monster bug," which is what we see on a few covers during the Gernsback era. It is a monster with "bug-like" or bulging eyes, and rarely insectoid.) The giant arachnid appears in "Dark Moon" by Charles Willard Diffin, his most imaginative story to date. The dark moon is a newcomer from space and has peculiar qualities that affect light. There's light enough when you land there, but the body cannot be seen from outside its atmosphere. The formula plot is redeemed by the author's inventiveness. In "When Caverns Yawned" by Captain S. P. Meek, artificial earthquakes are Saranoff's latest means of trying to destroy the United States.

During the four months we've just covered, two issues of a new science-fiction title appeared: *Miracle Science and Fantasy Stories*, published by Harold Hersey and dated April/May and June/July respectively. Douglas Dold was the editor, whilst the covers and interior artwork were by his brother Elliott. I looked through them at the time, and seeing them again in the fifties confirmed my first reaction—they were the shoddiest-looking SF magazines of the period. I bought the second issue because of the cover, but could not bring myself to read it. Other fans who had read both assured me later that I had not missed anything. I do remember an announcement in the second issue that the third would contain a surprise story—a great science fiction novel. The title and author were not revealed and the third issue never appeared; but the promised story was published in another magazine later, as we shall see when we consider 1932's issues.

The year for *Weird Tales* had opened on an ominous note. The first issue was dated February/March, and editor Farnsworth Wright announced in "The Eyrie" that henceforth the magazine would be bi-monthly. It did return to monthly publication in the summer, but it was a sign that all was not well. There was not much by way of weird-scientific stories in *Weird Tales* during these months apart from the regular appearances of Edmond Hamilton. He contributed "The Horror City" (February/March), involving giant intelligent octopi, and "Ten Million Years Ahead" (April/May), an adventure in futurity. Fans of Edgar Rice Burroughs's stories, though, would have been delighted at Otis Adelbert Kline's new serial, *Tam, Son of the Tiger*, which ran for six episodes from the June/July issue. His Tarzan-style adventure, *Jan of the Jungle*, had just been running in the April and May weekly issues of *Argosy*. The only real piece of science fiction in *Argosy* during these months was Harl Vincent's novelette, "Beyond the Dark Nebula."

MAY-AUGUST 1931

Paul's cover for the June *Wonder Stories*, shows an Earthman holding a Martian at weaponpoint in the communications room of a spaceship. It illustrates "In the Spacesphere" by Charles Cloukey, essentially a story of international intrigue aboard an ocean liner translated into interplanetary intrigue. A new author, Frank K. Kelly, appears with "The Light Bender," dealing with a device that bends light and warps space. The writing is excellent and an astonishing achievement for one sixteen years old at the time. Kelly would become a favorite with the readers.

In "The Man Who Changed the Future" by R. F. Starzl, the protagonist has his consciousness sent forward a century. He can see and hear, but is invisible and intangible to those in the future. Supergangsters are now the rulers of cities. At the end of the story our hero's body is accidently sent forward instead of his consciousness returning to the present.

The Cloukey and Starzl stories both illustrate a complaint surfacing in the letters column about the number of stories that are little more than ordinary western, crime, or adventure tales, placed in the future or on another world. The editor agrees with the fault and replies that the staff is trying to remedy it. Forrest J Ackerman raises an interesting time paradox. What if someone visited the future, picked up copies of *Wonder Stories* on sale then, returned to the present, and simply plagiarized them for today's *Wonder Stories*? The editor admits that he cannot be positive that some stories he buys might not be from future issues!

The cover for the July *Wonder Stories* has a fantastic scene from "The City of Singing Flame" by Clark Ashton Smith, showing the temple of the great purple flame and the weird aliens about to plunge into it. Two Earthmen, much dwarfed by the size of the other creatures, are present, and one is trying to restrain the other from immolating himself. Here is the first science fiction tale by Smith that makes full use of both his imagination and the poetic style that he used in *Weird Tales*.

Editor David Lasser collaborated with Dr. David H. Keller on the two-part novel, *The Time Projector*, starting in this issue. Keller's view of the question of whether the future is fixed or fluid is that knowledge of the future may make changes possible; in other words, the machine projects visions of what will happen if no action is taken to prevent it. It projects that Los Angeles will be destroyed by an earthquake and fire, just as San Francisco had earlier in the century. Though it cannot be averted, the forewarning may save many lives. However, people do not want to know the truth, and the time projector is destroyed.

"The Red Spot of Jupiter" by Dennis McDermott, presents the first anti-hero to appear in the magazines. Lem Gulliver is a criminal who shows no socially redeeming qualities, but wins out in the end due to strength and determination. We also have "A Daring Trip to Mars" by Max Valier, published as a memorial to the distinguished German rocket experimenter who had been killed by an explosion during testing in 1930.

Particularly interesting is Hugo Gernsback's extra-long editorial, "Wonders of the Machine Age." Here Gernsback's point is that while technological progress may result in some immediate unemployment, the new machines will in time create more jobs than they destroy.

Announced in the editorial in the Summer 1931 *Wonder Stories Quarterly* were the seven interplanetary plot contest winners, and a notice that the contest would continue. Five of the winners were unknown, and remained so. The other two were Allen Glasser and John Michel. What was not known at the time, outside a small circle, was the Glasser's third-prize winning plot, had been the idea of Mortimer Weisinger. He made the mistake of telling the idea to Glasser under a promise of silence, but Glasser wrote it up and submitted it as his own.

The lead novel is *Vandals of the Void* by Australian author J. M. Walsh. The inhabitants of Earth, Mars, and Venus collaborate in tracking down mysterious and invisible brigands preying upon all interplanetary ships. Earthmen and Martians are enough alike to allow intermarriage. The heroine is a Martian girl who, like all other Martians, is black. No one at any time makes an issue of that fact. I didn't realize, upon first reading, that here was a genuine anti-racist story. The essence of racism *is* that an issue is made of a person's color or race, and those elements are considered more important than the worth of any individual.

"The Machine of Destiny" by Ulysses George Mihalakis, is based upon the immutable-future philosophy. It's handled like a weird tale but is strictly science fiction. The author would later appear in *Unknown Worlds* as Silaki Ali Hassan. P. Schuyler Miller's "The Man from Mars" deals with a supposed fake on exhibit at a circus, but who is actually the real thing. The Martian is handled sympathetically. Clark Ashton Smith's "The Amazing Planet," the cover story, is a sequel to "Marooned on Andromeda." The imaginative aspects triumph over a routine story line.

The August *Wonder Stories* features Benson Herbert's sequel to "The World Without." At the end of that story, one of the two explorers had made his way back. In "The World Within," he returns to rescue his companion. Here he finds himself in the bloodstream of the giant creature, but in neither tale do the explorers get any idea of what the creature looks like as a whole. "The Island of the Giants" by A. Rowley Hilliard deals sympathetically with a scientifically created super-race, even though it is destroyed at the end.

A new contest centers upon "Twelve Hours to Live" by Jack Williamson. At the end, the hero and his wife are marooned on the beach of a desert island by the pirate Black Hawk, along with two heavy metal chests. The wife, currently in a coma, is enclosed in one of them, which also contains a radio through which help can be obtained, and a supply of food and water. The other chest is packed with deadly spores, fatal to anyone opening it. The hero has seen what the spores do, so he knows it is no bluff. The only visible difference between the two chests is that one bears the inscription, *THE OTHER ONE*. Our hero has twelve hours to decide which one to open, because the air in the chest containing his wife will then be exhausted. There the story ends, and $50 in prizes are offered to readers who come up with the most convincing solutions.

The September issue starts a three-part serial, *Exiles of the Moon* by Nathan Schachner and Arthur L. Zagat. One episode in the story makes it memorable. At the end of the first installment, one character is outside the spaceship without protection. There will be a surprise for readers at the start of part two, which I'll describe later.

"The Mutiny in Space" by Gawain Edwards is essentially a retelling of the voyage of Columbus in 1492, translated to a single spaceship en route to Venus. The crew is terrified and convinced that there is not enough fuel, and that they are off course. The captain is killed in the ensuing mutiny, but he has left a message urging them to continue and assuring them that they will see the planet before them in a short time. They do—Venus had been obscured by the Sun.

J. Harvey Haggard's "An Adventure on Eros" is not what it appears to be, but was an ideal Gernsback gadget story, especially when one recalls his hypnobioscope. The protagonist of the story turns out to be a student taking a study course under sleep that teaches by putting him in the situation described.

The June *Amazing Stories* features "The Power Planet" by Murray Leinster, telling of an interworld power station and the attempt by an unspecified Earth nation to capture it. More memorable is "The Incredible Formula" by Paul Ernst. Here we read of a scientific means of reviving the dead as mindless zombies, controllable by radio. The results are unpleasant, but Ernst shows why the so-called "livies" become essential to the economy.

The July *Amazing* presents the first episode of Dr. E. E. Smith's three-part serial, *Spacehounds of IPC*. It's independent of the Skylark stories and everything takes place within our solar system. I was somewhat disappointed, although here is the first example of Smith's genius for portraying sympathetic but utterly non-human beings. "Cleon of Yzdral" is a Merrittesque fantasy by P. Schuyler Miller, dealing with a legend of the world described in "Through the Vibrations." Most memorable, however, is "The Jameson Satellite" by Neil R. Jones, the first story in what would prove to be a long and popular series. Professor Jameson arranges to have his body placed in a coffin without having been embalmed, and the coffin enclosed in a space vehicle that is put in orbit immediately upon his death, so that his body will never decay. Millennia later, the coffin-ship is discovered by a race of semi-immortal machine creatures, the Zoromes, who revive the professor and make him one of them. The stories can be read with enjoyment today.

August's lead story, "Submicroscopic" by Captain S. P. Meek, was presented by Isaac Asimov in his anthology of personal favorites, *Before the Golden Age*. The story is enjoyable, but by that time many of us no longer found tales of reducing one's size to the microscopic level and encountering complete worlds and human beings, in any way credible.

The Summer *Amazing Stories Quarterly* features "The Blue Barbarians" by Stanton A. Coblentz, another of his satires. One outstanding touch is the Venusian equivalent of gold: green glass, called "gulgul." Once two of the Earthmen, having escaped confinement as inferior forms of humanoid life, stumble upon a mass of broken green glass, they are immediately hailed as millionaires, and referred to as "large-letter"-men, denoting the highest order in the society. Morey has a charming cover for "Cosmic Menace" by A. W. Bernal, whereon we see Earth itself transformed into a vast rocket ship and plunging out of its orbit. The "menace" was a vast dust cloud that the solar system as a whole was approaching; it would have blocked Earth off from the light and heat of the sun. Keller is back again, telling of "Half-Mile Hill," wherein a man strikes back at the constant roar of traffic noise around his home, by inventing a device that interferes with automobile transmission.

The September *Amazing* has one of Morey's poorer covers, illustrating "Awlo of Ulm," the sequel to "Submicroscopic." It looks as if it had been cut out and pasted on to a white background. (Morey should be forgiven, however; it was that cover which attracted the attention of a young woman named Catherine L. Moore; she was immediately converted, and a couple of years later made a tremendous hit with her first-published story, "Shambleau," in *Weird Tales*.) The issue also marked Wesso's final appearance in the monthly *Amazing* during the Gernsback era, though he would continue to illustrate novels in the *Quarterly* for another year. Henceforth, with a single exception, all the artwork in the monthly was to be by Leo Morey, who was now Art Director for the Teck Publishing Company. Considering the times, that was probably a good deal for him, and an economic way of handling art expenses for the company. It costs less to hire one man to do everything, than pay several artists piecemeal. The result, however, was that the illustrations were confined to the limits of Morey's abilities, and increased deadline pressures meant that he had to do many of his drawings in a hurry. Now and then there were examples of his best work, both for covers and interiors, but on the whole we saw him below par. That explains why critics like Damon Knight, who started following the magazines in 1933 or later, could not find a kind word to say for Morey. When Damon visited me in the mid-seventies, I pulled out my 1932 *Amazing*s and showed him some of Morey's best covers. Then he found kind words.

Although not listed on the contents page, David H. Keller's "The Steam Shovel" is in the September issue. It's the last in the Wing Loo series, and here the doctor is entirely benevolent. His experiment consists of putting the brain of an elephant into a steam shovel, which is thereafter controlled by it. The outstanding story in the issue, however, is "The Arrhenius Horror" by P. Schuyler Miller, dealing with a fantastic and rather fearful life-energy form that grew from spores from space.

From the scene on the cover of the June 1931 *Astounding Stories*, you'd think that it was a jungle-adventure magazine. A great ape swings between the trees, carrying an unconscious man, and is fighting off a leopard, while a girl looks on from the bole of a tree. It illustrates "Manape the Mighty" by Arthur J. Burks, a story that aroused many objections from the readers. They did not mind the implausibility of ape and human brains being switched (something *Weird Tales* readers had read about in stories by Bassett Morgan as far back as 1927). Their complaint was that it was all too much like a Tarzan story. John Hanson appears in "The Man from 2071" by S. P. Wright, which tells of a man in Commander Hanson's future coming back to try to change the past. "The Earthman's Burden" is another IFP tale of R. F. Starzl, located on Mercury, with the Mercutians looking like the traditional representation of the Christian's Devil: horns, hooves, and spiked tails. Frank R. Paul makes his debut in *Astounding* illustrating that story, and was immediately hailed by the readers, who wanted to see more of his drawings there (without dropping Wesso); he did appear a few times later until the magazine died.

The July cover contains something we'd never seen before on the front of *Astounding*: the date. Wesso's picture more than atones for his jungle job. It shows a naked man confronting an intelligent and malignant-looking machine, on a small island, atop of which is a building surrounded by a mysterious purple glow. It illustrates "The Doom from Planet 4" by Jack Williamson. The title tells the story; we all know that the attempted invasion from Mars will be foiled. Much better is "The Revolt of the Machines" by Schachner and Zagat. Here, a decadent world culture, entirely dependent upon machines, is terminated when the master machine decides to take over. The story deals with the efforts of a few humans, who escaped the general massacre, to survive on their own. It anticipates John W. Campbell's Teacher series, some years later.

Charles W. Diffin's sequel to "Dark Moon," *Brood of the Dark Moon*, starts in the August issue, and is the best of the three serials he had in the Clayton *Astounding*. Here is another example of imagination and alien atmosphere more than compensating for a familiar plot-line.

That was the first issue of *Astounding* that I bought after the disappointment of those two 1930 issues. I couldn't resist Wesso's cover, showing a tiny man, naked except for a loincloth, on a makeshift raft into which a jacknife, looking huge by comparison, is pinned. He is being menaced by a hawk. It illustrates "The Midget from the Island" by H. G. Winter (a pseudonym of

Harry Bates and Desmond Hall). In the latest Dr. Bird story, "The Port of Missing Planes," Bird, Carnes, and Saranoff all encounter a peaceful but scientifically superior race of giant moles living beneath the ground. For me, it is the best of Meek's Bird-Saranoff series.

Either I had changed, or the magazine had really improved. At any rate, I was looking forward to the September issue which bore (for my eyes) Wesso's best cover during the Clayton period. Illustrating "The Sargasso of Space" by Edmond Hamilton, we see two spacesuited figures dueling with steel bars, with the object of smashing the opponent's glassite helmet.

The big news of the issue, however, was a full-page advertisement announcing *Strange Tales*, and offering a three-issue subscription for fifty cents. (The cover price was twenty-five cents, five cents more than *Astounding's*.) It would have the same format as *Astounding*, but appear bi-monthly. The first issue, dated September, appeared in the middle of August, and soon proved to be excellent competition to *Weird Tales*, which I started buying at the same time. The magazine did not carry much science fiction, though there is an occult-science rationale to the lead novelette in the first issue, "The Dead Who Walk" by Ray Cummings.

There was some good science fiction in *Weird Tales* at this time, especially in the August 1931 issue, which contained "The Earth Owners" by Edmond Hamilton (a Charles Fort type, "we are property" tale), Ralph Milne Farley's "The Time Traveler," "Moon Madness" by Wallace West and, most memorable of all, "The Whisperer in Darkness" by H. P. Lovecraft. The September issue had "The Immeasurable Horror" by Clark Ashton Smith, a tale of Venusian exploration. The "horror" is a giant amoeboid creature that devours everything in its path.

The main science fiction in *Argosy* was Ray Cummings's serial, *Tama, Princess of Mercury*, which began in the June 27 issue. It was the sequel to *Tama of the Light Country*, and delivered much of the same.

SEPTEMBER-DECEMBER 1931

Sam Moskowitz once showed me a carbon-copy letter signed by David Lasser addressed to authors' agent Julius Schwartz. It announced that *Wonder Stories* would cease publication with the October 1931 issue, but that a new science fiction magazine would be substituted in a few months. There's no way of telling how many such letters were sent out. However, when the October isue appeared, plans had evidently been changed. The editorial page contained an announcement that, with the next issue, *Wonder* would resume the old large-size format. There would be other surprises for the readers.

The October cover shows a man being lifted by a strange machine, and illustrates "Between Dimensions" by J. E. Keith. The narrator is caught in a dimensional trap whereby he shuttles between this world and another dimension with its machine culture. One of the most powerful short stories of the entire period, "Death from the Stars" by A. Rowley Hilliard, appears here. It tells of a strange and horrible disease brought to Earth by a meteor. There is no cure or treatment, and we do not know whether the expedient of destroying its victim by fire checks the disease's spread. Morrison F. Colladay's sequel to "The Cosmic Gun," "The Return of the Cosmic Gun," deals with the further possibilities of that invention, none of them pleasant.

At the start of part two of Schachner and Zagat's serial, *Exiles of the Moon*, Dore Swithin, who was outside the spaceship without any protection, is brought back inside. Everyone assumes he's dead, until someone mentions that he was out there for four minutes. The protagonist declares that he may not be dead and resuscitation is possible. He has neither exploded nor frozen solid. Our hero explains that, (a) you lose heat in a vacuum by radiation—the victim was not exposed long enough to freeze, (b) the victim was not out long enough to suffocate, and (c) the comparison between deep-sea fish exploding when brought to the surface is inappropriate. The difference there is between thousands of pounds to the inch and fifteen. People on Earth have survived a loss of half of fifteen pounds pressure without harm. Thus, while Dore Swithin is suffering from shock, partial suffocation, and some damage from total loss of outside pressure, he recovers. In 1935, when Stanley G. Weinbaum made the same essential point in "The Red Peri," he would be acclaimed as being the first to do so, as by then the Schachner/Zagat story had been generally forgotten.

For some reason the Fall 1931 *Wonder Stories Quarterly* went on sale on September 1, but subsequent issues reverted to the former fifteenth-of-the month on-sale date. The cover featured one of Paul's most original spaceships, and it's painful to see a massive meteor-torn hole in the lower section. It illustrates a routine adventure story, "The Asteroid of Death" by Neil R. Jones. Another translation from the German makes up the lead novel, The Cosmic Cloud by Bruno H. Burgel. It's a well-written mainstream novel with science fictional aspects. The Earth encounters a dust cloud in space which brings about a new ice age. Outstanding among the short stories is "The Man-Beast of Toree" by Ralph T. Jones, telling of an intelligent man from another world, made into a beast when captured by a non-human species. His thumbs are amputated and he is treated like an animal, the equivalent of a race horse, until he sinks to that level. I cannot imagine a more vivid illustration of the human thumb's importance. The story remains chilling today.

The first two winning entries in the plot competition appeared in this issue. William Thurmond's first-prize plot was turned over to Ray Cummings. The result, "The Derelict of Space," is among Cummings's best short stories of the period. E. M. Johnston was the second prize-winner and Clark Ashton Smith wrote the story, "The Planet Entity," around the idea that what we have assumed to be the canals of Mars are actually the physical extension of a single living and intelligent creature. It struck me as a real winner at the time, but re-reading shows that it is much too preachy, unlike any of Smith's other stories, which get points across in a less direct manner.

The November issue was not only large-size, but printed on a thinner, high-quality, white paper. And we saw an announcement that Frank R. Paul would now be the exclusive illustrator. Despite his particular faults, he was a better choice than Morey had been for *Amazing*, and most of his work during the time that he remained exclusive at *Wonder* was well done.

Featured in the issue was P. Schuyler Miller's "Tetrahedra of Space," which describes the non-violent means through which the eponymous silicon beings are persuaded that Earth is not a good place for them to settle. "The Superman of Dr. Jukes" by Francis Flagg is a warm, human account of a man who, temporarily, becomes a superman. Clark Ashton Smith presented "Beyond the Singing Flame," the sequel to "The City of Singing Flame." Many readers found the story too fantastic, but others were enthusiastic. It is to Gernsback's credit that Smith continued to be welcome at *Wonder Stories* with tales he wanted to write, however controversial his style might be.

The prize-winning letters in the "Twelve Hours to Live" contest were written by the active fan Walter L. Dennis, reader M. Gittleman, and author Frank K. Kelly. Dennis's solution uses the fact that whilst the chests are too heavy to lift, one is tightly packed with spores, and the other is not. A little jiggling should reveal the presence of objects moving inside. The hero should scoop out a hole in the sand beneath each chest, large enough so that it could be moved up and down. Then each could be jiggled and the one from which the sound is heard is the right one.

Gittleman's solution is to wait for sounds to come from within the chest containing the woman. When her air supply is gone, she will awaken and pound on the sides of the chest.

Kelly's solution is psychological. He follows the Black Hawk's reasoning. When the hero first sees the inscription, *THE OTHER ONE*, he will assume a trick. But, reasons the Black Hawk, "If he is subtle enough he will realize that I know his opinion of me; he will think that my twisted sense of humor may lead me to put the wife in the uninscribed chest, but more probably as a crowning sardonicism, to do the unexpected and place the wife in the carved chest. Carrying my reasoning a final step, a step that the captain is not cunning enough to follow, I will, while he hesitates between doubt and indecision, put his wife in the chest with the mock warning. He will not dare to open it because of the warning." Elegant reasoning, but physical experimentation is more likely to bring peace of mind, and success, than dialectic discourse.

The December issue starts one of the best science fiction novels of the period, *The Time Stream* by John Taine, a complex but masterful story of an attempt to change the past. It was announced for three installments, but was extended to four. The story moves slowly and goes deeply into character exploration. Those readers who demanded fast action and adventure did not like it, but it was highly praised by the more literary minded, many of whom also enjoyed action stories.

Two authors make their debut here: Arthur K. Barnes with "Lord of the Lightning" (the title tells the story), and Clifford D. Simak with "The World of the Red Sun." In Simak's story we again encounter a vast brain in a globe, ruling decadent humanity, but there's a twist at the end. The two travelers want to see the farther future, then return to the world they've delivered from the brain. When they try, they find that time travel is one-way only, and they're stranded at the end of the world.

It was a jolt to see a vivid blue background on Paul's lunar-scene cover for the January 1932 *Wonder Stories*, illustrating "Martian Guns" by Stanley Bell, but otherwise the picture of the giant cannon bombarding Earth is effective. So is the story. A surprise awaits the reader in "The Derelicts of Ganymede" by John W. Campbell, Jr. Not only are the scientific explanations briefer than usual, but the story is romantic and humorous. We'd never encountered a female in Campbell's stories before, or ever suspected that he could be funny.

"The Duel on the Asteroid" by Dennis McDermott and P. Schuyler Miller, is a sequel to "The Red Spot of Jupiter," featuring the anti-hero Lem Gulliver. The authors wanted to make this a series, gradually humanizing Gulliver, even as he is brought to justice. The editors were apparently agreeable, but no further tales in the series appeared.

The Winter 1932 *Wonder Stories Quarterly* features "The Onslaught from Rigel" by Fletcher Pratt. Here, Earth is invaded by superior, elephant-like beings, and all humans are somehow transmuted into metal without being harmed. I wasn't convinced by that then, and am still not, but it was fun to read. Paul's cover illustrates "The Moon Destroyers" by Monroe K. Ruch. We see a fleet of spaceships focusing disintegrating rays upon our satellite. It has been calculated that the Moon's gravitation pull is setting up increasing stresses and strains in Earth's crust leading to more and more earthquakes, so the moon has to be destroyed.

The third-prize winner in the plot contest is "The Martian" by A. Rowley Hilliard, based on Allen Glasser's/Mort Weisinger's idea. It is the very moving story of a stranded Martian treated as a circus freak, who pines away in his loneliness.

Morey's covers for the October and November *Amazing Stories* illustrate scenes from *The Stone from the Green Star* by Jack Williamson, the only two-part serial in the SF magazines of this period to cop a cover for both its installments. It was Williamson's first interplanetary novel, and it struck me as one of his best, simply because it was more rooted in science than fantasy. A new series of science fiction mysteries started in the October issue with "The Master of Mystery" by Bob Olsen. The whole series was good.

More memorable, in the November *Amazing*, was the debut of Abner J. Gelula with "Automaton." It starts out like the usual super-robot-that-takes-over story, then takes a new turn. The robot triumphs and becomes ruler of the world, and the heroine joins forces with it against her lover.

The Fall *Amazing Stories Quarterly* features *Seeds of Life* by John Taine, a particularly powerful novel of the effects of nuclear radiation. It isn't credible today, but remains an excellent story. The issue also introduced my own nomination for the all-round worst author of the period: Joseph W. Skidmore. "Dramatis Personae" is written down to the (then) ten-year-old level. Needless to say, Skidmore was well-liked by younger readers.

Morey's cover for the December *Amazing* is altogether better than the three preceding, illustrating part one of *The Inevitable Conflict* by Paul H. Lovering. The cover shows a fleet of futuristic aircraft bombing New York City, and we see the entire panorama of the area from the viewpoint of one of the attackers. The conflict is invasion from the East, in a future where the West has become a matriarchy. One short story, "Trial by Television," by Fred Kennedy, is memorable, and remains possible.

The January 1932 issue introduces a science fiction character who would be very popular in "Tumithak of the Corridors" by Charles R. Tanner. Earth has been conquered by the Shelks of Venus, and the remnants of humanity live underground on sufferance by the conquerors, who also use humans for food. The issue also contains the first of a series by J. Lewis Burtt, "The Lemurian Documents," which retells various stories from Greek mythology as if actual events in a scientific past. The first, "Pygmalion," follows the original myth so closely as to make one wonder why it should have been retold as science fiction.

Apart from the continuation of Charles W. Diffin's serial, *Brood of the Dark Moon*, the high spot of the October *Astounding Stories* is an amusing one—the cover. It aroused denunciations from one reader as being a sex picture. The girl in the picture wears a sheer gown with no underclothing and the outlines of her breasts and buttocks are apparent. It illustrates Paul Ernst's less than memorable "The Red Hell of Jupiter."

The November issue introduced one of the most popular characters of the period in "Hawk Carse" by Anthony Gilmore. There would be three more stories about this future equivalent of an old-West gunfighter in *Astounding*. Fans soon began to ask, "Who is Anthony Gilmore?" but it would be some years before his identity was revealed as Harry Bates and Desmond Hall.

By a curious coincidence, Wesso's December cover also shows a scene high over New York City. It illustrates *The White Invaders* by Ray Cummings, which is a shorter rewrite of his earlier novel, *Into the Fourth Dimension*. The new two-part serial is *Giants on the Earth* by S. P. Meek. This had been announced to start in the November issue but, as editor Bates explained, "an unpredictable concatenation of fortuities prevented our getting the first installment . . . in this issue." It was not a great story, but was a welcome relief from the Dr. Bird series. The "giants" are Jovians who have conquered Earth.

The outstanding content in the December issue is "Morale" by Murray Leinster, a story of the war of 1941-43. It deals with a super-tank, known as the Wabbly, which invades New Jersey in 1942. It seems to be invincible, but our protagonists figure out the Wabbly's weak spot and how to exploit it. "Out Around Rigel," a short story by Robert H. Wilson, has an illustration showing two men in spacesuits dueling with swords. The story is charming, although the relativity aspect (a seemingly short interstellar trip that proves to have taken centuries when the hero returns to a now-dead Luna) isn't exactly a new idea. dr. Miles J. Breuer did it earlier in "The Fitzgerald Contraction."

There is another giant ape on the cover of the January 1932 *Astounding*. This one is climbing a skyscraper in New York City, holding a terrified man by one heel. It illustrates Arthur J. Burks's two-part sequel to "Manape the Mighty," *The Mind Master*. Here the super-scientist of the first story makes his way to New York to create an army of apes with human brains—all for something less than humanitarian purposes. "Creatures of Vibration" by Harl Vincent is a sequel to "Wanderers of Space," and Francis Flagg's "The Seed of the Toc-Toc Birds" is an imaginative tale of menace from the microcosm.

A few other science fiction tales appeared in the non-SF pulps during these months. The most memorable is "Wolves of Darkness" by Jack Williamson in the January 1932 *Strange Tales*. It isn't a werewolf story, but a tale of invasion from another dimension by beings that take over the bodies of humans and animals alike. It is in no way related to Williamson's later novel, *Darker Than You Think* (*Unknown* December 1940). In the same issue, "The Door to Saturn" by Clark Ashton Smith, puts two fugitive magicians from one of Smith's far-past locales on to the planet Saturn, but it's more satire than science fiction. Smith had another such tale in the January 1932 *Weird Tales*,

"The Monster of the Prophecy," describing the adventures of a terrestrial poet on a strange world in the system of Antares. The Earthman discovers that he himself is the prophesied monster.

1931 saw no particular trends. It was still dominated by the super-science adventure, but a glimmering of realism was dawning over frivolity. My selection of the best stories from 1931 are grouped as before.

From the *Wonder* group, the best serials and novels were *The Outpost on the Moon* by Jocelyn Maxwell, *Utopia Island* by Otfrid von Hanstein, and *The Cosmic Cloud* by Bruno H. Burgel. The best shorter fiction was "The War of the Giants" by Fletcher Pratt, "The City of (the) Singing Flame" by Clark Ashton Smith, "The Island of the Giants" and "Death from the Stars" by A. Rowley Hilliard, and "The Man-Beast of Toree" by Ralph T. Jones.

From the *Amazing* group, the best serials and novels were *Across the Void* by Leslie F. Stone, *Spacehounds of IPC* by E. E. Smith, *The Blue Barbarians* by Stanton A. Coblentz, and *Seeds of Life* by John Taine. Best shorter fiction was "Through the Vibrations" and "The Arrhenius Horror" by P. Schuyler Miller, "The Incredible Formula" by Paul Ernst, "The Jameson Satellite" by Neil R. Jones, and "Automaton" by Abner J. Gelula.

There was a somewhat better variety of choices from *Astounding* in 1931, but the quality was still limited. The best serials were *The Exile of Time* by Ray Cummings and *Brood of the Dark Moon* by Charles W. Diffin, and best novelettes "Hawk Carse" by Anthony Gilmore and "Morale" by Murray Leinster. I'd nominate no short story.

For the first half of 1931 *Amazing Stories* and its companion *Quarterly* gave *Wonder Stories* good competition, but by the end of the year *Wonder* was clearly the better magazine. *Astounding* remained in last place.

40.

MARKING TIME

The February *Wonder Stories* features another unusual story by Edmond Hamilton. "A Conquest of Two Worlds" is not about saving the Earth; on the contrary, it shows Earthmen as greedy, ruthless exploiters and destroyers of the harmless inhabitants of Mars and Jupiter. One Earthman, sickened by it all, defects to the native Jovians to help them defend their culture. He is treated as a renegade and finally killed, his mission unaccomplished.

In Jack Williamson's "The Moon Era," the cover story, the protagonist's time machine goes back to the time when our moon was inhabitable, and the home of strange but not entirely alien beings. It remains a charming, science-directed fantasy. "The Challenge of the Comet" by Arthur K. Barnes is based upon an actual event of 1931. A fog of some unknown poison gas swept over part of Belgium, killing scores of peasants; the nature and source of the gas was never discovered. Barnes's story makes the gas a vital part of the environment of creatures inhabiting a passing comet. They want to move to Earth, and Earth's atmosphere will have to be permeated with the gas before they can live here.

With "The Radium World," Frank K. Kelly became a frequent contributor to *Wonder Stories*, mostly with tales of otherworld adventure and intrigue. They were all well written, but not outstanding. This one is about a treasure planet.

The March and April issues featured a short novel, *The Final War*, by Carl W. Spohr, who had been an artillery officer in the German army during 1914-1918. As the editor notes, "in this story, there is no attempt to show one side as wrong and the other as right. The thing that is uppermost in his mind is to show so completely the suicide of another great war that nations will simply refuse to fight." It was an outstanding anti-war science fiction novel, and time has not eroded its effectiveness as fiction. Of course, we all know that it did not prevent the Second World War.

Paul's March cover shows three small aero-warships producing a ball of energy, the ray from which destroys a large aero-battleship. It illustrates "Red April, 1965" by Frank K. Kelly, which suffers from being in the same issue as Spohr's novel. It is also marred by comic-relief black characters. (We must remember, however, that at this time, a war movie featuring the "Two Black Crows" was very popular.) Clark Ashton Smith takes us beyond time and space in his fantastic "The Eternal World," and Raymond Z. Gallun's "Waves of Compulsion" deals with an attempted conquest by an alien creature making use of mass hypnotism.

Two stories stand out in the April issue, in addition to Spohr's serial: "The Reign of the Star-Death" by A. Rowley Hilliard, where the only hope of saving millions of people from the plague described in "Death from the Stars" is through ruthlessly exterminating thousands who have been infected; and

"The Last Woman" by Thomas S. Gardner, wherein the final female of the human species (which has achieved non-sexual means of reproduction) is a museum exhibit.

The Spring 1932 *Wonder Stories Quarterly* features "The Vanguard to Neptune" by J. M. Walsh, an enjoyable interplanetary adventure. More memorable are "The Woman from Space" by Richard Vaughan, telling sympathetically of a super-female; "The Voice in the Void" by Clifford D. Simak, wherein we learn that the "God" of the "superior" Martian race was actually an Earthman from a long-vanished human civilization; and "The Sterile World" by Warren E. Sanders, wherein humanity faces extinction. Plot-winning stories also appeared, but they were very ordinary by comparison with the three earlier tales.

Brood of Helios by Bertin was the new three-part serial starting in the May *Wonder Stories*. It tells of two men and a woman, suddenly transported into the far future where the world is peopled by savages and evolved humans. The latter have a high technology but are total pacifists. They are incapable of defending themselves against any form of hostility.

Captain S. P. Meek is here with "Vanishing Gold," wherein we encounter Dr. Bird and Saranoff. One cannot be sure whether this story was the last one written, or whether "The Great Drought" in the May *Astounding* was the final one. Both leave the usual opening for further adventures in the series. But why did "Vanishing Gold" appear in *Wonder Stories*? We'll return to that question later.

Also memorable in the May issue were "The Venus Adventure" by John Beynon Harris, dealing with the decadence of a human colony on Venus, and a most amusing satire on free-wheeling super-science, "Why the Heavens Fell" by Epaminondas T. Snooks, D.T.G. The heavens fell because the law of inverse squares was repealed by the United States Congress. The results throughout American territory are immediate, shattering, and final. It would be a number of years before we learned that "Snooks" was *Wonder Stories*'s associate editor, C. P. Mason, and that the D. T. G. stood for "Don't Tell Gernsback!" The story, which was not science fiction in the conventional sense, was perfect in Gernsback's sense, because not only did it reflect his sense of humor, it was instructive about the inverse square law.

Troyana, Captain S. P. Meek's sequel to *The Drums of Tapajos*, began serialization in the February 1932 *Amazing Stories*. It's of the same quality as the first story, introduces new material plausibly, and remains a first-class science-adventure story. Also featured is the second in Neil R. Jones's Professor Jameson series, "The Planet of the Double Sun." It inspired an excellent cover by Morey. In fact some of Morey's best work would be the covers for Jameson stories.

Murray Leinster presents an uncomfortable portrayal of criminals seizing a new invention in "The Racketeer Ray," and Dr. David H. Keller's short-short, "The Pent House," was long acclaimed as among his best. Re-reading affirms its charm, but credibility is no part of it. We're asked to believe that a newly married young couple could spend five years together in a single apartment, which they may not leave during that period, and not go stir-crazy or begin to hate each other murderously.

The feature novel in the Winter 1932 *Amazing Stories Quarterly* is *A*

Voice Across the Years by Fletcher Pratt and I. M. Stephens (his wife, Inga). It tells of an alien, forced to land on Earth, and an Earthman who assists him and goes with him to his own world. Though in many ways it is a superior culture, there is room for satire, and Pratt's touch is more subtle than Coblentz's. "Blue Waters" by William Lemkin, Ph.D., is about a lake filled with gold in colloid form. It isn't an exciting story, but remains fascinating. "Moss Island" by Carl Jacobi, who had just made his debut in *Weird Tales*, is weird, but still science fiction. "Naval Control" by John Shamus O'Donnell, may be the first in the magazines to deal with a near-human robot. This one is a housemaid who falls in love with a sailor; the consequences are most amusing.

Morey's cover for the March *Amazing* is disappointing. We have a scene that seems to have been cut out an pasted on to the background color. It illustrates "The Light from Infinity" by L. A. Eshbach, a formula fantasy. The lead story, "The Cities of Ardathia" by Francis Flagg, was praised for its socially conscious qualities at the time, but does not take re-reading very well. We also have "The Gorgons" by J. Lewis Burtt, the second of his Lemurian Documents. The Gorgons are shown as a monstrous life form on another world.

Morey's cover for the April *Amazing*, illustrating "The Lost Machine" by John Beynon Harris, remains one of my favorites. It shows a silvery spaceship in the sky above a park area in New York City and, on the ground, a mechanical being. The "lost" machine destroys itself in what seems to be despair, after telling its story of being marooned on Earth.

"Mechanocracy" by Dr. Miles J. Breuer, is a rewarding cautionary tale of world government by machines, where any citizens may be subjected to euthenasia if they're likely to make waves. "Seven Sunstrokes" by Bob Olsen is the second in his Master of Mystery series—the solution is ingenious.

"The Return of the Tripeds," in the May issue, is the third Professor Jameson story, and concludes the adventure started in "The Planet of the Double Sun." It has a first-class cover illustration by Morey. Another sequel, in the same issue, is "Worlds Adrift" by Stephen G. Hale, relating what happened after Earth was split in two at the end of "The Laughing Death." There was also the third in Burtt's Lemurian series, retelling the legend of "Daedalus and Icarus." However, the star of the issue is the opening installment of Dr. Keller's three-part serial, *The Metal Doom*. What would happen if *all* metals were suddenly attacked by a disease that quickly turned them to rust? The story concentrates on the consequences in the United States, and is a powerful account of disaster and survival.

The next issue of *Amazing Stories Quarterly* bore the date Spring-Summer on the cover. That was the first shock of the year in the science-fiction world, as the effects of the Depression started to take hold. The feature novel is *Invaders from the Infinite*, the last of the Arcot, Wade, and Morey stories by John W. Campbell. It's as cosmic in scope as anything we'd seen from "Doc" Smith, and is a thriller, despite the overlong scientific discussions. It's also very similar in plot to *Skylark Three*. For example, the evil malignant invaders' planet is destroyed, and our heroes have to chase a single escaping spaceship for the final confrontation.

Bob Olsen's "The Ant with a Human Soul" tells of a man's consciousness transferred to an ant. It's one of Olsen's best. We learned later that this was the story originally planned for the unpublished third issue of *Miracle Science and Fantasy Stories.*

Wesso's cover for the February 1932 *Astounding Stories*, for "The Pygmy Planet" by Jack Williamson, shows a miniature planet balanced between two vertical and one horizontal rays. It is hanging there in a laboratory, and we see a miniature airplane taking off from the floor. Both the cover and the story retain their fantastic charm.

Wandl, the Invader, a four-part sequel to *Brigands of the Moon* by Ray Cummings, starts here. It is the final Cummings novel to have any freshness, even though the plot is predictable. We would not see any further stories from Cummings in the SF magazines during the Gernsback period. The issue also has a strong novelette by H. G. Winter, "Seed of the Arctic Ice," dealing with intelligent seals. Wesso's March cover shows a spaceship encountering a swarm of red leech-like creatures in the depths of space. It illustrates "Vampires of Space," a John Hanson story by Sewell Peaslee Wright. The vampires are known as "electites" and feed on metal.

The feature novelette is "The Affair of the Brains" by Anthony Gilmore, the second in the Hawk Carse series. Here, the basic idea of Dr. Keller's "The Cerebral Library," is brought to effect. A series of human brains are linked together to form a living library. The detached brains remember their lives as humans and are in torment. Carse is trapped into revealing the whereabouts of his friend, Elliot Leithgow, whose brain the sinister oriental Ku Sui wants to add to his living library. The story ends with Carse's escape and his vow to return to liberate the brains.

The April *Astounding* has the most unusual cover yet seen on a science fiction magazine. On a purple background, off-white, demon-like creatures with black, bat-like wings, are carrying a huge net containing a space-suited man. It illustrates "The Finding of Haldgren," last in the Dark Moon series by Charles W. Diffin. The story takes place on our own Moon where Chet Bullard finds and rescues a scientist and his daughter, long believed to have been lost in an early attempt to reach the moon. Dr. Miles J. Breuer appears with an amusing dimensional tale, "The Einstein See-Saw," involving a safe filled with scientific data that has been made to shuttle between dimensions.

The May issue contained a surprise short Hawk Carse story, not announced as forthcoming in the previous issue. "The Bluff of the Hawk" deals with Carse's escape from the cohorts of Ku Sui after the conclusion of "The Affair of the Brains."

The issue presents the final Dr. Bird story to appear in *Astounding*, "The Great Drought" by S. P. Meek. It ends with Saranoff defeated but still alive. in the late 1950s or early '60s, I was corresponding with Meek—by then Colonel Meek, Retired—over a reprint of *The Drums of Tapajos* and *Troyana* for Avalon Books. I asked him why the Dr. Bird series had stopped so abruptly. He told me that the "Fellow Travelers" (Communist sympathizers, not Party Members), had gotten to Harry Bates and persuaded him to stop running such virulent anti-Russian propoganda. It may be, then, that Bates rejected "Vanishing Gold" and Meek immediately sent it to Hugo Gernsback, and it was sheer coincidence that both appeared in the May 1932 issues. Bates, though, did run one more story in which a Soviet super-scientist threatens the world; we'll note that later.

One story stood out in *Weird Tales* during these four months and that was "The Earth-Brain" by Edmond Hamilton in the April issue. A man decides that Earth is a living entity and has a brain, which he finds, much to his misfortune. There was more on offer in *Argosy* with the six-part serialization of A. Merritt's *The Dwellers in the Mirage* starting in the January 23 issue, and a new Ray Cummings serial, *The Insect Invasion* starting in the April 16 issue. For Burroughs fans there was a new Tarzan serial, *Tarzan and the City of Gold* starting in the March 12 issue. Murray Leinster and R. F. Starzl were also present with stories during this period. Science fiction was clearly still a feature of *Argosy*'s content.

MAY-AUGUST 1932

With the June issue, *Wonder Stories* returned to using ordinary pulp paper, but otherwise the magazine was unchanged. However, with other layout changes that had started with the November 1931 issue, *Wonder* was now the most modern-looking of the three magazines. *Amazing* and *Astounding* continued to look exactly as they had since 1930.

Paul's cover illustrates a scene from "The Invisible City," another of Clark Ashton Smith's fine science fantasies. The issue's memorable story is "The Hell Planet" by Leslie F. Stone, which has a realistic touch seldom found in interplanetary stories of the period. The mythical planet Vulcan (once thought to exist between Mercury and the Sun) is not only alien but in nearly every way deadly to human beings. The story remains chilling.

The July issue gives further indication that all is not well with the magazines. The cover does not illustrate a story but is a simple presentation of what looks like colored balls on a white background. It's a contest cover with prizes offered for the best letter giving a scientific explanation of the cover—but they are not big prizes, $15 being the top, and the fourth to tenth prize-winners receiving only a year's free subscription to the magazine.

Starting in this issue is Otfrid von Hanstein's three-part novel, *In the Year 8000*, another translation. I must confess I rather liked it in 1932, but rereading it appalled me. It is ferociously racist. In 8000 a.d., we have the superior white race controlling what we think of as the civilized world. It is confronted by the "evil" and "inferior" black and yellow races. Among the whites, all emotion has been bred out except for an atavism here and there. And to top it off, at the end of the story, the warm-hearted (atavistic) hero is dying, and the leader of the white race is on the verge of death from an incurable heart condition. Our hero donates his heart to the other man, and the operation is successful. Upon recovery, the heretofore emotionless leader immediately becomes the same type of compassionate person that the hero had been. No, I'm not making that up!

The best story in the issue is "The Time Conqueror" by L. A. Eshbach, about a brain that survives through centuries.

"The Reader Speaks" column in this issue contained a letter signed, "R. W. Lownder" from Darien, Connecticut. I learned my lesson from that misprint in my first-published letter, and henceforth I typed out my name below my signature!

Paul's cover for the Summer 1932 *Wonder Stories Quarterly* is from "The Menace from Mercury," a plot-winning story written by Raymond Z. Gallun from an idea supplied by John Michel, who would become well known in the fan world later. Featured is *Beyond Pluto*, a well-written, light-hearted novel by John Scott Campbell, who would not be seen again during the period. Laurence Manning appears for the first time alone with "The Voyage of the Asteroid," a well thought-out and plausible story of interplanetary exploration on a Venus that we now know never was.

With the August issue, there's a further streamlining of interior layouts, and we have a true sense-of-wonder cover, showing a man in a cylinder far above the Earth. It illustrates "The Space Coffin," a future crime adventure by A. Rowley Hilliard. Two novelettes, "Tyrant of the Red World" by Richard Tooker, wherein one member of an exploration team seeks to conquer the "natives" of an alien planet, and "Flight Into Super-Time," one of Clark Ashton Smith's imaginative science-fantasies, stand out.

The September cover repeats the device used on the July issue. This time we see arcs of color, and again prizes are offered for the best scientific explanations. The new three-part serial is a translation from the French, *The Death of Iron* by S. S. Held. While having the same basic theme as Dr. Keller's "The Metal Doom," this is a mainstream-type novel, and here the progress of the metal-attacking disease is gradual. Fletcher Pratt, who translated it, was living in France during the period, and never saw copies of the magazine containing it. He asked me, sometime in the 1950s, whether Gernsback had published the story, adding that, ". . . there was a lot of screwing in that story." I replied that, aside from one sentence, "Painted prostitutes sold their well-worn bodies," there was no apparent sex. But even bowdlerized, it remains an outstanding novel.

Francis Flagg's "After Armageddon" deals with the survivors of a war that has destroyed civilization; and Hendrik Dahl Juve makes his final appearance with "In Martian Depths," a realistic story of encounter with aliens.

Morey's cover for the June 1932 *Amazing Stories* shows sailboats out on the water, and in the sky two huge globes, just barely visible in the clouds. Some form of gas is issuing from them. It's one of his loveliest paintings. Unfortunately, the story illustrated, "Masters of the Earth" by John Edwards, is a routine invasion tale. The Lemurian series continues with "Phaeton" by J. Lewis Burtt. More memorable is "A Matter of Nerves" by Dr. William Lemkin. As the result of surgical error, the victim's senses are scrambled so that he feels heat as cold and vice versa.

The Martian city we see on the July cover is also lovely to look at, but the buildings don't look much different from New York's skyscrapers, although there are two moons in the sky. It illustrates Harl Vincent's interplanetary adventure tale, "Thia of the Drylands." I found J. Lewis Burtt's latest Lemurian tale, "The Sacred Cloak of Feathers," more interesting than the others because I've never been able to identify the specific myth upon which it is based.

Morey said at one time that his cover for the August 1932 *Amazing* was his personal favorite. It's well done, showing at the top two spaceships colliding in a blinding flash of light so that they can hardly be seen, and spacesuited figures hurled into the void. The story illustrated, "Beyond the Planetoids" by Edwin K. Sloat, is a routine space-pirate tale.

The Swordsman of Sarvon, a three-part serial by Charles Cloukey, begins here. (None of us suspected at the time that Cloukey had died before the story was published.) It's a wild tale of planetary and interplanetary intrigue, involving two nations on Venus, one friendly to Earth, the other out for conquest. Sarvon is the friendly nation, and one Meriden is the swordsman of the title. We're involved in invisibility, devices that enable you to walk through walls (although why you don't also fall through floors is never explained), and personality transference. It's fun to read.

"The Last Evolution," telling of machines succeeding rather than revolting against man, was a different story, not only for author John W. Campbell, Jr., but for its time. Re-read today, it seems overlong and clumsily written. Nonetheless, the theme of machines naturally supplanting, rather than overthrowing, human beings still comes across strongly. "Room for the Super Race" by Walter Kateley, tells of an invading asteroid peopled by super humans. In the author's quiet manner, pulp heroics are soft-pedalled, although the invasion is foiled.

The September cover is for "Prometheus," the final tale in J. Lewis Burtt's Lemurian series. It shows Prometheus in his spaceship, nearing the sun, in his search for the secrets of atomic power. It's marred by the artist's usual difficulty in drawing an attractive facelity to draw an attractive face. Jack Williamson's "The Lady of Light" is one of his science-fantasies, and "Suicide Durkee's Last Ride" by Neil R. Jones, is one of the few future-sports stories of the period; this one deals with auto-racing. Most memorable, unfortunately, is "The Romance of Posi and Nega," the first of a series by Joe W. Skidmore. The tone of the series is set with the opening paragraphs:

> Posi and Nega came into existence far out in the vast voids of space. Mothered they were by the cosmic rays of interstellar space; fathered by that mysterious energy that gives life and impulsion to electrons.
>
> What mighty force, what vast intelligence dominates and actuates the Universe, even to the marvellous and intricate scheme of atoms and electrons? One cannot contemplate the composition of matter and tolerate atheistic thoughts.

Of course, many can—and do. And while I am not an atheist myself, I can certainly tolerate atheistic thoughts in others who contemplate the composition of matter. So here we have just one out of many examples of Skidmore's sloppy thinking.

Throughout, Posi explains and explains and explains everything to Nega, who is consistently portrayed as a typical "beautiful but dumb" female. She's more curious about what those strange human beings call "love" and "marriage" than the tiresome wonders of matter and the Universe—and if anyone can make them seem tiresome, Skidmore can! The stories are frequently interrupted with quotations from the classics and from great thinkers, to illustrate some point or other. It all adds up to inspirational drivel, but I found the stories moderately entertaining at the time. Others liked them very much, judging by the letters published in "Discussions."

The June 1932 *Astounding Stories* carried the first episode of Charles W. Diffin's four-part serial, *Two Thousand Miles Below*. A race of humanoid beings sought safety within Earth at the onset of one of the glacial ages. Now they seek to repossess Earth's surface. We also have a kindly race of true humans living still farther below. The story wasn't bad, but was a disappointment after "Brood of the Dark Moon," and the development pattern was all too familiar. Much better was "The Raid on the Termites" by Paul Ernst. Two men reduce themselves in size and enter a termitary. From that point on, it's strict entomology, except that the author does suggest the possibility of something like a central intelligence ruling each termitary. He never becomes as fantastic, however, as Dr. Keller did in "The Human Termites." Mark Marchioni joins the art staff with this issue illustrating "Hellhounds of the Cosmos," a dimensional story by Clifford D. Simak. John Hanson is with us in "Priestess of the Flame" by Sewell Peaslee Wright. Here we have one of Commander Hanson's well-liked subordinates defect upon falling in love with the ruling "priestess" of an alien planet.

The June 1932 issue of *Astounding*'s companion, *Strange Tales*, contained one item of science fiction, "Dread Exile" by Paul Ernst, wherein a humanoid Martian exchanges bodies with an Earthman.

Astounding Stories was published on the first Thursday of every month, but no issue appeared on the first Thursday of June or July. Around the middle of July the September issue suddenly appeared, with the announcement that publication was now bi-monthly. Aside from an excellent cover illustrating "Raider of Universes" (mistakenly pluralized on the cover) by Donald Wandrei, the only memorable item is "Disowned" by Victor Endersby. The blurb: "The tragic misadventure of a man to whom the sky became an appalling abyss, drawing him ever upward," describes the tale accurately without giving any essential details away.

Weird Tales contained a few scientific tales, amongst them Edmond Hamilton's "The Terror Planet" set on Uranus, and Clark Ashton Smith's "The Vaults of Yoh-Vombis" set on Mars, both in the May issue. Frank Belknap Long provided a tale of an invasion by nasty beings from another dimension in "The Brain-Eaters" for the June issue.

The main feature in *Argosy* was the appearance of the sequel to *The Blind Spot*, *The Spot of Life*, written solo by Austin Hall (Homer Eon Flint had died in the interim). Hall's writing abilities had not improved in the intervening years, but his imagination was as vivid, and the sequel held a certain fascination.

SEPTEMBER-DECEMBER 1932

The cover for the October *Wonder Stories* shows a wrecked spaceship that has plunged so deeply into the surface of an asteroid that the exit port is buried. A single, trapped man looks out of a window port at strange, semi-transparent creatures. It illustrates "Master of the Asteroid," an ironic tale by Clark Ashton Smith. Featured is "The Planet of Youth" by Stanton A. Coblentz, a satire involving the apparent discovery of a youth-restoring agent on Venus, and the resultant frenzied rush to get there. A short story, "The Man of Stone" by Hazel Heald, was actually a revision by H. P. Lovecraft, and thus his second appearance in a Gernsback publication.

This was the final issue of *Wonder Stories* to carry portraits of the authors. There was no explanation of why the feature was dropped, but I heard later that many authors had protested about the sketches of them. Having met some of the authors not too many years later, I can say that the sketches were often inadequate and sometimes positively misleading.

The cover for the November *Wonder Stories* again featured a design rather than an illustration. This time it was not a contest, and it was also the only cover for the Wonder group not done by Frank R. Paul. Gernsback's editorial, "Wonder of the Colors," explains what we see: it's the dot over the letter "i" in the word *Stories* in the logo, magnified sixty times. Of more importance is the big splash of red in the center of the cover on which "NOW 15¢" is printed in yellow, with black outlines. The magazine had a flat appearance, and for a good reason. There was no longer a spine; it was saddle-stitched and the number of pages reduced to sixty-four. Gernsback tried to explain that this change would be an improvement: authors would have to write more tightly and eliminate unneeded descriptions, so we would all gain from it. I wonder if anyone was convinced; I was not.

One immediate result was that *The Death of Iron* was extended to four installments; another was that the average number of stories per issue was reduced from six to five. The one memorable short story in the issue is "The Dimension of Chance" by Clark Ashton Smith. That was the first story to describe a world in which anything could happen—there was no cause-effect relationship. The trouble with such stories is that if anything can happen, then what we read in the story happens only because the author wanted it to. Given the circumstances, anything else could have happened just as plausibly.

A couple of weeks after the November issue, the Fall *Wonder Stories Quarterly* presented another shock. It was now the thickness that the monthly had been, which meant that feature novels would be shorter, or there would be fewer additional stories. Paul's cover shows a small spaceship taking off from a planetoid that is slowly being consumed by atomic fire; it illustrates "The Atom Flame" by Jack Williamson. The lead novel is "Emissaries of Space" by Nathan Schachner. Alien beings come to Earth, offering to help humanity solve its social and political problems. The offer is accepted and, too late, Earthmen learn the price they must pay.

The December cover is among Paul's most striking. Within a futuristic building we see a huge ball of water in the air, in which people are swimming. It illustrates "The Time Express" by Nathan Schachner. The new serial, *The Wreck of the Asteroid* by Laurence Manning, is clearly a novella divided into three installments for the monthly but originally intended to run complete in the *Quarterly*. (This is clear from the number of illustrations we find in part three, *Wonder Stories*, February 1933. In the monthly we do not find more than one illustration per story other than in the early 1929 issues.) It continues the adventures of the crew now stranded on Mars.

Most interesting in this issue is "Space Rays" by John W. Campbell, because it elicited a special introduction by Hugo Gernsback, "Reasonableness in Science Fiction." Gernsback applauds Campbell's take-off on absurd rays, and considers it an excellent burlesque. Campbell, himself, was not at all pleased. He hadn't intended it as a spoof!

The January 1933 cover shows a spaceship under construction and apparently complete externally, being riven in two by what appears to be a superdense liquid falling from above. My first reaction was, "What a mean thing to do!" and I still feel that way. it illustrates "The Messenger from Space," an interplanetary mystery by D. D. Sharp. The substance that splits the ship is a super-dense liquid found on the planetoid 1932-HA—now called Reinmuth—that is approaching Earth. A spaceship from Reinmuth has come to Earth, then departed, leaving one human-type crew member to prevent Earthmen from flying to Reinmuth. Spaceflight is in its early stages, and the peculiar orbit of Reinmuth makes it, in effect, a trolley that runs around the solar system.

Sharp is also credited on the contents page as author of "The Synthetic Entity" but that is a misprint. Inside we see it is by Captain S. P. Meek. That tale, of a seemingly indestructible super-amoeboid creature, was Meek's final appearance in the science fiction magazines. We also have "The Memory of the Atoms" by Nathan Schachner and R. Lacher (who remains unidentified), wherein the cure for a worldwide plague is found in a woman's hidden memory. Readers were also delighted to find in this issue a photograph and brief profile of Frank R. Paul.

Just after the monthly went on sale, the Winter 1933 issue of *Wonder Stories Quarterly* appeared, which was to be the final number. The cover shows Earth as seen from the port of a spaceship, and illustrates a translation from the German on "Interplanetary Bridges" by Ludvig Anton, telling of a German expedition to Venus shortly after the end of the Great War. Some readers objected to the intensely nationalistic tone, but why shouldn't Germans feel patriotic? Such readers didn't object to the USA always presented as top nation. There was room for only one other story, "Exiles on Asperus" by John Beynon Harris, which is an interesting speculation on behaviorism. The descendants of a lost expedition to Asperus are found; they are apparently enslaved by the rather monstrous natives of that world, but they have been brought up from infancy to regard those natives as benevolent and loving, and are so attached to them that they cannot be rescued.

The October 1932 *Amazing Stories* features "Space-Rocket Murders" by Edmond Hamilton. The motive for the deaths proves to be an attempt on the part of the Venusians to keep Earthmen earthbound. They don't want to conquer Earth, but they are determined not to let Earthmen pollute Venus.

At that time, the name Howard Melvin Fast had no special meaning. "Wrath of the Purple" is the fiction debut of an author who would become world-famous as Howard Fast, for his sociological novels and for *Spartacus*. We would not see any further stories by him in the SF magazines for decades. The "purple" is a form of life, or semi-life, accidently created by a researcher in cellular activity, that destroys everything else living. Another debut is that of Eando Binder with "The First Martian," a story of first contact and resultant commerce with the friendly Martian culture. There is no villainy in the tale. "Eando" was a linkage of the initials of brothers Earl and Otto Binder.

In "The Man Who Fought a Fly" by Leslie F. Stone, we don't have a giant fly, but a reduced human. "Infra-Calorescence" by R. I. Melhorn is a solid, scientific mystery tale. This issue contained the only illustration in the monthly between October 1931 and April 1938 that was not by Leo Morey. It was credited to B. Bamont, who never appeared again—which was no loss.

September 23, 1932 was the publication date of the Fall-Winter *Amaz-*

ing Stories Quarterly, which was nearly a month earlier than we expected. It was pleasant to see that it remained the same size, but semi-annual publication was something else. Further issues would appear, but at unpredictable intervals. Morey's cover shows a giant aircraft flying over a battlefield. On its underpart is a super electromagnet which is attracting all the metal beings used by the combatants. It illustrates "The King and the Pawn" by Seven Anderton, a well-known writer for *Blue Book* and other adventure magazines. The "King" is a super-scientist who has proclaimed himself "King of the World." he isn't a madman but a genuine humanitarian, and his first move is to put an end to brush wars over the world.

The feature novel is *Faster Than Light*, a sequel to "Venus Liberated" by Harl Vincent. Here the characters of the first tale, both Earth and Venus dwellers, unite on a voyage of exploration to Procyon, as a means of traveling faster than light has been discovered. It has all of the author's charm, and fewer of his plot-routine defects than some of the shorter tales. Also in this issue was "Beyond the Veil of Time" by B. H. Barney. It was a lost-race fantasy about a hidden part of Peru which was very reminiscent of A. Merritt. I was to find out why a few months later.

The November *Amazing* issue starts a two-part serial, *World of the Living Dead* by Ed Earl Repp, which was very similar to "The World at Bay." An inner-Earth culture breaks through to the surface, bent on conquest with super-scientific weapons. The earlier story was far better. Bob Olsen offers "Captain Brink of the Space Marines," the first of an intended new series. The title tells the story, and Morey has a good cover, showing two of the marines in the grips of aerial entities on another planet.

The December issue presents Morey's first under-water scene on the cover, and it's better than the two previous ones by Paul for the June 1930 *Wonder Stories* or Wesso for the February 1931 *Astounding*. You really get a murky feeling and, for a change, the two divers are not up against an octopus; it's a shark that menaces them. Unfortunately you have to study the cover to find anything amazing about it. When you do you'll see that one of the two divers is firing an electric discharge from a tube at the shark. There's one outstanding story in the issue, "No More Tomorrows," one of David H. Keller's best grotesque tales. The protagonist has discovered an elixir that destroys all sense of the future in anyone who drinks it. "The Call to Migrate" by H. M. Crimp deals with controlling insect swarms, a fascinating idea but treated as ridiculously melodramatic in its plot.

On the contents page, instead of the usual announcement of stories planned for the next issue, was a notice that *Amazing* would have a different kind of cover. Instead of story illustrations, we will see designs symbolizing science fiction. When the January 1933 *Amazing* appeared, the cover was indeed different. I remember going to my newsstand and seeing it at the top of a bundle of magazines that had just been opened. When I told the dealer that I wanted a copy of the new *Amazing Stories* I had to point to it; he was amazed. We see a symbolic spaceship and two globes symbolizing planets. The entire cover is in tones of blue, none of them bright, and the comet-tail logo is gone. At the upper left we read "SCIENTIFIC FICTION" and "Amazing Stories" is redesigned and centered. There are no story titles or authors' names.

A. Hyatt Verrill's *The Treasure of the Golden God* is the new two-part serial. It's an adventure story based on speculative anthropology relating to South America. Bob Olsen's Master of Mystery makes his final appearance in "The Pool of Death," another good story ruined by an illustration that shows the solution. Memorable this month is "Omega, the Man" by Lowell Howard Morrow, telling of the last human couple on Earth and the final depletion of Earth's water supply. It was Morrow's final appearance in the magazines, and his last was his best.

Two stories aroused reader protests. "The Last Earl" by Franklin W. Ryan was a traditional weird tale, and not a good one, and "Delilah" by Margarette W. Rea, was good, but not science fiction. It's a story about somnambulism and presented only facts known at the time.

The question in readers' minds as the year ended was, would the more respectable covers help or harm *Amazing's Stories*?

Only two issues of *Astounding* appeared in the last third of the year. The November issue features "The Passing of Ku Sui" by Anthony Gilmore, wherein Hawk Carse closes the case of the living-library brains and puts an end to Ku Sui's activities. A short-short story, "A Scientist Rises" by D. W. Hall, was acclaimed because the scientist sacrifices himself rather than allow a discovery that might be misused to become public.

November brought the only happy surprise of the year. The January 1933 issue restored the original title, *Astounding Stories of Super-Science*, and upon opening the issue, readers found a scientific editorial by Harry Bates, a question-and-answer department by an accredited scientist, and a promise from the editor that henceforth there would be more science in the stories. And even better; we were told that a new novel by Dr. Edward Elmer Smith, *Triplanetary*, would begin in the next issue.

The cover was one of Wesso's most charming, showing the golden city in Murray Leinster's "The Fifth-Dimension Tube," a sequel to "The Fifth-Dimension Catapult," which enhances the original story. The same can be said of "Under Arctic Ice" by H. G. Winter, a sequel to "Seed of the Arctic Ice." In the sequel, the problem is to rescue a submarine trapped by the seal-creatures.

The only science fiction in the October 1932 *Strange Tales* was "In the Lair of the Space Monsters" by Frank Belknap Long, a better tale than the title leads you to suspect: the space monsters are sympathetic creatures. There was no further science fiction in *Strange Tales*. The January 1933 issue, which went on sale in October 1932, had none, and it proved to be the final issue.

Argosy rounded out a good year of science fiction with two rousing serials, *Pirates of Venus* by Edgar Rice Burroughs starting in the September 17 issue, and *Burn, Witch, Burn* by A. Merritt in the October 22 issue. The Burroughs novel began a new series of interplanetary adventure, and was paralleled by his closest imitator, Otis Adelbert Kline, whose *Buccaneers of Venus* began as a six-part serial in the November *Weird Tales*. Fans of rousing space opera were thus well catered for in 1932.

Another interesting event of the year had started with an announcement in the September 1932 *Amazing Stories*. Under the headline "SCIENCE FICTION" was the following advertisement:

"The Advance Guard of Future Civilization." Masterful tales of fantastic adventure!!! Stirring action stories of astonishing science! Interplanetary voyages; atomic adventure; time traveling, etc. Masterpieces of pseudo-science by R. F. Starzl, David H. Keller, Ed Earl Repp, Hugh Langley, Ray Palmer, Edwin K. Sloat, Jerome Siegel, Bernard J. Kenton and others. Price: 15 cents per copy; $2.50 a year. Scientific fiction novelty presented with every yearly subscription. *Magazine is not sold on newsstands.* Send money order or cash at once to: SCIENCE FICTION, 10622 Kimberley Ave., Cleveland, Ohio.

I sent them a money order and did receive the promised bonus for a yearly subscription, although I forget what it was. But the first issue, which arrived shortly thereafter, was a shock. What I saw was a poorly mimeographed magazine with poorly drawn illustrations, and not a single known name on the contents page. The editorial apologized for the appearance of the magazine, but assured me that I would be enthralled by the fiction. I tried to read one clumsily written story and gave up. Thereafter, I just glanced at each issue as it came in, and noted that the art work by Joseph Schuster showed some talent, at least. But I refused to strain my eyes on the text. Siegel and Shuster would make their mark in the comics later, when they introduced a character called Superman. It was the first attempt to inaugurate a science fiction magazine produced by fans. There would be further misfire attempts later.

Here are my nominations for the best stories of 1932.

In the *Wonder* group, the best serials and novels were *The Time Stream* by John Taine, *The Final War* by Carl W. Spohr, *Brood of Helios* by John Bertin, and *The Death of Iron* by S. S. Held. The best novelettes and short stories were "The Reign of the Star-Death" by A. Rowley Hilliard, "A Conquest of Two Worlds" by Edmond Hamilton, "The Last Woman" by Thomas S. Gardner, "The Eternal World" by Clark Ashton Smith, "The Hell Planet" by Leslie F. Stone, and "The Planet of Youth" by Stanton A. Coblentz.

In the *Amazing* group, the best serials and novels were *Troyana* by S. P. Meek, *The Metal Doom* by David H. Keller, *A Voice Across the Years* by Fletcher Pratt and I. M. Stephens, and *Invaders from the Infinite* by John W. Campbell, Jr. The best novelettes and short stories were "Tumithak of the Corridors" by Charles R. Tanner, "No More Tomorrows" by David H. Keller, "The Ant with a Human Soul" by Bob Olsen, and "The King and the Pawn" by Seven Anderton.

In *Astounding* the best serial was *Wandl, the Invader* by Ray Cummings. The best novelettes and short stories were the Hawk Carse series, "The Affair of the Brains," "The Bluff of the Hawk" and "The Passing of Ku Sui" by Anthony Gilmore, "Hellhounds of the Cosmos" by Clifford D. Simak, and "Disowned" by Victor Endersby.

By the end of the year, even in its reduced size, *Wonder Stories* was the leading SF magazine.

41.

THE DARK DAYS, 1933

JANUARY-JUNE 1933

Statistically, 1933 was a bleak year for science fiction. The total number of magazine issues published in 1932 had been 39, exclusive of *Weird Tales* and *Strange Tales*. The equivalent for 1933 was 24. No science fiction monthly had twelve issues, although *Weird Tales* managed to produce twelve issues dated 1933. However, as the year seemed to spiral into darkness at the start, it ended on an optimistic note, as we shall see.

The year got off to an unauspicious start with the final issue of *Astounding Stories of Super-Science*. Dated March, it contained a good mix of stories. "The End of Time" was a wild and woolly but fascinating tale by Wallace West. When time stops, everyone goes into suspended animation! "The Death-Traps of FX-31" by Sewell Peaslee Wright was the last John Hanson story, and is up to the level of the series. (The "traps" are the dwelling places of a form of trapdoor spider on an alien planet.) Whether Wright wrote further tales in the series and was rejected, or whether he simply gave up is open to question. My guess is that he did not feel like carrying the series any further now that the Clayton *Astounding* was gone. "Wanderer of Infinity" by Harl Vincent is memorable for his characterization of the wanderer, a super-scientist with indefinitely extended mortality, who is atoning for former misdeeds when he was super-ambitious. And Murray Leinster's "Invasion" would be memorable if only for the fact that it tells of the struggle of the United Nations against Soviet aggression.

For all its shortcomings *Astounding Stories* had become well-liked, even by many who put it in last place, as I did. Its disappearance was considered a heavy blow. It did not fail because of poor sales. On the contrary, according to what Harry Bates told me in the '50s, the magazine had gone into the black in 1932. It was the publisher himself who failed. With *Astounding* gone, there were only two monthlies and one now misnomered *Quarterly* to stagger through the year.

The cover of the February *Wonder Stories* shows an enormous Moon close to Earth. It illustrates "The Moon Doom" by Nathaniel Salisbury, which was a deliberately unfinished story forming the basis for a new contest. Three further installments, between 3000 and 4000 words each, were to be written by the readers and the contest was open to all, amateurs and professionals. Each further installment would carry the story forward and parts two and three had to have cliff-hanging endings. It was planned for the second part to appear in the March issue but the time allowed was too short.

The memorable story in the February issue is "The Eternal Dictator" by Nathan Schachner, telling of a man with an infinitely extended lifetime. He eventually becomes world ruler simply because he is the oldest and wisest candidate; there is no seizure of power.

On the March cover, illustrating John Beynon Harris's novelette "Wanderers of Time," the slogan has given away to a story title: "The Robot Technocrat." The author, Nathan Schachner, is not mentioned there. The "technocrat" is a machine that predicts first-order probabilities, not inexorable futures. "The Man Who Awoke" by Laurence Manning, is a well-written and thought-out tale beginning a series. The protagonist travels to the future through suspended animation and first finds himself living in a world-forest civilization upon awakening. At the end of each episode, except for the final one, he goes back into time-suspension.

The April issue offered the first good news of the year: *Wonder Stories* resumed its former 100-page thickness and the price returned to 25¢. The cover story, "The Fatal Equation" by Arthur G. Stangland, is a murder mystery wherein the "solve" key of the integrator is gimmicked to give a fatal bolt of electricity to the operator. "Master of the Brain" is the second in Manning's "Man Who Awoke" series, telling of a society ruled by a great brain. Another series, "The Revolt of the Scientists," by Nathan Schachner, starts in this issue. The insurrectionary scientists are Technocrats, out to destroy the Price System and inaugurate Technocracy. Clark Ashton Smith's "The Light from Beyond" deals with a consciousness-raising drug which allows the taker to meet super-beings. Forrest J Ackerman, writing in Charles Hornig's *The Fantasy Fan*, expressed dislike of the story, though stressing that he regarded Smith's other stories highly. That set off *ad hominem* attacks on Ackerman from both the author and his friend and colleague, H. P. Lovecraft. Neither of the two authors show up well in the fray; Ackerman did not attack Smith, but only said he did not like a particular Smith story and said why, clearly enough. While I disagreed with Ackerman on that point, my sympathies were with him, and Smith and Lovecraft should have apologized for their intemperance after they had cooled down. Neither did, and Lovecraft bore a permanent grudge against Ackerman.

"The Forgotten Man of Space" by P. Schuyler Miller concentrates on a human, rather than scientific, aspect of interplanetary exploitation. The contest winner for part two of "The Moon Doom" was William Lichtenstein. None of the winners would be known writers, or would appear in the magazines again.

The May cover illustrates "The Visitors from Mlok" by Clark Ashton Smith. Aliens visit Earth, capture a man and, taking him back to their own world, operate on him so that he can live there and communicate with them. When they release him and send him back to Earth, he is completely unsuited for living there. "The City of Sleep" is the third in Laurence Manning's "Man Who Awoke" series and explores more fully the situation first described in "The City of the Living Dead" by Manning and Pratt. Leslie F. Stone's "Gulliver, 3000 AD" tells of an Earthman who lands in a Lilliputian-like culture on Jupiter. The second in Nathan Schachner's "The Revolt of the Scientists" series is "The Great Oil War," where the revolutionaries strike at the energy industry. Edmond Hamilton's "The Isle of Unreason" deals with a society where the rulers consider any sort of dissidence "unreasonable," and those who transgress are banished to a small island filled with other "unreasonables" who are given supplies, but must otherwise care for themselves. The story was very popular, but an important aspect of the theme would be handled better by Robert A. Heinlein in "Coventry" (*Astounding SF*, July 1940).

Paul's cover for the June *Wonder*, illustrating "Captive of the Crater" by D. D. Sharp, is among his finest. We see a spacesuited man falling headfirst into a Lunar crater. The crater goes beyond the Moon's center of gravity, and the man becomes a pendulum. "The Final Struggle" by Nathan Schachner concludes "The Revolt of the Scientists," wherein the Technocrats win and set about to build a new scientific civilization. In "The Individualists" by Laurence Manning, the fourth in "The Man Who Awoke" series, we find a totally anarchic culture made possible by super-science. No person is bound in any way to any other person, aside from mutual agreements, and there is no law applicable to all.

"Men of the Dark Comet" by Festus Pragnell deals with an encounter between two Earthmen and the intelligent, super-scientific beings of a passing comet. The aliens are friendly and co-operative, and the conflict in the story comes from the attitudes of the humans, one of whom accepts the comet-beings as benevolent while the other sees them as evil.

A new serial, *The Radio Terror* by Eugène Thebault, translated from the French, starts here. The "terror" is a misanthropic scientist who declares on French radio that he is the master of unknown forces and waves possessing an infinite power of destruction. He makes no demands, but simply announces that he is going to annihilate humanity and destroy Earth.

The following issue had no cover-date, but on the spine it is given as July-August, whilst only August appears on the contents page. Inside, an announcement informs us that the two issues have been combined because sales go down during the summer months. The cover shows a spaceship battered by meteors, with small lifeboats emerging from it, illustrating "Castaways on Deimos," a space adventure tale by J. Harvey Haggard.

In "The Elixir," Laurence Manning brings "The Man Who Awoke" series to a close, telling of a far-future society that has discovered a means of immortality. The level of invention and writing in the series was excellent and it is amongst the best works of its period. In "The Mystery of Planet Deep," by George A. Dye, a strange, deserted city is discovered under the sea. Super-scientific devices are still working, but the irruption of the explorers has a disastrous effect upon them. The machines manage to seal off the city against any further discovery. Upon escaping, the explorers decide to report officially that they hadn't discovered anything unusual.

"The Cosmic Horror" by Richard Searight deals with ball lightning, about which little was known at the time. Here a form of intelligent life in the form of ball lightning comes to Earth via a meteor and becomes a real menace. Although H. P. Lovecraft helped Searight with some of his writing, it is not believed that he had a hand in this one.

The concurrent issues of *Amazing Stories* were not as memorable overall as *Wonder*'s. The contents of *Amazing* remained the same, readable in general, but rarely offering anything new to long-standing readers. Letters commenting on the new-style covers began to appear in the March issue and most comments were favorable. The editor says that more readers approved of the new covers than disapproved. One reader suggests that symbolic covers alternate with the older-type illustrations, feeling that Sigmond would run out of ideas after a while. (He was right; they soon began to show a family resemblance to each other, even though each one was acceptable by itself.

The cover for the February *Amazing* is two-color, as all were after the first. This one shows globular spaceships encountering a symbolic dragon. The effect is pleasing. Aside from the conclusion of *The Treasure of the Golden God* by Verrill, one story in the February issue is memorable, though for the wrong reason. I recall thinking, when I first started to read "The Ho-Ming Gland" by Malcolm Afford, that here was a sequel to "The Gland Men of the Island" in the January 1931 *Wonder Stories*. But after reading another page or so I began to wonder. I put the magazine down and pulled out my copy of the original story. What we had here was not a sequel. It was the same story under a slightly different title.

What had happened? In his book *Reflections on the Moon Pool*, Sam Moskowitz relates the circumstances. Afford had submitted his manuscript to *Amazing Stories*, possibly in late 1929, certainly no later than early 1930. He heard nothing and, after a year, decided that the manuscript had been lost, and sent another copy to Gernsback's *Wonder Stories*. Either Dr. Sloane paid no attention to his competition, or, if "The Ho-Ming Gland" was the original title, he did not realize that he was reading a story that had already been published. Sloane, at this time, had no efficient staff, as Gernsback did, and was close to eighty years old. Memory failure may be the answer rather than ignoring the other magazines. Nevertheless, it was another embarrassing incident following the Merritt plagiarism. Letters had started to arrive at *Amazing*'s office about B. H. Barney's "Beyond the Veil of Time," including one from Merritt himself, who had objected to the story, stating that a great deal of it had been taken from "The Moon Pool" and "The Snake Mother." Sloane published an announcement of the fact in the June 1933 *Amazing* without either an apology or an explanation.

The Spring-Summer issue of *Amazing Stories Quarterly*, which went on sale early in January, also had a symbolic cover design by A. Sigmond, showing three spaceships setting off in different directions. The feature novel, *The Man from Tomorrow* by Stanton A. Coblentz, tells of a man from the twenty-third century brought accidently to the present by a fourth-dimensional device. He is a little man with a large head and claims superior intelligence. It's an amusing satire, but suffers from the necessary absence of Coblentz's strongest suit: imaginative descriptions of alien worlds and societies. Among the short stories is "The Valley of the Blind" by Abner J. Gelula, a spin-off from the better H. G. Wells story, "The Country of the Blind." At the end, the protagonist is blinded and starts a new life.

The March *Amazing* sees the first of two parts of *Beyond the End of Space* by John W. Campbell, Jr. Even at the time, it struck me as a minor work, and the plot is very reminiscent, in places, of *The Skylark of Space*. I suspect that the manuscript had been gathering dust at *Amazing*'s office for a number of years. "The Tomb of Time" by Richard Tooker is an enjoyable tale of interior-Earth exploration, for all its similarities to Jules Verne's *Journey to the Center of the Earth*. There's nothing new in Jack Williamson's "In the Scarlet Star," either. Here the mysteries of space-time results in one minute of our time equaling five year's subjective time to the explorer who returns alive but decidedly worn.

Two stories in the April issue are worth mentioning. "The Memory Stream" by Warren E. Sanders deals with racial memory, and is well written.

The other is Mike Ashley's nomination for the all-round worst story of the period, "Universal Merry-Go-Round" by Roger Bird. I can't think of a rival for that dubious honor; by comparison, any story by Joseph W. Skidmore comes across as competent. The first three pages suffice to give an impression of the whole. Professor Witherton invites his young assistant (the narrator) to look at a new planet which Witherton discovered a year ago but hasn't mentioned to anyone before. Witherton's plan to visit the planet is rooted in his theory that the ether of space is stationary aside from the so-called ether-drift that is too small to be relevant:

> "I have invented a machine that has the unusual ability to stand still in a world of motion. In reality, it will be pinned to the solid ether. We will sit perfectly still, while the Earth moves off and leaves us. Then we will wait just here where we are till, in the course of its cycle, the new planet X comes round and crosses our path."

They'll have to sit still for a year and three days, sealed in a big metal ball. "Unless we take every precaution, the monotony will drive us mad." But the two are not going alone. "We must have a girl along," he insisted, "a girl who can play a violin and keep us company through those long, quiet hours ..." The girl he has in mind is his attractive daughter. Unbeknown to our narrator the professor has been building his traveling sphere for a whole year. "Much of it was done in pieces out in the laboratory. But you could never have guessed that they were parts meant as parts of this." There are no windows in the sphere. Witherton explains: "You see, I realized that it would not be wise for us to look at the sights off in space, while we were shut up in here. They would be so strange and frightening that we could not look at them without becoming insane ..." How will they get the great ball out of the room? Oh, it will crash through the walls as the Earth moves away from it; they'll feel a slight shock, that's all. Thus, sanity is assured and the story continues, getting sillier as it goes along. Sometimes I wonder if the author intended it as a burlesque. Within the restrictions of the time, the Monty Python team could not have done better.

By comparison, the May issue has three outstanding stories. "Martian and Troglodyte" by Neil R. Jones, tells of a peaceful and mutually helpful encounter between visiting Martians and sub-humans. P. Schuyler Miller's "Jeremiah Jones, Alchemist" is a humorous tale about a scientific hoaxer, and "The Death Drum" by A. Hyatt Verrill tells of a deadly weapon invented by a South American Indian tribe based on the properties of sound.

The June issue features "Tumithak in Shawm" by Charles R. Tanner. In this sequel to "Tumithak of the Corridors," the hero's efforts have liberated the underground corridors from the invading Venusian, called Shelks, which occupy Earth, and are still in control on the surface. Tumithak now leads an expedition to the surface to challenge them. We would have to wait until 1941 for the next story in the series. We also see John Russell Fearn's debut with the start of a two-part serial, *The Intelligence Gigantic*, which displays his special imaginative qualities very well.

The July issue has two memorable stories. "Hibernation" by Abner J.

Gelula deals with a means of human hibernation that has been discovered, and is used by the government to deal with dissenters. "Unto Us a Child Is Born" by David H. Keller tells of a future wherein a couple must obtain permission to have a child.

The July issue also has the last, and most fascinating, of the symbolic covers. We see Earth at the lower right, with a tower on it topped by a radiant ball, from which circles of light are emerging. At the lower right is a spaceship, and at the upper right is a fish. Sigmond's signature does not appear on it and I read later in *Science Fiction Digest* that three other artists, including Leo Morey, had worked the original over.

Amazing Stories had deteriorated considerably, and I suspect that what kept it alive was the reduction in competition. Those of us who could afford to buy more than one magazine—and *Wonder Stories* was the favored one during the first half of the year—were so desperate for more science fiction, that we would not think of not buying each issue of *Amazing*.

The first half of the year was thus a sad one for science fiction fans. Many who hadn't bothered before turned to *Weird Tales*, which consistently ran weird-scientific stories, and to *Argosy*, which continued to run science fiction serials and novelettes, especially by Edgar Rice Burroughs, Ralph Milne Farley, and Murray Leinster. *Argosy* science fiction wasn't much like Gernsback SF, but offered enjoyable to excellent fantastic adventure, sometimes better written and plotted than was seen in either *Wonder Stories* or *Amazing*.

Weird Tales changed its cover date from one month ahead to concurrent. The May issue, due on sale on April 1, did not appear until April 15, and the June issue went on sale on June 1. Followers of the magazine feared, at first, that the delay meant either a folding or the return to bi-monthly publication, but the monthly schedule was maintained steadily after June 1, and for the rest of the Gernsback period. The best stories in *Weird Tales* in the first half of the year, was a rousing new serial from Jack Williamson called *Golden Blood* (April to September), "The Star-Roamers" by Edmond Hamilton (April), and "The Iron Man," about a giant robot, by Paul Ernst (June). Somehow, though, they were all substitutes for the real thing, which was very sadly lacking.

JULY-DECEMBER 1933

July 1933 saw only one science fiction issue: the August-September *Amazing Stories*. Morey is back on the cover illustrating "The Meteor-Men of Plaa" by Henry J. Kostkos, which deals with beings of the upper atmosphere. Walter Kateley appears with "Children of the Great Magma," telling of the discovery of the Garden of Eden and of a lost race dwelling there. "The Essence of Life" by Festus Pragnell, tells of friendly visiting Jovians and a serum that prolongs life and increases intelligence. "Across the Ages" by Allen Glasser tells of a man suddenly finding himself in imperial Rome. It was good reading, but I learned later, in *Science Fiction Digest*, that the story was an outright plagiarism. Glasser's career, both as a leading fan, and as a writer, ended with that exposure.

There's an announcement revealing that the next issue of *Amazing* will be dated October and appear on September 11. I also learned from *Science Fiction Digest* that with that issue *Amazing* would switch to pulp size.

Only one SF magazine appeared in August, the September-October issue of *Wonder Stories*. It maintained the magazine's standard. *The Radio Terror* ends, and there are three, strong complete stories. "Monsters of Callisto" by Edward H. Hinton tells of adventures on a Jovian satellite which is an aquasphere. "Spheres of Hell" by John Beynon Harris at first appears to be about a scientific menace from the East, but ends, convincingly, in comedy. "The Moon Tragedy" by Frank K. Kelly, his best since "The Light Bender," is the personal tragedy of two Earthmen, among the many sent to the Moon to start building homes for the people of overcrowded Earth.

There was an announcement that the next issue would be dated November, implying a return to a monthly schedule. Again, *Science Fiction Digest* brought the news of a reversion to pulp size with that issue.

Morey's cover for the October *Amazing Stories* illustrates Stanton A. Coblentz's novelette "The Men Without Shadows." They are superior but benevolent beings from Saturn, who come to Earth solely to help humanity solve its problems. The new serial is the two-part *When the Universe Shrank* by J. Lewis Burtt. The title indicates the course of the story, wherein the cultures of Earth and Mars, now closer together, clash.

A welcome surprise was the return of Professor Jameson and the Zoromes in "Into the Hydrosphere" by Neil R. Jones. The series would continue for the rest of the period. All the stories were novelettes, and the standards set by the first three in 1932 were maintained. Here was one extended series that did not run into the ground. Jones's imagination, and ability to make the faceless Zoromes interesting, make the series enjoyable reading still.

Two rather odd stories are also memorable. "Theft of the Washington Monument" by Robert Arthur tells how the entire structure is made to travel into the future. "The Tree Terror" by David H. Keller tells of a variety of club moss which grows sixty feet high and spreads.

With the October issue, *Amazing* resumed reprints, though usually only a short story per issue, but classic authors were favored and reader response was not enthusiastic.

September did bring a pleasant surprise, though. Completely unannounced, *Astounding Stories* appeared on the newsstands on the third Wednesday, under the Street & Smith banner. The first issue, dated October, was not overwhelming. I procrastinated several days before buying a copy. The cover scene suggested a lost-race adventure, not science fiction. Inside there were no familiar illustrators and only one of them, Paul Orban, showed any feeling for science fiction.

Worse still, several of the stories were clearly supernatural. In all there would be ten weird tales spread over the first three issues of the revived *Astounding*. The first thought is that these were left over in the inventory of the defunct Clayton *Strange Tales*. But that is very doubtful. The final issue of *Strange Tales* announced three stories as coming in the next issue: "The Valley of the Lost" by Robert E. Howard, "The Seed from the Sepulchre" by Clark Ashton Smith, and "The Case of the Crusader's Hand" by Gordon MacCreagh. Howard's story was returned to him—I ran a reproduction of Harry Bates's accompanying letter in *Magazine of Horror*. Smith's story appeared in the October 1933 *Weird Tales*, and "The Hand of St. Ury" by MacCreagh in the January 1951 *Weird Tales* certainly suggests that the author had revised his unpublished *Strange Tales* novelette for resubmission. It's difficult to believe that other manuscripts were not also returned to their authors when *Strange Tales* folded.

What's the explanation, then, for the weird stories in *Astounding*? Perhaps they decided to see if a mix of science fiction and weird tales would work. But I have another suggestion. It may be that they originally planned to revive *Strange Tales* as well, having purchased the title, and started to buy material for the first new issue. Then the plans were changed, and *Strange Tales*'s revival was aborted. But the purchased stories had to be used, so they were transferred to *Astounding*, and spread out over the first three issues.

The October *Astounding* was hardly memorable. There are four known names on the contents page: Paul Ernst, Donald Wandrei, Anthony Gilmore, and Nat Schachner. Gilmore's story, "The Coffin Ship," is an interplanetary adventure, and a distinct disappointment when we were hoping for more Hawk Carse stories. The single memorable item in the issue is "A Race Through Time" by Donald Wandrei, well illustrated by Orban. Here we have two time machines. The villain kidnaps the girl and sets out for the future with her, to the year one million a.d. The hero pursues and realizes too late that his rival had set his own time machine a million years ahead starting from the year 1, while he himself had started counting from the day he left in 1950. Both machines work one-way-only; neither can return to the past, so our hero is stranded on a dying Earth and his beloved has long since died.

In October 1933, we were back to three monthly science fiction magazines. With its November dated issue, *Wonder Stories* returned to monthly publication and also back to pulp size. That would be its final format change. On the editorial page we saw that David Lasser had been replaced as editor by Charles D. Hornig. Hornig was a young fan of the day, who had just started his own magazine, *The Fantasy Fan*. He was my age, 17, in 1933, and would have started his senior year in High School that September. I had graduated in June of that year because of a rapid shift from the first to the second grade when I started school—they found my reading ability was on the second-grade level. When Hornig started work (on August 7, 1933), the September-October issue of *Wonder Stories* had just gone on sale, and he had sufficient time to put the November isue together.

The new serial is Sidney Patzer's two-part *The Lunar Consul*, dealing with a scientific organization aiming at world rule. The Consul, who is its head, is never seen and is believed to have solved the secret of invisibility. In fact he has, though it's not what you assume. It's simply hypnotism, and its works perfectly. If people are told under hypnosis that they cannot see something or someone, then that thing or person becomes invisible to them. The fantastic element here is that of *mass* hypnotism, which has not yet proven to be 100% efficient, as it is in Patzer's story.

A new series by Laurence Manning begins here with "The Call of the Mech-Men." The stories center around the members of the Stranger Club whose motto is "Truth is Stranger than Fiction." No single member is common to all of the stories. The Mech-Men are an enclave of a race of intelligent machines stranded for centuries on the Boothia Peninusula.

Two fans writing in collaboration, make their debut: A. Fedor and Henry Hasse, with "The End of Tyme," a humorous tale of a man from the future who wants to make important changes in the events of the year 1932 and calls upon the editor of a science fiction magazine. Its title is *Future Fiction*.

The November *Amazing Stories* offers a novelette by John W. Campbell, Jr., dealing with an industrialist's attempts to destroy a new invention (and its inventor) which would put him out of business. Mortimer Weisinger makes his first appearance with "The Price of Peace," about a superweapon which, upon demonstration, terrifies the nations of the world into disarmament. At the end, after peace is triumphant, we learn that the weapon was a hoax, and the demonstration rigged. The theme would reappear twice in later issues of *Astounding* but Weisinger really pre-empted it.

The cover of *Astounding*'s November issue looks more like science fiction. Here we see a man dressed in the military costume of ancient Greece holding what looks like a Gorgon's head in his hand with some kind of rays emanating from it. They are trained on an aviator who is covered from head to toe, and is wearing a gas mask, while there is a scantily clad girl next to him. It illustrates "Beyond the Sphinx's Cave" by Murray Leinster, which has the theme that the gods of ancient Greece are real beings, still dwelling within Earth. No more plausible, but more fun to read, is "Plane People" by Wallace West, wherein a group of humans find themselves transported to an world where the inhabitants are two-dimensional. Their third dimension is so slight that they have no awareness that height or depth exists. Most popular in the issue was "Dead Star Station" by Jack Williamson, dealing with an old inventor at a space station, and his device which saves a ship from capture by the gravity of a dead star. And, though out of place in the magazine, "My Lady of the Tunnel" by Arthur J. Burks, is one of the most powerful weird tales of the year.

The December *Wonder Stories* starts a two-part serial, *Evolution Satellite*, by J. Harvey Haggard. Some mysterious force on the little world causes all life forms to advance then revert to simpler forms in a relatively short period of time. Noticeable differences can be observed in a few days, sometimes sooner. Clifton B. Kruse makes his debut with a future-war tale, "The Heat Destroyers." John Beynon Harris's "Invisible Monsters" is effectively done, but more memorable is "The Mole-Men of Mercury" by Arthur K. Barnes. That story has a protagonist who is not only a coward but loathsome in every other way. Events push him into action which proves to be valuable, and in the end he is considered a great hero by those who knew nothing else about him.

The December *Amazing Stories* has no serial, but readers welcomed "Time's Mausoleum," wherein Professor Jameson's adventures continue directly from Neil R. Jones's October novelette. Bob Olsen's "Four Dimensional Escape" is another in his series, and a short story, "A Vision of Venus" by Otis Adelbert Kline, was appreciated by those familiar with his Venus novels. It's a charming vignette set in the same background.

Also in November appeared the Winter 1934 issue of *Amazing Stories Quarterly*. I no longer have a copy, but memory will suffice. The cover illustrated the reprint of *The Second Deluge* by Garrett P. Serviss, which was most welcome to me and others who had heard of it but had not been able to obtain copies of the 1926-1927 issues where it had previously appeared. All the interior illustrations were new drawings by Morey, and most of them well done. Also welcome was the reprint of "The Menace" by Dr. David H. Keller from the Summer 1928 issue. The third reprint, "A Winter Amid the Ice" by Jules Verne, had not previously appeared in either the monthly or quarterly. I never got to reading it.

The December 1933 *Astounding Stories* was the last to contain weird tales, and the first to offer a type of story that the editor, F. Orlin Tremaine, labeled "thought variant." That label was to be confined to stories either presenting a new idea in science fiction, or a really new twist on a familiar one. The thought variant for this issue is "Ancestral Voices" by Nat Schachner which was heralded in the previous issue as being the most controversial story to be published in a science fiction magazine; Tremaine anticipated arguments about it continuing for years. Howard Brown's cover illustrated the Schachner story, and was decidedly science-fictional, as all covers would be from now on. We see the protagonist in his time machine, which has arrived in ancient Rome at a time when barbarians are attacking the city. A barbarian has entered the machine and our inventor is about to shoot him. He kills the barbarian. Because that did not happen in our history, where the man lived to breed, all his descendants suddenly vanish. Back in the twentieth century, thousands of people of all races and cultures disappear. Schachner's point is that nowadays there is no such thing as a "pure" race anywhere; we are all mixtures. The story did not raise even a modicum of the controversy expected. There were a few desultory arguments about whether one could go back into time and kill someone living then, but that was hardly a new objection.

A serial began in the issue, Charles Willard Diffin's two-parter *Land of the Lost*, dealing with a stratosphere world where matter, changed by cosmic energy, is invisible to surface dwellers a hundred miles below. In "Farewell to Earth" by Donald Wandrei, the protagonist finds the remnants of humanity, all of whom are descendants of his lost beloved and her kidnapper. They are about to abandon Earth for the planet of another sun.

The January 1934 *Wonder Stories* offered the start of one of the best-loved novels of the period, *The Exile of the Skies* by Richard Vaughan. In an unspecified future, where a world government controls earth, a super-scientist, Knute Savary, plans to overthrow it and become dictator. He is not a madman, and his plan is discovered and foiled bloodlessly. He is sentenced to perpetual exile from Earth, and the balance of the story tells of his wanderings, his regret over his folly, and his final salvation of Earth in a duel against deadly super-mental entities. He was joined in exile by a woman who initially sought vengeance against him, but then became his true and loving companion. The story has the cosmic sweep of Dr. Smith's Skylark tales, but with much better writing and characterization. It was reprinted in the Summer 1950 issue of *Fantastic Story Quarterly*, and in the late fifties, Thomas Bouregy wanted to publish it in hardcover. He even had a cover jacket done for it, which was later used for a different novel. What stopped him was that he could not make contact with the author or his estate and could therefore obtain no rights to reprint it. The story retains its excellence, but is now too outdated a form of science fiction for present-day publishers. Some oldtimers, like me, would buy it lovingly, but there are not enough of us!

Donald A. Wollheim made his debut in this same issue with "The Man from Ariel," telling of an alien visitor who is mortally wounded when his one-person ship crashes on Earth, but through mental communication manages to tell his story before he dies.

Dr. Edward Elmer Smith himself, competed against Vaughan in the January issue of *Amazing Stories*, where his four-part serial, *Triplanetary* began. It would later be subsumed into what became the first book in his complete "Lensman" series. I am among the minority who prefer the original, non-Boskonian, version. There is no doubt that the Smith serial was a boost to *Amazing*'s sagging reputation at the time. "The Lost Language" by Dr. David H. Keller, is another of his moving character studies that are only marginally science fiction. A little boy grows up speaking a language that no one understands, and no linguist can trace, and refuses to learn any other.

"Colossus" by Donald Wandrei was the thought variant in the January 1934 *Astounding*, and brought forth more controversy in the "Brass Tacks" letter column than did "Ancestral Voices." Many readers considered it a masterpiece; others considered it bad or nothing special. Since the theme of a man irrupting into another gigantic universe of which ours is but an atom was far from new, going back to "The Man from the Atom" by G. Peyton Wertenbaker ten years earlier, and the plot is sheer pulp formula, I side with the naysayers. Brown's cover, though, showing the golden space-ship undergoing lengthwise expansion as it speeds out into galactic space, is one of his most striking efforts.

Nat Schachner's "Redmask of the Outlands," a tale of the year 5000, where the inhabited world is a mixture of medieval city states and super-science, was well-liked and long remembered. Also in the issue is the first in a non-connected series of mundane short satires by Stanton A. Coblentz, all set on Earth. They were all more or less amusing, but all do not require specific comment. The first was entitled, "The Confession of Dr. De Kalb."

Science fiction had continued to appear in the non-SF pulps, though to a lesser degree. Edmond Hamilton continued to provide regular fare in *Weird Tales* such as "The Fire Creatures" (July) and "The Horror on the Asteroid" (September), matching Jack Williamson's "The Plutonian Horror" (October). But the big news of the year in that pulp was the debut of C. L. Moore with "Shambleau" (November), the first in a series dealing with interplanetary adventurer Northwest Smith and his Venusian sidekick, Yarol. All were highly imaginative and well written, and it would be some time before it was known that the initials masked the identity of a young lady, Catherine L. Moore. *Argosy*'s offerings were less impressive, though they included a new serial by Ray Cummings, *The Fire Planet* (September 23 start), and a new serial by Otis Adelbert Kline, *The Outlaws of Mars* (November 25 start).

1933 had also seen increased activity in the fan magazine field. Recovering from my disappointment with Siegel's *Science Fiction*, I took a chance and subscribed to *Science Fiction Digest*, ads for which had been running in *Amazing Stories* for some time. I was not disappointed. This magazine was printed, and all about science fiction and fantasy. The first issue I received included part two of the satirical "Alicia in Blunderland" by Nihil, who proved to be P. Schuyler Miller. The next issue brought forth a true novelty: the first part of a round-robin science fiction serial, *Cosmos*, each installment by a different author. Most were by known authors, who cheerfully donated their talents, amongst them David H. Keller, A. Merritt, E. E. Smith, Ralph Milne Farley, Otis Adelbert Kline, Arthur J. Burks, John W. Campbell, and Edmond Hamilton, who wound it all up at the end.

The Fantasy Fan, though started as a competitor to *Science Fiction Digest*, shifted its main concentration to weird and fantastic literature with the second issue, after Hornig became editor of *Wonder Stories*. Hornig proved to be both literate and tasteful, presenting fiction and poetry by Clark Ashton Smith (one story, "The Kingdom of the Worm," is among his best), H. P. Lovecraft, August Derleth, and others. The magazine endured into 1935, and old-timers consider it among the very best of the early fan magazines.

With fewer issues and thus fewer stories, there are less to choose from for the year's best. As Vaughan's *The Exile of the Skies* is predominantly a 1934 serial, I have excluded it from the following nominations, which means there are no novel-length works worthy of consideration.

From *Wonder Stories*, the best stories and novelettes were "The Visitors from Mlok" by Clark Ashton Smith, "Men of the Dark Comet" by Festus Pragnell, "The Moon Tragedy" by Frank K. Kelly, "The Call of the Mech-Men" by Laurence Manning, "The Mole-Men of Mercury" by Arthur K. Barnes, plus the series, "The Man Who Awoke" by Manning.

From *Amazing Stories*, "Omega, the Man" by Lowell Howard Morrow, "The Death Drum" by A. Hyatt Verrill, "Tumithak in Shawm" by Charles R. Tanner, and "The Men Without Shadows" by Stanton A. Coblentz.

From *Astounding Stories*, "Invasion" by Murray Leinster, "A Race Through Time" and "Farewell to Earth" by Donald Wandrei, "Plane People" by Wallace West, and "Ancestral Voices" by Nat Schachner. Honorable mention should go to two outstanding weird stories, "My Lady of the Tunnel" by Arthur J. Burks and "The Demon of the Flower" by Clark Ashton Smith.

42.

SCIENCE FICTION REBORN, 1934

JANUARY-JUNE 1934

The calendar year 1934 was the first stable one for science fiction magazines since 1928. Each of the three monthlies had twelve issues without changes in format, title, or price. Covers this year became more individual trademarks than before. For *Wonder Stories*, Paul's covers were always bright, presenting fantastic and usually thrilling scenes. Morey's for *Amazing Stories* had subdued colors and quiet scenes. Howard Brown also used subdued colors for *Astounding Stories* though his scenes were usually more exciting than Morey's. His human figures were generally good, although his females all seemed to be wearing clothes of a style around 1919, even in futuristic scenes. Frank R. Paul was the leader in the covers department.

The February *Wonder Stories* continued *The Exile of the Skies* by Richard Vaughan and offered two short stories with new ideas. "The Sublime Vigil" by Chester D. Cuthbert tells of the mysterious disappearance of a girl while she is climbing a small mountain with her fiancée. A "space warp" is offered as an explanation, but it is the writing and characterization that makes the story memorable. A new interior artist, Lumen Winter, who could draw human figures very well, shows the bereaved lover, now elderly. He is standing on the mountain at the point of his beloved's disappearance, hoping that some day the "warp" will bring her back. "The Spore Doom" tells of humans forced to build an underground civilization because Earth's surface has become uninhabitable. The author, Eando Binder, would became a "name" writer this year.

Less original, but notable, is "The Vengeance of a Scientist" by Abner J. Gelula, where invisibility is the means of a protagonist's revenge on those who had destroyed his medical career with false charges against him. The story is similar to W. F. Hammond's "The Grey Shadow" in the July 1930 *Amazing Detective Tales*.

"Xandulu," by Jack Williamson, begins in the March issue, and is another of his Merrittesque science fantasies, dealing with a lost race and a super-scientific menace. It's more a series of novelettes, the first two have pseudo-endings. "Martian Madness," by British author P. E. Cleator, is a story of a disastrous trip to Mars and an encounter with its hostile life-forms, from which only only one member of the expedition returns. It is memorable for being the last instance in the period where an author was charged with plagiarism. It was not until the July 1935 issue that we read in "The Reader Speaks" about the accusation. D. W. Holland of London, wrote:

> In March 1934 you published a story called "Martian Madness" by P. E. Cleator. You called it a gem. I recommend for your perusal a story written by Basil Tozer, "The Pioneers of Pike's Peak." In short, your "gem" is one of the worst pieces of literary

piracy that I have ever come across.

The editor replied:

> When "Martian Madness" by P. E. Cleator was first pub-
> lished, we received a letter from an Englishman stating that it
> was a plagiarism of "Pioneers of Pike's Peak." We had Mr.
> Cleator, also an Englishman, visit the fan who made the asser-
> tion, and it turned out that the latter party, who had stated that
> the story was a "word for word" copy, had greatly exaggerated
> and had not, in fact, even seen "Pioneers of Pike's Peak" for at
> least a couple of decades.
>
> The editors had been unable to get a copy of the story itself, so
> it remains unknown how much similarity there really is between
> the stwo stories. The charges of plagiarism went no further.

Kenneth Sterling was the youngest author (13) ever to sell a science fiction story to Hugo Gernsback. "The Brain-Eaters of Pluto" was sheer slapstick, compounded of puns and gags. Example:

> He was completely surrounded by Martians who were closing
> in. Being patriotic, they were all singing their national anthem,
> "Martian Through Georgia." Suddenly, Ray was struck with an
> idea. Quickly, he took out his oofus-woofus machine and shouted,
> "Quick, Henry, the Flit!" Immediately a flit gun appeared with
> which he sprayed the insect-men of Mars. The Martians, being
> insects, perished.

Gernsback and Hornig evidently considered it hilarious. They even went
to an unabridged dictionary to dig up peculiar-looking adjectives about it in
the blurb. Being a pun-lover, I got a number of laughs out of it at the time, and
Sterling had an instant reputation as a top science fiction humorist.

Outstanding in the March issue are Laurence Manning's "Caverns of
Horror," telling of Stranger Club members encountering some nasty survivals
in caverns underground, and "The Literary Corkscrew" by David H. Keller,
about a writer whose output was on the genius level when he was in any sort
of pain, but vapid nonsense when he felt well.

Paul's April cover is one of his effective Lunar scenes. It shows a spaceship surrounded by big-chested humanoids carrying boulders. Clearly, they
mean the ship no good. It illustrates "The Moon Devils," an adventure story
by John B. Harris. Somewhat stronger is "The Message from Space" by John
Edwards, about a message from Venus which enables Earth's peoples to protect themselves from cosmic disaster. This could pass well as an example of
Hornig's "new story" policy, but not so "The Land of Mighty Insects" by A. C.
Stimson. There was nothing new about an unexpectedly warm pocket in the
Arctic area, or about giant insects.

Most important in the April issue was the editorial announcing the formation of the Science Fiction League, and promising full details in the next issue. There is a reproduction of the League emblem showing Paul's drawing of

the spaceship *Geryon* (from his cover for "The Shot into Infinity") plunging through space with Earth in the background. From here on, every issue of *Wonder Stories* had a special department devoted to the League and its members' activities. It was, in effect, a fan magazine within a professional one, and did not displace "The Reader Speaks" which remained open to all and became larger in the Hornig period. It did, however, become fan-centered, although arguments about scientific aspects of various stories continued. Most of the published letters now were from readers on the High School or early college level.

Another excellent German novel, *Druso* by Friedrich Freksa, begins in the May issue. It tells of a group of people in the future traveling into the still-farther future by way of suspended animation. When they awaken, they find that the great civilization they left behind has been shattered by insectoid conquerors from the planet Druso. Earthmen are enslaved, with but a remnant trying to rebuild a scientific culture and to overcome the invaders. Epaminondas T. Snooks is back with "Traders in Treasures," not slapstick, but an ironic tale of the Antarctic. The activities of human explorers and a form of life there result in mutual benefit, though neither ever become aware of the others' existence.

The June issue features a long novelette by Kaye Raymond, "Into the Infinitesimal." There's nothing new about it—an excursion into the microcosm, where a world of humans like us is found. The world is doomed, and the story becomes a fantasy wherein the inhabitants are transformed into a kind of energy-life. And while "The Doorbell" by Dr. David H. Keller is one of his most effective scientific horror stories, it cannot be called science fiction—the device described could be constructed at the time by anyone with enough money.

The new serial in the July issue, *Enslaved Brains* by Eando Binder, takes an idea that isn't new in itself, but works out its implications thoroughly. A man who has been away from the United States for many years returns to find that technology has increased enormously, and that all the great machines are run by human brains, detached from the deceased. But, as in the "Hawk Carse" stories, the brains retain the consciousness of their former selves and suffer agony in their new condition.

Hornig's outstanding discovery is seen in this issue, a new author named Stanley G. Weinbaum, with "A Martian Odyssey." This humorous tale of a Martian expedition is the first to present aliens fully equal in intelligence to humans, but who do not think like humans. Tweel immediately became a favorite character, and many readers pleaded for a sequel.

"Voice of Atlantis" by Laurence Manning is a Stranger Club tale and tells of dimensional goggles which enable the user to see into the far past when the high and scientific civilization of Atlantis existed. Scientists of that time have also invented such goggles and are communicating with our far future. "The Last Shrine" by Chester D. Cuthbert deals with a lost race and the possibilities of hypnotism, without repeating the sort of plot one would expect.

While Charles D. Hornig sought out new writers and worked with them, and F. Orlin Tremaine aggressively went after all the well-known writers, offering better terms for new ideas, T. O'Conor Sloane, now in his 80s, apparently just read the stories that came in, selected those he thought would please his readers, and put them in his pile of manuscripts to be published when he could fit them in. *Amazing Stories* was well liked in England, but offered little competition to its lively rivals here. Nonetheless, many oldtime authors remained faithful to *Amazing* and continued to send in manuscripts, despite the long wait for publication and payment. The general tone of the magazine remained old-fashioned and there were no changes in format to give it the fresh appearance of the other two.

Terror Out of Space by H. Haverstock Hill (J. M. Walsh) started in the February *Amazing*. A slow-moving story, it tells of the coming of the Martians to Earth on a friendly mission. They take two Earth couples back to Mars with them and we learn of the "terror" that menaces both planets from an unknown world named Ados. "The Regenerative Wonder" by Winthrop W. Hawkins tells of a medical discovery whereby people can regrow accidently amputated parts, like a crustacean. W. Alexander had used the idea in 1929, but Hawkins does it better. Phil Nowlan's short story, "The Time Jumpers," takes a couple back to earlier times in American history; they see a landing of the Vikings, and later try unsuccessfully to warn General Braddock of what he's up against in his disastrous attempt to take Fort DuQuesne.

The March issue features a long novelette, "Peril Among the Drivers" by Bob Olsen, wherein an adventure-seeking young woman has her consciousness transferred to an ant. It maintains the enjoyable level of Olsen's other "ant" stories, but offers nothing new. Outstanding is "A Job of Blending," a short-short tale by Victor A. Endersby, wherein a Chicago tailor, harrassed by racketeers, uses his study of optics to make new and fantastic suits for them. The racketeers are all shortly thereafter killed crossing the streets: the suits make a perfect camouflage against the surroundings.

In the April issue, Francis Flagg's "The Mentanicals" tells of a future wherein the human race has been reduced to the animal level and the world is ruled by mechanical cylinder-shaper creatures.

The May issue has a symbolic cover. Morey made a painting of the line-cut illustration that used to appear on the contents page of the large-size *Amazing*, showing Jules Verne's tomb. His rendition is fuzzy, where the original was sharp and clear, and is on a flat, cobalt blue background. It remains my nomination for Morey's all-time poorest cover of the period.

Two new serials start in this issue: *The Lost City* by Milton R. Peril, in three parts, and *Measuring a Meridian* by Jules Verne, three parts extended to four. I must confess that I enjoyed the Peril novel at the time, but re-reading it was a shock. I didn't realize in 1934 how poor Peril's writing was. Randall Garrett told me about having read a short article that Charles R. Tanner wrote about the novel. His title was "A Peril of Great Price," whereupon Randy burst out laughing but, alas, couldn't recall any specific details. You might say, however, that where A. Hyatt Verrill's stories show a good *command* of English, Peril's work shows a great *commandeer* of English.

Fletcher Pratt makes his final appearance in this period as a writer (he continued to provide translations) with "Dr. Grimshaw's Sanatorium." The doctor's speciality was changing ordinary humans into three-foot midgets.

Walter Kateley makes his final appearance in the June issue with "Subjugating the Earth," wherein the centaur-like conquerors from another world are finally overcome. Abner J. Gelula's "Peace Weapons" tells of how a war was brought to a stop by releasing giant insects in the battle areas, which forced all military activity into killing the insect monsters instead of fellow humans.

A two-part serial by Dr. David H. Keller, *Life Everlasting*, starts in the July issue and is one of his best stories. A doctor discovers a serum that not only cures any disease that the patient may have, but restores youth and gives immunity to any further infection. It may even confer immortality, although we never find out for sure. The side effect is that it sterilizes the recipients. Bob Olsen's final fourth-dimensional tale is his humorous "The Fourth-Dimensional Auto Parker," a lovely idea which, of course, doesn't work out as well as it should. New author, George H. Scheer, Jr., is introduced with "Beam Transmission," the first of a series. It's a form of transmission which results in interplanetary travel without spaceships; but the plot is over-familiar, with the visiting Earthmen helping Good Guys against Bad Guys on another world.

The interior makeup of both *Amazing* and *Wonder* was standard in that all illustrations were full page. But in *Amazing* no effort was made to have every illustrated story start on the left-hand page. Many started with right-hand pages of type, and you had to turn the page to see the artwork. It didn't make looking through a new issue very exciting.

Wonder Stories's streamlined layouts were eye-catching and every illustrated story did start on a left-hand page, so that you saw the artwork at once. To do that, the endings of some stories had to be jumped to the back of the magazine, but that wasn't too annoying. There was a lively appearance to *Wonder Stories*, while *Amazing* looked rather drab. *Astounding*'s layouts were fluid. There might be full-page illustrations, or double-spreads, or part-page ones. You couldn't know in advance, and that added to the pleasure of leafing through a new issue. There was an Editor's Page, and it appeared where convenient for makeup purposes. It contained a short pep-talk by Tremaine and was always interesting, though never an instructional essay on an aspect of science. And there was a variety of illustrators, though not all first rate. Mark Marchioni started to appear in the February issue, and a couple of months later he would be joined by Elliot Dold, whose imagination and individual style soon made him a favorite. After a few months, Dold would dominate the magazine, but he never appeared exclusively in any issue.

The February *Astounding* starts a two-part serial, *Rebirth* by Thomas Calvert McClary, who was hitherto known as a western and adventure story writer. It tells of a scientific experiment whereby everyone in the world loses all memory of his or her past. Civilization falls to pieces at once, and the story is about building a new one from scratch, as the more intelligent people begin to comprehend what they see around them. It was immediately regarded as a classic, and still upholds its reputation.

McClary also had a short story in the issue, under the name of Calvin Peregoy. In "Shortwave Castle," the first of a series, Dr. Conklin has created a race of microscopic, intelligent non-human creatures and evolved them to the super-scientific stage of existence. From them he hopes to learn the solution to important problems in his own world. The tale is unexpectedly moving, with a tragic finale.

Tremaine showed that he appreciated good science-fiction humor when he ran "Scandal in the Fourth Dimension" by A. R. Long. Ms. Long describes the misadventures of a mathematics professor who manages to project himself into the fourth dimension—partly. His lower half is invisible, although he can still stand and walk, and his footsteps can be heard.

The March issue brought the only change in all three magazines this year. *Astounding* increased its size to 160 pages and now offered the most reading matter at the lowest price.

There are two thought-variants in addition to the conclusion of *Rebirth*. "Born of the Sun" by Jack Williamson is based on the occult concept that the planets are eggs of living creatures, which will some day hatch. The other, "The Man Who Stopped the Dust" by John Russell Fearn, is thought out very well. What would it be like if all the dust in Earth's atmosphere were removed? At first it seems to be a blessing, but Fearn then shows the liabilities of the action and why we need that dust.

"Manna from Mars" is Stanton A. Coblentz's satirical offering for the issue and is among his better ones. The Martians offer to send a wonder-food to Earth, which will solve all hunger problems. The very announcement has sharp repercussions, and in the end it remains uncertain as to whether or not it was a hoax. Also satirical is "The Retreat from Utopia" by Wallace West, telling of the future when all manner of prohibition laws against harmful substances—foods, drink, tobacco—as well as uncivil behavior, are strictly enforced.

Brown's April cover shows the most unusual-looking spaceship yet to appear on a science-fiction magazine. The rightly described "squat, monstrous" ship from Yarkand looks like a huge, black, pot-bellied stove on runners, with forward and rearward projections. A boom is projecting from the ship from which hangs a red box with a great eye in its center and gas fumes emanating from the bottom. It illustrates *The Legion of Space*, a six-part serial by Jack Williamson. That epic of the four-man expedition to Yarkand to rescue a girl who alone could assemble the weapon to destroy the monstrous Medusae that inhabit that world, was tremendously popular. There would be two sequels, and the character Giles Habibula, an old, ever-complaining, and seemingly cowardly soldier of the Legion who nevertheless comes through in a crisis, became an immediate favorite with the readers.

The thought variant is "He from Procyon" by Nat Schachner. The being from Procyon is a *deus ex machina* and appears only at the beginning and end. He instills into six humans, chosen at random, a temporary power: everyone who hears their voices is under irrestistible compulsion to obey them literally. Of course, one of them seeks to become a dictator.

"The Green Plague" by Stanton A. Coblentz is an anti-war cautionary tale. The plague is perfected for restricted use against the enemy, then gets out of hand. This issue also starts a reprint of Charles Fort's book *Lo!* which assembles together alleged events that are unexplainable by science as we know it. Tremaine considered the book a factual thought-variant! Reader response was varied and few shared the editor's enthusiasm.

There are two regular thought-variants in the May *Astounding*. "The Brain of Light" by John Russell Fearn, deals with super light-entities, beings of light itself, in the upper atmosphere. "The Blinding Shadows" by Donald Wandrei, tells of an experiment resulting in the irruption of three dimensional shadows of fourth-dimensional beings into our world. The results are not happy. Fearn's story was his first to be soundly criticized for elementary errors in science— optics, in this instance. Much better, and more worthy of being called a thought-variant, is "The Wall" by Howard W. Graham, Ph.D. (Donald Wandrei's brother). Here we have a paint with the quality of total impenetrability; it presents a wall that cuts off part of New York City from the rest.

Leading off the June *Astounding* is "Sidewise in Time" by Murray Leinster, entirely worthy of being called a thought-variant. It tells of a journey through different times, some real, others that might have been. It's the first "worlds of if" story and includes an episode in a triumphant Confederate States of America. The theme really demanded novel length treatment, but the story remains effective despite its sketchiness. Outstanding in this issue are "The World Wrecker" by Raymond Z. Gallun and "Rex" by Harl Vincent. Gallun tells of an experiment in exchanging objects between Earth and an alien world; it results in the unintentional destruction of that other world. In "Rex" we have a robot that is almost human. At the end it destroys itself in despair at not being able to achieve human traits, but that very act shows that it had actually done so.

July's thought-variant is "Before Earth Came" by John Russell Fearn, which reveals that our universe was constructed by an ancient race of superbeings and was intended to be the home of perfect people in a perfect world. The difficulty is that, in order to account for existing imperfections on Earth, the creators have to behave like idiots at crucial moments. "Dr. Lu-Mie" by Clifton B. Kruse is more worthy of the thought-variant label. It tells of an entomologist who is so sympathetic to termites that he becomes as one with them. No brief description can convey the feeling of the story, which is one of the finest of the period.

Weird Tales published one of its most popular serials in 1934, *The Solitary Hunters* by Dr. David H. Keller (January to March), which dealt with giant wasps. Each of the three installments was voted by the readers as the best item in each issue, the only time that ever happened with a serial. *Weird Tales* published a larger number of good SF stories in the first part of 1934 than at most other periods of its long history. Amongst them were "Explorers of the Ice Age" (January) and "Wizard's Isle" (June), both by Jack Williamson. Edmond Hamilton had "Thundering Worlds" (March) and the last of his Interplanetary Patrol series, "Corsairs of the Cosmos" (April). C. L. Moore continued her Northwest Smith series with "Black Thirst" (April) and "Scarlet Dream" (May), both top quality. *Argosy* was publishing less science fiction, though it did present one memorable item in "The Radiant Enemies" by R. F. Starzl (February 10), telling of a treasure in radium on a comet, and the weird beings there that guard it.

The fan magazines also lived up to their promise in 1934. In 1933, many fans had received material from William L. Crawford announcing a new magazine, *Unusual Stories*, for which he solicited subscriptions. It would be printed and contain unusual stories of high quality that the professional magazines would not print. After many months subscribers received an "advance issue," dated March 1934. It was not complete. It had an editorial, a profile of science fiction author Richard Tooker, and most of a story by Cyril G. Wates, "When the Waker Sleeps." That issue was never completed. The next we saw was a digest-sized magazine entitled *Marvel Tales*. The first issue included non-SF stories "Binding de Luxe" by David H. Keller and "Celephaïs" by H. P. Lovecraft, both of which had been announced for *Unusual Stories*. It was not, then, a rip-off like *Science Fiction*; readers did get a measure of the material advertized.

Science Fiction Digest changed its title to *Fantasy Magazine* at the start of the year. The name change was to allow it to cover the entire fantasy and SF world, including the whole of *Weird Tales*. In the April issue we saw "The Dead Woman" by David H. Keller. Harry Bates had written to Keller, betting him that he could not write a true horror story. Keller responded with "The Dead Woman," which Bates immediately accepted for *Strange Tales*. That magazine folded before it could be used and Bates sadly returned the manuscript. Keller sent it to *Weird Tales*, but Farnsworth Wright found it much too horrible. It finally saw magazine publication in America in the April 1939 *Strange Stories*.

With all this activity and promise, 1934 was shaping up to be the most exciting period in science fiction since the beginning.

JULY-DECEMBER 1934

In July we saw the final issue of *Amazing Stories Quarterly*, dated Fall 1934. It was again all reprint, but this time reprinting the original illustrations. Only Morey's cover shows new art work, and is a rather poor copy of one of Paul's drawings for the feature novel, *The Sunken World* by Stanton A. Coblentz. The short stories selected to fill the issue were neither poor nor notable.

There are two stories in the August 1934 *Wonder Stories* that are worth mentioning. In "The Return of Tyme" by A. Fedor and Henry Hasse, the editor of *Future Fiction* is again visited by the man from the future just as he is about to end it all in despair. *Future Fiction* is in dire straits, but Tyme brings with him a stack of future issues of the magazine to assure him that all is not lost; the magazine will survive and flourish. There's an amusing postscript by Mohammed Ulysses Socrates Fipps, head office boy of *Wonder Stories* (Gernsback himself) giving a different ending to the story and making it even more of a paradox. "The Men from Gayln" by E. Mantell, deals with an invasion by beings who prove to be our own distant descendants. Not a new idea, but nicely done.

The contents pages of *Wonder Stories* were always well filled, giving at first glance an impression that there were many stories in the issue. But not only all four departments, but also brief fillers, were listed. At times that could be misleading, especially when there were sometimes only four stories in an issue.

The September issue starts with a translation from the French, *The Fall of the Eiffel Tower*, a three-part serial by Charles de Richter. All over France buildings are collapsing, and ships falling to pieces and sinking. Notes are received from an unknown claiming credit for the disasters and warning that the world will be destroyed unless France and all other nations disarm at once. John Beynon Harris makes his final appearance for the period with "The Man from Beyond," which provides one of Paul's most colorful and pleasing covers. The "man" is an Earthman (a criminal) who is rescued in a bizarre way by the native Venusians. Taine of San Francisco reappears in "The Tree of Evil" by David H. Keller. The leaves of the tree are a form of narcotic that destroys the eater's sense of morality. Laurence Manning has an unusual short story in "The Living Galaxy"—a galaxy which is a single entity.

The October issue presents the most unpopular story of Hornig's editorship, "The Final Struggle" by Francesco Bivona. Not a single published letter had anything good to say about it, and all berated Hornig on his claim to be offering only "new" stories. The story was nothing but a hamhanded variation on *Frankenstein*. Much better is Eando Binder's novelette "The Thieves from Isot," telling of a Plutonian expedition to Earth which neither contacts nor menaces us, but simply sets up mining operations to obtain metals of which their home planet is short.

The November *Wonder Stories* is memorable for "Valley of Dreams," the sequel to "A Martian Odyssey" by Stanley G. Weinbaum, where again earthmen encounter the somewhat ostrich-like Tweel and his fellows. It was an excellent continuation of the first story. Starting this issue is *Dawn to Dusk*, in three parts, by Eando Binder. Several men go into suspended animation in order to see the future and two of them survive to meet the Last men on a dying Earth. It was well handled.

"Twenty-Five Centuries Late" by Philip Jacques Bartel is the first of a series, dealing with the far future, when all human beings are dwarfs with big heads. All were light-hearted tales that made pleasant reading but were otherwise unmemorable. Also light-hearted, but somewhat more memorable, is "One Prehistoric Night" under the name Philip Barshofsky. It tells of a Martian expedition to Earth in prehistoric times and its defeat by the local fauna. Paul's cover shows the Martian spaceship attacked by small, leaping dinosaurs that the diminutive Martians are trying to fend off with rayguns.

It was pleasing to see a conical spaceship taking off into a blue sky in snowy mountainous reaches on the December *Wonder Stories*. It was less pleasing to read the story, "The Alien Room" by W. P. Cockroft, and find that the cover had given the story away. We weren't supposed to know in advance that the mysterious room buried in the snows was part of an alien spaceship. Laurence Manning's "The Moth Message" is another Stranger Club tale, and while not as good as others in the series, is still engrossing. A message from the past is preserved on the wings of a certain species of moth. The message leads explorers to the remnants of a lost civilization. Also in this issue was the second most unpopular story from the Hornig period: "House of Monstrosities" by Edsel Newton, blurbed on the contents page as a tale of "hybrid horrors." It was another stale variation on the *Frankenstein* theme.

The January Science Fiction League department offered the first science fiction test for League members and announced that those who had a grade of 70 or higher would be awarded the degree of B.Stf. (Bachelor of Science Fiction). I joined the League then and sent in my test.

The Hidden Colony by Otfrid von Hanstein, the new serial, was a precursor to *Electropolis*, which had run in the Summer 1930 *Wonder Stories Quarterly*. There's a reference in that story to the mechanical farm of Wenzel Aporius, and that is what this story is about. It takes place in Yucatan, during the Great War, and was the last story to be translated by Fletcher Pratt, who was in France attending the Sorbonne during those years. He did not know until he asked me in the '50s that Gernsback had published his translation.

Dr. Keller's "One Way Tunnel" is well illustrated on the cover whereon Paul shows a futuristic New York covered in a glass dome. Saurian-like monsters swim in the water around it and rest on top of the dome, which is being attacked by a bomber. At the lower right we see the Statue of Liberty entirely cut off from the City. The story was one of Keller's wild but fascinating ones.

"Master of the Genes" by Edmond Hamilton is about a not-quite-mad-but-certainly-irresponsible scientist who experiments with gene control in the Amazon, producing monstrosities among the natives. There may be similarities here to the Bivona and Newton tales, but there is a difference. The monsters do not revolt, and the story derives from Wells's *The Island of Dr. Moreau* rather than from *Frankenstein.*

Morey's cover for the August 1934 *Amazing Stories* is a symbolic representation of *Life Everlasting.* We see a swarm of enticing nude female bodies spiralling skybound. In the lower lefthand corner, a doctor in a white coat apparently exhorts a woman with a baby. The issue presents the final installment of Keller's poignant and human story. When people realize that the wonderful panacea also sterilizes them, they decide that the price is too high to pay for possible immortality in perfect health. "The Velocity of Escape" is the first of a series by Joe W. Skidmore dealing with the duel between good super-scientist Donald Millstein and the evil super-scientist "The Falcon." I mention it only because the final story in the series is memorable.

Two new serials start in the September *Amazing Stories. The Moon Pirates* by Neil R. Jones, a two-parter, is the kind of story you'd expect to find in the early Clayton *Astounding*, momentarily exciting but nothing substantial. *Through the Andes*, a three-parter by A. Hyatt Verrill, is another of his enjoyable stories about lost civilizations in South America.

The feature novelette introduces new author, W. K. Sonneman, with "The Master Minds of Venus." The superior Venusians come to Earth to help us in our struggle against War, but take no action aside from furnishing equipment to an anti-war couple. By means of that they overcome the warmongers. The invention is a device whereby everyone who thinks of perpetrating violence against his or her fellow humans, on either a large or small scale, immediately gets a crippling headache.

The October issue has a memorably crude cover depicting the chief villain in *The Moon Pirates* training a ray on a prisoner, and melting his skull. However, the feature novelette, "The Pool of Life" by P. Schuyler Miller, is a powerful and original story of a hidden pool which attracts creatures of past eras of evolution. The proto-men emerging present a real menace.

Morey's November cover illustrates part three of *Through the Andes*, showing the protagonist up against the "god" of the secluded civilization. It proves to be a surviving dinosaur. Memorable, for the wrong reason, is the feature novelette "The Moon Waits," by H. L. G. Sullivan. The Lunarians seek to discourage flights to the Moon because of the nature of Earthmen. Fine idea, but what's wrong is that it involves a fixed tube between Earth and Moon through which the Lunarians travel. That carried poetic license in scientific matters too far and many readers objected. Dr. Sloane responded that he had wondered how many readers would catch that flaw! A new serial, *Land of Twilight* by Robert Page Preston, starts here. It's an *Argosy*-type adventure of a trip to Mercury and exploits amongst the primitive human civilization there.

Professor Jameson returns in the December issue in "The Sunless World" by Neil R. Jones. Henry J. Kostkos has a fascinating idea in "Men Created for Death"—human beings designed to mature at great speed, but who die of old age much sooner. They are the solution to the problem of a war in which America is otherwise outnumbered and outfought. The story drips with sentiment but the idea remains novel. "The Million Dollar Gland," wherein through gland operations a wealthy miser becomes a spendthrift, is W. Alexander's final appearance.

John W. Campbell, Jr.'s *The Contest for the Planets* is the new three-part serial starting in the January 1935 issue. The title would change to *The Conquest of the Planets* with the next issue, and we finally learned that it was supposed to be a series with the overall title "The Conquest of the Planets." The first episode was titled "Mother World" as it dealt with Earth. It tells of the overthrow of a cruel and corrupt world civilization by scientists working under cover, and is not among Campbell's best efforts.

The feature novelette is "The World Aflame" by Isaac R. Nathanson, telling of an attempt to unlock atomic power; the result is the destruction of Earth as one unlocked atom fires off others. That was indeed the main fear before events showed that exploding one type of atom would not set off a chain reaction amongst other kinds. "An Epos of Posi and Nega" is the latest in that series by Joe W. Skidmore. He had, no doubt from humility, dropped the more imposing name "Joseph," but he did not lose his pretentiousness. "Epos" should refer to poetry not prose!

Just how well versed F. Orlin Tremaine was in scientific matters remains debatable, but there's no doubt that he did not consider science fiction as a means of instructing people in science. Nor was he particularly concerned about the accuracy of the science in his stories. Hugo Gernsback looked at his new rival not so much with envy at the magazine's increasing popularity as with disdain at its disregard for what he considered worthwhile in science fiction. "Fairy tales for adults" was his opinion of many of the stories in *Astounding*. In one way Gernsback's contempt was valid, but Tremaine was making the first steps toward a type of science fiction wherein the science, while essential to the extent that you wouldn't have a story without it, was sublimated.

The August 1934 *Astounding* presented a new type face that was slightly thinner and allowed more characters per line. It was easy to read and looked more attractive, and most of all gave readers more words per page. The cover shows E. E. Smith's massive *Skylark III*. Brown's portrayal follows the one that Wesso had done for the final installment of that story, although Brown's is marred by what looks like rows of bolts around sections: Wesso's illustration in the October 1930 *Amazing Stories* showed the *Skylark Three* as completely seamless. But few readers cared enough to complain—or, as in my own case, were not able to compare the two illustrations at that time. At last we had another cosmic tale of Seaton and Crane versus DuQuesne, who was resurrected in a believable manner. *The Skylark of Valeron* would run for seven installments, but that annoyance was partly offset by the excellent illustrations by Dold.

"Dr. Conklin, Pacifist" by Calvin Peregoy, was the second in that series. Here Conklin discovers that the source of all man's vices lies in certain sections of the brain, and he invents a ray that interferes with their action. Does a perfect world result? Well, yes, in one way, but Conklin and everyone else discovers that the side effects, such as utter lack of ambition, are too much.

"Stratosphere Towers" by Nat Schachner is the first of an unconnected series about great super-scientific projects to benefit humanity but which some dictator or would-be dictator tries to take over; the resulting struggle sometimes ends with the annihilation of both the enemy and the project. In the first, the towers are efficient sources of solar energy. "The Last Men" by Frank Belknap Long is the first in a series about different far-future types of humanity subservient to some other form of life. In this tale the masters are giant insects, and great moths hunt humans as art objects. All the stories in the series are well done and moving.

The thought-variant for the September issue is "The Living Equation" by Nat Schachner, wherein the symbols in a super-computer take on a life of their own. "Famine on Mars" by Frank K. Kelly portrays the dying Martian civilization in its struggle to survive. It's not an Earth-Mars war tale, but a moving portrayal of altruism versus greed. "Dragon's Teeth" by Wallace West is a humorous story of ancient times wherein we learn that the gods of Greece were really members of an expedition from Mars. The idea was not new, but this version of Cadmus and the dragon's teeth, is delightfully done. Later West would expand his theme into a novel, *Lords of Atlantis* (1960), but this episode did not fit in. With the September issue the type in "Brass Tacks" was reduced allowing more letters to be published. It was a strain on the eyes, but few readers complained.

"Inflexure," the thought variant in the October issue, is the debut of Clyde Crane Campbell. Here a scientific experiment results in all times existing simultaneously on Earth. It's one of the few occasions when Tremaine published a story containing long footnotes. We would learn much later that the author's real name was H. L. Gold. Street & Smith would buy stories from an author who was Jewish, but not allow a Jewish-looking name to appear on its contents pages. That touch of anti-Semitism would remain in force until John W. Campbell managed to oust it from his magazines.

"The Vapor Death" by Frank Belknap Long is the second in his Last Men series. Here the Masters of Humanity are giant mechanical brains. "The Truth About the Psycho-Tector" is one of Stanton A. Coblentz's most biting short satires. The device is designed to reveal what your real talents are, and the inventor hopes to aid humanity by helping round pegs out of square holes, as it were. But few people want to know the truth about themselves and their potential. They seek out the "tester" so that they can be told that, however lowly their actual positions, they were really supposed to be great artists, authors, entertainers, scientists or leaders of men.

"The Bright Illusion" is C. L. Moore's first appearance in a science fiction magazine. It should have been labelled a thought-variant, as it presents a new idea: that beings of totally different types can experience love with each other, even though each looks repulsive to the other. E. E. Smith wrote in to say that he considered the story excellent, even though he did not agree with the idea.

Outstanding in the November issue is the debut of Don A. Stuart, whom no reader at the time suspected of being John W. Campbell, Jr. "Twilight" is the first appearance of a new direction in science fiction: the mood story, stressing character or vision with the scientific element subdued, though important. It became instantly popular. The thought-variant is "The Mole Pirate" by Murray Leinster. An important scientific discovery is hijacked by a master criminal. The "mole" is a vehicle which can interpenetrate matter and travel through apparently solid substance without touching it. Thus it can pass through the walls of a bank in its intangible mode, then solidify, so that those inside can emerge and loot the bank. "The Great Thirst" by Nat Schachner is the first story about heavy water, details of which had just come to light in the popular press. More on that later.

The December *Astounding* has three stories by John W. Campbell, Jr., and one of them, "The Irrelevant" (as Karl Van Campen) proved to be *the* controversial story that Tremaine thought he had when he published "Ancestral Voices" a year earlier. Arguments over whether or not the story disproves the law of conservation of energy started immediately in "Brass Tacks" and long letters pro and con appeared each issue for six months into 1935. The thought variant is the new serial, *The Mightiest Machine* by Campbell, and is my nomination for his best super-science novel, with a cosmic sweep rivalling E. E. Smith's. This story of exploration, wherein the protagonists irrupt into a different universe and help humans in their war of extermination against an alien form of intelligent life, is the first by Campbell in which specific plot elements are not immediately traceable to the earlier Skylark stories by Smith. Campbell's third story is "Atomic Power" by Don A. Stuart, wherein the conquest of the atom's energy involves unforeseen interferences with the universe.

Yet, despite those three blockbusters, most memorable in the issue is the novelette "Old Faithful" by Raymond Z. Gallun. A Martian scientist in a dying culture seeks communication with Earth and sets out to cross space. There is not even a suggestion of invasion or chicanery. The Martian, whom the humans call Old Faithful, is portrayed with compasion and readers mourned when his voyage to Earth proved fatal.

It is little surprise that many oldtimers regard the December 1934 *Astounding* as the single best issue of the science fiction pulps.

Frank K. Kelly makes his final appearance for the period in the January 1935 *Astounding* with "Star Ship Invincible" wherein a comparison is drawn between a supposed indestructible starship and the so-called unsinkable *Titanic*. It's an intensely warm tale of disaster, and Brown's cover illustration shows the weird distortions that two of the characters undergo when the ship enters the "sink hole" of space.

"Green Glory" by Frank Belknap Long is another of his Last men series; here the Masters of Humanity are great ants. Stanley G. Weinbaum had also now been lured to *Astounding*, and presented "Flight on Titan," an adventure tale of survival on that unfriendly world, that includes the author's touches of humor. It isn't up to the level of Weinbaum's first two stories, but is still top drawer. "Osa, the Killer" by Clifton B. Kruse tells of exploring the consciousness of a preying mantis. It lacks the punch of "Dr. Lu-Mie," but is nonetheless well done.

Weird Tales continued to run a number of quality weird-science stories. There was a further Northwest Smith story from C. L. Moore, "Dust of Gods" (August). "Through the Gates of the Silver Key" (July) by H. P. Lovecraft and E. Hoffmann Price can be considered a science-directed fantasy, while both "The Beast-Helper" by Frank Belknap Long and "The Distortion Out of Space" by Francis Flagg (both August) are science fiction.

The outstanding story of the year, however, outside the specialist pulps, was the fantastic *Creep, Shadow* by A. Merritt, his final complete novel, which ran in *Argosy* for September 8. It has a touch of the Merritt poetry without the incessant purple prose of his earlier stories.

All that made 1934 a phenomenal year and difficult to limit my choice for the best stories, but here they are.

Wonder Stories: serials, *The Exile of the Skies* by Richard Vaughan and *Druso* by Friedrich Freska. Short stories and novelettes: "A Martian Odyssey" and "Valley of Dreams" by Stanley G. Weinbaum, "The Sublime Vigil" by Chester D. Cuthbert, and "Caverns of Horror" by Laurence Manning.

Amazing Stories: serials, *Triplanetary* by Dr. E. E. Smith and *Life Everlasting* by Dr. David H. Keller. Short stories and novelettes: "A Job of Blending" by Victor A. Endersby, "Peril Among the Drivers" by Bob Olsen, and "The Pool of Life" by P. Schuyler Miller.

Astounding Stories: serials, *Rebirth* by Thomas Calvert McClary, *The Legion of Space* by Jack Williamson, and *The Skylark of Valeron* by Dr. E. E. Smith. Short stories and novelettes: "Short Wave Castle" by Calvin Peregoy, "Dr. Lu-Mie" by Clifton B. Kruse, "The Last Men" by Frank Belknap Long, "Famine on Mars" and "Star Ship Invincible" by Frank K. Kelly, "The Bright Illusion" by C. L. Moore, "Twilight" by Don A. Stuart, and "Old Faithful" by Raymond Z. Gallun.

Wonder Stories did offer some fine material in its 1934 issues but it remained substantially the same, issue after issue, except for the new excitement of the Science Fiction League. *Astounding*, however, offered a continuous surprise, growing each month so that, by September when the first anniversary issue of the Street & Smith magazine appeared, the difference between it and the October 1933 issue was truly astounding! For many readers it was now the leading science fiction magazine.

43.

WONDER'S DWINGLING LIGHT, 1935

JANUARY-JUNE 1935

There would be but one change during the first half of 1935, and even so it looked as if the stable period were here for good. Both *Wonder Stories* and *Amazing Stories* remained much as before, while *Astounding Stories* continued to grow.

The February *Wonder Stories* features "The Robot Aliens" by Eando Binder, and Paul's cover shows three of the massive creatures routing the United States army, though not apparently attacking them. They were not in fact hostile, but humankind had panicked at the sight of them. "The Fatal Glance" by Derwin Lesser (Charles D. Hornig), tells of a device that allows the viewer to see the surface of Mars as it really is. The sight proves so horrifying that one viewer dies on the spot and two others go insane. We're not told what they saw. The theme would be presented again, at greater length, by Nat Schachner two years later, in "Beyond Which Limits" (*Astounding Stories* February 1937). "The Truth Gas" by Edmond Hamilton is one of his rare comedies. A scientist has discovered a gas which, upon being inhaled, makes the subject incapable of saying anything that he or she does not believe to be the truth. The results are amusing. "The Life Detour" by Dr. David H. Keller, is the second story based upon heavy water. There would be one more, and I'll comment upon all three when we get to it.

The March issue starts one of Stanton A. Coblentz's best satires, *In Caverns Below*. While it takes place underground, here on Earth, we are able to encounter two bizarre human cultures that allow the author full sway for his imaginative descriptions and comments. "The Eternal Cycle" by Edmond Hamilton is more of a sketch than a story, but it still tells a story. A scientist has built a device through which he can go into the future and see the end of the universe. He kidnaps his rival and forces him to join him. They see the end of the universe, and immediately see a new universe begin. Eventually, though only a few hours to them subjectively, they return to what seems to be the same Earth they left, just in time to see themselves setting out.

"Pigments Is Pigments" by Mortimer Weisinger, is an amusing tale of scientific vengeance. Our protagonist, who has been swindled by a big industrialist, has developed a serum that can turn a white man black and vice versa. He succeeds in injecting his victim without him knowing and the next day the industrialist wakes up as black as the Ace of Spades. Our protagonist is now ready to make him an offer he cannot refuse.

"The Elixir of Progress" by Philip J. Bartel in the April issue, is the second in his twenty-fifth century series and deals, among other things, with the rediscovery of coffee. Dr. Thomas S. Gardner returns with a short tale, "The Insect World." Written as a report by the leader of an interstellar voyage of exploration to his superiors at home, it tells of a world nearly balanced between insect and mammal life and how he and his crew turn the balance in favor of the mammals. There is no description of the aliens; we know only that they are neither mammalian or insectoid themselves, and they're astonished to find signs of intelligence in the mammals of our Earth, millennia past.

Most interesting in the issue is "The Prophetic Voice" by Laurence Manning. A united and progressive humanity has learned how to communicate with its own descendants in the future. Suddenly comes a strange warning. Some kind of cataclysm is about to occur in our present within a few years. The communicator has no idea what it may be; he knows only that there is a long blank period, and that some people did survive. He suggests that humankind take refuge in caves and go into suspended animation, which they do. Eighty years later the world's peoples awake and return to the surface to rebuild such ravages that time has made. But they find no clue whatsoever to what happened on the surface during those eighty years. Was it all a hoax? The author leaves it up to the reader to decide.

The May issue starts *The Waltz of Death* by P. B. Maxon, a novel that had received an honorable mention in a prize contest run by *Liberty* magazine. It's borderline science fiction at best, but a good story with a scientific puzzle behind a mysterious death. In "The Living Machine," Dr. David H. Keller solves the problem of drunken or just careless driving by perfecting an automobile with a brain. There is no driver; the chief passenger gives oral commands for starting, stopping and turning, but cannot affect the speed.

With the June issue, the price of *Wonder Stories* was again dropped to fifteen cents, but this time without a reduction in pages. It was now the least expensive science fiction magazine, and a fair buy for the price. Paul's cover shows plant-like beings surrounding a man seated at a table and preventing him from pouring another drink. It illustrates "Seeds from Space," the last of the Stranger Club series by Laurence Manning, and generally considered the best. The "seeds" were from those giant, intelligent plants, which constitute a menace to humanity. It may not be the first story wherein humanity was saved from an alien menace by a drunk, but it's certainly the first where the protagonist was able to turn the trick precisely because he was a drunk.

"Pygmalion's Spectacles" by Stanley G. Weinbaum tells of an experiment wherein the subject believes he is living in a drama set up by the experimenter. More powerful is "Death from Within" by Sterling S. Cramer. What appears to be an unknown plague in an isolated community is actually an irruption of nasties from the fourth dimension. There are no heroics, or conquests on either side. The humans have to abandon the area in the end.

The July issue presents the final cover contest in a Gernsback science fiction magazine. Paul's scene is as strange as those on any of his other contest covers. We see the surface of a small planetary body on which there is a superscientific machine pointed at Earth in the sky. From a spaceship comes bolts of energy that are striking the machine and we see the strange, small alien beings suffering from the effects. If you look carefully at Earth you see that only the Americas are depicted. The prizes for the contest are another sign of the times. Only $25 is offered for the best short-short story written around the scene, with $10 in cash for the second prize, and $7.50 for third. (It is doubtful whether any of the prize-winners received their prizes.)

The new serial, *The Green Men of Graypec* by Festus Pragnell, is an adventure story wherein the consciousness of the narrator is transferred to that of a simian male on a microcosmic world, Kilsonia. Nothing new there. But the author's imagination is such that the story is fresh and new and the plot unpredictable. Kilsonia is inhabited by intelligent simians, human beings, and alien creatures currently dominating it, each with its own type of civilization. The story was deservedly popular and was published in hardcover in England as *The Green Man of Kilsonia* (1936).

Amazing Stories remained the same during the first six months of 1935 with a few stories worth mentioning. The February issue offers the final adventure of Taine of San Francisco to appear in the SF magazines, "Island of White Mice" by Dr. David H. Keller. It tells of a ruthless scientific experiment wherein the subjects (college men and women) would have been the victims, had it not been for Taine.

One thing that T. O'Conor Sloane could never be accused of was sensationalism. The Keller story is exciting and the situation unusual. But how does Sloane introduce the story? Thus:

> This is a narration in Dr. Keller's best vein. The author's many years of professional work in the realm of psychology gives the touch of authenticity to it. It is a study of human character under what may be termed difficult circumstances, and will be found an entertaining, almost cynical story of weak human nature, but the author's good humor pretty well disposes of any such aspect.

Breathtaking, isn't it? But Sloane wasn't always that enthused. More typical is this one for "Zora of the Zoromes" in the March issue:

> In presenting another of Neil R. Jones' "Jameson" series stories, we are acceding to the desires of many readers who have expressed the wish for more of Professor Jameson and the Zoromes. Again we are with these strange beings and we follow Professor Jameson in his adventures with them, who seems to be quite content with the strange society with which fate has thrown him into contact.

Princess Zora is a member of the humanoid race that inhabits Zor itself, most members of which become "machine-men" when death approaches. Zor is at war with another race of beings, the Mumes. When Zora's lover, Bext, is "killed," revived and made into a machine-man, Zora elects to become one herself immediately. The Zoromes add to their number constantly by adopting as machine men any other intelligent beings who are willing to join them.

A two-part serial, *Earth Rehabilitators, Consolidated* by Henry J. Kostkos, starts in the March issue. In the far future Earth has been abandoned and the remnants of humanity live on Saturn under the domination of the Saturnians. The Earthmen plan to reclaim their original world. Kostkos's imaginative touches lift the story above the simple "Good Earthguys vs. Bad Saturnians" plot and occasional mediocre writing.

The idea behind "Interference" by Max C. Sheridan retains its fascination, based as it is on wave mechanics, and a plot by the Japanese to send an invading army over a "solid" ocean. But the wisecracking style, which more or less pleased me in 1935, now makes the story less readable.

In the April issue we have a sequel to "The Call to Migrate" by H. M. Crimp. "The Mosquito Army" shows how control of insect migration defeats an attempted invasion of the United States when the invaders find that they have to fight not the unprepared Americans but millions of hungry mosquitos, well prepared to feed.

Liners of Time by John Russell Fearn, another serial announced as being in three episodes but extending to four, starts in the May issue. This is one of Fearn's best all-out fantasies, and no fault can be found with his science because it's all made up for the occasion. "The White City" by David H. Keller is a tale of attempted conquest of New York via weather control. Snow falls day after day on the city without let-up until it is banked two-hundred feet high. Everywhere else the winter is milder than usual.

A. Hyatt Verrill makes his last appearance in the period with a three-part serial, *The Inner World*, starting in the June issue. It deals with the report of a man who found his way into the interior of the Earth and discovered an insectoid civilization there. The creatures are friendly, but he finds that there is no way back for him. It's well written and the plot isn't predictable.

"Space War" by Neil R. Jones leads off the July issue and is a direct sequel to "Zora of the Zoromes." The war with the Mumes is concluded here. Most interesting in this issue is "Parasite" by Harl Vincent, telling of invisible alien creatures which attach themselves to humans and take control. Here is the prototype for Robert A. Heinlein's novel, *The Puppet Masters* (1951).

The February 1935 *Astounding Stories* is the strongest issue of any of the magazines in the first half of the year. Brown's cover is one of his best. It shows a huge multi-colored building that towers above the others, and is surrounded by glowing rings at its top. It illustrates "The Ultimate Metal" by Nat Schachner. The great skyscraper has been built of that super-metal, which proves to be unstable.

Two new series start in this issue. "Parasite Planet" by Stanley G. Weinbaum introduces Ham Hammond and Pat Burlingame in an adventure on Venus, filled with the author's floral and faunal inventiveness and humor. More serious is "The Machine" by Don A. Stuart, first of an unconnected series which develops a theme. Humanity is entirely dependent upon machines. However, the Master Machine shuts itself off forever and people must now take care of themselves. The results are immediate breakdown of society and a brutal period of savagery.

Two series end in this issue. The final story in Frank Belknap Long's Last Men series is "The Great Cold" telling of tiny human beings living in the sea, the Masters of which are the great crustaceans. Calvin Peregoy's Dr. Conklin series ends with "Shortwave Experiment," wherein the doctor combines experiments on peanut brittle with an attempt to raise his daughter's intelligence level.

No story is labelled thought variant in the March issue, although "Proxima Centauri" by Murray Leinster deserves it. This is the first tale of a generations-long voyage to a star. "Mind of the World" by Nat Schachner tells of an invention which allows all minds to be joined in the body of one man who will be the living library of the world, so that the combined knowledge of the world will be accessible to all for tapping. However, the man who volunteers to sacrifice his individuality has his own plans as to how he'll use his position. "Blindness" by Don A. Stuart is an ironic tale of a scientist who loses his eyesight in an expedition to venture near the Sun and learn the secret of atomic power. When he returns he finds that others have found a different source of abundant energy.

The Einstein Express, a two-part serial by J. George Frederick, is the thought variant for the April issue. it deals with galactic space exploration through dissociating human bodies and broadcasting them around the universe and back for re-assembly. "The Lotus Eaters" is the second in Stanley G. Weinbaum's Hammond-Burlingame series, notable for the character of the intelligent plant-like being, Oscar. In "Prowler of the Wastelands," Harl Vincent returns with the story of the creation of a super-evolved feline called Miracle. For once we do not have a disastrous ending to a great experiment, although Miracle deserts humanity to go back to the wild.

"Age" by Clyde Crane Campbell is the final story about heavy water to appear in the magazines. In the first, Nat Schachner's "The Great Thirst," we find that drinking heavy water is dehydrating leaving a terrible thirst. The villains in the story filter heavy water into the drinking supply of a small community and then profit from having the only source of fresh water. In Keller's "The Life Detour," drinking heavy water brings death within a short time. In "Age" the immediate effects of drinking heavy water are beneficial. It restores youth and vigor and accelerates the physical and mental abilities of the young. Then, suddenly, all who have taken it grow old immediately—burnout, as it were. The story proved to be quite controversial, and one of the fans who tore it to pieces was Ramon Alvarez del Rey, who would later become famous as Lester del Rey.

The May issue, again, does not list any story as a thought variant, although Eando Binder's "Set Your Course by the Stars" deserves the label. The first space-flier finds that he cannot orient himself once out of the Earth's atmosphere because there are so many more stars visible that space is not dark but filled with blinding light. We now know that such is not the case, but it was a plausible idea at the time.

The other outstanding story in the May issue is "The Escape" by Don A. Stuart, a tale of love and the lovers' attempt to escape the rigid rules of a future society. They run off together but are captured and psychologically conditioned to accept and love the mates that have been chosen for them. Campbell defied his readers to prove that that was not a happy ending.

The new serial is Twelve Eighty-Seven by John Taine and is the first novel to deal with an atomic war, but unlike any war that had occurred before. There are no overt hostilities. It's a war between chemists and relates to a form of nuclear dust that has the property of making any kind of soil enormously fertile. But there are side-effects. The dust is radio-active and everyone working with it comes down with fatal radiation sickness. It was not one of Taine's most popular stories—there is hardly any action—but it remains a powerful novel however outdated it may be.

When the June issue appeared with again no story being labelled as a thought variant, readers began to suspect that Tremaine had abandoned the label, which indeed, he had. Featured is "Alas, All Thinking" by Harry Bates, dealing with a time traveler from the far future wherein humans have become grotesque creatures with enormous heads and tiny, impotent bodies.

"The Invaders" is the second in Don A. Stuart's Machine series. We would learn later that it should be called "The Teachers" series. It takes place a century or so after "The Machine" when the alien Tharoo come to Earth and set out to restore the savage remnants of humanity to their potential. "The Orb of Probability" by Nat Schachner is another "anything can happen" type of story. Here, bored rebels in a too-perfect future world reintroduce uncertainty.

The July issue features "The Son of Old Faithful" by Raymond Z. Gallun, wherein the "son" of the Martian of the first story carries on his father's work successfully. Peaceful relations with Mars are established. "The Accursed Galaxy" is Edmond Hamilton's first appearance in the Tremaine *Astounding*, and he would not appear there frequently. It could have been called a thought variant. The reason for what appears to be the expanding universe is that the other galaxies are fleeing from ours which is accursed with the plague of life!

"Liquid Power" introduces a new author, Warner Van Lorne, who would appear as frequently in *Astounding* as Joseph W. Skidmore did in *Amazing*. The comparison is not inapt, as both were very poor writers, but Van Lorne occasionally had an idea that triumphed over his limitations. It would not be until many years later that it was established that Van Lorne was actually Nelson Tremaine, F. Orlin's brother. With one exception, all the Van Lorne stories were by Nelson.

A new series by Clifton B. Kruse starts in this issue with "Menace from Saturn." Kruse has a team of spacehounds caught up in various adventures and he tries to make them memorable, but all the stories read like modest imitations of Weinbaum and Williamson. They continued for nearly a year without arousing enthusiasm.

There was noticeably less science fiction outside the specialist pulps. *Weird Tales* ran one serial, *Rulers of the Future* (January to March), a powerful short novel by Paul Ernst, whilst *Argosy* ran two short stories by Ray Cummings, "The Moon Plot" (February 16) and "The Polar Light" (April 13). It was almost as if science fiction had at last found a strong and safe home in *Astounding*.

July-December 1935

The August *Wonder Stories* brought the first in a new series of humorous stories by Stanley G. Weinbaum, dealing with super-genius Van Manderpootz, who admits to being the greatest scientist the world has ever known. The narrator is a playboy and the professor's one-time student, Dixon Wells. Van Manderpootz has no interest in developing his inventions. Once he has proven his point he dismantles the device and goes on to another. The fun in the story comes from how Wells tries to use each invention to help him redeem a romantic failure. The results always turn out to be a fiasco. In the first, "The Worlds of If," the subjunctivizer will show the viewer what would have happened at any time in his or her life if he or she had done something different at a critical moment.

Another view of alternate realities is given in "The Branches of Time" by David R. Daniels, which deals with the actual exploration of possible time-worlds of the future. It's little more than a sketch, but well done. "The Reign of the Reptiles" by A. Connell, tells of a time-travel expedition into prehistory when reptiles not only ruled the Earth but had a super-scientific explanation. We learn that the human race was created in the reptiles' laboratory.

Weinbaum's Van Manderpootz returns in the September issue with "The Ideal." This device, the idealizator, enables one to view in detail what he or she is most attracted to, and see it in its ideal form. Naturally, Dixon Wells uses it to win his ideal woman, but fails. Philip J. Bartel's last twenty-fifth century story for this period is "The Hundredth Generation." An attempt is made to recreate human beings as they were in the past. The results are a winged race of cannibals. One final story in this series, "The Infinite Eye," appeared in the November 1939 *Future Fiction.*

The new serial is *World of the Mist* by Laurence Manning, a well-done variant on the theme of breakthrough into another dimension. "The Space Lens" by Millard Verne Gordon tells of a world which seems to be a replica of Earth. In fact, due to a spacewarp, the Lens gathers light from Earth as it was thousands of years ago. The by-line was a pseudonym for Donald A. Wollheim who had not been paid for his earlier story, now a year over due. Stories Wollheim had submitted under his own name after he began pestering *Wonder Stories* for payment had been rejected. So he used the Gordon alias and arranged to have the story mailed from a different address. The story was accepted promptly, but no money was forthcoming. The story of how Wollheim took legal and other action against Gernsback and his magazines is detailed in Ashley's section. Gernsback may have forgiven Wollheim in time, but his friend Louis H. Silberkleit never did. When I went to work for Columbia Publications in 1940 as a free-lance science fiction editor, I soon learned that the name Wollheim was anathema there. Silberkleit made it clear, without specifically saying so, that Wollheim's name was never to appear on Columbia's contents pages. That was why all of Don's stories that I used at Columbia were run under pseudonyms.

A new serial, *The Perfect World*, started in the October issue. Having read other stories by Benson Herbert I expected a good tale. The idea was good: the "perfect world" on which the Earth explorers land is actually a spaceship. What I did not expect was the way the story was written. It reads like a clumsy translation from the German, and nothing at all like his previous stories. "The Martian Gesture" by Alexander M. Phillips tells of a peaceful visit to Earth by the Martians, just after world civilization has been destroyed by War. The visitors find one living human being.

The next issue of *Wonder Stories* was dated December instead of November, and while the indicia still states the magazine is published monthly, box copy at the end of a story tells us that the November and December issues have been combined. The cover shows a scene from the top of the Empire State Building in New York City where a crowd is staring at a warship floating upside down in the air. It illustrates "Dream's End" by A. Connell, a fantasy based on the occult theory that what we consider reality is only the continuous dream of some godlike superbeing. The dreamer is on the point of awakening and reality begins to fragment.

The first prize winner from the July cover contest is "The Rays from the Asteroid" by R. D. Parkinson. It does not account for everything we saw on the cover. "Three from the Test Tube" by Raymond A. Palmer may be the first story to deal with children developed artificially from a fertilized human egg. It's sheer pulp melodrama.

December saw the February issue of *Wonder Stories*, again with the simple announcement of two issues being combined, with no explanation. The new serial, in two parts, is *A World Unseen* by Joseph W. Skidmore, and here his imagination and careful scientific study overcome his usual faults. The heroine has been shot by the Falcon. The bullet has lodged in her spine and attempts to remove it will almost certainly result in permanent paralysis. But our hero, Donald Millstein, has invented a means of size reduction and he and the doctor make themselves small enough to enter the girl's bloodstream, with all the equipment they need, and travel to the site of the bullet, there to work on it without severing crucial nerves. This was a brand new concept which would surface again, decades later, as the film *Fantastic Voyage*.

Weinbaum's third Van Manderpootz tale, "The Point of View," deals with his attitudinizer. With this device you can see the world exactly as some other person sees it. Again Dixon Wells manages to use it to frustrate himself. Had Weinbaum lived, there might have been at least one more story in the series before he ran out of ideas suitable for Van Manderpootz. As it is, the series ended before anyone grew tired of it. Kenneth Sterling's "The Bipeds of Bjhulu" is the second prize story from the July cover contest. it's an amusing satire on human history, a narrative rather than a story, and doesn't explain all we saw on the cover. It can be enjoyed without reference to its source. The best complete story in the issue, however, is "Isle of Gargoyles" by Dr. William Lemkin, dealing with hyperthyroidism and a small enclave of people suffering from it.

Amazing Stories for August 1935 features two novelettes. "The Kingdom of Thought" by Lloyd A. Eshbach was a fantastic adventure in the antarctic dealing with lost races and thought control. "The Golden Planetoid" by Stanton A. Coblentz is another satire dealing with benevolent super-beings who try to help Earthmen improve themselves and the victory of human stupidity over all odds. To someone who started reading SF with this issue, it could come across as effective, despite the idiocies of the narrator. It inspired an attractive cover illustration showing men protecting their eyes with shields, approaching a huge, glowing, spaceship-like mass.

On August 1, the new issue of *Amazing* had a small red rectangle cut out between the title and the price at the upper right which declared the date October 1935 instead of September. *Amazing* had gone bi-monthly. The cover is especially appealing, showing one of Morey's attractive spaceships cutting across the full face of the Moon. It illustrates "Another Dimension" by George H. Scheer, a sequel to "Beam Transmission." In this tale, the protagonists save Earth from invading aliens by going into another dimension.

All stories are complete in this issue and it leads with "A Legend of Posi and Nega" by Joseph W. Skidmore, the last published tale in that series, though others were planned before Skidmore's death in a car accident in January 1938. Outstanding in the issue is an anti-war story, "World Gone Mad" by Nat Schachner.

The December issue also presents all stories complete. The feature novelette is "The Fall of Mercury" by Leslie F. Stone, dealing with a degenerate

Saturnian culture on Mercury that seeks interplanetary conquest, and the co-operation between the home Saturnians and earthmen to quell it.

"The Meteor Miners" by L. A. Eshbach offers a new idea. No one had thought of the asteroid belt as a source of metals before. Years later, when Eshbach asked Dr. E. E. Smith where he got the idea for the meteor-miner sequence in *Gray Lensman*, Smith replied without hesitation, "I got it from you!"

The February 1936 contents page now acknowledges that the magazine is published bi-monthly, with this issue appearing on December 1, 1935. A new two-part serial, *The Maelstrom of Atlantis* by Joseph W. Skidmore, starts here. It tells of deep-sea exploration in a super-bathysphere which becomes disconnected from the mother ship. Lost Atlantis is found on the ocean floor. Morey at last gets the chance to portray a giant octopus on the cover! Outstanding in the issue is "When the Top Wobbled" by Victor A. Endersby, dealing with chaos and recovery in civilization when earth shifts markedly on its axis. "The Lurking Death" by Dr. Walter Rose is an effective tale of giant trap-door spiders which had escaped from a super-entomologist's laboratory in London.

Against the darkening glow of *Wonder* and *Amazing*, *Astounding* shone like a beacon. The August 1935 issue features "The Galactic Circle" by Jack Williamson, about an expedition around the "universe of size." The "ship" expands into infinity and finally returns to its starting place. With "Rebellion," Don A. Stuart's Teacher series ends. The humans overthrow Tharoo rulership, expel the aliens, and start their own super-scientific human civilization. "The Upper Level Road" is the single Warner Van Lorne story not written by Nelson Tremaine. F. Orlin Tremaine himself wrote that one. It's a dimensional story that many readers thought to be a new idea, but older readers recognized it as a spin-off of "The Gostak and the Doshes" by Miles J. Breuer from the March 1930 *Amazing Stories*. Tremaine's version, though, is more of an adventure than Breuer's, and not a satire.

Two authors make their debut here: R. R. Winterbotham with "The Star That Would Not Behave"—it proves to be a mirage, and Ross Rocklynne with "Man of Iron," about an attempt to make it possible for a man to penetrate metal. Both newcomers would become well known and well liked.

"The Son of Redmask" by Nat Schachner is a sequel to his "Redmask of the Outlands." It's an "overthrow-the-evil-Emperor" tale and lacks the charm of the first story. Outstanding in the issue is a short story, "The Phantom Dictator," wherein Wallace West anticipates the theme of Vance Packard's *The Hidden Persuaders*. A series of animated movies is design to put viewers into hypnotic sleep, at which point they are given commands for political action. West told me, years later, that his story had come out of an actual experiment made by some Hollywood animators. They made one such film and tested it on each other. It worked so well that they were horrified. They destroyed the film and refused to tell how they obtained the hypnotic effect.

Islands of the Sun, a two-part serial by Jack Williamson, starts in the September issue. It tells of human civilizations within the Sun's envelope before the planets were born, and has the over-familiar Williamson plot of one protagonist against an apparently invincible enemy. "W62 to Mercury" by Clifton B. Kruse continued the adventures of of Kar, Mardico, and Prock that began with "Menace from Saturn." The series is generally known as the W62 series, because all the stories, after the first, center around the small spaceship which conveys them around the solar system.

In "Earth Minus" by Donald Wandrei, an experiment which seeks to find the primal form of matter succeeds all to well and results in Earth and everything on it melting into primal form. Outstanding is "Greater Glories," a science fantasy by C. L. Moore, telling of an encounter with a composite, alien being.

The new serial starting in the October issue is *I Am Not God* by Nat Schachner. While the plot is the familiar one of humanity trying to survive a cloud of lethal gas from space, Schachner poses an important problem. Given that only a fraction of those who have succumbed to the gas can be restored, because supplies of the antidote are limited, who should be chosen to live?

"Night" by Don A. Stuart, is a sequel to "Twilight." Now we see the wonderful mechanical culture of the far-future continuing its operations after the last human being has died. The machines will run until they finally break down without any consciousness of what they are doing or why. Ham Hammond and Pat Burlingame appear in their third and last story, "The Planet of Doubt" by Stanley G. Weinbaum. That adventure takes place on Uranus and has the usual enjoyable mix of adventure, humor, and an ingenious solution to the scientific problem.

Charles Willard Diffin returns in the November issue with a four-part serial, *Blue Magic*. It is his best-plotted novel, dealing with time and far-flung worlds. At the end, back on Earth, we find that during the entire adventure, starting when a shipload of aliens kidnap the hero and heroine, only ninety minutes have elapsed.

"The Red Peri" by Stanley G. Weinbaum is the story which has been erroneously credited as the first to show that one could live for a few minutes in a total vacuum. That credit should go to Schachner and Zagat's "Exiles of the Moon" which we discussed in the 1931 chapter. It was clearly intended as a series about the female pirate known as the Red Peri, and the Earthman who loves her, but must capture her and bring her to justice.

Outstanding in this issue is "The Adaptive Ultimate" by John Jessel, telling of an experiment which makes the subject invulnerable. The girl involved can instantly adapt to anything, and part of the adaptation is transforming herself from a plain-looking waif into a stunning beauty. There is, of course, an Achilles's heel. Had not Weinbaum died at the year's end, it might have been longer before we discovered that he was Jessel.

In the December issue, Tremaine announced, regretfully, that Elliot Dold had been forced, by reasons of health, to retire from illustrating for the time being.

Two stories stand out in the issue: "The Mad Moon" by Stanley G. Weinbaum, filled with more of his fantastic and funny aliens, and "The Fourth-Dimensional Demonstrator" by Murray Leinster, about what turns out to be a duplication machine, and the amusing results of demonstrating it.

"Davy Jones's Ambassador" by Raymond Z. Gallun tells of an intelligent and scientific race of fish and a man whom they rescue from a wrecked submarine and put under observation. The one memorable point about "Forbidden Light" by James Montague, which Tremaine blurbed as "a tale of medieval science," is that it started a controversy in "Brass Tacks" as to whether lightning strikes down from the sky or up from the Earth. (I don't recall that any reader came up with the correct answer—namely, that an initial upward flash sets the path for the downward strike.) The story involves a "secret" science of the Middle Ages and the artificial monster which it creates.

The January 1936 issue features "Strange City" by Warner Van Lorne. The protagonist finds himself in a strange city indeed, with no idea of where he is or how he got there. Despite the clumsy writing, it remains a gripping story, one which requires a sequel because, while the hero wins over the opposition at the end, the fundamental question of where he is has not been answered.

Wesso returns to *Astounding* with this issue and his illustrations here and later would generally be very good. Here he illustrates "The Isotope Men" by Nat Schachner, about an experiment whereby the two warring elements in every person are split into two separate individuals, the dominant and the recessive. It's reminiscent of *Dr. Jekyll and Mr. Hyde* by Robert Louis Stevenson, but the origins do not matter; Schachner wrote an original story here.

The issue presents a collaboration between Stanley G. Weinbaum and Ralph Milne Farley, "Smothered Seas." There are Weinbaum touches, to be sure, but the story is essentially a Farley one, dealing with international intrigue and a scientific menace to the United States.

Hardly noticed was a short story dealing with future medicine, "Laboratory Co-Operator #3" by B. L. Bowen. It tells, very effectively, of an experiment in telepathic transfer, which saves the life of the patient.

The number of SF stories outside the specialist pulps continued to dwindle through 1935. Edmond Hamilton appeared frequently in *Weird Tales*. "The Six Sleepers" (October) tells of men from various periods who have entered a certain cave, gone into suspended animation from the gas there, and who all awake in the distant future. Nat Schachner would make better use of that idea in his "Past, Present and Future" series that started in the September 1937 *Astounding*. Hamilton's "The Great Brain of Kaldar" (December) concludes a swashbuckling interplanetary series that had started in *Weird Tales*'s short-lived companion *The Magic Carpet Magazine*.

Murray Leinster was the mainstay scientifictioneer in *Argosy* with two stories, "The Morrison Monument" (August 10), an interesting twist on the time travel theme, and "The Extra Intelligence" (November 30).

In the fan field, Charles D. Hornig was forced to discontinue *The Fantasy Fan*, despite its excellence, as it was becoming too expensive. *Fantasy Magazine* saw its third anniversary with the September issue which featured another round-robin experiment, *The Challenge from Beyond*. This time there were two stories, one weird, one SF, both based on the same title. The SF version was written by Stanley G. Weinbaum, Donald Wandrei, Edward E. Smith, Murray Leinster, and Harl Vincent. The weird version was by A. Merritt, C. L. Moore, H. P. Lovecraft, Robert E. Howard, and Frank Belknap Long. I remember Donald A. Wollheim drawing my attention in 1936 to how much better the writing was in the weird version. (Rereading today sustains that impression. What is interesting about the science-fiction version, is that it is more fantasy than science fiction, and could have appeared in *Weird*

Tales.)

My selection of the best stories of 1935 are as follows.

Wonder Stories: serials, *In Caverns Below* by Stanton A. Coblentz, *The Green Man of Graypec* by Festus Pragnell, and *World of the Mist* by Laurence Manning. Short stories and novelettes, "The Robot Aliens" by Eando Binder, "Seeds from Space" by Laurence Manning, the Van Manderpootz series by Stanley G. Weinbaum, and "The Martian Gesture" by Alexander M. Phillips.

Amazing Stories: no serials. Short stories and novelettes, "The Island of White Mice" by David H. Keller, "Parasite" by Harl Vincent, and "World Gone Mad" by Nat Schachner.

Astounding Stories: serials, *The Mightiest Machine* by John W. Campbell, Jr., and *Twelve Eighty-Seven* by John Taine. Short stories and novelettes, the Teacher series, "The Escape" and "Night" all by Don A. Stuart, "The Phantom Dictator" by Wallace West, "Greater Glories" by C. L. Moore, and "The Adaptive Ultimate" and "The Mad Moon" both by Stanley G. Weinbaum.

As 1935 ended *Astounding* now shone as the leading light in science fiction, and everything else around seemed darkness.

44.

THE END, 1936

With its February issue, *Astounding Stories* had trimmed edges, the first science fiction pulp to give its readers what so many had been asking for since 1930. It did so without raising its price or reducing the number of pages. Brown's cover for the new serial, *At the Mountains of Madness* by H. P. Lovecraft, shows two antarctic explorers fleeing from a green, jelly-like mass that is reaching out for them. The story itself was botched by Tremaine's cuts and by breaking Lovecraft's long paragraphs into short ones, which did not make easier reading; it just read as if the author did not know how to paragraph his long thoughts.

John Russell Fearn's novelette "Mathematica" is as wild as any of his other stories, but only a mathematician could find errors in it. A super-mathematics machine takes explorers into strange dimensions where super-alien cultures are found. The story remains fun to read and a sequel, "Mathematica Plus" in the May issue, would make it more fun.

Frank Belknap Long's "Cones" is a vivid picture of a strange life form, with which contact is fatal to humans, though the beings themselves are not hostile. "The Psycho-Power Conquest" by R. R. Winterbotham is an ironic tale of attempted conquest of Earth by aliens using a clever ploy that fails because they do not understand a particular human trait—greed.

The March 1936 *Astounding* features a long novelette, "Entropy" by Nat Schachner, dealing with a means to conquer space and time. Brown's cover shows part of the results: the protagonist and the girl are floating along a huge red beam. Each is encased in a bubble and neither can reach the other. Tremaine announces the death of Stanley G. Weinbaum and presents the first of his stories to be published posthumously, "Redemption Cairn." It has the feeling of a Western story. A framed man proves his innocence of charges of cowardice. "The Roaring Blot" by Frank Belknap Long tells of a mass of negative electrons and the havoc they cause upon striking Earth. While not one of its best issues, the March *Astounding* was still the best of the three magazines that appeared in February 1936.

The April 1936 *Amazing Stories* had an especially pleasing cover for "Labyrinth," a Professor Jameson novelette by Neil R. Jones. There was also an amusing novelette, "A Modern Comedy of Science" by Isaac R. Nathanson which tells how corruption in a small town was overcome by the Utopian Reformer, a retired schoolteacher who has worked out a means of invisibility. He calls on various malfeasors in the town's government and applies his cane vigorously to the proper area of their anatomies until they agree either to resign from office, restore what they've stolen, or both. They can neither see nor grapple with him. No one is killed or permanently injured, and the story is still fun to read. "The Intelligence Undying" by Edmond Hamilton deals with a future ruled benevolently by a man whose memories have been inherited entire from his predecessor, and so on back to the twentieth century.

It seems fitting that the final issue of a science fiction magazine published by Hugo Gernsback in this period should be dated almost exactly ten years after the April 1926 *Amazing* began it all. Paul's cover shows a spaceship emanating green rays which are boring a hole into the surface of a planetoid and lifting a small mass of material. It illustrates "World of Singing Crystals" by Thomas S. Gardner, a sequel to his "The Insect World." The alien explorers are removing a meteor that is poisoning the crystalline life. Nine complete short stories round out the issue, plus the conclusion of *A World Unseen*. Two of the tales are humorous. "The Cosmic Cocktail" by Siegfried Wagener deals with a device that concentrates moonlight; "The Imperfect Guess" by Philip Barshofsky tells about the ordeal of a hack science-fiction author who is visited by other dimensional beings he has described in his stories and who consider themselves libelled.

"Earth's Lucky Day" by Forrest J Ackerman and Francis Flagg tells of super-beings who come to Earth and prevent an impending war by confiscating all the important long-range weapons. All that people see of the aliens are giant hands reaching down and removing the weapons. "The Duplicate" by A. Connell anticipates cloning. A scientist makes an exact duplicate of himself except for the contents of his brain. It is completely under its creator's control. "Fate" by Alan Conn is a reader-cheater; the subject of the story, who has had his youth restored and is about to be protected against any possible disease, has a fatal accident just when the story is supposed to begin.

"Emotion Solution" by Arthur K. Barnes deals with an attempt to improve humanity by eliminating all emotion. The "solution" works as intended and the results are horrifying. The issue also contains "The Emotion Gas" by George F. Gatter, about a gas which can induce whatever emotion might be wanted. On the whole the final issue was a good one, though it could not compete with *Astounding*.

Why did *Wonder Stories* fail?

The economic condition had much to do with it, of course. Hugo Gernsback had run a small company, centered in technical magazines. None of them, nor all of them together, were sufficiently profitable to support a "hobby" magazine like *Wonder Stories* through long periods of loss, the way that Clayton had carried *Astounding Stories* at a loss for over two years. Liquid capital was short, but printers, engravers, office rent and staff had to be paid and on time. The authors and illustrators had to wait. If a particular writer stopped sending in manuscripts because he had not received payment for stories published a year or more ago, there were dozens of eager amateurs to take his place. Their stories could be put in shape by the editor. And eager young illustrators could be found, too.

But beyond that, Gernsback would have been in serious difficulties anyway. Once other pulp publishers discovered that a science fiction magazine could make money, they simply took the game away from him. They were not concerned about what science fiction meant to Gernsback, or to Gernsback's earlier readers. The public would buy action-adventure stories with pseudo-scientific trimmings.

The new authors discovered by Gernsback in *Amazing's* early years were mostly trained professionals who wrote in their spare time and were not primarily concerned with getting money for their manuscripts. But by the mid-thirties new writers were either professional pulp authors who occasionally turned to SF, or young men who had been reading the Gernsback magazines from their teens. Few of either group had thorough scientific educations, but fan writers knew science fiction and had imagination. They worked out innumerable variations on the stories they'd read and loved and often came up with reasonably plausible new ideas. As Donald A. Wollheim once noted, science fiction feeds on science fiction. And those newcomers expected to get paid for their efforts.

The story rooted in sound speculation on genuine scientific possibilities has never disappeared but, by 1936, it was becoming a minority exhibit in the magazines. In his later years, Gernsback felt that he had made a mistake bringing out science fiction magazines when he did, and that the public was not really ready for what he considered true science fiction.

If he had decided against it in 1926, would someone else have brought out such a magazine? Farnsworth Wright had certainly considered a magazine devoted entirely to weird-scientific tales. Had Wright persisted instead of Gernsback, it would have meant that the first "science fiction" magazine would have been a pulp, action-adventure title, with little or no emphasis on science. It's very doubtful that *The Skylark of Space* would have appeared in it, and there certainly would have been no vehicle for John W. Campbell, Jr. Nor would such a magazine have coined the term science fiction, and another phrase entirely may have come into common usage.

I think we can be sure that if Hugo Gernsback had not done it, no one else would have done it as thoroughly or so well.

APPENDIX I

MEMORIES OF WONDER

by Charles D. Hornig

The driving snow was stinging my face as I walked down West Grand Street in Elizabeth, New Jersey that mid-December morning in 1933. I was heading for the railroad station a half-mile away. The large black overcoat kept me quite snug—though its sinister appearance had caused me to be stopped and questioned by the officers in a police car only days before, while on the way to the home of a friend for an evening of good recorded music.

At the station I would pay two cents for a copy of the *New York Times* which I would peruse carefully for a half-hour on the train to New York City—facing another half-mile in the blizzard straight toward the Woolworth Building, that imposing Edwardian structure now cowering behind giant black monoliths. However, my destination was *behind* the Woolworth Building, at 98 Park Place, into the crowded loft offices of Gernsback Publications. Greeting me was a row of cluttered cubicles with little outside light—but to me it was paradise—for, at 17, I was Managing Editor of *Wonder Stories*, a science-fiction magazine with a circulation embracing the world! I could still not fully believe it. Not only was I doing the most fascinating and wonderful thing in the world, but I had the daily company, in my own cubicle, of the editors of the Gernsback science magazines: friendly, loud and Slavic Joe Kraus, and enigmatic C. P. Mason, with a voice reminiscent of Lionel Barrymore doing Dr. Gillespie. Between the smelly cigars of Joe Kraus and the equally offensive pipes of C. P. Mason, I had little in the way of fresh air to breathe, and to this day I am allergic to smoke.

C. P. Mason was an associate editor of *Wonder Stories*, but all he did was make his vast knowledge available to me for my "Science Questions and Answers" department. Occasionally I would trick him: for instance, there was the time I asked him which was the better fuel—lignite or anthracite. After a lengthy explanation to me as to why anthracite was best, I said, "Well, I guess it's true that there's no fuel like an old fuel." He chased me (playfully, thank goodness) with a pair of large shears for several minutes. We all had lots of fun. At this time, few people knew that Mason had written a few short science-fiction items under the name, "Epaminondas T. Snooks, D.T.G." Mason intended the latter to stand for "Death's Too Good," but it soon got converted to "Don't Tell Gernsback"!

The great Gernsback himself had the larger office at the far end of the hall. I seldom entered this inner sanctum, except to put manuscripts on his desk for final approval. What mysterious things went on in that office? I was especially puzzled one day when I heard the emissions of some contraption that made me very, very sleepy. It was all I could do to finish the afternoon's work. I learned later that he had been working further on his earlier invention, the "hypnobioscope," a device which was intended to teach students whilst they slept, but which also had a tendency to put one to sleep through the use of infra-low vibrations. This was used at the University of Florida in conjunction with recorded lessons so that students could learn while sleeping. The device was later discarded when it was learned that the students were as exhausted the next day as they would have been had they stayed awake and studied!

The artists for the Gernsback publications—including soft-spoken and always-smiling Frank R. Paul—worked in an even more dungeon-like loft on the floor above. At times I watched the miracles take place as Paul painted the next *Wonder Stories* cover, or dashed off a line-drawing. He enjoyed reading the stories in manuscript form, especially those he was to illustrate. Frequently, he would decide himself which scenes to use for his work.

I have always looked older than my age, and no one in the Gernsback office (except Mr. H. himself) knew my age until my article, "How to Write a Science Fiction Story," appeared in *Author and Journalist* in the spring of 1934. There it stated flatly that I was seventeen. C. P. Mason and Joe Kraus saw this and chided me as a "child prodigy." I assured them I had attained eighteen by then.

But where did it all start. How did I become "a child prodigy"? It was a fluke—or a combination of flukes—maybe a kind of synchronicity.

It's difficult to determine the exact moment when a great event enters one's life—in this case, science fiction? I guess I could date it from the thrill I experienced watching *The Golem* come to life at the turn of a key in an old silent movie my mother took me to see when I was seven, in 1923. It was certainly there in 1926 when I sat open-mouthed through the great *Metropolis* of Fritz Lang, and excitement hitherto unknown. Later, my elder sister bought a copy of *Weird Tales*, in June 1928, and then discarded it in disgust, a victim of lack of imagination. I retrieved it from the trash and read it with complete absorption, and to this day remember many of the stories in that issue in detail. But I was not old enough at twelve, to be hooked—and, of course, *Weird Tales* was only partly science fiction. Oddly enough, one of the ghost stories in that issue was written by a man who later became my sister's brother-in-law—Capwell Wycoff. I met him only once. His career was as a minister of some protestant church, and served as a missionary in the state of Kentucky. He was a very serious person and not interested in science-fiction.

On August 12, 1930, my mother gave me a quarter to go to the movies. But I had seen all of them then showing and sought a new form of amusement. By chance, I glanced at a local newsstand and found myself staring at a picture of a New York skyscraper being torn from its roots in a sea of flames. This captured me immediately, and I found myself buying the September 1930 issue of *Amazing Stories*. I was now fourteen and ready to be addicted. It worked. After avidly perusing the entire issue, I forced one of my friends to sit quietly while I read him one of the stories aloud.

Quarters were hard to come by in 1930, the beginning of the Great Depression, but I took whatever work I could find—delivering suits for a tailor, selling candy, peddling magazines door-to-door—anything, to get my hands on every issue of *Amazing Stories*, *Wonder Stories*, *Astounding Stories*, and *Weird Tales* as it was published. I was soon familiar with the entire field.

All during 1931 I lived in a science-fiction dream, all of my spare time devoted to securing, reading and carefully cataloging and cross-filing information on every bit of science fiction that was available. I had little money to acquire back issues, but I did find some marvelous used-magazine stories in New York City, even some specializing in science fiction, and they got all my spare cash. Slowly my collection grew. Eventually I secured every science fiction and fantasy publication in print at the time.

In the beginning, there was Fandom. It grew through young men (mostly) writing letters to the magazines and then to each other. The cradle of the movement was the readers' departments of the professional magazines. I was soon in touch with some of the leading fans of New York, having learned first of their initial fan magazine effort, *The Time Traveler*, printed by the hand-set method in Jamaica, New York, by Conrad H. Ruppert. Living close to new York, I frequently attended impromptu meetings of the first New York group, which included such early fans as Julius Schwartz, Mortimer Weisinger, Milton Kaletsky, and Connie Ruppert. We had no regular meeting place, though we usually spent hours on the balcony of some mid-town Automat Cafeteria, until we were thrown out by the management.

By the spring of 1933 it came to me, as it does to all good fans, that I should make the effort to publish a fan magazine of my own. Contacting many of the leading writers of the day—H. P. Lovecraft, Clark Ashton Smith, David H. Keller, Seabury Quinn, August W. Derleth, Eando Binder—I soon had on hand a large number of short stories. Fans contributed articles about writers and the field, and with the promise of Connie Ruppert to hand-set twelve pages and print two hundred and fifty copies for only ten dollars, I put together my first issue of *The Fantasy Fan*, dated September 1933. It ran for eighteen issues, ending with February 1935. I was so proud of that first number.

In order to obtain subscribers to *The Fantasy Fan*, I sent free copies to fans with letters in the prozines, and to all the editors of science-fiction magazines, including Hugo Gernsback.

In July 1933 I was working a full week for five dollars for a local lawyer, filling on while his secretary was on vacation. (It was an airless office in an old building in Elizabeth—the spot where, the year before, I had first been called "Mister." I was sixteen, and a passing shoe-shine boy asked, "Shine, Mister?" Now, time has a way of telescoping, and it doesn't seem that many years since I was first called a "dirty old man" and then, by someone with more manners, an "elderly gentleman." But all this is beside the point.) Anyway, I went home after work one day late in July 1933 and found a telegram under my door. It was from Hugo Gernsback, and it said, "If you can come into my office, I believe I have a proposition that will interest you." From here on it became like a Walter Mitty (or Horatio Alger) dream.

I was heralded in to the inner office of the great Hugo Gernsback with a lump in my throat. What could he possibly want me for? He showed a little disappointment. "I didn't think you were so young," he said. He went on to explain that his current editor of *Wonder Stories*, David Lasser, had become so involved in Socialism that he didn't have enough time to do his job properly and so Gernsback was looking for a new editor. (I found out later that he had another motive—to save considerable money on editing expenses.) He said that he liked my efforts in *The Fantasy Fan* and that he wanted someone like me, an enthusiastic fan, to do the job—but he now had some doubts about me, because of my age. I somehow assured him that I would be a good, faithful editor, completely devoted. There was no mention of talent. So, he gave me a novel in manuscript plus a mimeographed sheet listing proof-reading rules, and told me to go home and edit it over the week-end, and to check with my parents to see whether I could leave High School and go to work. We shook hands. He smiled slightly, and told me to come back on Monday morning.

I walked out of his office in a daze. I could not believe that it had happened. I had to tell someone about it right away. The first thing I did was to get on a north-bound L-train (the elevated railroad) and visit Allen Glasser in the Bronx. Allen was dutifully amazed. (You don't hear much about Allen Glasser now, because he was soon drummed out of science fiction as a plagiarist, but at the time he was one of the leading fans.) Leaving Glasser, I went across the Bronx to the home of Julius Schwartz. By this time I was beginning to believe it myself. Don't ask me why I didn't telephone instead of visiting—I was too confused to know *what* I was doing! My parents, being practical people (and poor), eagerly encouraged me to take the job and quit High School (which I did, making up one-and-a-half years of day-school in four years of night-school).

On Monday morning, Hugo Gernsback told me that he had decided to give me a chance, and asked me how much salary I would expect, reminding me that I was young and inexperienced. This being the depression, I meekly suggested twenty-five dollars a week. He said, "Let's say twenty to start." Had I known at the time about Gernsback's tight financial policy, I would have asked for $35 and maybe got $30. He had been paying Lasser $65 per week.

(Regarding salary: within six months I knew that I had been doing a good job, so I wrote Gernsback a note suggesting that I should now be paid a *real* salary, at least $50 per week. He called me in. We had a good laugh over my suggestion, and he increased me to $25. Another six months, and I was receiving $27.50—a lordly sum for those days, more than many a man was earning to support a family.)

Gernsback has long been known as a scientific genius and the father of modern science fiction, all of which is true. But he had a reputation among his employees and writers as a poor payer. He paid as little as he possibly could, and as late as he could, so that he had been sued many times. This was one deplorable fact about him that many believe kept him from going much further. So, why did anyone work for him? Because, aside from money, it was a joy. He allowed almost complete freedom of operation to his editors and encouraged innovation.

Having become Managing Editor of *Wonder Stories* I decided a change of policy was necessary on my own *The Fantasy Fan* to avoid conflict. *The Fantasy Fan* would henceforth emphasize weird and fantasy literature, with a minimum of science-fiction. This fanmag (like most), never made money—it wasn't intended to—but did consistently cost more to publish than it brought in. My professional editorship guaranteed that I would have the income to continue it (for eighteen issues), but it also almost meant its early demise. I had no occasion to present later issues to Gernsback, and he just took it for granted that I had discontinued publication of *TFF*. By the time it occurred to him to ask me about it, saying that he did not think it would be proper for me to have a fanmag on the side, *TFF* had already given up its ghost.

However, I cherish the memories of those marvelous Saturdays during that year and a half when I would visit Connie Ruppert in Jamaica, joined by Julius Schwartz and often Mort Weisinger. We would together collate and fold and staple the two hundred and fifty copies of the latest *TFF*. It's not only the fellowship I recall, but also Connie's father's secret-recipe German potato salad—the most marvelous I have ever tasted! Then, afterwards, lovingly guarding that little package of *TFF*s on the subway and train back to Elizabeth, there to address envelopes to the fifty or so subscribers. A. B. K. Goree of Austin, Texas, bought up most of the remainders. I wonder where they are now? My last full set went to Forrest J Ackerman to celebrate his fifty years in science fiction.

There has been some controversy about *The Fantasy Fan* insofar as I never copyrighted it. Everything I published, therefore, came into the public domain, which means anyone is free to reprint anything without permission or fee to anyone else. I used this fact as a ploy, once, to get under the skin of August W. Derleth, inheritor of H. P. Lovecraft material, who jealously guarded all rights to Lovecraft. Back in the fifties, I became miffed at Derleth's possessive attitude, and told him that I planned to publish an anthology of Lovecraft material, solely from the old *Fantasy Fan* files. It could include a lot of good stuff that I was first to print without copyright. Knowing he could not bully me out of it, or threaten to sue (infringing on his rights), he gave me a long, sad story of how unprofitable it would be for me to carry out this project—how I would lose my shirt, as he had done. Needless to say, I had no serious intention of putting out such a book—but I did get a rise out of Derleth!

Later issues of *The Fantasy Fan* were special issues, sporting a slick cover and dedicated to some writer or subject—H. P. Lovecraft, Clark Ashton Smith, fantasy poetry, short stories, and so on. I regretted that I was only able to publish, in serial form, half of Lovecraft's marvelous *Supernatural Horror in Literature* before the demise of *TFF*. This article was published in entirety previously in a small New England publication, *The Recluse*, but Lovecraft was updating it for *TFF*.

Life behind the Woolworth Building lasted only nine months. In May of 1934, Gernsback Publications moved to more spacious quarters at a newer building at 99 Hudson Street, about a mile further uptown. So, goodbye to the atmosphere of Lower Broadway, Wall Street, the Battery, and those lovely lunches with Frank R. Paul and other artists in the basement Automat across from the City Hall, when twenty-five cents would buy a most adequate meal.

Moving to the spacious offices at 99 Hudson Street was like being taken out of a dungeon and put on parole. I guess it was not unique to Gernsback Publications that we should, at times, be honored by the employment of European royalty—many such people would come through New York. The office secretary (whose services I never needed to use), was at one time a Russian count (who called himself Henry Roberts, and at times put on proper royal airs), and at another time a lovely Italian countess. She was twenty-one and ready for me, but alas, I was not ready for her.

Soon after we moved uptown, I was surprised to find myself visited by an unsmiling John W. Campbell, Jr. This was in 1934, and before he had become editor of *Astounding Stories*, though he was already quite famous in the field as a writer. In fact, by this time, he was so well known, that he felt it time to try and unload, again—this time to a new market (me)—many of his early unsaleable short stories. I was quite flattered by the pile of manuscripts he threw on my desk. He made it quite clear, in a most business-like way, that I could only have these stories if I paid him one cent per word—unheard of for Gernsback, who only paid his good friend Laurence Manning three-quarters of a cent, and that was tops. However, I told him I would tell Gernsback that nothing less than a cent would do for John W. Campbell. I perused the manuscripts, finding them all very amateurish and quite unusable, even for *Wonder Stories*, and so I returned them to Campbell, who never forgave me for this. Forever after he ostracized me, ignoring me completely at all future conventions and meetings, or would say something hostile. I lived to grovel before him some years later when I needed a job and suggested that I could be of some help to him on *Astounding Stories*—providing him with a cherished opportunity to reject *me*.

Two other authors were regulars at Gernsback's offices. Laurence Manning was a favorite of Gernsback's and the only one ever to receive three-quarters of a cent per word for his stories. He was a slight, though tallish, mild-mannered man, and quiet, and I don't think made a deep impression on anyone. David H. Keller was a favorite of everyone—very friendly, and full of fun. However, his manuscripts were the most difficult to edit—full of strike-overs and cross-outs with bad, if any, punctuation. I did visit him once in his home in Stroudsburg, Pennsylvania, straight across New Jersey about fifty miles from new York City.

I should say something about the New Policy that was instigated at *Wonder Stories* shortly after my arrival. This was my idea, and not Gernsback's. What I had in mind was the presentation of stories that lived up to the expectations of the magazine's name—*Wonder*. I wanted that essential sense of wonder in each yarn—that which distinguishes science fiction from every other kind of fiction. I did not want stories that merely transplanted western or detective stories to another planet. To my mind, a western transferred to Mars is not science fiction; it is still a western. Also, I wanted stories that were scientifically plausible, or at least possible, not pure fantasy. I remember turning down one yarn because it dealt with a tree that kept growing until it was thousands of times larger than the Earth. The author had not provided for the source of the physical material for this tree. I did not object to stories that contained logical flaws, such as time-travel or diminunization, because these themes were already in the core of the genre.

The full impact of the New Policy is difficult to judge. Most of the manuscripts received were unusable, but I always wrote letters of rejection explaining in detail why each story had to be turned down. This seemed to encourage a few to do better work and write material that was quite usable.

By pure luck, I was honored to introduce the work of Stanley G. Weinbaum. He sent me his story, "A Martian Odyssey," for my consideration, and I immediately recognized it as something superior. I raved about it to Mr. H., who liked it so much himself that he wrote for blurb for it. Poor unsuspecting Weinbaum was not aware of the marketing situation, and by pure chance sent his first manuscripts to the magazine paying the least—*Wonder*'s one-half-cent per word. Had he sent it to *Astounding*, he would certainly have received a cent a word, and perhaps a bonus. In fact, I was surprised to learn, only recently, that Weinbaum had never been paid for "A Martian Odyssey"!

Subsequently, I received more from Weinbaum, but I was soon approached by my friend, Julius Schwartz, who had by now turned authors' agent. He said he would like to correspond with Weinbaum, all of us being fans, and asked me for his address. I suspected he wanted this information for more than friendship, but I did have to feel sorry for the low payment Weinbaum was getting from us. Of course, as soon as Julie had the address he appealed to Weinbaum to let him market the stories at higher rates with other publications. So I lost sole control over Weinbaum. But I was not sorry, because I was firstly on the side of the writer. Fandom is thicker than editorship!

Which reminds me of the Science Fiction League. By 1934, Hugo Gernsback had formed the Radio league to help spread the good word about his radio publications and the rapid growth of radio. It was so successful that he decided to do the same thing for *Wonder Stories*, so he called me in one day and told me to start a Science Fiction League. He left it all up to me. So, a new department appeared in *Wonder Stories*, announcing it and offering to provide handsome chapter certificates free to any three or more fans who could get together in any one place. (Incidentally, I don't think it is generally known that these certificates were designed, in old English scroll, by Frank R. Paul.) Nothing else was free from *Wonder Stories*. We charged nominal rates for stationery, labels, and lapel buttons. From there on down, everything was voluntary, free, and democratic. But at the top, I made all the decisions. This became a sore point with the rival International Cosmos Science Club, who wanted to decide things for us. When you get right down to it, all we had was a nice bunch of young boys getting together to discuss science fiction in one of the world's first such clubs—spreading and growing rapidly with the sponsorship by *Wonder Stories*, whose prime motive was to sell more copies of the magazine.

Each member was given a number, according to the order in which his application was received. I remember that a George Gordon Clark of Brooklyn was member Number One and that Forrest J Ackerman became Honorary Member Number One.

During the following years I attended the meetings of a number of chapters, not only in New York and New Jersey, but also in Pennsylvania and California. California boasted the most famous chapter, the fastest growing and the oldest: the Los Angeles Science Fantasy Society, an outgrowth of the Los Angeles Science Fiction League, which still meets today. The last time I went to an LASFS meeting, I didn't know a soul there, and I didn't hear a word about science fiction. This is a far cry from 1938 and surrounding years when the LASFS and its members were practically my life-blood. We met weekly in the Little Brown Room at the rear of Clifton's Cafeteria at 7th and Broadway in the heart of Los Angeles. I spent many a glorious meeting there, and also Saturdays at the home of Russ Hodgkins where a number of us worked on the fanmag *Imagination* (I did an entire issue as guest editor in 1938). It was a true Mecca for the faithful.

It was in that Little Brown Room that I met Pogo—no, not the possum of the comic strip, but Mary Corinne Patti Gray. Pogo was an Esperanto diminutive for the initials P. G. Otherwise she was called Patti. During the thirties science fiction was a realm belonging to fans who were mostly teenage boys, so to find a *girl* in our midst, and actually interested in science fiction, was a novelty. She was the niece of Myrtle Douglas (Esperanto Morojo) and came from Gila Bend, Arizona. Patti was only sixteen in 1938, but fair game for the lonely introverted fans of the day, so many fell in love with her. I (a New York editor!) swept her off her feet for a few weeks until she came to her senses. I remember the night she let me know that our romance was over—I went off in dejection and wallowed in a double-malted. Today, I think there are enough female fans to go round!

The year 1934 saw me begin to travel, sporting the lordly salary of $25 per week. In June I took a special rail tour to Chicago with Connie Ruppert, there to visit with the local fans, including my first contact with Walt Dennis, Clifford Kornoelje (Jack Darrow), Earl Korshak, and others. Together we saw the great World's Fair of 1933-34. Connie was chided on the train by fellow tourists for revealing that he not only read Buck Rogers in the comic strips every day, but that he cut them out and pasted them in an album.

A couple of months later, Mort Weisinger decided to visit Chicago again with me, but this time on a "week-end rail excursion" from Philadelphia. First we had to get to Philadelphia by bus, and then find the railroad that was offering a special fair of $12 for the 1800-mile round-trip to Chicago. When we got to Philly we found that particular tour had already left, and we had to pay $16.50 each. Well, I had enough money, but Mort didn't, so he pawned a ring for $5 and I loaned him another $5. That still left us with not enough for food. We were on trains for most of the weekend, with about twelve hours in Chicago. When we got to the Midwest, Jack Darrow met us at the station—but he could only spare a dollar or two. We dropped in on Paul Ernst, but he was much too formal to mention money to. However, at the home of Otto, Earl, and Jack Binder, we found a jovial atmosphere (though their parents had pictures of Hitler on the walls), and we were soon in their basement drinking beer from a keg. This was the first time I had ever enjoyed a glass of beer, and two glasses on an empty stomach made me quite carefree. Further, Otto was good for a $5 loan. Mort and I finally travelled the thousand miles back home on two ham sandwiches and two cups of coffee each. It was a minimum voyage in every way, and not a bed for our heads the whole trip!

Aside from trips taken during vacation time, I found another way of sneaking in time-out for extra wanderings—"good-will tours." Gernsback was always willing for me to take off a few days to visit writers, artists and fans in other parts of the country. One ten-day trip taken at the end of 1935 I have documented with a few old-time black-and-white photos taken with a Brownie 2 box camera. A couple of pleasant days were spent with Clay Ferguson, fan and fan artist in Roanoke, Virginia. There I sampled his mother's *real* southern-friend chicken. I recall Clay's father was a policeman. Further south I dropped in on Thomas S. Gardner, popular author, who showed me over the campus of the University of Tennessee at Knoxville.

A shorter trip, during which I drove my ancient 1926 Nash well over a thousand miles (stopping every hundred to put in another quart of oil), I was accompanied by my good friend Julius Schwartz. This was over Labor Day, 1935. We spent the first night with Lloyd Eshbach at his home in Reading, PA, then spent a short time with the female author Amelia Reynolds Long at her place in Harrisburg, capital city of Pennsylvania. She was garbed in clothing from at least a half-century earlier, with long dress and laced boots, and we noted she could not seem to focus her eyes which were constantly shifting. Later in the same day we met for the first time, William Crawford, then beginning to publish his semi-pro publications in Everett, PA, and Richard A. Frank, a visiting fan from Millheim, PA. Both later became close friends, most particularly Rich Frank, whose little town of Millheim I returned to many times in the next few years. The next day, after a fitful night in a cheap railside hotel in Steubenville, Ohio, a glorious drive down the Ohio river through West Virginia, we wound up in the evening in Washington, DC to chat for several hours with female writer Leslie F. Stone and her husband. By the time we left the Stone's apartment it was after midnight and, Congress being in session, there were no hotel rooms available in the city. By two in the morning we had found a room in Alexandria, Virginia.

The most glorious trip I took while with Gernsback was in the summer of 1935, when I decided to go all the way to California: bus to Chicago, special rail tour to Los Angeles, Portland, Seattle, Minneapolis and home. Of course, I was most anxious to visit L.A. with all its fans, and see Hollywood and the stars. The first person I phoned in L.A. was Forrest J Ackerman, already, at nineteen, the World's Number One Science-Fiction Fan, and with a collection to overrun his grand-parents' apartment in Hollywood. We saw a lot of L.A. together, and even haunted the studios to get movie-stars' autographs.

And so the years went pleasantly by with Gernsback—well, the two-and-a-half years—and I enjoyed every minute of them. New artists, like Charles Schneeman, came looking for work, and I eagerly introduced several of them. I have often wondered how much I have missed out in human relationships as the editor on the bottom of the pile—the one who could pay the least, and then only after long delays, even to the point of lawsuit. I know that consciously no one blamed me for Gernsback's poor financial behavior, but nevertheless many authors must have thought of me in a negative connotation because I was in the middle of it all. A remark would be made to me once in a while, but only once was I threatened.

This happened at a meeting of the New York Science Fiction League in the High School of Commerce in Manhattan in December 1935. We had, by that time, a large number of members in the city, and I had called the meeting. Shortly after we began we heard a large number of determined footsteps in the corridors and in burst William S. Sykora, Donald A. Wollheim, and about a dozen tough-looking non-science-fiction-looking characters. The toughs went directly to the rear of the classroom and sat down. Wollheim took a seat near the front. Bill Sykora walked up to me at the desk and said: "Okay, Charlie, just take a seat and you won't be hurt." Taken completely by surprise, and not being a hero in any case, I did what I was told.

Donald A. Wollheim then stood before the meeting and read a long diatribe against Gernsback, denouncing him for not paying his authors. Some months earlier I had accepted a story by Wollheim and published it. He was due twenty-five dollars and he had not yet received his money. When all this was over, Sykora came up to me and said, very friendly, "Okay, Charlie, you can go ahead with your meeting." Then both he and Wollheim took seats, saying nothing during the remainder of the rather tense evening.

When the meeting was over, Sykora and his gang left first. Schwartz was with me and as we were about to leave—the last ones to go—Julie noticed that Sykora and his toughs were hanging around the front of the school. Julie turned a little pale. I'm sure I did too, but I could not directly observe it! Fortunately the school janitor then arrived. He sized up the situation and led us to a basement exit onto another street. Julie and I made for the nearest subway entrance, a little uneasy waiting for the first train. We could picture that gang descending the subway stairs while we were still on the platform.

Not many exciting things happened while I was working for Gernsback, but I don't think I (or anyone else) has ever mentioned the evening when someone brought in some "stag" movies, and showed them to the men in the office after close of business at 5.00 p.m. They were projected on a translucent door of a stock room. It should be mentioned that Gernsback did not attend. We later learned that some of the girls in the next office were also enjoying the movies on the other side of the translucent door!

And so it went. Late in 1935 I received a request from a publisher in Finland to translate and issue some of our work. I went to Irving Mannheimer, our business manager, with the letter. He agreed the proposition and, as I left, I punned: "Well, I guess this is the Finnish of *Wonder Stories!*" Mannheimer, without a smile, looked up at me and said, "You bet it is!" A few months later, *Wonder Stories* was gone. Gernsback could not make it pay and, desperately tried to save it by offering to sell it only by mail, thus saving distribution costs. I believe that Gernsback killed it himself through his bad financial policies. Had he paid the writers enough, and promptly, we could have received much better material. Also, we were in depression times, and magazines were an unavailable luxury for many.

So, Standard Magazines offered to buy the title and Gernsback jumped at it. Mannheimer suggested that perhaps Standard would be willing to hire me as editor, and so I talked to Leo Margulies, the chief editor. However, it was not that simple. In the first place, Standard operated on a different editorial policy. They published many kinds of pulps—western, detective, love, action—and they had a staff of editors, all on an equal level under Margulies. All stories would go the round of all editors and, of course, I was not familiar with the other types of pulps. Secondly, my good friend Mort Weisinger was already on their staff. So, if they did need a specialist in science-fiction, they already had one.

I did not have much hope of going to Standard, but I gave Margulies a call anyway, and was much encouraged by him. He said that he felt sure that they could add me to their staff, and to call him back later that week. My hopes were greatly raised. I was making plans to transfer. Then, on Friday, when I called him back, Margulies was no longer friendly, but quite curt. "Sorry, we can't use you." I blundered a response. "What did Mort have to do with it?" He shouted, "None of your business, son!" and hung up. My *Wonder* days were over.

I had later professional dealings with science fiction—with the magazine *Science Fiction* for a couple of years between 1939 and 1941, and with Gernsback's *Superworld Comics* in 1940—but I have hardly qualified as an active fan for over forty years. But it remains my first literary love, and I do see the old-timers from time to time, even occasionally visiting a convention. This is the Future I wondered about in 1930—and I have seen men walk on the Moon!

APPENDIX II

*Index to Scientific Fiction and Speculative
Articles in the Gernsback Publications*

Appendices II-V provide an issue by issue listing of all of the science fiction and speculative articles in Gernsback's magazines in the period 1908 to 1936. This Appendix covers specifically *Modern Electrics, The Electrical Experimenter/Science and Invention, Radio News,* and *Practical Electrics/The Experimenter* for their period under Gernsback's control, 1908 to 1929. In order to show the development of science fiction in Gernsback's magazines, this listing includes all stories regardless of speculative content. Those which are not recognizable as science fiction are identified as "non-SF" after the title.

Each index follows the same format although this first one is necessarily abbreviated since much that was published was straight scientific news and articles, and these are not themselves listed. The top line states first the volume number and issue number within that volume, with the whole number of issues in brackets. That is followed by the cover date, the item illustrated on the cover and the cover artist. These are listed only when the cover illustrates a scene from a science-fiction story or is itself of a speculative nature. The issue entries then list the title, author, and illustrator's name in brackets. An asterisk after the title indicates the item is a reprint, and the original source is given following the entry. The index only lists those issues containing a relevant story or article.

Throughout these appendices, the following abbreviations are used: a, non-fiction article; ed, editorial; ged, guest editorial; ill, illustrative feature; n, novel (over 40,000 words); na, novella (20-30,000 words); nt, novelette (10-20,000 words); s, short story (up to 10,000 words); sn, short novel (30-40,000 words); sr, serial (followed by the number of episodes, *e.g.*, 1/2 means part one of a two-part serial); trans, translated; v, verse.

MODERN ELECTRICS
[April 1908-March 1913]

Editor: Hugo Gernsback, April 1908-March 1913. *Assistant Editors:* A. C. Austin, Jr., October 1910-January 1911; A. C. Lescarboura, October-December 1911; C. A. LeQuesne, Jr., October 1911-December 1913. *Associate Editor:* H. Winfield Secor, October 1910-January 1911.

1/9 (9) December 1908

"Harnessing the Ocean" (a), Hugo Gernsback
"The Wireless Screech," spoof column by Fips [Gernsback]. It appeared in all subsequent issues.

2/9 (21) December 1909

"Television and the Telephot" (a), Hugo Gernsback

4/1 (37) April 1911.

"The Telephot" (Westcott?)

"Ralph 124C 41+" (sr1/12), Hugo Gernsback

[Note: all covers, April 1911-March 1912, illustrate Ralph 124C 41+; titles have been given to those episodes which did not bear a title on the cover.]

4/2 (38) May 1911.

["The Avalanche"] (Westcott?)

"Ralph 124C 41+" (sr2/12), Hugo Gernsback

4/3 (39) June 1911.

"The Hypno-Bioscope" (Westcott?)

"Ralph 124C 41+" (sr3/12), Hugo Gernsback

4/4 (40) July 1911.

"The Radiumizer" (Westcott?)

"Ralph 124C 41+" (sr4/12), Hugo Gernsback

4/5 (41) August 1911.

"New York A.D. 2660" (Westcott?)

"Ralph 124C 41+" (sr5/12), Hugo Gernsback

4/6 (42) September 1911.

"A Helio-Dynamophore Plant" (Westcott?)

"Ralph 124C 41+" (sr6/12), Hugo Gernsback

4/7 (43) October 1911.

"Alice 212B 423" (Weadon)

"Ralph 124C 41+" (sr7/12), Hugo Gernsback

4/8 (44) November 1911.

["The Clue"] (Weadon?)

"Ralph 124C 41+" (sr8/12), Hugo Gernsback

4/9 (45) December 1911.

"The Space Flyer" (Wrenn)

"Ralph 124C 41+" (sr9/12), Hugo Gernsback

4/10 (46) January 1912.

"Fernand and Llysanorh" (Wrenn)

"Ralph 124C 41+" (sr10/12), Hugo Gernsback

4/11 (47) February 1912.

["The Pursuit"] (Weadon?)

"Ralph 124C 41+" (sr11/12), Hugo Gernsback

4/12 (48) March 1912.

["Alice Restored"] (Wrenn)

"Ralph 124C 41+" (sr12/12), Hugo Gernsback

5/7 (55) October 1912

"The Scientific Adventures of Mr. Fosdick: 1. The Feline Light and Power Company Is Organized" (s), Jacque Morgan

5/8 (56) November 1912

"The Scientific Adventures of Mr. Fosdick: 2. Mr. Fosdick Invents the Seidlitzmobile" (s), Jacque Morgan

5/9 (57) December 1912

"The Scientific Adventures of Mr. Fosdick: 3. The International Electro-Galvanic Undertaking Corporation" (s), Jacque Morgan

5/10 (58) January 1913

"The Scientific Adventures of Mr. Fosdick: 4. The Afro-American Cataphoretic Process Co. Ltd." (s), Jacque Morgan

5/11 (59) February 1913

"The Scientific Adventures of Mr. Fosdick: 5. Mr. Fosdick Goes In For Synthetic Chemistry" (s), Jacque Morgan

THE ELECTRICAL EXPERIMENTER
[May 1913-April 1929]

Editor[-in-Chief]: Hugo Gernsback, May 1913-April 1929. *Associate Editors:* H. Winfield Secor, May 1913-June 1925; T. O'Conor Sloane, May 1922-August 1931; *Managing Editor:* H. Winfield Secor, July 1925-February 1930; *Field Editor:* Joseph H. Kraus, July 1925-October 1930; *Radio Editor:* A. P. Peck, July 1925-June 1926; Joseph Liebowitz, July-August 1926; James Francis Clemenger, September 1926-April 1927; Paul Welker, May 1927-December 1929; *Art Director:* J. Kelly Burleigh, July-December 1925; M. Essman, January 1926-January 1927; K. H. Joy, February-April 1927; William Romaine, May 1927-September 1928; Norman J. Stone, March 1929-September 1930.

2/2 (14) June 1914

"Mysterious Night" (non-SF s), Thomas N. [sic] Benson [*Wireless Wizz*]

2/3 (15) July 1914

"Olga's Surprise Party" (non-SF s), Thomas N. [sic] Benson [*Wireless Wizz*]

2/5 (17) October 1914

"The Midnight Chase" (non-SF s), Thomas W. Benson [*Wireless Wizz*]

3/1 (25) May 1915.

"Baron Münchhausen's New Scientific Adventures" (Thomas N. Wrenn)

"Baron Münchhausen's New Scientific Adventures: 1. I Make a Wireless Acquaintance" (sr1/13), Hugo Gernsback

3/2 (26) June 1915.

"Baron Münchhausen's New Scientific Adventures" (Wrenn)

"Baron Münchhausen's New Scientific Adventures: 2. How Münchhausen and the Allies Took Berlin" (sr2/13), Hugo Gernsback

3/3 (27) July 1915.

"Baron Münchhausen's New Scientific Adventures" (Wrenn)

"Baron Münchhausen's New Scientific Adventures: 3. Münchhausen on the Moon" (sr3/13), Hugo Gernsback

3/4 (28) August 1915

"Baron Münchhausen's New Scientific Adventures: 4. The Earth as Viewed from the Moon" (sr4/13), Hugo Gernsback

3/5 (29) September 1915

"Omegon" (s), George Frederick [sic] Stratton (Wardell)

3/6 (30) October 1915

"Baron Münchhausen's New Scientific Adventures: 5. Münchhausen Departs for the Planet Mars" (sr5/13), Hugo Gernsback

"The Gravitation Nullifier" (s), George Frederic Stratton (Wardell)

3/7 (31) November 1915.

"The Radium Destroyer" (Wrenn)

"The Electro-Magnetic Gun and its Possibilities" (ed), Hugo Gernsback

"Baron Münchhausen's New Scientific Adventures: 6. Münchhausen Lands on Mars" (sr6/13), Hugo Gernsback

"Warfare of the Future" (ill)

3/8 (32) December 1915.

"A Canal Scene on Mars" (Wrenn)

"Baron Münchhausen's New Scientific Adventures: 7. Münchhausen is Taught Martian" (sr7/13), Hugo Gernsback

"How the Wireless Wizz Celebrated Xmas" (non-SF s), Thomas W. Benson (Wardell?)

"The Electrical Burglar of the 20th Century" (ill)

3/9 (33) January 1916

"The Poniatowski Ray" (s), George Frederic Stratton (Wardell)

"Baron Münchhausen's New Scientific Adventures: 8. Thought Transmission on Mars" (sr8/13), Hugo Gernsback

"How Wireless Wiz Welcomed the New Year" (non-SF s), Thomas W. Benson (Wardell?)

3/10 (34) February 1916.

"An Electro-Gyro-Crusier" (Wrenn)

> "The Electro-Gyro-Crusier" (a), Eric R. Lyon, A.B.
> "The Shirikari Tentacle" (s), George Frederic Stratton (Wardell)

3/11 (35) March 1916.

"The Tesla Destroyer" (Wrenn)

> "The Utilization of the Sun's Energy" (ill),
> "The Tesla High-Frequency Oscillator" (a), H. Winfield Secor
> "Baron Münchhausen's New Scientific Adventures: 9. The Cities of Mars" (sr9/13), Hugo Gernsback

3/12 (36) April 1916

> "Baron Münchhausen's New Scientific Adventures: 10. The Planets at Close Range" (sr10/13), Hugo Gernsback

4/1 (37) May 1916.

"The Anti-Gravitation Ray" (Vincent Lynch)

> "The Mystery of Gravitation" (a), H. Winfield Secor
> "When Gyro-Cruiser Meets Land Dreadnaught" (ill) in "Warfare of the Future" feature.
> "The Wireless Wizard's Ghostly Conspiracy" (non-SF s), Thomas W. Benson

4/2 (38) June 1916.

"Electric Bomb Firer" (Wall)

> "Dropping Bombs Thru a Cone of Light" (a), no credit.
> "Baron Münchhausen's New Scientific Adventures: 11. Martian Amusements" (sr11/13), Hugo Gernsback
> "The Wireless Wiz Plays War Lord" (non-SF s), Thomas W. Benson (artist unknown)

4/3 (39) July 1916.

"Gyro Land-Flyer" (no credit)

> "A Long-Distance Electro-Mobile of the Future" (a), E.J. Christie
> "Trailing Aravilla" (s), George F. Stratton (Wardell).

4/4 (40) August 1916

> "The Wireless Wiz Turns Detective" (non-SF s), Thomas W. Benson (artist unknown)

4/5 (41) September 1916.

"Saturn and Ultra-Violet Light" (R. Burnside Potter)

> "Energy Direct from the Sun" (ed), Hugo Gernsback
> "The Electrical Mechanism of the Ether" (a), A. Press, B.Sc.

4/7 (43) November 1916

> "Baron Münchhausen's New Scientific Adventures: 12. How the Mar-

tian Canals Are Built" (sr12/13), Hugo Gernsback

4/8 (44) December 1916

"A Giant Torpedo That Eats Thru the Earth" (a), no credit.
"How the Wireless Wiz Turned Evangelist" (non-SF s), Thomas W. Benson (artist unknown)

4/10 (46) February 1917.

"Trench Destroyer" (Wall)

"The Trench Destroyer" (a), Hugo Gernsback
"Electric Power from Ocean Waves" (a), H. Winfield Secor
"Baron Münchhausen's New Scientific Adventures: 13. Martian Atmosphere Plants" (sr13/13), Hugo Gernsback

4/11 (47) March 1917.

"Electric Flyer Makes 500 Miles an Hour" (George Wall)

"Tapping the Earth's Heat" (ed), Hugo Gernsback
"Traveling at 500 Miles Per Hour in the Future Electric Railway" (ill)

4/12 (48) April 1917

"The Wireless Wiz and the Card Sharks" (non-SF s), Thomas W. Benson (artist unknown)

5/1 (49) May 1917.

"Electric Torpedo Destroyer" (Wall)

"Combating the Submarine"* (a), Hugo Gernsback [*Sunday New York American*, April 15, 1917]
"Eddy Currents" (s), C.M. Adams (Pearsall)

5/2 (50) June 1917.

"Electrocuting the Enemy" (Wall)

"Shooting with Electricity" (a), Hugo Gernsback
"Joe's Experiment" (non-SF s), C.M. Adams (Pearsall)

5/3 (51) July 1917

"Ham Jones)Scientist" (non-SF s), Harlan A. Eveleth

5/4 (52) August 1917

"The Radio Bomb" (non-SF s), C.M. Adams

5/11 (59) March 1918

"At War with the Invisible" (sr1/2), R. & G. Winthrop (Paul)

5/12 (60) April 1918.

"At War with the Invisible" (Vincent Lynch)

"At War with the Invisible" (sr2/2), R. & G. Winthrop (Paul)

6/1 (61) May 1918.

"Television and the Telephot" (Vincent Lynch)

"Coming Inventions 1: Television and the Telephot" (a1/2), Hugo Gernsback

"A Tight Squeeze for Uncle George" (non-SF s), Thomas Reed

6/2 (62) June 1918

"The Making of an Electrical Man"

"Coming Inventions 1: Television and the Telephot" (a2/2), Hugo Gernsback

6/3 (63) July 1918.

"Will the Germans Bombard New York?" (George Wall)

"Will the Germans Bombard New York?" (a), Hugo Gernsback

6/4 (64) August 1918.

"Aerial Mono-Flyer of the Future" (George Wall)

"Aerial Mono-Flyer of the Future" (a), H. Winfield Secor

"The Magnetic Storm" (s), Hugo Gernsback (Paul)

6/11 (71) March 1919

"How Jimmy Saved the Bank" (non-SF s), F. W. Russell

7/1 (73) May 1919.

"The Thought Recorder" (Howard Brown)

"The Thought Recorder" (a), Hugo Gernsback (Paul)

7/3 (75) July 1919

"How Don Flashed the S.O.S." (non-SF s), Mabel M. Davis (Wardell?)

7/5 (77) September 1919.

"You Too Can Do This on Eros" (George Wall)

"Interesting Phenomena of Gravitation" (a), Isabel M. Lewis (illus)

7/7 (79) November 1919

"Interplanetary Communication" (a), Dr. C.S. Brainin

"Plan T" (s), John White (illus)

7/10 (82) February 1920.

"Suspended Gravitation" (Howard Brown)

"The Goddard Moon Rocket" (a), [Hugo Gernsback] (Pearsall?)

"Suspended Gravitation" (a), Hugo Gernsback (Paul)

"The Golden Vapor" (s), E. H. Johnson (Paul)

7/11 (83) March 1920

"Power Transmitted by Wireless" (Brown)

"The Moon Rocket" (ed), Hugo Gernsback

"The Airship of Tomorrow" (a), George Wall (Wall)

"Wireless Transmission of Power Now Possible" (a), Thomas W. Benson

"Whispering Ether" (s), Charles S. Wolfe (Paul)

7/12 (84) April/May 1920

"Hello Mars!" (a), H. Winfield Secor (Paul)
"The Educated Harpoon" (s), Charles S. Wolfe (Paul)

8/1 (85) May/June 1920

"Aladdin's Lamp" (s), Charles S. Wolfe (Paul)

8/2 (86) June/July 1920.
"Sea-Going Ferris Wheel" (Howard Brown)

"A Sea-Going Ferris Wheel" (a), Hugo Gernsback (Wardell?)
"Inter-Planetary Communication" (a), Albert V.T. Day
"The Phantom Arm" (s), Charles S. Wolfe (Paul)

8/3 (87) July 1920

"Alarm Number 18" (s), Charles S. Wolfe (Paul)
"My Message to Mars" (s), Clement Fezandié (Paul)
"Overcoming Gravitation" (a), George S. Piggott

[magazine retitled: SCIENCE AND INVENTION]

8/4 (88) August 1920

"Jules Verne, The World's Greatest Prophet" (a), Charles I. Horne, Ph.D.
   (Paul)
"The Ultimate Ray" (a), Ray Whitcomb (Paul)
"The Master Key" (s), Charles S. Wolfe (Paul)

8/5 (89) September 1920

"The Unknown Avenger" (s), Harold F. Richards, Ph.D. (Paul)
"The Airplane of the Future" (a), Hugo Gernsback
"The Whirling Eye" (s), Thomas W. Benson & Charles W. Wolfe

8/6 (90) October 1920

"The Loaded Line" (s), Charles S. Wolfe (Paul)
"An American Jules Verne" (a), no credit, but may be Gernsback himself.
   [Profile of Luis Senarens]
"The Electric Shoes" (s), J. Mac-Richard

8/7 (91) November 1920

"Dr. Pringle Discusses Life" (non-SF s), John DeQuer (Paul)
"Applied Chemistry" (s), Charles S. Wolfe (Paul)

8/8 (92) December 1920

"Einstein and the Fourth Dimension" (a), Hugo Gernsback
"A Prophet of Science" (non-SF s), John DeQuer (Paul)
"Life or Death" (s), Charles S. Wolfe (Paul)

8/9 (93) January 1921

"The Elixir of Life" (s), H. L. Johnstone (Paul)

8/10 (94) February 1921.

"Can We Make Ourselves Invisible?" (Howard Brown)

"A Radiogenes" (s), Charles S. Wolfe (Paul)

"Can We Make Ourselves Invisible?" (a), Hugo Gernsback

8/11 (95) March 1921

"The Movie Theater of the Future" (a), Hugo Gernsback

"The Devil's Understudy" (s), Charles S. Wolfe (Paul)

"Dr. Pringle Discusses Mind" (non-SF s), John DeQuer (Paul)

8/12 (96) April 1921.

"Can We Visit the Planets?" (Howard Brown)

"Flying in Space" (a), Hugo Gernsback

"The Love Machine" (s), Charles S. Wolfe (Paul)

"In 1999" (s), B. Franklin Ruth (Paul)

"A Trip to the Moon" (a)

9/1 (97) May 1921

"Dr. Hackensaw's Secrets: No.1. Secret of Artificial Reproduction" (s), Clement Fezandié (Paul)

9/2 (98) June 1921

"The Deflecting Wave" (non-SF s), Herbert L. Moulton (Paul)

9/3 (99) July 1921.

"To Europe in Sixteen Hours" (Howard Brown)

"The Aerohydrotor)a 200 Mile-an-Hour Ocean-Going Craft" (a), Edwin F. Linder

"Dr. Hackensaw's Secrets: No.2. The Atom" (s), Clement Fezandié (Paul)

9/4 (100) August 1921

"The Red Vote" (s), Harold F. Richards (Paul)

9/5 (101) September 1921

"The Transformation of Professor Schmitz" (s), George R. Wells (Paul)

9/6 (102) October 1921.

"Dr. Hackensaw's Secrets: No.3. The Secret of Suspended Animation" (s), Clement Fezandié (Paul)

"A Scientist's Dream of Future Movies" (a)

9/7 (103) November 1921

"Life on Mars" (ed), Hugo Gernsback

"Have We Neighbors in Space?" (a), Ivan L. Smith

"The Filled Tooth" (s), Charles S. Wolfe (Paul)

9/8 (104) December 1921.
"Learn and Work While You Sleep" (Howard Brown)
"Without Residue" (s), Charles S. Wolfe (Paul)
"The Glass City of Tomorrow" (a), William Walsh
"Crops on the Moon" (a)
"Learn and Work While You Sleep" (a), Hugo Gernsback

9/9 (105) January 1922
"Wheel-less Subways of Tomorrow" (a)
"The Vibrator of Death" (s), Harold F. Richards, Ph.D. (Paul)

9/10 (106) February 1922.
"Flying 10,000 Years Hence" (Howard Brown)
"10,000 Years Hence" (a), Hugo Gernsback (Paul)
"An Excursion Into the Past" (s), Ernest K. Chapin (Paul)

9/11 (107) March 1922
"The Ninth Spool" (s), Charles S. Wolfe (Paul)
"The Psychic Lens" (s), Carl S. Wallace (Paul) [not in ToC]

9/12 (108) April 1922.
"The Super-Nose" (Howard Brown)
"Dr. Hackensaw's Secrets: No.4. The Super-Nose" (s), Clement Fezandié (Paul)
"The Gravity King" (s), Clelland J. Ball (Paul) [not in ToC]

10/1 (109) May 1922
"Dr. Hackensaw's Secrets: No.5. The Secret of Invisibility" (s), Clement Fezandié (Paul)
"If New York City Were the Whole World" (a), Charles Nevers Holmes
"The Radio Explorers" (s), Robert C. Parker (Paul)
"A Tropical North Pole)A Scheme for Melting or Reclaiming All the Ice from the Polar Regions" (a), C. S. Corrigan, C.E.

10/2 (110) June 1922
"Dr. Hackensaw's Secrets: No.6. The Secret of the Telautomaton" (s), Clement Fezandié (Paul)
"The Ray of Hercules" (s), Russ Simonton (Paul)

10/3 (111) July 1922.
"Television by Radio" (Howard Brown)
"A Tunnel Thru the Earth!" (a), Clement Fezandié
"Dr. Hackensaw's Secrets: No.7. The Secret of Life" (s), Clement Fezandié (Paul)
"The Radiophot)Television by Radio" (a), Hugo Gernsback

10/4 (112) August 1922
"Vacuum Cleaned Cities of Tomorrow" (a)
"Unlimited Destruction" (s), Ernest K. Chapin (Paul)

10/5 (113) September 1922

"Dr. Hackensaw's Secrets: No.8. Secret of Electrical Transmission" (s),
Clement Fezandié (Paul)

"Restoring the Moon" (s), Burnie L. Bevill (Paul)

"The End of the World)How Soon?" (a), Ivan L. Smith

"Flying Around the World in Twenty-Four Hours" (a)

10/6 (114) October 1922

"A Sub-Conscious Murderer" (s), Nellie E. Gardner (Paul)

"Dr. Hackensaw's Secrets: No.9. The Secret of Television" (s), Clement
Fezandié (Paul)

10/7 (115) November 1922

"Dr. Hackensaw's Secrets: No.10. The Secret of Tel-Hypnotism" (s),
Clement Fezandié (Paul)

10/8 (116) December 1922

"The Warship of 1950" (a), Graser Schornstheimer

"Dr. Hackensaw's Secrets: No.11. A Journey to the Year 2025" (s), Clement Fezandié (Paul)

10/9 (117) January 1923

"Dr. Hackensaw's Secrets: No.12. The Secret of the Philosopher's Stone"
(s), Clement Fezandié (Paul)

10/10 (118) February 1923.
"The Stellar Express" (Wardell)

"Navigating Interstellar Space" (a), Charles Frederick Carter

"The New Accelerator"* (s), H. G. Wells (Paul) [*The Strand Magazine*,
December 1901]

"Dr. Hackensaw's Secrets: No.13. The Secret of the Artificial Gills" (s),
Clement Fezandié (Paul)

10/11 (119) March 1923

"The Submarine of Tomorrow" (a), Graser Schornstheimer

"The Star"* (s), H. G. Wells (Paul) [*The Graphic,* Christmas 1897]

"Dr. Hackensaw's Secrets: No.14)The Secret of the Motorless Airplane"
(s), Clement Fezandié (Paul)

10/12 (120) April 1923

"The Thing from Outside" (s), George Allan England (Paul)

"Dr. Hackensaw's Secrets: No.15. The Secret of the Sixth Sense" (s),
Clement Fezandié (Paul)

11/1 (121) May 1923.
"The Automobile of 1973" (no credit)

"Dr. Hackensaw's Secrets: No.16. The Secret of the Earthquake" (s),
Clement Fezandié (Paul)

"Hunting Criminals in 2,000 A.D." (s), Felix Leo Goeckeritz (Pearsall)

"The Automobile of 1973" (a), Hugo Gernsback (Pearsall)

11/2 (122) June 1923

"The Great Food Panic" (s), Burnie L. Bevill (Paul)

"Dr. Hackensaw's Secrets: No.17. The Secret of the Walking Radiobile" (s), Clement Fezandié (Paul)

11/3 (123) July 1923

"Around the Universe" (sr1/6), Ray Cummings (Paul)

"Dr. Hackensaw's Secrets: No.18. The Secret of the Talking Ape" (s), Clement Fezandié (Paul)

"Skyscrapers of Tomorrow" (a), H. Winfield Secor

11/4 (124) August 1923.

"The Man from the Atom" (Howard Brown).

Cover labelled SCIENTIFIC FICTION NUMBER

The Man from the Atom" (s), G. Peyton Wertenbaker (Pearsall?)

"Dr. Hackensaw's Secrets: No.19. The Secret of the Super Telescope" (s), Clement Fezandié (Paul)

"Around the Universe" (sr2/6), Ray Cummings (Paul)

"Advanced Chemistry" (s), Jack G. Huekels (Paul)

"The Electric Duel" (s), Hugo Gernsback (Paul)

"Vanishing Movies" (non-SF s), Teddy J. Holman (Paul)

11/5 (125) September 1923

"Around the Universe" (sr3/6), Ray Cummings (Paul)

"Dr. Hackensaw's Secrets: No.20. A Car for the Moon" (s), Clement Fezandié (Paul)

11/6 (126) October 1923

"Our Cities of the Future" (a), Hugo Gernsback

"Dr. Hackensaw's Secrets: No.21. Dr. Hackensaw's Trip to the Moon" (s), Clement Fezandié (Paul)

"Around the Universe" (sr4/6), Ray Cummings (Paul)

11/7 (127) November 1923

"Around the Universe" (sr5/6), Ray Cummings (Paul)

"Dr. Hackensaw's Secrets: No.23 *[sic, there was no No.22]. What Dr. Hackensaw found on the Moon" (s), Clement Fezandié (Paul)*

11/8 (128) December 1923.

"A Floating Railroad" (no credit)

"Dr. Hackensaw's Secrets: No.24. The Secret of the Memory Obliterator" (s), Clement Fezandié (Paul)

"Around the Universe" (sr6/6), Ray Cummings (Paul)

"Invisible Elevated Railway" (a), Edwin F. Linder (illus)

11/9 (129) January 1924

"The Airplane of the Future" (a), H. Winfield Secor

"The Man on the Meteor" (sr1/9), Ray Cummings (Paul)

"Dr. Hackensaw's Secrets: No.25)The Secret of the Submarine City" (s), Clement Fezandié (Paul)

11/10 (130) February 1924.

"The Submarine-Land Dreadnought" (Brown)

"Can We Visit the Planets?" (a), Don Home *[pseudonym for Donald H. Menzel]*

"Submersible Dreadnought of Tomorrow" (a), no credit

"The Man on the Meteor" (sr2/9), Ray Cummings (Paul)

"Space Camera Photographs Earth" (a), Raymond F. Yates

"Dr. Hackensaw's Secrets: No.26. The Secret of the Perpetual Youth" (s), Clement Fezandié (Paul)

11/11 (131) March 1924.

"Speaking to Mars Over a Light Beam" (no credit)

"How I Would Speak to Mars" (a), Hugo Gernsback

"Can We Signal Mars?" (a), Charles T. Dahama *[pseudonym for Donald H. Menzel]*

"The Man on the Meteor" (sr3/9), Ray Cummings (Paul)

"Dr. Hackensaw's Secrets: No.27. The Secret of the Mermaid" (s), Clement Fezandié (Paul)

11/12 (132) April 1924

"Traveling on a Light Wave" (a), Ernest Brennecke

"The Man on the Meteor" (sr4/9), Ray Cummings (Paul)

"Dr. Hackensaw's Secrets: No.28. The Secret of Size" (s), Clement Fezandié (Paul)

12/1 (133) May 1924.

"The Radio Police Automaton" (no credit)

"The Radio Police Automaton" (a), Hugo Gernsback (illus)

"Beauty Culture of Tomorrow" (a), Dorothy Gernsback (illus)

"The Infinite Vision" (s), Charles C. Winn (Paul)

"The Man on the Meteor" (sr5/9), Ray Cummings (Paul)

"More Interstellar Communication" (a), Chevalier De Terrail

12/2 (134) June 1924.

"The End of the World" (no credit)

"The End of the World" (a), Charles T. Dahama *[Donald H. Menzel]* (Paul)

"The Man on the Meteor" (sr6/9), Ray Cummings (Paul)

"Dr. Hackensaw's Secrets: No.29. Around the World in Eighty Hours" (s), Clement Fezandié (Paul)

12/3 (135) July 1924

"The Man on the Meteor" (sr7/9), Ray Cummings (Paul)

"Dr. Hackensaw's Secrets: No.30. The Secret of the Flying Horse" (s), Clement Fezandié (Paul)

"Railroads of Tomorrow" (a), George F. Murphy (illus)

"Artificial Creation of Life" (a), Dr. E. Bade & J. F. Mazur, M.B.

12/4 (136) August 1924.

"Evolution on Mars" (Paul)

"The Diabolic Ray)Is It Possible?" (a), C. A. Olroyd, H. W. Secor & J. H. Kraus

"Evolution on Mars" (a), Hugo Gernsback (Paul)

"The Man on the Meteor" (sr8/9), Ray Cummings (Paul)

"Dr. Hackensaw's Secrets: No.31. The Secret of the Dream Machine" (s), Clement Fezandié (Paul)

12/5 (137) September 1924

"The Man on the Meteor" (sr9/9), Ray Cummings (Paul)

"Dr. Hackensaw's Secrets: No.32. The Secret of the Gravitation Screen" (s), Clement Fezandié (Paul)

12/6 (138) October 1924

"The Living Death" (sr1/9), J. Martin Leahy (Paul)

"Dr. Hackensaw's Secrets: No.33. The Secret of the Microscopic World" (s), Clement Fezandié (Paul)

12/7 (139) November 1924

"The Living Death" (sr2/9), J. Martin Leahy (Paul)

"Dr. Hackensaw's Secrets: No.34. The Secret of Perpetual Motion" (s), Clement Fezandié (Paul)

"Homo Artificialis" (a), Joseph H. Kraus & H. Winfield Secor (Pearsall?)

12/8 (140) December 1924

"The Living Death" (sr3/9), J. Martin Leahy (Paul)

"Dr. Hackensaw's Secrets: No.35. The Secret of the Extinct Microbe" (s), Clement Fezandié (Paul)

12/9 (141) January 1925

"The Dirigible of the Future" (ill), no credit

"The Living Death" (sr4/9), J. Martin Leahy (Paul)

"Dr. Hackensaw's Secrets: No.35. *[sic, there were two no.35s, correcting the omission of no.22]. A Journey to the Year 3000" (s), Clement Fezandié (Paul)*

12/10 (142) February 1925.

"Diagnosis by Radio" (Brown)

"The Radio Teledactyl" (a), Hugo Gernsback

"The Living Death" (sr5/9), J. Martin Leahy (Paul)

"Dr. Hackensaw's Secrets: No.36. The Mystery of the Z-Ray Spectacles" (s), Clement Fezandié (Paul)

12/11 (143) March 1925

"New York City 100 Years Hence" (a), H. Winfield Secor (Wardell)

"The Living Death" (sr6/9), J. Martin Leahy (Paul)

"Dr. Hackensaw's Secrets: No.37. The Mystery of the Walking Skeleton" (s), Clement Fezandié (Paul)

12/12 (144) April 1925

"The Living Death" (sr7/9), J. Martin Leahy (Paul)
"Dr. Hackensaw's Secrets: No.38. The Mystery of the Radio Cipher Machine" (s), Clement Fezandié (Paul)

13/1 (145) May 1925

"The Living Death" (sr8/9), J. Martin Leahy (Paul)
"Dr. Hackensaw's Secrets: No.39. The Mystery of Atomic Energy" (s), Clement Fezandié (Paul)

13/2 (146) June 1925

"The Living Death" (sr9/9), J. Martin Leahy (Paul)
"Dr. Hackensaw's Secrets: No.40. A Journey to the Center of the Earth" (sr1/4), Clement Fezandié (Paul)

13/3 (147) July 1925

"Tarrano the Conqueror" (sr1/14), Ray Cummings (Paul)
"Dr. Hackensaw's Secrets: No.41. A Journey to the Center of the Earth" (sr2/4), Clement Fezandié (Paul)

13/4 (148) August 1925

"Tarrano the Conqueror" (sr2/14), Ray Cummings (Paul)
"Dr. Hackensaw's Secrets: No.42 A Journey to the Center of the Earth" (sr3/4), Clement Fezandié (Paul)

13/5 (149) September 1925.
"Life Suspended in Ice" (Brown)

"Life Suspended in Ice" (a), Hugo Gernsback (Brown?)
"Tarrano the Conqueror" (sr3/14), Ray Cummings (Paul)
"Dr. Hackensaw's Secrets: No.43. A Journey to the Center of the Earth" (sr4/4), Clement Fezandié (Paul)

13/6 (150) October 1925

"Tarrano the Conqueror" (sr4/14), Ray Cummings (Paul)
13/7 (151) November 1925
"Tarrano the Conqueror" (sr5/14), Ray Cummings (Paul)
13/8 (152) December 1925
"Tarrano the Conqueror" (sr6/14), Ray Cummings (Paul)
13/9 (153) January 1926
"Tarrano the Conqueror" (sr7/14), Ray Cummings (Paul)
"Air Transportation Station of 1950" (ill), no credit

13/10 (154) February 1926.
"The Light-Beam Piano" (no credit)

"The Light-Beam Piano" (a), A. B. Peck (illus)
"Tarrano the Conqueror" (sr8/14), Ray Cummings (Paul)

13/11 (155) March 1926

"Tarrano the Conqueror" (sr9/14), Ray Cummings (Paul)

13/12 (156) April 1926

"Can the Dead be Reunited?" (Brown?)

"Can the Dead be Reunited?" (a), Hugo Gernsback

"Tarrano the Conqueror" (sr10/14), Ray Cummings (Paul)

14/1 (157) May 1926

"Tarrano the Conqueror" (sr11/14), Ray Cummings (Paul)

14/2 (158) June 1926

"Tarrano the Conqueror" (sr12/14), Ray Cummings (Paul)

14/3 (159) July 1926

"Tarrano the Conqueror" (sr13/14), Ray Cummings (Paul)

14/4 (160) August 1926

"Tarrano the Conqueror" (sr14/14), Ray Cummings (Paul)

14/5 (161) September 1926.

"The Dream Recorder" (Brown?)

"The Dream Recorder" (a), Hugo Gernsback

"The World's Greatest Cataclysm" (a), Donald H. Menzel (Reavis)

"Into the Fourth Dimension" (sr1/9), Ray Cummings (Paul)

14/6 (162) October 1926

"Into the Fourth Dimension" (sr2/9), Ray Cummings (Paul)

14/7 (163) November 1926

"Into the Fourth Dimension" (sr3/9), Ray Cummings (Paul)

14/8 (164) December 1926

"Into the Fourth Dimension" (sr4/9), Ray Cummings (Paul)

14/9 (165) January 1927

"Life on Other Worlds" (ed), Hugo Gernsback

"Into the Fourth Dimension" (sr5/9), Ray Cummings (Paul)

14/10 (166) February 1927

"Into the Fourth Dimension" (sr6/9), Ray Cummings (Paul)

14/11 (167) March 1927

"Into the Fourth Dimension" (sr7/9), Ray Cummings (Paul)

14/12 (168) April 1927

"Into the Fourth Dimension" (sr8/9), Ray Cummings (Paul)

15/1 (169) May 1927

"In the Year 2026" (a), staff writer based on predictions of Von A.B. Henninger (Bate)

"The Canal-Geometers of Mars" (a), Donald P. Beard

"Into the Fourth Dimension" (sr9/9), Ray Cummings (Paul)

15/2 (170) June 1927

"After Television)What?" (ed), Hugo Gernsback

"Can We Fly to the Planets?" (a), translated from the German (Wardell)

"The Dynamo Terror" (s), Charles Magee Adams (Wardell)

15/3 (171) July 1927

"Tales from the Scientific Club: A Bar of Poisoned Licorice" (s), Ray Cummings (Wardell)

15/4 (172) August 1927.

"Is This Possible?" (W. E. Reinecke)

"The Impossible is Possible" (a), Hugo Gernsback

"Tales from the Scientific Club, No.2)What the Typewriter Told" (s), Ray Cummings (Paul)

15/5 (173) September 1927.

"Gravitation Conquered at Last" (W. E. Reinecke)

"Twenty Years Hence" (ed), Hugo Gernsback

"To the Moon via Tunnel" (a),

"Ocean Islands for Aircraft" (a), E. Zeloni

"Gravity Nullified" (a), [exposé published in the following issue]

"The Radio Séance" (s), Karyl Kanet (Paul)

15/6 (174) October 1927

"The Metal Emperor"* (sr1/11), A. Merritt (Paul) [revised version of "The Metal Monster," *Argosy*, August 7-September 25,1920]

15/7 (175) November 1927.

"Is This Possible?" (W. E. Reinecke)

"Is This Possible?" (a), Joseph H. Kraus

"The Metal Emperor"* (sr2/11), A. Merritt (Paul)

15/8 (176) December 1927

"The Metal Emperor"* (sr3/11), A. Merritt (Paul)

15/9 (177) January 1928

"The Metal Emperor"* (sr4/11), A. Merritt (Paul)

15/10 (178) February 1928

"The Metal Emperor"* (sr5/11), A. Merritt (Paul)

15/11 (179) March 1928

"The Metal Emperor"* (sr6/11), A. Merritt (Paul)

15/12 (180) April 1928

"The Metal Emperor"* (sr7/11), A. Merritt (Paul)

16/1 (181) May 1928

"A Coming Discovery" (ed), Hugo Gernsback *[about the search for a trans-Neptunian planet]*

"The Metal Emperor"* (sr8/11), A. Merritt (Paul)

16/2 (182) June 1928

"Inter-Planetary Communication" (ed), Hugo Gernsback

"The Metal Emperor"* (sr9/11), A. Merritt (Paul)

16/3 (183) July 1928

"The Metal Emperor"* (sr10/11), A. Merritt (Paul)

16/4 (184) August 1928

"The Metal Emperor"* (sr11/11), A. Merritt (Paul)

16/5 (185) September 1928

"From the Earth to the Moon via Rocket" (a),

16/6 (186) October 1928

"The Unfinished Radio" (s), Edna Becker

16/8 (188) December 1928

"Cities of Tomorrow" (a), Lee deForest & Harvey Wiley Corbett

Gernsback's last issue was dated April 1929. Science & Invention *ran till its August 1931 issue, and, although it occasionally ran speculative articles, the only piece of science fiction that it published was "The Invisible Incendiary" by F. N. Linton in the August 1929 issue.*

RADIO NEWS

[First issue, July 1919. Entitled *Radio Amateur News* for volume one only]

Editor [-in-Chief]: Hugo Gernsback, July 1919-April 1929; *Associate Editors*: Pierre H. Boucheron, June-December 1920; Robert E. Lacault, January 1921-June 1925; Sylvan Harris, July-December 1925; C. P. Mason, October 1928-April 1929. *Managing Editor*: Sylvan Harris, January-September 1926; Robert Hertzberg, October 1928-February 1929.

1/5 (5) November 1919

"The Third Pill" (non-SF s), J. K. Henney (Paul)

1/7 (7) January 1920

"A Case of Nerves" (non-SF s), Julian K. Henney (Paul)

1/8 (8) February 1920

"Interplanetarian Wireless" (ed), Hugo Gernsback

1/9 (9) March 1920

"When the Lights Grew Dim" (non-SF s), Robert W. Allen (Paul)

2/1 (13) July 1920

"Radio in 1945" (ed), Hugo Gernsback

"The President's Special" (non-SF s), Thomas W. Benson & Charles S. Wolfe

2/2 (14) August 1920

"The Simplest Hook-up" (non-SF s), Thomas W. Benson & Charles S. Wolfe

2/3 (15) September 1920

"Mystic Waves" (non-SF s), Robert W. Allen

2/4 (16) October 1920

"The Radio Man's Code" (non-SF s), Erald A. Schivo (Paul)

2/5 (17) November 1920

"The Man Who Stands By" (non-SF s), Erald A. Schivo (Paul)

2/6 (18) December 1920

"The Spirit of Christmas" (non-SF s), Erald A. Schivo (Paul)

"Raided by Radio" (non-SF s), Herbert Warren Dodge (Paul)

2/7 (19) January 1921

"A Phony Phone" (non-SF s), Volney G. Mathison (Paul)

"The Mystery of the Dampt-Undampt Messages" (non-SF s), Herbert L. Moulton (Paul)

2/8 (20) February 1921

"The Phantom Call" (non-SF s), R.A. Chath (Paul)

2/9 (21) March 1921

"The Phantom and the Circuit" (non-SF s), Charles Osborne Parks (Paul)

"Martian Madness" (non-SF s), Erald Schivo (Paul)

2/10 (22) April 1921

"Found by Radio" (non-SF s), Harry Welton (Paul)

2/11 (23) May 1921

"The Death Dash" (non-SF s), "Sparks" (Paul)

2/12 (24) June 1921

"The Thirteenth Tap" (non-SF s), Bernard S. Greensfelder (Paul)

"Married via Radio" (non-SF s), Erald A. Schivo (Paul)

3/1 (25) July 1921

"The Mystery of the V.T." (non-SF s), W. Andrews

"The Acid Test" (non-SF s), George L. Sharp (Paul)

3/2 (26) August 1921

"When Romance Meets Up with Science" (non-SF s), Harold Van Riker (Paul)

"The Derelict of the Storm" (non-SF play), Charles Reberger

3/3 (27) September 1921

"Radiomania" (non-SF s), Charles S. Wolfe (Paul)

"Power by Radio" (non-SF s), Kenneth Warner (Paul)

3/4 (28) October 1921

"High Voltage" (non-SF s), Richard E. Morris (Paul)

"Ghosts by Radio" (non-SF s), George M. Bramann (Paul)

3/5 (29) November 1921

"The Wireless Third Degree" (non-SF s), George A. Gibson (Paul)

"Inland Castaways" (non-SF s), Elliot Marner (Paul)

3/6 (30) December 1921

"So This is Wireless" (non-SF s), Stanley Edgar (Paul)

"World's Record" (non-SF s), Clyde C. Young (Paul)

3/7 (31) January 1922

"The Fable of the Ham and the 4KW" (non-SF s), Chas. K. Fulghum (Paul)

"Over the Wireless Phone" (non-SF s), Erald Schivo (Paul)

3/8 (32) February 1922

"Mr. Sparks at Sea" (non-SF s), Raymond F. Guy (Paul)

"Larry Doyle's Wireless" (s), R. O'Head (Paul)

3/9 (33) March 1922

"There's Nothing Too Good for the Man with Brains" (non-SF s), Armand C. Ross (Pearsall)

"The Ordeal" (non-SF (s), Erald A. Schivo (Pearsall)

3/10-11 (34) April-May 1922

"The Crystal" (non-SF s), Bernard Greensfelder (Paul)

3/12 (35) June 1922

"Too Much Efficiency" (non-SF play), Bernard Greensfelder (Paul)

4/1 (36) July 1922

"Gunbarrel Radio" (non-SF s), H.M. Sutherland (Paul)

4/2 (37) August 1922

"A Hill Billy's Radio" (non-SF s), Monroe Worthington (Paul)

4/3 (38) September 1922

"The Detective Detector" (non-SF s), Perry Poorman (Paul)

4/4 (39) October 1922

"One Way or Another" (non-SF play), Erald A. Schivo (Paul)

4/5 (40) November 1922

"The Radio King" (sr1/2), adapted by George Bronson Howard from the movie serial by Robert Dillon

4/6 (41) December 1922

"The Radio King" (sr2/2), adapted by George Bronson Howard from the movie serial by Robert Dillon

4/7 (42) January 1923

"Mr. Murchison's Radio Party" (non-SF s), Ellis Parker Butler (Paul)
"Mr. Trip in the Electron Bottle" (spoof a), L. Hectron

4/8 (43) February 1923

"Mr. and Mrs. Brownlee Hold Hands" (non-SF s), Ellis Parker Butler (Ward)

4/9 (44) March 1923

"Mr. Bimberry Hears the Banquet" (non-SF s), Ellis Parker Butler (Paul)

4/10 (45) April 1923

"Mr. Brownlee's Loudtalker" (non-SF s), Ellis Parker Butler (Paul)
"C.W."* (s), William A. Griffith, Jr. (Paul)

4/11 (46) May 1923

"Mr. Bink's Radio" (non-SF s), Ellis Parker Butler (Paul)

4/12 (47) June 1923

"Mr. Filbert Tunes In" (non-SF s), Ellis Parker Butler (Paul)

5/1 (48) July 1923

"Casey's High-Voltage Cat" (non-SF s), Ellis Parker Butler (Paul)

5/2 (49) August 1923

"Hetterby's Set" (non-SF s), Ellis Parker Butler (Paul)

5/3 (50) September 1923

"The McNoodle Brothers' Radio Mystery" (non-SF s), Ellis Parker Butler (Paul)

5/4 (51) October 1923

"The Celebrated Pilkey Radio Case" (non-SF s), Ellis Parker Butler (Paul)

5/5 (52) November 1923

"The Great Radio Message from Mars" (non-SF s), Ellis Parker Butler (Paul)

5/6 (53) December 1923

"Solander's Radio Tomb" (non-SF s), Ellis Parker Butler (Paul)

5/7 (54) January 1924

"The Proof" (non-SF s), Allison Phelps (Paul)
"Toll of the Sea" (non-SF s), Howard S. Pyle (Paul)

5/8 (55) February 1924

"The Warning" (non-SF s), S. P. Wright (Paul)

5/9 (56) March 1924

"The Sad Story of AZZ" (non-SF s), Ellis Parker Butler (Paul)

5/10 (57) April 1924

"The Golden Rabbit" (non-SF s), Ellis Parker Butler (Paul)

5/11 (58) May 1924

"What Station Do You Want?" (non-SF s), Howard Wilmot (Paul)

5/12 (59) June 1924

"Too Much Waves" (non-SF s), Ellis Parker Butler (Paul)

6/1 (60) July 1924

"Lucy's Radio Present" (non-SF s), Warren Ordway (Paul)

6/2 (61) August 1924

"Allez, Houpla!" (non-SF s), Robert Francis Smith (Paul)

6/3 (62) September 1924

"Regulate or Bust" (non-SF s), Ellis Parker Butler (Paul)

6/4 (63) October 1924

"The Wail of the Lonesome Shrine" (non-SF s), Robert Francis Smith (Paul)

6/5 (64) November 1924

"Cent from Heaven" (non-SF s), Robert Francis Smith (Paul)

6/6 (65) December 1924

"A First Night with a First Set" (non-SF s), Jason C. Grant (Paul)

6/7 (66) January 1925

"Books in the Air" (non-SF s), Warren Ordway (Paul)

6/8 (67) February 1925

"The Master Puts One Over" (non-SF s), Robert Francis Smith (Paul)

6/9 (68) March 1925

"The Insurrecto Hook-Up" (non-SF s), Robert Francis Smith (Paul)

6/10 (69) April 1925

"The Great Bedtime Story Conspiracy" (non-SF s), Robert Francis Smith (Paul)

6/11 (70) May 1925

"The Strong Arm Circuit" (non-SF s), Robert Francis Smith (Paul)

6/12 (71) June 1925

"A Midsummer Night's Scheme" (non-SF s), Robert Francis Smith (Paul)

7/1 (72) July 1925

"The Juice Hangs High" (non-SF s), Robert Francis Smith (Paul)

7/2 (73) August 1925

"Drink To Me Only with Thine Ears" (non-SF s), Robert Francis Smith (Paul)

7/3 (74) September 1925

"The Poor Fish" (spoof), M. U. S. Fips [Gernsback]
"Ride and Seek" (non-SF s), Robert Francis Smith (Paul)

7/4 (75) October 1925

"The Times Flies (non-SF s), Marius Logan (Paul)

7/6 (77) December 1925

"Justice is Deaf" (non-SF s), Robert Francis Smith (Paul)

7/7 (78) January 1926

"The Master Laughs it Off" (non-SF s), Robert Francis Smith (Paul)

7/9 (80) March 1926

"Radio Beats the Ticker" (non-SF s), Marius Logan (Paul)

7/10 (81) April 1926

"So's Your Old Ghost!" (non-SF s), Marius Logan (Paul)

7/11 (82) May 1926

"The Radio Burglar" (non-SF s), Ernest M. Thompson (Paul)

7/12 (83) June 1926

"S.O.S.)Searchin' Out Sadie" (non-SF s), Marius Logan (Paul)

8/1 (84) July 1926

"Sam Jones, Radio Tube Bootlegger" (non-SF s), Volney G. Mathison (Paul)

8/2 (85) August 1926

"Budge Puts it Through" (non-SF s), Armstrong Perry (Paul)

8/3 (86) September 1926
"Echoing Silence" (non-SF sr1/2), George B. Ludlum (Clark)

8/4 (87) October 1926
"Echoing Silence" (non-SF sr2/2), George B. Ludlum (Clark)

8/5 (88) November 1926
"Came the Dawn" (scenario), C. Sterling Gleason (Paul)

8/7 (90) January 1927
"The Invisible Net" (s), Charles Magee Adams (Paul)

8/8 (91) February 1927
"The 'Ham'" (non-SF s), Armstrong Perry (Paul)

8/9 (92) March 1927
"Horatio at the Bridge" (non-SF s), Robert Francis Smith (Paul)

8/10 (93) April 1927
"Gentlemen Prefer Broadcasts" (non-SF s), Robert Francis Smith (Pearsall)

8/12 (95) June 1927
"The Face That Vamped a Thousand Guys" (non-SF s), Robert Francis Smith (Paul)

9/1 (96) July 1927
"He Bloops to Conquer" (non-SF s), Robert Francis Smith (Paul)

9/2 (97) August 1927
"Radio Revenge" (non-SF s), Armstrong Perry (Paul)

9/3 (98) September 1927
"Silent Dynamite" (non-SF s), C. Sterling Gleason (Paul)

9/4 (99) October 1927
"Listen, My Children" (non-SF s), Robert Francis Smith (Paul)

9/5 (100) November 1927
"The Voice of the People" (non-SF s), Joseph D. Mountain & C. Sterling Gleason (Paul)

9/6 (101) December 1927
"Till the Clouds Roll Dry" (non-SF s), Robert Francis Smith (Paul)

9/7 (102) January 1928
"Love in the Air" (non-SF s), A. M. Jones (Paul)

9/8 (103) February 1928
"The Switch Engine of the Air" (non-SF s), Joseph D. Mountain & C. Sterling Gleason (Paul)

9/9 (104) March 1928

"Roasted by Radio" (non-SF s), C. Sterling Gleason (Paul)

9/10 (105) April 1928

"The Old Dray Mare" (non-SF s), Robert Francis Smith (Paul)

9/11 (106) May 1928

"In the Bright Darkness" (non-SF s), C. Sterling Gleason (Paul)

9/12 (107) June 1928

"The Radio Gun)The Silent Weapon of the Future" (a), Joseph Riley
"The Port of Missing Airplanes" (s), C. Sterling Gleason (Paul)

10/1 (108) July 1928

"The Passing of the Third-Floor Quack" (non-SF s), Robert Francis Smith (Paul)

10/5 (112) November 1928

"Rays of Justice" (s), C. Sterling Gleason (Paul)

10/7 (114) January 1929

"The Dark Side of Radio" (non-SF s), Dorothy Gernsback (Paul)

10/9 (116) March 1929

"The Wings of Death" (s), C. Sterling Gleason (Paul)

PRACTICAL ELECTRICS
[November 1921-February 1926]

Editor and Publisher: Hugo Gernsback, all issues. *Associate Editor*: T. O'Conor Sloane, all issues (last three redesignated *Managing Editor*).

1/1 (1) November 1921

"Fifty Years Hence" (a), Hugo Gernsback (illus)

2/1 (12) November 1922

"The Electric Maid" (a), Hugo Gernsback (illus)

3/4 (27) February 1924

"Sam Graves' Electric Mind Revealer" (s), George Frederic Stratton (Paul)

3/5 (28) March 1924

"Sam Graves' Gravity Nullifier" (s), George Frederic Stratton (Paul)

3/6 (29) April 1924

"Premonitions" (s), J. Kay London (A. Stahle)

3/7 (30) May 1924

"The Man Who Saw Beyond" (s), James Pevey (A. Stahle)

3/8 (31) June 1924

"Specs" (s), Charles Magee Adams (A. Stahle)

3/9 (32) July 1924

"The Rain Maker" (s), J. Kay London (A. Stahle)

3/10 (33) August 1924

"When Sound Was Annihilated" (s), Robert Joergensen (artist unknown)

3/11 (34) September 1924

"An Electrocution That Failed" (s), Robert Rollins (artist unknown)

3/12 (35) October 1924

"The Radio Vision" (s), H. P. Clay (Paul)

[magazine retitled: THE EXPERIMENTER]

4/1 (36) November 1924

"The Ark of the Covenant"* (sr1/15), Victor MacClure (Rowley) [Harrap, London, 1924, as *Ultimatum*]

4/2 (37) December 1924

"The Ark of the Covenant"* (sr2/15), Victor MacClure (Rowley)

4/3 (38) January 1925

"The Ark of the Covenant"* (sr3/15), Victor MacClure (Rowley)

4/4 (39) February 1925

"The Ark of the Covenant"* (sr4/15), Victor MacClure (Rowley)

4/5 (40) March 1925

"The Ark of the Covenant"* (sr5/15), Victor MacClure (Rowley)

4/6 (41) April 1925

"The Ark of the Covenant"* (sr6/15), Victor MacClure (Rowley)

4/7 (42) May 1925

"The Ark of the Covenant"* (sr7/15), Victor MacClure (Rowley)

4/8 (43) June 1925

"The Ark of the Covenant"* (sr8/15), Victor MacClure (Rowley)

4/9 (44) July 1925

"The Ark of the Covenant"* (sr9/15), Victor MacClure (Rowley)

4/10 (45) August 1925

"The Ark of the Covenant"* (sr10/15), Victor MacClure (Rowley)

4/11 (46) September 1925
"The Ark of the Covenant"* (sr11/15), Victor MacClure (Rowley)

4/12 (47) October 1925
"The Ark of the Covenant"* (sr12/15), Victor MacClure (Rowley)

5/1 (48) November 1925
"The Ark of the Covenant"* (sr13/15), Victor MacClure (Rowley)

5/2 (49) December 1925
"The Ark of the Covenant"* (sr14/15), Victor MacClure (Rowley)

5/3 (50) January 1926
"The Ark of the Covenant"* (sr15/15), Victor MacClure (Rowley)

APPENDIX III

Index to Amazing Stories, Amazing Stories Annual *and* Amazing Stories Quarterly, *1926-1929*

This Appendix provides an issue by issue listing of contents to Gernsback's Experimenter family of science-fiction magazines whilst under his editorial control. The format and abbreviations used are the same as those in Appendix II. To save repetition, in all cases the cover artist is Frank R. Paul.

AMAZING STORIES

Editor and Publisher: April 1926-April 1929. *Managing Editor*: T. O'Conor Sloane, April 1926 only. *Associate Editors*: T. O'Conor Sloane, May 1926-October 1929; Miriam Bourne, October 1928-October 1929. *Literary Editors*: Wilbur C. Whitehead, July 1926-March 1929; C. A. Brandt, July 1926-December 1931.

1/1 (1) April 1926.

"Off on a Comet"

"A New Sort of Magazine" (ed), Hugo Gernsback

"Off on a Comet"* (sr1/2), Jules Verne (Paul) [Hachette, 1877; first US, Scribner's, 1878]

"The New Accelerator"* (s), H. G. Wells (Paul) [*The Strand Magazine*, December 1901]

"The Man from the Atom"* (s), G. Peyton Wertenbaker (Paul) [*Science & Invention*, August 1923]

"The Thing from)Outside"* (s), George Allen England (Paul) [*Science & Invention*, April 1923]

"The Man Who Saved the Earth"* (nt), Austin Hall (Paul) [*All-Story Weekly*, December 13,1919]

"The Facts in the Case of M. Valdemar* (s), Edgar Allan Poe (Hynd) [*American Review*, December 1845]

1/2 (2) May 1926.

"The Crystal Egg."

"Thank You!" (ed), Hugo Gernsback

"A Trip to the Center of the Earth"* (sr1/3), Jules Verne (MFC?) [Hachette, 1864; first US, Shepard, 1874]

"Mesmeric Revelation"* (s), Edgar Allan Poe (Paul) [*Columbian Lady's & Gentleman's Magazine*, August 1844]

"The Crystal Egg"* (s), H. G. Wells (Paul) [*The New Review*, 1897]

"The Infinite Vision"* (s), Charles C. Winn (Paul) [*Science & Invention*, May 1924]

"The Man from the Atom: Part 2" (s), G. Peyton Wertenbaker (Paul)

"Off on a Comet"* (sr2/2), Jules Verne (Paul)

1/3 (3) June 1926.

"A Trip to the Center of the Earth"

"The Lure of Scientifiction" (ed), Hugo Gernsback

"A Trip to the Center of the Earth"* (sr2/3), Jules Verne (Paul)

"The Coming of the Ice" (s), G. Peyton Wertenbaker (Paul)

"Mr. Fosdick Invents the Seidlitzmobile"* (s), Jacque Morgan (Paul) [*Modern Electrics*, November 1912]

"The Star"* (s), H. G. Wells (Paul) [*The Graphic*, Christmas 1897]

"Whispering Ether"* (s), Charles S. Wolfe (Paul) [*The Electrical Experimenter*, March 1920]

"The Runaway Skyscraper"* (nt), Murray Leinster (Paul) [*Argosy*, February 22, 1919]

"An Experiment in Gyro-Hats"* (s), Ellis Parker Butler (Paul) [*Hampton's Magazine*, June 1910]

"The Malignant Entity"* (s), Otis Adelbert Kline (Hynd) [*Weird Tales*, May-June-July 1924]

"Dr. Hackensaw's Secrets)Some Minor Inventions" (s), Clement Fezandié (Paul)

1/4 (4) July 1926.

"The Eggs from Lake Tanganyika"

"Fiction Versus Facts" (ed), Hugo Gernsback

"Station X"* (sr1/3), G. McLeod Winsor (Paul) [Lippincott, 1919]

"The Man Who Could Work Miracles"* (s), H.G.Wells (Hynd) [*Illustrated London News*, July 1898]

"The Feline Light and Power Company is Organized"* (s), Jacque Morgan (Paul) [*Modern Electrics*, October 1912]

"The Moon Metal"* (na), Garrett P. Serviss (Paul) [*All-Story*, May 1905]

"The Eggs from Lake Tanganyika"* (s), Curt Siodmak (Paul) [first US trans; German source: *Scherl* magazine, date unknown]

"The Magnetic Storm"* (s), Hugo Gernsback (Paul) [*The Electrical Experimenter*, August 1918]

"The Sphinx"* (s), Edgar Allan Poe (Paul) [*Arthur's Magazine*, January 1846]

"A Trip to the Center of the Earth"* (sr3/3), Jules Verne (Paul)

"The Secret of the Invisible Girl" (s), Clement Fezandié (Paul)

1/5 (5) August 1926.

"The Talking Brain."

"Impossible Facts" (ed), Hugo Gernsback

"A Columbus of Space"* (sr1/3), Garrett P. Serviss (Wardell) [*All-Story*, January-June 1906]

"The Empire of the Ants"* (s), H. G. Wells (Paul) [*The Strand Magazine*, December 1905]

"The International Electro-Galvanic Undertaking Corporation"* (s), Jacque Morgan (Paul) [*Modern Electrics*, December 1912]

"Dr. Ox's Experiment"* (na), Jules Verne (Paul) [Hachette, 1872; first US, Osgood, 1874]

"The Talking Brain" (s), M. H. Hasta (Paul)
"High Tension" (s), Albert B. Stuart, M.D. (Paul)
"Station X"* (sr2/3), G. McLeod Winsor (Paul)
"Aspiration" (v), Leland S. Copeland

1/6 (6) September 1926.

"In the Abyss."

"Editorially Speaking" (ed), Hugo Gernsback
"In The Abyss"* (s), H. G. Wells (Paul) [*Pearson's Magazine*, August 1896]
"A Columbus of Space"* (sr2/3), Garrett P. Serviss (Wardell)
"The Purchase of the North Pole"* (sr1/2), Jules Verne (Wardell?) [Hachette, 1889; first US, Once a Week Library, 1891]
"Station X"* (sr3/3), G. McLeod Winsor (Paul)
"The Moon Hoax"* (nt), Richard Adams Locke (Hynd) [*The New York Sun*, August 25-31 1835]
"A Psalm of Light" (v), Beta

1/7 (7) October 1926.

"Beyond the Pole"

"Imagination and Reality" (ed), Hugo Gernsback
"Beyond the Pole" (sr1/2), A. Hyatt Verrill (Paul)
"A Columbus of Space"* (sr3/3), Garrett P. Serviss (Wardell)
"The Purchase of the North Pole"* (sr2/2), Jules Verne (Wardell)
"Hail and Good-By" (v), Leland S. Copeland
"The Island of Dr. Moreau"* (sr1/2), H. G. Wells (Paul) [Heinemann, 1896]
"Blasphemer's Plateau" [nt], Alexander Snyder (Paul)
"Lullaby" (v), Leland S. Copeland

1/8 (8) November 1926.

"The Mad Planet"

"Plausibility in Scientifiction" (ed), Hugo Gernsback
"The Second Deluge"* (sr1/4), Garrett P. Serviss (Paul) [*The Cavalier*, July 1911-January 1912]
"The Island of Dr. Moreau"* (sr2/2), H. G. Wells (Paul)
"Beyond the Pole" (sr2/2), A. Hyatt Verrill (Paul)
"The Mad Planet"* (na), Murray Leinster (Paul) [*The Argosy*, June 12, 1920]
"A Drama in the Air"* (s), Jules Verne (Paul) [*Musée des Familles*, 1851]
"Stars" (v), Leland S. Copeland

1/9 (9) December 1926.

[Story contest cover]

"$500.00 Prize Story Contest" (ed), Hugo Gernsback
"The First Men in the Moon"* (sr1/3), H. G. Wells (Wardell?) [*The Strand Magazine*, November 1900-August 1901]
"The Man Higher Up"* (s), Edwin Balmer & William B. MacHarg (Paul) [*Hampton's Magazine*, September 1909]

"The Time Eliminator" (s), Kaw (Paul)
"Through the Crater's Rim" (nt), A. Hyatt Verrill (Paul)
"The Lord of the Winds" (s), Augusto Bissiri (Paul)
"The Telepathic Pick-Up" (s), Samuel M. Sargent, Jr. (Hynd)
"The Educated Harpoon"* (s), Charles S. Wolfe (MEC?) [*The Electrical Experimenter*, April 1920]
"The Diamond Lens"* (nt), Fitz-James O'Brien (Paul) [*The Atlantic Monthly*, January 1858]
"The Second Deluge"* (sr2/4), Garrett P. Serviss (Paul)
"Ascension" (v), Leland S. Copeland

1/10 (10) January 1927.

"The Man Who Could Vanish"

"Incredible Facts" (ed), Hugo Gernsback
"The Red Dust"* (nt), Murray Leinster (R?) [*The Argosy*, April 2, 1921]
"The Man Who Could Vanish" (nt), A. Hyatt Verrill (Wardell?)
"The First Men in the Moon"* (sr2/3), H. G. Wells (Wardell?)
"The Man with the Strange Head" (s), Miles J. Breuer (Hynds)
"The Second Deluge"* (sr3/4), Garrett P. Serviss (Paul)
["Discussion" letter column starts this issue]

1/11 (11) February 1927.

"The Land That Time Forgot"

"Interplanetary Travel" (ed), Hugo Gernsback
"The Land That Time Forgot"* (sr1/3), Edgar Rice Burroughs (Paul) [*Blue Book*, August 1918]
"On the Martian Way"* (s), Capt. H. G. Bishop, U.S.A. (Hynd) [*The New Broadway Magazine*, November 1907]
"The First Men in the Moon"* (sr3/3), H. G. Wells (Paul)
"New Stomachs for Old" (s), W. Alexander (artist unknown)
"The Eleventh Hour"* (s), Edwin Balmer & William B. MacHarg (artist unknown) [*Hampton's Magazine*, February 1910]
"The Thought Machine" (s), Ammianus Marcellinus (Paul)
"The Second Deluge"* (sr4/4), Garrett P. Serviss (Paul)
"H.G.Wells Hell of a Good Fellow Declares His Son"* (interview with Frank Wells), H.G. Robison [*New York World*, 1926]

1/12 (12) March 1927.

"The Green Splotches"

"Idle Thoughts of a Busy Editor" (ed), Hugo Gernsback
"The Green Splotches"* (na), T. S. Stribling (Gambee) [*Adventure*, January 3, 1920]
"Under the Knife"* (s), H. G. Wells (Paul?) [*The New Review*, January 1896]
"The Hammering Man"* (s), Edwin Balmer & William B. MacHarg (Paul) [*Hampton's Magazine*, May 1910]
"Advanced Chemistry"* (s), Jack G. Hueckels (artist unknown) [*Science & Invention*, August 1923]
"The People of the Pit"* (s), A. Merritt (Gambee) [*All-Story Weekly*, Jan-

uary 5, 1918]

"The Land That Time Forgot"* (sr2/3), Edgar Rice Burroughs (Paul) [*Blue Book*, October 1918]

2/1 (13) April 1927.

"The Man in the Room"

"The Most Amazing Thing" (ed), Hugo Gernsback

"The Plague of the Living Dead" (nt), A. Hyatt Verrill (Paul)

"The Remarkable Case of Davidson's Eyes"* (s), H. G. Wells (Dean) [*The Pall Mall Budget*, March 28, 1895]

"John Jones's Dollar"* (s), Harry Stephen Keeler (Paul?) [*Black Cat*, August 1915]

"The White Gold Pirate" (nt), Merlin Moore Taylor (Hynd)

"The Man in the Room"* (s), Edwin Balmer & William B. MacHarg (Dean) [*Hampton's Magazine*, May 1909]

"The Automatic Self-Serving Dining Table" (s), Henry Hugh Simmons (Paul)

"The Balloon Hoax"* (s), Edgar Allan Poe (Paul) [*The New York Sun*, April 13, 1844]

"Superstar" (v), Leland S. Copeland

"The Land That Time Forgot"* (sr3/3), Edgar Rice Burroughs (Paul) [*Blue Book*, December 1918]

2/2 (14) May 1927.

"The Star of Dead Love"

"Amazing Creations" (ed), Hugo Gernsback

"The Moon Pool"* (sr1/3), A. Merritt (Paul) [book version, Putnam, 1919]

"The Man Who Died by Proxy" (s), Frank Gates (Paul)

"The Time Machine"* (sn), H. G. Wells (Paul) [book version, Heinemann, 1895]

"The Singing Weapon" (s), Bent Prout (Paul)

"Light of Life" (v), Leland S. Copeland

"The Man Who Was" (nt), Walter Burch (de Aragon)

"The Star of Dead Love" (s), Will H. Gray (Paul)

2/3 (15) June 1927.

"The Moon Pool"

"The $500 Cover Prize Contest" (ed), Hugo Gernsback

"The Visitation" (nt), Cyril G. Wates (Paul)

"A Remarkable Drawing" (ill), J.M. de Aragon

"The Electronic Wall" (s), Geo. R. Fox (Paul)

"The Fate of the *Poseidonia*" (s), Clare Winger Harris (Paul)

"The Story of the Late Mr. Elvesham"* (s), H. G. Wells (Paul) [*The Idler*, May 1896]

"Secrets Never Told" (v), Leland S. Copeland

"The Lost Comet" (s), Ronald M. Sherin (Paul)

"Solander's Radio Tomb"* (s), Ellis Parker Butler (Paul?) [*Radio News*, December 1923]

"The Moon Pool"* (sr2/3), A. Merritt (Paul)

"The Four-Dimensional Roller-Press" (s), Bob Olsen (Paul)

2/4 (16) July 1927.
"Radio Mates"

"Surprising Facts" (ed), Hugo Gernsback
"The Ether Ship of Oltor" (nt), S. Maxwell Coder (Paul)
"The Voice from the Inner World" (s), A. Hyatt Verrill (Paul)
"The Lost Continent" (s), Cecil B. White (Paul)
"The Gravitomobile" (s), D.B. McRae (Paul)
"The Plattner Story"* (s), H. G. Wells (Paul) [*The New Review*, April 1896]
"Von Kempelen and his Discovery"* (s) Edgar Allan Poe (Paul) [*Flag of Our Union*, April 14, 1849]
"Radio Mates" (s), Benjamin Witwer (Paul)
"The Moon Pool"* (sr3/3), A. Merritt (Paul)
"Planet Neptune to Mother Sun," "Alone" and "Of Their Own Have We Given Them" (v), Leland S. Copeland

2/5 (17) August 1927.
"The War of the Worlds"

"A Different Story" (ed), Hugo Gernsback
"The War of the Worlds"* (sr1/2), H. G. Wells (Paul) [*Pearson's Magazine*, April-December 1897]
"The Tissue-Culture King"* (s), Julian Huxley (Paul) [*Cornhill Magazine*, April 1926]
"The Retreat to Mars" (s), Cecil B. White (Paul)
"Electro-Episoded in A.D. 2025" (s), E.D. Skinner (Paul)
"The Ultra-Elixir of Youth" (s), A. Hyatt Verrill (Paul)
"The Chemical Magnet" (s), Victor Thaddeus (Paul)
"The Automatic Apartment" (s), Henry Hugh Simmons (Paul)
"The Shadow on the Spark" (nt), Edward S. Sears (de Aragon)

2/6 (18) September 1927.
"The Malignant Flower"

"The Mystery of Time" (ed), Hugo Gernsback
"The Malignant Flower" (s), Anthos (Paul) [trans. from the German]
"The Radio Ghost" (nt), Otis Adelbert Kline (Paul)
"The Electric Duel"* (ss), Hugo Gernsback (Paul) [*Science & Invention*, August 1923]
"The Tide Projectile Transportation Co." (s), Will H. Gray (Paul)
"The Stone Cat" (s), Miles J. Breuer (de Aragon)
"The Colour Out of Space" (nt), H. P. Lovecraft (de Aragon)
"The War of the Worlds"* (sr2/2), H. G. Wells (Paul)
"A Link to the Past" (s), Charles G. Blandford (Paul)

2/7 (19) October 1927.
"Around the Universe"

"Amazing Youth" (ed), Hugo Gernsback
"Around the Universe"* (nt), Ray Cummings (Paul) [*Science & Inven-*

tion, July-December 1923]

"Aepyornis Island"* (s), H. G. Wells (Paul) [*The Pall Mall Budget*, December 27, 1894]

"The Winged Doom" (s), Kenneth Gilbert (Paul)

"The Treasures of Tantalus"* (sr1/2), Garret Smith (Paul) [*The Argosy*, December 11, 1920-January 8, 1921]

"The Paradise of the Ice Wilderness" (s), Jul. Regis (Paul) [trans. from the Norwegian]

2/8 (20) November 1927.

"The Machine Man of Ardathia"

"Space Flying" (ed), Hugo Gernsback

"A Story of the Stone Age"* (na), H. G. Wells (Paul) [*The Idler*, May-August & November 1897]

"The Astounding Discoveries of Doctor Mentiroso" (nt), A. Hyatt Verrill (Paul)

"Treasures of Tantalus"* (sr2/2), Garret Smith (Paul)

"The Machine Man of Ardathia" (s), Francis Flagg (Paul)

2/9 (21) December 1927.

"Below the Infra Red"

"Strange Facts" (ed), Hugo Gernsback

"Robur the Conqueror, or The Clipper of the Air"* (sr1/2), Jules Verne (Paul) [Hachette, 1886; first US, G. Munro, 1887]

"The Country of the Blind"* (s), H. G. Wells (Paul) [*The Strand Magazine*, April 1904]

"The Electro-Hydraulic Bank Protector" (s), Henry Hugh Simmons (Paul)

"The Author's Explanation of 'The Astounding Discoveries of Dr. Mentiroso'" (a), A. Hyatt Verrill

"The Undersea Express" (s) J. Roaman (Paul)

"Crystals of Growth" (s), Charles H. Rector (Paul)

"The Riot at Sanderac" (s), Miles J. Breuer (Hynd?)

"Below the Infra Red" (na), George Paul Bauer (Paul)

2/10 (22) January 1928.

"The Comet Doom"

"Our Unstable World" (ed), Hugo Gernsback

"The Comet Doom" (nt), Edmond Hamilton (Paul)

"The Man on the Bench" (s), W. J. Campbell (Paul?)

"The Psychological Solution" (nt), A. Hyatt Verrill (Paul)

"Rice's Ray" (s), Harold A. Lower [mistakenly by-lined Harry Martin, the lead character] (DEA)

"Robur the Conqueror"* (sr2/2), Jules Verne (Paul)

"The Stolen Body"* (s), H. G. Wells (de Aragon?) [*The Strand Magazine*, November 1898]

2/11 (23) February 1928.

"Baron Münchhausen's Scientific Adventures"

 "New Amazing Stories Quarterly" (ed), Hugo Gernsback

 "The Master of the World"* (sr1/2), Jules Verne (Paul) [Hachette, 1904; first US, V. Parke, 1911]

 "Worlds Unknown" (v), Leland S. Copeland

 "The Revolt of the Pedestrians" (nt), David H. Keller, M.D. (Paul)

 "Baron Münchhausen's Scientific Adventures: 1. I Make a Wireless Acquaintance; 2. How Münchhausen and the Allies Took Berlin"* (sr1/6), Hugo Gernsback (Paul) [*The Electrical Experimenter*, May & June 1915]

 "Pollock and the Porroh Man"* (s), H. G. Wells (Paul) [*The New Budget*, May 23, 1895]

 "Four Dimensional Surgery" (s), Bob Olsen (Paul)

 "The Disintegrating Ray" (s), David M. Speaker (Paul)

 "Cosmic Ciphers" (v), Leland S. Copeland

 "The Fourteenth Earth" (s), Walter Kateley (Paul?)

 "The Fighting Heart" (s), W. Alexander (de Aragon)

 "Ourselves" (v), Leland S. Copeland

 "Smoke Rings" (s), George McLociard (Paul)

2/12 (24) March 1928.

"Lakh-Dal, Destroyer of Souls"

 "Amazing Thinking" (ed), Hugo Gernsback

 "Ten Million Miles Sunward" (na), Geoffrey Hewelcke (artist unknown)

 "Baron Münchhausen's Scientific Adventures: 3. Münchhausen on the Moon; 4. The Earth as Viewed from the Moon"* (sr2/6), Hugo Gernsback (Paul) [*The Electrical Experimenter*, July & August 1915]

 "The Flowering of the Strange Orchid"* (s), H. G. Wells (Paul) [*The Pall Mall Budget* August 2, 1894]

 "The Master of the World"* (sr2/2), Jules Verne (Paul)

 "Lakh-Dal, Destroyer of Souls" (nt), W. F. Hammond (Paul)

 "Sub-Satellite" (s), Charles Cloukey (Paul)

3/1 (25) April 1928.

[Scientifiction Symbol contest]

 "$300.00 Prize Contest, Wanted: A Symbol for Scientifiction" (ed), Hugo Gernsback

 "A Story of the Days to Come"* (sr1/2), H. G. Wells (Paul) [*Pall Mall Magazine*, June-October 1899]

 "The Fallacy in 'Ten Million Miles Sunward'" (a), Prof. W.J. Luyten

 "The Yeast Men" (s), David H. Keller, M.D. (Paul)

 "The Way of a Dinosaur" (s), Harley S. Aldinger (Paul)

 "Baron Münchhausen's Scientific Adventures: 5. Münchhausen Departs for the Planet Mars; 6. Münchhausen Lands on Mars"* (sr3/6), Hugo Gernsback (Paul) [*The Electrical Experimenter*, October & November 1915]

"The Miracle of the Lily" (s), Clare Winger Harris (de Aragon)
"When Hearts Remember Home" (v), Leland S. Copeland
"The Ancient Horror" (nt), Hal Grant (Paul)
"The Master Key"* (s), Charles S. Wolfe (Paul) [*Science & Invention*, August 1920]
"The Return of the Martians" (nt), Cecil B. White (Paul)

3/2 (26) May 1928.
"The Octopus Cycle"

"Facts Outfictioned" (ed), Hugo Gernsback
"Four Dimensional Robberies" (s), Bob Olsen (Lawlor)
"The Octopus Cycle" (nt), Irvin Lester & Fletcher Pratt (Paul)
"Dr. Brittlestone's Method" (s), Samuel M. Sargent, Jr. (artist unknown)
"The Thousand-and-Second Tale of Scheherazade"* (s), Edgar Allan Poe (Paul) [*Godey's Lady's Book*, February 1845]
"A Story of the Days to Come"* (sr2/2), H. G. Wells (Lawlor)
"Our Little Neighbor" (v), Leland S. Copeland
"Baron Münchhausen's Scientific Adventures: 7. Münchhausen is Taught Martian; 8. Thought Transmission on Mars"* (sr4/6), Hugo Gernsback (Paul) [*The Electrical Experimenter*, December 1915 & January 1916]
"The Master Ants" (nt), Francis Flagg (de Aragon)
"A Visitor from the Twentieth Century" (s), Harold Donitz (Paul)

3/3 (27) June 1928.
"The Blue Dimension"

"Our Amazing Minds" (ed), Hugo Gernsback
"The Invisible Man"* (sr1/2), H. G. Wells (Lawlor) [*Pearson's Weekly*, June 12-August 1, 1897]
"The Blue Dimension" (s), Francis Flagg (Paul)
"A Biological Experiment" (s), David H. Keller, M.D. (Paul)
"Baron Münchhausen's Scientific Adventures: 9. The Cities of Mars; 10. The Planets at Close Range"* (sr5/6), Hugo Gernsback (Paul) [*The Electrical Experimenter*, March & April 1916]
"The Golden Girl of Munan" (nt), Harl Vincent (Lawlor)
"The American Jules Verne"* (a), no credit (photos) [*Science & Invention*, October 1920]

3/4 (28) July 1928.
"Super-Radio"

"Our Amazing Senses" (ed), Hugo Gernsback
"Super-Radio" (s), Charles Cloukey (Paul)
"Vandals from the Moon" (na), Marius (Lawlor)
"The Invisible Man"* (sr2/2), H. G. Wells (Lawlor)
"Baron Münchhausen's Scientific Adventures: 11. Martian Amusements; 12. How the Martian Canals Are Built; 13. Martian Atmosphere Plant"* (sr6/6), Hugo Gernsback (Paul) [*The Electrical Experimenter*, June, November 1916, February 1917]
"Just Around the Corner" (play), Raymond Knight (Lawlor)

"The Educated Pill" (s), Bob Olsen (Paul)

3/5 (29) August 1928.
"The Skylark of Space"

"The Amazing Unknown" (ed), Hugo Gernsback
"The Skylark of Space" (sr1/3), Edward Elmer Smith & Lee Hawkins
Garby (Paul)
"The Head" (s), Joe Kleier (Lawlor)
"Armageddon)2419 A.D." (na), Philip Francis Nowlan (Paul)
"The Perambulating Home" (s), Henry Hugh Simmons (Paul)
"The Moth"* (s), H. G. Wells (Lawlor) [*The Pall Mall Gazette*, March 28,
1895]

3/6 (30) September 1928.
Scientifiction Symbol Prize Winning Entry.

"Our Amazing Universe" (ed), Hugo Gernsback
"The Ambassador from Mars" (na), Harl Vincent (Paul)
"Life" (v), Leland S. Copeland
"The Invisible Bubble" (s), Kirk Meadowcroft (Paul)
"Unlocking the Past" (s), David H. Keller (Paul)
"Results of $300.00 Scientifiction Prize Contest"
"The Great Steel Panic" (s), Irvin Lester & Fletcher Pratt (Paul)
"The Skylark of Space" (sr2/3), Edward Elmer Smith & Lee Hawkins
Garby (Paul)

3/7 (31) October 1928.
"To the Moon by Proxy"

"New Amazing Facts" (ed), Hugo Gernsback
"The Menace of Mars" (nt), Clare Winger Harris (Paul)
"To the Moon by Proxy" (nt), J. Schlossel (Paul)
"The Skylark of Space" (sr3/3), Edward Elmer Smith & Lee Hawkins
Garby (Paul)
"Reprisal" (s), Thomas Richard Jones (Paul?)
"The Voyage to Kemptonia" (nt), E.M. Scott (Paul)

3/8 (32) November 1928.
"The Moon Men"

"Amazing Life" (ed), Hugo Gernsback
"The World at Bay" (sr1/2), B. & G.C. Wallis (Paul)
"The Ananias Gland" (s), W. Alexander (Paul)
"The Psychophonic Nurse" (s), David H. Keller, M.D. (Paul)
"The Moon Men" (nt), Frank Brueckel, Jr. (Paul)
"The Eye of the Vulture" (s), Walter Kateley (Paul)
"The Living Test Tube" (s), Joe Simmons (Paul)

3/9 (33) December 1928.
"The Metal Man"

"An Amazing Phenomenon" (ed), Hugo Gernsback
"The Appendix and the Spectacles" (s), Miles J. Breuer, M.D. (Paul)

"Flight to Venus" (nt), Edwin K. Sloat (Paul)
"The Metal Man" (s), Jack Williamson (Paul)
"The World at Bay" (sr2/2), B. & G.C. Wallis (Paul)
"The Fifth Dimension" (s), Clare Winger Harris (artist unknown)
"Before the Ice Age" (s), Alfred Fritchey (artist unknown)
"Monorail" (s), George McLociard (Paul)
"The Space Bender" (nt), Edward L. Rementer (Paul)

3/10 (34) January 1929.

"The Sixth Glacier"

"Amazing Reading" (ed), Hugo Gernsback
"The War of the Planets" (na), Harl Vincent (artist unknown)
"The Sixth Glacier" (sr1/2), Marius (Paul)
"Cauphul, The City Under the Sea" (nt), George Cookman Watson (Paul)
"Absolute Zero" (s), Harold Moorhouse Colter (Paul)
"The Roger Bacon Formula" (s), Irvin Lester & Fletcher Pratt (Paul)

3/11 (35) February 1929.

"The Death of the Moon"

"Life, the Amazing Puzzle" (ed), Hugo Gernsback
"The Captured Cross-Section" (s), Miles J. Breuer, M.D. (Paul)
"The Lord of the Dynamos"* (s), H. G. Wells (Paul) [*Pall Mall Budget*,
    September 6, 1894]
"The Sixth Glacier" (sr2/2), Marius (Paul)
"Mernos" (nt), L.C. Kellenberger [mistakenly by-lined Henry James, the
    lead character] (Paul)
"Phagocytes" (s), A. H. Johnson (Paul)
"The Death of the Moon" (s), Alexander Phillips (Paul)
"The Last Man" (s), Wallace G. West (Paul)

3/12 (36) March 1929.

"The Airlords of Han"

"Our Amazing Stars" (ed), Hugo Gernsback
"Into the Green Prism" (sr1/2), A. Hyatt Verrill (Paul)
"The Face of Isis" (nt), Cyril G. Wates (Paul)
"The Worm" (s), David H. Keller, M.D. (Paul)
"The Airlords of Han" (sn), Philip Francis Nowlan (Paul)

4/1 (37) April 1929.

"The Revolt of the Atoms"

"The Amazing Einstein" (ed), Hugo Gernsback
"The Revolt of the Atoms"* (nt), V. Orlovsky (Paul) [trans. from *Mir
    Priklyuchenniv*, March 1927]
"The Terror of the Streets" (nt), George McLociard (Paul)
"Buried Treasure" (s), Miles J. Breuer (Mackay)
"Into the Green Prism" (sr2/2), A. Hyatt Verrill (Paul)

This was the last Gernsback issue

AMAZING STORIES ANNUAL and *QUARTERLY*
[*Editorial staff as per* Amazing Stories]

AMAZING STORIES ANNUAL

[Summer] 1927,
"The Master Mind of Mars"

"Editorial" (ed), Hugo Gernsback
"The Master Mind of Mars" (n), Edgar Rice Burroughs (Paul)
"The Face in the Abyss"* (sn), A. Merritt (Paul) [*Argosy Weekly*, September 8, 1923]
"The Man Who Saved the Earth"* (nt), Austin Hall (Paul) [*All-Story Weekly*, December 13,1919]
"The People of the Pit"* (s), A. Merritt (Gambee) [*All-Story Weekly*, January 5, 1918]
"The Man Who Could Vanish"* (nt), A. Hyatt Verrill (Wardell?)
"The Feline Light and Power Company is Organized"* (s), Jacque Morgan (artist unknown) [*Modern Electrics*, October 1912]
"Under the Knife"* (s), H. G. Wells (Paul) [*The New Review*, January 1896]

AMAZING STORIES QUARTERLY

1/1 (1) Winter 1928,
"When the Sleeper Wakes"

"Preface" (ed), Hugo Gernsback
"The Moon of Doom" (n), Earl L. Bell (Paul)
"The Atomic Riddle" (nt), Edward S. Sears (Paul)
"When the Sleeper Wakes"* (n), H. G. Wells (Lanos*) [book version, Harper, 1899]
"The Golden Vapor"* (s), E.H. Johnson (Paul) [*The Electrical Experimenter*, February 1920)
"The Puzzle Duel" (s), Miles J. Breuer, M.D. (Paul)
"The Terrors of the Upper Air" (s), Frank Orndorff (Paul)

1/2 (2) Spring 1928,
"The Second Swarm"

"The Rise of Scientifiction" (ed), Hugo Gernsback
"A Modern Atlantis" (n), Frederick Arthur Hodge (Paul)
"The Nth Man" (sn), Homer Eon Flint (Paul)
"The King of the Monkey Men" (na), A. Hyatt Verrill (Paul)
"The Vibrator of Death" (s), Harold F. Richards, Ph.D. (Paul)
"The Second Swarm" (nt), J. Schlossel (Paul)
1/3 (3) Summer 1928, "Out of the Sub-Universe"
"The Sunken World" (n), Stanton A. Coblentz (Paul)

"Out of the Sub-Universe" (s), R. F. Starzl (Paul)

"The Menace" (4 connected stories: "The Menace," "The Gold Ship," "The Tainted Flood," "The Insane Avalanche"), David H. Keller, M.D. (Paul)

"Ten Days to Live" (nt), C.J. Eustace (Paul)

1/4 (4) Fall 1928,

"The World of the Giant Ants"

"Scientifiction, Searchlight of Science" (ged), Jack Williamson

"The World of the Giant Ants" (n), A. Hyatt Verrill (Paul)

"Stenographer's Hands" (s), David H. Keller, M.D. (Paul)

"Four Dimensional Transit" (na), Bob Olsen (Paul)

"When the World Went Mad" (s), Ronald M. Sherin (Paul)

"The Gravity King" (s), Clelland J. Ball (Paul)

Editorials from Our Readers: "Beyond the Realm of Known Possibilities," Victor L. Osgood; "Title Purposes of Scientifiction," W. Melvin Goodhue; "Pioneers," B.S. Moore; "History of Scientific Fiction," James T. Brady, Jr.; "Words," C.E. Caulkins; "Science," H.A. Frazier; "Scientifiction, 20th Century Prophet and Historian," R.C. Smith; "Is Progress Destructive," J.A. Coomes; "Scientifiction, An Inspiration for Future Scientific Progress," Gilson Willets; "The Future of Scientifiction" Daryl McAllister.

2/1 (5) Winter 1929,

"The Beast-Men of Ceres"

"Why We Believe in Scientifiction" (ged), Frederick Dundas Stewart

"Ralph 124C 41+"* (n), Hugo Gernsback (Paul) [book version, Stratford, 1925]

"The Seventh Generation" (nt), Harl Vincent (Paul)

"The Evolutionary Monstrosity" (s), Clare Winger Harris (Paul)

"The Murgatroyd Experiment" (nt), Capt. S. P. Meek, U.S.A. (Paul)

"The Beast-Men of Ceres" (nt), Aladra Septama (Paul)

"The Hollister Experiment" (s), Walter Kateley (Paul)

"What the Sodium Lines Revealed" (nt), L. Taylor Hansen (Paul)

Editorials from Our Readers: "The Boundaries of Knowledge," C. William Smith; "Advanced Truth," Robert N. Slate; "The Prophecies of Science," Judson W. Reeves; "Scientifiction, the Highway to Constructive Thinking," Henry Hasse; "The Emancipation of Literature," Raymond P. Henze; "The Amazing Work of Wells and Verne," Jack Williamson; "Scientifiction and Literature," Harold Donitz; "Scientifiction)the Literature of Science and Life," Robert S. Withers; "Scientifiction, Synthetic Interpretation," Decima Azuley; "Scientifiction)a Mirror of the Future, Literature)the Mirror of Knowledge," L. Taylor Hansen; "Imagination Linked to Science," F.D. Harris; "Man as a Prophet," Purcel G. Schube; "Progress and the Spirit of Scientifiction," Alfred H. Weber.

[This was the last Gernsback issue]

APPENDIX IV

Index to Gernsback's Wonder magazines, 1929-1936

This Appendix provides an issue by issue contents listing to *Wonder Stories* and its companions. The format and abbreviations are the same as in Appendix II. All covers are by Frank R. Paul unless otherwise stated.

AIR WONDER STORIES

Editor-in-Chief: Hugo Gernsback, July 1929-May 1930. *Literary Editor*: David Lasser, July 1929-May 1930. *Art Director*: Frank R. Paul, July 1929-May 1930. *Associate Editors*: C. P. Mason, February-May 1930; A. L. Fierst, February-March 1930; M. E. Dame, April-May 1930.

1/1 (1) July 1929.
"Islands in the Air"

"Air Wonder Stories" (ed), Hugo Gernsback
"The Ark of the Covenant"* (sr1/4), Victor MacClure (Paul) [Harrap, London, 1924; as *Ultimatum*]
"Islands in the Air" (s), Lowell Howard Morrow (Paul)
"The Beacon of Airport Seven" (s), Harold S. Sykes (Paul)
"The Bloodless War" (s), Dr. David H. Keller (Paul)
"Men with Wings" (na), Leslie F.Stone (Paul)

1/2 (2) August 1929.
"The Silent Destroyer."

"Future Aviation Problems" (ed), Hugo Gernsback
"The Silent Destroyer" (nt), Henrik Dahl Juve (Paul)
"Beyond Gravity" (nt), Ed Earl Repp (Paul)
"The Ark of the Covenant"* (sr2/4), Victor MacClure (Paul)
"The Planet's Air Master" (na), Edward E. Chappelow (Paul)

1/3 (3) September 1929.
"Flight in 1999"

"Rocket Flying" (ed), Hugo Gernsback
"The Airplane of the Future" (a), Hugo Gernsback (Wall)
"The Yellow Air-Peril" (nt), Harl Vincent (Paul)
"Where Gravity Ends" (s), Robert H. Leitfred (Paul)
"The Ark of the Covenant"* (sr3/4), Victor MacClure (Paul)
"Flight in 1999" (s), Bob Olsen (Paul)
"The Air Terror" (s), Lowell Howard Morrow (Paul)

1/4 (4) October 1929.

"Through the Air Tunnel"

"Airship vs Airplane" (ed), Hugo Gernsback
"The Sky Maniac" (nt), Henrik Dahl Juve (Paul)
"Around the World in 24 Hours" (s), R. H. Romans (Paul)
"Through the Air Tunnel" (s), Harl Vincent (Paul)
"The Air Spy" (s), Edward Lee Harrison (Paul)
"The Ark of the Covenant"* (sr4/4), Victor MacClure (Paul)
"The Invisible Raiders" (s), Ed Earl Repp (Paul)
"The Robot Master" (s), O. Beckwith (Paul)

1/5 (5) November 1929.

"Cities in the Air."

"Airplanes MUST Have Radio" (ed), Hugo Gernsback
"Cities in the Air" (sr1/2), Edmond Hamilton (Paul)
"10,000 Years Hence"* (ill), text by Hugo Gernsback (Paul) [*Science & Invention*, February 1922]
"When Space Ripped Open" (nt), Ralph W. Wilkins (Paul)
"Suitcase Airplanes" (s), E.D. Skinner (Paul)
"Beyond the Aurora" (nt), Ed Earl Repp (Paul)
"The Second Shell" (s), Jack Williamson (Paul)
"The Crystal Ray" (s), Raymond Gallun (Strother)

1/6 (6) December 1929.

"The Flight of the Eastern Star."

"Glider Flying" (ed), Hugo Gernsback
"The Blue Demon" (nt), Lowell Howard Morrow (Nutter)
"Flight of the *Eastern Star*" (s), Ed Earl Repp (Paul)
"The Phantom of Galon" (nt), J.W. Ruff (Paul)
"Freedom of the Skies" (nt), Edsel Newton (Paul)
"Flannelcake's Invention" (s), H. McKay (Winter)
"Cities in the Air" (sr2/2), Edmond Hamilton (Paul)

1/7 (7) January 1930.

"The Thunderer"

"One Thousand Miles an Hour" (ed), Hugo Gernsback
"The Flying Legion"* (sr1/4), George Allan England (Paul) [*All-Story Weekly*, November 15-December 20, 1919]
"Airports for World Traffic"* (a), H. Dominik (Henninger) [trans. from German by F.M. Currier]
"The Storm Buster" (nt), Ed Earl Repp (Paul)
"The Death's Head Meteor" (s), Neil R. Jones (Winter)
"The Thunderer" (nt), A. H. Johnson (Paul)

1/8 (8) February 1930.

[Story contest cover]

"$300.00 Prize Story Contest" (ed), Hugo Gernsback
"The Vanishing Fleet" (nt), Henrik Dahl Juve (Paul)

"The Red Ace" (nt), Eugene George Key (Paul)
"Liners of Space" (nt), Jim Vanny (Ruger)
"The Flying Legion"* (sr2/4), George Allan England (Paul)
"Berlin to New York In One Hour"* (a), Max Valier (artist unknown)
[trans. from German by F.M. Currier]

1/9 (9) March 1930.
"The Return of the Air Master"

"Future Aviation Problems" (ed), Hugo Gernsback
"The Return of the Air Master" (sn), Edward E. Chappelow (Paul)
"The Space Visitors" (s), Edmond Hamilton (Paul)
"The X Gas" (s), Cyril Plunkett (Win)
"A Test of Airplane Lightning Hazards" (a), Walter E. Burton (photos)
"The Flying Legion"* (sr3/4), George Allan England (Paul)

1/10 (10) April 1930.
"The Flying Buzz-Saw"

"Stations in Space" (ed), Hugo Gernsback
"Through the Meteors" (nt), Lowell Howard Morrow (Paul)
"The Heat Ray" (s), O.L. Beckwith (Leonard)
"The Flying Buzz-Saw" (s), Harold B. McKay (Paul)
"Evans of the Earth Guard" (s), Edmond Hamilton (Winter)
"The Meteoric Magnet" (s), Moses Schere (Paul)
"The Flying Legion"* (sr4/4), George Allan England (Paul)
"How High Can Man Fly?" (a), Lieut. Apollo Soucek as told to Walter Raleigh (photo)

1/11 (11) May 1930.
"The Air Trap"

"The Air Trap" (s), Edward E. Chappelow (Paul)
"The Arctic Rescue" (s), Walter Kateley (Winter)
"Women with Wings" (nt), Leslie F. Stone (Leonard)
"The Invisible Destroyer" (s), L. A. Eshbach (Paul)
"The Sky Ruler" (nt), Ed Earl Repp (Paul)
"The Bat-Men of Mars" (sr1/3), Wood Jackson (Paul)

Thereafter merged with Science Wonder Stories *to form* Wonder Stories *from June 1930*

SCIENCE WONDER STORIES
[Editorial staff as per Air Wonder Stories*]*

1/1 (1) June 1929.
"Warriors of Space"

"Science Wonder Stories" (ed), Hugo Gernsback
"The Reign of the Ray" (sr1/2), Irvin Lester & Fletcher Pratt (Paul)
"The Diamond Maker"* (s), H. G. Wells (Paul) [*The Pall Mall Budget,*

1894]

"Warriors of Space" (nt), James P. Marshall (Paul)

"The Marble Virgin" (s), Kennie McDowd (Paul)

"The Threat of the Robot" (nt), Dr. David H. Keller (Paul)

"The Making of Misty Isle" (s), Stanton A. Coblentz (Paul)

"What Science Fiction Means To Me" contest winners: 1. "The Door to the World of Explanation," B.S. Moore; 2. "Tremendous Contribution to Civilization," Jack Williamson; 3. "A Scientist-Author Speaks," Edward E. Smith, Ph.D. Other entries by R.P. Tooker, Frank H. Dunfee, George P. Trayer, S. Weinberg, Roy Wicks, Edward Alpert, Michael Cangelosi, C.A. Livingston, J. Lawrence Collier, Neil H. Tasker, Sanford Gordon, Tom Olog.

1/2 (2) July 1929.

"Wonders of Gravitation"

"The Wonders of Gravitation" (ed), Hugo Gernsback

"The Alien Intelligence" (sr1/2), Jack Williamson (Paul)

"The Reign of the Ray" (sr2/2), Irvin Lester & Fletcher Pratt (Paul)

"The Boneless Horror" (s), Dr. David H. Keller (Paul)

"The Menace from Below" (na), Harl Vincent (Paul)

"The Problems of Space Flying"* (a1/3), Capt. Hermann Noordung (illus) [orig. Germany, 1928; trans. by Francis M. Currier]

"What Science Fiction Means To Me" contest winners: 1. "The Gift of the Master Mentality," Tom Olog; 2. "An Escape from the Monotony of Life," James P. Marshall; 3. "Directing the Way to Truth," Michael Hnatko. Other entries by Byron W. Dunlavey, Louis H. Scher.

1/3 (3) August 1929.

"The Problems of Space Flying"

"The Wonders of Space" (ed), Hugo Gernsback

"The Moon Beasts" (nt), William P. Locke (Paul)

"The Radium Pool" (sr1/2), Ed Earl Repp (Paul)

"The Eternal Man" (s), D. D. Sharp (Paul)

"The Alien Intelligence" (sr2/2), Jack Williamson (Paul)

"The Feminine Metamorphosis" (nt), Dr. David H. Keller (Paul)

"The Problems of Space Flying"* (a2/3), Capt. Hermann Noordung (illus)

"What Science Fiction Means To Me" contest winners: 1. "The Story of Humanity," F.P. Swiggett, Jr.; 2. "The Perfect Entertainment," J. Roy Chapman; 3. "Crosses the Chasm of Impossibility," Al Browne. Other entires by Nicholas Mizibrocky, James O. Walker.

1/4 (4) September 1929.

"The Onslaught from Venus"

"Hidden Wonders" (ed), Hugo Gernsback

"The Human Termites" (sr1/3), Dr. David H. Keller (Paul)

"The Cubic City" (s), Rev. Louis Tucker, D.D. (Paul)

"The Onslaught from Venus" (nt), Frank Phillips [Philip Francis Nowlan] (Paul)

"The Radium Pool" (sr2/2), Ed Earl Repp (Paul)
"The Problems of Space Flying"* (a3/3), Capt. Hermann Noordung (illus)

1/5 (5) October 1929.

"Into the Subconscious"

"Wonders of Space" (ed), Hugo Gernsback
"The Metal World" (s), Ed Earl Repp (Paul)
"The Ancient Brain" (s), Allen G. Stangland (Paul)
"The Human Termites" (sr2/3), Dr. David H. Keller (Paul)
"Into the Subconscious" (s), Ray Avery Myers (Paul)
"From Eros to Earth" (nt), Walter Kateley (Paul)
"In Two Worlds" (s), Edward E. Chappelow (Winter?)

1/6 (6) November 1929.

[Story contest cover]

"$300.00 Prize Story Contest" (ed), Hugo Gernsback
"The Phantom Teleview" (s), Bob Olsen (Paul)
"My Little Martian Sweetheart" (v), The Planet Prince [J. Harvey Haggard]
"The Killing Flash" (ss), Hugo Gernsback (Paul)
"The Stellar Missile" (nt), Ed Earl Repp (Winter)
"The Gold Triumvirate" (s), Walter Kateley (Paul)
"The Space Dwellers" (s), Raymond Gallun (Lieberman)
"The Human Termites" (sr3/3), Dr. David H. Keller (Paul)
"The Green Intelligence" (s), Harley S. Aldinger (Paul)

1/7 (7) December 1929.

"The Time Oscillator"

"The Wonders of Interstellar Flight" (ed), Hugo Gernsback
"The Conquerors" (sr1/2), David H. Keller (Paul)
"The Rocket Comes to the front Page" (a), no credit
"The Time Oscillator" (nt), Henry F. Kirkham (Paul)
"The Radiation of the Chinese Vegetable" (s), C. Sterling Gleason (Winter)
"The Super Velocitor" (nt), S.C. Carpenter (Blythe)
"Life in the Cosmos"* (a) [editorial from *New York Sun*, October 5, 1929]
"The Lost Martian" (nt), Henry Harbers (Paul)

1/8 (8) January 1930.

"The Vapor Intelligence"

"Wonders of Other Worlds" (ed), Hugo Gernsback
"The Fitzgerald Contraction" (nt), Miles J. Breuer, M.D. (Paul)
"The Red Dimension" (s), Ed Earl Repp (Winter)
"The Vapor Intelligence" (s), Jack Barnette (Paul)
"The Conquerors" (sr2/2), David H. Keller (Paul)

1/9 (9) February 1930.

"The Land of the Bipos"

"Can Man Free Himself from Gravity?" (ed), Hugo Gernsback

"The Horrible Transformation" (s), J. Stallworth Daniels (Paul)

Thereafter merged with Air Wonder Stories *to form* Wonder Stories *from June 1930*

WONDER STORIES

Editor-in-Chief: Hugo Gernsback, June 1930-April 1936. *Managing Editor*: David Lasser, June 1930-October 1933; Charles D. Hornig, November 1933-April 1936. *Associate Editor*: C. P. Mason, June 1930-April 1936. *Literary Editor*: C. A. Brandt, January-November 1932. *Art Director*: Frank R. Paul, June 1930-April 1936.

2/1 (13) June 1930.
"Trapped in the Depths"

"The Wonders of Sleep" (ed), Hugo Gernsback
"A Subterranean Adventure" (sr1/3), George Paul Bauer (Paul)
"The Incredible Monstrosity" (nt) Walter Kateley (Paul)
"Trapped in the Depths" (s), Capt. S. P. Meek (Paul)
"The Time Ray of Jandra" (nt), Raymond A. Palmer (Leonard)
"Waves of Death" (s), Wesley Arnold (Paul)
"The Bat-Men of Mars" (sr2/3), Wood Jackson (Leonard)

2/2 (14) July 1930.
"The Flight of the Mercury"

"Wonders of the Unknown" (ed), Hugo Gernsback
"The Time Valve" (nt), Miles J. Breuer, M.D. (Paul)
"The Flight of the Mercury" (s), Charles R. Tanner (Paul)
"The Bat-Men of Mars" (sr3/3), Wood Jackson (Paul)
"After 5000 Years" (s), Victor A. Endersby
"The Master Allegory" (v), The Planet Prince [J. Harvey Haggard]
"The War of the Great Ants" (s), Jim Vanny (Leonard)
"A Subterranean Adventure" (sr2/3), George Paul Bauer (Paul)
"The Red Plague" (s), P. Schuyler Miller (Paul)
"Advance of Science" (v), The Planet Prince [J. Harvey Haggard]
"Whose Flight Was the More Hazardous?" (a), John Randolph

2/3 (15) August 1930.
"The Radium Master"

"Wonders of Memory" (ed), Hugo Gernsback
"The Martian Revenge" (nt), Henrik Dahl Juve (Paul)
"The Annihilator Comes" (nt), Ed Earl Repp (Leonard)
"When the Moons Met!" (s), Clyde F. Beck (Miller)
"The Radium Master" (nt), Jim Vanny (Paul)
"A Subterranean Adventure" (sr3/3), George Paul Bauer (Miller)

2/4 (16) September 1930.

"The Tragedy of Spider Island"

"The Wonders of Space-Matter" (ed), Hugo Gernsback
"The War Lord of Venus" (sr1/3), Frank J. Bridge [Frank J. Brueckel] (Marchioni)
"In 20,000 A.D.!" (nt), Nat Schachner & Arthur L. Zagat (Paul)
"The Tragedy of Spider Island" (s), Captain S. P. Meek, U.S.A. (Paul)
"The King of the Black Bowl" (nt), R. F. Starzl (Miller)
"A Rescue in Space" (s), Lowell Howard Morrow (Miller)
"The Torpedo Terror" (s), Edsel Newton (Leonard)

2/5 (17) October 1930.

"Marooned in Andromeda"

"Marooned in Andromeda" (nt), Clark Ashton Smith (Paul)
"The Lizard-Men of Buh-Lo" (nt), Francis Flagg (Marchioni)
"The Empire in the Sky" (s), Ralph W. Wilkins (Paul)
"The City on the Cloud" (s), L. Taylor Hansen (Marchioni)
"Faster Than Light" (s), J. Harvey Haggard (Marchioni)
"The Man Who Laughs" (s), Norman J. Bonney (Marchioni)
"The War Lord of Venus" (sr2/3), Frank J. Bridge [Frank J. Brueckel] (Marchioni)

2/6 (18) November 1930.

"The Time Annihilator"

"The Wonders of Flight" (ed), Hugo Gernsback
"The Time Annihilator" (nt), Edgar A. Manley & Walter Thode (Paul)
"The House in the Clouds" (s), Ulf Hermanson (Paul)
"The Invulnerable Scourge" (s), John S. Campbell (Marchioni)
"Lords of the Deep" (nt), Henry F. Kirkham (Marchioni)
"Hornets of Space" (s), R. F. Starzl (Marchioni)
"The War Lord of Venus" (sr3/3), Frank J. Bridge [Frank J. Brueckel] (Marchioni)

2/7 (19) December 1930.

"The Synthetic Men"

"Life on Other Planets" (ed), Hugo Gernsback
"The Outpost on the Moon" (sr1/3), Joslyn Maxwell [Max J. Irland] (Paul)
"The End of Time" (nt), Henry F. Kirkham (Marchioni)
"The Silent Scourge" (s), Morrison Colladay (Marchioni)
"The Synthetic Men" (s), Ed Earl Repp (Paul)
"The Struggle for Venus" (nt), Wesley Arnold (Marchioni)
"The Air-Plant Men" (nt), Roger Wulfres (Marchioni)

2/8 (20) January 1931.

"The Soulless Entity"

"Wonders of the Vacuum" (ed), Hugo Gernsback
"The Satellite of Doom" (nt), D. D. Sharp (Marchioni)

"The Flaming Cloud" (s), Edsel Newton (Marchioni)
"Death from the Seas" (s), Joseph Kennelly (Anderson)
"The Gland Men of the Island" (s), Malcolm R. Afford (Marchioni)
"The Soulless Entity" (s), Anthony Pelcher (Paul)
"The Outpost on the Moon" (sr2/3), Joslyn Maxwell [Max J. Irland]
(Paul)

2/9 (21) February 1931.

"Dust of Destruction"

"The Wonders of the Simple" (ed), Hugo Gernsback
"Dust of Destruction" (s), P. Schuyler Miller (Paul)
"The Great Transformation" (s), Ray Cummings (Marchioni)
"A Flight into Time" (s), Robert H. Wilson (Marchioni)
"The Murders on the Moon-Ship" (nt), George B. Beattie (Wilson)
"The Sleeping War" (s), David H. Keller, M.D. (Marchioni)
"The World Without" (s), Benson Herbert (Marchioni)
"The Outpost on the Moon" (sr3/3), Joslyn Maxwell [Max J. Irland]
(Paul)

2/10 (22) March 1931.

"The Green Torture"

"Wonders of the Future" (ed), Hugo Gernsback
"The Return from Jupiter" (sr1/2), Gawain Edwards [G. Edwards
Pendray] (Paul)
"The World Without Name" (s), Edwin K. Sloat (Marchioni)
"The Terrors of Aryl" (s), R. F. Starzl (Marchioni)
"Back to 20,000 A.D." (nt), Nathan Schachner & Arthur L. Zagat
(Marchioni)
"The Synthetic Monster" (s), Francis Flagg (Marchioni)
"The Green Torture" (s), A. Rowley Hilliard (Paul)
"From Out of the Earth" (s), Ed Earl Repp (Marchioni)

2/11 (23) April 1931.

"The Man Who Evolved"

"The Wonders of Creation" (ed), Hugo Gernsback
"The Emperor of the Stars" (s), Nathan Schachner & Arthur L. Zagat
(Marchioni)
"An Adventure in Futurity" (nt), Clark Ashton Smith (Marchioni)
"The Sargasso Monster" (s), Edsel Newton (Paul)
"The Man Who Evolved" (s), Edmond Hamilton (Paul)
"The Conquest of Gola" (s), Leslie F. Stone (Marchioni)
"Great Green Things" (s), Thomas H. Knight (Marchioni)
"The Return from Jupiter" (sr2/2), Gawain Edwards [G. Edwards
Pendray] (Paul)

2/12 (24) May 1931.

"Through the Purple Cloud"

"Telepathy" (ed), Hugo Gernsback
"Utopia Island" (sr1/2), Otfrid von Hanstein (Paul) [orig. German, 1927,

by Francis M. Currier]
"Through the Purple Cloud" (s), Jack Williamson (Paul)
"The Cosmic Gun" (s), Morrison F. Colladay (Marchioni)
"Worlds to Barter" (s), John B. Harris (Marchioni)
"The War of the Giants" (s), Fletcher Pratt (Marchioni)
"The Beasts of Ban-du-Lu" (s), Ed Earl Repp (Lane)

3/1 (25) June 1931.

"In the Spacesphere"

"Wonders of the Human Body" (ed), Hugo Gernsback
"In the Spacesphere" (nt), Charles Cloukey (Paul)
"The Light Bender" (s), Frank K. Kelly (Marchioni)
"The Eye of Two Worlds" (s), Arthur G. Stangland (Marchioni)
"The Man Who Changed the Future" (s), R. F. Starzl (Fisher)
"The Exiles of Venus" (s), Jim Vanny (Marchioni)
"Utopia Island" (sr2/2), Otfrid von Hanstein (Paul) [trans. from the German by Francis M. Currier]

3/2 (26) July 1931.

"The City of Singing Flame"

"Wonders of the Machine Age" (ed), Hugo Gernsback
"The Time Projector" (sr1/2), David Lasser & David H. Keller, M.D. (Paul)
"The Planet of Despair" (s), R. F. Starzl (Marchioni)
"The City of Singing Flame" (s), Clark Ashton Smith (Paul)
"The Red Spot of Jupiter" (s), Dennis McDermott [P. Schuyler Miller & Walter L. Dennis] (Marchioni)
"Rebellion)5000 A.D.!" (nt), Garth Bentley (Marchioni)
"A Daring Trip to Mars"* (s), Max Valier (Marchioni) [trans. from German by F.M. Currier]

3/3 (27) August 1931.

"The 35th Millennium"

"Wonders of the Void" (ed), Hugo Gernsback
"Venus Mines, Incorporated" (s), Nathan Schachner & Arthur L. Zagat (Marchioni)
"The World Within" (s), Benson Herbert (Marchioni)
"The 35th Millennium" (nt), Arthur G. Stangland (Paul)
"Twelve Hours to Live!" (s), Jack Williamson (Marchioni)
"The Island of the Giants" (nt), A. Rowley Hilliard (Leonard)
"The Time Projector" (sr2/2), David Lasser & David H. Keller, M.D. (Paul)

3/4 (28) September 1931.

"An Adventure on Eros"

"Wonders of the Earth's Interior" (ed), Hugo Gernsback
"Exiles of the Moon" (sr1/3), Nathan Schachner & Arthur L. Zagat (Paul)
"A 20th Century Medusa" (nt), R. F. Starzl (Marchioni)

"The Mutiny in Space" (nt), Gawain Edwards [G. Edwards Pendray] (Leonard)
"The Disc-Men of Jupiter" (nt), Manly Wade Wellman (Marchioni)
"An Adventure on Eros" (s), J. Harvey Haggard (Paul)

3/5 (29) October 1931.

"Between Dimensions"

"The Return of the Cosmic Gun" (nt), Morrison F. Colladay (Marchioni)
"Death from the Stars" (s), A. Rowley Hilliard (Marchioni)
"Between Dimensions" (s), J. E. Keith (Paul)
"Beyond the Star Curtain" (s), Garth Bentley (Marchioni)
"After 1,000,000 Years" (s), J. M. Walsh (Marchioni)
"Exiles of the Moon" (sr2/3), Nathan Schachner & Arthur L. Zagat (Paul)

3/6 (30) November 1931.

"Tetrahedra of Space"

"Wonders of the Stars" (ed), Hugo Gernsback
"Tetrahedra of Space" (nt), P. Schuyler Miller (Paul)
"The Superman of Dr. Jukes" (s), Francis Flagg (Paul)
"Beyond the Singing Flame" (s), Clark Ashton Smith (Paul)
"Emperors of Space" (nt), Jerome Gross & Richard Penny (Paul)
"Exiles of the Moon" (sr3/3), Nathan Schachner & Arthur L. Zagat (Paul)

3/7 (31) December 1931.

"Reign of the Robots"

"Wonders of Life" (ed), Hugo Gernsback
"The Time Stream" (sr1/4), John Taine (Paul)
"The Reign of the Robots" (nt), Edmond Hamilton (Paul)
"The Andromeda Menace" (s), Joseph F. Houghton (Paul)
"Lord of the Lightning" (s), Arthur K. Barnes (Paul)
"The World of the Red Sun" (nt), Clifford D. Simak (Paul)
"The Terror from the Sea" (s), Robert Arthur, Jr. (Paul)
"At the End of the Spectrum" (v), The Planet Prince [J. Harvey Haggard]

3/8 (32) January 1932.

"Martian Guns"

"The Wonders of Space Radiation" (ed), Hugo Gernsback
"Martian Guns" (nt), Stanley D. Bell (Paul)
"The Derelicts of Ganymede" (nt), John W. Campbell, Jr. (Paul)
"The Duel on the Asteroid" (s), P. Schuyler Miller & Dennis McDermott [Walter L. Dennis & Paul McDermott] (Paul)
"The Crystal Empire" (s), Sidney D. Berlow (Paul)
"The Time Stream" (sr2/4), John Taine (Paul)

3/9 (33) February 1932.

"The Moon Era"

"The Wonders of 2031" (ed), Hugo Gernsback
"The Moon Era" (nt), Jack Williamson (Paul)
"The Challenge of the Comet" (s), Arthur K. Barnes (Paul)

"A Conquest of Two Worlds" (nt), Edmond Hamilton (Paul)
"The Radium World" (nt), Frank K. Kelly (Paul)
"The Time Stream" (sr3/4), John Taine (Paul)

3/10 (34) March 1932.

"Red April, 1965"

"What is Life?" (ed), Hugo Gernsback
"The Final War" (sr1/2), Carl W. Spohr (Paul)
"The Eternal World" (s), Clark Ashton Smith (Paul)
"Waves of Compulsion" (nt), Raymond Gallun (Paul)
"Red April, 1965" (nt), Frank K. Kelly (Paul)
"Mutiny on Mercury" (s), Clifford D. Simak (Paul)
"The Time Stream" (sr4/4), John Taine (Paul)

3/11 (35) April 1932.

"50th Century Revolt"

"The Wonders of Light-Time?" (ed), Hugo Gernsback
"50th Century Revolt" (nt), Arthur G. Stangland (Paul)
"The Reign of the Star-Death" (nt), A. Rowley Hilliard (Paul)
"The Last Woman" (s), Thomas S. Gardner (Paul)
"The Electronic Siege" (s), John W. Campbell, Jr. (Paul)
"The Man Who Shrank" (s), George B. Beattie
"The Final War" (sr2/2), Carl W. Spohr (Paul)

3/12 (36) May 1932.

"The Moon Mistress"

"Wonders of Atomic Power" (ed), Hugo Gernsback
"Brood of Helios" (sr1/3), John Bertin (Paul)
"Vanishing Gold" (s), Capt. S. P. Meek (Paul)
"The Moon Mistress" (nt), Raymond Gallun (Paul)
"When the Earth Tilted" (s), J. M. Walsh (Paul)
"The Venus Adventure" (nt), John B. Harris (Paul)
"Why the Heavens Fell" (s), Epaminondas T. Snooks, D.T.G. [C. P. Mason] (Paul)

4/1 (37) June 1932.

"The Invisible City"

"Wonders of the Commonplace" (ed), Hugo Gernsback
"The Invisible City" (s), Clark Ashton Smith (Paul)
"The Hell Planet" (nt), Leslie F. Stone (Paul)
"The Message from Mars"* (nt), Ralph Stranger (Paul) [previously published in a British magazine]
"Under Arctic Ice" (nt), Walter Kateley (Paul)
"The Power Satellite" (s), R. F. Starzl (Paul)
"Brood of Helios" (sr2/3), John Bertin (Paul)

4/2 (38) July 1932.

(contest cover)

"The Wonders of Distance" (ed), Hugo Gernsback

"In the Year 8000" (sr1/3), Otfrid von Hanstein (Paul) [trans. from German by Konrad Schmidt & Laurence Manning]
"Castaways of Space" (s), Arthur G. Stangland (Paul)
"The Time Conqueror" (nt), Lloyd A. Eshbach (Paul)
"The Master of Storms" (s), Edwin K. Sloat (Paul)
"Brood of Helios" (sr3/3), John Bertin (Paul)

4/3 (39) August 1932.

"The Space Coffin"

"The Wonders of Knowledge" (ed), Hugo Gernsback
"Tyrant of the Red World" (nt), Richard Tooker (Paul)
"Flight into Super-Time" (nt), Clark Ashton Smith (Paul)
"The Space Coffin" (nt), A. Rowley Hilliard (Paul)
"The Platinum Planets" (nt), George B. Beattie (Paul)
"In the Year 8000" (sr2/3), Otfrid von Hanstein (Paul) [trans. from German by Konrad Schmidt & Laurence Manning]

4/4 (40) September 1932.

[story contest cover]

"The Wonder of Dreams" (ed), Hugo Gernsback
"The Death of Iron"* (sr1/4), S. S. Held (Paul) [orig. France, 1931; trans. by Fletcher Pratt]
"Crossroads of Space" (s), Arthur G. Stangland (Paul)
"In Martian Depths" (nt), Henrik Dahl Juve (Paul)
"After Armageddon" (s), Francis Flagg
"Red Flame of Venus" (nt), P. Schuyler Miller (Paul)
"In the Year 8000" (sr3/3), Otfrid von Hanstein (Paul) [trans. from German by Konrad Schmidt & Laurence Manning]

4/5 (41) October 1932.

"Master of the Asteroid"

"Wonders of Sight" (ed), Hugo Gernsback
"The Planet of Youth" (nt), Stanton A. Coblentz (Paul)
"Outcasts from Mars" (s), Arthur G. Stangland (Paul)
"Chicago, 2042 A.D." (nt), Paul Bolton (Paul)
"Master of the Asteroid" (s), Clark Ashton Smith (Paul)
"The Man of Stone" (s), Hazel Heald (Paul)
"The Death of Iron"* (sr2/4), S. S. Held (Paul)

4/6 (42) November 1932.

[design by art department]

"Wonders of Colors" (ed), Hugo Gernsback
"The Venus Germ" (nt), R. F. Starzl & Festus Pragnell (Paul)
"The Lake of Life" (s), Arthur G. Stangland (Paul)
"The Asteroid of Gold" (s), Clifford D. Simak (Paul)
"The Dimension of Chance" (s), Clark Ashton Smith
"The Death of Iron"* (sr3/4), S. S. Held (Paul)

4/7 (43) December 1932.

"The Time Express"

"Wonders of the Universe" (ed), Hugo Gernsback
"The Wreck of the Asteroid" (sr1/3), Laurence Manning (Paul)
"The Time Express" (nt), Nathan Schachner (Paul)
"The Planetoid of Doom" (s), Morrison Colladay (Paul)
"Space Rays" (s), John W. Campbell, Jr. (Paul)
"Reasonableness in Science Fiction" (a), Hugo Gernsback *[inset into Campbell's story]*
"The Death of Iron"* (sr4/4), S. S. Held (Paul)

4/8 (44) January 1933.

"The Messenger from Space"

"Wonders of Mars" (ed), Hugo Gernsback
"The Memory of the Atoms" (nt), Nathan Schachner & R. Lacher (Paul)
"The Messenger from Space" (s), D. D. Sharp (Paul)
"The Synthetic Entity" (s), Capt. S. P. Meek (Paul)
"The Last of the Lemurians" (s), Arthur G. Stangland (Paul)
"The Wreck of the Asteroid" (sr2/3), Laurence Manning (Paul)
"Presenting Paul" (a), *photo and brief text on Frank R. Paul*

4/9 (45) February 1933.

"The Moon Doom"

"Wonders of Intelligence" (ed), Hugo Gernsback
"The Eternal Dictator" (nt), Nathan Schachner (Paul)
"Escape from Phobos" (s), Neil R. Jones (Paul)
"At Bay in the Void" (s), D. D. Sharp (Paul)
"The Moon Doom" (sr1/4), Nathaniel Salisbury
"The Wreck of the Asteroid" (sr3/3), Laurence Manning (Paul)

4/10 (46) March 1933.

"Wanderers of Time"

"Wonders of Technocracy" (ed), Hugo Gernsback
"The Robot Technocrat" (nt), Nathan Schachner (Paul)
"The Man Who Awoke" (nt), Laurence Manning (Paul)
"Dweller in Martian Depths" (s), Clark Ashton Smith (Paul)
"Wanderers of Time" (nt), John Beynon Harris (Paul)

4/11 (47) April 1933.

"The Fatal Equation"

"Wonders of Interplanetary Life" (ed), Hugo Gernsback
"Revolt of the Scientists" (nt), Nathan Schachner (Paul)
"The Light from Beyond" (s), Clark Ashton Smith (Paul)
"The Fatal Equation" (s), Arthur G. Stangland (Paul)
"The Man Who Awoke, II. Master of the Brain" (nt), Laurence Manning (Paul)
"Giants in the Earth" (s), Morrison Colladay (Paul)
"The Moon Mines" (nt), Eando Binder (Paul)

"The Forgotten Man of Space" (s), P. Schuyler Miller (Marchioni)
"The Moon Doom" (sr2/4), William Lichtenstein
"The Dimension Twister" (s), Hugh King Harris

4/12 (48) May 1933.

"The Visitors from Mlok"

"Wonders of Thought" (ed), Hugo Gernsback
"Gulliver, 3000 A.D." (na), Leslie F. Stone (Paul)
"The Man Who Awoke, III. The City of Sleep" (nt), Laurence Manning (Paul)
"The Third Vibrator" (s), John Beynon Harris (Paul)
"Brahma-Kalpa)or the Expanding Universe" (ss), Epaminondas T. Snooks, D.T.G. [C. P. Mason]
"The Revolt of the Scientists, II. The Great Oil War" (nt), Nathan Schachner (Paul)
"The Visitors from Mlok" (s), Clark Ashton Smith (Paul)
"The Island of Unreason" (s), Edmond Hamilton (Paul)
"The Moon Doom" (sr3/4), Wesley P. Baird
"Men Without Sleep" (s), Edwin Bruell

5/1 (49) June 1933.

"Captive of the Crater"

"Wonders of Touch" (ed), Hugo Gernsback
"The Radio Terror" (sr1/3), Eugene Thebault (Paul) [trans. from French by Fletcher Pratt]
"Captive of the Crater" (s), D. D. Sharp (Paul)
"The Revolt of the Scientists, III. The Final Triumph" (nt), Nathan Schachner (Paul)
"Men of the Dark Comet" (nt), Festus Pragnell (Paul)
"The Man Who Awoke, IV. The Individualists" (nt), Laurence Manning (Paul)
"The Moon Doom" (sr4/4), Clinton Earle Fisk
"The Dead World" and "The Robot" (v), Clarence Edward Flynn

5/2 (50) August 1933.

"Castaways on Deimos"

"Wonders of Space Flight" (ed), Hugo Gernsback
"The Mystery of Planet Deep" (nt), George A. Dye (Paul)
"The Cosmic Horror" (s), Richard F. Searight (Paul)
"Castaways on Deimos" (s), J. Harvey Haggard (Paul)
"The Isotope Men" (nt), Festus Pragnell (Paul)
"The Man Who Awoke, V. The Elixir" (s), Laurence Manning (Paul)
"The Radio Terror" (sr2/3), Eugene Thebault (Paul) [trans. from French by Fletcher Pratt]

5/3 (51) October 1933.

"The Moon Tragedy"

"Wonders of World Speeds" (ed), Hugo Gernsback
"Monsters of Callisto" (na), Edward H. Hinton (Paul)

"Spheres of Hell" (s), John Beynon Harris (Paul)
"The Moon Tragedy" (nt), Frank K. Kelly (Paul)
"The Last of the Swarm" (s), Henry E. Lemke (Paul)
"The Radio Terror" (sr3/3), Eugene Thebault (Paul) [trans. from French
    by Fletcher Pratt]

5/4 (52) November 1933.

"The Call of the Mech-men"

"Oxygen on Mars" (ed), Hugo Gernsback
"The Lunar Consul" (sr1/2), Sidney Patzer (Paul)
"The End of Tyme" (s), A. Fedor & Henry Hasse (Burian)
"Death Between the Planets" (s), James D. Perry (Paul)
"The Tomb from Beyond" (s), Carl Jacobi (Paul)
"The Call of the Mech-men" (s), Laurence Manning (Paul)
"The Man with X-Ray Eyes" (s), Edmond Hamilton (Lumen Winter)
"Through the Einstein Line" (s), J. Harvey Haggard (Lumen Winter)

5/5 (53) December 1933.

"Evolution Satellite"

"The Wonders of Motion)Matter" (ed), Hugo Gernsback
"Evolution Satellite" (sr1/2). J. Harvey Haggard (Paul)
"The Inquisition of 6061" (s), Arthur Frederick Jones (Lumen Winter)
"Invisible Monsters" (s), John Beynon Harris (Burian)
"The Heat Destroyers" (s), Clifton Bryan Kruse (Saaty)
"The Mole-Men of Mercury" (s), Arthur K. Barnes (Lumen Winter)
"The Lunar Consul" (sr2/2), Sidney Patzer (Paul)

5/6 (54) January 1934.

"The Moon Plague"

"Wonders of Micro-Life" (ed), Hugo Gernsback
"The Exile of the Skies" (sr1/3), Richard Vaughan (Paul)
"The Man from Ariel" (s), Donald A. Wollheim (Paul)
"Today's Yesterday" (s), Rice Ray [Russell Blaiklock] (Lumen Winter)
"When Reptiles Ruled" (s), Duane N. Carroll (Paul)
"The Secret of the Microcosm" (s), F. Golub (Lumen Winter) [trans. from
    German by F.M. Currier]
"The Moon Plague" (s), Raymond Z. Gallun (Lumen Winter)
"Garfield's Invention" (s), Leo Am Bruhl (Lumen Winter) [trans. from
    German by F.M. Currier]
"Evolution Satellite" (sr2/2). J. Harvey Haggard (Paul)
"Impressions of the Planets)Venus" (v), Richard F. Searight
"The Riddle" (v), Al Browne

5/7 (55) February 1934

"The Spore Doom"

"Wonders of Our Color Sense" (ed), Hugo Gernsback
"The Spore Doom" (nt), Eando Binder (Paul)
"The Sublime Vigil" (s), Chester D. Cuthbert (L. Winter)
"The Vengeance of a Scientist" (nt), Abner J. Gelula (L. Winter)

"An Episode on Io" (s), J. Harvey Haggard (L. Winter)
"The Shot from the Sky" (ss), Benson Herbert (Paul)
"The Exile of the Skies" (sr2/3), Richard Vaughan (Paul)

5/8 (56) March 1934.

"Children of the Ray"

"Wonders of Radio Waves" (ed), Hugo Gernsback
"Xandulu" (sr1/3), Jack Williamson (Paul)
"The Brain-Eaters of Pluto" (s), Kenneth Sterling (Paul)
"Children of the Ray" (s), J. Harvey Haggard (Paul)
"Martian Madness" (s), P. E. Cleator (L. Winter)
"Caverns of Horror" (s), Laurence Manning (Bulow)
"The Literary Corkscrew" (s), David H. Keller, M.D. (Paul)
"The Exile of the Skies" (sr3/3), Richard Vaughan (Paul)
"To a Spaceship" (v), August W. Derleth
"Luna" (v), H.S. Zerrin

5/9 (57) April 1934.

"The Moon Devils"

"The Science Fiction League: An Announcement" (ed), Hugo Gernsback
"The Land of Mighty Insects" (nt), A. C. Stimson (Paul)
"The Moon Devils" (s), John Beynon Harris (L. Winter)
"The Menace from Space" (nt), John Edwards (Paul)
"The End of the Universe" (ss), Milton Kaletsky
"The Last Planet" (s), R. F. Starzl (L. Winter)
"Xandulu" (sr2/3), Jack Williamson (Paul)
"Passing of the Planets)Venus" (v), H.S. Zerrin

5/10 (58) May 1934.

"Earthspot"

"The Science Fiction League" (ed), Hugo Gernsback
"Druso"* (sr1/3), Friedrich Freksa (Paul) [orig. Germany, 1931; orig. German, 1924; trans. by Fletcher Pratt]
"Traders in Treasures" (s), Epaminondas T. Snooks, D.T.G. [C. P. Mason] (Paul)
"Earthspot" (s), Morrison Colladay (Paul)
"The Tone Machine" (s), Chester G. Osborne (L. Winter)
"The Green Cloud of Space" (s), Eando Binder (L. Winter)
"Xandulu" (sr3/3), Jack Williamson (Paul)

6/1 (59) June 1934.

"Into the Infinitesimal"

"The Wonders of Time" (ed), Hugo Gernsback
"Into the Infinitesimal" (na), Kaye Raymond (Schneeman)
"The Doorbell" (s), David H. Keller, M.D. (L. Winter)
"Ode to Arrhenius" (v), Charles D. Hornig
"Cosmic Calamity" (ss), W. Varick Nevins, III
"Adrift in the Void" (s), John Pierce, B.S. (Paul)
"Druso"* (sr2/3), Friedrich Freksa (Paul)

6/2 (60) July 1934.

"Voice of Atlantis"

"Wonders of Automatism" (ed), Hugo Gernsback
"Enslaved Brains" (sr1/3), Eando Binder (Paul)
"Voice of Atlantis" (s), Laurence Manning (L. Winter)
"A Martian Odyssey" (s), Stanley G. Weinbaum (Paul)
"A Hair-Raising Tale" (ss), W.L. Sheppard, Jr.
"The Last Shrine" (s), Chester D. Cuthbert (L. Winter)
"Druso"* (sr3/3), Friedrich Freksa (Paul)

6/3 (61) August 1934.

"Dimensional Fate"

"Wonders of Reality" (ed), Hugo Gernsback
"Dimensional Fate" (s), A.L. Burkholder (Paul)
"A Visit to Venus" (nt), Festus Pragnell (Paul)
"The Return of Tyme" (s), A. Fedor & Henry Hasse (L. Winter)
"Postscript to 'The Return of Tyme'" (ss), Mohammed Ulysses Socrates
    Fips [Hugo Gernsback]
"The Sense Twister" (s), W. Varick Nevins, III
"The Man from Gayln" (s), E. Mantell (L. Winter)
"Enslaved Brains" (sr2/3), Eando Binder (Paul)

6/4 (62) September 1934.

"The Man from Beyond"

"Wonders of the Planets" (ed), Hugo Gernsback
"The Fall of the Eiffel Tower"* (sr1/3), Charles de Richter (Paul) [trans.
    from French by Fletcher Pratt]
"The Man from Beyond" (s), John Beynon Harris (Paul)
"The Living Galaxy" (s), Laurence Manning (Saaty)
"The Wanderer" (v), L. A. Eshbach
"The Tree of Evil" (s), David H. Keller, M.D. (L. Winter)
"Enslaved Brains" (sr3/3), Eando Binder (Paul)

6/5 (63) October 1934.

"The Thieves from Isot"

"Wonders of Pressure" (ed), Hugo Gernsback
"The Thieves from Isot" (nt), Eando Binder (Paul)
"The Final Struggle" (s), Francesco Bivona (L. Winter)
"The Brain of Ali Kahn" (s), L. A. Eshbach (L. Winter)
"The Fall of the Eiffel Tower"* (sr2/3), Charles de Richter (Paul)

6/6 (64) November 1934.

"One Prehistoric Night"

"The Wonders of Bio-Mechanics" (ed), Hugo Gernsback
"Dawn to Dusk" (sr1/3), Eando Binder (Paul)
"The Control Drug" (s), Benson Herbert (L. Winter)
"Valley of Dreams" (s), Stanley G. Weinbaum (Paul)
"Omega" (v), August W. Derleth

"One Prehistoric Night" (s), Philip Barshofsky (Paul)
"The Growth Promoter" (ss), Paul K. Chapple
"Twenty-Five Centuries Late" (s), Philip J. Bartel (L. Winter)
"The Fall of the Eiffel Tower"* (sr3/3), Charles de Richter (Paul)
"The Martian Cry" (v), L. A. Eshbach

6/7 (65) December 1934.
"The Alien Room"

"Wonders of Fiction" (ed), Hugo Gernsback
"The Alien Room" (s), W. P. Cockroft (Paul)
"Higher Jurisdiction" (ss), D. D. Sharp
"The Black River" (s), John M. Corbett (Paul)
"House of Monstrosities" (s), Edsel Newton (Marchioni)
"The Moth Message" (s), Laurence Manning (Saaty)
"The Time Tragedy" (s), Raymond A. Palmer (Paul)
"The Waterspout" (s), Eugene H. Scheftleman (L. Winter)
"Sleep Scourge" (s), Henry J. Kostkos (Paul)
"Dawn to Dusk" (sr2/3), Eando Binder (Paul)

6/8 (66) January 1935.
"One-Way Tunnel"

"Wonders of Space-Distances" (ed), Hugo Gernsback
"The Hidden Colony"* (sr1/3), Otfrid von Hanstein (Paul) [trans. from
     the German by Fletcher Pratt]
"The Prenatal Plagiarism" (ss), Mortimer Weisinger
"One-Way Tunnel" (nt), David H. Keller, M.D. (Paul)
"The Emotion Meter" (s), W. Varick Nevins, III
"Master of the Genes" (s), Edmond Hamilton (Paul)
"Cosmic Joke" (s), Leslie F. Stone (Paul)
"Dawn to Dusk" (sr3/3), Eando Binder (Paul)

6/9 (67) February 1935.
"The Robot Aliens"

"Wonders of Your Body" (ed), Hugo Gernsback
"The Robot Aliens" (nt), Eando Binder (Paul)
"The Fatal Glance" (ss), Derwin Lesser [Charles D. Hornig]
"The Truth Gas" (s), Edmond Hamilton (Paul)
"The Life Detour" (s), David H. Keller, M.D. (Paul)
"The Hidden Colony"* (sr2/3), Otfrid von Hanstein (Paul)

6/10 (68) March 1935.
"The Eternal Cycle"

"Wonders of Weight" (ed), Hugo Gernsback
"In Caverns Below" (sr1/3), Stanton A. Coblentz (Paul)
"The Eternal Cycle" (s), Edmond Hamilton (Saaty)
"The Celestial Visitor" (s), Lilith Lorraine (Paul)
"Pigments is Pigments" (s), Mortimer Weisinger (L. Winter)
"The Hidden Colony"* (sr3/3), Otfrid von Hanstein (Paul)

6/11 (69) April 1935.

"Phantom Monsters"

"Wonders of Progress" (ed), Hugo Gernsback
"The Elixir of Progress" (s), Philip J. Bartel (Paul)
"Phantom Monsters" (ss), Joseph H. Kraus
"Lunar Dawn" (v), L. A. Eshbach
"A Suitor by Proxy" (s), Harry Collier (Paul)
"The Insect World" (s), Thos. S. Gardner (Paul)
"The Missing Hours" (s), Morton Brotman (L. Winter)
"The Prophetic Voice" (s), Laurence Manning (Paul)
"In Caverns Below" (sr2/3), Stanton A. Coblentz (Paul)
"Man and the Cosmos" (v), August W. Derleth

6/12 (70) May 1935.

"The Living Machine"

"Disembodied Thought" (ed), Hugo Gernsback
"The Waltz of Death" (sr1/3), P.B. Maxon (Schneeman)
"Human Ants" (s), J. Harvey Haggard (Paul)
"The Moaning Lily" (s), Emma Vanne (Schneeman)
"The Living Machine" (s), David H. Keller (Paul)
"In Caverns Below" (sr3/3), Stanton A. Coblentz (Paul)
"The Planeteer" (v), Stark Robertson

7/1 (71) June 1935.

"Seeds from Space"

"Wonders of Orientation" (ed), Hugo Gernsback
"Seeds from Space" (s), Laurence Manning (Paul)
"Pygmalion's Spectacles" (s), Stanley G. Weinbaum (L. Winter)
"The Mystery of the -/-" (s), W. Varick Nevins, III (Paul)
"Death from Within" (s), Sterling S. Cramer (Saaty)
"The Waltz of Death" (sr2/3), P.B. Maxon (Schneeman)

7/2 (72) July 1935.

[Story Cover Contest]

"Wonders of Suspended Life" (ed), Hugo Gernsback
"The Green Man of Graypec" (sr1/3), Festus Pragnell (Paul)
"Justice of the Atoms" (s), Charles B. Pool (L. Winter)
"The Memory Machine" (nt), Bernard Sachs (Marchioni)
"A Thief in Time" (ss), Raymond A. Young
"The Waltz of Death" (sr3/3), P.B. Maxon (Schneeman)

7/3 (73) August 1935.

"The Reign of the Reptiles"

"Wonders of Transportation" (ed), Hugo Gernsback
"The Reign of the Reptiles" (s), A. Connell (Paul)
"The Worlds of If" (s), Stanley G. Weinbaum (Paul)
"The Man with the Four-Dimensional Eyes" (s), Leslie F. Stone (Marchioni)

"The Branches of Time" (s), David R. Daniels (Paul)
"The Green Man of Graypec" (sr2/3), Festus Pragnell (Paul)

7/4 (74) September 1935.
"The Ideal"

"Wonders of Transplanted Organs" (ed), Hugo Gernsback
"World of the Mist" (sr1/2), Laurence Manning (Paul)
"The Ideal" (s), Stanley G. Weinbaum (Paul)
"One Hundred Generations" (nt), Philip Jacques Bartel (Saaty)
"The Space Lens" (s), Millard Verne Gordon [Donald A. Wollheim] (Paul)
"The Green Man of Graypec" (sr3/3), Festus Pragnell (Paul)

7/5 (75) October 1935.
"The Cosmic Pantograph"

"Wonders of Extravagance" (ed), Hugo Gernsback
"The Perfect World" (sr1/3), Benson Herbert (Paul)
"The Cosmic Pantograph" (s), Edmond Hamilton (Paul)
"Martian Gesture" (nt), Alexander M. Phillips (Schneeman)
"The Sex Serum" (s), H.O. Dickinson (L. Winter)
"World of the Mist" (sr2/2), Laurence Manning (Paul)

7/6 (76) December 1935.
"Dream's End"

"Wonders of Mystery Rays" (ed), Hugo Gernsback
"Dream's End" (s), A. Connell (Paul)
"The Isle of Madness" (s), Lilith Lorraine (Schneeman)
"Red Moon" (s), Kenneth Sterling (Paul)
"Three from the Test-Tube" (nt), Raymond A. Palmer (Paul)
"The Rays from the Asteroid" (ss), R. D. Parkinson
"The Perfect World" (sr2/3), Benson Herbert (Paul)

7/7 (77) February 1936
"The Mad World"

"Wonders of Space Flight" (ed), Hugo Gernsback
"A World Unseen" (sr1/2), Joseph W. Skidmore (Paul)
"The Mad World" (s), A.L. Burkholder (Paul)
"The Point of View" (s), Stanley G. Weinbaum (Marchioni)
"The Biped of Bjhulu" (ss), Kenneth Sterling
"Isle of the Gargoyles" (nt), William Lemkin, Ph.D. (Saaty)
"The Perfect World" (sr3/3), Benson Herbert (Paul)

7/8 (78) April 1936.
"The World of Singing Crystals"

"Wonders of Distribution" (ed), Hugo Gernsback
"The World of Singing Crystals" (s), Thos. S. Gardner (Paul)
"The Cosmic Cocktail" (s), Siegfried Wagener (L. Winter)
"Earth's Lucky Day" (s), Francis Flagg & Forrest J Ackerman (Paul)
"The Duplicate" (s), A. Connell (L. Winter)
"The Imperfect Guess" (s), Philip Barshofsky (Winter)

"Fate" (ss), Alan Conn [Alan Connell]
"Emotion Solution" (s), Arthur K. Barnes (Schneeman)
"Futility" (s), Gerald H. Adams
"The Emotion Gas" (s), George F. Gatter (L. Winter)
"A World Unseen" (sr2/2), Joseph W. Skidmore (Paul)

SCIENCE WONDER QUARTERLY
(Editorial staff as per [Science] Wonder Stories)

1/1 (1) Fall 1929.

"The Shot into Infinity"

"$500.00 in Prizes" (ed), Hugo Gernsback
"The Shot into Infinity"* (n), Otto Willi Gail (Paul) [orig. Germany, 1925; trans. by F.M. Currier]
"The Artificial Man" (s), Clare Winger Harris (Paul)
"The Hidden World" (n), Edmond Hamilton (Paul)
"The Gravitational Deflector" (s), Harry D. Parker (Paul)

1/2 (2) Winter 1930.

"The Moon Conquerors"

"What I Have Done to Spread Science Fiction" (ed), Hugo Gernsback
"The Moon Conquerors" (n), R. H. Romans (Paul)
"The Osmotic Theorem" (nt), Capt. S. P. Meek, U.S.A. (Barker)
"Into the 28th Century" (nt), Lilith Lorraine (Paul)
"Underground Waters" (s), A. C. Webb, M.D. (Paul)

1/3 (3) Spring 1930.

"The Stone from the Moon"

"What I Have Done to Spread Science Fiction" (ed), Hugo Gernsback
"The Stone from the Moon"* (n), Otto Willi Gail (Paul) [orig. Germany, 1926; trans. by F.M. Currier]
"Within the Planet" (s), Wesley Arnold (Leonard)
"Via the Hewitt Ray" (nt), M. F. Rupert (Winter)
"The Mechanical Bloodhound" (s), Frank Bridge [Frank J. Brueckel] (Ruger)
"The Ape Cycle" (nt), Clare Winger Harris (Winter)
"The Mad Destroyer" (s), Fletcher Pratt (Ruger)
"The Thought Materializer" (s), F.B. Long, Jr. (Paul)

[magazine retitled: WONDER STORIES QUARTERLY]

1/4 (4) Summer 1930.

"The Monsters of Neptune"

"What I Have Done to Spread Science Fiction" (ed), Hugo Gernsback

"The War of the Planets" (sn), R. H. Romans (Paul)
"The Tower of Evil" (nt), Nathan Schachner & Arthur Leo Zagat (Paul)
"Electropolis"* (n), Otfrid von Hanstein (Paul) [orig. Germany, 19278.
    Trans. by F.M. Currier]
"The Monsters of Neptune" (nt), Henrik Dahl Juve (Paul)
"The Eternal Man Revives" (s), D. D. Sharp (Volga)
"The Moon Rays" (s), David H. Keller, M.D. (Imler)

2/1 (5) Fall 1930.
"Between Earth and Moon"

"Science Fiction vs Science Faction" (ed), Hugo Gernsback
"Between Earth and Moon"* (n), Otfrid von Hanstein (Paul) [orig. Ger-
    many, 1928; trans. by F.M. Currier]
"An Atomic Adventure" (nt), William Lemkin, Ph.D. (Marchioni)
"The Island of Terror" (nt), Ransome Sutton (Marchioni)
"The Struggle for Neptune" (nt), Henrik Dahl Juve (Paul)
"The Secret of the Tomb" (na), R. Crossley Arnold (Miller)
"The Revenge of the Chosen" (s), Thomas H. Knight (Marchioni)

2/2 (6) Winter 1931.
"The Mark of the Meteor"

"Wonder Facts" (ed), Hugo Gernsback
"The Scarlet Planet" (n), Don Mark Lemon (Paul)
"The Man of Bronze" (nt), A. L. Fierst (Miller)
"The Mark of the Meteor" (s), Ray Cummings (Paul)
"Pithecanthropus Island" (s), Isaac R. Nathanson (Marchioni)
"The Martian Nemesis" (nt), George B. Beattie (Marchioni)
"The Hour the Conqueror Came" (s), Edsel Newton (Marchioni)
"Three Worlds to Conquer" (nt), D. D. Sharp (Marchioni)

2/3 (7) Spring 1931.
"Into Plutonian Depths"

"Interplanetary Plot Contest" (ed), Hugo Gernsback (includes plot ex-
    ample, "The Meteor Pest")
"Into Plutonian Depths" (n), Stanton A. Coblentz
"The Empire of Glass" (s), Frank Milloche (Marchioni)
"The Avenging Ray" (nt), A. Rowley Hilliard (Marchioni)
"The Inverted World" (s), J. Rogers Ullrich (Volga)
"When Planets Clashed" (nt), Manly Wade Wellman (Marchioni)
"The Winged Menace" (nt), Packard Dow (Marchioni)

2/4 (8) Summer 1931.
"The Amazing Planet"

"Results of Interplanetary Plot Contest" (ed), Hugo Gernsback
"Vandals of the Void" (n), J. M. Walsh (Paul)
"The Machine of Destiny" (s), Ulysses George Mihalakis (Marchioni)
"The Man from Mars" (s), P. Schuyler Miller (Marchioni)
"The Amazing Planet" (nt), Clark Ashton Smith (Marchioni)
"The Great Invasion" (s), Sidney Patzer (Marchioni)

"Outcast in Space" (s), Arthur G. Stangland (Marchioni)

3/1 (9) Fall 1931.

"The Asteroid of Death"

"Wanted: More Plots" (ed), Hugo Gernsback
"The Cosmic Cloud" (n), Bruno H. Burgel (Paul) [trans. from German by Konrad Schmidt & Fletcher Pratt]
"The Asteroid of Death" (s), Neil R. Jones (Paul)
"The Man-Beast of Toree" (nt), Ralph T. Jones (Marchioni)
"The Derelict of Space" (nt), Ray Cummings from a plot entry by William Thurmond (Paul)
"Zina the Killer" (ss), Walter Livingston Martin
"The Planet Entity" (nt), Clark Ashton Smith from a plot entry by E. M. Johnston (Marchioni)
"The Struggle for Pallas" (s), J. M. Walsh

3/2 (10) Winter 1932.

"The Moon Destroyers"

"Wanted: More Plots" (ed), Hugo Gernsback
"The Onslaught from Rigel" (n), Fletcher Pratt (Paul)
"The Moon Destroyers" (s), Monroe K. Ruch (Paul)
"The Revolt of the Star Men" (na), Raymond Gallun (Paul)
"The Metal Moon" (nt), R. F. Starzl from a plot entry by Everett C. Smith (Paul)
"Shipwrecked on Venus" (s), Neil R. Jones (Paul)
"The Martian" (nt), A. Rowley Hilliard from a plot entry by Allen Glasser (Paul)

3/3 (11) Spring 1932.

"Vanguard to Neptune"

"Wanted: Still More Plots" (ed), Hugo Gernsback
"Vanguard to Neptune" (n), J. M. Walsh (Paul)
"Rebels of the Moon" (s), Manly Wade Wellman from a plot entry by Max Jergovic (Paul)
"The Woman from Space" (nt), Richard Vaughan (Paul)
"The Voice in the Void" (s), Clifford D. Simak (Paul)
"Red Slag of Mars" (nt), Jack Williamson from a plot entry by Laurence Schwartzman (Paul)
"The Sterile World" (nt), Warren D. Sanders (Paul)

3/4 (12) Summer 1932.

"The Menace from Mercury"

"Wanted: Still More Plots" (ed), Hugo Gernsback
"Beyond Pluto" (n), John Scott Campbell (Paul)
"Some Day The Moon" (v), Robert Friend
"Epilog to the Rubaiyat" (v), J.Z. Howard
"Plea to Science Fiction" (v), Don Fernando
"Exiles of Mars" (s), Frank K. Kelly (Paul)

"Rebellion on Venus" (nt), John Bertin from a plot entry by Edward Morris (Paul)

"The Voyage of the Asteroid" (sn), Laurence Manning (Paul)

"The Menace from Mercury" (s), Raymond Gallun from a plot entry by John Michel (Paul)

"The Jovian Horde" (nt), Al H. Martin (Paul)

4/1 (13) Fall 1932.

"The Electron Flame"

"Good News for our Readers" (ed), Hugo Gernsback

"Emissaries of Space" (n), Nathan Schachner (Paul)

"The Crisis with Mars" (nt), Frank K. Kelly (Paul)

"Guardians of the Void" (nt), Arthur K. Barnes (Paul)

"The Electron Flame" (s), Jack Williamson (Paul)

4/2 (14) Winter 1932.

"Interplanetary Bridges"

"On Reprints" (ed), Hugo Gernsback

"Interplanetary Bridges"* (n), Ludwig Anton (Paul) [orig. Germany, 1922; trans. by Konrad Schmidt]

"Exiles on Asperus" (na), John Beynon Harris (Paul)

APPENDIX V

Index to SCIENTIFIC DETECTIVE MONTHLY

Editorial Chief: Hugo Gernsback, January-October 1930. *Editorial Commissioner*: Arthur B. Reeve, January-October 1930. *Editorial Deputy*: Hector G. Grey, January-May 1930; David Lasser, June-October 1930. *Editorial Inspector*: A. L. Fierst, January-March 1930; M. E. Dame, April-October 1930. *Scientific Criminologist*: C. P. Mason, January-October 1930.

1/1 (1) January 1930.

"The Fast Watch" [Ruger]

"Science vs. Crime" (ed), Hugo Gernsback

"What Are the Great Detective Stories and Why?" (a), Arthur B. Reeve

"The Mystery of the Bulawayo Diamond" (s), Arthur B. Reeve (Winter)

"The Campus Murder Mystery" (s), Ralph W. Wilkins (Winter)

"The Fast Watch"* (s), Edwin Balmer & William B. MacHarg (Ruger) [*Hampton's Magazine*, June 1909]

"The Perfect Counterfeit" (s), Captain S. P. Meek, U.S.A. (Winter)

"The Eye of Prometheus" (s), R. F. Starzl (Paul)

"A Message from the Ultra-Violet" (a), H. Ashton-Wolfe

"The Bishop Murder Case"* (sr1/3), S. S. Van Dine (Blythe) [bookform, 1929]

1/2 (2) February 1930.

"The Man Higher Up" [Ruger]

"Scientific Crime Detection" (ed), Hugo Gernsback

"The Bacteriological Detective"* (s), Arthur B. Reeve (Winter) [*Cosmopolitan*, February 1911]

"A Scientific Widowhood" (s), David H. Keller, M.D. (Blythe)

"The Man Higher Up"* (s), Edwin Balmer & William B. MacHarg (Ruger) [*Hampton's Magazine*, September 1909]

"The Man with the Silver Disc" (s), L. A. Eshbach (Winter)

"True Adventures of a Super-Scientific Detective" (a), Joseph Gollomb (Ruger)

"The Bishop Murder Case"* (sr2/3), S. S. Van Dine (Ruger)

1/3 (3) March 1930.

"The Robot Terror" [Ruger]

"Science and the Criminal Mind" (ed), Hugo Gernsback

"The Seismograph Adventure"* (s), Arthur B. Reeve (Winter) [*Cosmopolitan*, April 1911]

"The Power Ray" (s), Jack Barnette (Ruger)

"The Robot Terror" (s), Melbourne Huff (Ruger)

"The Man in the Room"* (s), Edwin Balmer & William B. MacHarg (Winter) [*Hampton's Magazine*, May 1909]

"Test-Tube Bloodhounds" (a), H.H. Dunn
"The Bishop Murder Case"* (sr3/3), S. S. Van Dine (Ruger)

1/4 (4) April 1930.

"Rays of Death" [Paul]

"Crime in Business" (ed), Hugo Gernsback
"The Terror in the Air"* (s), Arthur B. Reeve (Winter) [*Cosmopolitan*, August 1911]
"The Invisible Master" (nt), Edmond Hamilton (Ruger)
"The Hammering Man"* (s), Edwin Balmer & William B. MacHarg (Winter) [*Hampton's Magazine*, May 1910]
"A Denizen of the Underworld" (s), Walter Kateley (Winter)
"Black Light" (s), Henry Leverage (Winter)
"Science, the Police)and the Criminal" (a), Ashur van A. Sommers
"Rays of Death" (sr1/2), Tom Curry (Paul)

1/5 (5) May 1930.

"The Electrical Man" [Ruger]

"The Subconscious Mind and Crime" (ed), Hugo Gernsback
"The Murder in the Clinic" (s), Edmond Hamilton (Winter)
"The Electrical Man" (nt), Neil R. Jones (Ruger)
"The Azure Ring"* (s), Arthur B. Reeve (Ruger) [*Cosmopolitan*, June 1911]
"The Eleventh Hour"* (s), Edwin Balmer & William B. MacHarg (Ruger) [*Hampton's Magazine*, February 1910]
"Hunting Vipers" (a), Dr. Edmond Locard
"Rays of Death" (sr2/2), Tom Curry (Paul)

[magazine retitled: *AMAZING DETECTIVE TALES*]

1/6 (6) June 1930

[Story Contest cover by Ruger]

"Radio and the Criminal" (ed), Hugo Gernsback
"The Diamond Maker"* (s), Arthur B. Reeve (Winter) [*Cosmopolitan*, May 1911]
"A Matter of Mind Reading"* (s), Edwin Balmer & William B. MacHarg (Ruger) [*Hampton's Magazine*, October 1910]
"The Flashlight Brigade" (s), Ralph Milne Farley (Ruger)
"The Gland Murders" (s), S. P. Meek (Ruger)
"Burning Water" (s), David H. Keller, M.D. (Winter)
"The Double Lightning" (s), A.C. Webb (Winter)
"The Blue Spangle" (s), R. Austin Freeman (Lieberman)
"The Sealed Room" (s), Henry Leverage (Ruger)
"The Telegraphic Finger Print" (a), Hector G. Grey

1/7 (7) July 1930.

"Horror House" [Ruger]

"How Criminals Are Identified" (ed), Hugo Gernsback

"The Tower Mystery" (s), Ernest Zorbas (Ruger)

"The Grey Shadow" (s), W. F. Hammond (Winter)

"Horror House" (s), Walter Livingston Martin (Ruger)

"Traced by a Scratch" (a), H.H. Dunn (Winter)

"The Mystery of the Phantom Shot" (s), Amelia Reynolds Long (Winter)

"The Private Bank Puzzle"* (s), Edwin Balmer & William B. MacHarg (Ruger) [*Hampton's Magazine*, August 1909]

"The Mind Machine" (s), George Eugene Key (Winter)

"The White Slave"* (s), Arthur B. Reeve (Ruger) [*Cosmopolitan*, June 1912]

"The Impossible Crime" (s), Ralph W. Wilkins (Jay Gould)

"Arrested by Radio" (a), Hector Gavin Grey

"Police Checkmate New Move of Scientific Criminals" (a), Ashur Van Dusen

1/8 (8) August 1930.

"Vapors of Death" [Ruger?]

"When is a Confession?" (ed), Hugo Gernsback

"The Painted Murder" (s), Eugene de Reszke (Jay Gould)

"The Astounding Clue" (s), Sam Weiner (Jay Gould)

"The Scientific Cracksman"* (s), Arthur B. Reeve (Jay Gould) [*Cosmopolitan*, December 1910, as "The Case of Helen Bond"]

"The Stamp of Doom" (s), Jerry E. Cravey (Jay Gould)

"The Vanishing Man" (s), Ralph Milne Farley (Jay Gould)

"Vapors of Death"* (s), Edwin Balmer & William B. MacHarg (Jay Gould) [*Hampton's Magazine,* December 1909]

"The Saxe Murder Case" (s), Eugene V. Brewster (Romaine)

"The Phantom Killer" (s), Morton Brotman (Ruger)

"Tracked by the Ultra-Violet" (a), Hector Gavin Grey

1/9 (9) September 1930.

"Menacing Claws" [Ruger]

"Crime Prevention" (ed), Hugo Gernsback

"The Temple of Dust" (s), Eugene George Key (Ruger)

"The Black Cabinet" (s), Henry Leverage (Romaine)

"Winged Death" (s), O.L. Beckwith (Wilson)

"The Duel in the Dark"* (s), Edwin Balmer & William B. MacHarg (Wilson) [*Hampton's Magazine*, November 1909, as "The Empty Cartridges"]

"Menacing Claws" (s), David H. Keller (Jay Gould)

"The Body That Wouldn't Burn"* (s), Arthur B. Reeve (Wilson) [*Cosmopolitan*, July 1911, as "The Spontaneous Combustion Case"]

"The Carewe Murder Mystery" (sr1/2), Ed Earl Repp (Jay Gould)

"Undertones of Death" (s), Frank Carter (Wilson)

"What Price Clues" (a), Herbert Mills

1/10 (10) October 1930.

"The Flower of Evil" [Ruger?]

"The Clasp of Doom" (s), Eugene de Reszke (Gould)

"Death in a Drop" (s), Ralph W. Wilkins (Marchioni)

"Shadows of the Night" (s), Neil R. Jones (Marchioni)
"The Man Who Was Dead"* (s), Arthur B. Reeve (Marchioni) [*Cosmopolitan*, October 1911, as "The Artificial Paradise"]
"The Flower of Evil" (s), C. R. Sumner (Marchioni)
"Murder in the Fourth Dimension" (s), Clark Ashton Smith
"The Man in Room 18" (s), Otis Adelbert Kline (Marchioni)
"The Man No One Could Lift" (s), Fred Ebel
"The Carewe Murder Mystery" (sr2/2), Ed Earl Repp (Gould)
"The Most Dangerous of Forgeries" (a), Edmund Lociard

NOTES

Preface

1. Blish, James, *More Issues at Hand* (Chicago: Advent, 1970), p. 118-119; see also Damon Knight, *In Search of Wonder* (Chicago: Advent, 1967), p. 283.
2. Aldiss, Brian W. *Billion Year Spree* (London: Weidenfeld & Nicolson, 1973), p. 209. The first phrase is repeated in *Trillion Year Spree* (London: Gollancz, 1986), p. 202.

Chapter 1

1. O'Neil, Paul, "Barnum of the Space Age," *Life Magazine* 55:4, July 26, 1963, p. 64.
2. Sam Moskowitz, in his *Explorers of the Infinite* (Cleveland: World, 1963) p.229, states that Gernsback learned of this by reading Lowell's *Mars as the Abode of Life*. However, as Gary Westfahl has pointed out in his article "'An Idea of Significant Import': Hugo Gernsback's Theory of Science Fiction" (*Foundation* 48, Spring 1990, p.32), Lowell's book was not published until 1908, and though Lowell had an earlier book, *Mars*, published in 1895, this did not apparently have a German translation prior to 1900. Although Gernsback's memory was at fault somewhere, the fact almost certainly remains that, at sometime around 1894, Gernsback became acquainted with the concept that Mars might be the home of intelligent life. It would have been surprising if he had not learned of the idea. Following the announcement by the Italian astronomer Giovanni Schiaparelli, in 1877, that he had discovered the presence of "canals" on Mars, there had been much speculation in the press about the possibility of intelligent life there. This idea had fascinated the French astronomer Camille Flammarion, with whose works Gernsback may have become acquainted, but it had been taken most strongly to heart by the American astronomer Percival Lowell. Lowell went so far as to build his own observatory in Arizona so as to study Mars in more detail, and this was opened in 1894. So, although Gernsback could not have read Lowell's book in that year, he could easily have read newspaper reports of Lowell's beliefs and activities.
3. More details about this unpublished work can be found in Sam Moskowitz's introduction to Gernsback's *Ultimate World* (New York: Walker, 1971).
4. "Practical Science," *The Electrical Experimenter* 7:73, May 1919, p. 2.
5. *Life Magazine, op.cit.*

Chapter 2

1. See Moskowitz, *Explorers of the Infinite, op. cit.*, p. 230-231 as the basic source for this period of Gernsback's life. Other data is drawn from the O'Neil interview in *Life* (*op.cit.*) and from documents made available from their files by the U.S. Department of Justice Federal Bureau of Investigation.

2. Gernsback, Hugo, "50 Years Hence," speech delivered at the Henry Ford Auditorium, Dearborn, Michigan, April 5, 1957 (see bibliography).

3. Gernsback, Hugo, *ibid.*

Chapter 3

1. *Modern Electrics* 1:1, April 1908, p. 10.
2. *ibid.*
3. *op.cit.* 1:10, January 1909, p. 342.
4. *op.cit.* 2:10, January 1910, p. 471.
5. *op.cit.* 3:12, March 1911, p. 698.
6. *op.cit.* 4:11, February 1912, p. 784-785.

Chapter 4

1. *Modern Electrics* 3:10, January 1911, p.570.
2. *Modern Electrics* 3:12, March 1911. This description reminds me of the headquarters of Doc Savage, atop the tallest skyscraper in New York. The Doc Savage stories were written by Lester Dent. I have no evidence that Dent had read *Ralph 124C 41+*, though it's possible. It's even more possible it was read by Henry Ralston and John Nanovic, the business manager and editor, respectively, at Street & Smith, which published *Doc Savage Magazine*. These two created the basic character and premise of Doc Savage, and may have recalled the home of Ralph during their creative session.
3. In *Science-Fiction: The Gernsback Years*, Everett Bleiler speculated that he may be New York businessman Jacque Lloyd Morgan (b. 1873).

Chapter 7

1. Aldiss, Brian W. *Penguin Science Fiction* (Middlesex: Penguin, 1961).
2. Gernsback, Hugo, "Imagination versus Facts," *The Electrical Experimenter* 3:12, April 1916, p.675.
3. Stratton, George F., *The Electrical Experimenter* 3:6, October 1915, p.250.
4. *ibid.*
5. Stratton, George F., *The Electrical Experimenter* 3:9, January 1916, p.473.
6. Gernsback, Hugo, *The Electrical Experimenter* 3:9, January 1916, p.473.
7. Gernsback, Hugo, *The Electrical Experimenter* 3:5, September 1915, p.177.
8. *The Electrical Experimenter* 8:3, July 1920, p.279, (unsigned).
9. Gernsback, Hugo, *Science and Invention* 8:4, August 1920, p.355.

Chapter 8

1. Gernsback, Hugo, "The Impact of Science Fiction on World Progress," *Science-Fiction Plus* 1:1, March 1953, pp.2, 67.
2. Senarens, Luis, interviewed in *Science and Invention* 8:6, October 1920, p.665.
3. Gernsback, Hugo, "Guest Editorial," *Amazing Stories* 35:4, April 1961, p.7.

4. *ibid.*

Chapter 9

1. Schomburg, Alex in *Chroma: The Art of Alex Schomburg* by Jon Gustafson (Poughkeepsie: Father Tree Press, 1986) p.13.

Chapter 10

1. *Practical Electrics* 3:4, February 1924, p.175.
2. *Science and Invention* 12:5, September 1924, p.476.
3. For more details on Macfadden's publishing and his role in the early days of science fiction, see Sam Moskowitz's series "Bernarr Macfadden and his Obsession with Science Fiction" in *Fantasy Commentator* detailed in the bibliography.
4. Isaacson, Charles D., "WRNY Starts Broadcasting Innovation," *Radio News* 7:5, November 1925, p.599.

Chapter 11

1. The quotes in this paragraph come from "A New Sort of Magazine," editorial in *Amazing Stories* 1:1, April 1926, p.3.
2. *Amazing Stories* 1:1, April 1926, p.96.
3. *Amazing Stories* 1:1, April 1926, pp.4-5.
4. *Amazing Stories* 1:12, March 1927, "Idle Thoughts of a Busy Editor," p.1085. I have sometimes wondered whether the word "bulky," though appropriate, was a misprint for "bulkly," as Gernsback's printers were Bulkly, Dunton & Co., and they may have registered the weave as a trade name.
5. Schomburg did paint a number of covers for Gernsback's technical magazines, especially *Radio-Craft*, in the thirties. Gernsback also selected him as his main technical artist after Paul's death in 1963.
6. *Amazing Stories* 1:2, May 1926, "Thank You!," p.99.
7. *ibid.*
8. *Ayer's Directory* for 1928 gave *Amazing's* circulation in 1927 as 104,117 based on the publisher's report.
9. *Amazing Stories* 1:4, July 1926, p.297.

Chapter 12

1. Gernsback, Hugo, "The Impact of Science Fiction on World Progress," speech reprinted in *Science-Fiction Plus* 1:1, March 1953, pp.2,67.
2. *Amazing Stories* 2:3, June 1927, p.309.
3. *Amazing Stories* 3:10, January 1929, p.957.
4. *Amazing Stories* 1:8, December 1926, p.773.
5. *Amazing Stories* 2:3, June 1927, p.213.
6. *ibid.*
7. *Amazing Stories* 1:12, March 1927, p.1085.
8. *Amazing Stories* 2:5, August 1927, p.421.
9. Correspondence between Hugo Gernsback and H. G. Wells held on file at the University of Illinois Library at Urbana-Champaign.

Chapter 13

1. *Amazing Stories* 2:2, May 1927, p.111.

2. *Amazing Stories* 2:2, May 1927, "The Moon Pool," p.140.

3. *op.cit.*, pp.286-287.

4. Gernsback, Hugo, *Amazing Stories* 2:2, May 1927, "Amazing Creations," p.109.

5. Panshin, Alexei, *The World Beyond the Hill* (Los Angeles: Tarcher, 1989), p.149.

6. *Amazing Stories* 1:4, July 1926, "Fiction versus Facts," p.291.

7. *ibid.*

8. *Science Wonder Stories* 1:2, July 1929, p.188.

9. *Amazing Stories* 2:6, September 1927, p.557.

10. *Amazing Stories* 3:4, July 1928, p.370.

11. *ibid.*

12. *Amazing Stories* 2:7, October 1927, p.625.

13. *Amazing Stories* 3:3, June 1928, p.269.

14. Gernsback, Hugo, "The Impact of Science Fiction on World Progress," reprinted in *Science-Fiction Plus* 1:1, March 1953, pp.2,67.

15. *Amazing Stories* 3:7, October 1928, p.662.

16. *op.cit.* p.667.

17. *Amazing Stories* 4:1, April 1929, p.80.

18. *Amazing Stories* 3:5, August 1928, p.465.

Chapter 14

1. *Amazing Stories* 2:10, January 1928, p.945.

2. *Amazing Stories* 2:11, February 1928, p.1025.

3. *Amazing Stories Quarterly* 1:3, Summer 1928, p.432.

4. Gunn, James, *The Road to Science Fiction #2* (New York: New American Library, 1979), p.169.

5. Keller, David H., "The Folly of Writing," unpublishing ms, made available by courtesy of Paul Spencer.

6. Lovecraft, H.P., *Selected Letters II* (Sauk City: Arkham House, 1968), p.149, HPL to Long, July 1, 1927.

7. Keller, David H., *op.cit.*

8. *Haverford News* 23:17, October 5, 1931, p.1.

9. *Amazing Stories* 2:7, October 1927, p.719.

Chapter 15

1. *Amazing Stories* 1:3, June 1926, p.195.

2. *Wonder Stories* 4:12, May 1933, p.987.

3. *Amazing Stories* 2:7, October 1927, p.719.

4. *Amazing Stories* 2:7, October 1927, p.708.

5. *Science Wonder Stories* 1:3, August 1929, p.283.

6. *ibid.*

Chapter 16

1. *New York Times*, June 16, 1928, p.10.

2. *New York Times*, August 22, 1928, p.10.

3. *Radio News* 10:2, August 1928, p.103.

Chapter 17

1. Lovecraft, H.P., *Selected Letters IV* (Sauk City: Arkham House, 1976),

p.343, HPL to F. Lee Baldwin, January 13, 1934.

2. Copies of the Gernsback-Wells correspondence is provided by courtesy of the University of Illinois Library at Urbana-Champaigne.
3. This letter is provided from the files of Robert E. Weinberg.
4. These details come from Irwin Porges's *Edgar Rice Burroughs: The Man Who Created Tarzan* (New York: Ballantine, 1976), pp.638, 1182.
5. Verrill, A. Hyatt, letter to Forrest J Ackerman, November 19, 1932, provided by courtesy of Forrest J Ackerman.
6. West tells this story in full in *The Weird Tales Story* by Robert E. Weinberg (West Linn: Fax, 1977), pp.53-54. His memory is not at fault as the facts were also recounted to Robert A.W. Lowndes in the fifties, and the basic details are in a letter from West to Forrest J Ackerman dated May 4, 1934.

Chapter 18

1. *Amazing Stories* 4:2, May 1929, p.103.
2. "An Interview with Stanton Coblentz" by Lawrence Davidson and Richard A. Lupoff, *Locus* 12:11, December 1979, p.10.
3. Biographical details are drawn from "The Age of Wonder: Gernsback, *Wonder Stories*, and David Lasser, 1929-1933" by Eric Leif Davin, *Fantasy Commentator* 6:1, Fall 1987.

Chapter 19

1. *Air Wonder Stories* 1:1, July 1929, p.5.
2. *Science Wonder Stories* 1:1, July 1929, p.5.
3. *ibid.*
4. *Air Wonder Stories, op.cit.*
5. Menzel to M. Harvey Gernsback, July 5, 1970, private letter.
6. De Forest, Lee, "Introduction," *Ralph 124C 41+* by Hugo Gernsback (New York: Frederick Fell, 1950) p.15.
7. *Science Wonder Stories* 1:4, September 1929, p.379.
8. *Amazing Stories* 1:10, January 1927, p.973. I ought to have spotted this usage in my detailed reading of the letter columns, but somehow I missed it. Credit for its discovery must go to Gary Westfahl (see bibliography).

Chapter 20

1. *Science Wonder Stories* 1:1, June 1929, p.53.
2. Letter, Gernsback to Hamilton, August 13, 1929; provided by courtesy of the Eastern New Mexico University Library.
3. Letter, Gernsback to Eshbach, August 29, 1929; provided by courtesy of The Temple University Library.
4. Eshbach, L.A., *Over My Shoulder* (Philadelphia: Oswald Train, 1983), p.40.
5. Gernsback, Hugo, "Hugo Gernsback Tells," *Writer's Digest*, April 1930, p.18.
6. *op.cit.*, p.66
7. Gallun's recollection comes from his interview with Eric Leif Davin, "Pioneer in the Age of Wonder," *Fantasy Commentator* 6:2, Fall 1988.
8. *Amazing Stories* 1:4, July 1926, p.382.

Chapter 21

1. Bates, Harry, "To Begin," *A Requiem for Astounding* by Alva Rogers (Chicago: Advent, 1964), p.*x*.
2. Black, Jr., R. Jere, "The Pseudo-Scientific Field," *Author and Journalist*, May 1930, p.8.
3. *Scientific Detective Monthly* 1:5, May 1930, p.464.
4. *Air Wonder Stories* 1:11, May 1930, p.1041.
5. *Science Wonder Stories* 1:12, May 1930, p.1099.
6. *Wonder Stories* 2:5, October 1930, p.389.

Chapter 22

1. "Hugo Gernsback Tells," *Writer's Digest* April 1930; "The Pseudo-Scientific Field," *Author and Journalist*, May 1930.
2. Letter, Smith to Lovecraft, January 27, 1930; reprinted in *Clark Ashton Smith: Letters to H. P. Lovecraft* edited by Steve Behrends (West Warwick: Necronomicon Press, 1987), p.7.
3. *ibid*, Smith to Lovecraft, August 22, 1930, p.10.
4. *ibid*, Smith to Lovecraft, January 1931, p.23.
5. *Wonder Stories* 2:11, April 1931, p.1340.
6. *ibid*.

Chapter 23

1. *Science Wonder Quarterly* 1:1, Fall 1929, p.4.
2. *Air Wonder Stories* 1:10, April 1930, p.953.
3. *Wonder Stories* 5:7, February 1934, p.796.
4. *Wonder Stories* 2:9, February 1931, p.1054.
5. *Wonder Stories* 3:2, July 1931, pp.278, 280.
6. *Wonder Stories* 3:6, November 1931, p.806.

Chapter 24

1. *The Electrical Experimenter* 7:11, March 1920, p.1098.
2. *Wonder Stories* 2:1, June 1930, p.78.
3. *ibid*.
4. *Clark Ashton Smith: Letters to H. P. Lovecraft, op.cit*, p.29; Smith to Lovecraft, August 1931.

Chapter 25

1. Quoted from the reproduction of the letter in Sam Moskowitz's "Henrik Dahl Juve and the Second Gernsback Dynasty," *Extrapolation* 30:1, Spring 1989.
2. In fact the editor was Douglas Dold and Hersey's memory must have been at fault.

Chapter 26

1. *Wonder Stories* 2:9, February 1931, p.1052.
2. *Wonder Stories* 2:9, February 1931, p.1046.
3. *Wonder Stories* 2:10, March 1931, p.1189.
4. *Science Wonder Stories* 1:8, January 1930, p.752.
5. *Science Wonder Stories* 1:10, March 1930, p.951.
6. *ibid*., p.952.

7. *Wonder Stories* 2:7, December 1930, p.754.
8. *Wonder Stories* 2:10, March 1931, p.1190.
9. *Wonder Stories* 3:12, May 1932, p.1353.
10. *Wonder Stories* 3:9, February 1932, p.1047.
11. *Wonder Stories Quarterly* 3:4, Summer 1932, p.509.
12. *Wonder Stories* 4:11, April 1933, p.892.
13. Keller, David H., interviewed by Julius Schwartz and Mort Weisinger in *Science Fiction Digest* 1:11, July 1933, p.4.
14. Gallun, Raymond Z., private communication, October 16, 1990.

Chapter 27

1. David, Eric Leif, *op.cit.* (chapter 20).
2. Williamson, Jack, *Wonder's Child* (New York: Bluejay, 1984), p.78.
3. In an editorial comment in "Discussions" (*Amazing Stories* 10:2, May 1935, p.140), Sloane remarked, "The Quarterly will be somewhat irregular in dates of publication. We have sometimes felt like discontinuing it definitely." Clearly, Sloane's feelings won.
4. *Wonder Stories* 4:10, March 1933, p.741.
5. *Wonder Stories* 3:2, July 1931, p.151, 284.
6. Robert A.W. Lowndes reminds me that David H. Keller's "The Metal Doom" (*Amazing Stories*, May-July 1932) deals with the same subject; but whereas S. S. Held treats it in the manner of a mainstream novel, Keller's characters cope with the situation in a true science-fictional manner. The Held novel is more literary, but Keller's is certainly more stimulating and fun to read.
7. *Wonder Stories* 3:6, November 1931, p.802.
8. *ibid.*
9. *Wonder Stories* 4:7, December 1932, p.569.
10. *Wonder Stories* 4:10, March 1933, p.744.
11. *Wonder Stories* 4:10, March 1933, p.763.
12. Interview with Eric Leif Davin, *Fantasy Commentator* 6:1, Fall 1987.
13. Moskowitz, Sam, *Seekers of Tomorrow* (Chicago: World, 1966), p.357.

Chapter 28

1. Letter, Olsen to Ackerman, March 16, 1932.
2. Letter, Flagg to Ackerman, July 6, 1933.
3. There have been several claims that the character of Superman was drawn from the Man of Bronze, Doc Savage. See *Bigger Than Life* by Marilyn Cannaday (Popular Press, 1990, p. 21-22). However, one of the forgotten footnotes of history is whom Joseph Schuster used as his model for the Man of Steel. Walt Dennis recalls that at this time, Schuster asked if he might use his profile for Clark Kent.

Chapter 29

1. Madle, Robert A., "Science Fiction's Greatest Year," *World Science-Fiction Convention Programme*, 1977.
2. *Wonder Stories* 5:6, January 1934, p.655.
3. Letter, Hornig to Hamilton, January 4, 1934, provided by courtesy of Eastern New Mexico University Library.
4. Letter, Smith to Ackerman, March 3, 1934.

Chapter 30

1. This book had an enduring popularity. It was published in bookform by Ward Lock in 1949, and reprinted in 1958 and again in 1961.
2. *The Daily Express*, July 12, 1932.
3. *Vision of Tomorrow* 1:4, January 1970, p.29, in "The Impatient Dreamers" by Walter Gillings.
4. *ibid.*
5. *Wonder Stories* 7:8, April 1936, pp.1017-8.

Chapter 31

1. *Wonder Stories* 5:9, April 1934, p.933.
2. *Wonder Stories* 5:10, May 1934, pp.1061-2.
3. *ibid*, p.1062.
4. Pohl, Frederik, *The Way the Future Was* (New York: Del Rey, 1978), p.21.

Chapter 32

1. private communication, February 1, 1988.
2. Williamson, Jack, *Wonder's Child, op.cit.*, p.97.
3. letter, Weber to Smith, May 24, 1934.

Chapter 33

1. *Wonder Stories* 7:8, April 1936, pp.921-4. *Ayer's* reports *Wonder's* circulation in 1934 as 50,628 dropping slightly to 48,356 in 1936. This seems high in light of Gernsback's comment and I suspect are based on copies printed rather than sold.
2. *ibid.*, p.907.

Chapter 34

1. Temple's was printed as "Mr. Craddock's Amazing Experience" in *Amazing Stories*, February 1939; Rocklynne's "Into the Darkness" appeared in *Astonishing Stories*, June 1940; and Kyle's "Golden Nemesis" in *Stirring Science Stories*, February 1941.

SELECTED BIBLIOGRAPHY

In the last thirty years of my reading about science fiction, I have probably lost track of the totality of items I have read about Hugo Gernsback and the early evolution of magazine science fiction. Much of this would certainly have influenced me in my thoughts about Gernsback and the period even though, in my research for this book, I tried to remain totally objective and not take for granted previously published data without endeavouring to check them out from prime sources wherever possible. The following bibliography sets out to list the relevant items that I know, by or about Hugo Gernsback and his publications, and about the science fiction and fantasy movement of the period, 1908 to 1936. It is not intended to be complete, but serves as an indication of some of the sources I used, and will also help researchers in widening their knowledge of the subject.

—Mike Ashley.

[Anon], "The Double Life of Dr. Bell," *Engineering & Science Magazine*, November 1951, p.14-15. A portrait of John Taine.

Adkins, Patrick H., "David H. Keller as Pulp Writer," introduction to *The Human Termites* by David H. Keller, New Orleans: P.D.A. Enterprises, 1979, p. 5-15.

Aldiss, Brian W. with **Wingrove, David**, *Trillion Year Spree*, London: Victor Gollancz, 1986, especially p.202-205.

Ashley, Mike, "Gernsback at Sea," *Pulp Vault* #6, November 1989, p.3-8; includes an index to *Pirate Stories* and *High-Seas Adventures*.

Ashley, Mike, *The History of the Science Fiction Magazine: Part 1, 1926-1935*, London: New English Library, 1974.

Ashley, Mike, "The Immortal Professor," *Astro-Adventures* #7, April 1989, p.3-7.

Ashley, Mike, "Mr. H. and Mr. H.G.," *Fantasy Commentator* 6:4, Winter 1989/90, p.263-274.

Ashley, Mike, "The Perils of Wonder: Clark Ashton Smith's Experiences with *Wonder Stories*," *The Dark Eidolon* 1:2, July 1989, p. 2-8.

Behrends, Steve, *Clark Ashton Smith: Letters to H. P. Lovecraft*, West Warwick: Necronomicon Press, 1987.

Behrends, Steve, "Foreword" to *The Dweller in the Gulf* by Clark Ashton Smith, West Warwick: Necronomicon Press, 1987, p. 5-7.

Black, R. Jere, Jr., "The Pseudo-Scientific Field," *The Author & Journalist*, May 1930, p.8-10.

Blackbeard, Bill, "Hugo Gernsback," *Twentieth-Century American Science-Fiction Writers, Part 1: A-L*, ed. David Cowart, Detroit: Gale Research, 1981, p.186-189.

Bleiler, Everett F., *Science-Fiction: The Early Years*, The Kent State University Press, 1990.

Bleiler, Everett F., *Science-Fiction: The Gernsback Years,* The Kent State University Press, 1998.

Carter, Paul A., *The Creation of Tomorrow: Fifty Years of Magazine Science Fiction*, New York: Columbia University Press, 1977.

Clareson, Thomas D., *Science Fiction in America, 1870s-1930s*, Westport, Connecticut: Greenwood Press, 1984.

Clarke, Arthur C., *Astounding Days*, London: Victor Gollancz, 1989.

Clarke, Arthur C., "Looking Into the Future," *Radio-Electronics*, May 1987, p.81-83.

Coblentz, Stanton A. with **Elliot, Jeffrey M.**, "In the Beginning," *SFWA Bulletin* 17:2, Summer 1983, p.9-11, 23.

Cockcroft, T. G. L., *Index to Fiction in Radio News and Other Magazines*, Lower Hutt, New Zealand: private, 1970.

Davin, Eric Leif, *Pioneers of Wonder*, New York: Prometheus Books, 1999.

Davidson, Lawrence & Lupoff, Richard A., "An Interview with Stanton A. Coblentz," *Locus* 12:11, December 1979, p.10-11.

Davin, Eric Leif, "The Age of Wonder: Gernsback, *Wonder Stories*, and David Lasser, 1929-1933," *Fantasy Commentator* 6:1, Fall 1987, p.4-25, 38-47. Includes interviews with David Lasser and Charles Hornig.

Davin, Eric Leif, "The Optimistic Pessimist: An Interview with Frank K. Kelly," *Fantasy Commentator* 6:3, Summer 1989, p.195-207.

Davin, Eric Leif, "Pioneer in the Age of Wonder: An Interview with Raymond Z. Gallun," *Fantasy Commentator* 6:2, Fall 1988, p.78-97.

Day, Donald B., *Index to the Science-Fiction Magazines, 1926-1950*, Portland, Oregon: Perri Press, 1952.

de Camp, L. Sprague, *Science-Fiction Handbook*, New York: Hermitage House, 1953.

De Forest, Lee, "Foreword" to *Ralph 124C 41+* by Hugo Gernsback, New York: Frederick Fell, second edition, 1950, p.15-18.

del Rey, Lester, *The World of Science Fiction*, New York: Garland Publishing, 1980.

Edwards, Malcolm J., "Hugo Gernsback" entry in *The Science Fiction Encyclopedia* ed. Peter Nicholls, London: Grafton, 1979, p.252.

Elkin, Deborah, "Hugo Gernsback's Ideas of Science and Fiction, 1915-1926," *Fantasy Commentator* 6:4, Winter 1989/90, p.246-258.

Elliot, Jeffrey M., "Charles D. Hornig: A Question of Conscience" in *Science Fiction Voices #4*, San Bernardino: Borgo Press, 1982, p.11-25.

Elliot, Jeffrey M., "Interview: Raymond Gallun," *Thrust* #17, Summer 1981, p.6-13; reprinted in *Pulp Voices*, San Bernardino: Borgo Press, 1983, p.52-63.

Eshbach, Lloyd Arthur [ed], *Of Worlds Beyond*, Chicago: Advent, 1964.

Eshbach, Lloyd Arthur, *Over My Shoulder: Reflections on a Science Fiction Era*, Philadelphia: Oswald Train, 1983.

Farley, Ralph Milne, "It's Too Juvenile," *The Author & Journalist*, January 1932, p.8-11.

Gallun, Raymond Z., "The Making of a Pulp Writer" in the series, "The Profession of Science Fiction," *Foundation* 22, June 1981, p. 35-48.

Gernsback, Hugo, *The Collected Works of Mohammed Ullyses* [sic] *Fips*, New York: Gernsback Publications, 1986.

Gernsback, Hugo, *Evolution of Modern Science Fiction*, New York: privately published, 1952. Includes checklist of science fiction in *Modern Electrics, The Electrical Experimenter, Science and Invention, Practi-*

cal Electrics and *The Experimenter* compiled by Theodore Engel.

Gernsback, Hugo, "50 Years Hence," address delivered before the joint meeting of the Michigan Institute of Radio Engineers and the American Radio Relay League at the Henry Ford Museum, Dearborn, Michigan, April 5, 1957.

Gernsback, Hugo, "50 Years of Home Radio," *Radio-Electronics*, March 1956.

Gernsback, Hugo, "Guest Editorial," *Amazing Stories* 35:4, April 1961, p.5-7, 88. [Entitled in manuscript "Science Fiction That Endures."]

Gernsback, Hugo, "How to Write 'Science' Stories," *Writer's Digest*, February 1930.

Gernsback, Hugo, "Hugo Gernsback Tells)," *Writer's Digest*, April 1930, p.17-18, 66.

Gernsback, Hugo, "The Impact of Science Fiction on World Progress," speech delivered at the Tenth World Science Fiction Convention in Chicago, August 31, 1952. Printed in *The Journal of Science-Fiction* 1:4, 1953, p.22-25; reprinted in *Science-Fiction Plus* 1:1, March 1953, p.2, 67. ·

Gernsback, Hugo, "New Name for Science Fiction?," *The Twilight Zine* 7, September 29, 1962; reprinted in *Forecast 1963*, Christmas 1962, p.12-15, 31.

Gernsback, Hugo, "The Prophets of Doom," address delivered before the Massachusetts Institute of Technology Science Fiction Society, October 25, 1963; printed in *Science Fiction Times* 409/410, December 1963, p.3-6.

Gernsback, Hugo, "Science Fiction vs. Reality," an address presented to the Massachusetts Institute of Technology Science Fiction Society on October 21, 1960; printed in *Science Fiction Times* 350, November 1960, p.1-5.

Gernsback, Hugo, *Space Review*, special edition of *Forecast 1958*, Christmas 1957, in which Gernsback considers all of his predictions relating to space flight, reprinting selected extracts and illustrations from his magazines.

Gernsback, Sidney, *Radio Encyclopedia, 1927*, reprinted by Palos Verdes Peninsula, California: Vintage Radio, 1974.

Gillings, Walter [as Thomas Sheridan], "Galactic Roamer," an interview with Dr. E. E. Smith, *Fantasy Review* 2:8, April-May 1948, p.4-6.

Gillings, Walter [as Thomas Sheridan], "Hugo Gernsback, Pioneer of Scientifiction," *Science-Fantasy Review* 4:18, Spring 1950, p.6-9, 17. ·

Gillings, Walter, "The Impatient Dreamers," first five episodes, *Vision of Tomorrow* 1:1, August 1969)1:5, February 1970.

Gillings, Walter [as Thomas Sheridan], "The Story of *Astounding*," in two parts, *Fantasy Review* 2:9, June-July 1948, p.4-6, and 2:10, August-September 1948, p.6-8.

Gillings, Walter [as Thomas Sheridan], "The Story of *Wonder*," in four parts, *Fantasy Review* 2:12, December 1948/January 1949, p.4-6 to 3:16, Autumn 1949, p.9-11.

Goulart, Ron, *Cheap Thrills*, New Rochelle: Arlington House, 1972; retitled *An Informal History of the Pulp Magazines*, New York: Ace Books, 1973, especially chapter eleven, "Super Science."

Gruber, Frank, *The Pulp Jungle*, Los Angeles: Sherbourne Press, 1967, especially chapter seven.

Gunn, James, *Alternate Worlds*, Englewood Cliffs, NJ: Prentice-Hall, 1975.

Gustafson, Jon, *Chroma: The Art of Alex Schomburg*, Poughkeepsie, NY: Father Tree Press, 1986.

Harbottle, Philip, *The Multi-Man: a bibliographic study of John Russell Fearn*, Wallsend: private, 1968.

Hartwell, David, *Age of Wonders: Exploring the World of Science Fiction*, New York: Walker & Co., 1984.

[Hasse, Henry], *Index to Fantasy & Science Fiction in Munsey Publications*, Los Angeles: FPCI, [nd].

Hersey, Harold, *Pulpwood Editor*, reprinted, Westport: Greenwood Press, 1974.

Hersey, Harold, "Looking Backward Into the Future," *Golden Atom* 11, 1955, p.45-68. (Part 1 only published.)

Hornig, Charles D., "Novelty)The Essential of Science Fiction," *The Author & Journalist*, July 1934, p. 11-13.

Jones, Robert K., *The Shudder Pulps*, West Linn, Oregon: Fax Collector's Editions, 1975.

Joshi, S.T., *An Index to the Selected Letters of H. P. Lovecraft*, West Warwick: Necronomicon Press, 1980.

Keller, David H., "Hugo Gernsback," *Fantasy Times* 100, February 1950, p.5-7.

Kelly, Frank K., "My Interplanetary Teens," *The Atlantic Monthly* 180, July 1947, p.102-103; reprinted in *Fantasy Commentator* 6:3, Summer 1989, p.192-194.

Knight, Damon, *The Futurians*, New York: John Day, 1977.

Knight, Damon, *In Search of Wonder*, Chicago: Advent, 2nd edition, 1967.

Kraft, David Anthony, *The Compleat OAK Leaves*, Clayton, GA: Fictioneer Books, 1980. The bound volume of issue 1-12 of *OAK Leaves*, the official journal of Otis Adelbert Kline and his works.

Kyle, David A., *A Pictorial History of Science Fiction*, London: Hamlyn, 1976.

Kyle, David A., *The Illustrated Book of Science Fiction Ideas and Dreams*, London: Hamlyn, 1977.

Lesch, Paul & Muller, Jean-Claude, "Hugo Gernsback: le père de la science-fiction moderne," untranslated.

Lillian III, Guy H., "Strange Schwartz Stories," *Amazing World of DC Comics* #3, November 1974, p.2-11.

Lowndes, Robert A.W., "Hugo Gernsback: A Man with Vision +," *Radio-Electronics*, August 1984, p.73-75.

Lowndes, Robert A.W., "Hugo Gernsback, Prophet of Science," unpublished typescript, in progress.

Lowndes, Robert A.W., "Hugo Gernsback's Science Fiction League" in

"Understandings," *Outworlds* p. 1621-1634.

Lowndes, Robert A.W., "Yesterday's World of Tomorrow: 1927," serialized in *Future Science Fiction*: #33, Summer 1957, p.72-75; #34, Fall 1957, p.83-88; #35, February 1958, p.65-69.

Lowndes, Robert A.W., "Yesterday's World of Tomorrow: 1928," serialized in *Future Science Fiction*: #36, April 1958, p.21-23, 127-130; #37, June 1958, p.77-82; #38, August 1958, p.69-72; #39, October 1958, p.100-109; #40, December 1958, p.89-99, 130; #41, February 1959, p.104-108.

Lowndes, Robert A.W., "Yesterday's World of Tomorrow: 1929," serialized in *Future Science Fiction*: #42, April 1959, p.23, 101-106; #44, August 1959, p.82-89.

Lundwall, Sam, *Science Fiction: An Illustrated History*, New York: Grosset & Dunlap, 1978. One section from this volume has been abstracted and revised as "Adventures in the Pulp Jungle," *Foundation* 34, Autumn 1985, p. 5-15.

Lundwall, Sam, *Science Fiction: What's It All About*, New York: Ace Books, 1971, especially chapter 9, "The Magazines," p. 199-215.

Lupoff, Richard A., *Edgar Rice Burroughs: Master of Adventure*, New York: Ace Books, 1968 (revised edition).

Madle, Robert A., "Science Fiction's Greatest Year," *World Science Fiction Convention Program*, 1977.

Magill, Frank N., *Survey of Science Fiction Literature*, Englewood Cliffs, NJ: Salem Press, 1979.

Morgan, Chris, *The Shape of Futures Past*, Exeter, Devon: Webb & Bower, 1980.

Moskowitz, Sam, *A. Merritt: Reflections in the Moon Pool*, Philadelphia: Oswald Train, 1985.

Moskowitz, Sam, "Amazing Encounter: Macfadden's Takeover of Gernsback's Company," in two parts, *Fantasy Review* 9:2, February 1986, p.8-10, 38, 40, to 9:3, March 1986, p.8-10, 40.

Moskowitz, Sam, "Anatomy of a Collection: The Sam Moskowitz Collection," *Science/Fiction Collections: Fantasy, Supernatural and Weird Tales* ed. Hal W. Hall, New York: The Haworth Press, 1983, p.79-110.

Moskowitz, Sam, "Bernarr Macfadden and His Obsession with Science Fiction," serialized in *Fantasy Commentator* as follows: 1. "The Early Struggles" 5:4, Fall 1986, p.261-279; 2. Macfadden Seeks His Avalon" 6:1, Fall 1987, p.49-59; 3. "Science-Fiction in *True Story Magazine*" 6:2, Fall 1988, p.98-106; 4. "Enter Fulton Oursler" 6:3, Summer 1989, p.162-175.

Moskowitz, Sam, *Explorers of the Infinite*, Cleveland: World Publishing Co., 1963.

Moskowitz, Sam, "The Gernsback Magazines No One Knows," *Riverside Quarterly* 4:4, March 1971, p.272-274

Moskowitz, Sam, "Henrik Dahl Juve and the Second Gernsback Dynasty," *Extrapolation* 30:1, Spring 1989, p.5-52.

Moskowitz, Sam, "A History of the Scientific Romance in the Munsey Magazines, 1912-1950," *Under the Moons of Mars*, New York: Holt, Rinehart & Winston, 1970, p.289-433.

Moskowitz, Sam, "How Science Fiction Got Its Name," *The Magazine of Fantasy & Science Fiction* 12:2, February 1957, p.65-77; reprinted in *The Origin of the Term Science Fiction*, New York: Hugo Gernsback, [1957]; revised and reprinted in *Explorers of the Infinite*, Cleveland: World Publishing Co., 1963, p.313-333.

Moskowitz, Sam, "Hugo Gernsback: Father of Science Fiction," New York: Criterion, 1959; revised as "Mr. Science Fiction: A Profile of Hugo Gernsback," *Amazing Stories* 34:9, September 1960, p.xx-xx; revised and reprinted as "Hugo Gernsback: Father of Science Fiction," in *Explorers of the Infinite*, Cleveland: World Publishing Co., 1963, p.225-242.

Moskowitz, Sam, *The Immortal Storm: A History of Science Fiction Fandom*, Westport, Connecticut: Hyperion Press, 1974.

Moskowitz, Sam, "The Origins of Science Fiction Fandom: A Reconstruction," *Foundation* 48, Spring 1990, p.5-25.

Moskowitz, Sam, "P. Schuyler Miller," memoriam, *Analog* 95:2, February 1975, p. 162-166; expanded as *A Canticle for P. Schuyler Miller*, Newark, New Jersey: private, 1975.

Moskowitz, Sam, "Road to Avalon: the Grand Old Man of Science Fiction," *Fantasy Times* 58, November 1947, p.2-5.

Moskowitz, Sam, *Seekers of Tomorrow*, Cleveland: World Publishing Co., 1966.

Moskowitz, Sam, "Setting the Record Straight: A Response to Lundwall's 'Adventures in the Pulp Jungle'," *Foundation* 36, Summer 1986, p.57-67.

Moskowitz, Sam, *Strange Horizons*, New York: Scribner's, 1976.

Moskowitz, Sam, "The Ultimate Hugo Gernsback," introduction to *Ultimate World* by Hugo Gernsback, New York: Walker, 1971, p.7-18.

Moskowitz, Sam, "The Willy Ley Story," *Worlds of Tomorrow* 3:7, May 1966, p.30-42.

O'Neil, Paul, "Barnum of the Space Age," *Life Magazine* 55:4, July 26, 1963, p.62-68.

Panshin, Alexei, "The Short History of Science Fiction," *Fantastic* 20:4, April 1971, p.109-115; reprinted in *SF in Dimension*, Chicago: Advent, 1976.

Panshin, Alexei & Cory, *The World Beyond the Hill*, Los Angeles: Jeremy Tarcher, 1989.

Parente, Audrey, *Pulp Man's Odyssey: The Hugh B. Cave Story*, Mercer Island, WA: Starmont House, 1988.

Parrinder, Patrick, *Science Fiction: Its Criticism and Teaching*, London & New York: Methuen, 1980.

Perry, Tom, "Experiment in Bankruptcy," *Amazing Science Fiction* 51:3, May 1978, p.101-116. [This was a follow-up to "Mythology Deluxe" by Perry in the July 1977 *Amazing* which provides some additional data, but is generally less useful.]

Pohl, Frederik, "Astounding Story," *American Heritage*, September/October 1989, p.42-54.

Pohl, Frederik, *The Way the Future Was: A Memoir*, New York: Del Rey Books, 1978, in particular the first five chapters.

Porges, Irwin, *Edgar Rice Burroughs: The Man Who Created Tarzan*, New York: Ballantine Books, 2 vols, 1976.

Pratt, Fletcher, "Foreword" to *Ralph 124C 41+* by Hugo Gernsback, New York: Frederick Fell, second edition, 1950, p.19-24.

Riach, Colin, "Science Fiction: Science Fact," programme in the television series *Horizon*, London: BBC-2, July 28, 1965, with filmed contributions by Hugo Gernsback, Sam Moskowitz, Arthur C. Clarke, Isaac Asimov, Dr. John R. Pierce and Stanford Neal. Transcript available in the BBC Written Archives.

Rogers, Alva, *A Requiem for Astounding*, Chicago: Advent, 1964.

Sampson, Robert, *Yesterday's Faces*, Bowling Green, Ohio: Popular Press, 4 vols, 1983-1987, especially Vol. 2, *Strange Days* (1984), Part IV: "Shadows of Other Suns."

Sampson, Robert, *Deadly Excitements: Shadows & Phantoms*, Bowling Green, Ohio: Popular Press, 1989, especially p. 127-131 on *Scientific Detective Monthly*.

Sanford, Julius, "Have You Been Hypnobioscoped?," *Cavalcade*, November 1950, p.12-15.

Sapiro, Leland, "Clichés in the Old Super-Science Story," *Riverside Quarterly*

[Schwartz, Julius], "Titans of Science Fiction: Hugo Gernsback," *Science Fiction Digest* 1:4, December 1932, p.3-4.

Schwartz, Julius & Weisinger, Mortimer, "David H. Keller, M.D.," interview in *Science Fiction Digest*, July 1933, p.3-4, 14.

Schweitzer, Darrell, "Keeper of the Flame," *Algol* 15:1, Winter 1977/78, p.22-27.

Shaftel, Oscar, "The Social Content of Science Fiction," *Science & Society* 17:2, Spring 1953, p.97-118.

Siegel, Mark, *Hugo Gernsback, Father of Modern Science Fiction*, San Bernardino: Borgo Press, 1988.

Smith, R. Dixon, *Lost in the Rentharpian Hills: Spanning the Decades with Carl Jacobi*, Bowling Green, Ohio: Popular Press, 1985.

Stableford, Brian, "Science Fiction Between the Wars: 1918-1938," *Anatomy of Wonder*, 3rd edition, ed. Neil Barron, New York: R.R. Bowker, 1987, p.49-88.

Stashower, Daniel, "A Dreamer Who Made Us Fall in Love with the Future," *The Smithsonian* 21:5, August 1990, p.45-54.

Tuck, Donald H., *The Encyclopedia of Science Fiction and Fantasy*, Chicago: Advent, 3 vols., 1974, 1978, 1982.

Tymn, Marshall B. & Ashley, Mike, *Science Fiction, Fantasy, and Weird Fiction Magazines*, Westport, Connecticut: Greenwood Press, 1985.

Warner, Jr., Harry, *All Our Yesterdays*, Chicago: Advent, 1969.

West, Wallace, "'The Last Man' Mess," *WT50* ed. Robert Weinberg, Oak Lawn, Illinois: Weinberg, 1974, p.41-42.

Westfahl, Gary, "On *The True History of Science Fiction*," *Foundation* #47, Winter 1989/90, p.5-27.

Westfahl, Gary, "An Idea of Significant Import: Hugo Gernsback's Theory of Science Fiction," *Foundation* 48, Spring 1990, p.26-50.

Westfahl, Gary, *The Mechanics of Wonder,* Liverpool University Press, 1998.

Whitman, Howard, "Truth Catches Up with His Fiction," *Coronet,* July 1944.

Williamson, Jack, "As I Knew Hugo," *Extrapolation* 11:2, May 1970, p. 53-55.

Williamson, Jack, "The Way it Was," in the series "The Profession of Science Fiction," *Foundation* 26, October 1982, p. 46-55.

Williamson, Jack, *Wonder's Child: My Life in Science Fiction,* New York: Bluejay Books, 1984, especially chapters 8-13.

Winter, Frank H., *Prelude to the Space Age: The Rocket Societies, 1924-1940,* Washington: Smithsonian Institute Press, 1983.

Wollheim, Donald A., *The Universe Makers,* New York: Harper & Row, 1971.

GENERAL INDEX

This index covers all references in the main text and in Appendix 1, but not the indices in appendices 2 to 5. Page references for magazines relate to a discussion about that magazine or its contents, and not if it is cited solely as a source for a story. Wherever possible author's birth-death dates are provided.

Y

Your Body 144, 190, 205, 251

Z

Zagat, Arthur Leo (1895-1949) 184, 193, 208, 250, 309, 310, 319-20, 322, 326, 328, 330
Zworykin, Vladimir (1889-1982) 120

Printed in the United Stat
19756LVS00003B/105

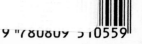